DATE DUE

DEMCO 38-296

CONTEMPORARY MUSICIANS

ISSN 1044-2197

CONTEMPORARY MUSICIANS

PROFILES OF THE PEOPLE IN MUSIC

LUANN BRENNAN, Editor

Leigh Ann DeRemer, Assistant Editor

VOLUME 26
Includes Cumulative Indexes

GALE GROUP

Detroit
San Francisco
London
Boston
Woodbridge, CT

STAFF

Luann Brennan, *Editor*
Leigh Ann DeRemer, *Assistant Editor*

Mary Alice Adams, Barry Alfonso Carol Brennan, Gerald E. Brennan, Gloria Cooksey, Linda Dailey Paulson, Evelyn Hauser, Lloyd Hemingway, K. Michelle Moran, Brenna Sanchez, Ann M. Schawlboski, B. Kim Taylor, Gretchen A. Van-Monette, *Sketchwriters*

Bridget Travers, *Managing Editor*

Maria Franklin, *Permissions Manager*
Edna Hedblad, *Permissions Associate*
Keryl Stanley, *Permissions Asstant*

Mary Beth Trimper, *Production Director*
Dorothy Maki, *Manufacturing Manager*
Cindy Range, *Buyer*

Robert Duncan, Michael Logusz, *Imaging Specialists*
Randy Bassett, *Image Database Supervisor*
Pamela A. Reed, *Imaging Coordinator*
Gary Leach, *Graphic Artist*
Cover illustration by John Kleber

ISBN 0-7876-3251-1
ISSN 1044-2197

10 9 8 7 6 5 4 3 2 1

Contents

Introduction ix

Cumulative Subject Index 233

Cumulative Musicians Index 261

Walter Afanasieff 1
    Hardly a household name

Chet Atkins 4
    Mr. Guitar

Florence Austral 7
    Operatic soprano

Avalon 11
    Ministry of voices

Erykah Badu 14
    Exceptionally gifted talent

Mandy Barnett 17
    Compelling, sophisticated voice

Bill Wyman & the Rhythm Kings 18
    Brain-child of a rolling stone

Chris Blackwell 22
    Laid back businessman

Pierre Boulez 25
    Modernist conductor and composer

Peter Brötzmann 29
    Powerhouse multi-reedman

William S. Burroughs 32
    Writer influences musicians

Captain Beefheart and His Magic Band 35
    Weird Renaissance Band

D Generation 39
    Hybrid of punk and glam rock

Dixie Chicks 41
    New age country music

Dropkick Murphys 44
    Blue collar punk music

Jacqueline DuPré 46
    Passionate cello performer

Five Iron Frenzy 49
    Zany punks with Christian focus

Fountains of Wayne 51
    Solid pop songwriting team

John Eliot Gardiner 53
    Accomplished British conductor

Gilberto Gil 56
    Contemporary Brazilian musician

Allen Ginsberg 59
    Highlyenthusiastic singer

Greater Vision 62
    Southern gospel harmonists

Gus Gus 65
    Icelandic techno ensemble

Gwen Guthrie 67
    Songwriter with flair

Tom T. Hall 70
    Master storyteller

Roger Hodgson 73
    Gave Supertramp its distinctive sound

John Lee Hooker 76
    Modern electronic bluesman

Cissy Houston 80
    Gifted gospel singer

Imperial Teen 83
Engaging post-punk sound

Blind Willie Johnson 86
Electrifying religious music

Howard Jones 89
Humanizer of techno-pop

Montell Jordan 92
Soared to stardom

Joy Electric 94
Christian rock with punk attitude

Phil Keaggy 96
Christian guitar virtuoso

Lenny Kravitz 99
Consistent hitmaking style

Ben Lee 102
Australian rock prodigy

Julian Lennon 105
Legacy comes into his own

Furry Lewis 108
Personifies the Memphis blues

Mark Linkous 111
Impressionistic songwriting style

Kevin Mahogany 113
Standard bearing jazz vocalist

Ricky Martin 116
Peurto Rican pop sensation

Lila McCann 119
Stands on her own

Jo Dee Messina 121
High-spirited redhead

Pat Metheny 124
Grammy winning jazz fusion guitarist

Mojave 3 127
Moody atmospheric sound

Monica 129
Talented chanteuse

Little Brother Montgomery 131
Timeless blues pianist

Oakland Interfaith Gospel Choir 134
Promoters of cultural understanding

Beth Orton 137
Folk music of a different vein

Maria João Pires 140
Portuguese pianist and musical purist

The Pretty Things 143
Tenacious British rock band

Propellerheads 146
Big beat electronica purveyors

Thomas Quasthoff 144
German child prodigy

Ralph Sharon Quartet 150
Work spans decades

Rasputina 153
Ladies cello society

Ray Condo and His Ricochets 155
Electric country musicians

André Rieu 157
Spirited violinist and conductor

Gabrielle Roth 161
Band leader with a steady beat

Tom Russell 164
Working class storyteller

Rusted Root 167
Unique electric rock group

Rebecca St. James 170
Australian Christian singer

Sebadoh 172
Mature indie rock

Bola Sete 175
Father of New Age music

Silk 178
Smooth vocal group

Sixpence None the Richer 180
  Christian pop-alternative act

Will Smith 183
  G-rated rapper

Sonic Youth 186
  No wave rock

Kim Stockwood 189
  Irresistable Canadian pop singer

Sweet Honey In The Rock 191
  Artistic and cultural activists

Steve Taylor 195
  Evangelical rock's court jester

Yuri Temirkanov 197
  Celebrated Russian conductor

Tom Petty and the Heartbreakers 200
  No burned-out gang of geezers

Underworld 204
  Cutting edge alternative music

Vanessa-Mae 207
  Unpredictable violin prodigy

Waddy Wachtel 210
  High-energy guitar player

Jody Watley 213
  Complete artist of the nineties

Wendy O. Williams and The Plasmatics 215
  Raw, raucous punk band

Paul Westerberg 218
  Brash punker continues singing

Paul Williams 221
  Multitalented entertainer

Cassandra Wilson 224
  Down-home singer

XTC 227
  British rock with cult following

Introduction

Fills the Information Gap on Today's Musicians

Contemporary Musicians profiles the colorful personalities in the music industry who create or influence the music we hear today. Prior to *Contemporary Musicians,* no quality reference series provided comprehensive information on such a wide range of artists despite keen and ongoing public interest. To find biographical and critical coverage, an information seeker had little choice but to wade through the offerings of the popular press, scan television "infotainment" programs, and search for the occasional published biography or exposé. *Contemporary Musicians* is designed to serve that information seeker, providing in one ongoing source in-depth coverage of the important names on the modern music scene in a format that is both informative and entertaining. Students, researchers, and casual browsers alike can use *Contemporary Musicians* to meet their needs for personal information about music figures; find a selected discography of a musician's recordings; and uncover an insightful essay offering biographical and critical information.

Provides Broad Coverage

Single-volume biographical sources on musicians are limited in scope, often focusing on a handful of performers from a specific musical genre or era. In contrast, *Contemporary Musicians* offers researchers and music devotees a comprehensive, informative, and entertaining alternative. *Contemporary Musicians* is published three times per year, with each volume providing information on over 80 musical artists and record-industry luminaries from all the genres that form the broad spectrum of contemporary music—pop, rock, jazz, blues, country, New Age, folk, rhythm and blues, gospel, bluegrass, rap, and reggae, to name a few—as well as selected classical artists who have achieved "crossover" success with the general public. *Contemporary Musicians* will also occasionally include profiles of influential nonperforming members of the music community, including producers, promoters, and record company executives. Additionally, beginning with *Contemporary Musicians 11,* each volume features new profiles of a selection of previous *Contemporary Musicians* listees who remain of interest to today's readers and who have been active enough to require completely revised entries.

Includes Popular Features

In *Contemporary Musicians* you'll find popular features that users value:

- **Easy-to-locate data sections:** Vital personal statistics, chronological career summaries, listings of major awards, and mailing addresses, when available, are prominently displayed in a clearly marked box on the second page of each entry.

- **Biographical/critical essays:** Colorful and informative essays trace each subject's personal and professional life, offer representative examples of critical response to the artist's work, and provide entertaining personal sidelights.

- **Selected discographies:** Each entry provides a comprehensive listing of the artist's major recorded works.

- **Photographs:** Most entries include portraits of the subject profiled.

- **Sources for additional information:** This invaluable feature directs the user to selected books, magazines, newspapers, and online sources where more information can be obtained.

Helpful Indexes Make It Easy to Find the Information You Need

Each volume of *Contemporary Musicians* features a cumulative Musicians Index, listing names of individual performers and musical groups, and a cumulative Subject Index, which provides the user with a breakdown by primary musical instruments played and by musical genre.

Available in Electronic Formats

Diskette/Magnetic Tape. *Contemporary Musicians* is available for licensing on magnetic tape or diskette in a fielded format. The database is available for internal data processing and nonpublishing purposes only. For more information, call (800) 877-GALE.

Online. *Contemporary Musicians* is available online as part of the Gale Biographies (GALBIO) database accessible through LEXIS-NEXIS, P.O. Box 933, Daton, OH 454012-0933; phone: (513)865-6800, toll-free:800-543-6862.

We Welcome Your Suggestions

The editors welcome your comments and suggestions for enhancing and improving *Contemporary Musicians*. If you would like to suggest subjects for inclusion, please submit these names to the editors. Mail comments or suggestions to:

The Editor
Contemporary Musicians
Gale Group, Inc.
27500 Drake Rd.
Farmington Hills, MI 48334-3535

Or call toll free: (800) 347-GALE

Walter Afanasieff

Producer, songwriter

Though they rarely become stars themselves, producers and songwriters are often crucial in making stars of others—or at least enabling established talents to remain in the spotlight. This certainly seems to be the case with Walter Afanasieff. While he has been an enormously successful songwriter, producer and musician, working with some of the biggest pop music names in the last two decades, Afanasieff is hardly a household name—even to the fans of the artists he is closely associated with (most notably, Mariah Carey). Nevertheless, Afanasieff's stamp appears on many of the top popular hits of the 1990s.

Born Vladamir Nikitich in Brazil in 1958, his Russian parents Nikita and Tatiana moved to San Francisco when Afanasieff was five years old. By then, he had already been studying classical piano for two years. Even as a child Afanasieff, who was exposed early on to a variety of musical styles, knew he wanted a career in the music industry. As he recounted to David Farinella in a 1998 Billboard article, "I would sit there as a little kid, rocking on my bed, listening to the Beatles, and know that this is what I wanted to do. I wanted to make music . . . . I had this internal clock, this musical rhythm, this music inside of me from day one." A young Afanasieff enrolled at the Conservatory of Music in San Mateo, California, before heading to Europe for additional schooling in classical music. Returning to California in 1978, he developed an interest in jazz that would lead to work with violinist Jean-Luc Ponty and Narada Michael Walden. Before becoming a producer, Afanasieff was a well-known session musician and composer in the San Francisco area, spent time in a number of bands, and backed vocalists such as James Brown, Aretha Franklin, and Whitney Houston. He got his start playing with Ponty, and later Walden, with whom he worked for approximately 10 years and who gave him the nickname "Babylove." His time with Walden, Afanasieff told Farinella, was particularly important to his career development. "I think the greatest teacher was Narada, because he truly is a magnificent producer," Afanasieff said. "He's very talented, he's very creative and improvisational. The one thing I really learned from him is how to do vocals."

After working with Walden for a decade, Afanasieff was appointed an executive staff producer for Sony Music in late 1990. Early on in his tenure at Sony, Afanasieff was involved with several successful projects including the Celine Dion-Peabo Bryson duet "Beauty and the Beast" for the Disney movie of the same name, and Carey's *Emotions* album. "I just happened to get lucky having a bunch of great artists to work with," Afanasieff told *Billboard*'s Susan Nunziata in a 1992 article.

If he isn't famous in his own right, though, Afanasieff's credits are legion. Among his many songwriting credits alone are his collaborations with fellow songwriters Walden, Preston Glass, and Kenny Williams on "Don't Make Me Wait For Love," a single on Kenny G's 1986 album *Duotones*. With John Bettis, he co-wrote the title track from Peabo Bryson's 1991 album *Can You Stop the Rain,* which was nominated for a Grammy Award for Best Rhythm and Blues Song of the Year. The same year Afanasieff co-wrote "Missing You Now" with Michael Bolton and legendary songwriter Diane Warren, which appeared on Bolton's best-selling *Time, Love and Tenderness* album. Afanasieff and Bettis also collaborated on "If You Go Away," a 1992 song which appeared on greatest hits album from NTKOB (formerly New Kids on the Block). With David Foster and Linda Thompson, he co-wrote the 1997 Celine Dion-Barbra Streisand duet "Tell Him," which appeared on both singers' albums that year.

Afanasieff is probably best known, however, for his work with Carey. He has had a hand in writing, producing, and arranging on the bulk of Carey's work, beginning with her self-titled 1990 debut album. Afanasieff produced subsequent releases by Carey, including hit singles such as 1993's "Hero" and "One Sweet Day," the 1995 duet with Boyz II Men. Besides working behind the scenes with Carey, Afanasieff has had occasion to share the spotlight with her as well. He backed Carey on piano during her May 20, 1992 performance on MTV's "Unplugged"

For the Record . . .

Born Vladamir Nikitich, 1958 in Brazil to Russian parents Nikita and Tatiana; studied music at Conservatory of Music in San Mateo, California; married Corinne, 1988, three children: Christina, Isabella, and Andrei.

Worked as a session musician and composer in the San Fransisco area backing artists such as James Brown, Aretha Franklin, and Whitney Houston; worked with jazz violinist Jean-Luc Ponty; worked with Narada Michael Walden; appointed executive staff producer of Sony Music, 1990; wrote and produced songs for Michael Bolton, Mariah Carey, Celine Dion, Kenny G, Kenny Loggins, and others.

Awards: Nominated for Grammy Award for "Can You Stop the Rain," a 1991 Peabo Bryson song he co-wrote with John Bettis.

Addresses: *Record company*—Sony 550 Music, 550 Madison Ave., New York, NY 10022.

show, which was later released as an EP. His reputation as a top producer caught the attention of Hollywood, as well. Afanasieff worked on a number of movie soundtracks, including 1991's *Beauty and the Beast, Aladdin* and *The Bodyguard* in 1992, and *Hercules* in 1997. With Walden he co-wrote, co-produced, and arranged the title track for the 1989 James Bond film *A License to Kill,* which was performed by Gladys Knight.

While he has worked on a number of high profile projects and with a number of well-known artists, Afanasieff said he enjoys the challenge of working with new performers as well. "In a pure, honest sense," he told *Billboard* in 1998, "I would prefer an artist who is an unknown, unheard artist." One of the newer artists he was working with in 1999 was the Australian pop duo Savage Garden (Darren Hayes and Daniel Jones).

His musical craftsmanship and skill did not gone unnoticed by the music community. In a 1998 tribute in *Billboard,* Carey praised Afanasieff as a "knowledgeable musician," and collaborator Bettis added that Afanasieff

"can literally play, write, or produce anything." Sony Music head Thomas Mottola told *Billboard* for the tribute, "One of the things I respect most about Walter is that, for him, a great record is about feeling, about emotion, and each element of his productions serves to bring that out of the songs. You know when you work with him he's going to dig deep and come up with something that sounds classic and brand new at one and the same time. And he achieves these results with very different artists."

For Afanasieff, producing is apparently ultimately something of an organic process. "I wasn't a guy who studied the engineers and studio techniques and 'miking' and what consoles everybody was using . . . I'd always read that, but that wasn't what I was interested in," he told Farinella. "I was into pure music, what moved me musically, what sounds the best, what keyboard sound work with that bass line, the chord changes, the vocals, the harmonies, the orchestra."

Selected discography

"Night Train," Lionel Richie, Motown, 1986.
"Missing You Now," Michael Bolton, Columbia, 1991.
"Hero," Mariah Carey, Columbia, 1993.
"My Heart Will Go On," Celine Dion, 550 Music, 1997.

Sources

Books

Popular Music, 1980-89: A Revised Cumulation, Gale Research, 1995.
Popular Music, 1991, Gale Research, Inc., 1992.
Popular Music, 1992, Gale Research, Inc., 1993.
Popular Music, 1993, Gale Research, Inc., 1994.
Popular Music, 1994, Gale Research, Inc., 1995.
Popular Music, 1995, Gale Research, Inc., 1996.
Rees, Dafydd, and Luke Crampton, *Encyclopedia of Rock Stars,* DK Publishing, 1996.

Periodicals

Billboard, May 16, 1992; December 12, 1998.
Detroit News, January 9, 1992; May 2, 1997.
Parade, May 9, 1999.

—*K. Michelle Moran*

Chet Atkins

Guitar, singer, songwriter

Chet Atkins may have first made his mark in country music, but his legacy has spread far, his style influencing jazz, blues, and rock guitarists. Atkins' jazz-tinged country guitar once got him dismissed from the Grand Ole Opry, the premier showcase for country music. His style turned out to be so influential, though, that he became the youngest person ever inducted into the Country Music Hall of Fame. He earned the honor in part because of his work as a producer, which some say kept country music from being overrun by rock and roll in the 1950s. More important, though, was his unique style of playing, which earned him the nickname "Mr. Guitar."

Born June 20, 1924, near Luttrell, Tennessee, Chester Burton Atkins grew up in a poor rural area amid a variety of musical influences. The son of a classically-trained gospel singer, Atkins avidly listened to the sounds around him, as he explained to *Billboard* magazine, "[I]f anybody came through the area playing something I didn't know, I'd steal it, take it over, and make it my own." His first instrument was a ukulele, which he strung with

For the Record . . .

Born Chester Burton Atkins, June 20, 1924, near Lutrell, TN; son of James Arley (a music teacher, piano tuner, and evangelical singer), and Ida (maiden name, Sharp) Atkins; married Leona Pearl Johnson (a singer), July 3, 1946; children: one daughter, Merle.

Played fiddle in the street for small change as a child; during the 1940s played fiddle and/or guitar for various radio stations and radio shows, including "The Jumpin' Bill Carlisle and Archie Campbell Show" and "Midday Merry-Go-Round" at WNOX, Knoxville, TN; member of staff band, WLW, Cincinnati, OH; performed on the Grand Ole Opry, 1946; signed with RCA, 1947; recorded hit single "Main Street Breakdown," 1949; performed again on the Grand Ole Opry during the late 1940s and 1950s with the Carter Family and Homer and Jethro; served in multiple capacities for RCA Victor Records, 1949-82; signed with Columbia, 1982.

Awards: Elected to the Country Music Hall of Fame, 1973; several Grammy Award winning recordings, including Me and Jerry, 1970, Chet Atkins Picks the Best, 1971, "Snowbird," 1971, Chester and Lester, 1976, "Cosmic Square Dance," 1985, Neck and Neck, 1990; named top guitarist several times by Cash Box Magazine; Humanitarian Award, 1972, from National Council of Christians and Jews; received Century Award, 1997, from Billboard magazine.

Addresseses: Record company—Columbia Records, 51 West 52nd St, New York, NY 10019.

during the 1940s. Although there always seemed to be work for him, he would frequently get fired for mixing in jazz with his country. He earned a brief stint with the Grand Ole Opry in 1946, and also cut his first record that same year for Bullet records. Atkins didn't stay put in Tennessee, though, and Steve Sholes of RCA records had to track him down in Denver, Colorado to sign him to a contract in 1947. He received some attention for such songs as "Canned Heat" and "Bug Dance" from his first sessions. In 1949, though, Atkins established an audience for his style with "Main Street Breakdown."

Atkins' stature as a solo artist continued to grow with the release of two albums in 1951. He continued playing as a session man, though, recording with country music legend Hank Williams, among others. Atkins' effective suggestions in the studio earned him a position as producer. In that role he specialized in recordings that relied more on string arrangements than on fiddles and steel guitars, which brought country music to a new audience. Atkins also had a keen ear for talent, and he was the first to sign such future country stars as Waylon Jennings, Dolly Parton, and Willie Nelson to recording contracts. Speaking of his success as a producer to Noel Holston of the Minneapolis Star-Tribune, Atkins said, "It's not that I'm so smart or anything, it's that I'm a square."

Atkins' production work didn't keep him from recording. His hit version of "Mr. Sandman" in 1955 displayed his gift for interpreting music written by others. He also began to draw on his varied musical background in his recordings, releasing albums such as the classically influenced Chet Atkins in Three Dimensions. Atkins' musical tastes weren't stuck in the past, though, as he kept up with the latest musical trends, some of which he inspired. When Chet Atkins Picks on the Beatles was released in 1966, it came with an endorsement in the liner notes from one of his more famous fans, Beatles guitarist George Harrison. The music industry also recognized the quality of Atkins' work throughout the 1960s and 1970s. He was repeatedly named the top guitarist of the year by Cash Box magazine and won several Grammy awards. Some of Atkins' most highly praised recordings were collaborations with his guitar heroes. He recorded The Atkins-Travis Travelin' Show with Travis in 1974, and his 1976 effort with Les Paul, Chester and Lester, won a Grammy. Atkins explained the appeal of such duets to Kevin Ransom of Guitar Player: "Playing with other guitarists inspires me to play better than I normally would, because it's kind of competitive."

Although his legend was secure, the 1980s brought changes in Atkins' place in the music industry. In 1982

wire from a screen door. He also learned to play the fiddle, and when he was nine, he traded a gun for a guitar. Besides learning classical music from his father and gospel from his neighbors, Atkins learned other styles from listening to the radio. He taught himself guitar trying to imitate what he heard, especially the finger picking style of Merle Travis. He didn't realize that Travis played with just his thumb and one finger, so from reading his father's classical music magazines, Atkins learned to play with his thumb and three fingers, which became his signature style.

Atkins started playing professionally on radio stations while still in high school. He dropped out of school and played at several radio stations throughout the country

he left RCA, where he was a vice-president, to sign with Columbia. Country music was changing, too, and Atkins' songs were more likely to be heard on New Age radio than on country stations. As always, though, Atkins successfully ranged across the musical spectrum. Two collaborations with rock guitarist Mark Knopfler won Grammies: the 1985 track "Cosmic Square Dance" and the 1990 album *Neck and Neck.* Throughout the 1990s, Atkins continued to record with guitarists who had learned from listening to him. The albums *Read My Licks* and *The Day Finger Pickers Took Over the World* showcased Atkins playing with such diverse performers as Knopfler, jazz guitarist George Benson, country performer Steve Wariner, and young Australian guitar phenomenon Tommy Emmanuel.

Surgery for a benign brain tumor and a stroke in 1997 slowed Atkins, but he remained active. He told Jim Patterson of the Associated Press, "I can play with feeling. But technically, I can't hook it like I used to." Still, he practiced daily and kept busy in the studio, putting together the 1998 album *Tribute to Tradition,* a collection of classic country songs performed by contemporary artists. He even played on one of the tracks, a version of "O Lonesome Me," which was a number-one hit when he produced it for Don Gibson in 1959. Another of Atkins' projects was been the annual Chet Atkins' Musician Days, a week of concerts and seminars for musicians. With all his attention to younger performers, Atkins showed that his legacy existed not only in the body of work that he has produced, but also in the knowledge and encouragement that he passed down to new generations.

Selected discography

Chet Atkins Plays Guitar, RCA, 1951.
Chet Atkins in Three Dimensions, RCA, 1951.
Hi-Fi in Focus, RCA, 1957.
At Home, RCA, 1958.
In Hollywood, RCA, 1959.
Mister Guitar, RCA, 1960.
Workshop, RCA, 1961.
Down Home, RCA, 1962.
Our Man in Nashville, RCA, 1963.
Guitar Country, RCA, 1964.
Progressive Pickin', RCA, 1964.
My Favorite Guitars, RCA, 1965.
Chet Atkins Picks on the Beatles, RCA, 1966.
From Nashville, RCA, 1966.
Guitar World, RCA, 1967.
(With Jerry Reed) *Me and Jerry,* RCA, 1970.
This is Chet Atkins, RCA, 1970.
For the Good Times, RCA, 1971.
Welcome to My World, RCA, 1971.
Pickin' My Way, RCA, 1971.
Now & Then, RCA, 1972.
Chet Atkins Picks on the Hits, RCA, 1972.
(With Merle Travis) *The Atkins-Travis Travelin' Show,* RCA, 1974.
Atkins String Band, RCA, 1975.
(With Les Paul) *Chester and Lester,* RCA, 1976.
Stay Tuned, Columbia, 1985.
Chet Atkins, C.G.P., Columbia, 1989.
(With Mark Knopfler) *Neck and Neck,* Columbia, 1990.
(With Jerry Reed) *Sneakin' Around,* Columbia, 1992.
Read My Licks, Columbia, 1994.
The Day Finger Pickers Took Over the World, Columbia, 1997.

Sources

Books

Contemporary Musicians, vol. 5, Gale Research, Inc., 1991.

Periodicals

Billboard, December 6, 1997.
Chicago Sun-Times, October 6, 1998, p. 33.
Florida Times Union (Jacksonville), July 12, 1998, p. E3.
Guitar Player, October, 1994.
Star Tribune (Minneapolis), May 22, 1998, p. 3E.

—Lloyd Hemingway

Florence Austral

Operatic soprano

Florence Austral is among the many twentieth century opera stars of born in Australia. Although well known internationally during the late 1920s and early 1930s, after her career reached its zenith fame seemed to quickly vanish. "Examining Florence Austral's life is a little like wandering through a garden maze," wrote biographer James Moffat. "One constantly encounters false starts and dead ends in the form of half truths, evasions, and even the occasional bare-faced lie." Both Austral and various publicists are reputed to have perpetuated these myths and lies.

Born Florence Mary Wilson in Melbourne, Australia, Austral used her stepfather's name, Fawaz, before being urged to take a stage name. Like other Australian divas of the era, the name was derived from her birthplace. To add to the confusion, her birth certificate was reportedly forged using the Fawaz name. The year her birth has been variously given as 1892, 1894, and 1896, with 1894 being the most commonly reported year of birth.

Her childhood and upbringing were apparently a source of embarrassment for Austral. She was born to William Wilson and Helena Mary Harris. Wilson was a Scandinavian-born carpenter who Anglicized his given name of Wilhelm Lindholm after successfully stowing away on an Australian-bound ship in the 1870s. Harris was a partner in a dressmaking firm. The couple married in September 1884. Their first child, Walter Stanley Wilson, was born in July 1885.

Austral's parents divorced in 1895. Wilson maintained custody of his son, while Florence remained in her mother's care. To lessen the stigma of the divorce and maintain her position as a businesswoman, Helena said her husband died. It was a lie then 3-year-old Florence Wilson repeated. According to Moffat, this early lesson in deception reinforced "that if some element of her life displeased her she had only to colour the facts ... and the unpleasant truth would disappear." Her mother remarried to a Syrian clothing manufacturer and devout Methodist, John Fawaz, in 1903.

Austral studied voice in Melbourne but precisely with whom remains in question. Austral was trained as a soprano, mezzo-soprano and contralto. Oddly she maintained throughout her life that she did not hear opera performed until 1919. This claim is questionable as it suggests she never saw Nellie Melba perform. At the time, Melba was the most prominent operatic performer in Australia and was also internationally renown. The two sopranos would later have a bitter rivalry.

Austral won the prestigious South Street Eisteddfod competition in 1913 as a mezzo-soprano. In 1919 she left the country to study with Gabriella Sibella in New York. Although her trip to America was ostensibly to capture the attention of the Metropolitan Opera, when offered a contract at the Met, she did not accept. She auditioned for the Chicago Opera Company during that period, as well.

Instead, she tried her fortunes in London, auditioning for the Grand Opera Syndicate in 1921. Her pieces included "Elisabeth's Greeting" from Wagner's *Tannhauser* and "Ritorna Vincitor" from Verdi's *Aida*. She was promptly given a contract and counseled regarding her professional name. Linking one's stage name to the area of their birth was considered a conceit common among Australian opera stars of the day. It was said to distinguish them from British operatic stars and distinctly announce their origins.

Austral made her debut at Covent Garden with the British National Opera Company May 16, 1922, as Brünnhilde in *Die Walkure/The Valkyrie*. She was reportedly given a standing ovation as well as 11 curtain calls. She would later sing the part in the entire "Ring" cycle and would be forever associated with Wagnerian roles. This is perhaps not terribly odd, given her father's Scandinavian heritage.

"For sheer vocal quality Florence Austral had few equals until Kirsten Flagstad came upon the scene," wrote critic

---

For the Record . . .

Born Florence Mary Wilson, 1892 in Melbourne, Australia; died May 11, 1968, Newcastle, New South Wales, Australia; parents, William Wilson and Helena Mary Harris; stepfather, John Fawaz; married John Amadio, 1925.

Operatic soprano trained in Australia and New York; debuted at London's Covent Garden with the British National Opera Company May 16, 1922, as Brünnhilde in *Die Walkure/The Valkyrie*; associated with Wagnerian roles throughout her career; made American debut in 1925. Recorded for British recording company HMV, 1926-31; diagnosed as having multiple sclerosis, 1930; lost voice during her last performance, 1942; returned to Australia and taught voice and adjudicated vocal competitions throughout 1950s; final radio interview, and diagnosed with breast cancer, 1964.

Cedric Wallis, who was in attendance at the Covent Garden debut. "I shall always remember the quality of Austral's voice. As an instrument in Wagner's orchestral patterns she was of the highest quality; a vocal phenomenon that does not happen very often. Perhaps the critic who summed it up the best was the one who wrote; 'If there is a greater Brünnhilde in the world she has not sung in London.'"

Despite raves following her debut, Austral seemed continually overshadowed by Melba. She made an appearance at Covent Garden during the 1922-23 season after which she pled with the audience to keep opera alive in England and help the "brave little band of singers" in the British National Opera Company. Austral received little but scorn from her countrywoman early in her career. This has been attributed primarily to Melba having injured her voice while attempting to sing Wagner. This became a lifelong frustration to Melba.

"Any Australian soprano who made a name in Wagner, or even seemed likely to, never inspired Melba's affection," according to John Hetherington's *Melba: A Biography*. "In a gala performance one night Melba sang in a scene from *Bohème* in the first half and Austral in a scene from *Aida* in the second half. Next morning Austral was talking with the stage manager when Melba came in." After a polite introduction, Melba pretended not to know Austral.

After some off handed comment, Melba rudely acknowledged her and abruptly walked off. Despite the Wagnerian rivalry, the aging Melba in 1924 said Austral had "one of the wonder voices of the world, especially in Wagner." That Austral was associated with Wagner "to the exclusion of almost all other music, was pretty much her own doing," according to Moffat. "She saw no danger in appearing in Wagner's operas so early in her career, but in the face of her own predilection, she was at least aware of the dangers of typecasting." Certainly Austral performed the works of other composers, including operas and songs by Handel, Richard Strauss, Verdi, Weber, Rossini, and Arthur Sullivan.

In 1924, Austral severed all connection with her family. Austral and her publicists constructed an elaborate facade to project the carefully crafted image they desired. The following year, she married to flautist John Amadeo.

Austral made her American debut in 1925 and toured throughout America in 1926. Cities where she performed included New York, Boston, Los Angeles, Denver and Cleveland. Her experiences in the United States were not pleasant, neither at this time nor during her tutelage by Sibella. Her isolation and failure to understand the culture colored her opinion of the United States.

She was most frequently associated with British opera and had a British recording contract with HMV. Austral recordings for the label span the years from 1926 to 1931. Of her 78-RPM recordings, some were reissued on LP; some of her work appears on compact disc reissues, primarily on compilations. Again, many of these are of Wagner selections.

Austral was acknowledged to be at the peak of her career between 1926 and 1931. "To judge from contemporary accounts," according to *Opera News*, "in her peak years her voice packed a wallop in the theater. She was noted for opulence of tone rather than for fire, nuance or interpretive depth, or for acting." Her voice was said to be "less forceful and more lyrical than that of many Wagnerian dramatic sopranos," according to *The New Grove Dictionary of Opera*. "[S]he maintained a consistent beauty and evenness of tone through the arduous parts."

But in 1929 her fortunes radically changed. She became ill with the flu after a performance at Covent Garden that season and canceled her remaining appearances. Later that year, she was invited to sing at the Berlin State Opera, reportedly the first British opera star to sing Wagner there since World War I. She then became ill again. With looming questions about her health and ability to perform, Austral was sent to a doctor for a comprehensive examination. The diagnosis was vague, but the Berlin State Opera management was convinced Austral could not fulfill her obligations. She was paid and sent home.

Among Austral's few confidantes was Dame Clara Butt, who suggested Austral might have multiple sclerosis (MS). Butt had MS and referred Austral to her physician. He confirmed the lay diagnosis in 1930. Like Butt, Austral was advised to give up her career, however, Austral's engagements extended through 1931. In that era little was known about MS, which was often called Disseminated Sclerosis. Austral kept her condition a secret.

Austral continued performing until 1943, but gave her last professional performance in Australia in 1936. On the eve of World War II, Austral abandoned plans to tour South Africa and instead volunteered with the Entertainment National Service Association in England. Her last BBC broadcast was an October 1942 performance of "The Vesper Hymn."

Her final career performance, the role of the Countess in *The Marriage of Figaro*, brought an embarrassing end to a magnificent career. She endured the humiliation of losing her voice on stage. "Her voice returned shortly after the collapse but her decision never to sing in public again was irrevocable. It was the most dismal and inappropriate of endings to a great career," wrote Moffat. "There would be no farewell performances, no gala send-offs."

Austral spent her final years teaching voice at the Melbourne University Conservatorium and Newcastle Conservatorium. She was also a consultant to the National Theatre for a few seasons in the late 1940s and judged numerous vocal competitions, including some in which the young Joan Sutherland performed. In some circles, Austral is considered the link between Melba and Sutherland.

Austral finally announced publicly that she had MS in April of 1962. Her health deteriorated more markedly after Amadio's death in 1964. After a diagnosis and operation for breast cancer, she moved to Sidney to be cared for by a professional nurse. In March of 1967, she was admitted to a nursing home in Newcastle. She died May 15, 1968 in Newcastle, New South Wales, Australia.

Selected discography

Florence Austral, Rubini, 1983.
Recorded Rarities I, Sanctus.
Ring Des Nibelungen/Ring Motiv, Pearl /Koch.
History of Covent Garden on Record, Pearl Gemm.
Florence Austral, Pearl.

Sources

Books

Burbank, Richard, editor, *Twentieth Century Music*, Facts on File, 1984.
Hetherington, John, *Melba: A Biography*, 1967.
Moffat, James, *Florence Austral: One of the Wonder Voices of the World*, National Library of Australia, 1995.
Mordden, Ethan, *A Guide to Opera Recordings*, Oxford University Press, 1987.
Sabin, Robert, editor, *The International Cyclopedia of Music and Musicians*, Ninth Edition, 1964.
Sadie, Stanley, editor, *The Grove Concise Dictionary of Music*, first edition, 1988.
Sadie, Stanley, editor, *The New Grove Dictionary of Opera*, 1992.

Periodicals

Opera News, April 13, 1996.

—*Linda Dailey Paulson*

Avalon

Christian vocal group

In March of 1999, the members of the Christian vocal group Avalon had every reason to be frazzled. Their third album, *In a Different Light*, was released the day before the Dove Awards — Christian music's equivalent to the Grammys—for which they'd been nominated in six categories; the night before the awards, they taped their first TV special; and one member of the four-person group got married that month. In Christian legend, after long searching for the Holy Grail, King Arthur, at the end of his life, sailed off to a mythical island paradise of Avalon, or Heaven. It may not have been Heaven, but after over 200 performances in 1998 and recording *In a Different Light*, the band needed the break the honeymoon afforded them.

Avalon came together in Nashville in 1995 at the hand of Christian record label Sparrow Records' producer Norman Sinclair. Looking for people who were interested in Christian ministry, as well as people who wanted to work in a group, he found vocalists Nikki Hassman, Jody McBrayer, Michael Passons and Janna Potter to form Avalon. Shortly after coming together, and still a year

Sparrow Media Relations. Reproduced by permission.

For the Record . . .

Members include **Nikki Hassman** (1995-98), vocals; **Jody McBrayer** (born in Tampa, FL), vocals; **Cherie Paliotta** (born in Johnston, RI), (joined, 1998), vocals; **Michael Passons** (born in Yazoo City, MS), vocals; **Janna Potter** (born in Baltimore, MD), vocals.

Group formed in Nashville by Sparrow Records producer Norman Miller, 1995; released debut, *Avalon*, 1996; released *A Maze of Grace*, 1997; "Testify to Love" was number one on the Contemporary Christian Music Update AC Chart for six weeks; Nikki Hassman left band, 1998; released *In A Different Light*, 1999.

Awards: Three Dove Awards, including Pop/Contemporary Song of the Year for "Testify to Love," 1999; two Dove Awards, including New Artist of the Year, 1998; two Christian Research Report awards, including Group of the Year, 1998; two American Songwriter Professional Songwriter Awards, including Artist of the Year and Song of the Year for "Testify to Love," 1998.

Addresses: *Record company*—Sparrow Records, P.O. Box 5085, 101 Winners Circle, Brentwood, TN 37024-5085.

before their first release, the group was a last-minute addition to the successful *Young Messiah Farewell* tour in 1995. The addition was so last-minute that it was too late for their names to be added to the programs, which had already been printed. Although unknown, the group still garnered good responses from audience and other artists. Their debut album, *Avalon*, was released on Sparrow in 1996. The album produced four number one Christian radio singles, including "Give it Up," "This Love," and "Picture Perfect World."

The group's second release, *A Maze of Grace*, in 1997, was a strong follow up to its debut. The single "Testify to Love" was the longest-running number one Christian single of the 1990s. Its success only grew when country star Wynonna selected it to sing on the *Touched by an Angel* soundtrack. One episode of the popular television show was written around the song. In 1998, the song was chosen the number one Song of the Year by Christian Research Report.

After being offered a solo deal with Sony in the spring of 1998, Nikki Hassman amicably left the group. "It wasn't an easy time for Avalon or for Nikki," Janna Potter told *Billboard*, "but she felt going into another area of music was where God was calling her . ... how do you fault somebody for doing what they feel God has called them to do?" Finding Hassman's replacement was no easy feat. After listening to 100 audition tapes, Avalon still had found no one. It was on the recommendation of friends and members of their band that Avalon found Cherie Paliotta — who had no audition tape — to fill the gap in the group. After an informal session around the piano with Paliotta—and an agreement between them to pray about the issue—Avalon knew they'd found their girl. "When it fits, it fits," Janna Potter told *The Tennessean*. Said Paliotta about the change, in the Avalon biography: "It was a big change for me when I came into Avalon, there were days when I didn't think I could get up there and remember one more lyric. But God came through for me in those moments and gave me the courage to anchor on to Him and move forward. And I think that was just the same for the others during the transition."

After pairing Avalon with producer Charlie Peacock for their first two, Sparrow hired Christian super-producer Brown Bannister for its third release. Bannister put the group through its paces, pushing the vocalists to keep recording the same song again and again, even when they thought it was as good as it could get. "Guys, that's great," Cherie Paliotta jokingly imitated Bannister for *The Tennessean*. "Let's try on more take, take 1,175." The band knew the hard work was worth it, and their proof was that they thought was a more R&B-style Avalon pop. "[Bannister] loves texture and harmony," Michael Passons told *New Christian Music Spotlight* in 1999, "and putting those together working in ways to make it truly pop." They also were aware of their producer's history. "I kept thinking, I'm singing for the guy who made Amy Grant famous," Cherie Paliotta told *Billboard* in 1999.

A major break for the group—who'd been on CNN *Headline News* twice, in addition to appearing on more than a dozen morning and syndicated Christian TV programs—was their first TV special, "Avalon Live at the Factory," taped at an old mattress factory the day before the Dove Awards. The next day, they walked away with three 1999 Dove Awards, including one for Pop/Contemporary Song of the Year for "Testify to Love." Amid all the chaos, Jody McBrayer got married.

Ultimately, Avalon wouldn't have minded a cross over into mainstream pop. There is a record of Christian artists making the move and, though their message is Christian, their sound is pure pop. In the 1990s, acts like Kirk Franklin, dc Talk, Bob Carlisle and Jars of Clay each made their marks in the Christian market, but then moved on to the next, more mainstream, level. Their "bubble-gum tendencies" have caused at least one critic to liken them to nineties pop heartthrobs Backstreet Boys, wrote *The Tennessean* in 1999, and their 50/50 coed split have garnered them comparisons to '70s Swedish pop stars Abba. Michael Passons told *New Christian Music Spotlight* in 1999 that the band wasn't out to get a mainstream hit, "But if for some reason pop wanted to play one of our songs…I'd be all for it. Because it would be just more people that would hear the song…. I think it's a tremendous ministry opportunity. I'd be lying if I said it wasn't a career opportunity as well." Cherie Paliotta had a bigger vision: "I really believe in my heart that we're not only going to minister to the Christian market," she told *The Tennessean*. "I truly believe that in my heart, or else I wouldn't be here."

Selected discography

Avalon, Sparrow, 1996.
A Maze of Grace, Sparrow, 1997.
In A Different Light, Sparrow, 1999.

Sources

Periodicals

Billboard, March 13, 1999.
Grand Rapids Press (Michigan), March 15, 1999.
Dallas Morning News, February 6, 1999.
New Christian Music Spotlight, Spring, 1999.
The Tennessean, April 1, 1999.

Online

"Avalon," *All-Media Guide,* http://www.allmusic.com (April 28, 1999).
Avalon Homepage, http://avalonlive.com (May 13, 1999).

Additional information was provided by Sparrow Records publicity materials, 1999.

—*Brenna Sanchez*

Erykah Badu

![separator]

Singer, songwriter

Erykah Badu released her first album, *Baduizm*, in 1997 to a rare degree of popular and critical acclaim. The Brooklyn-based singer/songwriter was hailed as an exceptionally gifted talent who effortlessly fused jazz singing styles of the past with 1990s-style R&B and hip-hop. Her fluent, highly individual vocalizing and spiritually-tinged songwriting were welcomed as something fresh and compelling. Badu's voice drew comparisons with that of Sarah Vaughan, Ella Fitzgerald and, in particular, Billie Holliday. Writing for the online All-Media Guide, John Bush noted that her "languruous, occationally tortured vocals" and "delicate phrasing immediately removed her from the legion of cookie-cutter female R&B singers." In concert, she cultivated a mystical persona that drew upon African and New Age sources for inspiration. "Habitually attired in a long dress, silver bracelets, necklaces and rings, and a head wrap that juts up like a crown, Badu works the stage—lighted by candles and surrounded by incense—like a woman on a mission," wrote Kevin Powell in Rolling Stone.

From Badu's own perspective, her music synthesized a wide range of influences, from jazz artists like Holliday through such R&B figures of the 1960s and 1970s as Marvin Gaye, Stevie Wonder and Chaka Khan. "Everything on the album [*Baduizm*] is a mixture of all those things I heard growing up as a black youth," she told *New York Times* writer Natasha Stovall. Later in the same interview, she stated, "I don't know the rules — what you're supposed to sing or what category you're supposed to be in— so I don't have any. I can't stand for someone to tell me, 'Well, we can't do that'."

Badu benefitted from growing up in a home that nurtured her creativity. Born Erica Wright in Dallas, Texas, she was raised by her mother Kolleen Wright and grandmother, both actresses involved in local theater. They both encouraged Erica to develop her artistic leanings, which included painting, dancing and acting as well as music. "I remember the first time I was in a show," she told the *New York Times.* "I was in the first grade. It was a Christmas play, and I sang 'Somebody Snitched On Me.' That's when I knew I could *command* the stage."

At age 14, she tried her hand at freestyle-rapping for a local radio station, KNON. After being accepted at Dallas' arts magnet high school, she gained notoriety as half of a female rap crew under the name MC Apples. "We were even better than a lot of the guy groups," Badu told *Rolling Stone.* "Shoot, I'm always going to be a freestyle fool. Rap is like the jazz of Billie Holiday's day." It was during her high school years that she decided to discard her "slave name." She changed the spelling of her first name to Erykah, which contained the Egyptian word "kah," meaning "inner light" or "inner self." Later, she

For the Record . . .

Born Erica Wright, February 26, 1972 (some sources say 1971) in Dallas, TX.

Formed duo Erykah Free with cousin Robert "Free" Bradford c. 1993; signed with Universal/Kedar Entertainment as solo artist, recorded duet "Your Precious Love" with singer D'Angelo in 1996; released albums *Baduizm* and *Live* in 1997; appeared in the film *Blues Brothers 2000*, 1998.

Awards: Grammy Awards for Best R&B Album and Best Female R&B Performance, 1998.

Addresses: *Record company*—Universal Records, 1755 Broadway, 7th Floor, New York, NY 10019.

changed her surname as well, taking "Badu" from a favorite scat-singing phrase. She subsequently learned that "badu" means "to manifest light and truth" in Arabic.

After high school, Badu enrolled at Louisiana's Grambling State University as a theater student. Before completing her studies, she returned to Dallas in 1993 and supported herself as a waitress and dance instructor while pursuing a music career. She initially formed a hip-hop duo called Erykah Free with her cousin, Robert "Free" Bradford. The pair soon earned local opening slots for such touring acts as the Wu-Tang Clan, D'Angelo, A Tribe Called Quest, Arrested Development and Mobb Deep, among others. Several recording offers followed, but the one Badu ultimately accepted from Kedar Entertainment was for her alone. Although Bradford eventually received production and songwriting credits on *Baduizm*, his relations with Badu became unavoidably strained. Badu relocated to Brooklyn after her recording deal with the Universal Records distributed label Kedar Entertainment was secure. Label founder Kedar Massenberg began promoting her by distributing advance copies of her recordings at the 1996 Soul Train Music Awards. He arranged for Badu to record a remake of the Marvin Gaye/Tammi Terrell duet "Your Precious Love" with R&B singer D'Angelo for the soundtrack to the 1997 film *High School High*. Her first single, the sensual, hypnotic "On & On," was released in January, 1998 and quickly became a number 12 pop hit. A month later, *Baduizm* appeared, rising to number two on the pop album charts and eventually topping the triple-platinum sales mark. An outstanding debut effort, the album was co-produced by the Roots, a hip-hop duo, and featured such stellar session players as jazz bassist Ron Carter. "On & On" was followed up by "Next Lifetime," which also became a hit.

Making the most of her career momentum, Badu received praise as the co-director of videos for "On & On" and "Next Lifetime," the latter featuring her mother, brother and grandmother as extras. She dabbled in acting by appearing in a September 1997 episode of ABC-TV's *One Life To Live* and portraying a jazz-singing Creole sorceress in the 1998 film *Blues Brothers 2000*. During the summer of 1997, she joined forces with funk pioneer George Clinton and hip-stars Cypress Hill, the Pharcyde and Outkast on the Smokin' Grooves Tour across the U.S. That fall, Badu released her *Live* album, which featured her in an intimate concert setting with a three-piece band and a trio of background singers. In addition to live versions of songs found on *Baduizm*, the album included the new tune "Tyrone," a scathing portrait of a soon-to-be-former boyfriend set to a slow-burning beat. *Live* also featured Badu's covers of songs by her R&B forerunners, including Chaka Khan's "Stay."

Badu was honored in 1998 with Grammy Awards for Best R&B Album and Best Female R&B Performance. She spent the summer of that year on tour with Lillith Fair, the all-female concert series launched by singer Sarah McLachlan. In the midst of all this activity, she also found time for a personal life with Outkast member Andre "Dre" Benjamin and their son, Seven, born in November of 1997. (The child's name was chosen because seven is a prime number.)

With two acclaimed albums behind her, Badu established herself as a major artist with no end to her success in sight. In interviews, she balanced self-confidence with a sense of her overall role in pop music. "It's a blessing, really," she told *Billboard*'s Shawnee Smith as *Baduizm* began its ascent up the charts. "I can't take all the credit for it. It's my energy and my voice, but it was a team effort. I'm just a midwife aiding in the rebirthing process of music."

Selected discography

Baduizm, Kedar Entertainment/Universal, 1997.
Live, Kedar Entertainment/Universal, 1997.

Sources

Books

Larkin, Colin, editor, *The Encyclopedia of Popular Music*, Muze, 1998.

Periodicals

Billboard, March 15, 1997.
New York Times, April 6, 1997.
Rolling Stone, February 20, 1997; March 20, 1997.

Online

"Erykah Badu," *All-Music Guide*, http://www.allmusic.com
    (May 21, 1999).
Erykah Badu Biography," *Rolling Stone Network*, http://
    www.rollingstone.com (March 13, 1999).
"Erykah Badu," *Wall Of Sound*,http://wallofsound.go.com
    (May 21, 1999).

—*Barry Alfonso*

Mandy Barnett

Singer

Tennessee-born Mandy Barnett has earned a rare degree of acclaim for her compelling, sophisticated voice and ability to interpret classic country material. Her smooth yet powerful singing style has been compared to that of country legend Patsy Cline, whom Barnett portrayed on stage for two years. The glowing reviews that Barnett has received have not translated into impressive record sales, due in part to her unwillingness to dilute her brand of country balladry to meet commercial standards.

Barnett's affinity for music was displayed at an early age. Growing up in Crossville, Tennessee, she was introduced by her mother and grandmother to pop and jazz stylists like Sarah Vaughn, Ella Fitzgerald, as well as country singers like Ray Price and Webb Pierce. She first began singing gospel in church, then started performing at talent shows and nightclubs under her mother's supervision. At age 12, she won a talent contest at East Tennessee's Dollywood theme park. This earned her a spot on *The Ernest Tubb Midnight Jamboree* radio program, which in turn led to an appearance at Nashville's renowned Grand Ole Opry.

Two years later, Barnett signed a recording contract with Capitol Records and began an ultimately frustrating six-year relationship with the label. Various producers tried to push her in a more contemporary country-pop direction, which Barnett resisted. "I think they were trying to turn me into a Wynonna type," she told *USA Today* after leaving the label. "I was listening to some stuff [from her Capitol sessions] the other day, and there's all this stuff where I'm just growling. It's almost rock 'n' roll." Capitol failed to complete an album to their satisfaction, and Barnett was dropped from their artist roster after she turned 18.

A year passed before Barnett made her real career breakthrough. A friend suggested she audition for the lead role in *Always...Patsy Cline*, a theatrical production to be staged at the Ryman Auditorium in downtown Nashville. "There were 450 people, and I was the only one who wasn't wearing a vintage cocktail dress," she recalled in an interview with Michael McCall for the *Nashville Scene*. "I was 109th in line. Everyone else sang 'Crazy' or 'I Fall To Pieces' or 'Walkin' After Midnight.' I figured they were sick of hearing those songs, so I chose 'Someday You'll Want Me To Want You,' because it was one of her obscure songs."

Barnett got the role and went on to star in *Always...Patsy Cline*, singing the songs Cline made famous while dressed in a wig and cowgirl suit. The musical enjoyed a two-year run to sell-out crowds, and sparked interest enough interest in Barnett to secure her a new contract with Asylum Records in 1996. That same year, Asylum

For the Record . . .

Born September 28, 1975 in Crossville, TN.

Performed at Grand Ole Opry, 1987; signed with Capitol Records, 1989; left Capitol, began two-year engagement as star of stage production *Always...Patsy Cline*, 1994; signed with Asylum, released *Mandy Barnett*, 1996; signed with Sire, began work with producer Owen Bradley, 1997; released *I've Got A Right To Cry*, 1999.

Addresses: *Record company*—Sire Records, 936 Broadway, New York, NY 10010. *Management*—Dan Cleary Management Associates, 1801 Avenue Of The Stars, Suite 1105, Los Angeles, CA 90067.

released *Mandy Barnett*, a song collection that attempted to balance the singer's natural style with current country hit standards. One of its songs, "Now That's All Right With Me," gained some airplay as a single, but the album proved a sales disappointment. Barnett began to feel pressured to conform to the country market, and she parted company with Asylum before a second album was recorded.

Things took a turn for the better when Barnett attracted the interest of record executive Seymour Stein, who was then in the process of reactivating his Sire label. Among other credits, Stein had been instrumental in launching the careers of Madonna, the Pretenders, Talking Heads and k.d. lang. He and Barnett met while she was recording three songs for the film *Traveller*. Stein was impressed enough to sign her to Sire.

An even more important association began when Barnett convinced veteran country music producer Owen Bradley to work with her. The pairing was a natural one, as Bradley was most famous as Patsy Cline's mentor and producer. In addition, he had produced hits for Ernest Tubb, Brenda Lee, Loretta Lynn, Conway Twitty and many other country stars of the 1950s and 1960s. At 81, he had long since retired from the music industry when Barnett approached him. Bradley agreed to producer her provided that he had a free hand in the studio. Stein agreed, and work on the album eventually titled *I've Got A Right To Cry* began.

Each week for nearly a year, Barnett and Bradley worked closely together searching out songs and working up arrangements. "Owen spent a lot of time trying to figure me out," Barnett told *No Depression*'s Bill Friskics-Warren. "And not just looking for songs for the record, but talking and sitting around playing and singing songs that we liked.... he learned very quickly that I liked ballads with a lot of range—songs that say things that pull at your heartstrings or make you sadder, songs that evoke some sort of emotion." Bradley had completed a four-song recording session with Barnett before his death on January 7, 1998. It was left to his brother Harold and nephew Bobby to complete the album, guided by notes that Owen had left behind. Continuing on was difficult at first, but the remaining sessions were finished to everyone's satisfaction.

Released in 1999, *I've Got A Right To Cry* placed Barnett's voice in the sophisticated country setting that Bradley had created for Cline nearly 40 years earlier. Her sure vocal touch on bittersweet ballads like "Mistakes" and the album's title song came through convincingly. Other tunes, such as "Give Myself A Party" and "Falling, Falling, Falling," were in an upbeat vein, but also effective. Critics debated whether the album was in step with the more rock-influenced country styles of the 1990s. But critical praise was widespread nonetheless. "More timeless than retro, this is an album that closet country fans can play without shame and pop purists should go out of their way to discover," wrote Andrew Boorstyn in *Interview*.

As a live performer, Barnett won similarly high marks. Reviewing her appearance at Madison Square Garden as part of a Women In Music concert, critic Jon Pareles wrote in the *New York Times*, "Ms. Barnett had the vocal finesse: the husky dives, the controlled slides and the timing to make her voice break just as she confessed 'I don't know what to do.' Surrounded by showboating, she made understatement persuasive."

I've Got A Right To Cry indicated to many that the 23 year-old Barnett had a long and rewarding career ahead of her. Though the "classic country" label seemed to confine her, she expressed the desire to go beyond easy categories. "Just because you pay homage to something doesn't mean that it's retro," she told *No Depression*. "Owen always told me that there are only two kinds of music: good and bad."

Selected discography

Mandy Barnett (includes "Now That's All Right With Me"), Asylum, 1996.
I've Got A Right To Cry, Sire, 1999.

Sources

Billboard, April 17, 1999.
Interview, April 1999.
Nashville Scene, May 13, 1999.
Nashville Tennessean, January 29, 1999.
Newsweek, April 19, 1999.
No Depression, May-June 1999.
USA Today, April 16, 1999.

Additional information was provided by Sire publicity materials, 1999.

—*Barry Alfonso*

Bill Wyman & the Rhythm Kings

Blues band

The British blues band Bill Wyman & the Rhythm Kings is an assemblage of some of the greatest names of 1960s and 1970s rock and roll. The Rhythm Kings was the brainchild of long-time Rolling Stones bassist Bill Wyman, who produced much of the band's material and provided continuity and structure for the group. The band's line up, though constantly changing, included Beverley Skeete on guitar and vocals, Gary Brooker on keyboards, and vocalist Georgie Fame. Cameo appearances from artists such as Peter Frampton and Eric Clapton added to the band's roll call of great rock and roll talent. The band signed with Velvel records and released two albums beginning in 1997, and toured between recording sessions.

Rhythm Kings leader Bill Wyman grew up in war-torn Europe, in one of the tougher neighborhoods of London's southeast side. He was born William George Perks, Jr. on October 24, 1936 in Lewisham Hospital in London. Wyman was the eldest of six children of Kathleen May "Molly" and William Perks, Sr. His father was a bricklayer by trade, who worked very hard to support his large

Photo by C. Roy Tee. AP/Wide World Photos. Reproduced by permission.

For the Record . . .

Members include **Bill Wyman** (born William George Perks, Jr., on October 24, 1936 in London, England), bass, keyboards; **Gary Brooker** (born on May 29, 1949), keyboards; **Georgie Fame** (born Clive Powell in Lancashire, England on June 26, 1943), vocals; **Beverley Skeete**, vocals.

Formed in 1997 by Bill Wyman; contracted with Velvel Records to record a trilogy of albums, including *Struttin' Our Stuff* in 1998, and *Anyway the Wind Blows* in 1999; toured Europe in 1999.

Addresses: *Management*—Ripple Productions Ltd., 344 Kings Road, London, SW3 5UR, England.

family. For Wyman, childhood was an eventful stream of childish pranks intermingled with the terror of German air raids, the distress of poverty, cramped living quarters, and childhood diseases. In spite of the hard times caused by the Great Depression and World War II, Wyman's parents stayed attentive to their children and supervised the brood under a watchful eye. The Perks children received strict discipline and were raised with a strong sense of morality; none of them were spoiled or indulged. Wyman and his siblings regarded simple treats like chewing gum and a glass of lemonade among the finest of pleasures during their formative years.

In1941 after the Japanese attack on Pearl Harbor, Wyman's father joined the British army and was stationed in Norwich. He sent the family to live near his in-laws' home in Penge. From time to time as a youngster Wyman lived at the residence of his maternal grandmother, Flora Jeffery. These intermittent stays at his grandparents' home were in part to ease the burden on his parents who were overwhelmed by their large family. In part Wyman stayed because of problems at school, which he generally disliked despite his high intelligence. It was from his grandmother that Wyman learned basic reading and math skills. It was with further assistance from his grandparents that Wyman took piano lessons and became involved in singing in the choir at the Holy Trinity Church near his grandmother's home.

His antipathy for academics notwithstanding, in September of 1947 Wyman received a scholarship to the Beckenham and Penge Grammar School, an honor that proved bittersweet for him because he spoke with a thick cockney accent and otherwise failed to fit into the elite student body at the prestigious school. He became trapped between two worlds—his family and friends admonished him not to become a snob, while his new friends and teachers at school kept him under continual derision for what were considered to be low-class ways. Just after 1950, only two months before what would have been the end of Wyman's curriculum, his father pulled the boy from school and sent him to work due to the family's dwindling economic resources. Wyman took his first job, with a bet-maker, until January of 1955 when he received a draft notice from the Royal Air Force (RAF). It was in the service, while stationed at Oldenburg, that Wyman developed a close camaraderie with an RAF cohort named Lee Whyman, who would eventually become the namesake for William Perks, Jr.

Wyman first began to pay attention to popular music as a youngster, and by 1950 he was very conscious of each new artist that came to the forefront, from Bing Crosby and Nat King Cole, to Jerry Lee Lewis and Elvis Presely. Wyman eagerly welcomed the inauguration of the British pop chart in 1953 and bought himself a record player in July of that year. Four years later, while serving in the RAF, Wyman bought himself an acoustic guitar and began to recruit a band. His first combo was a skiffle group. After two years of military service Wyman worked for a meat importer and then as a storekeeper. For social life he frequented dance halls and ballrooms, where eventually he met his future wife, Diane Maureen Cory. The couple married on October 24, 1959, Wyman's 23rd birthday. In 1960 Wyman bought a Burns electric guitar and started up another group which eventually became known as the Cliftons. Soon afterward he switched to bass guitar. Slowly the Cliftons dissolved, and its members went on to play with other bands.

Diane and Bill Wyman's son, Stephen Paul Wyman, was born on March 29, 1962, just months before Wyman embarked on one of the most unique adventures in the history of rock and roll. In December of 1962 Wyman was invited by a musician friend to meet a band called the Rollin' Stones, a blues group in need of a bass player. Wyman met the band, but found that he was a clean-cut contrast to the scruffy Rollin' Stones. He and the band were in fact mutually disinterested in each other until the Stones got a look at Wyman's powerful amplifiers and other sound gear. According to rock and roll legend, good sound gear was a commodity so prized that the band accepted Wyman into the group because they liked his amplifiers. Wyman played his first gig with the Rollin'

Stones on December 15, 1962. The band changed its name to Rolling Stones in 1963, and in 1964 Wyman changed his name legally from William George Perks, Jr., to William George Wyman, in honor of his friend Lee Whyman from the military. Around that same time Wyman, who was considerably older than most of the other members of the band, shaved five years off his age for publicity purposes, by adopting a birth date of October 24, 1941. For the next 30 years Wyman played as a member of one of the most famous and controversial rock-and-roll bands in history.

Wyman released a number of solo albums during his years with the Rolling Stones, including *Monkey Grip* in 1974 and *Stone Alone* in 1976. He starred in the movies *Sympathy for the Devil* and *Gimme Shelter,* both in 1970, and he published his memoirs in an autobiography called *Stone Alone* with Ray Coleman in 1990. Additionally Wyman dabbled as a restaurateur, an author, and a student of archaeology and medieval history. When Wyman left the Stones in 1993 he was already the owner of Ripple Records, Ripple Music, Ripple Publications, and Ripple Productions.

Apart from a string of marriages and other questionable shenanigans, Wyman retained a generally conservative lifestyle in comparison to his fellow Rolling Stones. He divorced his first wife in 1969 and remarried amid a flurry of scandal, in June of 1989 to Mandy Smith, a fashion model and a singer whom he first dated when she was only 13 years old. Wyman and Smith spent only five days together. They separated in May of 1990 and divorced in 1991. In 1993 Wyman married his third wife, ex-model Suzanne Accosta.

Wyman left the Rolling Stones in 1993, and in 1997 he formed Bill Wyman and the Rhythm Kings. The members of the Rhythm Kings typically varied between one performance and the next, but always included a collection of the biggest names in rock and roll and R&B. Rhythm Kings royalty includes keyboard artist Gary Brooker, former Rolling Stones guitarist Mick Taylor, the late pianist Nicky Hopkins, former Squeeze vocalist Paul Carrack, and blues artist Beverley Skeete. Rock legends Eric Clapton and Peter Frampton performed on Rhythm Kings recordings. The band released two albums; *Struttin' Our Stuff* in 1998 and *Anyway the Wind Blows* in 1999, both on Velvel.

Keyboard player Gary Brooker, formerly of Procol Harum, was born on May 29, 1949. Brooker, a founding member of Procol Harum, was raised in a middle class family in London, the son of a musician. Brooker took piano lessons as a child and went away to school as a teenager to study classical composition. During the course of his education he experimented with modern, jazz-related musical styles including boogie-woogie. In 1966 Brooker met Keith Reid through a mutual friend who recognized the possibility that the two musicians might collaborate, which they did. The two wrote songs together—Brooker wrote the music while Reid wrote the lyrics. Eventually Denny Cordell, who managed Joe Cocker, produced Brooker and Reid's songs as played by Brooker's band Procol Harum. Procol Harum peaked in the late 1960s and early 1970s following such chart-topping hits as "A Whiter Shade of Pale" in 1967.

Rhythm Kings vocalist Georgie Fame was born Clive Powell in Leigh (Lancashire), England on June 26, 1943. Fame was the son of a cotton spinner who played and sang as a hobby. Fame himself sang in the church choir in grade school and was a self-taught piano player. Fame began to play the piano professionally in his late teens at a London ballroom, but his show business "break" came when *Oliver* composer Lionel Bart discovered Fame and referred him to British music producer Larry Parnes. Parnes changed Clive Powell's name to Georgie Fame and used the teenager as a backup musician with assorted bands, until 1961. Fame appeared on the popular television shows, "Hullabaloo" and "Shindig," and toured with the Tamla Motown Review in 1965. Fame is accompanied on Rhythm Kings vocals by English blues singer Beverley Skeete.

Several of rock music's most famous guitarists have recorded with the Rhythm Kings including Wyman's former Rolling Stones mate, Mick Taylor, Eric Clapton, Peter Frampton, and Albert Lee. Intermittent contributors on drums include Procol Harum veteran Graham Broad. Broad, along with percussionist Ray Cooper added spice to the first Rhythm Kings recording, *Struttin' Our Stuff*, in 1998. Other Rhythm Kings contributors include Chris Rea, who was professionally involved with Wyman on more than one occasion prior to the formation of the Rhythm Kings; ex-Squeeze vocalist, Paul Carrack, and guitarist Terry "Tex" Taylor. The Rhythm Kings' album, *Anyway the Wind Blows,* secured a slot in the top five jazz-blues album chart in England.

Selected discography

Albums

Struttin' Our Stuff, Velvel, 1998.
Anyway the Wind Blows, Velvel (released in Europe), 1999.

Sources

Books

Wyman, Bill, with Ray Coleman, *Stone Alone: the Story of a rock 'n' Roll Band,* Viking, 1990.

Stambler, *Encyclopedia of Pop, Rock and Soul,* St. Martin's Press, New York, 1974.

Periodicals

Entertainment, April 28, 1995, p. 14.

Independent on Sunday, October 19, 1997.

London Free Press, February 18, 1999.

Newsday, March 1, 1998, p. D21.

People, March 8, 1999.

Time, December 3, 1990, p. 123; April 12, 1993, p. 81.

Online

"All-Music Guide," *All-Media Guide,* http://www.allmusic.com (June 29, 1999).

"Graham 'the' Broad," http://www.procolharum.com/ procolgrb.htm (June 29, 1999).

—*Gloria Cooksey*

Chris Blackwell

Record label founder

Chris Blackwell may have come across as a laid-back businessman enjoying the good life in the Caribbean, but as *Rolling Stone* wrote in 1999, he was "responsible for the most important music of the last forty years." Founder of Island Records and Palm Pictures, Blackwell nurtured and promoted the careers of a diverse group of artists including Bob Marley, Roxy Music, Steve Winwood, U2, Inner Circle, and The Cranberries. He also brought reggae music to international attention during his tenure at the helm of Island.

Born in London to an Irish father and Jamaican mother in 1937, Blackwell spent his early years in Jamaica, from the age of six months. His mother, Blanche Lindo, was part of the Jamaican aristocracy who traced their roots in Jamaica back to the late 1600s. The Blackwells socialized with a crowd that included actor Errol Flynn and authors Noel Coward and Ian Fleming.

Blackwell returned to England to be educated after repeatedly missing school due to childhood asthma. There he attended private school, but was asked at 17 to leave for trafficking cigarettes and liquor to fellow students. Blackwell then embarked a checkered career that included gambling, teaching water skiing, and working as location manager on the first James Bond film, *Dr. No*.

Trips to the United States to visit his father and stepmother changed Blackwell's life. It was here, in the jazz clubs of Chicago and New York, that his passion for music was sparked. Upon returning to Jamaica, he heard a jazz ensemble in Montego Bay that he wanted to record. *Lance Hayward at the Half Moon* was released in 1959 and became the first Island Records release.

In 1960, Blackwell opened an office in Kingston, Jamaica and recorded two consecutive hit songs. Within two years he would produced 26 singles. Eventually, Island releases were selling well on another island—the United Kingdom. Blackwell chose to move his company's headquarters to London in 1962, the same year Jamaica gained its independence. From that period through the mid-1960s Island's main focused was on Ska, a new Jamaican music that found acceptance among London's Mod teen subculture.

It was also during this period that Blackwell and two other producers formed BPR Music to concentrate on pop music. He discovered 15-year-old Jamaican singer Millie Small and brought her to England in 1963 to record "My Boy Lollipop." Blackwell felt that the popularity this record would generate would far outpace the fledgling company's ability to keep up with sales. Thus, he licensed the song to Fontana and sure enough, six million records were sold worldwide in 1964, marking his entry into the mainstream pop music business.

Soon after, Blackwell discovered another teen sensation at a London nightclub. The Spencer Davis Group, fronted by young Stevie Winwood, was immediately signed by Blackwell and licensed to Fontana as well. They soon had a hit with "Keep On Running," and followed with "Gimme Some Lovin'" and "I'm a Man."

The Spencer Davis Group broke up, but Winwood formed a new group—Traffic. The band debut release, *Mr. Fantasy* was Island's entry into rock music in 1967. Soon, the company added other rock artists and groups including Free, Emerson Lake & Palmer, Mott The Hoople, Jethro Tull, Cat Stevens, and Robert Palmer. Island also entered the British folk rock genre with a roster including Sandy Denny, Richard Thompson, and Nick Drake.

In the 1970s Island inked to a contract a group that continues to influence music: Bob Marley & The Wailers. Marley's group brought reggae and Rastafari, a Jamaican music form and a black religion tied to the back-to-Africa movement, to mainstream attention. "Bob Marley was a gamble," Blackwell told Nigel Williamson of the *Los Angeles Times Magazine*. "I gave him £4,000 upfront to make the first album. Everybody said I was mad and I'd never see the money again. I took the risk and trusted him and it paid off many times over." Bob

Born June 22, 1937 in London, England; son of Middleton Joseph and Blanche Lindo Blackwell; immigrated to Jamaica at six months; returned to England to attend school; children: two; grandchildren: one.

Formed Island Records in 1959, which would propel reggae music to international attention; moved to UK, 1962; discovered Minnie Small's "My Boy Lollipop;" became first ska hit, 1963; diversified roster with rock groups such as Traffic, Spooky Tooth and Jethro Tull, 1970s; scored rock hits with Cat Stevens and Roxy Music; and introduced Bob Marley & The Wailers to the world, 1980s; scored additional success with groups and artists including U2, Steve Winwood, Robert Palmer and Grace Jones; entered film industry, and produced hits including Kiss of the Spiderwoman and Mona Lisa; sold label to PolyGram for $300 million, and continued to head company, 1989; formed hotel and resort company Island Outpost, 1991; 1990s: left PolyGram's Island Entertainment Group, 1997; formed Islandlife, 1998.

Addresses: *Office*—Palm Pictures, Four Columbus Circle, Fifth Floor, New York, NY 10019.

Marley & The Wailers released *Catch a Fire* in 1972. The group toured the United Kingdom and United States in support of the album.

It was also his association with Marley that caused Blackwell to lend financial support to the film *The Harder They Come*, which starred reggae artist Jimmy Cliff. Through these relationships, he was attracted to other Jamaican reggae groups including Toots and the Maytals, Burning Spear, and Inner Circle. The Mango subsidiary was formed in 1973 by Blackwell solely to promote Jamaican music in the United States.

Although Blackwell and Island Records would become legendary for exporting reggae from Jamaica to the rest of the world, his part in this export would come into question. Was Blackwell, a white Jamaican, continuing a traditional of black exploitation? Blackwell, himself, was acutely aware of racial and class differences. As a child, he reportedly saw a servant chastised for breaking some trinket. "I didn't like the ruling society of Jamaica, didn't relate to it," he told *Conde Nast Traveler*. "And I didn't want to be part of it."

That resolve continued into his adulthood. According to a 1999 account in *Rolling Stone*, when returning to Jamaica with Millie Small in the 1960s following a world tour, he accompanied her to her family home in Kingston, Joe Boyd recounted that Small's mother came to the door, then bowed to Blackwell as she backed away. "At that point,' says Boyd, echoing Blackwell's embarrassment, 'Chris realized he wasn't a genius but an idiot'."

Blackwell's relationship with Marley was a different story, though. According to an interview with Marley republished in *Reggae, Rasta, Revolution: Jamaican Music From Ska to Dub*, their relationship was strictly business. "Chris Blackwell didn't help me," Marley had told *Melody Maker*. "I had to work *hard* while Blackwell flew out and enjoyed himself. But he had the contacts at the time that we felt we needed, and perhaps we did. But Blackwell did a lot for himself. I remember a time when he had nineteen Jamaican acts signed, and before my days he wouldn't touch one." Marley did record 10 albums on Island Records, each one of them gold, including *Rastaman Vibrations* and *Uprising*.

After Marley's death, producer Lee "Scratch" Perry, "swore that Island Head Chris Blackwell was a vampire and responsible for Bob Marley's death," according to another article re-published in *Reggae, Rasta, Revolution: Jamaican Music From Ska to Dub*. These comments severed his relationship with the label.

Another reggae producer held a contrary opinion of Blackwell. Bunny Lee said, "Chris Blackwell [made] all the other companies get involved, after he [made] Bob Marley a star." Blackwell's relationship with Marley continues. After his death, Blackwell formed Blue Mountain Music to oversee the rights to Marley's considerable musical heritage. According to a 1999 *Rolling Stone* article, attorneys for Marley's widow Rita reported she was pleased with their sometimes-tenuous relationship.

Another important signing for Blackwell and Island in the 1970s was Roxy Music, adding another groundbreaking group to the label's roster. The group is credited as the first "glam rock" band. This subspecies of rock was noted for flashy on-stage attire—which included sequined costumes and outrageous makeup—as much as for it's unique sound.

The 1980s were no different than the 1970s for Blackwell. Island signed new artists who were continually reached new heights of popularity while simultaneously producing great music. These included recordings by reggae artists Gregory Isaacs, Sly & Robbie, and Black Uhuru. Rock continued to be a successful genre for Island Records throughout the 1980s, as well. Among the groups signed early in the decade was the Irish band U2, who had previously been rejected by every major label in the UK. By 1987, U2 was atop the world with its universally hailed recording *The Joshua Tree*. 1986 was another watershed year for Island rock artists. Winwood's album *Back in the High Life* reached number one, and Palmer's "Addicted to Love" was the number one single. Other artists to achieve plaudits during this period were Tom Waits—whose albums *Swordfishtrombones, Rain Dogs,* and *Bone Machine,* were critically praised—and Grace Jones.

Island Alive, Blackwell's film production subsidiary, mirrored the success of Island Records. In the 1980s the company produced and distributed Academy Award-recognized films such as *Kiss of the Spiderwoman, The Trip to Bountiful, Mona Lisa* and *Dark Eyes*. In 1989, Blackwell sold Island Records to PolyGram for $300 million. Blackwell decided to stay at the helm of his companies, which was renamed Island Entertainment Group.

Blackwell diversified his business interests further in the 1990s with the creation of a hotel and resort company called Island Outpost. In 1999, the company had seven hotels in Miami's South Beach district and six Caribbean resorts, including Pink Sands, Strawberry Hill. Among Blackwell's numerous holdings was Goldeneye, the house built by author Ian Fleming—the house where he had written the James Bond novels.

Blackwell left PolyGram in November of 1997 amid reports published in *Billboard* and the *Los Angeles Times* that he was "unhappy with his working relationship" with president and CEO Alain Levy. *The Los Angeles Times Magazine* said inappropriate racial comments by a PolyGram executive were in large part to blame for the irreconcilable differences between Blackwell and Poly-Gram management. *Rolling Stone,* in 1999, attributed it to a "mixture of corporate interference and apathy" that caused his departure "in a flurry of faxes." Blackwell is reported to have given million-dollar "surprise presents" to several people upon his departure.

Blackwell then formed Islandlife, an umbrella company for the Island Outpost properties and new entertainment-related businesses, staffed with many people who worked with Blackwell at Island Records. Even after more than 35 years of discovering and nurturing new musical talent, slowing down, it seemed, was not an option. "I don't live the life of somebody who figures out who they are going to have lunch with, going to cocktail parties and the theatre, he told *Rolling Stone* in 1999. "I just like causing things to happen and chasing ideas I'm excited about."

Sources

Books

Barnard, Stephen, *The Encyclopedia of Rock,* Macdonald & Co. Ltd., 1987
Potash, Chris, editor, *Reggae, Rasta, Revolution: Jamaican Music From Ska to Dub*, Schirmer Books, 1997.

Periodicals

Billboard, November 15, 1997; May 16, 1998.
Conde Nast Traveler, January 1996.
Los Angeles Times Magazine, ND.
Music Business International, October 1998.
Pulse! April 1999.
Rolling Stone, February 18, 1999.
Screen International, July 31, 1998.
Travel & Leisure, October 1997.

Additional information provided by liner notes for *Island 40th Anniversary: Vol. 5 * 1972-1995 * Reggae Roots*, Palm Pictures and Islandlife publicity materials, 1999.

—*Linda Dailey Paulson*

Pierre Boulez

Conductor, composer

Photo by Bernard Gotfryd. Archive Photos, Inc. Reproduced by permission.

Modernist conductor and composer Pierre Boulez jolted the world of classical music into the twentieth century with his sophisticated compositions and his presentations of both early and modern classics. For over 50 years, Boulez founded, co-conducted, and directed world-class musical organizations on two continents. Boulez is a recipient of many honors, including Commander of the British Empire, and a member of the Order of Merit of the Federal Republic of Germany. He holds a fistful of honorary doctorate degrees along with a Nobel Prize for Music. The recipient of 19 Grammy Awards and a host of other honors, Boulez distinguished himself as the composer of over two dozen major works of modern music. He possessed the poise and confidence prerequisite to the creation of new artistic genres.

A student of Messiaen and Leiowitz, and an admirer of Mondrian and Klee, Boulez flashed his modernist approach and affirmed his rejection of all things past. He personally likened his musical styles to a severed umbilical chord, yet for his modernist character Boulez remained always a slave to theory. Nothing in his style discounted structure. He is in fact widely acknowledged for the extensive organization displayed in the rhythms, dynamics, and other aspects of his music, which is further characterized by his use of clusters and extremes of register. His *Pli selon Pli and Structures* clearly display those particular characteristics of Boulez. At times controversial and, by his own admission, not always easy to listen to, Boulez established for himself a position of respect and authority at major concert halls and opera houses worldwide. He further earned recognition as the author of five French publications on the subject of contemporary music.

Pierre Boulez was born on March 26, 1925 in Montbrison in France, the son of Léon Boulez and Marcelle Calabre. In 1942, Boulez moved to Paris, where he enrolled at the Paris Conservatory (Conservatoire) in 1944. He studied under Olivier Messiaen, graduated in 1945, and went on to study privately with Andrée Vaurabourg-Honegger. In 1946, Boulez studied classic 12-tone technique under the guidance of René Leibowitz. As a student and afterward, Boulez assigned a great deal of admiration to modern artists of many disciplines, including Mondrian, Klee, Becket, and Joyce. Musically his favorites included Messiaen, Debussy, and Stravinsky; and Boulez freely acknowledged their influence upon art his art.

Professional Career

In 1946 at age 21, Boulez assumed a position as the music director of the Jean-Louis Barrault Theater Company. He remained in that capacity for ten years, during

for its modern repertoire and presentations. Marigny evolved over time to be called the Domaine Musical of Paris, a leading presenter of French avant-garde music. Boulez came to international prominence in 1955 with a composition called *Le Marteau sans Maître*. The chamber work, which Boulez revised in 1957 received praise from critics and musicians worldwide. Stravinsky lauded the work as a superlative example of modern composition.

In time Boulez came to appreciate the great artistic power of the orchestral conductor, at which point his career soared rapidly. He earned praise for his credible interpretations of the works of the Second Viennese School, including such composers as Schoenberg, Berg, and Webern. He earned further acclaim for his operatic productions, which encompassed works by Wagner, Mahler, Debussy, Ravel, Bartók, and Stravinsky. Boulez was invited in 1959 by Southwest German Radio to move to Baden-Baden where he conducted the *Südwestfunk* throughout the 1960s. During that decade his stature as a conductor took him beyond the confines of Germany and throughout Europe, where he conducted orchestras in London, Amsterdam, and Rome. He led orchestral festivals throughout Germany and taught at both Darmstadt and Basel. From 1962-63 he spent time as a visiting professor at Harvard University. He accepted a position as a professor at the Collège de France in 1976.

Cleveland and Los Angeles Orchestras

In March of 1965, Boulez spent time in Cleveland at the invitation of the Cleveland Orchestra's renowned conductor, George Szell. There, Boulez led the Cleveland Orchestra in the performance of his own composition, *Figure-Double-Prisme*, for the first time in the United States. Boulez's relationship with the Cleveland Orchestra, as with many world class groups, endured for decades. Together he and the Cleveland Orchestra taped award winning recordings, most notable among them were the works of Stravinsky, Debussy, and Messiaen. He served with the orchestra for five years as a guest conductor, and stepped into a position as the fist principal guest conductor in 1970 following the death of Szell. He remained as a musical advisor to the group during the 1971-72 orchestra season. From 1967-72 Boulez was credited with performing over 100 works with the Cleveland Orchestra.

Boulez fostered similar affiliations with the Los Angeles Philharmonic and the Chicago Symphony Orchestra. He first conducted the Los Angeles Philharmonic in January of 1969, performing Webern, Berg, and Bartók. In 1970 at the University of California in Los Angeles (UCLA) he

which time he aided in the founding of the Concerts Marigny in 1953, along with Barrault and Madeleine Renaud Barrault. Concerts Marigny became renowned

collaborated with that same orchestra in a "Contempo" concert, which they repeated later at the Ojai Festival. He worked with the group again on numerous occasions, including a performance of Carter's *Concerto* in February of 1975, and again at UCLA and at the Ojai Festival in 1984. His collaborations with that orchestra spanned nearly two decades, from Los Angeles, to Paris, to Salzburg, Germany. They were reunited in March and October of 1987 and again in 1992-94, and 1996. Their many memorable performances included pieces by Bartók, Berg, Mahler, Schoenberg, Stravinsky, and Webern. Boulez conducted the Los Angeles Philharmonic in productions of his own works as well, including the U.S. premiere of Livre *Pour Cordes* at Festival Boulez at UCLA in May of 1989.

Between 1971-75, Boulez served as the principal conductor of BBC Symphony Orchestra. For much of the 1970s, Boulez stepped in as the musical director of the New York Philharmonic, behind the eminent Leonard Bernstein. The early 1970s marked a self-imposed exile on the part of Boulez from his homeland of France. His extended absence, in protest for greater government sponsorship of the arts, ended in 1974, at which time he accepted a commission by then President Georges Pompidou to establish a musical research institute in Paris. The center, which was originally designated the Center Georges Pompidou, came to be called the Institute de Recherches et de Coordination Acoustique/ Musique (IRCAM). In 1975, Boulez took over the directorship of IRCAM, and under its auspices formed the Ensemble InterContemporain. As conductor and president of the ensemble, he brought that group to Los Angeles in 1976 where they performed Boulez's own composition, *Rèpons,* at the Philharmonic New Music Group series and at UCLA. Boulez took the group to the United States on other occasions in 1986, 1991, and in 1993. He remained in the directorship of IRCAM until early 1991 when he resigned from his active duties, but retained the title of honorary director of the institute.

A Man of Many Honors

The numerous affiliations throughout Boulez's career effected a barrage of award-winning performances and recordings over the years. He was first nominated for a Grammy award in 1966. He failed to win that year, although between 1967-97 he won an impressive 19 Grammys, including nine conductor's awards for Best Orchestral Performance. Those award-winning recordings included his *Debussy* recordings with the (Cleveland) New Philharmonia in 1968 and 1969. Other Grammy awards bestowed on Boulez included six for Classical Album of the Year, for the opera *Wozzeck* in 1967,

Concerto for Orchestra in 1973, *Lulu* in 1980, *The Wooden Prince* in 1993, *Concerto for Orchestra* in 1994, and *Debussy* in 1995. In 1996, Boulez and the Ensemble InterContemporain won the Grammy Award for Best Small Ensemble Performance for a rendition of "Explosante-Fixe" as performed on the album *Boulez Conducts Boulez.*

Boulez received further honors in the form of doctorate degrees from universities at Cambridge and Bâle in 1980, from Los Angeles in 1984, Oxford in 1987, and Brussels in 1988. In 1989, he received the Praemium Imperiale from the Japan Art Association. Boulez received a special honor in 1996 when King Carl XVI Gustaf of Sweden presented the Nobel Prize of Music (the Polar Prize) jointly to Boulez and folksinger Joni Mitchell.

During the late 1980s and through 1991, Boulez served as the vice-president of the Opéra Bastille. In 1989, he signed an exclusive recording contract with the Deutsche Grammophon label, and in 1991 he returned to Canada after a prolonged absence of 20 years. That year he served as the guest artistic director of the Scotia Festival. In 1992 Boulez took the Welsh National Opera on a European tour performing *Pellisande et Mélisande.* That same year at the Salzburg Festival he performed as a guest conductor with the Ensemble InterContemporain, the Los Angeles Philharmonic, and the Vienna Philharmonic. In 1995, after eight residencies with the Chicago Symphony Orchestra, he was honored by an appointment as the principal guest conductor of that organization. Boulez was only the third conductor ever to receive that distinction. His most memorable presentations with the Chicago Symphony included numerous performances of the works of Bartók.

From 1976-80, Boulez spent five seasons with the with the Bayreuth Festival Orchestra performing Wagner's operatic trilogy, *Der Ring des Nibelungen.* He and the orchestra recorded that work on the Philips label in 1981. Additionally, Boulez co-founded Cité de la Musique, which opened in Paris in 1995. He is the respected author of five published authoritative papers and essays on new music.

Selected discography

Berg: Wozzeck (with the Paris National Opera) Columbia, 1966.
(with the New Philharmonia Orchestra) *Boulez Conducts Debussy,* Columbia, 1967.
(with the New Philharmonia Orchestra) *Boulez Conducts Debussy, Volume 2: Images pour Orchestre,* Columbia, 1968.

(with the Cleveland Orchestra) *Stravinsky: Le Sacre du Printemps*, Columbia, 1969.

(with the New York Philharmonic) *Bartók, Concerto for Orchestra*, Columbia, 1972.

(with the New York Philharmonic) *Ravel: Daphnis et Chloé*, Columbia, 1974.

Berg: Lulu (Complete) (with Orchestre de l'Opéra de Paris), Deutsche Grammophon, 1979.

Wagner: Der Ring des Nibelungen (with Bayreuth Festival Orchestra), Philips, 1981.

(with the Chicago Symphony Orchestra) *The Wooden Prince and Cantata Profana*, Deutsche Grammphon, 1992.

(with the Chicago Symphony Orchestra) *Bartók: Concerto for Orchestra: 4 Orchestral Pieces, Op. 12*, Deutsche Garmmophon, 1993.

Boulez Conducts Boulez (with the Ensemble InterContemporain; includes "Explosante-Fixe"), Deutsche Grammophon, 1995.

(with the Cleveland Orchestra) *Berlioz: Symphonie Fantastique*, Deutsche Grammophon, 1997.

(with the Chicago Symphony Orchestra) *Stravinsky: The Firebird*.

(with the Chicago Symphony Orchestra) *Schoenberg: Pelleas and Mélisande*

Selected compositions

Domaines, Harmonia.

Improvisations sur Mallarmé I & II for Soprano & Instrumental Ensemble, Hungaroton.

Multiples for Orchestra, Sony Classical.

Notations 1-4 for Orchestra, Erato.

Sonatine for Flute & Piano, Erato.

Sources

Books

O'Neil, Thomas, *The Grammys: The Ultimate Unofficial Guide to Music's Hightest Honor*, Perigree, 1999.

Periodicals

American Record Guide, July-August 1995.
Atlantic Monthly, September 1995.
Nation, November 6, 1995.
New Statesman, February 12, 1999.

Online

"Pierre Boulez," *Chicago Symphany Orchestra,* http://www.chicagosymphony.org/bios/boulez.htm (May 20, 1999).

"Pierre Boulez," *Emory University 20th Century Music,* http://www.emory.edu/MUSIC/ARNOLD/boulez_content.html (May 20, 1999).

"Pierre Boulez,"http//www.cris.com/~jadato/boulez.htm (May 20, 1999).

"Pierre Boulez - Bio,"http://www.laphil.org/library/bios/BoulezP.html (May 20, 1999).

http://www.classicalinsites.com/li_e/featured/boulez/su_biograph.html (March 19, 1999).

"Pierre Boulez Selected Discography," http://www.eyeneer.com/CCM/Composers/Boulez/boulezdisc.html (May 20, 1999).

—Gloria Cooksey

Peter Brötzmann

Clarinet, saxophone, tarogato

Multi-reedman Peter Brötzmann has been called "The Loudest, The Heaviest Free Jazz Player of them All." It is a moniker he has earned. His trademark sound, often a blast that assaults the listener, is so ragged and rough as to appear almost without technique. John Litweiler wrote of it in *The Freedom Principle,* "Brötzmann's own tenor sound is always distorted into multi-phonics and screaming overtones ... his medium is screaming energy music with a deliberately manic edge." Such is the raw power of his blowing that, according to John Corbett's liner notes for the CD *The Dried Rat-Dog,* Brötzmann once broke a rib playing the saxophone. A prolific performer, Brötzmann has played in a wide variety of settings: from solo and duets to the large Global Unity Orchestra and almost everything in between. He plays a variety of saxophones and clarinets, as well as other more exotic reed instruments, including the tarogato, a double-reed instrument he came to favor. His performances have spanned the globe, from Europe to Asia to North America, although in the latter half of the 1990s the jazz scene in Chicago has been particularly congenial to his playing. He has appeared on some 100 records over the first 35 years of his career. As he approached his sixtieth birthday, he showed no sign of letting up; to the contrary, his vital, impassioned playing energized band mates half his age.

Brötzmann grew up in Remscheid, West Germany. His father kept the radio tuned to stations that played German and Russian classical music, but Brötzmann cultivated a taste for jazz as a teenager and would sneak downstairs after the family was in bed to listen to Willis Conover's midnight jazz broadcasts on American Armed Forces Radio. Becoming a jazz player was the farthest thing from his mind at that point. "My goal was always to be a professional artist," he told *Coda,* and after he finished high school, Brötzmann moved to the city of Wuppertal and entered the art academy.

He obtained his first instrument, a clarinet at 14 or 15. He taught himself the fingerings and practiced along with recordings by Louis Armstrong, Kid Ory, Sidney Bechet and other early jazz masters. With their lessons under his belt, he started playing in local Dixieland and swing bands. The idea of Brötzmann the powerhouse playing mannered music like Dixieland jazz seems a bit incongruent. But at the end of the 1990s, Brötzmann's sax heroes, Lester Young and Coleman Hawkins, were still masters of tone, control and invention. And Brötzmann was himself surprised, many years later, when he listened to a tape of himself playing in one of his early swing bands and realized that his early style was as raw as his mature one.

Eventually he bought a tenor sax and started playing hard-bop and other modern jazz styles. Around 1962, he

Born March 6, 1941 in Remscheid, Germany; married; children: one daughter, one son Caspar. *Education:* attended the Art Academy, Wuppertal, Germany.

Taught himself clarinet as a teenager; played in local Dixieland and swing bands in Wuppertal ; obtained a saxophone and began playing bop and other modern jazz forms; played regularly with bassist Peter Kowald, 1962; played with cutting edge musicians like Don Cherry, Steve Lacy, and Carla Bley, mid-1960s; began playing with trio Kowald and Sven-Ake Johansson, 1965; participated in founding of Globe Unity Orchestra; released two self-financed, self-produced albums, *For Adolphe Saxe* and *Machine Gun,*1967-68; founded Free Music Productions collective with Jost Gebers and Kowald, 1969; formed influential trio with Hans Bennink and Fred Van Hove, 1970-75; performed in *Last Exit* with Sonny Sharrock, Bill Laswell and Ronald Shannon Jackson, 1986-1988, played regularly with percussionist Hamid Drake, 1992-99.

Addresses: *Home*—Wuppertal, Germany; *Record company*—Free Music Production, Postfach 100 227, D-10562, Berlin, Germany; telephone: (49 30) 394 17 56; Okkadisk, PO Box 146472, Chicago, IL 60614.

hooked up with a young tuba player, Peter Kowald. Not long after that, Kowald switched to string bass and the two Peters started playing together regularly at Wuppertal's Jazz Club/Ader Street, a nightly gig that lasted nearly ten years. Their music was fueled by the music they were listening to, all the revolutionary post-bop developments in jazz: Miles Davis, Ornette Coleman, John Coltrane, Charles Mingus, Thelonious Monk, and Don Cherry. Wuppertal had a thriving cultural scene in the early 1960s. Most good American jazz musicians passed through town, and Brötzmann and Kowald played with most of them. Carla Bley invited them to join her band on a European tour; Steve Lacy and Don Cherry would stay with Brötzmann when they were in town. By 1964, Brötzmann and Kowald were playing free jazz. With Sven-Ake Johannsson, they formed an influential trio that helped establish it as a genre in Germany. That trio was instrumental in the development of the first Globe Unity Orchestra.

Brötzmann was also involved with the Fluxus group of artists like Naim June Paik, Yoko Ono, and Wolf Vostell. He had his first art exhibit in Wuppertal in the early-1960s. But neither art nor music was paying very well at the time and Brötzmann had a wife and two children to support. "I did whatever it took," he told *Coda's* Steven A. Loewy, "whether working in the local brewery, or helping in my father-in-law's blacksmith shop, or doing advertising work, or assisting my professor." He was still concentrating on his work as a visual artist when he won his first widespread recognition as a musician at the 1966 German Jazz Festival in Frankfurt.

Two years later, he cut an album that Loewy called "the most important recording of Brötzmann's career: *Machine Gun.* Taking its title from Don Cherry's nickname for Brötzmann, the record was financed by Brötzmann and released on his own BRÖ label. For *Machine Gun,* Brötzmann assembled an octet of Europe's leading improvisers, including Kowald on bass, Hans Bennink on drums, and Fred Van Hove on piano. *Machine Gun* was made in May of 1968, during a pivotal moment in European politics when cities across the continent were rocked by student uprisings. The sense of a revolution being born—in music as well as politics—was what turned Brötzmann once and for all to music. He believed deeply that the radical music he was creating could help foster change in the political and social realms, too. In the spring of 1999, he admitted that that belief about the power of music was an illusion. Nonetheless, that first Brötzmann record still retained its gut-wrenching power thirty years after it was made. It is the best-selling album on the FMP label and has been released twice as an album and once as a CD.

Following the success of *Machine Gun* Brötzmann, Kowald, and Jost Gebers formed Free Music Productions (FMP) in 1969. In the spirit of the times, FMP was formed as a democratic collective for recording and distributing the radical music being created. Eventually, as the group grew, collective decision-making became increasingly difficult and all authority was placed in Gebers's hands where it remained in mid-1999. Another lasting result of *Machine Gun:* the core of its band, Brötzmann, Van Hove and Bennink, went on to form an influential trio that performed and recorded through much of the 1970s.

The 1980s were a fertile period for Peter Brötzmann, a time of prolific recording in a variety of settings. *Alarm,* recorded in 1981, saw him return to the large group format after a decade of small combo and solo recording, this time with a nine-piece band. In the mid-1980s he formed the group Last Exit with New York downtown musicians Sonny Sharrock on guitar, Bill Laswell on bass, and Ronald Shannon Jackson on drums. Some purists considered Last Exit a sell-out to pop-rock commercialism, but Brötzmann defended the band in *Coda*: "At the time we formed Last Exit, the free music scene was almost dead—nothing was happening. Last Exit was an exciting concept, with great musicianship.... But no one became rich from Last Exit." The group released five recordings between 1986 until 1988. It only ended when Sonny Sharrock died.

If anything, the pace of Brötzmann's activities seemed to increase in the 1990s. He recorded *Last Home* with his son Caspar—a stunning, unclassifiable guitarist—in 1990 and *Machine Kaput* with the German trio Ruf der Heimat in 1995. He performed regularly with Chicago percussionist Hamid Drake—as a duo on *The Dried Rat Dog*, in a trio with Mahmoud Gania on *The Wels Concert*, as part of the Die Like a Dog Quartet, and with the 1998 Octet/Tentet gatherings. As evidenced by his work with the Octet/Tentet and Drake, Brötzmann found the Chicago free jazz scene and its players particularly genial, and he visited the city about twice a year in the latter half of the 1990s. Nonetheless, he maintained a furious pace of work and collaboration with artists including Haruhiko Gotsu, Tetsu Yahauchi and Shoji Hano in Japan, the Thomas Borgmann Trio, Kees Hazevoet, Borah Bergmann, and Anthony Braxton.

In the 1990s, critics claimed Brötzmann had lost his old fire, that "The Loudest, The Heaviest Free Jazz Player of them All" was mellowing out. The new prejudice judgement irritated him as much as the old one. "The problem with a lot of jazz critics," Brötzmann told Kurt Goergen in 1998, "is that these fools don't know how to listen properly. I've always included quiet and lyrical passages in my music. It's just that these critics—certainly, those in the old days too—can't or won't listen properly. They're only noticing them now. Before they only wanted to hear the screaming Brötzmann because it fit the times better." Still he confessed to Loewy in early 1999 that he might be changing a little with age. "Getting older has made me quieter, in some ways. The older you get the more personal your playing becomes. I would like to come to a point—like Coleman Hawkins—where I play a few notes, and those notes are as honest and serious as possible."

Selected discography

For Adolphe Sax, FMP 0080, 1967.
Machine Gun, FMP CD24, 1968.
Brötzmann, Van Hove, Bennink, FMP 0130, 1973.
Ein Halber Hund Kann Nicht Pinkeln, FMP 0420, 1977.
Alarm, FMP 1030, 1981.
Last Exit, Enemy 101, 1986.
Cassette recordings '87, Celluloid CELD 6140, 1987.
Low Life, Celluloid CELL 5016, 1987.
Last Home, Pathological, PATH04, 1990.
The März combo, FMP CD47, 1992.
Die like a dog; fragments of music, life and death of Albert Ayler, FMP CD64, 1993.
The dried rat-dog, Okka disk OD12004, 1994.
The Wels concert, Okka disk OD12013, 1996
Stalker songs, CIMP 160, 1997.
The Chicago Octet/Tentet, Okka disk OD12022, 1997.

Sources

Books

Litweiler, John, *The Freedom Principle*, William Morrow & Co, 1984.

Periodicals

Coda, March/April 1999.
Down Beat, April 1983; July 1984; January 1987 August 1987; August 1998.

Online

"Peter Brötzmann," *European Free Jazz Pages*, http://www.shef.ac.uk/misc/rec/ps/efi/index.html

—Gerald E. Brennan

William S. Burroughs

Novelist, multimedia artist

William S. Burroughs is one of the most significant writers of the twentieth century. Books like *Naked Lunch, Junky, The Soft Machine, Nova Express, The Ticket that Exploded, Cities of the Red Night,* and *The Western Lands* pushed the form of the novel to its outermost limits and introduced previously-unexplored or taboo themes such as drug addiction, homosexuality, and systems of control. Published to great critical and legal controversy—Burroughs' first books were routinely banned for obscenity—his work early on won a small audience of writers, critics and enthusiasts that quickly grew. By the 1970s, Burroughs' influence was being felt throughout the arts, by filmmakers, visual artists, and in particular musicians.

His affect on music was beginning to be felt early in the decade when groups like Soft Machine and Steely Dan took their names from Burroughs' books. Interestingly "heavy metal," the name given to the music of groups like Led Zeppelin, Deep Purple, and Black Sabbath, was an expression coined by Burroughs around 1960. But it was the punk and new wave movements that adopted Burroughs as their godfather. His highly critical view of government, the mass media and middle class life in general matched the rebellious sensibilities of groups like the Sex Pistols, the Clash, the Dead Kennedys, Caberet Voltaire and Throbbing Gristle. It eventually became *de rigueur* for rock stars to visit—and be photographed—with Burroughs. His guests ranged from Frank Zappa to Lou Reed and from Blondie, to U2.

Burroughs did not begin collaborating with popular musicians until the 1980s. However he began working systematically with tapes in the mid-1960s. The tape work grew out of writing techniques he developed, the fold-in and the cut-up: pages of writing would be folded or physically cut into pieces and recombined to form new juxtapositions of word and image. Burroughs took those ideas a step further with tape recordings. He recorded texts written by himself an other authors. He then rewound or fast-forwarded through the tape. At random points he inserted other texts, radio broadcasts, even noise recorded in the streets. Those tape "cut-ups"—like the written one—broke down the associational patterns of thought and enabled the creation of new, previously unthought patterns to emerge. Burroughs believed those associational patterns were largely imposed by outside powers like the mass media. Breaking down those patterns, Burroughs theorized, would be an important step in freeing man from the forces of control all around him. A selection of Burroughs' tape experiments was released in 1981 by Throbbing Gristle's Genesis P-Orridge on the album *Nothing Here Now but The Recordings.*

Burroughs' first album was a spoken word recording entitled simply *Call Me Burroughs.* On it he read from *Naked Lunch* and *Nova Express.* Unlike his friend Allen Ginsberg, who sang his own and others poems and songs at readings and on several recordings, reading was Burroughs' essential *modus operandi.* He read excerpts of his work on several Giorno Poetry Systems albums; at public appearances he usually read selections from published or work-in-progress. In his frequent collaborations with musicians, Burroughs only *sang* on two pieces—" 'T' Ain't No Sin" on Tom Waits' *The Black Rider* and a thoroughly bizarre version of the Marlene Dietrich hit "Falling in Love Again" on *Dead City Radio.* Music made its first appearance on a Burroughs' albums with *Breakthrough in the Grey Room,* which included pieces by the Master Musicians of Jajouka; one of his first appearances on a music album was the cut "Sharkey's Night" on Laurie Anderson's *Mister Heartbreak* released in 1983. Their association went back at least five years to their earlier work together with Giorno Poetry Systems and the Nova Conference. On "Sharkey's Night" Anderson's music provided the backdrop to Burroughs' deadpan monologue. He appeared later in Anderson's film *Home of the Brave,* in which he was her dance partner to the song, "Language is a Virus." That piece, based directly on theories formulated at the time of his cut-up experiments, was just one example of the influence Burroughs was beginning to have on music at the time.

For the Record . . .

Born as William Seward Burroughs, February 5, 1914, St. Louis, MO (died August 2, 1997); married Ilse Klapper, Joan Vollmer. *Education:* Attended Harvard University, received BA.

Met students Jack Kerouac and Allen Ginsberg in New York City, mid-1940s; published first book, *Junkie*, 1953; wrote *Queer*, early 1950s; first sections of *Naked Lunch* published, 1958; wrote cut-up novels, *The Soft Machine, The Ticket That Exploded,* and *Nova Express*, published, 1961-64; collaborated on series of films, including *Towers Open Fire*, with Anthony Balch, 1963; tape recorder experiments, 1964-68; appeared at Nova Convention, 1979; appeared on *Saturday Night Live*, 1981; published *Cities of the Red Night*, 1981; published *Queer*, 1985; appeared as old junkie in Gus Van Sant's film *Drugstore Cowboy*; published *The Western Lands*, 1987; released *Dead City Radio*, Island Records, 1990; released *Spare Ass Annie and Other Tales*, Island Records, 1993; released "The 'Priest' They Called Him," with Kurt Cobain, Tim/Kerr Records, 1993; released *The Black Rider*, with Tom Waits, Island Records, 1993.

A 1981 appearance on *Saturday Night Live* led to Burroughs first full-blown musical project. The last piece he read was "Twilight's Last Gleaming" from *Nova Express*. Music coordinator Hal Willner played "The Star-Spangled Banner" as background. The juxtaposition of the national anthem with Burroughs' blackly satiric version of the sinking of the Titanic worked. Six years later, at the suggestion of Allen Ginsberg, Willner approached Burroughs about recording an entire album of similar material. *Dead City Radio* would be "the image of a true and great American writer with 'The Star-Spangled Banner' behind him ... a timeless album that would sound as if it could have been recorded tomorrow," as Willner wrote in the album's liner notes. One of the high points on the record is Burroughs' reading of "A Thanksgiving Prayer." He gives thanks for everything most shameful in American life and history—the ruin of the environment, the slaughter of the Indians and buffalo, hate crimes—backed up with the kind of syrupy strings one is used to hearing behind inspirational platitudes mouthed on late night TV. In fact, Willner used old tapes of the NBC Symphony Orchestra on most of the cuts. Other

musical contributions were made by John Cale, Steely Dan's Donald Fagen, Sonic Youth, and Blondie's Chris Stein.

Willner also co-produced, *Spare Ass Annie and Other Tales,* which came out in 1993. Parts of the project closely resemble *Dead City Radio*'s string arrangements; the rest of the music was constructed by the Disposable Heroes of Hihoprisy, a collaboration suggested by Burroughs' secretary, James Grauerholz. The union of Burroughs and hip-hop suggests the extent of the writer's influence: just as in the 1960s Burroughs had openly appropriated texts by other writers for his cut-up novels, music like rap, hip-hop and electronica cut-up and appropriated the work of other musicians by means of sampling technology.

In 1993, Burroughs also released a record with Nirvana's Kurt Cobain, "The Priest They Called Him." The piece, originally published in the book *Interzone*, tells the story of a sick junky looking for a fix on Christmas Eve. Interestingly the piece appears under the title "The Junky's Christmas" on *Spare Ass Annie.* The two are a study in contrasts. "Junky's Christmas" is awash with nostalgia, sentimentality even. The sound behind "Priest" is the junk-sick feedback wall of Cobain's guitar doing to "Silent Night" what Jimi Hendrix did to "The Star-Spangled Banner," in the words of *Rolling Stone*'s Al Weisel. And six months before Cobain's violent suicide, according to Graham Caveney's *Gentleman Junkie*, Burroughs remarked of the Nirvana guitarist "There's something wrong with that boy. He frowns for no good reason."

Perhaps the most fruitful of Burroughs' musical collaborations was *The Black Rider,* a piece for stage directed by Robert Wilson with music and songs by Tom Waits. The premise for the play was an old German folk tale about a hapless marksman, Wilhelm, who makes a deal with the Devil to win a shooting contest and thereby the hand of the girl he loves. The Devil offers some magic bullets guaranteed to hit whatever the shooter desires. The catch: The Devil reserves the right to aim the last bullet however and without meaning to Wilhelm kills his new bride. The story has a sinister parallel to Burroughs' own life. In the early 1950s in Mexico, he killed his wife trying to shoot a wine glass off her head in a drunken game of William Tell. Burroughs wrote the libretto for the "opera" and his texts formed the basis of the songs Waits wrote. "William Burroughs was as solid as a metal desk and his text was the branch this bundle would swing from," Waits wrote in the *Black Rider* liner notes. "His cut up text and open process of finding a language for this story became a river of words for me to draw from...." In addition to his brilliant vocal on "'T' Ain't No Sin," he contributed the lyrics, drawn from his own hard experience, for "Crossroads:" "Now, George was a good straight boy ... but there was bad blood in him someway he got into magic bullets and that leads straight to Devil's work, just like marywanna leads to heroin You think you can take those bullets of leave 'em, do you? Just save a few for bad days." *The Black Rider,* unlike Burroughs earlier musical albums, was more than a hodgepodge selection of earlier writing. The pieces were new, they were unified by the play's story, and the music was composed by an artist as much as genius in his realm as Burroughs is in his, Tom Waits.

In the last four years of his life, Burroughs did not work on any other musical projects. Less than a year after his death in August 1997, a four-CD set of readings he did for Giorno Poetry Systems was released.

Selected discography

Call Me Burroughs, 1965, re-released on CD on Rhino 1999.
Nothing Here Now but The Recordings, Industrial Records, 1981.
Laurie Anderson: *Mister Heartbreak,* Warner Brothers, 1984.
Break Through In Grey Room, Sub Rosa, 1987.
Dead City Radio, Island, 1990

(with Kurt Cobain), "The 'Priest' They Called Him," Tim/Kerr Records, 1993.
Spare Ass Annie and Other Tales, Island Records, 1993.
(with Tom Waits), *The Black Rider,* Island, 1993
Best of William Burroughs—From Giorno Poetry Systems, Mouth Almighty/Mercury, 1998

Sources

Books

Caveney, Graham, *Gentleman Junkie,* Little Brown and Co., 1998.

Periodicals

Billboard, April 25, 1998.
New York Times, November 14, 1993.
Opera News, November 1993.
Rolling Stone, November 25, 1993.
Time, December 6, 1993.

Additional information obtained from the liner notes of *The Black Rider* and *Dead City Radio.*

—*Gerald E. Brennan*

Captain Beefheart and His Magic Band

Avant-garde group

Don Van Vliet, aka Captain Beefheart, is one of the most fascinating, most creative, most challenging, and just plain weirdest Renaissance men produced by rock music. His music is an amalgam of delta and Chicago blues, rock 'n roll, free jazz, sea shanties, spontaneous poetry, psychedelia, and various strains of the experimental, avant-garde, dada, and bizarre, thanks to his vision and the collaboration of a series of capable and sympathetic musicians. Like other unconventional composers—such as Harry Partch or Thelonious Monk—Van Vliet's music is unique, almost instantly recognizable, and has exerted a remarkable influence on other musicians interested in exploring the boundaries of musical sound.

Vliet—he only added "Van" in the latter half of the 1960s—was born in Los Angeles, California. An only child, by all accounts he had a strange childhood. "I never went to school," he claimed in a *Village Voice* piece by Lester Bangs. "I told [my mother] that I couldn't go to school because I was sculpting at that time a hell of a lot. That was kindergarten, I think. I used to lock myself in a room an sculpt when I was like three, five, six." His artistic talent was remarkable enough that he was offered a scholarship to study art in Europe. His parents disapproved and moved to the Mojave Desert town of Lancaster, California, when Vliet was 13. "They wanted to get me away from all the 'queer' artists,' he told Bangs, "isn't that awful?"

In Lancaster Vliet met a number of musicians, including Alex Snouffer, Jerry Handley, and Frank Zappa, who were playing in various local bands. Vliet and Zappa spent time together listening to R&B records. When Zappa eventually acquired a primitive recording studio in Cucamonga, he and Vliet collaborated there on different ideas, one of which was a script Zappa was writing entitled *Captain Beefheart vs. the Grunt People*. The first of many myths about Don Vliet, who Zappa wanted to play the lead in his movie, would claim that Zappa came up with the name because Vliet had a beef in his heart against the world.

Snouffer, meanwhile, was putting together a blues band with Handley and asked Vliet, who played blues harp, to be the singer. Snouffer and Handley had already settled on a name for the band: Captain Beefheart and his Magic Band (CB&HMB). With Vliet, Snouffer on guitar, Handley on bass, Doug Moon on guitar, and Vic Martenson on drums, CB&HMB quickly became popular in the towns around the Mojave Desert. Its first big break came when it played the Teenage Fair at the Hollywood Palladium in the spring of 1965. Besides being seen by Bill Harkelroad, Mark Boston, and John French, all of whom would later join the Magic Band, the performance led to a new manager who had contacts with A&M Records. In 1966, they recorded their first single, a heavy, pounding version of Bo Diddley's "Diddy Wah Diddy." The record quickly became a regional hit and seemed destined for the national charts. In a one-in-a-million coincidence, though, the Remains had a hit on the East Coast with the same song and the two records ended up canceling each other out. To make matters worse, A&M co-owner Jerry Moss decided that Beefheart's music was too negative and cancelled the band's contract.

By mid-1966, Don Vliet was getting into avant jazz performers, like Ornette Coleman and Roland Kirk; he had also begun writing the songs that would appear on the first Beefheart album, *Safe As Milk*. Drummer John French had joined the band by that time and recalled in his *Grow Fins* liner notes that while Vliet would provide lyrics, assembled from scraps he carried around in a shopping bag, the composition of the music was a collaborative effort in which the entire band took part. Legends to the effect that Don Vliet was able to access levels of perception and existence off limits to mere mortals began around this time. One night, for example, after the band had lost their A&M contract and moved to a house in Hollywood, a spaced-out Vliet collared French and drove aimlessly around town until Vliet finally pulled into a delicatessen. According to French, record producers Bob Krasnow and Richard Perry were there eating and asked "Are you Captain Beefheart? We've been looking for you." They had been impressed with "Diddy

For the Record . . .

Members include **Jimmy Carl Black** (India Ink); **Paul Blakely**, drums; **Mark Boston** (Rockette Morton) bass, guitar; **Ry Cooder**, guitar, bass; **Jeff Cotton** (Antennae Jimmy Siemens) guitar; **Roy Estrada** (Orejon) bass; **Eric Drew Feldman**, bass, keyboards; **Bruce Fowler**, (Fossil Fowler) trombone; **John French** (Drumbo), drums, guitar, bass, vocals; **Jerry Handley**, bass, vocals; **Bill Harkelroad** (Zoot Horn Rollo) guitar; **Victor Hayden** (The Mascara Snake) bass clarinet; **Rich Hepner**, guitar; **Sam Hoffman**, theremin; **Elliot Ingber** (Winged Eel Fingerling), guitar; **Gary Lucas**, guitar; **Vic Martensen**, drums; **Cliff Martinez**, drums; **Doug Moon**, guitar; **Richard Redus**, guitar; **Alex Snouffer** (Alex St. Clair) guitar, vocals; **Richard Snyder** (Midnight Hatsize Snyder), bass, guitar, vocals; **Jeff "Moris" Tepper**, guitar, vocals; **John Thomas**, piano; **Art Tripp** (Art Marimba) drums, marimba; **Don Van Vliet** (Captain Beefheart, born January 15, 1941, Los Angeles, CA), vocals, harmonica, soprano saxophone; **Dennis Whalley**, guitar; **Robert Williams**, drums.

Captain Beefheart and His Magic Band formed by Alex Snouffer in Lancaster, CA around 1964; play Teenage Fair at Hollywood Palladium in spring of 1965 where they meet Leonard Grant who became their manager; signs with A&M Records; debut A&M single, "Diddy Wah Diddy," 1966; released *Safe As Milk*, Buddah Records spring 1966; Van Vliet collapsed on stage at beginning of San Francisco concert and band is unable to appear at Monterey Pop Festival, 1967; released *Trout Mask Replica* with Frank Zappa, Straight Records, 1969; released *Lick My Decals Off Baby*, 1970; released *The Spotlight Kid*, 1972; released *Clear Spot*, 1972; Magic Band quits, 1974; Van Vliet released *Bongo Fury* with Frank Zappa and the Mothers, 1975; original *Bat Chain Puller* recorded but never released 1975; released *Shiny Beast (Bat Chain Puller)*, 1978; released *Doc At the Radar Station*, 1980; released *Ice Cream For Crow*, 1982; *Pearls before swine ice cream for crow* released with poetry CD, 1996; released *Grow Fins* (rarities set), 1999.

Wah Diddy" and wanted to make a record with Beefheart. "Afterwards," according to French, "Don explained ... that's why he was so spaced out. He knew he was

supposed to be somewhere and he didn't know where it was. He said 'You thought I was crazy but I knew what I was doing.'" Similar stories of Van Vliet's clairvoyance arose throughout his musical career.

The encounter with Krasnow led to a contract with Buddah [sic] Records, and in the spring of 1967 the band went to work making *Safe As Milk*. Vliet wanted guitarist Ry Cooder to join the Magic Band. He had seen Cooder at the Teenage Fair in 1965. Cooder, put off by the rowdy, out-of-control atmosphere generated by the bikers, booze and drugs around the Beefheart band, resisted. But he eventually agreed to join, at least long enough to make the album, and his slide and Vliet's growling voice open the record's first cut. *Safe As Milk*, with Vliet's virtuosic vocals, its slithery slide guitars, its thunderous bass and theremin, remained an exciting record nearly 35 years after it was made.

Not long after the record had been cut, the band was invited to perform at the 1967 Monterey Pop Festival, the show that made stars out of Jimi Hendrix and Janis Joplin, among others. It was the band's chance to show the larger public what it could do. In preparation, Beefheart and the Magic Band played a concert in San Francisco. They got through the first song, but as the second began, Vliet froze, turned around and walked off stage, and collapsed. The band finished the song without a singer, then left the stage as well. After the show, Ry Cooder quit the band. They did not play Monterey. "That was the end of it right there basically," French said, "from then on we were an avant-garde band who was never gong to make any money."

Krasnow managed to organize a European tour nonetheless, during which they recorded a session for John Peel, the English disk jockey who had fallen in love with the band's music while he was working in California. Upon their return to the United States, they recorded an album that would appear under the name *Strictly Personal*, a set of longer songs which included more instrumental jams. During the tour of Europe that followed, Krasnow presented them with the first copies of the album. To Vliet's dismay, Krasnow had added a dose of phasing to the mix to give the music a fashionably psychedelic sound. To make matters worse, according to French, Krasnow returned to the United States with all the band's money. Unable to pay for hotels or food, CB&HMB cut the tour short and returned home.

Back in the States, Van Vliet—he modified his name around this time—moved into his mother's house. The Magic Band entered a period of great change. Jeff Cotten had already replaced Ry Cooder. Alex Snouffer, fed up with the deceptions of the band's management, quit, followed by Jerry Handley who had a wife and children to support. They were replaced by guitarist Bill Harkelroad and bassist Mark Boston. To Van Vliet's good fortune, his old friend Frank Zappa had been given his own label by Warner Brothers Records, along with complete artistic license. Zappa offered Van Vliet the freedom to record an album as he wished. The stage was set for *Trout Mask Replica*.

The band settled into a house in the San Fernando Valley where recording gear had been set up. He had christened the Magic Band with surreal new names: Cotton became Antennae Jimmy Siemens, Harkelroad Zoot Horn Rollo, French Drumbo, and Boston Rockette Morton. An entire mythology has grown up around the songs on *Trout Mask Replica* and their compositions: Van Vliet supposedly composed every song on the album in a marathon eight and a half hour session at the piano and then single-handedly taught the Magic Band how to play them. The process of the songs' development, according to French and other members of the Magic Band, did not happen in an uninterrupted burst and Van Vliet was, in any case, incapable of teaching them to the band because his grasp of music was entirely intuitive and unschooled. He simply did not have the vocabulary to communicate his wants on his own. Instead he relied on the expertise of others, at first French then Harkelroad, to translate his ideas—communicated through piano, whistling, or evocative poetical images—about what he wanted into information the band members could use.

It wasn't only personal limitations that caused difficulties. The music Van Vliet was hearing in his head was completely unlike anything ever set to vinyl. It was jagged and rough in places, interrupted frequently by blasts of saxophone noise; the Magic Band musicians were often playing in completely different keys and time signatures *simultaneously!* The musicians rehearsed the charts French had developed for six months. Rarely during that time did Van Vliet practice with them. In the end, Van Vliet persuaded Zappa, who produced *Trout Mask Replica,* to cut the album in a recording studio instead of their house as originally planned. Zappa booked them six hours, normally enough time to lay down two to three songs. He was astounded when the Magic Band was able to record 14 tunes in four and a half hours.

About a year after *Trout Mask Replica* was completed, Captain Beefheart and the Magic Band returned to the studio to record *Lick My Decals Off Baby* for Warner Brothers. The album, which Van Vliet produced himself, is—except arguably for *Trout Mask Replica*—the purest, most difficult, exhilarating, and "Beefheartian" of all the band's recorded work. It is marked by the same unset-

tling rhythms and harmonies, but the sound is denser over all, its pace more intense and unrelenting than the previous record. The addition of Art Tripp's marimba gave Magic Band music a texture unlike any other in popular music. Except Captain Beefheart and the Magic Band was not particularly popular.

The band was not earning any money and their next record, the more bluesy *Spotlight Kid* (1972), was made in an atmosphere described by French as one of "drudgery and grinding poverty." When *Clear Spot* was released later the same year, its grooving heavy rock like "Low Yo Yo Stuff," mellow soul like "Too Much Time," and showstoppers like "Big Eyed Beans From Venus," made it appear as if Beefheart had finally found the long-elusive formula for commercial success. It wasn't to be. After the band returned from another European tour, Snouffer, back with the group, discovered hard evidence that Van Vliet's management company had cheated the musicians out of money owed them. There was a confrontation, the Magic Band quit and eventually formed Mallard. No one but French would ever play with Beefheart again.

The next two albums, *Unconditionally Guaranteed* and *Bluejeans & Moonbeams* represent the low water mark of Beefheart's recorded work. Again, Frank Zappa came to the rescue and, in 1975, Van Vliet appeared on *Bongo Fury,* essentially a Mothers of Invention album. The tour for *Bongo Fury* proved a serious strain on their friendship. Van Vliet's lax musical discipline and unpredictability clashed with Zappa's desire for control and structure. Despite Van Vliet's questionable treatment of his band musicians over the years, John French returned to the Beefheart fold in 1975 and set about putting together a new Magic Band which cut an album called *Bat Chain Puller*. The record, never released, has circulated for years as only a bootleg.

Bat Chain Puller provided material for the last three Beefheart records, which represented a renaissance of the career of the renaissance man, Don Van Vliet. *Shiny Beast (Bat Chain Puller)* (1978) and *Doc At the Radar Station* (1980) marked a return to the "hard" Beefheart style of *Trout Mask Replica* and *Lick My Decals Off Baby*. Van Vliet's dealings with the Magic Band seemed to have mellowed considerably though. In the late 1960s and early 1970s, he had been demanding, paranoid, and often distant. The attitude may have grown out of his experience with his first band, founded and led by Snouffer, which did not take him or his ideas seriously. By the time the 1970s were ending, Beefheart had proved to have a decisive influence on a whole generation of younger musicians, like Devo and Pere Ubu. The new Magic Band, with the exception of French, were all young and rabid fans of the earlier Beefheart recordings. Perhaps Van Vliet didn't feel as personally threatened by the new musicians as he had by the older ones. Or maybe it was just because he had gotten older.

Listening to much of the last Beefheart album, 1982's *Ice Cream For Crow,* one can almost hear Van Vliet bidding goodbye to music. Frantic, almost desperate music was still being played by the Magic Band. But it often seemed like Captain Beefheart himself was no longer interested in singing, like he'd rather just recite his poetry. As if to confirm his adieu the band did not tour for the record. They did release a video of the title track which, much to Van Vliet's disgust, MTV refused to air. *Ice Cream For Crow* remains a powerful recording. Cliff Martinez, speaking to French on *Grow Fins,* expressed what most members of the different Magic Bands felt: "I never played anything with more energy. I mean, I played with a bunch of punk bands which was supposed to be high energy and angry. But that was never quite as close as the Beefheart thing."

The release of *Ice Cream For Crow* began, to the dismay of his cargo of cult fans, the long musical silence Van Vliet. Not the artistic silence, though. Since then, he devoted his life to painting, splitting his time between the desert and redwood country. He showed his work regularly at galleries in New York and other great cities, and his paintings regularly sell for five figure prices. At the end of the 1990s he was said to be in poor health, evident on a small recording of a poetry reading released in Italy in 1996. The voice falters and is but a pale shadow of the sonic weapon Van Vliet wielded in previous years. But the frail voice merely amplifies the power of the words once hollered so mightily on *Trout Mask Replica:* "When I get lonesome the wind begin t' moan/ When I trip fallin' ditch/ Somebody wanna throw the dirt right down/When I feel like dyin' the sun come out/Stole my fear 'n gone/ Who's afraid of the spirit with the bluesferbones/Who's afraid of the fallin' ditch Fallin' ditch ain't gonna get my bones."

Selected discography

Safe As Milk, Kama Sutra, 1967; reissued, Buddha, 1999.
Strictly Personal, Blue Thumb, 1968.
Trout Mask Replica, Straight Records, 1969; reissued as CD.
Lick My Decals Off Baby, Reprise, 1970.
Mirror Man, Buddah, 1970; reissued as *The Mirror Man Sessions,* 1999.
The Spotlight Kid, Reprise, 1972; reissued as CD with *Clear Spot.*
Clear Spot, Reprise, 1972.
Unconditionally Guaranteed, Mercury, 1974.
Bluejeans & Moonbeams, Mercury, 1974.
Shiny Beast (Bat Chain Puller), Warner Brothers, 1978.
Doc At the Radar Station, Virgin, 1980.
Ice Cream For Crow, Virgin, 1982.
The Legendary A&M Sessions, A&M, 1984.
Grow Fins: Rarities 1965-1982, Revenant, 1999.
The Dust Blows Forward, Rhino, 1999.

Sources

Periodicals

Los Angeles Times, July, 22, 1999.
Rolling Stone, May 14, 1970.
San Francisco Chronicle, June 6, 1999.
Village Voice, October 10, 1980.

Additional information for this article was taken from the liner notes to *Grow Fins: Rarities 1965-1982.*

—*Gerald E. Brennan*

D Generation

Punk band

When D Generation formed in 1991, the band's members may not have had any idea what it was they were getting themselves into. Then again, perhaps they found exactly what they were looking for. After being together for less than a decade, the members of the band—who lived the hybrid life of the hardcore, punk and gritty glam rock they played—became familiar with getting thrown out of hotels and off stages, being dropped by a major record label even before their first release, and trouble making in general.

Three childhood friends—vocalist Jesse Malin, guitarist Danny Sage, and guitarist Richard Bacchus—started D Generation in New York City's East Village as a straight-ahead rock band. The exact moment in time that they made the switch to being "degenerate misfit deviants who might even be considered talented musicians"—as D Generation was described by imusic.com—is unclear, but the band made its name for being angry, yet dedicated, members of New York's punk scene.

Before they'd ever been signed, D Generation played sell-out concerts at such seminal New York City venues as CBGB and the Continental. Lorraine Ali described them in *Rolling Stone* in 1999 as "New York '90s punk that takes the best of the '70s Street-rat sneers, tight black pants and artfully messed-up hairdos: D Generation are the stuff that popped-up '70s punk was made

of.... tailor-made for grimy pinball arcades and Brand X beer-drinking binges."

D Generation finally earned the attention of the major labels and in 1994 signed with EMI. The band was geared up for its self-titled debut, but changes in the upper levels of the EMI left the band out in the cold. They'd gotten lost in the shuffle and left with none of the support they'd signed on for. Luckily, positive media exposure had brightened the band's prospects and, after a major-label bidding war, D Generation signed with Columbia Records in 1996.

D Generation's Columbia debut, *No Lunch*, was released in 1996. They chose the former front man of the 1980s rock band The Cars, Ric Ocasek, to produce the record. Ocasek had previously worked with long-time punk band Bad Brains, alternative pop band Weezer and rockers Bad Religion. *Spin*'s Charles Aaron rated the record an eight out of ten, writing, "D Generation defiantly believe in rock 'n' roll's burlesque. They just wanna wrap the dirty city up in (less than) three tumultuous minutes and stuff it in your back pocket," Aaron wrote, referring to the high-powered impact of the band's short songs.

In addition to giving the record a four-star review, *Rolling Stone* writer David Fricke wrote in 1996, "There is no better sales pitch for the snot-rock classicism and teenage-warfare spirit of D Generation than [the song] 'No Way Out.' Richard Bacchus' and Danny Sage's guitars spit bullets, singer Jesse Malin seethes with rabid impatience. Malin, Sage, Bacchus, bassist Howie Pyro and drummer Michael Wildwood embrace the values of aggressive brevity." Fricke went on the label the song a "stone classic" and predicted that D Generation would be able to produce more music in the *No Lunch* vein.

The video for "No Way Out," directed by Nigel Dick debuted on MTV's weekly alternative video show "120 Minutes" in October of 1996. Dick was behind the camera for Guns 'n' Roses' "Welcome to the Jungle" and "Sweet Child O' Mine," as well. In 1997, Richard Bacchus left the band and was replaced by guitarist Todd Youth. They also covered Iggy Pop's "I Got Nothing," which was included on the Iggy Pop tribute album, *We Will Fall*. D Generation had a knack for landing on high profile tours. They opened for such bands as Social Distortion, L7, Green Day, Cheap Trick, and The Offspring. The band also played on the Ramones' farewell tour and the KISS reunion tour.

Near the end of 1998, D Generation showed its support for Coney Island High, the nightclub on New York's Lower East Side that had helped launch the band. One of the club's owners performed a hostile takeover of sorts when he fired the staff and changed the locks. The band played at a benefit for the venue that raised enough money to buy the club. For the fundraiser, the quintessential 1960s girl-group singer Ronnie Spector sang her signature tune, "Be My Baby," with D Generation. In February of 1999, Todd Youth left the band and original guitarist Richard Bacchus returned to replace him. Drummer Michael Wildwood was replaced by Joe Rizzo that same year.

With its third release, *Through the Darkness*, D Generation seemed finally to be gaining the inertia to match its New York City following. "Glam rock, that pungent brew of high fashion, low morals and gender-bending outrageousness, has always found its earthiest practitioners on the streets of New York," wrote Ali in *The New York Times*. "This East Village-based band of veteran club punks carries the torch once held by the New York Dolls and.... could finally be headed for its 15 minutes."

On *Through the Darkness*, D Generation encouraged the Seventies side of their punk-rock sound by hiring producer Tony Visconti, who'd produced such high-level 1970s acts as David Bowie, T. Rex and Thin Lizzy. With simple three-chord melodies and lead singer Malin's "Marlboro-

ravaged" voice, the sound of the album was "naive and eager, yet defiant and dirty," Ali continued in her *New York Times* review.

The tracks on *Through the Darkness* showcased the band's bleak worldview. Chief songwriter Malin's lyrics dealt with the isolation of life in 1999, sorry relationships, discrimination, and the shallowness of modern entertainment and culture in the face of the new millennium. On the album's first track, "Helpless," Malin screams, "Our parents gave us television and vanished in their cars/ Teachers gave us bad religion, stomach aches and scars." The song also appeared on the soundtrack to the 1999 film of a group of demonic private school teachers called *The Faculty*. The band itself called the *Through the Darkness* "a soundtrack for the end of the world."

Selected discography

Through the Darkness, Columbia, 1999.
(contributor) *The Faculty* (soundtrack), Sony, 1998.
(contributor) *We Will Fall* , Royally, 1997.
No Lunch, Columbia, 1996.
D Generation, EMI, 1994.

Sources

Periodicals

The New York Times; March 19, 1999.
Rolling Stone, March 4, 1999.

Online

"D Generation,"*Rocket Online*, http://www.rocketonline.com (April 29, 1999).
"D Generation," *Rolling Stone Network*, http://rollingstone.com (March 12, 1999).
"D Generation," *Wall of Sound*, http://www.wallofsound.com (March 12, 1999).

Additional information was provided by Sparrow Records publicity materials, 1999.

—*Brenna Sanchez*

Dixie Chicks

Country group

Dixie Chicks hatched a new age of country music in 1998 with the release of their major label debut *Wide Open Spaces*. In less than a year, the hot country act was being presented gold albums, featured in fashion spreads, and given critical acclaim with the added benefit of industry recognition through numerous music award nominations and honors.

Sisters Emily Erwin and Martie Seidel were multi-instrumentalists from a young age. Encouraged by their parents, the girls began playing bluegrass music in a Dallas band. With Laura Lynch and Robin Macy, the sisters decided to play for tips on a downtown Dallas street corner in 1989. What started as a lark became serious business when they earned about $375 in one hour. Passersby asked how they could hire the group, which was soon performing at private parties and conventions. They became one of the region's favorite country groups. Early fans included high-profile businessman and former presidential candidate Ross Perot, and Texas politician George W. Bush.

Photo by Reed Saxon. AP/Wide World Photos. Reproduced by permission.

But the group didn't yet have a name. There exist several published variations recounting the origins of "Dixie Chicks." The official record company position is that the group heard Little Feat's "Dixie Chicken" on the radio, "only Martie didn't want to be a chicken ... so the name was shortened to Dixie Chicks."

The first incarnation of the Dixie Chicks tended toward rhinestone studded cowgirl drag, bluegrass-tinged country, and country swing. The group gained additional notice by opening for national country acts such as Garth Brooks, Alan Jackson, and Emmylou Harris; they also recorded commercials for McDonald's and Justin Boots. The group released three independent recordings between 1990 and 1994, which were sold at their shows. Sales of the three recordings totaled around 60,000.

"We've always known how to market ourselves," said Seidel to *Southwest Airlines Spirit*'s Eric Celeste. "Even in the beginning we would milk the novelty of our act. That's how we made our living. We were the 'Texas hometown girls,' and that's what they wanted to see at these conventions where we would play. We could play all the clubs we loved, but that's not where we made our money. We made it playing for the folks at IBM."

Natalie Maines, daughter of acclaimed steel guitarist Lloyd Maines, joined the group in 1995. Maines had been awarded a scholarship to the Berklee School of Music and changed her major four times. About the same time, Lloyd Maines had been regularly playing with the Dixie Chicks on their self-produced recordings. When the sisters sought a singer to front the band after Lynch's departure, he just happened to have Natalie's Berklee audition tape with him.

Maines' arrival marked the group's transformation into a mainstream country group with panache. "Natalie is sensitive to the fact that there was a long history of the Dixie Chicks before she got there," Seidel told Celeste. We played so many gigs for so many years where we were just there to look at, just musical wallpaper ... [Maines] deserves a lot of the credit, too. It's not like she is a newcomer. She's carrying on a third generation of Maines musicians." The group sites diverse musical influences including musicians from rock, country, and bluegrass: Bela Fleck, Bob Wills, Sam Bush, Bonnie Raitt, James Taylor, Dolly Parton, Indigo Girls, Emmylou Harris and Linda Ronstadt.

Dixie Chicks continued as an opening act for country music's elite, performed on the Grand Ole Opry, and on various country-oriented television shows. The group also reportedly showed up in the lobby of talk show host David Letterman's office building for an unsolicited audition, and was promptly kicked out of the building. The trio toured Europe and Japan in addition to performing throughout the Southern and Southwestern United States at venues including Dollywood and the Kerrville Folk Festival. They even played at a Presidential Inaugural Gala. All this *before* they had signed a contract with a major label.

The group started 1998 with three professional goals timed with the release of *Wide Open Spaces* in January:

to have a number one record, to earn a gold album, and to get a Country Music Association award nomination. They met all three goals by August.

Wide Open Spaces, their Monument/Sony debut, was a quadruple platinum selling record. The hit "There's Your Trouble" was widely acclaimed by critics as a saucy antidote to country's syrupy sweet sound, "making Garth Brooks look like a wheezing old man." Dislodging country's "boring pop-wannabes" from the charts was seemingly easy. *Wide Open Spaces* was the fastest entry into the country top 10 in the SoundScan chart's history.

Critics liked them, too. *Rolling Stone* called the group "country's finest proponents of high-spirited thrills." In 1999, with the success of the single "Tonight the Heartache's On Me," *Billboard* asked the rhetorical question "Can these girls do anything wrong? It seems not. Every single has shown impressive chart activity, and their Country Music Association and Grammy Award wins just continue to slather icing on the trio's sweet-tasting cake of success." *USA Today* selected both "There's Your Trouble" and "Wide Open Spaces" as country singles of the year in 1998 and credited Dixie Chicks with "single-handedly returning the sound of banjo to country radio."

It was initially felt that Maines' voice needed to be country-fied because she was said to sound too much like alternative rock diva Alanis Morrisette. The gals held their ground both in their musical direction and style choices. Dixie Chicks have been compared to country acts The Forester Sisters and Lee Ann Womack as well as to pop artist Lisa Loeb. The trio endured cutesy quips likening them to "a country Wilson Phillips," and *Rolling Stone*'s pronouncement as "the redneck answer to the Spice Girls."

Shirley Jinkins of the *Fort Worth Star-Telegram* took the trio to task, too, calling them "Shania-ized," referring to country-pop star Shania Twain. She wrote that girls were "dressing lean and trendy, showing a little skin and sporting uniformly platinum locks. It's a cohesive, if mainstream, look. The downside is a loss of distinctiveness that the former All-Cowgirl Band had in abundance." Responded Maines, "We might as well look twenty-something as long as we can."

Their cute looks, though helpful in gaining media attention, had a decided downside. "When you're three blond women in this industry, you're at a disadvantage as far as perceptions go," Seidel told *Seventeen*. In that same article, Erwin said some critics and fans might be curious as to who's playing on the CD. "A lot of people in Nashville sing over tracks laid down by studio musicians. I may not be the best banjo player in Nashville, but I can re-create our sound in a live show." She told *Country America* that fans attending their live shows clearly see that Dixie Chicks are the real deal.

Selected discography

Little Ol' Cowgirl, Crystal Clear, 1992.
Thank Heavens for Dale Evans, Crystal Clear, 1992.
Shouldn't a Told You That, Crystal Clear, 1993.
Wide Open Spaces, Sony, 1998.

Sources

Albany (Oregon) Democrat-Herald, July 10, 1998.
Atlanta Constitution, January 15, 1998.
Billboard, January 17, 1998; May 2, 1998; April 10, 1999.
Country America, September 1998.
Country Weekly, January 20, 1998.
Entertainment Weekly, December 25, 1998.
Harper's Bazaar, March 1999.
Music Row, July 8, 1998.
People, February 9, 1998; September 28, 1998; October 12, 1998; December 28, 1998.
Pollstar, March 30, 1998.
Rolling Stone, December 10, 1998; December 24, 1998.
Seventeen, April 1999.
Sophisticate's Hairstyleguide, October 1998.
Southwest Airlines Spirit, October 1998.
Tennessean (Nashville, TN), January 26, 1998; February 7, 1998; August 5, 1998.
TV Guide, February 20, 1999.
USA Today, January 27, 1998; September 23, 1998; September 24, 1998; December 29, 1998.
USA Weekend, November 27, 1998.
Washington Times, January 25, 1998.

Additional information provided by Monument/Sony Records publicity materials, 1999.

—*Linda Dailey Paulson*

Dropkick Murphys

Punk rock band

Amidst the late 1990s resurgence of ska and hardcore punk music, the Boston, Massachusetts, band Dropkick Murphys made a name for itself with its Irish influenced brand of Oi! punk anthems. The hard-working, heavy-touring Irish-American punk band have been known to occasionally play traditional Irish drinking songs along with their original songs about working class stiffs during their live shows. Band members say this blend of blue-collar punk music attracts a diverse fan base, from the latest generation of punk fans to their Irish grandparents.

The band formed on a lark in 1996 in the basement of a Boston barbershop. "We'd joked about it 'cos of us, me and Mike [McColgan] had never been in a band before and didn't know how to play," said bassist-songwriter Ken Casey. "The other two guys [Rick Barton and Bill Close] humored us and showed us a few things, and it developed quicker than we'd planned. We soon went from just playing some covers in a basement to touring."

Dropkick Murphys went through several drummers in their early days including Bill Close, their original drummer, and Jeff "The Shark" Erner, who played on the band's first recordings, the last of which was *Boys on the Docks*. Matt Kelly joined the band after a two-song audition just as the band began touring and recording. Casey told the *Boston Globe* in 1999, "The first gig, I'd been playing three weeks. But what we run on is the fire in our bellies. If it's more about music and less about the

passion, that's when no one wants to listen to you anymore and that's what happens to a lot of old punk bands."

Constantly touring, Dropkick Murphys quickly gained a reputation as true road warriors. Although they were first known only within the confines of their home state of Massachusetts, the band earned greater widespread popularity and attention through nearly three years of non-stop touring. From1997-99 Dropkick Murphys toured with numerous popular punk and ska bands including The Mighty Mighty Bosstones, The Swingin' Utters, Agnostic Front, The Working Stiffs and U.S. Bombs.

In the true spirit of the punk do-it-yourself ethos, the group recorded and released several seven-inch singles, many of them on their own Flat Records label. Flat Records has also recorded several seven-inch split recordsone record featuring two different groupsby other punk groups including The Cuffs, Vigilantes, Pressure Point and Terminus City. Dropkick Murphys also recorded for other labels including GMM Records, Pogo Records and TKO Records.

In 1997 Dropkick Murphys signed with Hellcat Records, the label owned by Tim Armstrong of the punk band Rancid. Lars Frederiksen, also of Rancid, first heard the band's EP *Boys on the Docks* at a friend's house, and immediately told Armstrong of his new discovery. Upon hearing that EP Armstrong quickly signed Dropkick Murphys to his label and included one of the band's songs on the Hellcat compilation *Give 'Em the Boot*. The band followed that up with two full length releases of their own on Hellcat, *Do or Die in 1998* and *The Gang's All Here* in 1999.

Casey said that although the success of *Do or Die* might have surprised some critics, it was no surprise to Dropkick Murphys, "because we laid the groundwork prior to the album and, when it came out, toured non-stop." It was at the end of the tour supporting *Do or Die* that singer McColgan decided to leave the band, citing the band's incessant touring as the main reason. Al Barr, a friend of the band, was the remaining members' first and only choice to replace McColgan. Barr joined as the band began recording *The Gang's All Here*.

The hectic tour schedule that led to McColgen's departure also led to an ever growing following for the band. Among the devoted was *Bikini's* J.R. Griffin, who called Dropkick Murphys "a wised-up handful of Irish-descended street thugs who grew up under the cloud of lower middle class blue collar drudgery, listened to The Business and Gang Green (and are pissed off about having

For the Record . . .

Members include **Al Barr**, vocals (joined, 1998); **Rick Barton**, guitar and vocals; **Ken Casey**, bass and songwriter; **Bill Close**, drums (1996-97); J**eff "The Shark" Erner**, drums (1997-98); **Matt Kelly**, drums (joined, 1998); **Mike McColgan**, vocals (1996-98).

Formed in Boston, MA, 1996; known for tireless touring; released numerous seven-inch records on a variety of labels including their own Flat Records, 1996-97; signed with Hellcat Records, 1997; released *Do or Die*, 1998; McColgan replaced by Barr, 1998; released *The Gang's All Here*, 1999.

Addresses: *Record company*—Hellcat Records, 2799 Sunset Blvd., Los Angeles, CA 90026.

to shovel too much snow), and who decided to do something other than swing away at life and miss. Combining what they know bestIrish drinking tales and hardcore Oi! musicthey drop tales of union strife, skinhead unity, and camaraderie with tight hardcore pumpers complete with side blows of tin whistles and bagpipes."

The Dropkick Murphys' music can best be described as a combination of 1977 era punk rock, Irish folk songs and "old-fashion working class rock 'n' roll," according to Hellcat Records publicity materials. The band is well known for its Irish sing-along pub tunes. Said Casey in an interview in *Lollipop Magazine*, "I think that's what we've gotten the most notoriety for because the style isn't heard too often. That part of us just comes out without us trying, those are the songs that just happen. The other songs we have to *try* to write. People say they want more of those songs, but on the other hand, we don't want to become cliche and play one specific style. We're a punk band, but out roots are in Irish folk."

The band's main influence is the punk band Stiff Little Fingers, although there are some similarities to the Ramones, the Pogues, and the Clash as well. They even have acknowledged throwing in a little AC/DC. "We wear our influences on our sleeve," Casey told the *Boston Globe*, "but we very much have our own agenda." That agenda is, in part, one that supports the blue-collar working man. Casey's grandfather was a union man whose story is told in "Boys on the Docks." The cover art for that EP is of his co-workers. Casey says his grandfather "organized most of the union workers down on the fish pier."

The members of Dropkick Murphys see their music as a sort of payback to their working class roots. Casey told *Bikini*'s Griffin, "In a way, I don't feel like a musician. I feel like we're carrying a torch for the working class. Maybe we're playing music, but we're like the spokespeople for a whole group of people. I feel like we're doing more for our type of people with this music that we could ever do working a nine-to-five."

Selected discography

Boys on the Docks (EP), Cyclone Records, 1998.
Do or Die, Hellcat Records, 1998.
The Gang's All Here, Hellcat Records, 1999

Sources

Boston Globe, March 14, 1999.
Rolling Stone, April 1, 1999.
Washington Post, February 27, 1998.

Additional source material provided by Hellcat Records publicity materials.

—*Linda Dailey Paulson*

Jacqueline DuPré

Cello

The career of young Jacqueline DuPré lasted a brief 12 years and during that time she graced the stages of the great concert halls of the world, with her passionate performances. Tragically, in October of 1973 she was diagnosed with multiple sclerosis, leaving her unable to play her cello. The extraordinary talent and charisma of young DuPré were fondly extolled in tributes from her friends and musical colleagues, both during her lifetime and after her death. Recordings of her emotive performances retained their appeal for decades afterward. She is perhaps best remembered by the strains of the Elgar Concerto—her signature musical and her numerous renditions of that composition.

DuPré sprang from a simple middle class background south of London. She was born on January 26, 1945 in Oxford, England and grew up in Purley (Surrey) and in London. She was the middle child and second daughter of Derek and Iris (Greep) DuPré. DuPré's older sister, Hilary, was also a gifted musician who played piano and flute. The two girls had one younger brother, Piers.

DuPre's father was an accountant who later became the editor of a trade magazine. Iris DuPré was a musician in her own right, a talented pianist and composer who once taught at the Royal Academy in London. Iris DuPré was widely recognized for her teaching skills, and it was she who taught her children about music and initially taught them to play their instruments. As a youngster, Jacque-line DuPré was not a prodigy in the traditional sense, although reportedly she was able to carry a tune at 18 months old—an age when most children are barely learning to speak. There were some critics who maintained that DuPré was the victim of overly ambitious parents who wanted her to succeed on the concert stage. Others believed, in contrast, that DuPré possessed an exceptional gift of empathy that was clearly manifest when she performed. It has been suggested further that she was unable to verbalize her emotions, and that facet of her character—combined with her ardent fondness for the tones of the cello—fueled her passionate music. What is known for certain is that DuPré was a cellist who was did not like to practice. The music came very easily to her. She enveloped her instrument with her own body as she played and swayed to the sounds that emanated from the cello strings. Additionally, she possessed an uncanny sense of hearing that augmented her innate talent.

DuPré was only four when she first heard the sounds of a cello on a children's program and immediately indicated that she wanted to learn to play the instrument. She received her first cello as a birthday gift when she turned five. At times, as a child, she seemed to be a misfit among her peers, in part because of her precocious talent, but also because of the huge cello that she lugged along with her to school and everywhere else. At six years of age she began to study at the London Cello School. Within three years, she was accepted as a student by the late and noted cellist William Pleeth at the Guildhall School of Music and Drama in London. She studied with Pleeth for seven years, then went on to study in Paris with Paul Tortelier for six months. She later studied with Pablo Casals in Zermatt, Switzerland, and for six months she studied with the great Mstislaw Rostropovich at the Conservatory in Moscow and graduated from the conservatory in 1966.

DuPré reportedly learned very quickly without enduring monotonous practice sessions, and her memorization skills were extremely sharp. Even as a student, DuPré began to perform in recitals. She made her solo debut in 1961 at London's Wigmore Hall, and four years later, on May 14, 1965 she made her American debut at Carnegie Hall in New York. There she performed the Elgar Concerto that came to be known as her signature piece. The event was her first mileston on the road to stardom. That same year, she made a recording of the Elgar Concerto with Sir John Barbirolli and the London Symphony Orchestra. Her teachers, as well as her audiences, were duly impressed by her performances. That fact was evidenced as early as 1964 when she received a gift of a Stradivari cello from an anonymous benefactor. The magnificent cello was made in 1712, and upon her death DuPré bequeathed the instrument to her colleague,

Born January 26, 1945 in Oxford, England, (died in London, October 19, 1987); daughter of Derek and Iris (Greep) Du Pre; *Education:* London Cello School; Guildhall School of Music, London, 1960; studied with William Pleeth, Paul Tortelier, Pablo Casals, Mstislaw Rostropovich; married Daniel Barenboim, June 15, 1967.

First public performance at age seven; performed in BBC concerts at age 12 and 13; first U.S. concert, Carnegie Hall, May 14, 1965; released many albums over the years including, *Jacqueline DuPré: Her Early BBC Recordings* (2 volumes), EMI, 1961; *Saint-Saëns: Le Cygne,* EMI 1962, 1969, 1992; *Schumann: Cello Concerto/Piano Concerto,* EMI, 1969; formed a trio with Daniel Barenboim and Pinchas Zuckerman; formed a quintet with Pinchas Zuckerman, Daniel Barenboim, Zubin Mehta, and Itzhak Perlman; extensive discography, released during her lifetime and posthumously.

Awards: Suggia-Cello Prize, an international competition at age 10; Gold Medal of the Guildhall School of Music, London, 1960; Queen's Prize for British musicians under 30, 1960.

Yo-Yo Ma. Later in her career, she was gifted with a second Stradivari that dated back to 1673.

Late in 1966, not long after she completed her studies in Moscow, DuPré met a talented pianist named Daniel Barenboim. The two were married in the city of Jerusalem, in June of the following year. Upon making each other's acquaintance, DuPré and Barenboim began a series of collaborations, including other prominent musicians of the times. The circumstances of their wedding occurred after she and Barenboim cancelled an engagement to perform in Israel early in 1967, because of a precarious political climate and an impending state of war. The war ended quickly and DuPré and Barenboim traveled immediately to Israel and performed a series of concerts to celebrate the peace. While in the Middle East, DuPré converted to Judaism and married Barenboim before returning home.

In 1968, still newlyweds, DuPré and her husband formed a trio with another young cellist, Pinchas Zuckerman. The Barenboims and Zuckerman performed around the world. They traveled extensively, along with Zucker-

man's wife, Eugenia—a talented writer and a flutist. After a time, noted violinists Itzhak Perlman and Zubin Mehta joined the group, which then became known as the Schubert "Trout" Quintet. The Trout quintet included talent so superb that it took on legendary proportions in the music world and eventually inspired a motion picture by Christopher Nupen. It was said of DuPré that she was especially brilliant as a chamber orchestra player because of her carefree and selfless character. She was in fact so admired for her sunny personality that those who knew her well endowed her with the nickname of "Smiley."

During her fleeting career, DuPré performed and recorded with the greatest musical organizations of her time, including the London Symphony Orchestra, the English Chamber Orchestra, the Chicago Symphony, New Philharmonia, the BBC Symphony Orchestra, and the Israel Philharmonic. Sadly, as the 1960s melded into the 1970s, DuPré began to experience a variety of physical and emotional symptoms that hampered and even impeded her performance. In retrospect it became known that she was suffering early symptoms of the onset of multiple sclerosis. By 1971, she was emotionally overwrought and sometimes suffered inexplicable depression. Within two years the physical symptoms were so severe that she commented that her limbs felt like lead, and she had little strength for anything, save playing her cello. In October of that year, she received the shocking diagnosis at St. Mary's Hospital in Paddington. DuPré was 28 years old when she learned she was suffering from multiple sclerosis and after that, she never again performed in public. Her body, overcome with disease, took on contorted proportions over time; and she suffered great physical ignominy. She used what energy she had left to teach music to others, but her physical constitution deteriorated rapidly. In 1983, in the throes of her illness, she moved to Notting Hill to spend her final years. She died in London on October 19, 1987 at 42. She was buried at Golders Green's Jewish Cemetery.

Before her death, in 1984, a group of her contemporaries expressed their love and admiration for her great talent in a publication edited by William Wordsworth entitled *Impressions.* Well wishers who knew her well filled the pages of the book with praise for the her talent and her spirit. Contributors to the book included her colleagues, Zubin Mehta and Pinchas Zukerman. Charles, Crown Prince of Great Britain, composed a forward to the book in which he confessed that he took up the study of the cello after he first heard DuPré's music. Later, in *American Record Guide* Tom Godell commented on a release of DuPré's *Don Quixote,* "... [She gave] the performance of a lifetime ... bold, dashing, almost reckless at the outset (just like Quixote himself)." Godell commented on another occasion regarding an anthology of cello concertos by DuPré, "No one before or since has played the cello quite like Jacqueline DuPré. The cello sang with a warmth and expressiveness usually achieved only by great vocalists."

During her lifetime DuPré won a series of awards, beginning at age 10 with the Suggia-Cello Prize in an international competition. In 1960, she received both the Gold Medal of the Guildhall School of Music in London, and the Queen's Prize for British musicians under 30. In 1976, DuPré was made an Officer of the Order of the British Empire. She was presented with honorary doctorate degrees from several fine schools including the Universities of Salford, London, Leeds, and Oxford. She was named a fellow at the Royal Academy of Music, Guildhall School of Music, and the Royal College of Music; and she received honorary fellowships from St. Hilda's College, and Oxford. *Country Living* reported in 1996 that a "milk-white" rose variety was named the "Jacqueline DuPré" in her honor, and in January of 1999, Julian Lloyd Webber released a piece called, "Jackie's Song," a tribute to DuPré. Jay Nordlinger of *National Review* called DuPré a "thrilling" cellist, and Eugenia Zuckerman's wife said of her in the *Washington Post;* "She was a musical lioness, ferocious and playful, uninhibited and passionate." An article in *Interview* reminisced of DuPré; "… [During her] legendary performances … she and her cello seemed as possessed as new lovers …"

After her death DuPré was eulogized widely. She was remembered as one of the greatest cello player of all time and was praised for the purity of her tones, her expression, and her ability to evoke shyness and boldness with equal facility. In 1998, cellist Elizabeth Wilson, a colleague of DuPré's, penned *Jacqueline DuPré: Her Life, Her Music, Her Legend.* A comment of DuPré's, quoted from Wilson's manuscript, was later reported in the *Post* by DuPré's good friend, Eugenia Zukerman, "Playing," DuPré commented, "lifts you out of yourself into a delirious place … "

Selected discography

Jacqueline DuPré: Her Early BBC Recordings (2 volumes), EMI, 1961.
Saint-Saëns: Le Cygne, EMI 1962, 1969, 1992.
Schumann: Cello Concerto/Piano Concerto, EMI, 1969.

with Daniel Barenboim

Jacqueline DuPré Impressions, EMI, 1965.
Strauss: Don Quixote/LALO: Cello Concerto, EMI 1968.
Schumann: Cello Concerto/Piano Concerto, EMI, 1969.
Beethoven: Piano Trios & 'Kakadu' Variations, EMI, 1970.
Beethoven: the Five Cello Sonatas, EMI, 1970.
Dvorák Cello Concerto/Haydn Concerto in C, (Barenboim conducting) EMI, 1971.
Chopin & Franck Cello Sonatas, EMI, 1972.
Haydn/Boccherini: Cello Concertos, EMI, 1967, 1969, 1998.
Dvorák: Cello Concerto, Waldesruhe, EMI, 1970, 1998.

Sources

Periodicals

American Record Guide, November-December 1994, p. 220; July-August 1996, p. 205(2).
Country Living, September 1996, p. 75.
Interview, January 1999, p. 52 (6).
National Review, February 22, 1999, p. 53.
New Statesman, January 29, 1999, p. 30.
Time, January 18, 1999, p. 79.
Wall Street Journal, January 5, 1999; March 12, 1999.
Washington Post, April 25, 1999.

Online

"Jacqueline du Pré", http://www.mindspring.com/--mmuelle/dupre/ (May 19, 1999).

—*Gloria Cooksey*

Five Iron Frenzy

Christian ska band

Denver's Five Iron Frenzy has managed the unlikely feat of combining a zany ska-hardcore punk sound with a positive Christian focus. Since its launching in 1995, this high-energy octet has toured at a furious pace in support of its CD releases, winning fans through both its music and its message. While on-stage antics and absurdly humorous lyrics are key elements of the band's appeal, Five Iron Frenzy also lace their music with serious expressions of the faith its members share. With the release of their 1997 CD, *Our Newest Album Ever!*, the band began to add more pop touches to their sound while retaining the rollicking edge that typifies 1990s ska revival bands.

Since their inception, Five Iron Frenzy sought to stay true to its Christian outlook even as it reached out to mainstream audiences. "I write most of the lyrics and can't be afraid to talk about what I believe," vocalist Reese Roper told *Billboard's* Jim Bessman, "but I'm not going up there with my Bible and beating people over the head either." The band sought to find a balance between the sacred and the secular in both their music and their lives. In an interview with Lou Carlozo for *CCM,* trombone player Dennis Culp noted that "When I was younger, contemporary Christian music did not appeal to me at all.... The time you praise God is definitely relevant, but that's not all there is to life. There's a need to be silly, a need to struggle, and that's always seemed more real to me. But our faith is definitely part of everything we do—we sing what's on our heart. There's no calculated formula."

Five Iron Frenzy began in the spring of 1995 as a side project for Roper with bassist Keith Hoerig and guitarists Micah Ortega and Scott Kerr, then members of an industrial rock unit named Exhumator. The roster was fleshed out with the addition of Culp, trumpeter Nathanel "Brad" Dunham. Saxophonist Leanor "Jeff" Ortega (Micah's cousin) joined a few months later. As for the origin of the band's name, Roper recounted in *CCM* that "a friend was joking around and grabbed a golf club and said he was going to use it to defend himself. Someone looked at him and said, 'Oh, it's going to be a five iron frenzy'!"

The band was a hard-working entity from the start, playing some 60 shows in eight months and sharing stages with Less Than Jake, Goldfinger and other neo-ska groups. From the beginning, it performed at both Christian music events like 1995 Cornerstone Festival and at shows with secular bands. The response they received was more enthusiastic than they anticipated. "For me personally, this [success] wasn't even a goal," Hoerig said in a *7ball* interview with Nancy VanArendonk. "My original goal for Five Iron was just to be a good local band — to be able to go as a Christian band and open for non-Christian bands at clubs in the Colorado area, just to do ministry there."

A 1995 Halloween show led to a recording contract with SaraBellum Records, a division of Christian music label 5 Minute Walk Records. Frank Tate, head of 5 Minute Walk, was impressed by the band's ability to reach a wide audience. "They're Christian to the core, but the focus is to show that being a Christian isn't weird — it's just having a friendship with Christ," Tate told *Billboard.* "And it's like with Michael Jackson: people say he's a performer, not a Jehovah's Witness performer.... They [Five Iron Frenzy] can cross over because they're not playing a game but writing really good songs — and being totally enchanting on stage."

Five Iron Frenzy's debut album, *Upbeats and Beat-downs*, was released by SaraBellum in November of 1996. One track, "When Zero Meets 15," dealt with homelessness in Denver and became a Christian modern rock chart hit. The band hit the road in its Ford van in support of the album, playing 150 concerts in 1997. In October of that year, it embarked on its five-week *Rock Your Socks Off* tour, which encouraged concert-goers to bring pairs of wool socks, to be donated to local homeless shelters.

For the Record . . .

Members include **Dennis Culp**, trombone; **Nathanel "Brad" Dunham**, trumpet; **Keith Hoerig**, bass; **Sonnie Johnston** (joined group, 1999), guitar; **Scott Kerr** (left group, 1999), guitar; **Leonor "Jeff" Ortega**, saxophone; **Micah Ortega**, guitar; **Reese Roper**, vocals; **Andy Verdecchio**, drums.

Group formed in Denver, CO in 1995; signed with SaraBellum as subsidiary of 5 Minute Walk Records, 1995; released debut album *Upbeats and Beatdowns*, 1996; released album *Our Newest Record Ever!*, 1997; appeared on Ska Against Racism tour, released EP *Quantity Is Job 1*, 1998.

Address: *Record company*—5 Minute Walk Records, 2056 Commerce Ave., Concord, CA 94520.

The band's second CD, *Our Newest Album Ever!*, appeared in November of 1998 and found it broadening and sharpening its sound. "Anyone who listens to the two albums can see that we've grown a little bit," Culp told *CCM.* "Now we've made a turn to more polished songwriting, better arrangements, more pop-oriented songs.... And the horn parts are more consistent. It's not just chords, there's a lot more riffing, a lot more orchestration." Much of the material on *Our Newest Album Ever!* displayed the band's penchant for unbridled silliness, but songs like "Superpowers" testified to its Christian outlook as well. The CD became a top ten Christian music chart hit, and entered the *Billboard* Top 200 pop album chart as well. Both *Upbeats and Beatdowns* and *Our Newest Album Ever!* sold upwards of 90,000 copies, a strong performance in the Christian pop music market.

November of 1998 saw the release of an EP, *Quantity Is Job 1.* "Since we've been on tour so much, it's been more difficult to write," Roper told *7ball.* "But we thought it'd be cool to get the songs we did have out there so people would have some new music." The EP ran the gamut from such expressions of Christian ideals as "All That's Good" and "Dandelions" to "These Are Not My Pants," a mini-rock opera that parodied heavy metal, swing, opera and other styles. Another highlight for the band in 1998 was taking part in the Ska Against Racism tour, performing alongside such secular ska notables as Reel Big Fish, Less Than Jake and the Toasters in venues across the United States.

By early 1999, Five Iron Frenzy had experienced its first line-up change, with former Jeffries Fan Club member Sonnie Johnston replacing Scott Kerr on guitar. The band continued on its ever-rigorous tour schedule with its new member in tow, and looked forward to the November 1999 release of a live album, *Proof That The Youth Are Revolting.* "I miss my friends when I'm on the road, but this is definitely something we feel is a ministry," Hoerig told *7ball.* "We hope we can serve the people we meet on the road, whether it be people at the shows ... or even just each other. We feel we need to serve people. I think it's a lot of fun."

Selected discography

Upbeats and Beatdowns, SaraBellum/5 Minute Walk, 1996.
Our Newest Album Ever!, SaraBellum/5 Minute Walk, 1997.
Quantity Is Job 1 (EP), SaraBellum/5 Minute Walk, 1998.

Sources

Billboard, October 7, 1997.
CCM, February 1998.
7ball, March/April 1999.
Ska-Tastrophe, Winter 1998.

Additional information was provided by 5 Minute Walk publicity materials, 1999.

—Barry Alfonso

Fountains of Wayne

Pop rock band

Named for a garden shop in Wayne, New Jersey, Fountains of Wayne was formed in December of 1995 by Adam Schlesinger and Chris Collingwood. The pair met in 1985 while they both attended Williams College, supposedly over learning chord progressions to an R.E.M. song. The duo is noted for its songwriting talents, and has been compared to numerous solid pop songwriting teams: John Lennon and Paul McCartney, Squeeze's Chris Difford and Glen Tillbrook, Alex Chilton and Chris Bell of Big Star and Andy Partridge and Colin Moulding of XTC.

During college the pair played in several improbably named bands including Wooly Mammoth, Are You My Mother?, and Three Men When Stood Side By Side Have A Wingspan Of Over 12 Feet. Shortly after graduation, they signed a record deal as the Wallflowers, a band name under which they never recorded and eventually sold to Jakob Dylan and crew. After college, Schlesinger moved to New York to concentrate on working with the band Ivy, a group that he continued to perform with even after starting Fountains of Wayne. Collingwood and Schlesinger continued to play together infrequently as Pinwheel.

Prior to forming Fountains of Wayne, Schlesinger wrote music for television shows including *House of Buggin'* and the short-lived *The Dana Carvey Show*, while Collingwood worked in a bank and played country music with Mercy Buckets in Boston. It was when he moved to New York that the pair began discussing a few songs that Collingwood had written. "We decided to get together and crank out a bunch more, and record them before we had time to think about it too much," Schlesinger told *Rolling Stone*.

The pair was together for a week when they recorded their debut album *Fountains Of Wayne* in 1996. Schlesinger played drums, bass guitar and keyboards, and produced the recording as well. Collingwood served as the group's guitarist and vocalist. "Radiation Vibe" hit number 14 on the *Billboard* Modern Rock Tracks in 1997. *Billboard* called the group's sound a "light-hearted, hook-heavy take on classic pop-rock verities." *Fountains Of Wayne* tied for second place in the magazine's 1996 Critics' Poll. When the time came to take Fountains of Wayne on the road, the pair hired Belltower guitarist Jody Porter, and former Posies drummer Brian Young to round out the band. The group opened for acts including Smashing Pumpkins and Lemonheads.

Fountains of Wayne was released at the same time as the soundtrack for the Tom Hanks film *That Thing You Do!* Schlesinger had been hired to write a song in the Beatles "Merseybeat" tradition for the film. The song "That Thing You Do" earned Schlesinger a Grammy nomination for Best Original Song. He was in the company of no less than Andrew Lloyd-Webber and Tim Rice as well as that of Grammy favorite Diane Warren.

Schlesinger told *Raygun* that both he and Collingwood are songwriting traditionalists. "Chris and I both write on acoustic guitars and piano, and that forces you to think about melody and lyrics. You can't rely on the drum track or the sound of the sample you pick to keep it interesting." In a *Rolling Stone Network* interview Schlesinger said, "We come from a point of view where you write melodies and lyrics, not just make a lot of noise or guitar riffs. We definitely come from more of a traditional songwriting place, you know, Beatles, '60s stuff, Zombies, Hollies, Beach Boys."

Collingwood lists Prefab Sprout and Aztec Camera as his influences, along with other early 1980s British bands like The Smiths and Everything But the Girl. "I don't really listen to anything but pop songs," Collingwood told *Billboard*'s Bradley Bab in 1997. "I've never liked anything that wasn't easily hummable right off. That sort of immediacy makes for an effective form of communication. In the right three minutes, you can get a real portrait of an emotion."

The group followed up with *Utopia Parkway* in 1999. "On *Utopia Parkway*, Fountains of Wayne create a pop

For the Record . . .

Members include **Chris Collingwood**, guitars and vocals; **Jody Porter**, guitar; **Adam Schlesinger**, (born in NJ; mother: publicist, father: horticulturist; both amateur musicians); bass and miscellaneous instruments; **Brian Young**, drums.

Group formed 1996 by Collingwood and Schlesinger as a duo; pair met while attending Williams College; played together in other bands prior to forming Fountains of Wayne; released *Fountains of Wayne*, Scratchie/TAG/Atlantic, 1996.; added Porter and Young in order to tour in support of album; recorded *Utopia Parkway*, 1999.

Addresses: *Record company*—Atlantic Records, 1290 Avenue of the Americas, New York, NY 10104.

masterpiece that makes them to '90s suburbia what the Kinks were to working class mores during the swinging '60s," wrote *Detour* critic Matt Diehl. An anonymous *Mademoiselle* critic gushed that "Their super simple, blatantly suburban, just-post-teenage tunes about crushing, cruising, lazing and loving have a head-boppy, deliberate rincky-dink quality: cheap and cheesy guitars, light and breezy harmonies, twinkly, New Wave-ish keyboards ... The feeling and imagery are so much fun, even the sad songs will make you smile."

Critics have noted similarities in the group's sound to a wide number of other successful pop acts from Beatles and Beach Boys to Cheap Trick and Marshall Crenshaw. "I'm much more comfortable being lumped in with Cheap Trick," Collingwood quipped. He told *Musician* that *Utopia Parkway* is filled with songs containing "absolutely none of ourselves and a lot of everybody else." And critics have made their own speculation about the group's pop inspirations, citing a diverse lot of artists including Billy Joel and The Romantics.

Collingwood told *Billboard* that *Utopia Parkway* is the band's chance to explore the depth of its abilities. "Typically, the first album is sort of a statement of purpose, to put it in ridiculous business terms," he said. "It's like, 'Here's what we are; here's what we do.' If you try to make it too complicated and too weird, it tends to muddle the vision. But once you've established that, I think it's a natural progression to do something a little more diverse."

The plaudits and songwriting team comparisons continued as "Denise" began airing on modern rock and college radio stations in the summer of 1999. However, Schlesinger contends, "College radio stations don't particularly care about our record," he told *TimeOut New York*. "We went straight to commercial radio with our first single."

The duo wanted to be known as songwriters rather than performers. Collingwood told *CMJ New Music Monthly* that Fountains of Wayne is "really more about having a forum for two songwriters that it is about four guys working on songs together." He told *TimeOut New York*, "I've never wanted to be known as a singer or a guitar player. I want to be known as a songwriter."

The art of songwriting is more difficult than it might seem according to Schlesinger. "If you sit around trying to write the perfect pop song, you really won't write anything," Schlesinger told *Pulse!* "I mean, we started just trying to write things that would entertain each other, more than trying to reach some kind of lofty goal with the songs. And I think sometimes that's what people respond to more than anything in a song—that even though you're using a kind of classic form, there's some little private joke or personal reference in it that keeps it from being a generic exercise."

Selected discography

Fountains of Wayne, Scratchie/TAG/Atlantic, 1996.
Utopia Parkway, Atlantic, 1999.

Sources

Alternative Press, June 1999.
Billboard, January 18, 1997; March 20, 1999.
CMJ New Music Monthly, May 1999.
Detour, April 1999.
Mademoiselle, April 1999.
Musician, January 1999.
New York Times, May 31, 1999.
People, March 3, 1997; March 17, 1997.
Pulse!, May 1999.
Raygun, May 1999.
Rolling Stone, November 28, 1996.
TimeOut New York, April 8, 1999.

Additional information provided by Atlantic Records publicity materials.

—*Linda Dailey Paulson*

John Eliot Gardiner

Conductor

Accomplished British conductor John Eliot Gardiner is noted for founding and directing the Monteverdi Choir in 1964 and its complement Monteverdi Orchestra in 1968. Although he conducted all types of music, he is a renowned authority in a variety of 17th and 18th century styles, and conducted Gluck's *Alceste* for the British Broadcasting Corporation (BBC) and *Iphigenie en Tauride* at Covent Garden in 1973. He founded the English Baroque Soloists in 1977, which he conducted in performances that featured original instruments of the Baroque era. Gardiner appeared in many of the major music centers of the world as a guest conductor. He was made an officer of the Ordre des Artes et des Lettres in 1988, and a Commander of the Order of the British Empire in 1989 in recognition of his long, illustrious, and varied career. Tim Page of the *New York Times* wrote, "Mr. Gardiner transcends syntax and goes directly to the heart of the music".

Gardiner was born on April 20, 1943, in Fontmell Magna, a town in southwestern England. He was raised on a farm and his parents, Rolf Gardiner and Marabel Hodgkin Gardiner, enlisted him in the local church choir as a child. Gardiner had learned some of the early-music repertoire by the time he was thirteen. His family members enjoyed singing at home, and that's where Gardiner developed a rudimentary knowledge of Renaissance and early Baroque-period choral music. He told *High Fidelity* magazine's Scott Cantrell, "It became quite a tradition in the house to attract other good amateur singers, and we actually did a concert tour in Germany and Austria and did some pretty good adventurous programs."

Gardiner's first major early musical influence was the material of Claudio Monteverdi. When he was six years old his parents took him to hear a lecture given by Nadia Boulanger on Monteverdi and to hear Walter Goehr conduct the composer's *Vespro della beata vergine* in Yorkminster. Gardiner listened to a taped radio broadcast of that work time and time again. He became a self-taught musician, and by the time he reached his teenage years he demonstrated an aptitude for conducting music. He attended the Bryanston School, and then worked with Palestinian refugees for the United Nations. Later, he studied Arabic, history, and medieval Spanish at King's College, Cambridge. As an undergraduate, he served as secretary of the King's College Music Society, and sang and played the violin in Berlioz-revival performances led by Colin Davis.

In 1964, as an extracurricular activity, he founded the Monteverdi Choir for a performance of the Vespers at King's College Chapel. He was granted music funding from the Musical Society, and hired well-known professional singers such as Robert Tear and John Shirley-Quirk as soloists. He told Cantrell, "It took quite a lot of gall. The challenge was to use the best singers of Cambridge, all of whom were beautifully schooled in the English choral tradition, which is very polite and disciplined, and to see if they were capable of singing this very difficult music with the appropriate elan and commitment and, above all, vocal color." The performance was considered a landmark event, and music critics foresaw a successful future for Gardiner's Monteverdi Choir.

After obtaining his master's degree in history, Gardiner decided he needed formal music training. He started by studying with harpsichordist and musicologist Thurston Dart. He earned a certificate of advanced studies in music from King's College in 1966, and moved to Paris where he studied with Nadia Boulanger for two years on a French government scholarship. He also studied with Antal Dorati and George Hurst—a protege of Pierre Monteux—and apprenticed himself to the BBC Northern Orchestra in Manchester for two years.

In the late 1960s the members of Gardiner's Monteverdi Choir—by now a mixture of professional and amateur singers—had reunited in London. Gardiner felt the secret of the choir's success was due to the fact that the professionals were kept on guard by amateurs who were just as accomplished, though unpaid—and the amateurs, in turn, were kept on guard by a fear of being the weak link. As a result, there was an atmosphere of

For the Record . . .

Born April 20, 1943, in Fontmell Magna, England; son of Rolf and Marabel (Hodgkin) Gardiner, farmers; married musician Elizabeth Suzanne Wilcock in 1981; children: three daughters. *Education:* King's College, Cambridge; studied with Nadia Boulanger, Antal Dorati, and George Hurst, apprenticed with BBC for two years.

Enlisted in the local church choir as a child; major early musical influence was the material of Caludio Monteverdi; became a self-taught musician; sang and played the violin in Berlioz-revival performances led by Colin Davis; founded the Monteverdi Choir for a performance of the Vespers at King's College Chapel in 1964; founded the Monteverdi Orchestra in 1968 to accompany the choir; prepared new editions of Jean Philippe Rameau's *Dardanus, Les fetes d'Hebe,* and *Les boreades* for London concert performances, 1973-75; principle conductor and music director, Canadian Broadcasting Corporation's Vancouver Orchestra, 1980-83; artistic director of the Gottingen Handel Festival in Germany from 1981-89; music director of the Opera de Lyon, founded Orchestre de l'Opera de Lyon, 1983; led symphony orchestras in New York, Dallas, San Francisco, Boston, Toronto, Montreal, and Detroit as a guest conductor; conducted the Philharmonic Orchestra, the Royal Philharmonic Orchestra, the Bournemouth Symphony Orchestra, the City of Birmingham Symphony Orchestra, and the Oslo Philharmonic; prolific recording career for the Erato, Philips, ARC, Argo, and London labels included annual releases of Bach's major choral works, the complete Mozart piano concertos, and a complete cycle of Beethoven concertos.

Awards: Grand Prix du Disque for *Israel in Egypt* (1979), Purcell's *The Fairy Queen* (1982), Handel's *Messiah* (1984), and Handel's *Solomon* (1985); accorded the Metropolitan Opera's Best Opera Recording honors in 1983 for Rameau's *Les boreades*; Voted Artist of the Year in 1994 by *Gramophone* magazine.

Addresses: *Office*—Monteverdi Choir and Orchestra, Ltd., Bowring Bldg., P.O. Box 145, Tower Pl., London EC3P 3BE, England; *Management*—IMG Artists Europe, Media House, 3 Burlington Lane, Chiswick, London, W42TH, England; *Home*—Gore Farm, Ashmore, Salisbury, Wiltshire, SP5 5AR, England.

friendly musical competition. Gardiner founded the Monteverdi Orchestra in 1968 to accompany the choir, but he chose not to use original-period instruments at first. He had used cornets and sackbuts in 1964 when he performed the Monteverdi Vespers, and viewed the result as discouraging. In 1978, though, Gardiner felt that he had gone as far as he could playing middle baroque and early classical music on modern instruments, and switched to original instruments

Gardiner prided himself on transcending academic concerns in music, but proved that he had an aptitude for scholarship when preparing new editions of Jean Philippe Rameau's *Dardanus, Les fetes d'Hebe,* and *Les boreades* for London concert performances between 1973-75. In order to mark the tenth anniversary of the Monteverdi Choir on April 19, 1975, Gardiner conducted Rameau's final opera, *Les boreades*, in London's Queen Elizabeth Hall for the first performance in modern times. *Les boreades* was subsequently presented as a fully staged production at the Aix-en-Provence Festival in 1982. By the late 1970s, Gardiner and his ensembles were in great demand throughout the United States and Europe. The Monteverdi Orchestra was renamed the English Baroque Soloists in 1978 after switching to original-period instruments.

From 1980-83 Gardiner served as the principle conductor and music director of the Canadian Broadcasting Corporation's Vancouver Orchestra, and from 1981-89 served as the artistic director of the Gottingen Handel Festival in Germany. In 1983 the Opera de Lyon hired him as music director and asked him to create an orchestra for the company. Gardiner, a British early-music specialist, didn't see a contradiction in leading the sixty-member Orchestre de l'Opera de Lyon, and told Michael Oliver of Gramophone, "Once you've defined the repertoire, the problems are identical: you take a score...and you start thinking about what sorts of sounds the composer was expecting to hear." After successful critical acclaim, Gardiner left the post in 1988 to pursue other projects, but remained "chef fondateur" (founder head) and conductor laureate. In April of 1983 he led the English Baroque Soloists and the Monteverdi Choir in a lauded performance of Handel's oratorio *Israel in Egypt* at Lincoln Center's Alice Tully Hall in New York City.

In 1989 Gardiner celebrated the silver anniversary of the Monteverdi Choir with an international tour that included the Unites States, India, Japan, and Australia. Gardiner also conducted the Philharmonic Orchestra at the Royal Festival Hall in London in 1989, in the premier of a new version of Debussy's *La mer*, as edited by Marie Rolf. A year later, he introduced—with little acclaim—a new period-instrument orchestra called the Orchestre Revolutionnaire et Romantique that was identical in personnel to the English Baroque Soloists. As a guest conductor, Gardiner led symphony orchestras in Dallas, San Francisco, Boston, Toronto, Montreal, and Detroit. He also led the New York Philharmonic, and the Orchestra of St. Luke's, with whom he made his Carnegie Hall debut in November 1988. In Europe he conducted the Philharmonic Orchestra, the Royal Philharmonic Orchestra, the Bournemouth Symphony Orchestra, the City of Birmingham Symphony Orchestra, and the Oslo Philharmonic.

Gardiner has also reached a wide audience through his many recordings. Incredibly prolific, he was averaging seventeen releases a year by 1989 for the Erato, Philips, ARC, Argo, and London labels. His output included annual releases of Bach's major choral works, the complete Mozart piano concertos, a complete cycle of Beethoven concertos, and the latter Mozart operas. He received the Grand Prix du Disque in 1979 for *Israel in Egypt*, again in 1982 for Purcell's *The Fairy Queen*, in 1984 for Handel's *Messiah,* and in 1985 for Handel's *Solomon*. He was also accorded the Metropolitan Opera's Best Opera Recording honors in 1983 for Rameau's *Les boreades*, and voted Artist of the Year in 1994 by *Gramophone* magazine.

Selected discography

Symphonie Fantastique, Berlioz, Philips, 1993.
Motetten, Johann Sebastian Bach, Erato, 1995.
Danny Boy: The Music of Percy Grainger, Philips, 1996.

Leonore, Beethoven, Deutsche Gramophone, 1997.
Fruehlings Sinf. Flower Songs, Britten, Deutsche Gramophone, 1997.
Jubilante, Philips, 1997.
Symphonische Taenze/Taras Bulba, Rachmoninoff, Deutsche Gramophone, 1998.
Sinfonien 1-4, Schumann, Deutsche Gramophone, 1998.

Sources

Periodicals

Boston Globe, February 17, 1989.
Boston Herald, February 18, 1989.
CD Review, September 1990.
High Fidelity, July, 1989.
London Observer, November 4, 1973.
London Times, December 12, 1989.
Los Angeles Times, February 27, 1989.
The New York Times, February 21, 1989; March 8, 1987; April 7, 1986.
The New Yorker, May 23, 1983.

Online

"John Eliot Gardiner" http://www.warner-classics/erato/ln/baroque/biogs/gardiner.htm (May 19, 1999).
"John Eliot Gardiner," http://www.dgclassics.com/artists/gardiner/gardiner.htm (March 19, 1999).

—B. Kimberly Taylor

Gilberto Gil

Singer, songwriter

A dominant force in contemporary Brazilian music, Gilberto Gil helped shape that nation's modern music in the twentieth century. His lasting influence could be seen beyond the borders of Brazil. Towards the end of the century he continued to exert his influence on new generations of musicians by discovering and nurturing new talent in, while continuing his schedule of recording and performing.

Gilberto Gil was born June 29, 1942 in Salvador, Brazil and spent his childhood in Bahia, in the Brazilian interior. As a child he began playing drums and showed interest in various forms of music. He started teaching himself to play trumpet by listening to radio programs at the age of seven. His family moved back to Salvador when Gil was in his teens. It was in 1950, after hearing the music of Luiz Gonzaga that he decided to learn to play the accordion. Gil played with a group Os Desfinados while still in high school. When he heard Joao Gilberto on the radio, he switched instruments again, this time to guitar.

Gil studied business at the University of Bahia and worked for a short time in Sao Paulo for Gessy-Lever, a huge multinational firm. In 1966 he decided to devote himself solely to a career in music. Early musical influences, in addition to Gonzaga and Gilberto, included Sivuca and Antonio Carlos "Tom" Jobim, the legendary Brazilian composer with whom he studied at the Goethe Institute. Gil had his first recording contract in 1966, and he had his first hit as a songwriter—Ellis Regina's version of "Louvaçáo" that same year.

It is truly difficult, if not entirely impossible, to write about Gilberto Gil without mentioning Caetano Veloso. Both were musicians shaped by almost identical influences. They were university students in Bahia and met at the Teatro Vila Velha in Salvador in 1963. Gil and Veloso competed in several music festivals—Gil's "Domingo no Parque" was one of his first songs to be widely recognized through participation in these competitions. "For their part, Gilberto Gil and Caetano Veloso," writes Tarik De Souza in a 1986 UNESCO Courier article, "picked up, each in his own way, the musical threads laid down by [Dorival "Dorri"] Caymmi and Joao Gilberto." They would become long-time friends and artistic collaborators.

As Mark Holston wrote in *Guitar Player*, that Brazilian musicians "owe their privileged status to a unique combination of factors present only in Brazil. Through imported African slaves came Brazil's most important musical ingredient, as Jobim describes: 'The striking feature of Brazilian popular music is the basic African rhythm.' Europeans, Jobim continues, also had an impact: 'The European contribution, as can easily be seen, is enormous: melody, harmony, and form, as well as instruments. The fact is that European culture found new and fertile ground here.'"

Gil and Veloso were among the artists attempting to amalgamate all these various influences, with the addition of electric guitars from British and American rock, while remaining politically and artistically relevant and uniquely Brazilian. The result was a movement called Tropicalismo. The movement has been described in various terms, often perceived as a counterpart to the American hippie movement. Bahian artists including Gil and Veloso, Tom Ze, Gal Costa, Maria Bethânia (Veloso's sister) and Jose Carlos Capinam were associated with the movement from 1967-69. The band Os Mutantes, composers Rogerio Duprat and Julio Medaglia, and poets Augusto and Haroldo de Campos were all associated with Tropicalismo, as well.

Tropicalismo was "a [cry] for moral and aesthetic liberty launched by Caetano Veloso and Gilberto Gil," explained Mario de Aratanha in the *UNESCO Courier*. "Political dissent invaded the realm of music, growing into full-blooded revolt against the military dictatorship set up in 1964. Under the new rulers, harsh artistic censorship joined up with police violence to silence a generation." "Their lyrics were socially-conscious and provocative,

Born June 29, 1942 in Salvador, Brazil.

Played various instruments in childhood and youth, including accordion, drums and trumpet; met Caetano Veloso in 1963; signed first recording contract, 1966; first noted hit "Domingo No Parque"; founded Tropicália movement in 1967 with Veloso and others; government censorship imposed in Brazil, Gil and Veloso arrested, jailed, and forced into exile in London1968; began exploring roots of Brazilian music; trip to Nigeria in 1977 results in recording Refavela; enters Bahian politics, successfully runs for city council, and is appointed to various cultural and social organizations, 1987; retired from politics, but remained involved in some organizations on a voluntary basis1992; continued to record throughout 1990s with Veloso, other musicians and as a solo artist. Awards: 1998 Grammy for Quanta Live; Knight of Arts and Letters (France) and Cruz da Ordem de Rio Branco (Brazil).

Addresses: *Record company*—Blue Jackel Entertainment, P.O. Box 87, Huntington, NY 11743. Website—http://www.gilbertogil.com.br.

but they also experimented with the electrifying rock sounds that emanated from England and the United States," wrote Christopher Dunn in *Americas*. "One particularly ingenious song by Gilberto Gil and poet Torquato Neto, 'Geleia Geral' (General Jelly), reconciles rock with traditional Brazilian popular culture." In that same article Gil told Dunn, "Tropicalismo opened the doors to all influences, it had a democratic attitude towards culture. It helped to reaffirm the popular culture of the streets, and influenced the re-africanization of Brazilian culture."

Around the same time, Brazil was entering a period of increased protests, political violence, military censorship and political and cultural repression. President Arthur da Costa e Silva, in December 1968, censored the arts and press with Institutional Act V. Under this legislation left-wing leaders, labor organizers and artists, including Veloso and Gil, were arrested. "We were very supportive of what was happening in the universities in the [U.S.] and in Paris, for instance," said Gil, "and reproduced those events for Brazilian students. So I wound up in jail for two months, then house arrest for six months. Then I was sent away to London, where I stayed for three years."

During his exile Gil made several trips to Africa and began exploring music of the diaspora throughout the Caribbean, particularly reggae. The most influential of these voyages was a trip to Nigeria in 1977. "When I went to Nigeria in '77, I met Fela, Stevie Wonder and King Sunny Ade. That trip really gave me the push toward blackness, toward really trying to understand the roots and spirit of the culture," explained Gil. "I made the links between Stevie Wonder and Miles Davis and Jimmy Cliff and Bob Marley: people speaking out, being proud of being black, understanding the difficulties of getting black culture into Western civilization. So when I got back to Brazil, I started doing music in a more black-oriented vein."

From Tropicalismo sprung Música Popular Brasileria (Brazilian Popular Music) or MPB. Gil is considered the first MPB musician to use an electric guitar. This wave of music in the 1970s introduced new Brazilian artists to the United States, but Gil's music was not widely recognized in American until the 1980s when Talking Heads founder David Byrne and other English-speaking musicians injected bossa nova and other Afro-Brazilian sounds into their own music.

In addition to being active as a recording artist throughout the 1980s and 1990s, Gil became politically active, particularly in Bahian cultural programs. He was a city councilman, elected with more votes than any other candidate and one of the few blacks in Brazil to hold public office in the late 1980s. He formed a group called Blue Wave and performed at events to raise funds and awareness for rainforest preservation. In 1995 he became part of the council for the Brazilian social program called Comunidad Solidaria. However, he decided against running for a second term saying, "I just couldn't adapt to the character of being a politician. The masks you wear. I'm not a warrior. I'm a humanist. And politics are not humanist at all."

Even after his short political career, Gil's popularity did not wane, and he continued to record and tour internationally. Gil's *Quanta Live* was recognized with a 1998 Grammy award. Gil told *Rhythm* "the most important thing to me is that I like the record, and that's the best point about receiving an award." Recorded live at the peak of the band's form in Brazil, Gil considered the Grammy as band achievement.

Towards the end of the century Gil—by now in his fifties— continued to grow musically. "I've always been a musician, and I have always tried to keep developing new ideas," said Gil in an interview for *O Sol De Oslo*. "Since I see change as a natural process, I think I've always been changing and developing my music. It's hard for me to state precisely which directions I took, but I have moved along using my feelings and intuition."

Selected discography

Refavela, Warner Music Brazil, 1977.
Personalidade, Polygram Brazil.
A Gente Precisa Ver o Lua, WEA Brazil, 1981.
(contributor) *Beleza Tropical: Brazil Classics Vol. I*, Luaka Bop, 1989.
(with Caetano Veloso) *Caetano y Gil: Tropicalia 2*, Nonesuch, 1994.
(contributor) *Red Hot + Rio* ("Refazenda"), PGD/Verve, 1996.
(contributor) *Tropicália 30 Anos* (five-CD set reissue), Mercury/Polygram Brazil, 1998.
Quanta Live, Atlanta/Mesa, 1998.
O Sol de Oslo, Blue Jackel Entertainment, Inc., 1999.
(contributor) *Beleza Tropical 2: Novo! Mais! Melhor!*, Luaka Bop, 1999.

Sources

Books

Broughton, Simon, et. al., editors, *World Music: The Rough Guide*, Penguin Books USA, Inc., 1994.
Schreiner, Claus, *Música Brasileira*, Marion Boyars Publishers, 1993.

Periodicals

Americas (English Edition), September-October 1993.
Guitar Player, December 1994; May 1999.
Knight-Ridder/Tribune News Service, August 12, 1993.
New York Times Magazine, April 25, 1999.
Philadelphia Inquirer, June 1, 1999.
Rhythm, June 1999.
The Nation, May 20, 1991.
Time, October 16, 1989.
UNESCO Courier, December, 1986; March 1991.

Additional information provided by Blue Jackel Entertainment, Inc., publicity materials.

—*Linda Dailey Paulson*

Allen Ginsberg

Poet, singer

Allen Ginsberg was arguably the most influential poet of the second half of the twentieth century. He was, with Jack Kerouac and William S. Burroughs, one of the leading figures of the Beat Generation of American writers, which alone would have guaranteed his fame. His public activity extended far beyond the composition of verse, however. Ginsberg was an ardent spokesman and publicist for the radical new writing of the 1950s and 1960s; he was an outspoken political dissident, critical of the abuses of power by governments of all stripes; he was the co-founder and director of the Naropa School of Disembodied Poetics in Boulder, Colorado; he was an early and highly influential gay rights advocate. And one of the most controversial aspects of his career, in the eyes of critics and his fans, was Allen Ginsberg's music. Untrained in composition or performance, Ginsberg was nonetheless a highly enthusiastic singer who, in the face of doubt and criticism, persevered to produce a small body of work that was well received, if poorly distributed, and quickly out-of-print.

Ginsberg grew up entertaining dreams of a career as a lawyer or writer, but apparently without giving a thought to becoming a musician. He enjoyed a wide variety of music ranging from Beethoven and opera, to George Gershwin, to Ma Rainey and Bessie Smith. Like his close friend Jack Kerouac, he was a fan of jazz in the late 1940s and early fifties, and later recalled listening to Symphony Sid's all-night radio show of non-stop bebop stars like Charlie Parker, Ben Webster, Lennie Tristano and Lester Young. It was in the middle 1950s when "Howl," a poem that captured the anger and discontent of his entire generation, made Ginsberg famous. He followed it up with other influential works, including poems like "America," "Sunflower Sutra," "Kaddish," and "Wichita Vortex Sutra" which were not overtly musical, but whose rhythms were based on Ginsberg's breath, much like the lines blown by a sax player. In 1954, traveling in Mexico, Ginsberg built his own set of log drums which he suspended from a tree and played. Bary Miles, in his biography Ginsberg, quotes one of Allen's letters of the time: "People come from miles around to hear my drumming. It really goes over big."

He discovered chanting as an aid to meditation in 1963, and chanted regularly from then on, both in private and at his public readings. In 1965 during one of Ginsberg's visits to Los Angeles, Phil Spector, who had produced hit singles for girl groups like the Ronnettes and the Crystals, offered not only to record an album of Ginsberg's chanting, but to make it a hit of it as well. The offer came at a time when Ginsberg was beginning to think seriously about the connections between popular music and poetry. Bob Dylan, a great admirer of Ginsberg's poetry, had proven time and again that one could write intelligent, even poetic song lyrics and still have hit records. The success of British invasion groups like the Beatles and Rolling Stones, only solidified Ginsberg's conviction that poetry could reach far more people through music and records than through traditional vehicles such as little magazines and books.

His first musical project involved setting some poems of William Blake to music. Ginsberg's interest in Blake went back as least as far as his student time at Columbia University. More significantly, though, Blake had been the center of a powerful, life-altering experience that Ginsberg had had in 1948. Depressed and aimless, Ginsberg was in his room reading Blake's *Songs of Innocence and Experience,* when a voice that he took to be Blake's began reciting two Blake poems, "The Sick Rose" and "The Little Girl Lost." Ginsberg experienced a deep, sudden insight into the eternal beauty of every detail of the world, "eternity in a grain of sand" as Blake had written in "The Tyger." The Blake vision set in motion, over the course of more than two decades, experiments by Ginsberg with drugs, religion, meditation, chanting and other forms of altered consciousness.

Ginsberg knew that Blake had sung these "songs" himself. No record of Blake's melodies survived, however, so Ginsberg set about writing his own, based on the sound of the words in the poems. He set "The Grey Monk"—a Blake poem not included in the *Songs*—to

Born Irwin Allen Ginsberg, June 3, 1926, Newark, NJ (died 1997); son of Louis and Naomi (Levy) Ginsberg. Education: attended Columbia University, New York, NY.

Began writing poetry as university student in the 1940s; experienced the voice of William Blake in a series of powerful visions, 1948; made first important impact his initial reading of *Howl* at the Six Gallery, October 13, 1955; "Kaddish" published, 1959; met Bob Dylan, 1963; began chanting to meditate as well as at his readings, 1963; set Blake's "The Grey Monk" to music, 1968; released *Wm. Blake's Songs of Innocence & Experience*, MGM Records, 1970; recorded group of songs with Bob Dylan, 1971; John Hammond recorded *First Blues* for Columbia Records but label refused to release it, 1976; Folkways released album of songs recorded by Harry Smith, 1981; performed on "Ghetto Defendant" on the Clash's *Combat Rock*, 1982; *First Blues* released on John Hammond Records, 1982; "Capitol Rock" single with Denver band The Gluons released in Rocky Mountain states, mid-1980s; *Collected Poems* published, 1984; released *The Lion For Real*, 1989; released *Holy Soul Jelly Roll—Poems And Songs* (box set), 1994.

Awards: National Book Award for Poetry, *The Fall of America*, 1974; Gold Medal, National Arts Club, 1979; member American Academy and Institute of Arts and Letters.

music in summer 1968. His plan to set more of Blake's work to music was given impetus when Paul McCartney asked Ginsberg to do something for the Beatles' new label, Apple Records. Ginsberg returned to his farm in upstate New York and, using an old pump organ, set about composing melodies for 19 Blake poems.

It was slow going. Ginsberg had no background or knowledge about composition, musical notation, or singing. "Ironically," wrote Michael Schumacher in his Ginsberg biography *Dharma Lion*, "his initial problem as a songwriter was not an inability to write melody, instead it was a lack of faith in his own capacity to write lyrics. The Blake poems provided him the lyrics—and the confidence." Ginsberg's friend Barry Miles, who was witness to the recording of the Beatles' *Sgt. Pepper's*

Lonely Hearts Club Band, came to assist with the recording. They worked all of June and July of 1969 on the project, eventually settling on eleven settings for the album, including "Ah Sunflower!" and "The Sick Rose," the two poems that had figured in Ginsberg's 1948 Blake visions.

Later Ginsberg would connect the visions and the recording sessions: "The mantra chanting all through the '60s deepened my voice so it sank deeper and deeper into my body," he wrote for the set *Holy Soul Jelly Roll—Poems And Songs (1949-1993)*. "In 'Nurse's Song' from the Blake record … my voice finally settled into some approximation of the voice I heard in 1948 … Sort of like experiencing what I would be like in the future." The album was released on MGM Records to favorable reviews, which encouraged Ginsberg to record another record's worth of material that was, unfortunately, never released.

In 1971, Bob Dylan heard Ginsberg improvising song lyrics at a reading. Impressed, he suggested recording together, which they did over two sessions in November of 1971 at the Record Plant in New York City. Ginsberg spent the first session getting comfortable with the setting and the musicians. The second session produced "CIA Dope Calypso" about covert government drug trafficking in Southeast Asia, "Going To San Diego" about Richard Nixon and the upcoming Republican National Convention, "Many Loves" about some of the men with whom he had had relationships, and "Whozat Jimmy Berman." Two takes of "September on Jessore Road," a song inspired by Ginsberg's experience of poverty in India, were also recorded. But much to his disappointment, neither track was usable. It didn't look like the other tracks would fare much better though. They went into a can and sat on a shelf for years before they were finally released.

In 1976, Ginsberg gave tapes of the 1971 sessions, along with a copy of his book *First Blues,* to John Hammond, the producer at Columbia who had discovered Leadbelly, Robert Johnson and scores of other brilliant musicians. Hammond liked what he heard and organized a session in June. The album they made included eight new songs along with three from the sessions with Dylan. Columbia executives were upset with Ginsberg's explicit references to homosexuality in some of the songs, however, and refused to release the record. The record, *First Blues,* would eventually be issued in 1983 on John Hammond's own label. Confusing Ginsberg's discography, Folkways released a completely different album in 1981 under the same title. That record was recorded by ethnomusicologist and eccentric, Harry Smith, in his room at New York's Chelsea Hotel in the mid-1970s.

Ginsberg's song writing tailed off in the 1980s, but he remained interested in the latest pop music trends. Attracted by their radical protest songs, Ginsberg visited the Clash backstage before one of their shows in New York in 1981. When they asked him to read a poem to the crowd, he offered instead to sing a song he had written with them. They spent ten minutes rehearsing then performed "Capitol Air," a song in which Ginsberg rejects both capitalism and communism. He was pleased at the enthusiastic response he got from the crowd. Six months later he visited the Clash again, this time in the studio, and was asked by Joe Strummer to look over and tighten up some of their new song lyrics. Ginsberg also provided the "voice of God" which appeared on the song "Ghetto Defendant" on the Clash album Combat Rock. Although he was not writing songs as much as he had earlier in his life and his recording had petty much stopped, Ginsberg never stopped singing, accompanied by his harmonium, at readings. He would also recruit local talent as back-up musicians when he traveled. The arrangement led to a recording of "Birdbrain" with the Denver band the Gluons, which was released in Colorado in the mid-1980s.

Despite his personal enthusiasm for music, Ginsberg had often gotten mixed reactions from audiences when he sang or chanted at readings. His voice was ordinary at best, and his harmonium provided just a simple background drone, not a true musical accompaniment. Preparing for his 1989 release The Lion For Real, Ginsberg asked friends, poets and musicians, how to approach the project. According to Michael Schumacher, vocalist Marianne Faithfull suggested "Maybe you shouldn't sing...." In response Ginsberg returned to a strength he had developed over the years, reading his poetry. Shorter works from all phases of his career are accompanied by musicians like Arto Lindsey, Bill Frisell, Marc Ribot, and G.E. Smith. Martha Bustin, writing in Rolling Stone, called The Lion For Real "an artful, affecting presentation of Ginsberg's work.... a virtual Ginsberg primer."

In the last years of his life, Ginsberg combined his reading with music on other recordings. He made "The Ballad of the Skeletons" with Philip Glass, Paul McCartney and Marc Ribot; the Kronos Quartet accompanied him on a reading of his landmark poem, "Howl." Ginsberg's recorded work was called "the most substantial offering of recorded works by any poet in history" by Schumacher. An enormous four-CD overview of it, entitled Holy Soul Jelly Roll—Poems And Songs, was released by Rhino Records in 1994.

Selected discography

Howl and Other Poems, Fantasy-Galaxy Records #7013, Berkeley, CA., 1959.
Kaddish, Atlantic Verbum Series #4001, New York, NY., 1966.
Wm. Blake's Songs of Innocence & Experience, MGM/Verse CTS 3083, 1970.
First Blues: Rags, Ballads and Harmonium Songs, Folkway Records FSS 37560, 1981.
First Blues, John Hammond Records W2X 37673, 1982.
The Lion for Real, Great Jones/Island Records CCD6004, 1989.
Holy Soul Jelly Roll—Poems And Songs, Rhino Records, 1994.

Sources

Books

Miles, Barry, Ginsberg: A Biography. Simon & Schuster, New York, 1989.
Schumacher, Michael. Dharma Lion: A Critical Biography of Allen Ginsberg, St. Martin's Press, New York, 1992.

Periodicals

Billboard, July 2,1994; October 26, 1996.
Rolling Stone, March 8, 1990.

Additional material provided by Bob Rosenthal and Peter Hale.

—Gerald E. Brennan

Greater Vision

Gospel group

Since its formation in 1990, Greater Vision has upheld the time-honored traditions of Southern gospel harmony singing. Lead singer Gerald Wolfe, baritone Rodney Griffin and tenor Jason Waldroup have become prominent in the Christian music community through their expert vocal blend and repertoire of standard hymns and original material. Committed to spreading their message of faith, Greater Vision has toured steadily in the United States and abroad since its formation, reaching a wide audience through both live shows and television appearances. "We try to offer listeners lots of variety, yet remain true to the traditional styling Greater Vision is known for," Wolfe commented in a Daywind Music press biography. "We sing to a broad audience, and because of that, there are people with a variety of needs. Some need encouragement and hope, while others need joyous songs.... That's why our programs are a mixture of both old and new. Sure, there are some great new songs out there, but casting aside the old hymns and convention style songs would be a big mistake."

Though the trio has gone through membership changes, Greater Vision has remained true to its original intentions. Founding member Wolfe grew up singing in church in his native East Tennessee, then went professional by joining the Dumplin Valley Boys in 1981. From there, he became a member of the famous Cathedral Quartet in 1986. Two years later, he left the group to pursue solo

church music ministry before deciding to launch a singing group of his own in December of 1990. Towards that end, he recruited baritone Mark Trammell, who had also sung with the Cathedrals years earlier. The trio was rounded out by tenor Chris Allman, formerly with the Allman Brothers (a gospel group, not the rock band of the same name). The group gained its name when Mark's wife LaResa noticed a church banner in Ohio that proclaimed "A Greater Vision for 1991."

Greater Vision quickly established itself on the Southern gospel performing circuit, winning fans through both its appealing sound and fervent Christian message. Signing a recording contract with Benson Music's Riversong label, the trio released its debut album On A Journey in 1991. The title song of the album reached the number one spot on gospel music charts, with its follow-up single "New Wine" reaching the top five. Greater Vision's next album, It's Just Like Heaven, yielded two more popular singles, "He Is Mine" and the title tune.

In December of 1993, Rodney Griffin replaced Mark Trammell, who joined the Gold City Quartet. A native of Somerset, Kentucky, Griffin had spent two years with the Dixie Melody Boys before joining Greater Vision. In addition to his strong baritone vocals, he added considerable songwriting talent as well. The trio continued to record, releasing The King Came Down in 1993 and, two years later, Take Him At His Word. The latter album expanded upon the group's traditional hymn repertoire by featuring such Griffin compositions as "Follow Me." "Oh, What A Friend," Take Him At His Word's first single, brought Greater Vision yet another gospel top ten hit.

The trio underwent another line-up change when Chris Allman left to embark on a solo career. His replacement was Jason Waldroup of Carrollton, Georgia. Waldroup was only 20 years old when he joined the group and youthful energy helped to make The Shepherd's Found A Lamb yet another successful album for the group in 1996. It yielded the singles "If There's No God" and "The Spirit Of Brokenness," the latter a Griffin original. Signing a new recording deal with Daywind Music, Greater Vision released When I See The Cross in 1997. The scope of this album was particularly broad, encompassing both Griffin originals like "He's Still Been God" and classic tunes like "The Glory Way," a gospel number from the 1920s. The single "All The Way" continued the trio's presence on gospel radio. When I See The Cross went on to receive a Dove Award and Southern Gospel Music Association Award nominations for Southern Gospel Album of the Year in 1998. That same year, Greater Vision also received three nominations at the fan awards sponsored by the gospel magazine Singing

For the Record . . .

Members include **Chris Allman** (left group in 1995), tenor; **Rodney Griffin** (joined group in 1993), baritone; **Mark Trammell** (left group in 1993), baritone; **Jason Waldroup** (joined group in 1995), tenor; **Gerald Wolfe**, lead vocals.

Group formed in 1990; signed with Riversong, 1991; released debut album *On A Journey*, 1991; recorded further for Riversong, 1992-1996; switched to Daywind, released *When I See The Cross* album in 1997; released *Far Beyond This Place*, recorded in Hungary with symphony orchestra, in 1999.

Addresses: *Record company*—Daywind Records, 128 Shivel Drive, Hendersonville, TN 37075. *Management*—Greater Vision, P.O. Box 1172, Morristown, TN 37816.

News, including Lead Vocalist of the Year, Baritone of the Year and Trio of the Year.

During this period of change, Greater Vision continued to tour, performing some 200 concerts per year and participating in cruises sponsored by Atlanta, Georgia's In Touch Ministries. Appearances on The Nashville Network, the Trinity Broadcasting Network, the Family Channel and other Christian and secular media outlets brought their music to millions. At times, they expanded their rich harmonies by working with a guest vocalist, such as lead singer Ivan Parker or bass singer Rex Nelson.

In October of 1998, Greater Vision received attention beyond the gospel music scene by performing and recording in Hungary. After giving a church concert in Budapest, the trio recorded an album's worth of songs with the Budapest Philharmonic Orchestra and Hungarian Radio Symphony. With arrangements by Daywind Music producer Wayne Haun, the recordings surrounded Greater Vision's traditional sound with classical and swing jazz-influenced orchestral backdrops to compelling effect. Working with an orchestra that was almost completely unfamiliar with American gospel music was a risky move, but ultimately a successful one."The players put their heart into it and played with so much emotion," Waldroup told *Singing News* writer Kimberly Ann Barshay. "Watching them try to play 'My Name Is Lazarus' [a gospel tune written by Griffin] was probably the funniest thing I've ever seen in my life! They were so accustomed to classic music. The string section attempted to play the fiddle parts on this Gospel 'barn burner,' and it took them a while to get it right."

The resulting album, *Far Beyond This Place,* was released in March of 1999. Most of the songs here benefitted from lush string settings, giving tunes like "Just One More Soul" and "Redemption Draweth Nigh" the feel of a film soundtrack. One number, "I Believe," had something of a swing feel to it, with jazz-flavored piano by Wolfe and a lively horn section. The closing number, "There's No Place Like Home," included a quote from "The Blue Danube Waltz" as an introduction. In assessing the album, Wolfe told Deborah Evans Price in a *Billboard* interview that "The truth is [,] gospel music fans hate change. They don't like a change in personnel or instrumentation. They want you to sound the same for 30 years, so we're careful not to go too far out on the edge, but at the same time I think this album will gain new listeners because it's such an unusual idea. It's not something you hear every day in our field."

Far Beyond This Place demonstrated that Greater Vision could adapt its sound to a new musical context. But whatever the style involved, putting the gospel message across has been the trio's primary goal. "Some people hear the word 'ministry' and automatically think someone is going to preach to them for an hour," Wolfe said in his group's Daywind press biography. "That's not what we do. We let the messages in our songs minister, but we also share our testimonials. People may just come to hear us sing, but when they leave they have no double WHO we represent. Ministry has to be the foundation a group is built on. If you do that, I believe God will honor your efforts."

Selected discography

On A Journey, Riversong, 1991.
It's Just Like Heaven, Riversong, 1992.
The Shepherd's Found A Lamb, Riversong, 1996.
When I See The Cross, Daywind, 1997.
Far Beyond This Place, Daywind, 1998.

Sources

Periodicals

Billboard, February 20, 1999.
Church Connection, April/May 1999.
Gospel Voice, March 1999.
Singing News, March 1999.
U.S. Gospel News, September 1997.

Online

"Greater Vision," http://members.aol.com/artistdnet/gv.htm (August 13, 1999).

Additional information was provided by Daywind Music publicity materials, 1999.

— *Barry Alfonso*

Gus Gus

Techno ensemble

For the Icelandic band Gus Gus, comparisons with their country's other great contribution to modern music, the Sugarcubes and their singer Bjork, are inevitable. Like their predecessors, Gus Gus also crafts delicate, structurally complex rhythms that owe much to current fashions in British electronic music and DJ/club culture. However, the band's numerous members are actually involved in several other different forms of creative expression, from cinematography to clothing design to photography. Gus Gus' live shows feature a barrage of visual elements programmed to interact with their trip-hop, lyrically poignant music.

Gus Gus originated in Reykjavik, Iceland around 1995 when Baldur Stefansson hired filmmakers Stefan Arni and Siggi Kjartansson to make a short film for Iceland's Social-Democratic Party. At the time, the Party employed Stefansson—who had studied political science at the University of Iceland—as a political strategist. He had initially attempted to direct his talents away from the performing arts since both of his parents were involved in film and theater as directors.

As a favor for the job, Stefansson agreed to be cast in a short film by Arni and Kjartansson. Six others cast to appear in the film, and they would eventually form the core of Gus Gus. They were singers Daniel Agust and Magnus Jonsson, singer-dancer Hafdis Huld—still in her teens—and three DJs: Steph, Biggi Thorarinsson, and Herr Legowitz. Agust was a veteran of several bands, Thorarinsson was a computer programmer by profession, and Legowitz was a dancer, producer, and DJ. Huld had several years of performing experience behind her, despite her youth, and had once formed her own circus troupe at the age of ten.

Financial problems brought the members of the project closer together, especially after Arni and Kjartansson asked Stefansson to act as producer. "I wound up putting the whole thing on my Visa card," Stefansson told Kieran Grant in the *Toronto Sun.* "It was probably one of the most stupid things I've ever done. But it worked out." The result was the short film *Pleasure,* which appeared in theaters in Iceland before the 1996 Drew Barrymore vehicle *Mad Love.* They also found they rather enjoyed working with one another. "After six weeks of shooting, everybody was in such good spirits that we decided to go to the studio and do an album together," Stefansson said.

Agust, Jonsson, and Huld began recording as T-World, but changed to Gus Gus by the time they released their self-titled 1995, Iceland-only debut. Pronounced "goos-goos," the name was borrowed from German cult film director Rainer Werner Fassbinder's 1972 movie *Fear Eats the Soul,* in which the North African culinary staple couscous figures suggestively. It was also designed to pay homage to American film director Gus Van Sant. *Gus Gus* landed in the hands of an associate at the legendary alternative label 4AD after Lewis Jamieson's London roommate visited Iceland and brought back the record. Jamieson then gave a tape to 4AD's founder, Ivo Watts-Russell, and as Jamieson told *Billboard's* Thom Duffy, "Ivo came back saying, `I love it,'" he recalled. "What I like about everything they do is the combination of their talents. They're at the cutting edge of dance and soul," Jamieson enthused.

The group's first release outside of Iceland was 1997's *Polydistortion,* which offered a surreal amalgamation of progressive electronica with ethereal sounds. "*Polydistortion* actually sounds like everything you've ever heard and, for the most part, all of it," assessed Mike Goldsmith in *New Musical Express,* "an irrepressible wig-out of the highest order." The record sold 150,000 copies globally, and Gus Gus became a favorite of the European music press.

The members of Gus Gus remained involved in their original passion, filmmaking. The videos made and directed by the band for "Believe" and "Polyesterday" were more reminiscent of their arty short films than standard showcase videos. Neither depicted the band performing and were saturated in lush colors using very

For the Record . . .

Members include **Daniel Agust**, vocals; **Stefan Arni**, vocals; **Hafdis Huld**, vocals (1995-99); **Magnus Jonsson**, vocals; **Siggi Kjartansson**; **Herr Legowitz**, DJ; **Baldur Stefansson**; Steph, DJ; and **Biggi Thorarinsson**, DJ.

Band formed in Reykjavik, Iceland, in 1995; released debut LP, *Polydistortion*, on 4AD in the United Kingdom, 1996; released *This Is Normal*, 1999.

Addresses: *Record company*—4AD Records, 8533 Melrose Ave., Suite B, Los Angeles, CA 90069.

long camera shots. "What's most important to us is to not make music videos [that look like] TV commercials," Kjartansson told *Billboard*'s Gina van der Vliet.

In 1997, the band signed with Los Angeles-based Satellite Films, and began working on a full-length feature film in Iceland for which they received a grant from the Icelandic National Film Fund. They also launched their own clothing line and became involved in making studio remixes of the works of several different artists, from Bjork to Depeche Mode to Joe Henry. They also contributed a song to the soundtrack of the motion picture *PI* and covered Depeche Mode's "Monument" for the tribute album *For the Masses*.

After touring for over a year, Gus Gus returned to the studio to record their sophomore release, *This Is Normal*, which arrived in the spring of 1999. Once again, the band earned deep critical accolades. Reviewing it for *Spin*, Barry Walters called *This Is Normal* "an extravagantly pretty album ... throbbing with the restless psychedelia of a culture lacking any modern identity but heaven-bent on crafting one." Writing in *Billboard*, Mark Solomons noted that the band "has recast itself in a more conventional pop mold; notwithstanding its amorphous and arty origins, this is a real band with real songs." Solomons went on to note that Gus Gus' *This Is Normal* "covers a wide beat-infested terrain that combines nuances from acts as diverse as Massive Attack and Lionrock, as well as elements of early `80s electro beats and late `80s house rhythms." Huld left the band just prior to embarking on a tour in support of *This Is Normal*.

Selected discography

Gus Gus, Skian Records, 1995.
Polydistortion, 4AD, 1997.
This Is Normal, 4AD/Warner, 1999.

Sources

Billboard, February 1, 1997; July 26, 1997; March 20, 1999.
New Musical Express, April 19, 1997; May 6, 1999.
Spin, June 1999.
Toronto Sun, July 24, 1997.
Village Voice, April 22, 1997.

—*Carol Brennan*

Gwen Guthrie

Singer, songwriter

During her nearly quarter-century career in music, Gwen Guthrie scored a series of R&B and dance-chart singles distinguished by their potent grooves and well-crafted lyrics. Her best-known song, "Ain't Nothing Goin' On But The Rent," brought her to a large pop audience in the United States for the first time. Known for her songwriting flair and independent spirit, she co-wrote most of her hits and managed to combine both American and Jamaican elements in her music. At the time of her passing at age 48 in February of 1999, she was remembered by her peers as a strong-willed artist who contributed much to the contemporary R&B scene.

Born in Newark, New Jersey, Guthrie began piano lessons at age eight and sang in the choir of the Mount Zion Baptist Church. In high school, she was a member of the Ebonettes, an all-girl vocal quartet that sported matching gowns and elbow-length gloves. She also performed with the Matchmakers alongside future Cameo lead singer Larry Blackmon. She went on to graduate from Newark State College and took a position teaching first grade in the New York City school system. During this time, she helped to establish herself in the music business by writing and singing commercial jingles. "Doing commercials is good and bad," she told writer Brian Chin in an interview for Billboard years later. "Financially, it's good. But you lose your imagination.... Later, you find it's all you can do. Now, I have my imagination back, and I don't want to lose it again."

Guthrie's career took a major leap forward when she sang background vocals on Aretha Franklin's 1974 hit "I'm In Love." Further singing assignments with Roberta Flack, Isaac Hayes and other artists followed. The mid-1970s also saw her active as a songwriter, composing Ben E. King's 1975 number one R&B single "Supernatural Thing." Around this time, CBS Records signed her as an artist, but disagreements between Guthrie and the label led to the cancellation of her album's release.

In 1978, she relocated to Jamaica and became involved with some of the island's top reggae musicians. She enjoyed a long working relationship with Jamaican singer/songwriter Peter Tosh, contributing vocals to his *Bush Doctor, Mystic Man* and *Wanted Dread And Alive* albums. The last-named album included a Tosh/Guthrie duet, "Nothing But Love." It was through Tosh that Guthrie met the famous reggae session duo of drummer Sly Dunbar and bassist Robbie Shakespeare, who asked her to sing lead vocals on an album they were recording for Island Records. The album was eventually released by Island in 1982 as Guthrie's self-titled solo debut. Combining American R&B with Jamaican production touches, *Gwen Guthrie* earned both pop and R&B airplay

For the Record . . .

Born July, 1950 in Newark, NJ, (died Feburary 4, 1999 in Orange, NJ); married Donald Wakefield (died 1995); children: Kamilah Ross and Iyana Wakefield.

Wrote hit single for Ben E. King, "Supernatural Thing," released in 1975; released duet with Peter Tosh, "Nothing But Love," in 1981; released debut album Gwen Guthrie on Island, 1982; released dance-oriented EP Padlock, 1983; signed with Polydor, released Good To Go Lover, 1986; signed with Reprise, released Hot Times, 1990; released reggae hit single "Girlfriend's Boyfriend," 1996.

with the songs "It Should Have Been You" and "For You (With A Melody Too)."

Portrait, a second album recorded with Dunbar and Shakespeare, followed in 1983, yielding the singles "Hopscotch" and "You're The One." A number of Guthrie's most dance-oriented tracks were gathered together on the 1983 EP Padlock, which included such danceclub hits as "Seventh Heaven," "Peanut Butter" and the title number. The recordings found on Padlock were remixed by Larry Levan, a DJ at the popular Paradise Garage club in New York. Guthrie's music was such a favorite at that venue that she became known as the "First Lady of Paradise Garage."

During the recording of her 1985 album Just For You, Guthrie had a falling out with Island president Chris Blackwell over creative control. The album failed to do as well as her two previous ones, and she left the label after its release. Looking back a year later in a Musician interview with Havelock Nelson, she claimed that Blackwell "tried to hold me back, not letting me realize my full potential. I don't believe in that. That's why I left. Slavery is over, honey."

Guthrie took a break from recording after the birth of her second child, Iyana. Signing with Polydor Records, she returned to record-making in 1986 with Good To Go Lover. Co-producing the album with David "Pic" Conley of the R&B group Surface, she was able to build upon her reggae and dance music base to reach a broader pop audience. The breakthrough track from Good To Go Lover was "Ain't Nothin' Goin' On But The Rent," a sarcastic look at the financial aspects of male/female

relations. Released as the album's first single, it became a number one R&B. It also reached number 46 on the pop charts as well. The song was inspired by a phrase her grandfather used to say, Guthrie told authors Adam White and Fred Bronson in an interview for The Billboard Book of Number One Rhythm & Blues Hits. She added that "the two biggest arguments in relationships are usually money and children. So I think people just related to it. And it had a good beat.... I was just saying it takes two. That both parties should be productive."

Though "Ain't Nothin' Goin' On But The Rent" became her only major pop hit, Guthrie enjoyed further dance club success with her remake of the Beatles' "Ticket To Ride" in 1988, and ventured back into reggae with "Friends And Lovers," a duet with singer Boris Gardner. Her work also appeared on soundtracks for such 1980s films Jumpin' Jack Flash and Disorderlies. In 1990, she moved in a more mainstream R&B direction with her debut album for Reprise, Hot Times. Though "Miss My Love" and the album's title track failed to do well as singles, she bounced back with the hit "Sweet Bitter Love." In 1993, she topped many of the international reggae charts with a Jamaican-produced single, "Girlfriend's Boyfriend."

Guthrie's career was sadly cut short when she was diagnosed with cancer in 1998. She passed away on Feburary 4, 1999 in Orange, New Jersey. Among those who recalled her with affection and respect was singer/producer Isaac Hayes, who told Billboard's Aliya S. King that "with her passing, a definite void has been placed in many of our lives. She loved this business, and she loved performing. When R&B music became mostly crossovers, Gwen remained a true R&B artist."

Selected discography

Gwen Guthrie, Island, 1982.
Portrait, Island, 1983.
Just For You, Island, 1985.
Good To Go Lover, Polygram, 1986.
Hot Times, Reprise, 1990.

Sources

Books

Larkin, Colin, editor, The Encyclopedia Of Popular Music, Muze, 1998.
White, Adam and Bronson, Fred, The Billboard Book Of Number One Rhythm & Blues Hits, Billboard Books, 1993.

Periodicals

Billboard, August 23, 1986; January 5, 1991; February 20, 1999.

Musician, October 1986.

Online

Garage Net Spotlight, http://www.garagenet.ndirect.co.uk/spotfebmar99 (June 9, 1999).

—*Barry Alfonso*

Tom T. Hall

Songwriter, singer, guitar

Photo by Mark Humphrey, AP/Wide World Photos. Reproduced by permission.

A master storyteller cut from the same cloth as Mark Twain and Edgar Lee Masters, Tom T. Hall's keen powers of observation and insight have helped him create some of country music's most poignant lyrics and vivid musical images. *Country Music* magazine's Bob Allan wrote, "In my estimation Tom T. Hall is one of the greatest country songwriters that ever lived. Maybe Hank Williams or Harlan Howard have written more hits, but in his heyday Hall took country music someplace it had never been before and has seldom been since." The characters he sings about are likable, and empathetic listeners find themselves humming along to homespun tunes such as "Old Dogs, Children, and Watermelon Wine," "Mama Bake a Pie," and "The Year that Clayton Delaney Died." Hall was nicknamed "The Storyteller" because of his narrative approach to music. Patrick Carr of *Country Music* wrote, "Hall has broadened and deepened the country river significantly, and is one of the major architects of the music's modern form." Whether writing songs for other artists, such as his famous "Harper Valley P.T.A.," or singing his own compositions, Hall has been a distinctive, successful part of country music scene since the 1960s, attracting fans such as author Kurt Vonnegut and former U.S. President Jimmy Carter.

Hall was born on May 25, 1936, in Olive Hill, Kentucky, one of eight children born to a bricklayer and part-time minister and his wife. His childhood home was made of pale gray boards and featured a porch with a view of a dusty road. Hall learned to play a schoolmate's guitar at the age of ten. His mother died of cancer when he was 13, and two years later, his father was shot—though not fatally—in an accident. As a result, Hall had to drop out of high school to help support his siblings by working in a factory. Hall's neighbor had a small traveling cinema show, and Hall began to accompany him when a teen, playing bluegrass with other musicians. He and his bandmates in The Kentucky Travelers were also featured on the local radio station WMOR, where Hall also worked as a disc jockey.

Hall did not consider a career in music because he aspired to be a writer or a journalist. He joined the U.S. Army in 1957, and earned a high school diploma while enlisted. After the Army, Hall enrolled at Roanoke College in Virginia to pursue writing. He admired Mark Twain and Ernest Hemingway, but discovered that he was actually better at writing country songs than stories or articles. While working as a disc jockey in Roanoke, he sent some of his compositions to Nashville, Tennessee, where music publishers liked his work. One company in particular, New Keys, urged Hall to relocate to Nashville. He did, and his first song recorded, "D.J. for a Day," was sung by Jimmy C. Newman. Hall married Iris

For the Record . . .

Born May 25, 1936, in Olive Hill, KY; one of eight children born to a bricklayer and part-time minister and his wife; married Iris "Dixie" Dean, 1964. Education: Attended Roanoke College after serving in the Army.

Began playing the guitar at the age of ten; performed in a local band and worked as a disc jockey while in high school; joined the U.S. Army in 1957; worked as a songwriter and performer from the early 1960s throughout the 1990s to the present; author of *The Storyteller's Nashville* and *The Laughing Man of Woodmont Cove.*

Awards: Grammy Award for *Tom T. Hall's Greatest Hits*; inducted into the Nashville Songwriter's Hall of Fame.

Addresses: *Record company*—RCA Records, 1133 Avenue of the Americas, New York, NY 10036, (212) 930-4000; 6363 Sunset Boulevard, #429, Los Angeles, CA 90028, (213) 468-4000; *Internet*—http://www.mercuryrecords.com.

"Dixie" Dean in 1964, an emigre from Weston-super-Mare, England, who worked as editor of *Music City News* in Nashville.

"D.J. for a Day" did well for Newman, but Hall's smash hit came in 1968 with "Harper Valley P.T.A.," which was recorded by Jeannie C. Riley. The song sold more than six million copies and inspired a television movie and a series. Like many of Hall's narratives, "Harper Valley P.T.A." was inspired by a real event: a woman in Hall's hometown who threw wild parties, which irked the town's more upstanding citizens. Her child was singled out for extra discipline at school, so the woman finally went to a P.T.A. meeting and pointed out the hypocrisy of these so-called upstanding citizens. By the time "Harper Valley P.T.A. was released, Hall had begun recording his own works on the Mercury label.

Hall resisted a recording contract for years, hoping to first gain a reputation in Nashville as a songwriter. Hall gave in, however, during the late 1960s, and the result was astounding: throughout the next two decades his musical output rivaled the most prolific country singers of that time. His earliest hits included "The Ballad of Forty Dollars" in 1968—which depicted the memorial service of a man who died without paying back the money he owed the song's narrator—and "A Week in a Country Jail" in 1969, which described the unusual conditions of the title's locale. One of Hall's most famous early releases was "The Year that Clayton Delaney Died." As with "Harper Valley P.T.A.," the song was gleaned from a true story; the song is a tribute to a drunken guitar player who fell on hard times and taught Hall how to play the guitar when he was a boy. Hall told Carr, "It started out with just me sitting down with a guitar and thinking, 'Well, I want to thank Clayton.' " Another of Hall's acclaimed songs, the philosophic "Old Dogs, Children, and Watermelon Wine," was drawn from a conversation he enjoyed with an elderly black man in a Miami bar. Hall's own favorite song was "I Love" in 1974, which lists all the things in life that he holds most dear.

Some of Hall's hit songs strayed from his trademark narrative style and became "sing-along" favorites. The gospel-tinged "Me and Jesus" advocates an individualistic approach to religion and is noted for being a toe-tapping, "feel good" song. The straightforward "I Like Beer" turned out to be more popular in Germany than in the United States, and at least 60 singers in Germany have recorded versions of Hall's song. He also garnered a loyal following in Poland. Hall switched from Mercury Records to RCA in the 1980s and fell into what could best described as a slump. He explained to Carr in 1989, "There are so many writers and publishers; *everybody's* writing songs. Where there were maybe a dozen guys who were really putting the hot tunes together when I started in Nashville, now there must be hundreds." Hall attributed his musical dry spell to changing tastes among country music fans. In response, Hall focused more intently on his prose, authoring the autobiographical *The Storyteller's Nashville* and the novel *The Laughing Man of Woodmont Cove.* He also continued to compose songs and told Carr, "I've got the songs, and one day next week someone will pick up that one tune that's just right for that one singer, and it'll be Number One."

Hall reemerged on the musical scene in 1996 with the release of *Songs from Sopchoppy,* an album recorded at his winter home on a Gulf Coast island. His timing seemed impeccable, as his reputation was enjoying a renaissance due to the fact that Alan Jackson had just released a hit with Hall's "Little Bitty," a song that appeared on *Songs from Sopchoppy,* and Deryl Dodd had recently taken Hall's classic "That's How I Got So Memphis" back up on the charts. Buddy Miller, too, offered an impressive version of the song on *Poison Love.* In 1995 Mercury released a 50-song retrospective called *Tom T: Hall: Storyteller, Poet, Philosopher.* Iris DeMent and other notable musicians agreed to work on an album-length tribute to Hall in 1998. In 1998 Hall released *Home Grown,* an all-acoustic album that recaptured much of the eloquence and brilliance of his earlier releases. Hall cowrote the bluegrass/gospel number "The Beautiful River of life" with his wife, Dixie. Hall—like many of the greatest storytellers, songwriters, and musicians of our time—illuminates the higher meaning in the small, familiar things that comprise our lives.

Selected discography

with Mercury

"The Ballad of Forty Dollars, 1968.
"A Week in a Country Jail," 1969.
(With Dave Dudley) "Day Drinkin,' "1970.
"The Year That Clayton Delaney Died," 1971.
"Me and Jesus," 1972.
"The Monkey That Became President," 1972.
"Ravishing Ruby," 1973.
"I Love," 1974.
"This Song is Driving Me Crazy," 1974.
"Country Is," 1974.
"I Care/Sneaky Snake," 1975.
"Deal," 1975.
"I Like Beer," 1975.
"Faster Horses (the cowboy and the Poet), 1976.
"Negatory Romance," 1976.
"It's All in the Game," 1977.

with RCA

"What Have You Got to Lose," 1978.
"There is a Miracle in You,"1979.
"You Show Me Your Heart (and I'll Show You Mine)," 1979.
"Son of Clayton Delaney," 1979.
"The Old Side of Town/"Jesus on the Radio (Daddy on the Phone)," 1980.
"Soldier of Fortune," 1980.

"Back When Gas Was Thirty Cents A Gallon," 1980.
"I'm Not Ready Yet," 1980.

Albums

Ballad of Forty Dollars, Mercury, 1968.
Ballad of Forty Dollars/Homecoming, Mercury, 1969.
Great Country Hits, Vol. 1 & 11, Mercury, 1972,
Great Country Hits, Vol. 111, Mercury, 1975.
I Witness Life/100 Children, Mercury, 1975.
Soldier of Fortune, RCA, 1980.
The Essential Tom T. Hall: The Story Songs, RCA, 1988.
Country Songs for Children, RCA, 1995.
Loves Lost & Found, RCA, 1995.
Tom T. Hall: Storyteller, Poet, Philosopher, RCA, 1995.
Songs From Sopchoppy, RCA, 1995.
Home Grown, RCA, 1998.

Sources

Books

Contemporary Musicians, Volume 4, Gale Research, 1991.

Periodicals

Country Music, January/February 1998; January/February 1989; March/April 1987.

Online

The Authorized Tom T. Hall Page, http://www.cnct.com/~tomthall (September 24, 1999).
"Tom T. Hall," *Yahoo Music,* http://musicfinder.yahoo.com/shop?d=p8id=halltomt&cf=11 (September 24, 1999).

—*B. Kimberly Taylor*

Roger Hodgson

Rock musician

Roger Hodgson collected credentials as one of the driving forces of the legendary rock group Supertramp. Together with Rick Davies he founded the band in 1969 and went on to write at least half of their songs. Hodgson's plaintive singing style, the bright melodies and the ironic yet introspective lyrics of his songs, and his staccato piano contributed a great deal to Supertramp's distinctive sound. After Supertramp's success had peaked, Hodgson, looking for new personal and musical directions, left the band to pursue a solo career. After leaving Supertramp he recorded three solo albums. Throughout 1998 he promoted his album *Rites of Passage* with live performances in the United States and Canada. By 1999, Hodgson was working on his new album *Open The Door*.

At age 12, Roger Hodgson played his own songs for his schoolmates at a private boarding school in Surrey, England. Soon after that he played in his first band, People Like Us, which recorded four demo songs, including one written by Hodgson. When Lionel Conway of Blue Mountain Music heard Hodgson's "Mr. Boyd," he

invited him to record a single, which was released under the name "Argosy" and contained "Imagine" on the B side. According to Hodgson's web site, one of the session musicians on the side was Elton John.

Supertramp

After Hodgson returned home from boarding school, his mother Jill encouraged him to respond to a "genuine opportunity" ad that English rock musician Rick Davies had placed in *Melody Maker*. Davies had found a wealthy sponsor to financially back up his new band and Hodgson was one out of hundreds of musicians who showed up to audition. He played acoustic guitar and sang Traffic's "Dear Mr. Fantasy." He had a beer with Davies during a break, and they soon became friends and formed the rock band Supertramp. When Supertramp's second album failed to sell, the band disintegrated and could have spelled the end of Supertramp. Hodgson and Davies remained together, however, and in 1973 they reformed the group with different musicians.

While Davies and Hodgson co-wrote songs on the first two Supertramp albums, they now wrote and sang their own songs but continued to share the songwriting credit for them. The well-educated optimist Hodgson was driven by dreams and aspirations for a better world, and his creative energy was not diminished by the lack of any musical equipment. According to Hodgson's web site, he even "recorded a demo of 'Dreamer' in his mother's back room, banging on boxes and over-dubbing all the voices and instruments." Hodgson wrote many of Supertramp's most popular songs, including "Dreamer," "Sister Moonshine," "Give a Little Bit," "The Logical Song," "Breakfast In America," "Take the Long Way Home," and "It's Raining Again."

Superior sound combined with films, slides and a computer-controlled light show became hallmarks of Supertramp's live performances. However, this perfectionism—primarily Hodgson's—led critics to complain about the band's overly polished sound. *Famous Last Words,* Supertramp's 1982 studio album, was released three years after their breakthrough album, *Breakfast in America*. Unhappy with the heavy blues influence and feeling that the band's creativity was vanishing, Hodgson left Supertramp in 1983.

Faced challenges as solo artist

After his departure from Supertramp Hodgson set up a 48-track studio in his home. Hodgson's first solo album was released in 1984 by A&M Records. *In The Eye of The Storm* included seven tracks, many of which had been written for Supertramp. The songs on the album covered wide stylistic ground, including "Had a Dream (Sleeping with the Enemy)" which some fans believed resembled Pink Floyd more than Supertramp.

Hodgson's search for a new beginning and new meaning in his life, as well as the challenges he was suddenly facing as a solo artist, were inspirations for these new songs. He performed, arranged and produced all of the songs on *In The Eye of The Storm* except for a few pieces on which Michael Shrieve played the drums, Jimmy Johnson fretless bass and Ken Allardyce harmonica. *In The Eye of The Storm* was frenetically embraced by the community of Supertramp fans and went platinum.

Hodgson's second solo album *Hai Hai* was released in 1987. Recorded during a 16-month period with seasoned Los Angeles session musicians, the album did not match Hodgson's expectations. The demanding perfectionist, according to his web site, "felt the album lacked focus and failed to express what he wanted as an artist. Unhappy with the outcome of *Hai Hai* and disillusioned by music industry pressures, Roger was further frustrated by his upcoming tour to promote an album that didn't meet his high standards." One week after *Hai Hai* was released Hodgson broke his wrists in an accident, and was not able to play piano for two years. It would take him a decade to recover physically and emotionally, until his comeback in 1997.

Back on Track

After Hodgson's numerous attempts to create satisfying results in his studio had failed, his wife Karuna took the initiative. Convinced that only live performing could enable her husband to overcome his self-doubt and perfectionism, and to re-awaken his joy in life and music, she conceived the idea of a live album that would get Hodgson back in touch with his music. Hodgson later told the Los Angeles Times: "She took the risk and was courageous enough to say, 'Roger, all you have to do is show up and play. I'll handle everything else.'" And that she did. Not only did she provide funding and successfully ensure that Hodgson and the band worked *together* instead of having the band work *for* him, she also founded her own record label to avoid the pressure that comes with contracting for a major label.

Physically weakened by post-infectious arthritis resulting from a trip to South America and emotionally exhausted from witnessing his sister Caroline's death from cancer, Hodgson managed to finish the work on the live album. A quickly assembled band including Hodgson's son Andrew and Supertramp saxophonist John Heliwell performed at six quickly organized concerts in August 1996 during his son's summer break from school. Although they planned to use the best recordings from all the performances for the album, all the songs on *Rites Of Passage* came from a concert performed in Hodgson's hometown Nevada City. They included six new Hodgson songs, three of his Supertramp classics, two songs by

band member Mikail Graham, and one by his son Andrew who also played drums, piano and harmonica.

Rites Of Passage was released in 1997, the same year Supertramp released its first studio album in a decade and reunited for a world tour. Hodgson went on his own tour called "Solo Tramp" in spring 1998. The national tour—his first in more than 14 years—took Hodgson to over 25 cities in the US and Canada. Like the album, the tour presented a mixture of Hodgson's Supertramp hits and new material that he performed alone on guitar, keyboards and the old pump organ on which he composed hits for Supertramp back in the 1970s. In interviews posted on his official Web site Hodgson commented on renewed musical energy: "My creative juices are flowing again and I feel the best is yet to come ... I'm very hungry to play for people again and I'm ready for a new love affair with my music and the world."

Selected discography

In The Eye of The Storm, A&M Records, 1984.
Hai Hai, A&M Records, 1987.
Rites of Passage, Unichord Productions, 1997.

Sources

Columbian, April 2, 1998.
Dallas Morning News, June 5, 1997.
Independent, September 17, 1997.
Los Angeles Times, August 16, 1997; April 11, 1998.
Rolling Stone, July 12, 1979; December 9, 1982.
St. Louis Post-Dispatch, May 07, 1998.

Additional information for this profile was provided by Karuna Hodgson.

—*Evelyn Hauser*

John Lee Hooker

Blues guitar

John Lee Hooker's presence in blues, past and present, is imposing. He is a living monument to the music. Often credited as a co-founder, with Muddy Waters, of modern electric blues, Hooker influenced three or more generations of players: Dr. Ross who saw him play in Detroit in the 1940s; the Animals, Yardbirds, Van Morrison and Canned Heat who fell under his spell in the 1960s; Stevie Ray Vaughan and Robert Cray who played with him in the 1980s. Hooker's own roots stretch back to Mississippi of the 1920s, the land and time when the blues were born. He recalls that as a child Charlie Patton, legendary as the "Founder of the Delta Blues," visited the house to see his stepfather. After a fifty-year career of remarkable staying power and flexibility, John Lee Hooker entered the period of his greatest popularity and influence after his seventieth birthday. At eighty-one he was still going strong.

Hooker was born on August 22, 1917 near Clarksdale, Mississippi. His parents, Minnie and William, were sharecroppers. Hooker was interested in music from an early age and as a boy built himself a one-string instru-

Photo by Jack Vartoogian. Reproduced by permission.

ment. Minnie's second husband, Will Moore, a popular local musician, began teaching the young boy how to play guitar. Eventually Moore even made him a present of one of his own instruments. More importantly, Hooker absorbed his stepfather's manner of playing, a hypnotic one-chord style that became an integral part of his recorded work. "Whatever I'm doin' is his style," Hooker told Billboard's Chris Morris in 1998. "My style is his style."

The Hottest Musician in Detroit

When he was barely in his teens Hooker left home in the early 1930s. "Where I came from in Mississippi was hell," he told Peter Watrous of the New York Times. "I wanted to be a star. I knew I couldn't make it in Mississippi, so I was working my way up north." His first stop was Memphis, whose Beale Street was the center of the blues universe at the time. Still too young for bars or nightclubs, Hooker played local house parties at the boarding house he was staying at. From Memphis he moved to Cincinnati where he sang in gospel groups, which gave him valuable experience singing in front of an audience, but his heart was with the blues. Unlike many other musicians, the switch from religious music to the Devil's music did not cause Hooker any crisis of conscience. "When I started singing blues the church didn't like it," he told Watrous, "but I was determined to be a musician and be a blues star, and I didn't care much what they thought."

In the mid 1930s, Hooker landed in Detroit. He took a day job as a janitor and by night played his blues in places like the Apex Bar or the Town Bar. "The town was booming, and I was playing three and four, sometimes five nights a week in small clubs," he told Watrous. "I got to be hot stuff, the hottest musician in Detroit."

"I Ain't Workin' No More"

After World War II had ended, Hooker got his first big break. Elmer Barbee, a Detroit record store owner, caught one of Hooker's shows. Impressed, he invited the singer down to his downtown store. Hooker took his guitar and ended up playing most of the night while Barbee recorded the songs on his disc-cutting machine. One of the tunes they came up with was "Boogie Chillen," based on a song he had once heard his stepfather Moore play. Barbee was wild for the number, convinced that they had a hit on their hands. He helped Hooker hook up with Bernard Bessman of Sensation Records. Hooker recorded the song for Sensation. "The thing caught fire," Hooker says in Robert Palmer's Deep Blues. "It was ringin' all around the country. When it come out every jukebox you went to, every place you went to, every drugstore, everywhere you went, department stores, they were playin' it in there ... And I was workin' in Detroit in a factory there for a while. Then I quit my job. I said, 'No, I ain't workin' no more!'"

About a year later Hooker signed a contract with Modern Records in Los Angeles for an advance of $1,000. Between 1949 and 1951, Hooker had three hits for Modern: "Hobo Blues," "In The Mood," and "Crawling

Kingsnake." He was suddenly in high demand, though, at other labels. When Modern failed to pay him royalties he was owed he began recording for other companies under a variety of pseudonyms: Johnny Williams, Delta John, Johnny Lee, Texas Slim, Birmingham Sam & His Magic Guitar, the Boogie Man, Sir John Lee Hooker, John Lee Booker, and John Lee Cooker. In 1955 he signed with Vee-Jay Records in Chicago, a label he would remain with for ten years. While there he abandoned his solo guitar accompaniment in favor of a full band. "Vee-Jay wanted the big sound," he told Chris Morris. "It was a good sound, a real good sound, a big fat sound." That fat sound led to another string of popular records for Hooker, including "Dimples" and "Boom Boom," which reached number 16 on the R&B charts and number 60 on the Pop charts in 1962.

Hooker wasn't about to be pigeonholed though, especially at a moment in history when musical tastes were undergoing major changes. He hit the folk circuit, and soon solo acoustic records for Riverside complemented his electric blues on Vee-Jay. He started playing the coffeehouse circuit and made appearances, beginning in 1960, at the Newport Folk Festival. In 1962 he toured Europe for the first time with the American Folk Blues Festival.

"People Got More Civilized"

There was already a John Lee Hooker renaissance of sorts underway in England as he made that tour. The Animals and the Yardbirds, deeply steeped in American blues, had their own hits with "Boom Boom." And other groups in the British blues revival had incorporated other Hooker songs into their repertoires. "I had no thought that British singers would start singing my songs," Hooker confessed to Watrous. "I had no idea what would come with that. People got more civilized." During the Sixties Hooker worked more and more with younger rock musicians who were his admirers. In England he played with John Mayall's Bluesbreakers and a young guitarist named Eric Clapton. In the U.S. at the end of the sixties, he teamed up with his boogie disciples, Canned Heat, with whom he cut two albums, *Hooker 'N Heat* and *Live At The Fox Venice Theater*—Influential collaborations that introduced Hooker's music to a new, younger generation. In 1972 he recorded *Never Get Out Of These Blues Alive* with another old fan, Van Morrison. During the rest of the seventies and for most of the eighties, Hooker's performing and recording tapered off, which wasn't surprising—he was pushing sixty and had worked at a frantic pace for the previous twenty years.

In 1989, when Hooker was seventy-two, he made the album that initiated what might be the most successful, productive periods of his career. *The Healer* was conceived by his agent Mike Kappus. It featured a star-studded line-up of guest artists including Carlos Santana, Robert Cray, Los Lobos, and Bonnie Raitt whose duet won Hooker his first Grammy, after being nominated in the Sixties, Seventies and Eighties. Other albums, equally successful followed, including 1991's *Mr. Lucky*, 1992's *Boom Boom*, and Grammy winners *Chill Out* (1995) and *Don't Look Back* (1997). The 1990s were Hooker's reward for his lifetime in music. He enjoyed unprecedented worldwide popularity, performing regularly at festivals and on television. In 1990 he was presented with an all-star tribute at Madison Square Garden in New York City, and in January 1991 he was inducted into the Rock & Roll Hall of Fame. He was a Charter Inductee to the Blues Hall of Fame. He even owns his own blues club, the Boom Boom Room, which opened in 1997 in San Francisco.

John Lee Hooker is proof of the power of the blues and its ability to transcend boundaries of generation and race. "The blues is the root of all music," he said. "People's heartaches, aches and pains, trouble and disappointment, money, no money, down-and-out, that causes the blues, and that affects everybody of every color, rich and poor. The blues has got more message than anything else. It's more flashy now, but it's the same thing as before. It's come down low and came back up, but it'll never die."

Selected discography

John Lee Hooker Sings the Blues, King, 1961.
The Real Folk Blues, Chess, 1966.
Live At The Cafe Au Go-Go, Bluesway/ABC, 1967.
Hooker 'N Heat, Liberty, 1971.
Never Get Out Of These Blues Alive, ABC, 1972.
The Healer, Chameleon/Silvertone, 1989.
Mr. Lucky, Silvertone, 1991.
The Ultimate Collection, Rhino, 1991.
Boom Boom, Pointblank/Virgin, 1992.
Chill Out, Pointblank/Virgin, 1995.
Don't Look Back, Pointblank/Virgin, 1997.
The Best Of Friends, Pointblank/Virgin, 1998.

Sources

Books

Palmer, Robert, *Deep Blues*, Viking Press, New York, 1981.
Russell, Tony, *The Blues—From Robert Johnson to Robert Cray*, Schirmer Books, New York. 1997.

Sonnier, Austin M., *A Guide to the Blues: History, Who's Who, Research Sources*, Greenwood Press, Westport, CT. 1994

Periodicals

Billboard, September 5, 1998; New York Times, October 16, 1990

Additional material and information provided by The Rosebud Agency and Mike Kappus.

—Gerald E. Brennan

Cissy Houston

Gospel and pop singer

Her stardom and commercial success may have far eclipsed that of her mother, but Whitney Houston isn't the only musical talent of note in her family. Having made a name for herself as a gifted singer of gospel, blues, and pop in a career that spanned more than 30 years, Whitney's mother Cissy can hardly be considered a slouch. From television and radio to theater and commercials, from gospel to secular, from backing vocals to solo work, Cissy's career has been long, rich, and varied.

The youngest of the eight children born to factory worker Nitch and homemaker Delia Drinkard, Cissy Houston started singing as a child. As a five-year-old, she began singing with siblings Anne, Nicky, and Larry in the family gospel act the Drinkard Singers in her hometown of Newark, New Jersey. Houston and nieces Dee Dee and Dionne Warwick—who were also Drinkard Singers for a time—later sang backing vocals for the likes of Wilson Pickett and Solomon Burke, among others.

From 1965 to 1970, Houston was the lead vocalist for the pop group Sweet Inspirations, which she formed with Sylvia Sherwell, Myrna Smith, and Estelle Brown. The group performed on hundreds of songs for other artists, including Neil Diamond, Aretha Franklin, and Elvis Presley before recording on its own. In 1968, the group released its only two albums—*Sweet Inspirations* and *What the World Needs Now is Love*—and earned a Top 20 hit and a Grammy nomination with the single "Sweet Inspiration." Houston soon left for a solo career, however, while her former bandmates continued as backup vocalists for other artists.

On her own Houston became the first singer to record "Midnight Train to Georgia," which later became a huge hit for Gladys Knight and the Pips. Houston teamed with Warwick again, joining her tour as one of three backing vocalists. She worked with Connie Francis and Nina Simone, as well, and recorded the songs "Think It Over" and "Tomorrow" from the hit musical *Annie*.

For a time, Houston scaled back her musical schedule to raise her three children—Gary, Michael, and Whitney—and spend more time with then-husband John. She returned to a more full-time music career in the late 1970s, when she released the albums *Cissy Houston* in 1977, *Warning—Danger* in 1979, and 1980's *Step Aside for a Lady*.

Besides her solo efforts, Houston also continued to lend her talents to other musicians. Throughout the late 1970s and early 1980s, she was probably most visible as a backing vocalist, working on Aretha Franklin's *Aretha, Love All the Hurt Away*, and *Jump to It*, and Chaka

Born Emily Drinkard, 1933, Newark, NJ, to Nitch (a Newark factory worker; died 1951) and Delia (a homemaker, died 1941), youngest of eight siblings; married first husband, 1954, (divorced); married second husband, John, 1959, (separated from John in 1980, divorced in 1993); children: three, Gary, born, 1958 (from first husband); Michael, born, 1962, Whitney, born August 9, 1963 (from second husband) .

Started singing with the family gospel group the Drinkard Singers in Newark, 1938; formed group Sweet Inspirations in 1960s (members alternately included Sylvia Sherwell, Myrna Smith, Estelle Brown, and nieces Dionne and Dee Dee Warwick); sang backup with Sweet Inspirations for Atlantic, Muscle Shoals, and New York Records; recorded two albums with Sweet Inspirations before leaving to pursue a solo career; backup singer for Elvis Presley, Dusty Springfield, Aretha Franklin, Dionne Warwick, among others; has recorded with Luther Vandross, David Bowie, and daughter Whitney Houston; subject of a 1988 Public Broadcasting Service program, Cissy Houston: Sweet Inspiration; performed on the 1989 television special, The Songwriters Hall of Fame 20th Anniversary: The Magic is Music; signed with House of Blues label and released gospel album Face to Face, 1996; published autobiography, How Sweet the Sound: My Life With God and Gospel, 1998.

Awards: Grammy Award, 1997, for Face to Face.

Addresses: Record company—House of Blues Music, 8439 Sunset Boulevard, Suite 404, West Hollywood, CA 90069.

Khan's Chaka. She recorded backup vocals for Luther Vandross' Never Too Much and For Always, For Love, as well as his 1991 album Power of Love. She also joined forces with Chuck Jackson for 1992's I'll Take Care of You, which raised funds for the Rhythm 'N' Blues Foundation. "She's worthy of any accolade thrown her way," Vandross told People in 1998. "I think she could have made a wonderful opera singer. Her voice is amazing."

Her life was the subject of a Public Broadcasting Service television program in 1988. Entitled Cissy Houston: Sweet Inspiration, the show featured her in sessions with artists including David Bowie, Vandross, and Warwick and demonstrated her impact on the music industry. She also brought her music to the public via nightclub performances, which earned her a good deal of critical praise. She was one of the performers on the 1989 television special The Songwriters Hall of Fame 20th Anniversary: The Magic is Music, joining a varied lineup that included Michael Bolton, Crystal Gayle, Patti LaBelle, k.d. lang, and Tommy Tune.

Houston encouraged her daughter's singing early on and took her on tour and to recording sessions. Houston also lent her backing vocals to the hits "How Will I Know" and "I Wanna Dance with Somebody (Who Loves Me)" from Whitney's first two albums.

1996's Face to Face on the House of Blues label came after Houston took a fairly lengthy hiatus from recording. The album marked a return to her gospel roots, and featured a 30-member Newark, New Jersey choir. Houston has a long history with Newark's New Hope Baptist Church choir, serving for periods as its music and choir director and hosting the weekly church radio broadcast. "I'm very proud of this album," she told Jet in 1996. "I did not want to go into a studio with music I wasn't in love with. I have so much to say through gospel songs, and I believe I write much better gospel lyrics and music than pop." Fellow music industry personnel apparently agreed, as Houston won her first Grammy award for the album.

Houston also contributed to the gospel soundtrack for the 1997 film The Preacher's Wife, in which Whitney starred. In a review of the album in People, the elder Houston was praised as one of the veteran singers who "[blew] Whitney away with their authority . . . [and] tempt you to seek out their albums for the gospel truth." Houston released a second solo gospel album on House of Blues in 1997.

In 1998 Houston shared her life story with How Sweet the Sound: My Life with God and Gospel, an autobiography she wrote with Jonathan Singer. The book chronicled her life and faith, including tragedies such as the death of her mother when she was only eight and the loss of her father to cancer when she was 18. Those expecting a gossipy tell-all were likely to be disappointed, however. As Houston told Jet in 1998, "I know people are so interested to know what you did on the road with this one and that one. I didn't want to write that because whatever I did on the road, I've forgotten ... I think it's lousy that people write about people who they worked with.... I did not want to do that. I said if I can write about my gospel and my faith and my experiences, then I would consider [writing a memoir]. So that's how this book came about."

Houston may never match her daughter Whitney in terms of fame, but the elder Houston seemed pleased with her career and the religious beliefs she instilled in her children. "A lot of things I've done have come late in life, and it's like a whole new career starting up," she told *Jet* in 1998. "I don't have any regrets about the way I planned and lived my life.... I am very proud of what I've become."

Selected discography

(with the Sweet Inspirations) *Sweet Inspirations,* Atlantic, 1968.
(with the Sweet Inspirations) *What the World Needs Now is Love,* Atlantic, 1968.
Cissy Houston, Janus, 1971.
Cissy Houston, Private Stock, 1977.
Warning—Danger, Columbia, 1979.
Step Aside for a Lady, Columbia, 1980.
(With Chuck Jackson) *I'll Take Care of You,* Shanachie, 1992.
Face to Face, House of Blues, 1996.

Sources

Books

Clarke, Donald, editor, *Penguin Encyclopedia of Popular Music,* Viking, 1989.
DeCurtis, Anthony and James Henke, editors, *Rolling Stone Album Guide,* Random House, 1992.
Larkin, Colin, editor, *Guiness Encyclopedia of Popular Music,* Vol. 3, Guiness Publishing, 1995.

Periodicals

Booklist, April 15, 1998.
Consumer's Research Magazine, December 1992.
Ebony, July 1991; May 1995.
Jet, May 13, 1996; June 15, 1998.
People, June 26, 1989; January 13, 1997; August 10, 1998.
Publisher's Weekly, December 16, 1996; April 27, 1998.

—*K. Michelle Moran*

Imperial Teen

Grunge group

San Francisco's pop-grunge group Imperial Teen mixes elements of punk, grunge, and "bubble gum" pop to create an engaging, individual, post-punk sound. CMJ said that the band's sound was "fueled by equal measurements of post-punk rattle and bubblegum hum accented by sexually provocative lyrics—traces of Sonic Youth, T-Rex, and even a little Blondie mingle within." A Rolling Stone review described the band as, "grown-up-and-proud Blondie fans," and Entertainment Weekly's said "there's something fundamentally warm and fuzzy about the mixed-gender quartet's seductive mix of indie-rock cliches (distorted guitar, diffident vocals) and hook-and-harmony informed popcraft." Imperial Teen's upbeat sound is supported by strong female backing vocals.

Imperial Teen was founded by Roddy Bottum in 1994, and was the second band he had played in. He continued to play keyboards for Faith No More after founding Imperial Teen, and viewed his new group as distinctly separate, not merely a "side project." Bottum founded the band in response to a particularly difficult time in his life; his father had terminal cancer, two of his friends had died, and he was addicted to heroin. Bottum took over guitar and vocal duties, and enlisted close friends Lynn Perko (drummer, formerly with The Wrecks and Sister Double Happiness), Jone Stebbins (bassist, also formerly of The Wrecks), and Will Schwartz (guitarist and vocalist). Imperial Teen's much-heralded debut album in 1996, *Seasick,* was produced by Steve McDonald of Red Kross. *Seasick* addressed the death of Bottum's friend Kurt Cobain of Nirvana with "Butch," Bottum's father with "Luxury," and Courtney Love with "Copafeelia." The angst and despair associated with so much loss at this time in Bottum's life was hidden beneath a veneer of cheery rock and pop riffs often dubbed "bubblegrunge," but *Seasick* was nevertheless a cathartic experience for Bottum.

Stebbins is originally from Reno, Nevada, and brought a healthy appreciation for mambo and lounge music to Imperial Teen. She played in an all-girl punk band with Perko called The Wrecks. Schwartz was born in New York City; he moved to Los Angeles where he met Bottum, and they decided to play together. Imperial Teen was his first experience playing in a band, though he knew from an early age that he wanted to be a performer. For Schwartz, the difficult part of choosing a career path was determining the medium in which to perform. When he started playing guitar and singing, he knew he had found his calling. Perko is a versatile musician who began playing in bands at the age of 16. Also a former member of The Wrecks, Perko plays drums, guitar, bass, and sings as well. She had originally wanted to be a teacher and live in Oregon, but moved to San Fran-

For the Record . . .

Members include **Roddy Bottum**, guitar, drums, vocals; **Lynn Perko**, drums, guitar, bass, vocals; **Will Schwartz** (born in New York, NY), guitar, vocals; **Jone Stebbins**, bass guitar, vocals.

Band founded by Roddy Bottum in 1994 while still with Faith No More; enlisted friends Perko (formerly with *The Wrecks* and *Sister Double Happiness*), Stebbins (formerly of *The Wrecks*), and Schwartz; released debut album *Seasick*, Slash, 1996; released *What Is Not To Love*, Slash, 1999.

Addresses: *Record company*—Slash Records, 7381 Beverly Boulevard, Los Angeles, CA 90067; (323) 937-4660.

cisco instead and joined the band The Dicks. The Dicks, originally from Texas, were a noted punk band who reestablished themselves in San Francisco. Perko toured extensively with The Dicks and honed her drumming skills to the point where she was quick, mean, and made drumming seem effortless. She then became the drummer for Sister Double Happiness before joining Imperial Teen. Her approach to drumming and personal style in Imperial Teen is more subtle than in previous bands, but no less artful.

Imperial Teen waited two years after forming before releasing their debut album *Seasick* on Slash Record, which contained eleven singles and included a Blondie cover delivered with passion and attitude. The album was recorded in approximately one week. Bottum has always maintained that playing with three of his best friends can be both comfortable and uncomfortable. The fact that it is not always comfortable gives the band an edge. Stebbins also enjoys the fact that band members maintain close friendships with one another, and feels the point of creating music is to have fun and to grow together musically. Schwartz views the band members as four distinctly different people who must find their common ground and explore it. All agree that the band is a positive force in their lives and a source of happiness.

Imperial Teen released *What Is Not To Love* in 1999. *Wall of Sound's* Spence Abbott said that the group's second album "was definitely worth the wait.... *What Is Not To Love* improves upon their theory of incorporating gentle, lilting pop melodies with tinges of forgotten youth, melancholy, aggressive guitar playing, propulsive drumming, and just the right amount of fuzz-enhanced psychedelic retro rush." *What Is Not To Love* offers eleven singles which mesh brooding, sonic undertones with catchy melodies and upbeat vocal injections. The first track, "Open Season," demonstrates this duality most aptly. "Yoo Hoo" demonstrates the band's guitar prowess, while "Lipstick" is reminiscent of the Violent Femmes in the early 1980s. A perfect example of the band's bubblegrunge lyric style can be found on "Lipstick" with, "Why do you have to be so proud? I'm the one with lipstick on." "Alone in the Grass" runs seven minutes, fifteen seconds—the longest track on the album, due in part to droning, extended guitar licks. The introspective "The Crucible" presents a stripped-down and rarely-seen side of the band, and "The Beginning" is a flat-out dance groove.

Abbott wrote, "Throughout the duration of the '90s, the term 'pop' has often been stigmatized; roughly equated with being vapid and unfulfilling.... Imperial Teen proves that pop can be engaging, intelligent, and well-crafted—knowing the lyrics, bobbing your head, and singing along is not only fun, but mandatory." Imperial Teen's contributions to the pop-rock-grunge-punk realm have been numerous; they combine the best aspects of numerous musical styles, create thoughtful, whimsical lyrics, and take their presentation into creative new territory. Band members explained at the *imusic* web site, "We're four people from varied backgrounds, influences and experiences. Imperial Teen is the pretty little baby rose that's growing like a bramble from our collective neurosis."

Selected discography

Seasick, Slash, 1996.
What Is Not To Love, Slash, 1999.

Sources

Periodicals

CMJ, February 1, 1999.
Entertainment Weekly, March 12, 1999.
Rolling Stone, March 4, 1999.

Online

"Imperial Teen," *iMusic Modern Showcase,* http://www.imusic.interserv.com/showcase/modern/imperialteen.html (March 1999).

"Imperial Teen Biography," *Imperial Teen Website,* http://www.imperialteen.com (March 12, 1999)

"What Is Not to Love," *Wall of Sound Review*, http://wallofsound.com (March 12, 1999).

—*B. Kimberly Taylor*

Blind Willie Johnson

Gospel singer, guitar

Blind Willie Johnson produced a series of ominous gospel recordings in 1920s and 1930s that combined virtuoso slide guitar, rough, powerful vocals, and songs that as often as not told of an angry God wreaking vengeance on a sinful world. Johnson's music electrified listeners during the depths of the Great Depression. Although Johnson recorded exclusively religious music, the earthy feel of his voice and guitar are the equal of any country blues artist recorded during his time. The music that electrified Johnson's contemporaries, black and white alike, continued to exert a powerful attraction at the end of the century.

Willie Johnson was born on a farm near Marlin Texas around 1901 or 1902. His mother died when he was about four years old, and his father George Johnson remarried, an act that would have dire consequences for the young boy. According to a story Willie's widow told researcher Sam Charters in the 1950s, a few years after his second marriage, George Johnson caught his second wife in the arms of another man. He gave her a severe beating and in retaliation, the woman threw a pan of lye in seven-year-old Willie's face, blinding him. The story may be mere fiction: other sources claim Willie Johnson told them he went blind from wearing borrowed glasses or from watching an eclipse of the sun through a piece of smoked glass.

Johnson's interest in both music and religion began at an early age. When he was only five, legend has it, he was telling folks he was going to become a preacher when he grew up. Around the same time his father him built a cigar box guitar. It is not known who taught him to play guitar, but he is said to have picked up his rough false bass singing style from a blind gospel singer in Marlin named Madkin Butler. By the time Johnson had reached his teens he was singing and playing guitar in the streets of Marlin, summer and winter alike, for the spare change passers-by might offer. In 1925 he was living in Hearne, Texas where his father did farm work. George would drive Willie into town each morning, where he would find a place under one of the awnings on the main street and perform. With three profitable brickyards Hearne's local economy was humming and Willie made good money there. It was so good that Blind Lemon Jefferson, the first great star of recorded country blues, would play the same streets at the same time Johnson was there.

At some point during the next two years Johnson moved to Dallas and was playing the streets there when he met his wife-to-be, Angeline. "A tall gangling man with a thin mustache; a dark intense man," as Sam Charters described him in *The Country Blues*, Johnson was singing "If I Had My Way" when Angeline saw him for the first time. When he left, she followed behind, singing the song herself until he finally noticed her. When he did she invited him to her house to sing hymns. Angeline later told Charters what happened next: she sat down at her piano and belted out a version of "If I Had My Way" that so impressed Willie that he urged her on shouting "Go on, gal, tear it up!" When she had finished singing, she made him a gumbo which he apparently enjoyed so much that he proposed marriage then and there. The gumbo was their courtship; the wedding was held June 22, 1927, the very next day.

Johnson 's first recording date took place later that year on December 3, 1927 for Columbia Records in Dallas. He recorded six sides, all religious songs, but infused with a passionate intensity that leapt from the lacquer grooves of the 78s. It was just Johnson's voice and his guitar. But his emotional slide playing, like a second vocalist, engaged in a beautiful call and response with his own singing. Johnson is said to have used a pocketknife when playing slide; however executed, it possessed a matchless precision. It is even more remarkable considering Texas has no bottleneck or slide guitar tradition—Johnson must have been essentially self-taught. He also sang with two distinct singing voices: one a soft tenor, the other, a growling false bass that quaked like the voice of an angry god. He contrasts them to beautiful effect on his version of "Let Your Light Shine On Me."

Willie's first release, in January 1928, was "I Know His Blood Can Make Me Whole" backed with "Jesus Make

Born Willie Johnson in 1901 (some sources say 1902), Marlin, TX; (died 1949); married Angeline, June 22, 1927.

Recorded six sides for Columbia, December 3, 1927; first record "I Know His Blood Can Make Me Whole" b/w "Jesus Make Up My Dying Bed" released late January of 1928; recorded four sides for Columbia in December of 1928; recorded ten sides in New Orleans for Columbia; recorded another ten titles in Atlanta April of 1930.

Up My Dying Bed;" his second which came out the following spring, was "Nobody's Fault But Mine" b/w "Dark Was the Night, Cold Was the Ground." A contemporary reviewer, quoted by Charters, enthused of the latter, "Blind Willie Johnson's violent, tortured and abysmal shouts and groans and his inspired guitar in a primitive and frightening Negro religious song 'Nobody's Business but Mine!'"

After his first session Johnson and Angeline moved a number of times, first to Waco, then Temple, before finally settling down and buying a house in Beaumont. In December 1928 he returned to Dallas to record once again for Columbia, this time four songs. The records, "I'm Gonna Run to the City of Refuge" b/w "Jesus Is Coming Soon" and "I Just Can't Keep From Crying" b/w "Keep Your Lamp Trimmed and Burning," were released in February and May 1929 respectively. It was long assumed that the female vocalist on these and later Blind Willie Johnson records was Angeline. However, David Evans's liner notes to *Sweeter As the Years Go By,* speculated that it might in actuality have been Willie B. Harris, a woman uncovered by blues researcher Dan Williams. Harris claimed not only to have been the sweet voice on most of Johnson's records, but also his wife—common-law presumably—when he proposed to Angeline! Interestingly, according to Evans in her 1950s interviews with Charters, Angeline never once claimed she had sung on any of her husband's recordings.

In December 1929 Columbia paid for Johnson to travel to New Orleans to record again and Angeline remained at home with the Johnson's new baby. For this session, a soprano from a local church was brought in to sing with Johnson. He remained in New Orleans nearly one month, playing for new audiences there. According to one story, Johnson was singing his passionate Sampson song "If

I Had My Way I'd Tear This Building Down" in front of the New Orleans Customs House and police nearly arrested him for attempting to incite a riot. Whether or not it is true, it testifies to the power and energy of Johnson's version of the song.

As Stephen Calt points out in his liner notes for *Praise God I'm Satisfied,* the fact that Columbia waited a full year between Johnson's recording sessions probably indicates that they were disappointed with his sales. In fact, in early 1929 Johnson sold about 5000 records. By contrast, Barbecue Bob and Bessie Smith Columbia's most popular artists, sold about 6000 and from 9000-10,000 respectively. As the depression deepened, however, and interest in religion surged, Blind Willie Johnson's popularity jumped, too. He continued to sell around 5000 records annually, but Barbecue Bob's sales dropped to 2000, and Smith's to 3000.

Johnson's session took place on April 30, 1930 in Atlanta Georgia. He cut ten sides on this last visit, concluding with the widely-copied "You Gonna Need Somebody On Your Bond." The Depression eventually cut drastically into Johnson's sales, but in November 1934 his was still the second largest listing in the Columbia race catalog, after Bessie Smith. That he continued to be popular is shown by the fact that four of his records were re-issued in 1935, a rare occurrence in race recordings of the time. Unusual also was Johnson's popularity among early white connoisseurs of black folk music.

Once his recording career had ended, Willie and Angeline Johnson continued to live in Beaumont with their children. He earned his living as a street musician, and when Charters called on them in the 1950s, store owners in town still remembered him as a dignified, neatly dressed man. Johnson sang regularly at the Mt. Olive Baptist Church and at regional religious gatherings, as well. In winter 1949 a fire broke out in the Johnson house. It destroyed Willie's guitar but the family managed to escape unharmed. They slept in the partially ruined home, on soaked mattresses that Angeline covered with newspapers. Willie tossed and turned that night. When he awoke, he was damp and sick, but went out in the streets singing anyway. He developed pneumonia, Angeline told Charters, and within a few days was dying. The local hospital was no help. "They wouldn't accept him. He'd be living today if they'd accepted him. They wouldn't accept him because he was blind."

Johnson's religious music exerted a potent influence on secular musicians, in particular blues artists like Mississippi Fred McDowell, Mance Lipscomb and Muddy Waters, as well as rock players such as Ry Cooder and

Alex Chilton. His music and popularity outlived him by decades. Bootlegs of the 1935 reissues, which appeared in the 1950s credited to "The Blind Pilgrim," sold well judging from the number that were subsequently found in private collections, according to David Evans. Even more remarkable, as late as the 1970s Columbia Records included a Blind Willie Johnson song on an anthology *The Gospel Sound.* Black gospel stations played the cut regularly and were deluged with calls from local churches who wanted to book the unknown artist to sing at church events. Little did they know he had been dead for twenty-five years.

Selected discography

Praise God I'm Satisfied, Yazoo, 1988
Sweeter As the Years Go By, Yazoo, 1990
The Complete Recordings of Blind Willie Johnson, Columbia/Legacy, 1993.

Sources

Books

Barlow, William, *Looking Up At Down: The Emergence of Blues Culture*, Temple University Press, Philadelphia, 1989.
Charters, Samuel, *The Country Blues*, Da Capo, New York, 1975.
Dixon, Robert and John Godrich, *Recording the Blues*, Stein & Day.

Additional information provided by the liner notes to *Praise God I'm Satisfied* by Stephen Calt and the liner notes to *Sweeter As the Years Go By* by David Evans.

—*Gerald E. Brennan*

Howard Jones

Composer, piano

Howard Jones was the first person to successfully humanize the 1980s musical genre of techno-pop, breathing new life into a style of music that had been previously characterized as cold, unemotional, and sterile. According to Ira Robbins in the fourth edition of the *Trouser Press Record Guide,* Jones used "instruments that in the mid '80s were generally favored for their musical anonymity, [creating] bouncy, warm hearted missives of personal encouragement and general goodwill. This likable ex-hippie may very well have been the new age's first pin up pop star."

John Howard Jones was born on February 23, 1955, in Southampton, England. He started to play the piano when he was seven years old. Jones and his parents moved around a lot when he was a young child. He spent part of his teenage years living in Canada and it was there that he began to play the organ in a progressive rock group called Warrior.

By the time he was old enough to study at the university, Jones was back in his native England where he enrolled in classes at the Royal Northern College of Music in Manchester. Jones did not last there long as the school's emphasis centered solely on classical music, quickly alienating and disenchanted Jones. After dropping out of the Royal Northern College of Music, Jones began to give piano lessons to interested students. He also worked with his wife as a produce distributor. Jones

kept his musical drive alive as he continued to perform in clubs, including stints in numerous jazz and funk ensembles.

He performed shows where he was accompanied only by drum machines and various keyboards and synthesizers. Also appearing at these shows was a mime named Jed Hoile who served to entertain the assembled audience with his interpretations of Jones' music. Jones received his big break when word of one of his one-man shows reached the attention of famed British DJ John Peel. Peel offered Jones the chance to record some of his music for a "Peel Session" radio broadcast on the British Broadcasting Corporation (BBC).

By 1983, Jones had already signed a recording contract with WEA for distribution rights for his material in both England and Europe. In America, however, he was signed to Elektra. In the autumn of that year, Jones released his first British single "New Song," which peaked at the number three spot on the British singles chart. A few months later he released his second British single, "What is Love," which managed to climb up to the number two slot on the British singles chart.

The spring of 1984 saw the release of his debut album, *Human's Lib. Human's Lib* quickly climbed up the British album chart and nested itself at the number one position. In America, however, things happened a little bit slower for Jones. It eventually took massive college radio airplay and constant MTV exposure of his videos before his debut album became a top 100 album. Later on that same year both "What is Love" and "New Song" finally managed to crack the American top forty singles chart, while his third single, "Pearl in the Shell" became the third British top ten single from Jones' debut album.

Jones released his second album, *Dream Into Action*, in 1985. This was the album that finally enabled him to make it big in America. *Dream Into Action* marked a departure for Jones. Gone was Hoile, the mime, and Jones' synthesized songs were augmented by the addition of horns, a cellist, and additional vocalists. The album managed to make its way to the number ten slot on the American album chart. The first single, "Things Can Only Get Better," peaked at number five on the American singles chart.

1986 brought continued success for Jones as he released *Action Replay*. This EP contained six songs including remixes or alternative versions of five previously released tunes. *Action Replay* produced Jones' biggest American hit single, the Phil Collins produced ballad "No One is to Blame," which managed to peak at number four. Later on that same year, Jones released

For the Record . . .

Born John Howard Jones, February 23, 1955, in Southampton, Hampshire, England. *Education:* attended Royal Northern College of Music.

Signed to Warner/Elektra, 1983; released *Human's Lib*, 1984; released *Dream Into Action*, 1985; released *Action Replay,* 1986; released *One to One,* 1986; released *Cross That Line,* 1989; released *In the Running,* 1992; released *Best of Howard Jones,* 1993; left Warner/Elektra and released *Working in the Backroom* on his Dtox label, 1993; signed to Plump Records and released *Live Acoustic America,* 1995; signed to Pony Canyon In and released *Angels and Lovers,* 1997; signed to Ark 21 and released *People,* 1998.

Addresses: *Record company*—Ark21 Records, 14724 Ventura Blvd., Penthouse Suite, Sherman Oaks, CA 91423.

One to One, which served to focus on Jones as a writer and singer while allowing a number of backing musicians to handle more of the chore of actually playing and performing the music.

Commenting on the change in pace on the Plump Records web site Jones said, "I started off as a one man band with Jed doing mime and dancing. Then I had a three piece band with bass drums and all of the keyboards and then I had a much bigger band with backing singers, horns and guitars. I think people are used to me doing different things and they seem to enjoy the various ways I present the music." Unfortunately, neither *One to One* nor its 1989 follow up *Cross That Line* were as successful as their predecessors, although *Cross That Line* did produce the modest hit "Everlasting Love."

For Jones' next album, 1992's *In the Running*, he changed his style yet again, touring with a single percussionist who accompanied him as he played the piano. Further commenting on his style shifts, Jones stated on the Plump Records web site that, " I keep up with technology as much as possible. But, I've played the piano since I was seven, and I studied piano at the Royal Northern College of Music in Manchester. Piano is the most natural thing for me. That's where my roots are." Unfortunately for Jones, going back to his roots and embracing them did not increase album sales as *In the Running* sold poorly.

1993 marked yet another change in the life of Jones. After the release of his greatest hits package *The Best of Howard Jones,* he was dropped by both his British and American record labels. Initially depressed and worried that he was already washed up and would never record again after, he soon came to realize that being dropped from his former labels was a blessing in disguise. Jones was now free produce whatever he wanted without the financial concerns of a large record company. He released his next record on his own label, UK Dtox. The collection of raw and unpolished out-takes and demos was called *Working in the Backroom.* Jones managed to sell 20,000 copies at his concerts.

His next record, *Live Acoustic-America* —released on Plump Records in 1995—highlighted a single show from Los Angeles in 1994. It would be another two years before Jones released another album. The 1997 Pony Canyon In release *Angels and Lovers* was Jones' first studio album since 1993. He would not wait that long before he released his next album, 1998's *People* on Ark 21.

Speaking about the role of creative people in greater society, Jones remarked in the Plump Records web site that " It's the job of an artist to articulate those feelings that people with busier, more hectic lives, haven't got the time or energy to express. I think that one should take that job seriously and realize that this is a way to positively contribute to society.... I like to encourage the idea of looking deeper into ourselves and finding out why we are and what we are."

Selected discography

Human's Lib, Warner/Elektra, 1984.
Dream Into Action, Warner/Elektra, 1985.
Action Replay, Warner/Elektra, 1986.
One to One, Warner/Elektra, 1986.
Cross That Line, Warner/Elektra, 1989.
In the Running, Warner/Elektra, 1992.
Working in the Backroom, UK Dtox, 1993.
Live Acoustic America, Plump Records, 1995.
Angels and Lovers, Pony Canyon In, 1997.
People, Ark 21, 1998.

Sources

Books

Robbins, Ira, ed. *Trouser Press Record Guide*, fourth edition, Macmillan, 1991.
Robbins, Ira, ed. *Trouser Press Guide to 90s Rock,* Fireside, 1997.

Romanowski, Patricia and Holly George Warren eds., *New Rolling Stone Encyclopedia of Rock and Roll*, Fireside, 1995.

Online

"Howard Jones," *AMG Biography*, www.allmusic.com/cg/x.dll (April 16, 1999).

"Howard Jones; About Howard," *The Plump Website*, www.plump.com/plump/hojobio.htm (February 9, 1999).

—*Mary Alice Adams*

Montell Jordan

Singer, songwriter, producer

Photo by Al Pereira. Michael Ochs Archive. Reproduced by permission.

Montell Jordan soared to stardom with the release of his first recording, "This Is How We Do It," a solid gold hit that topped the rhythm and blues charts for weeks. The cynics watched and waited for Jordan's popularity to wane as quickly as it appeared, but with each successive release new facets of his talent unfolded. A brief three years later there were few who could refute that Jordan was a solid and durable performer who would undoubtedly remain on the popular music scene for years to come. He released four gold-selling songs in succession. His first album was certified gold, and his second album featured three gold single releases. When Jordan's third album, *Let's Ride,* went platinum, the message was evident that Jordan was more than a one-hit performer. A capable songwriter and producer, he contributed his talents to the productions of other musicians who experienced similar success.

Born in 1972, Jordan was the oldest child of Delois Allen and Elijah Jordan. The family lived a lower middle class existence in South Central Los Angeles. With four children, financial survival was a day-to-day ritual, and both of Jordan's parents worked to make ends meet. His father was an accountant, and his mother was a business administrator.

Jordan was in grade school when his grandfather gave him a saxophone. The oddly shaped instrument captured Jordan's attention and sparked a keen interest for music in the boy. In time Jordan expanded his musical interests, learning to play the piano at age 10, and to sing by age 11. He joined the choir of his Baptist church congregation along with a close friend, and in time both were well-respected members of the group.

As Jordan matured he reached the imposing physical height of six-foot-eight-inches tall. He told Margena Christian in *Ebony Man* that he missed the obvious detour into an athletic career mainly because of financial limitations that kept him otherwise occupied as a teenager in private schools. In grade school and at an all-boy's high school, Jordan worked in the school cafeteria while his friends were playing ball and practicing their skills at recess. Jordan in turn pursued other interests, at home in his free time.

He nurtured his musical skills outside of school, even after he moved on to college. He attended Pepperdine University in Malibu, California, which proved to be an exceptional financial drain on both Jordan and his family. He determinedly worked at assorted jobs and completed a sensible curriculum in organizational communications, all the while relegating his love of music to the priority of a spare time hobby. After graduation in 1991, he considered enrolling in law school, but opted instead to work for an advertising agency.

Eventually the agency downsized and Jordan lost his job. He turned the misfortune into opportunity as it left him ample time to pursue his musical ambitions. He sold his car for the money to buy a keyboard and used the instrument to make a demonstration tape. He spent some time singing in a local nightclub until late in 1993, when he began negotiations with Def Jam records. *This is How We Do It,* his first album, went into production in January of 1994. He was still in his mid-twenties when his first single, "This Is How We Do It," hit the big time. The song not only earned a gold record for Jordan, but it hovered at first place on the charts for seven weeks. The album of the same name reached number 4 on the R&B charts.

In the spring of 1995 Jordan toured with Boyz II Men and TLC. In 1997 his second album *More* was released on Rush Associated Labels. That album hit number 2 on the R&B charts and featured three gold singles: "I Like," "Falling," and "What's on Tonight." "I Like," was also featured on the soundtrack of the Eddie Murphy film, *The Nutty Professor.* He produced his third album, *Let's Ride,* in collaboration with rapper Master P's production company, Beats by the Pound. *Let's Ride* features a variety of musical styles from gospel to funk. Jordan embraces hip-hop styles, clearly distinguished by his talent for romanticizing ghetto themes with a positive and upbeat sentiment.

Known as more than a performer, Jordan wrote much of his own material and has written hit songs for others, as

well. His "Nobody's Supposed to be Here," was a major hit for rhythm and blues diva Deborah Cox. The song hit number one of the R&B charts and surfaced as a crossover hit in the 10 on the pop charts. Jordan also produced albums for other groups on his M3 label

Jordan's escalating popularity as a fresh new face in the music industry made him a popular fixture at awards shows, as a presenter, nominee, and award winner. *Billboard* nominated Jordan for the *Billboard* Music Video Award as best new artist in 1995, and then invited him to be a presenter at the 1995 *Billboard* Music Awards.

In 1997 Jordan appeared at the Nation Association for the Advancement of Colored People 28th Image Awards, and he was a presenter at the 8th Annual Rhythm & Blues Foundation Pioneer Awards, at the NY Hilton. He was a presenter at the 1998 *Billboard* Music Video Awards and, a few weeks later, performed at the "Soul Train Lady of Soul Awards" in honor of Chaka Khan.

Jordan was as a delegate to Alan Roy Scott's 1997 Music Bridge song-writing sessions and conferences in Clifden, Ireland. Music Bridge holds sessions worldwide, and Jordan collaborated on songs and performed at the 1999 Music Bridge sessions in Havana, Cuba, as well.

Selected discography

This is How We Do It, 1995.
More (includes "Falling," "I Like," and "What's on Tonight"), Rush Associated Labels, 1996.
Let's Ride, Def Jam, 1998.

Sources

Periodicals

Billboard, February 22, 1997; February 21, 1998; June 27, 1998; September 12, 1998; December 26, 1998.
Ebony Man, May 1997.
Entertainment, June 2, 1995.
Essence, November 1998.
Los Angeles Times, Record Edition, March 29, 1999.
New York Amsterdam News, July 16, 1998.
People, June 19, 1995.

Online

"Montell Jordan," http://www.defjam.com/artists/montell/montell.html (May 9, 1999).

—*Gloria Cooksey*

Joy
Electric

Christian rock band

Ronnie Martin and Jeff Cloud are well aware that the music they make as Joy Electric strikes some as unusual. They play synthesizers, write pop melodies, have a punk attitude, and sing lyrics with a Christian message. Singer and songwriter Martin has noted that this blend of secular sound and religious message has made it difficult for them to get heard in either music market.

Addressing the difficulty of getting airplay on popular radio, Martin told Jeff Niesel of the *Orange County Register*, "It might be hard for the people at the label to have confidence in us, because I think we sound kind of weird to them." He went on to say; "The Christian rock industry avoids us like the plague. We are so baffling to them." In spite of the puzzled music industry, Joy Electric has found a devoted following. Todd Durant, an online music retailer, told David Richards of *Billboard*, "We sell-through our order in the first week. The band's fans are very dedicated." The band rewards this dedication by playing in music stores when touring in support of new releases. Besides offering intimacy, these performances allow fans to hear the duo on acoustic guitars instead of their usual electronic keyboards.

The band's sound in the studio and in large venues, though, draws on an electronic rock tradition that dates back to the 1970s. Martin has cited electronic bands such as Kraftwerk, Tangerine Dream, and Human League

as major influences. Martin grew up in Orange County, California and started recording with his brother Jason in 1992 as Dance House Children. In 1993 Cloud, another Orange County native, joined the brothers for an album titled *Rainbow Rider.* This effort got them a deal with Christian alternative-rock label Tooth and Nail, which gave them national distribution for their work for the first time. In the meantime, though, Jason had left the group for other ventures, so Ronnie and Cloud became Joy Electric, and their first album, *Melody,* came out in 1994.

Even by that time, Martin was frustrated by the pop music world's rejection of Christian music and the Christian music world's rejection of electronic pop. He admitted to Todd Brown of the *Lighthouse electronic Magazine* that the song "Never Be a Star" came from Martin's anticipation of a lukewarm reception for Joy Electric's first effort. "I had this aching feeling before Joy Electric came out that the reception to it was going to be less than low, and I was totally right, and I got more depressed about that." Their follow-up EP, *Five Stars for Failure,* was born of this low mood. Still, Joy Electric kept their religious perspective, citing scriptural sources for several songs on the CD's cover.

The band's commitment to their electronic sound continued to grow. Before their third release, *Melody Maker,* Martin worked on building his own analog synthesizers, wanting to rely exclusively on a single instrument without resorting to samples or drum machines to fill out the sound. Before the album came out, Martin told Brown, "The new record is just going to be the purest electronic synthesizer record ever released in the Christian market." While relying completely on synthesizers, Martin and Cloud also kept up their punk attitude. Martin described their 1997 album, *Robot Rock,* to Niesel as being "like our version of a punk album with synthesizers." Cloud added, "What we're doing is more punk than what the punk bands are doing."

Attempting to reach an audience that could appreciate such an attitude, they released the single, "Monosynth," a song about the power of synthesizers, and supported it by shooting a video for MTV. Martin and Cloud felt that openly expressing the religious beliefs helps make them punk. They called their 1999 album *Christiansongs,* which marked the first time they mentioned religion in an album title. Martin told Richards that the title had a double meaning: "It's a recognition by us that, yes, we are a Christian band. But ... it is meant to shock people a little. All the bands you see on MTV try to be alternative but seem uniformly bland."

Although Martin and Cloud have stayed busy with Joy Electric, releasing four albums and three EP's between

For the Record . . .

Members include **Jeff Cloud** (born 1974, Orange County, CA), synthesizers; **Ronnie Martin** (born 1970, Orange County, CA), vocals and synthesizers.

Signed with Tooth and Nail and released debut album, *Melody*, 1994; moved to BEC recordings and released *Robot Rock*, 1997; released the single and video "Monosynth," 1997; released their fourth album, *Christiansongs*, 1999.

Addresses: *Band*—Joy Electric, P. O. Box 30164, Santa Ana, CA 92735. *Website*—http://www.becrecordings.com/bands/joyelectric.

1994 and 1999, each has taken on other projects during that time. Cloud formed a band with Jason Martin called Pony Express. In the meantime, Ronny Martin expanded his role in the music business, forming his own label, Plastiq Musiq, to produce and record music by other electronic acts. The label's first release, *You Are Obsolete* by House of Wire, gained praise as one of the best electronic albums of 1998.

If the synthesizers, beliefs, and attitudes set Joy Electric apart from the MTV pack, their melodies put them firmly in the tradition of popular music. Martin considers his song writing as the crucial first step for Joy Electric. He composed on piano, looking for what he described to Brown as " three-and-a-half minute songs with catchy chord changes, melodies, and choruses that you don't forget." Next comes the electronic arrangement. Martin believed this emphasis on songwriting is what distinguished Joy Electric from electronica acts such as the Chemical Brothers, whom he described to Niesel by saying, "they have cool beats, but it's not like you can hum along with it."

Even as he continues to expand his role in the electronic scene, Martin has consistently been outspoken about the indifference of the Christian music industry to Joy Electric. Although they performed live at religious music festivals, they had trouble receiving airplay on contemporary Christian radio. He sees hypocrisy in the way the industry operates, telling Brown, "[Y]ou read in magazines, 'Christian musicians need to be more original.' Then, as soon as you get an act that is really trying to push down boundaries they reject it totally."

At least in the world of secular music, Joy Electric could get noticed just for being Christian. As he told Richards, "Mention that you're Christian and you get a reaction from people, sometimes negative, but a reaction nonetheless." No matter what reaction they got, Joy Electric remained committed to both their sound and their message.

Selected discography

Melody, Tooth and Nail, 1994.
Five Stars for Failure, Tooth and Nail, 1995.
We Are the Music Makers, Tooth and Nail, 1996.
Old Wive's Tales, Tooth and Nail, 1997.
Robot Rock, BEC, 1997.
The Land of the Misfits, BEC, 1998.
Christiansongs, BEC, 1999.

Sources

Periodicals

Orange County Register (Santa Ana, CA), January 9, 1998.
Billboard, March 13, 1999.

Online

Lighthouse electronic Magazine, http://tlem.netcentral.net (May 12, 1999).

—Lloyd Hemingway

Phil Keaggy

Singer, songwriter

Photo by Jon Sievert. Michael Ochs Archive. Reproduced by permission.

During a career that has spanned over three decades, Phil Keaggy has carved out a unique niche for himself in both the contemporary Christian and main-stream pop music worlds. His virtuosity on guitar has earned him wide admiration among afficionados of the instrument. It might be argued that his audience would be larger if his exceptional talents were applied to making records for a secular market. Nevertheless, Keaggy has remained true to his spiritual focus ever since becoming a solo artist, stretching the boundaries of Christian music over the course of some 26 albums.

Keaggy's mastery of the guitar transcends categories, Christian or otherwise. His acoustic playing is particular-ly fluent, utilizing unusual open tunings and deft finger-picking. As his career has progressed, he has incorpo-rated sampling and layering effects to extend his capa-bilities in concert. There are flashes of classic folk, baroque and jazz fusion in his approach that, taken together, make his style distinctly his own. As a song-writer, Keaggy has taken melodic inspiration from the Beatles and other secular pop/rock artists, as well as from Irish and American folk sources. His lyrics, rooted in Christian themes and Biblical references, touch upon spiritual struggles with a positive emphasis.

Born March 23, 1951, in Youngstown, Ohio, Keaggy began his musical apprenticeship with a 19 dollar Sears Silvertone guitar at age ten. He learned to play despite having lost most of his right-hand middle finger in an accident when he was four. By his mid-teens, he had became proficient enough to perform in local clubs. From there, he formed the band Glass Harp with bassist Daniel Pecchio and drummer John Sferra in the summer of 1968. Though they never entered rock's big leagues, the Ohio-based trio released three albums on Decca Records and shared the stage with Yes, Traffic, Chicago, Humble Pie and Iron Butterfly. Keaggy's fluent guitar touch won the admiration of such rock notables as Ted Nugent and, according to a persistent rumor, Jimi Hendrix.

On Valentine's Day, 1970, Keaggy's life was profoundly changed by tragedy. That night, he embarked on a harrow-ing LSD trip that left him physically and emotionally shaken. He later learned that, at that same hour, his mother had been killed in an automobile accident hundreds of miles away. The impact of her loss helped to lead him towards embracing Christianity. As he told interviewer Todd Hafer in *The Gazette*, "It was only in God that I could find something strong enough to replace the love I knew for her, and she had for me. She was a Roman Catholic woman, full of the spirit of God. She loved her children."

Keaggy's newly-found faith was reflected in his songwrit-ing. His first recorded Christian song, "The Answer,"

Born March 23, 1951 in Youngstown, OH.

Began recording career as member of band Glass Harp in 1970; released first solo album What A Day on New Song, 1974; released first all-instrumental album The Master And The Musicia, 1978; recorded for Sparrow and Nissi labels, 1980-1986; released landmark album The Wind & The Wheat on Maranatha Music/Myrrh, 1987; released further albums on Myrrh, Word/Epic, Sparrow and Canis Major labels, 1989-1997; returned to singer/songwriter recording with Phil Keaggy CD in 1998.

Awards: Dove Award for Instrumental Album of the Year for The Wind & The Wheat, 1988; Dove Award for Instrumental Album of the Year for Beyond Nature, 1992; Dove Award for Instrumental Album of the Year for Invention, 1998.

Address: Record company—Myrrh Records, Word Entertainment Inc., 3319 West End Avenue, Nashville, TN, 37203. Management—Proper Management, 2814 Kenway Rd., Nashville, TN 37215.

appeared on Glass Harp's second album, Synergy. In August of 1972, Keaggy quit the band and joined a Christian fellowship in upstate New York. Two years later, he re-emerged as a solo artist with What A Day, released on the small New Song label. The album marked a departure for him, both musically and spiritually. "What A Day was mild-mannered and soft," he recalled in an interview with Jas Obrecht in Guitar Player, "but at the same time it expressed my heart. With Glass Harp, I was striving for excellence and finding myself. I was not satisfied with simple things; I just pushed and pushed myself. Coming into Christianity, I found that I can express things in my heart in a very simple manner, and people are in a place to receive that."

From there, Keaggy went on to record further albums for New Song at a steady pace, releasing Love Broke Through in 1976 and Emerging in 1977. The Master And The Musician, appeared in 1978, was his first all-instrumental album. The 1980s found him switching labels to Sparrow, then moving over to Nissi and, later, to Myrrh. For Myrrh, he recorded his 1987 album The

Wind & The Wheat, an instrumental work that earned him his first Dove Award for Instrumental Album of the Year from the Gospel Music Association.

Keaggy's reputation began to spread to the secular music world during this period. In reviewing Keaggy's 1986 album Getting Closer, Guitar Player writer Jas Obrecht hailed his songs as "catchy and accessible, his playing superb. His solos tap the most modern techniques, from wild whammies to two-handed flash. He proves especially adept at legato lines, volume swells, and doubling.... The lyrical slant of each song is decidedly humanistic, if not overtly Christian."

The 1990s found Keaggy back on Sparrow, releasing both instrumental albums and singer/songwriter projects. A busy tour schedule in the U.S. and overseas helped to keep his following a strong one. He won further Dove Awards, including ones for Best Instrumental Album of the Year in 1992 for Beyond Nature and in 1998 for Invention. He also received Grammy Award nominations for Best Rock Gospel Album in 1991 for Find Me In These Fields and in 1994 for Crimson & Blue. In addition, he earned second place for the Best Acoustic Fingerstyle Guitarist Award from Guitar Player in 1995 and 1996.

In 1998, Keaggy returned to the Myrrh roster to release a critically-praised self-titled CD. Phil Keaggy was his first singer/songwriter album since 1995's True Believer, and tapped into his affinities with the pop/rock tradition of the Beatles. Such tracks as "Tender Love" and "A Sign Came Through A Window" recalled the rich melodies and arrangements of Paul McCartney's late 1960s work. "I don't mind the Beatles comparisons," Keaggy said in a Myrrh press biography. "They wrote the best songs of the rock era, period, and any comparison to them is a compliment." Among the sources for Phil Keaggy's lyrics were the poems of Christian writer H.A. Ironside and the writings of Fifth Century cleric St. John Chrysostom. The album was very much a family affair. Recording much of the album's basic tracks at his home studio, Keaggy enlisted his wife and daughter as background singers and set several lyrics by his sister Geri to music.

Keaggy's musical path has led him from mainstream rock 'n' roll into a secure place in contemporary Christian music. Slowly over the past several decades, he has begun to win fans among secular listeners. But, as he has repeatedly made clear in interviews, his commitment to spreading his spiritual message has not diminished with time. "The gift of music is not only something that you share with other people, it's something that you give back to your creator," he told Tom Gannaway in an interview for *Fingerstyle Guitar.* "To me, it has to express love and the gratitude that's in your heart, because that's ultimately what we're created to do. As it says in the book of Isaiah, 'The people whom I have formed for myself shall declare my praise.' That's the foremost reason I am a Christian musician."

Selected discography

What A Day, New Song, 1974.
The Master And The Musician, New Song, 1978.
Getting Closer, Nissi, 1985.
The Wind & The Wheat, Maranatha Music/Myrrh, 1987.
Beyond Nature, Myrrh/Epic, 1991.
Crimson & Blue, Myrrh, 1993.
Time-Collection, 1970-1995, Myrrh, 1995.
True Believer, Sparrow, 1995.
Phil Keaggy, Myrrh, 1998.

Sources

Billboard, March 3, 1989; March 11, 1989.
CCM, November, 1998.
Christian Musician, July/August 1998.
Fingerstyle Guitar, August 1998.
Gazette, August, 1998.
Guitar Player, May, 1986; June, 1995.

Additional information was provided by Myrrh Records and Proper Management publicity materials, 1999.

—*Barry Alfonso*

Lenny Kravitz

Singer, songwriter

Archive Photos, Inc. Reproduced by permission.

One of the first rock superstars to emerge at the start of the 1990s, Lenny Kravitz built his success out of elements of pop music's recent past. From his 1989 debut album Let *Love Rule* onwards, his deft ability to matched aggressive guitar-driven rock with smooth R&B rhythms proved to be a consistent hitmaking combination. His versatile vocal style and psychedelic-tinged "flower child" persona mixed the sensuality of classic soul singers with echoes of John Lennon and other 1960s-era rock icons. His lyrics frequently conveyed idealistic and spiritual sentiments, while his musical direction invited comparisons with the likes of the Beatles, Led Zeppelin and Jimi Hendrix.

From the start of his recording career, Kravitz's penchant for tapping into the sounds and clothing styles of his childhood stirred critical debate. As quoted in *Contemporary Musicians*, Volume 5; *Rolling Stone* reviewer Anthony DeCurtis described his first album as symptomatic of an untested generation "trying to capture the sound of young America sifting through the fragments of postmodern culture and creating childlike musical collages of no particular point ... as if the world were a kind of shopping mall in which this kind of music can be blended with that regardless of the inherent integrity of any particular genre." *Spin* critic Christian Wright appeared more sympathetic when he speculated that; "Maybe Lenny Kravitz is a new hippie with an old soul or maybe his neo-Bohemia is the supreme pretense. Either way he's convincing." The argument over whether Kravitz was an artist of substance or merely a facile revivalist began anew with the release of each new album.

Born May 24, 1964, Kravitz embraced show business as something of a birthright. The only child of NBC television news producer Sy Kravitz and actress Roxie Roker, who played Helen Willis on the TV sitcom *The Jeffersons,* he lived an idyllic city life while growing up in Manhattan's rich cultural atmosphere. As a child, he was introduced to many famous jazz and R&B musicians; on one occasion, he recalled sitting on Duke Ellington's lap while the legendary composer played the piano. In 1974, he moved to Los Angeles with his parents, where he joined the California Boys' Choir, with whom he recorded under the supervision of conductor Zubin Mehta. He also studied music dilligently during his teenage years, teaching himself to play guitar, bass, keyboards and drums. Drawn to a music career while a high school student, he left home at 16 and began to circulate demo recordings under the name of Romeo Blue. After an initial deal with IRS Records fell through, Kravitz secured a contract with Virgin Records under his own name in early 1989.

When his *Let Love Rule* album appeared in late 1989, Kravitz was more widely known as the husband of

For the Record . . .

Born May 24, 1964 in Brooklyn, New York; son of Sy Kravitz (NBC television news producer) and Roxie Roker (an actor); married Lisa Bonet (divorced); children: one daughter.

Began musical career as Romeo Blue, c. 1980; signed with Virgin Records, 1989; released debut album *Let Love Rule*, Virgin, 1989; co-wrote "Justify My Love," a number one single for Madonna, 1991; released album *Mama Said*, Virgin, 1991; recorded with Mick Jagger, released album *Are You Gonna Go My Way*, Virgin, 1993; released *Circus*, Virgin, 1995; released *5*, Virgin, 1998; released single "American Woman" from *Austin Powers: The Spy Who Shagged Me* (soundtrack).

Awards: MTV Video Music Award for Best Male Video, 1993; Grammy Award for Best Male Rock Performance, 1998.

Addresses: *Record company*—Virgin Records, 338 North Foothill Road, Beverly Hills, CA 90210.

---

actress Lisa Bonet than as a musician. But the swift success of his first album established him as a media figure in his own right. *Let Love Rule* featured Kravitz as the sole vocalist and instrumentalist on every track. His recording methods were deliberately antiquated, utilizing vintage tube amplifiers and favoring analog over digital technology. Though the album's title track only reached number 89 on the American charts as a single, touring and television appearances boosted Kravitz's profile in America and Europe. He enjoyed his greatest breakthrough in 1990 as the co-writer of Madonna's "Justify My Love," which went on to become a Number One single.

In response to America's impending conflict with Iraq, Kravitz recorded a new version of John Lennon's "Give Peace A Chance" in tandem with Yoko Ono, Sean Lennon and other luminaries, which rose to number 54 in the U.S. in March, 1991. He was quickly on the charts again with "It Ain't Over 'Til It's Over," the initial single from his second album, *Mama Said*. This soulful tune reached number two in the United States, helping *Mama Said* to eventually earn platinum certification. A number of the songs on the album dealt with the break-up of Kravitz's marriage to Bonet, and benifitted from a tough-

er rock-oriented sound overall. A second single from *Mama Said*, "Stand By My Woman," charted at number 76 in late 1991.

Amidst his rising success as an artist, Kravitz found time to produce an album by French singer Vanessa Paradis in 1992 and, in the following year, teamed up with Mick Jagger on "Use Me." He also co-wrote "Line Up" for Aerosmith's *Get A Grip* album. 1993 saw the release of his *Are You Gonna Go My Way* album, which went on to reach double platinum status. He continue to tour frequently, and had the honor of having one of his musical heroes, ex-Led Zeppelin singer Robert Plant, open shows for him in Europe. A renewed interest in sixties fashion and music around this time made Kravitz's backwards-looking style seem up-to-date. He commented to *Rolling Stone* writer Kim Neely that "When I came out with *Let Love Rule,* everybody was trippin' on the way it sounded and what I was talking about. They said I was this sweet little child, talking about love and understanding. You know, 'You can't say those things, that's childish.' Now, *they're* ready to accept it, so all of a sudden *I* am more mature.... When actually I'm the same musician."

Kravitz's next solo release, *Circus*, was released in 1995 and quickly reached gold certification. A move towards more contemporary sonic ideas, the album yielded the chart singles "Rock And Roll Is Dead" and "Can't Get You Off My Mind". As usual, critical reaction to *Circus* was mixed. Reviewing the album for *Musician*, Mac Randall praised Kravitz for "his ability to conjure up a magical late '60s/early '70s sonic world that never quite existed but should have" and hailed the album as "yet another demonstration of a classic equation: blistering rock guitar plus bruising funk rhythms equals excitement." On the negative side, *Rolling Stone* reviewer Mark Kemp opined that "Flagrant appropriation has been a hallmark for Kravitz since *Let Love Rule*, but on most of *Circus'* tracks, it finally becomes redundant, rendering the guilty pleasures few and far between."

Weathering the death of his mother in December of 1995, Kravitz took part in the 40-city H.O.R.D.E. American concert tour during the summer of 1996 before beginning work on his next album. Recording over an eight-month period, he embraced sampling and drum loops for for the first time and steered his sound in a distinctly modern R&B direction. "No tape, this time," he said of his recording methods in a Virgin Records press biography. "And 'Digital' used to be a dirty word for me. But by working instrument by instrument, building up the sound, I was able to construct the record like a puzzle. I was listening to a lot of New York hip-hop. I like that technique—the sparseness, the groove, the rhythm."

Released in 1998, *5* brought Kravitz yet another platinum album. Its single "Fly Away" reached number 12 on the pop charts and earned him a Grammy Award for Best Male Rock Performance of 1998. He was also fortunate enough to have his version of the Guess Who's 1970 hit "American Woman" featured on the soundtrack of the hugely popular 1999 film *Austin Powers: The Spy Who Shagged Me.* "American Woman" was included on later pressings of *5* and went on to become a high-charting single as well.

Whatever the sources of his music may be, Kravitz demonstrated artistic staying power throughout the nineties. For his part, he seemed not be overly concerned about issues of originality. "Do I have to make up a new form of music?", he asked in a *Rolling Stone* interview. "Is that my job? Everything's been done... I just play what comes out of me. Whether I'm innovative or not, I'm doing what's true to me, what's natural. Maybe someday I'll do something that no one's heard, I don't know. But at least I'm doing what God put in me to come out."

Selected discography

Let Love Rule, Virgin, 1989.
Mama Said, Virgin, 1991.
Are You Gonna Go My Way, Virgin, 1993.
Circus, Virgin, 1995.
5, Virgin, 1998.

Sources

Books

Contemporary Musicians, Volume 5, Gale Research, Inc., 1991
DiMartino, Dave, *Singer-Songwriters,* Billboard Books, 1994.
The Encyclopedia of Popular Music, Muze, 1998..

Periodicals

Musician, October 1995.
Rolling Stone, September 7, 1989; June 24, 1993; September 21, 1995; June 11, 1998.
Spin, July 1990.
Stereo Review, June 1993.

Additional information was provided by Virgin Records publicity materials.

—*Barry Alfonso*

Ben Lee

Singer, songwriter

Photo by Mitchell Gerber. Corbis-Bettmann. Reproduced by permission.

Although he was probably more widely known for his romance with young actress Claire Danes—of movies such as the *Mod Squad* and the television series *My So-Called Life*—Australian alternative rock prodigy Ben Lee earned admirable critical credibility at a relatively early age. His home-recorded single debut as a 14-year-old in the band Noise Addict attracted the interest of Sonic Youth's Thurston Moore and Beastie Boys' Mike D. The single earned Lee a record deal before he was even out of high school.

By that point, though, Lee had already been honing his craft for years, having written his first songs at the age of ten. At 13 the Sydney native had formed Noise Addict. It's not surprising that Lee's age was as much a topic of discussion as was his music. Reviewing his 1995 debut solo album, *Grandpaw Would* for *Rolling Stone,* Christina Kelly wrote, "it's hard to believe lyrics this dead-on were written by a kid this young. Then you realize that only a 15-year-old could write songs with such a perfect combination of innocence and cynicism."

"I Was I Was Him" brought immediate attention to Lee and Noise Addict—bass player Daniel Kohn and drummer Saul Smith. A tongue-in-cheek ode to Lemonhead Evan Dando "I Was I Was Him" included the oft-quoted lyrics, "He's got six different flannel shirts, Airwalks not thongs/He even understands the words to Pavement songs." Kathleen Hanna of Bikini Kill reportedly later covered the song. A new version of "I Wish I Was Him" first appeared on *The Taste in My Eyes,* a 1994 EP issued on the Australian label Fellaheen. When Noise Addict's American debut, the EP *Young & Jaded,* was released on the Beastie Boys' label Grand Royal in 1994, it included the original recording of "I Wish I Was Him," along with a cover version of the Jonathan Richman song "Back in Your Life." The same year, the band also released the EP *Def* on the Ecstatic Peace! label.

Although Noise Addict was often likened to fellow Australian teen rock band Silverchair, a number of writers noted that the primary similarity between the two bands was the age of their members. Unlike the grunge-oriented Silverchair, Lee and Noise Addict demonstrated more of a pop sensibility. As Sara Sherr wrote for the *Knight Ridder/Tribune News Service,* "Lee mixes elements of innocence and wisdom, catchy songs with witty, poignant lyrics about girls and pop music, and the struggle to be yourself in a world populated by interchangeable scenesters."

In 1995, Lee took a brief hiatus from Noise Addict to record *Grandpaw Would.* An engaging outing, *Grandpaw Would* was praised in the *Trouser Press Guide to '90s Rock* as "a joy: one catchy little pop song after another."

Born 1979 in Australia.

Formed trio Noise Addict in Australia, 1992; first self-recorded single with Noise Addict, 1993; released debut EP, *The Taste in My Eyes,* released on Australian label Fellaheen, 1994; first solo record, *Grandpaw Would,* released on Fellaheen/Grand Royal, 1995; left Noise Addict for solo career, 1996; debut solo album on Capitol, *Breathing Tornadoes,* in 1999.

Addresses: *Record company*—Capitol, 1750 North Vine, Hollywood, CA 90028-5274.

The album featured background vocals by Rebecca Gates of the Spinanes on "Pop Queen" and Liz Phair on "Away With the Pixies." Lee returned to Noise Addict—which now featured new guitarist Romy Hoffman—to record 1996's *Meet the Real You.* It would be the last album Lee would record with Noise Addict before splitting from the group to concentrate on a solo career.

The following year Lee issued his first post-Noise Addict album, *Something to Remember Me By,* which was recorded at the Beastie Boys' Grand Royal studio in Los Angeles. Writing for the *Detroit News,* Tom Long called the album "a personal, complex and affecting work that doesn't necessarily show a wisdom beyond his years; instead it shows a wisdom about his years, and may be one of the best albums of 1997." The album again teamed Lee with producer Brad Wood, who had worked on Lee's first solo record. Wood had also worked with alternative rock acts Veruca Salt and Liz Phair.

Something to Remember Me By featured some reasonably well known alternative rockers backing Lee, including Hole's Melissa Auf der Maur and That Dog's Anna Waronker on backing vocals. The album tackled more weighty themes than his previous outings, which Lee said he did consciously. "It's not a light album, something you can really put on in the background," Lee told Steve Appleford of *Rolling Stone* in 1997. "There's no reason to let people off lightly just because they've already paid for the record."

By the age of 20, he had already released his third solo outing, 1999's *Breathing Tornadoes.* The album, which incorporated more musical technology than previous efforts, demonstrated Lee's continuing musical growth

and garnered him even more critical accolades. *Newsweek* praised the record's "infectious electrofolk." Lee told *Billboard's* Carrie Borzillo, "I just feel I've been so literal so many times in the past; this was the first time I experimented with different degrees of abstraction. I wanted to talk about more complex feelings, and the only way to do that was with more complex lyrics." Evelyn McDonnell dubbed it "infectious" and "charming" in her review for *Interview,* while *Esquire* said the album "hit the pop-alternative nail on the head."

For his fourth solo album, *Breathing Tornadoes,* Lee worked with producer Ed Bueller, who was well known for his work with British acts like Suede and Pulp. "I didn't want to be in the situation where you fall into old habits, and before you know it, you're making the same jokes and using the same sounds," Lee told Borzillo. The album, Lee's first for Capitol Records, was recorded in a New York apartment and features the single "Nothing Much Happens."

To promote the album, Lee was slated to tour the Northeastern United States, as well as open several shows for the band Cracker. In a 1997 article in *Entertainment Weekly,* Lee exhibited his knack for digging beneath the surface of issues, which apparently extends beyond his songs, as he discussed his career. "I'm dealing with my soul and the souls of the people who listen to me," Lee told writer Matt Diehl. "However I'm judged, I'm gonna make it through and I'm gonna do it all."

Selected discography

Grandpaw Would, Fellaheen/Grand Royal, 1995.
Away with the Pixies EP, Fellaheen, 1995.
Something to Remember Me By, Grand Royal, 1997.
Breathing Tornadoes, Grand Royal/Capitol, 1999.

with Noise Addict

The Taste in My Eyes EP, Fellaheen, 1994.
Young & Jaded EP, Grand Royal, 1994.
Def EP, Ecstatic Peace!, 1994.
Noise Addict vs. Silver Chair (reissue of *The Taste in My Eyes),* Fellaheen, 1995.
Meet the Real You, Fellaheen, 1995; Grand Royal, 1996.

Sources

Books

Robbins, Ira, editor, *Trouser Press Guide to '90s Rock,* Fireside, 1997.

Periodicals

Billboard, February 20, 1999.
Detroit News, June 12, 1997.
Entertainment Weekly, April 28, 1995; February 2, 1996;
    May 23, 1997; May 30, 1997.
Esquire, March 1999.
Interview, February 1999.
Knight-Ridder/Tribune News Service, January 17, 1996.
Newsweek, April 12, 1999.
Rolling Stone, May 18, 1995; March 20, 1997.

—K. Michelle Moran

Julian Lennon

Singer, songwriter

Photo by Kathy Willens. AP/Wide World Photos. Reproduced by permission.

Being the son of a legend is hard. Living up to that legend is even harder. Continuing that legend's legacy is nearly impossible—especially when the legend/father is infamous ex-Beatle John Lennon. According to VH-1's *Behind the Music*, the elder Lennon "preordained what Julian was gonna be [when he asked baby Julian] who's gonna be a little rocker like his daddy?" John Lennon would never see his son fulfill his destiny, when in 1984, Julian Lennon became a big rocker with the release of his hit debut album, *Valotte*. Three albums and seven years later, Julian had had enough of life in the public and of critic's who had seen him both as a replacement for his father and, as stated by *Behind the Music*, "a pretender to the throne." In 1991 Lennon, tired of the ceaseless scrutiny and comparisons to his father, disappeared. As he stated in the 1985 concert film *Stand By Me*, "It's great to get recognition [for the music], but fame doesn't do anything for me whatsoever."

John Charles Julian Lennon was born on April 8, 1963 in Liverpool, England. Being the first Beatle baby, "Jules" received instant media attention. Attention from his father, however, was limited. While John Lennon was busy changing the face of pop music, Julian's mother Cynthia was left to care for him. And although he resented his father's lack of participation in his life, Julian was able to identify with his father's music, stating at www.julianlennon.com "My dad's music was a great inspiration to me."

It was Julian, however, who inspired the Beatles song "Hey Jude." *Behind the Music* described the song as, "an anthem of hope and longing—a song of comfort and concern. written by Paul McCartney to console a five year old boy devastated by his parents divorce." In 1999, Julian, as stated on his web site, still finds it, "hard to imagine this man [McCartney] was thinking about me and my life so much that he wrote a song about me. If I'm sitting in a bar and the song comes on the radio, I still get goose pimples." In 1968 John left Julian and Cynthia, moving from London to New York City with his new wife Yoko Ono, a Japanese performance artist. Julian would not see his father for the next four years.

Reconciliation Cut Short by Assassin's Bullet

Throughout the mid-Seventies, Julian and his father slowly began to repair their relationship. Julian even played drums on "Ya Ya," a song on his father's *Walls and Bridges* album. However, Julian recalled on *Behind the Music* that, "I didn't know how to react with him. He didn't know how to react with me." In 1975, with the birth of Sean Ono Lennon, John's second son, Julian contin-

For the Record . . .

Born John Charles Julian Lennon on April 8, 1963 in Liverpool, England; son of ex-Beatles singer/songwriter John Lennon and Cynthia Powell, a television host.

At eleven years old played drums on "Ya Ya" on father's *Walls and Bridges* album; taught himself to play piano; continued to rebuild his relationship with his father until 1980 when John Lennon was assassinated; signed with Atlantic Records, 1983; released debut album Valotte, (include hits "Too Late For Goodbyes" and "Valotte"), 1984; released The Secret Value of Daydreaming, 1986; released Mr. Jordon, 1989; released Help Yourself (included "Saltwater"), 1996; formed Music From Another Room label; released Photograph Smile, 1999.

Addresses: *Record company*—Music From Another Room; *Website*—www.julianlennon.com.

ued to find it hard to connect with his father, especially when John took five years off from the music business to stay at home with Sean. Julian further recalled that he felt "frustrated a bit... why couldn't he have recognized this and tried to make things better, try to change things in regards to his love or respect for me."

Yet, even with this frustration, Julian and John continued to try and rebuild their relationship. But Julian's deep seeded resentment for his father, to some degree, remained, as he told Elizabeth Grice of the *Daily Telegraph*, "He was a hypocrite. Dad could talk about peace and love out loud to the world, but he could never show it to the people who supposedly meant the most to him: his wife and son. How can you talk about peace and love and have a family in bits and pieces—no communication, adultery, divorce? You can't do it, not if you're being true and honest with yourself." Perhaps Julian and John would have had eventually come to some sort of understanding, but on December 8, 1980, John Lennon was assassinated. Julian was only seventeen years old.

For the next four years, Julian partied through London. All the while, he thought about becoming a musician and even began sending out demo tapes anonymously. However, as Elizabeth Thomas wrote in *Contemporary Musicians, Vol. 2*, "Julian was daunted by grief and the shadow of his father's immense talent." *Rolling Stone*'s

Elizabeth Kaye noted an ironic twist: "when he [Julian] was small, he worried that he could never write songs or sing them the way his father did. When he was older, he worried that anything he wrote or sang would sound too much like his father."

Some record companies did not care if Julian sounded too much like John, but rather wanted to cash in on the eerie resemblance. In the mid-Eighties, Thomas wrote, Julian "stumbled into a record deal designed to exploit John's memory by having the son sing an unreleased song stolen from his father's estate." Ironically, it was Lennon's stepmother Yoko Ono—the woman who Julian would later sue—who paid off the record company so Julian could get out of his contract.

Never "Too Late For Goodbyes"

In 1984, Atlantic Records signed Julian and released his debut album, *Valotte*. The album produced two hit singles, "Too Late For Goodbyes" and "Valotte." Lennon was embraced by fans and critics alike who may or may not have believed, as Julian told *Rolling Stone* in 1985, that he was not "trying to carry on a tradition—except maybe in the simplicity of Dad's writing." Moreover, Producer Phil Ramone commented in *Rolling Stone* that Julian, "can hit your heart with a lyric and be clever with a melody. Music is the joy of his life, no doubt about it." *Valotte* earned Lennon a 1985 Grammy Award nomination for Best New Artist.

Atlantic Records also realized that Lennon could not only continue his father's legacy, but also stuff their pockets with large amounts of money—and he was powerless to stop them. As Lennon told *San Francisco Chronicle* reporter Aidin Vaziri in 1999, "I was young and naive, so I signed my life away. Unfortunately, the first album will quite possibly never be mine, which sickens me to death. But when you're vying for your first album deal, you'd just about give up your mother." Following a massive 18 month tour, Lennon wanted time off to write; however, Atlantic reminded him that he was "contractually obligated" to release another album. Thus, in the spring of 1986 Atlantic released Lennon's second album, *The Secret Value of Daydreaming*. It was a disappointment, both critically and financially.

Three years later, though, he seemed to somewhat redeem himself with his third album, *Mr. Jordan*, which *People* called, "an unexpectedly striking and vigorous piece of work." With his fourth album, 1991s *Help Yourself*, Lennon continued on his path of public and critical redemption. That album produced the minor hit, "Saltwater," yet, Lennon felt that he was no longer receiving the support of his record company. He told *Behind the Music*, "they realized ... I couldn't be pressured to trying to write what they wanted to hear." Thus, after seven years and five and a half million albums sold, he decided that he had had enough of the music industry.

Not Just the "Son of"

For the next seven years Lennon traveled throughout Europe, did some acting, shopped for antiques—anything that did not involve the music business. He resurfaced in 1996 co-writing the score for the hit movie, *Mr. Holland's Opus* and purchasing $80,000 worth of Beatles memorabilia including a handwritten first draft of "Hey Jude." Julian had always felt that that the Beatles were more than just his father, as he explained to Jae-Ha Kim of the *Chicago Sun-Times*, "There are some people who say that Dad was the Beatles, but I disagree with that. Without Paul, there wouldn't have been the Beatles."

Julian had always wanted something to pass down to his children, as well—to continue the Lennon legacy. But as he told Kim, "I was never given anything from Dad or the estate... The thing is she's [Yoko Ono] got everything. She owns his name, his likeness, all his money. You name it. She's got it." Eventually Ono and Lennon agreed on a financial settlement in 1996 that guaranteed Julian and half brother Sean an even split in copyrights of John's songs.

In the midst of these financial settlements, Lennon was also fighting to get out of his record contract with Atlantic. He told Kim, "I didn't write (any songs) for years because I didn't want (the record company) to own them." It took five years for Lennon to dissolve his contract. After forming his own record label, Music From Another Room, he began writing again. This time, however, Lennon was writing "not for an album. It was for writing's sake. And for the sake of challenging myself. To prove my own self worth as a writer," as he told *Behind the Music*.

Lennon recorded those songs at his own expense, released them on his label, and established his own web site. The end result, *Photograph Smile* won rave critical reviews. *Rolling Stone*'s David Wild wrote, "the homespun, intimate feeling *Photograph Smile* sounds like the work of a man who has come to peace with ghosts of the past and gotten on with the business of writing some good new tunes."

Lennon was clearly pleased with such press, telling Daniel Durchholz of *Rolling Stone*, "the gratifying thing about this record is the reviews—which have been the best I've ever had in my life." Lennon, it seemed, had finally found a sort of inner peace. As he told *Milwaukee Journal Sentinel* reporter Steve Morse, "I've felt that I would [always] find a level of peace in life ... I think what keeps you going is that love inside you and the hope, the faith that things are going to bloody work out in the end."

Selected discography

Valotte, Atlantic, 1984.
The Secret Value of Daydreaming, Atlantic, 1986.
Mr. Jordan, Atlantic, 1989.
Help Yourself, Atlantic, 1991.
(contributor) *Mr. Holland's Opus*, (soundtrack) 1996.
Photograph Smile, Music From Another Room, 1999.

Sources

Books

Contemporary Musicians Vol. 2, Gale Research, Inc., 1989.

Periodicals

Chicago Sun-Times, March 9, 1999.
Denver Post, February 24, 1999.
The Guardian, May 23, 1998.
Milwaukee Journal Sentinel, February 27, 1999.
People, January 7, 1985; April 17, 1989.
Rolling Stone, June 6, 1985; February 25, 1999.
San Francisco Chronicle, February 21, 1999.

Online

"Julian Lennon," www.julianlennon.com (May 9, 1999).
"The Other Son." *Rolling Stone Network: Random Notes*, www.rollingstone.com (May 4, 1999).

Additional information provided by: *World Press Review*; the 1985 concert film/documentary, *Stand By Me: A Portrait of Julian Lennon*, produced and directed by Martin Lewis, and VH-1's *Behind the Music*, produced by Gay Rosenthal, originally broadcast, April 25, 1999.

—Ann M. Schwalboski

Furry Lewis

Bluesman

Furry Lewis, the bluesman who eventually came to personify the Memphis blues, was born Walter Lewis in Greenwood Mississippi in the last decade of the 1800s—March 6, 1893 is usually given as his birthday. His father disappeared completely before his birth and little Walter was raised by his mother. When he was about six years old, he and his mother moved to Memphis where he attended school until the fifth grade. His childhood friends in Memphis gave him the nickname "Furry", but by the time he was rediscovered in the 1950s not even Furry himself could remember why.

His interest in music began at an early age, possibly in part because of exposure to a guitarist named Blind Joe who Lewis frequently saw around his home on Brinkley Street in Memphis. Lewis later recorded two of the songs Blind Joe played, "Casey Jones" and "John Henry." Like so many black children of the time who loved music, Furry made himself a primitive instrument. "I loved guitar," Lewis later told Bengt Olsson, in *Memphis Blues,* "[I] made my own guitar. I taken [sic] a cigar box and cut a hole in the top of it and taken another little piece of thin wood like beaverboard and made the neck. And I taken some nails and nailed them in the end of the neck and bent them down and taken wire off a screen door. And that's what I made my strings out of. Of course, I wasn't playing nothing, but that's just the way I got a start."

Eventually he obtained a real guitar, but in the meantime he learned harmonica and began playing in the streets of Memphis. Lewis told Olsson that his first professional job had been with the W.C. Handy band sitting in for absent musicians. He also credited Handy—composer of the "St. Louis Blues," known as the "Father of the Blues," and probably the most well known black musician of the day—with giving him his first good guitar. "I kept that guitar until I absolutely wore it out completely. I kept it for twenty-five or thirty years. It was a Martin."

Lewis played his way from town to town up and down the Mississippi River as a young man. In the course of his travels, around 1916, he suffered a debilitating accident. Train hopping near Du Quoin, Illinois, his foot got stuck in a railroad coupling and a train ran him over, severing his leg. "I had just caught a freight," he later told blues researcher Samuel Charters, in *Sweeter Than The Showers Of Rain,* "'cause I didn't feel like spending the money for a ticket."

Around 1920 Lewis got an important break when he met Jim Jackson. Jackson was a popular performer in the medicine shows—variety shows that traveled from town to town selling patent medicine—and with his help, Furry joined the Dr. Willie Lewis medicine show. By 1923, though, he had settled back in Memphis and found a secure job with the city sweeping streets. When he returned, he formed a band of his own and before long he had made a place for himself in the Beale Street musical scene that was just beginning to thrive. It was a period on intense cross-fertilization in Memphis blues. Besides Lewis and Jim Jackson, Memphis Minnie, Gus Cannon, Frank Stokes, and Will Shade and the Memphis Jug Band were actively performing. Musicians accompanied one another in street concerts, at house parties, on medicine show trips and eventually on records. Lewis played regularly with the Memphis Jug Band before it started recording, and he continued to perform with Jim Jackson. Lewis later told Bengt Olsson that he had played at one time or other with most of the blues greats of the 1920s, including, Memphis Minnie, Texas Alexander, Blind Lemon Jefferson, and Bessie Smith—but it is impossible to establish just how accurate these claims are.

Lewis' association with Jim Jackson seems to have led to his first opportunity to record. After being contacted by Vocalion Records, Lewis took the train to Chicago in May 1927 for his first session. He recalled the hospitality he received, "I made two or three records for Mr. Jack Kapp," he told Charters, "he know'd [sic] what I like and so he had a whole gallon of whiskey sitting there." Somehow the session came off despite the alcohol and the following fall Vocalion called him back for a second session.

Although blues was very much in vogue in 1927 Lewis did not limit himself to recording just blues. In addition to "Rock Island Blues," "Jelly Roll," "Everybody's Blues," and "Mr. Furry's Blues," he recorded old-time popular ballads that pre-dated blues music. And his versions brought a unique sensibility to songs that were already chestnuts by the 1920s. For example, in "John Henry" and "Kassie Jones," songs about larger than life figures whose ambition leads to their deaths, he sings from the perspective of the dead men's wives and children. It was an approach that made their deaths less heroic but ultimately more tragic.

Lewis was unique among bluesmen in the way he prepared his songs before a recording session in that he never improvised his lyrics on a particular theme in the studio. "I used to get me a tablet," Lewis is quoted by Stephen Calt in the liner notes to *Furry Lewis In His Prime*, "and attempt to sit down and make up verses. Then after I do [sic] that, I used to take it down to Johnson's Printing Shop and he'd typewrite it out for me." When performing, he fingerpicked his accompaniments on a guitar tuned to an open G or D chord. He was one of the rare Memphis musicians who used a bottleneck or pocketknife when he played, one reason he may have made the farfetched claim that he "invented" slide guitar.

Lewis' records apparently did not have high sales and Vocalion did not ask him to record in 1928. In August of that year, however, Ralph Peer, a representative of the Victor Record Company, came to Memphis and Lewis recorded eight sides, including "Kassie Jones Part 1," "Kassie Jones Part 2," and "I Will Turn Your Money Green." Those records didn't sell any better than the earlier ones and he did not record for Victor again. He cut his last 78s in the fall of 1929, just before the Great Depression decimated the blues industry. After that last session he faded into the utter obscurity known only to the poor. He continued to work his street-cleaning job, and before long that was how his neighbors in Memphis knew him; his musical past was obliterated. He played his guitar for his own entertainment—when he had one. As often as not though, the instrument sat in the pawnshop, traded for money to buy a bottle.

The next time Lewis' name surfaced was on Harry Smith's monumental *Anthology of American Folk Music*, a set released in 1952 which included "Kassie Jones, Part 1 & 2." The *Anthology* inspired folklorists and musicians to search out the musicians who had recorded on the other side of the great divide created by the Depression and World War II. In 1958, Charters was in Memphis visiting Will Shade, whom Charters had recently tracked down. Shade's wife mentioned to Charters that Lewis lived in the same neighborhood and that she frequently met him working out on the street. Charters called around to some Memphis city departments and eventually found Lewis. Shortly afterwards he was in Furry's small furnished room, listening to the long-lost bluesman play "John Henry."

Lewis began making records again almost immediately. Charters recorded him first in February and October 1959, and the result, songs and story telling, was released by Folkways on *Furry Lewis Blues*. In 1961 he signed a contract for two albums with Prestige Records. Recorded at the Sun Studios in Memphis, and like in the 1920s Lewis had to take time off from his street cleaning job, or go to the studio after work. Finding Lewis inspired Charters to make his film, *The Blues*. In *Sweeter Than The Showers Of Rain*, he wrote "mostly because of Furry and the flashing pattern of his fingers as he picked 'John Henry.' It seemed that film was the only way to capture what he was doing." Charters filmed Lewis at work cleaning Memphis streets, then at home playing a guitar decorated with a colorful ribbon.

Like other old-time musicians, like Mississippi John Hurt and Sleepy John Estes, Lewis discovered a brand new career in the 1960s and beyond. He began regularly recording albums, appearing at folk and blues festivals, and playing clubs. Most of his life Lewis believed he had been born in 1900 and kept his city job until 1960 when he believed he had reached retirement age. Afterwards, a student searching through old school records to help Lewis qualify for Medicaid, uncovered evidence that he had in fact been born seven years earlier.

In 1972 he was the featured performer in the Memphis Blues Caravan, which included the likes of Bukka White, Sleepy John Estes & Hammy Nixon, Memphis Piano Red, Sam Chatmon, and Mose Vinson. Around the same time he had a role in the Burt Reynolds movie, *W.W. and the Dixie Dance Kings.* Lewis was the opening act on one of Leon Russell 1970s tours, and performed and recorded with the rock group, Alabama State Troupers. He lived out the last decades of his life as the pre-eminent representative of the old-time blues. He died in Memphis on September 14, 1981.

Selected discography

Furry Lewis Blues, Smithsonian/Folkways, 1959.
Back on My Feet Again, Prestige/Blues, 1961.
When I Lay My Burden Down, Biograph, 1970.

Fourth & Beale, Lucky Seven, 1975.
In His Prime (1927-1928), Yazoo, 1988.
Complete Works (1927-1929), Document, 1990.
Blues Magician, Lucky Seven, 1999.

Sources

Books

Barlow, William, *Looking Up At Down: The Emergence of Blues Culture*, Temple University Press, Philadelphia, 1989.
Charters, Samuel, *The Country Blues.* Da Capo, New York, 1975.
Charters, Samuel, *Sweeter Than The Showers Of Rain*, Oak Publications, New York, 1977.

Additional information provided by the liner notes to *Furry Lewis: In His Prime* by Stephen Calt.

—*Gerald E. Brennan*

Mark Linkous

Singer, songwriter

Alternative pop band Sparklehorse was formed in 1995 by native Virginian Mark Linkous, who survived a near-death experience in 1996 after releasing his debut album, *Vivadixiesubmarinetransmissionplot*. He went on to release *Good Morning Spider* in 1998. *Rolling Stone* magazine's Mark Binelli described the album as "a weird and wonderful record that combines the idiosyncrasies of Southern folk art with the sweeping drama of Radiohead's *OK Computer*." Jonathan Perry at www.rollingstone.com wrote, "For all its haunted reflections, *Good Morning Spider* sounds not like the work of a man who's fallen down to die, but rather like a man who somehow, against all odds, has gotten to his feet to live."

Mark Linkous was born and raised in Richmond, Virginia, but left his native state while still in his teens in search of a record deal. With dreams of stardom, he moved to New York City and then to Los Angeles, joined various struggling bands, and eventually grew weary of waiting for a career break; success seemed elusive and fickle. But he heard a Tom Waits recording , and it inspired him to move back home to Virginia and to follow his own individual muse. In Richmond, he joined a band that played, as he told Perry, "nothing but 300-year-old Irish songs." He attempted to discard everything he knew about music in order to start over with a fresh, more honest perspective. He told Perry that that particular time of his life was dedicated to abandoning everything and "learning how to make art out of pain or clay." Linkous had felt that modern rock at the time was missing the crucial elements of innocence,

honesty, and purity of purpose. So, back in Virginia, Linkous began recording unusual sounds that echoed in his mind: he sang through toilet paper rolls, recorded with his grandmother's washing machine running in the background, and utilized the odd sounds of various toys. This novel, whimsical approach led to a contract with Capitol Records in 1995 and the release of his debut album, *Vivadixiesubmarinetransmissionplot*.

Members of the alternative band Radiohead, whose members share a similar musical perspective with Linkous, heard his debut release while riding around in a cab in Egypt, and promptly invited him to join them on tour. Linkous explained to Binelli, "So I made a band out of these motorcycle buddies" in order to tour with Radiohead. Linkous and his friends formed a band and forged a friendship with Radiohead while touring; Linkous toured again with Radiohead the following year in 1996.

During that second tour with Radiohead, Linkous accidentally overdosed on anti-depressants and Valium. He passed out in a London hotel room for more than 12 hours with his legs pinned underneath him, cutting off circulation to his legs. When paramedics arrived and attempted to straighten his legs, the procedure triggered a heart attack. Linkous had seven operations to save his legs and required a three-month stay at St. Mary's Hospital in London. Doctors said his legs would have to be amputated, and he was confined to a wheelchair for six months. Linkous was in a morphine-medicated state for two years after the accident and ended up wearing leg braces. He told Perry, "For a while there, I was really scared that when I technically died—which I guess I did for a few minutes—that the part of my brain that allowed me my ability to write songs would be damaged." While Linkous was confined to the hospital, he received numerous cards and letters from fans who told him how much his debut release had meant to them. His hospital walls were covered with these letters, and they lifted his spirits and helped him make it through the ordeal.

Linkous not only survived, he eventually returned to his Virginia farmhouse to create *Good Morning Spider*, which contained, as Perry wrote, music "as old as it is new, as bare as it is busy." His sophomore release was rife with a cacophony of peculiar sounds, improbable instruments, and unexpected delights. Taken in total, the music Linkous created on *Good Morning Spider* was a type of restless-sounding dreamscape that rustled with Appalachian flavors, rustic folk music, and mid-fi pop. The result was material with a timeless quality. Jonathan E. Segel of Camper Van Beethoven played guitar, keyboards, violin, and glockenspiel while on tour in 1998 and 1999 with Linkous in Australia, New Zealand, and the U.S. in support of *Good Morning Spider*. David Lowery of

For the Record . . .

Born and raised in Richmond, VA; left home in his teens and moved to New York City, then to Los Angeles.

Joined various struggling bands; moved back home to Virginia; joined a band that played traditional Irish music; began recording unusual sounds such a vocals rendered through toilet paper rolls, the sound of a washing machine, the odd sounds of various toys; signed with Capitol Records, 1995; released debut album *Vivadixiesubmarinetransmissionplot*, 1995; toured with Radiohead, 1995-96; accidentally overdosed on anti-depressants and Valium in London, 1996; survived to record and release *Good Morning Spider*, 1998.

Addresses: *Record company*—Capitol Records, 810 Seventh Avenue, 4th floor, New York, NY 10019; (212) 603-8600; 1750 North Vine Street, Hollywood, CA 90028-5274; (213) 462-6252.

Cracker, formerly with Camper Van Beethoven, is a frequent Linkous collaborator, and the Lowery-Linkous single "Sick of Good-byes" from Cracker's 1993 album *Kerosene Hat* was tapped by Capitol Records as *Good Morning Spider*'s first U.K. single. The single was also featured on the television show *Felicity* in 1999. In addition to multi-instrumentalist Segel, Linkous's touring band also included cellist Sophie Michalitsianos, drummer Scott minor, and bassist Scott Fitzsimmons.

Although the material on *Good Morning Spider* is largely a product of Linkous's accident and its aftermath, he has always displayed an impressionistic songwriting style. His post-accident, sophomore release was more intro-spective than his debut release, and all of the songs on *Good Morning Spider* examined the fragile, fleeting, delicate quality of life—as well as its tangle of conflicting emotions. The coronet-laced "Painbirds," the gentle acoustics of the nursery rhyme prayer "Saint Mary," and the memorable "Chaos of the Galaxy/Happy Man" were especially poignant and written with great sensitivity. The single "Pig," noisy and rambunctious, was reminiscent of Linkous's punk rock days in New York City and Los Angeles. He told Binelli that he credits the strong creative showing on his sophomore release less to his close brush with death than to his beautiful and awe-inspiring surroundings at home in Virginia. He said, "When I first moved back here, I was able to appreciate the open spaces and just make the music. It didn't matter if it ever got recorded. That's when I started doing good music, I think."

Selected discography

with Sparklehorse

Vivadixiesubmarinetransmissionplot, Capitol, 1995.
Chords I've Known, EP, Slow River, 1996.
Good Morning Spider, Capitol, 1998.

Sources

Periodicals

Calgary Sun, February 28, 1999.
Rolling Stone, March 18, 1999.

Online

"Sparklehorse," http://www.rollingstone.com/sections/news/text/ (September 24, 1999).

—B. Kimberly Taylor

Kevin Mahogany

Jazz vocalist, bandleader

Kevin Mahogany's childhood dream was not to be a jazz singer. Born in Kansas City, Missouri, in 1958, he began playing baritone saxophone in junior high school. He studied with saxophonist Ahmad Alaadeen at Kansas City's Charlie Parker Academy and, at age 12 started playing in Eddie Baker's New Breed Jazz Orchestra, an 18-piece big band. By the time he was 14, he was teaching clarinet and had become interested in other woodwind instruments, percussion instruments, and piano. It wasn't until his senior year of high school that he became interested in singing.

While attending Baker University in Baldwin, Kansas Mahogany formed a jazz choir, became interested in Broadway-style shows, and earned Bachelors of Fine Arts degree in Music and English Drama. After graduation in 1981, he put down his saxophone for the last time and concentrated solely on his vocal career. His biography from Warner Brothers states that Mahogany finally made the switch "out of frustration. The euphonious interpretations created by his saxophone could not keep up with the solos playing in his head." But having the instrumental background gave him an edge as a vocalist and bandleader. "I've been on both sides of that, as an instrumentalist and vocalist," he said in his bio. "What I see the instrumentalists saying is, 'If you're going to be a vocalist you need to know what's going on here.'"

And he did. He founded a group, originally called Mahogany and The Apollos, and later known simply as Mahogany, which performed R&B, crossover jazz and popular music in Kansas City and developed a regular following over the next 10 years. It was around that time when, working as a booking agent scheduling national artists in Kansas City venues, the Montana-based group NRE Trio heard him sing and asked him to tour with them. During this tour a producer from the German label Enja Records heard Mahogany sing and signed him to a recording contract.

Mahogany established his talent for performing a wide range of styles and material with his debut release *Double Rainbow* in 1993. With this release he impressed critics with his versatility by taking on a selection of seldom-heard ballads, bop tunes and blues songs. "The ballads—always a test of any jazz talent—are appropriately touching but never overly sentimental," wrote Bob Brownlee in Mahogany's Enja Records bio. "And while it can be an acquired taste, only a handful of vocalists have ever scatted with the overwhelming power of Kevin Mahogany."

Mahogany released two more albums on Enja, *Songs & Moments* in 1994 and *You Got What It Takes* in 1995, before signing a major-label contract with Warner Broth-

Born Kevin Mahogany, July 30, 1958, Kansas City, MO. *Education:* Attended Charlie Parker Foundation academy, Kansas City, 1970;

Played baritone saxophone in Eddie Baker's New Breed Jazz Orchestra, 1970; attended Baker University, Baldwin, Kansas, 1976-81; earned Bachelors of Fine Arts degree in Music and English Drama, 1981; signed by Enja, 1993; released debut album, *Songs & Moments*, 1994; signed by Warner Bros., 1995; released *Kevin Mahogany*, 1996; released *Another Place, Another Time*, 1997; played on *Eastwood After Hours: Live at Carnegie Hall*, 1997; played in the Robert Altman film *Kansas City*, 1997; released *My Romance*, 1998.

Awards: *Jazziz* magazine Critics' Pick, 1998; Best Male Vocalist Readers' Poll awards from *Jazzis* and *Down Beat*, 1998.

Addresses: *Record company*—Warner Bros. Records, 3300 Warner Blvd, Burbank, California 91505.

ers. 1995 was also the year he made his big-screen debut, playing a character based on Big Joe Turner in Robert Altman's film about jazz in Mahogany's hometown, *Kansas City*, starring Jennifer Jason Leigh.

Mahogany's 1996 Warner Brothers debut, *Kevin Mahogany*, garnered high praise from a number of high-profile sources. *Newsweek* called him "the standout jazz vocalist of his generation." In the *New Yorker*, jazz writer Whitney Balliet—who dubbed him "The Baronial Baritone" for his deep, rich voice—wrote, "There is little Mahogany cannot do." And *JazzTimes* writer Willard Jenkins wrote in a review of *Kevin Mahogany*, "Mahogany sounds relaxed and in high spirits, poised to take his place as the standard-bearing male jazz vocalist [he] works this material with a great deal of spirit, care for the lyrics, and abundant feeling."

Mahogany released his sophomore Warner Brothers album, *Another Time, Another Place*, in 1997 to more critical praise. "With his full-bodied, deeply masculine voice," wrote *Stereo Review*'s Phyl Garland, "he makes the past come alive again by drawing from the rich traditions of blues, R&B and jazz." In 1997 Mahogany became involved with two projects by film star Clint

Eastwood: the *Eastwood After Hours: Live at Carnegie Hall* CD, an ensemble organized by the Hollywood star and the soundtrack for the film *Midnight in the Garden of Good and Evil*, which Eastwood produced and directed.

Mahogany's third album for Warner Brothers, *My Romance* in 1998, was a collection of ballads. The album featured covers of contemporary songs and old standards, including the works of such present-day artists as James Taylor, Lyle Lovett and Van Morrison. Warner Brothers likened him to Billy Eckstine, Nat King Cole and Johnny Hartman in his approach to such classics as Arthur Prysock's "How Did She Look?" and Eckstine's "Everything I Have is Yours," and the title track. "I am a huge fan of both these artists and have wanted to do a tribute to them for a long time," Mahogany said of Prysock and Eckstine in his bio. "No one does these songs anymore."

Warner Brothers capitalized on what they called "his interpretation without overblown sentimentality, capturing the delicacy and nuance of every word." The critics agreed, and Mahogany again was most lauded for his versatility in performing both old and new material, be it R&B, blues, soul, gospel, jazz or country. "While he could be called a crossover artist, he's no sellout," wrote John Janowiak for *Down Beat* in 1998. "The harmonies and style of these interpretations are in the jazz tradition, and they're done with taste." That same year, *Down Beat* highlighted Mahogany as Male Vocalist of the Year in its reader's poll.

Mahogany took the praise in stride and was quoted by his German management company, B.H. Hopper Management, as drawing his ability to perform such a wide variety of material from his youth. "I listened to everything while I was coming up," he said. "If all that is your background, you should be able to sing anything." In addition to the 1998 *Down Beat* title, Mahogany earned Best Male Vocalist of the Year in the *Jazziz* reader's poll and *Another Time, Another Place* was a *Jazziz* Critics' Pick that year.

Selected discography

My Romance, Warner Bros., 1998.
(contributor) *Eastwood After Hours: Live at Carnegie Hall*, Warner Bros., 1997.
Another Time, Another Place, Warner Bros., 1997.
(contributor) *Midnight in the Garden of Good and Evil* (soundtrack), Warner Bros.,1997.
Kevin Mahogany, Warner Bros., 1996.
You Got What It Takes, Enja, 1995.
Songs & Moments, Enja, 1994.
Double Rainbow, Enja, 1993.

Sources

Periodicals

Down Beat, December 1998.
Stereo Review, January 1998.

Online

"Kevin Mahogany," Hopper Management, http://www.hopper-management.com (April 29, 1999).
"Kevin Mahogany," Enja Records, http://www.enjarecords.com (April 29, 1999).
"Kevin Mahogany," Jazz Central Station, http://www.jazzcentralstation.com (April 29, 1999).
"Kevin Mahogany," All-Media Guide, http://www.allmusic.com (April 28, 1999).
"Kevin Mahogany," CD Now, http://www.cdnow.com (April 29, 1999).

Additional information was provided by Warner Bros. Records publicity materials, 1998.

—*Brenna Sanchez*

Ricky Martin

Singer, actor

Photo by John Riley. AP/Wide World Photos. Reproduced by permission.

On the edge of the new millennium, Puerto Rican pop sensation Ricky Martin—almost by himself—gave Latino music an international face. An electrifying performance at the 1999 Grammy Awards launched Martin into worldwide super-stardom. As *Entertainment Weekly*'s Andrew Essex reported, "his leather-pants, electro-pelvis version of "La Copa de la Vida single-handedly goosed a very dull [Grammy] telecast, earning him a standing ovation." It earned him a legion of fans, as well, who quickly snapped up copies of Martin's CDs the next day.

Born Enrique Martin on December 24, 1971 in San Juan, Puerto Rico, Ricky was not an over night success. Martin, the only child of Enrique Martin, a psychologist and Nereida Morales, an accountant who were divorced when Martin was two, began his climb into stardom at age eight by acting. In 1983 at age 12, Ricky—after auditioning three times—was finally accepted as a member of the Latin boy band, Menudo. Menudo's manager, Edgardo Diaz, told *Time*, "He [Martin] was small, not a big singer, and his voice was not so good then. But we thought he could learn a lot by being with the group." For the next five years Martin toured dozens of countries with Menudo, including Spain, Italy, Guam, and Japan.

At least one ex-member of Menudo has publicly described his experience with the group as, in Essex's words, "abusive, exploitative, and unsavory." In spite of this, Essex continues, "[Martin] focuses on the lessons Menudo instilled in him: 'I learned what discipline was. For me, it's been easy to forgive.'" However, Martin did tell *People*'s Peter Castro and Lynda Wright that, "our [the band's] creativity was stifled we were told [the songs we wrote] were no good."

And because Martin constantly was on tour, his family relationships—especially with his father—suffered. As Martin recalled in *People*, "When my dreams started coming true, my parents started fighting. I had everything I ever wanted, but my family was falling apart." His father, Martin continued, "wanted me to choose between him and my mother. How do you ask a child that?" Castro and Wright wrote that in 1985, "[Martin] so resented his father that he changed his name from Enrique [to Ricky]." It would take almost ten years for father and son to repair their relationship.

Acting, Accidents, and Albums

In 1988, Martin left Menudo, graduated high school, and moved to New York City. In 1992, Martin moved again, this time to Mexico City where he restarted his acting

For the Record . . .

Born Enrique Martin on December 24, 1971 in San Juan, Puerto Rico.

Began acting at age eight; joined Latin pop band, Menudo at age 12, 1983; was dismissed from Menudo, 1988; released first album, *Ricky Martin*, 1992; released second album, *Me Amaras*, 1993; resumed acting on the popular soap opera, *General Hospital* and on Broadway in *"Les Miserables,"* 1994; released third album, *A Medio Vivir*, 1995; provided voice for *Hercules* in the Spanish language version of the Disney film, *Hercules*, 1997; released fourth album, *Vuelve*, which included the smash hit, "La Copa de la Vida," 1998; performed at 1999 Grammy Awards; released his first English-language album, Ricky Martin, 1999

Awards: Best New Latin Performer, *Billboard* Video Awards, 1993; Best Actor, Heraldo Award, 1993; Grammy Award for Best Latin Pop Performance, 1999; Best Selling Latin Artist, World Music Awards, 1999.

Addresses: *Record Company*—C2 Records/Columbia Records; *Management*—Angelo Medina Enterprises, 1406 Georgetti Street, Santurce, Puerto Rico, 00910; *Fan Club*—Ricky Martin International Fan Club, P.O. Box 13345, Santurce Station, San Juan, Puerto Rico.

career. Martin earned a Heraldo—the Mexican Academy Award for his work in the film adaptation of *Alcanzar una Estrella* (Reach for a Star), a Spanish or soap opera. Also, in 1992, Martin signed to Sony and released his first solo album, *Ricky Martin*. Sony Music CEO Tommy Mottola saw the future of Latin pop music telling *Time*'s Christopher John Farley, "The heart and soul of the music will be able to break down barriers easily. It's undeniable." Also undeniable was Martin's burgeoning popularity. After a sold out tour of South America and being named *Billboard* Video Awards' Best New Latin Artist of 1993, Martin released his second album, *Me Amaras* and moved to Los Angeles, California.

In 1994 Martin earned a role on the ABC soap opera, *General Hospital*. Martin told *Hispanic* magazine reporter Rosie Carbo that, "For me, *General Hospital,* has been an incredible way of learning and growing as an actor. I look at it as a training school that's going to help my acting career [however], I think this will even help me in

my musical career." Martin's confidence continued to grow with his performance as "Marius" in the Broadway play, *Les Miserables*. Martin also continued to record music and in 1995 released his third album, *A Medio Vivir.*

As Martin began to grow ever more popular, he became aware of being stereotyped. As he told Essex, "It's all about breaking stereotypes. For me, the fact that people think Puerto Rico is *Scarface*, that we ride on donkeys to school—that has to change." Martin began to break stereotypes by becoming Puerto Rico's national tourism spokesman, by voicing "Hercules" for Disney's Spanish-language version of the 1997 animated film, *Hercules*, and by releasing his fourth album, *Vuelve*. *Vuelve* hit number one in 22 countries on the strength of the smash single, "La Copa de la Vida" (The Cup of Life). In 1998 this single became the anthem for soccer's World Cup, thus raising Martin's international popularity. It also became the anthem for Governor Pedro Rossello's campaign to have Puerto Rico named United States' fifty-first state. However, Martin did not authorize the use of the song. Martin's manager Angelo Medina told *Billboard*'s Karl Ross, "Music doesn't choose sides. It belongs to everyone." And that's the message Martin wanted American audiences to embrace. However, it would take a memorable performance by Martin at the 1999 Grammy Awards for the United States to open its arms.

Created a "Loca" Audience

Martin performed "La Copa de la Vida" (The Cup of Life) at the 1999 Grammy Awards. Martin told *Billboard*'s John Lannert and Carrie Bell, "[I was] glad to let 2 million people all over the world in different cultures know who I am and what kind of music I make." Audiences were glad too. About two hours into a boring show, *Time*'s David E. Thigpen wrote, "[Martin] performed the musical equivalent of CPR." Martin's performance—and leather pants—gave the Grammy audience something to remember. Joey Guerra of the *Houston Chronicle* quoted one record store manager as saying, "Ever since he appeared on the Grammies, [Martin's albums have been] blowing out the door. I don't know what those leather pants did. It just like turned everybody on." According to *Rolling Stone* Martin's Grammy appearance, "increased sales of *Vuelve* by 500 percent." In May 1999, Martin released *Ricky Martin*—his first English-language album. Reporters, fans, and critics alike asked Martin why he had apparently left behind his Latin roots. As *Entertainment Weekly*'s David Browne commented, "The danger of leaving behind one's home turf, especially for world-music artists lies in the loss of [their] identity." However, as Martin told *USA Today*'s Arlene

Vigoda, "I will never stop singing in Spanish, but this a communications business, and it's all about getting closer to cultures." Martin further stated when he accepted the 1999 World Music Award for Best Selling Latin Artist that, "To create music is to unite countries." *Ricky Martin*, however, retains a Latin quality while also showing Martin's diversity, including a duet with pop music icon, Madonna. But, as *St. Louis Post-Dispatch* reporter Kevin C. Johnson commented, "before anyone can accuse Martin of selling out by singing in English, there's a Spanish version of 'Livin' La Vida Loca' and 'Bella,' where Martin flip-flops between the two languages."

Confronted Sex Symbol Image

However, it was not merely a number one hit single that created such a successful album, but Martin's image as a leather-pants-wearing sex symbol. When asked by *Rolling Stone*'s David Wild if he felt comfortable with that image, Martin replied, "Sex symbol is equal to no credibility. That's something I don't want to fight with. Sexuality and sensuality are completely different things. Sensuality is something that you're born with. Am I sensual? Well, a lot of people say I am. But sexuality is something I leave for my own mirror. I don't share that with anyone." Martin continued his worldwide tour throughout the summer of 1999, telling Vigoda, "I need the immediate reaction I get from performing my music." Vigoda further quoted Martin as saying, "I want to do this forever. I don't want to be the hit of the summer, and hopefully, with a lot of humility, we can talk in 10 years and I'll still be here." Little Judy of LaMusica.com, for one, seems to think he will: "Martin is much more than a pop idol. In possession of natural talent and quiet intelligence, he is a young man discovering his soul as an artist. What he learns and shares with the world in the future, is what art, in the truest sense of the word, is all about."

Selected discography

Ricky Martin, Sony Discos, 1992.
Me Amaras, Sony Discos, 1993.
A Medio Vivir, Sony Discos, 1995.
Vuelve, C2/Columbia, 1998.
Ricky Martin, C2/Columbia, 1999.

Sources

Periodicals

Billboard, March 17, 1997; September 5, 1998; March 13, 1999.
Entertainment Weekly, April, 23, 1999; May 14, 1999.
Hispanic, September 1994.
Hispanic Times Magazine, October/November, 1996.
Houston Chronicle, March 8, 1999.
Los Angeles Times, December 5, 1995; May 12, 1999.
Milwaukee Journal Sentinel, May 2, 1999.
People, May 15, 1995.
Rolling Stone, May 3, 1999; May 13, 1999; June 10, 1999.
San Francisco Chronicle, May 9, 1999.
St. Louis Post-Dispatch, May 16, 1999.
Time, March 15, 1999; May 24, 1999.
USA Today, March 1, 1999.

Online

"Ricky Martin Soul of a Young Artist," www.LaMusica.com (May 6, 1999).
"Ricky Martin," *Rolling Stone Random Notes*, www.RollingStone.com (May 20, 1999).

Additional information was provided by the liner notes from the album *Ricky Martin*.

—*Ann M. Schwalboski*

Lila McCann

Country singer

Lila McCann has established herself as a hit-making country artist while still in her teens. Her debut album appeared in the wake of singer LeAnn Rimes' enormous success and comparisons between the two teenaged vocalists have been frequently made. But McCann has stood on her own by virtue of her All-American cheerleader image and polished vocal abilities. She has been able to shape a convincing identity by recording material appropriate for her age, choosing more mature songs as her career has progressed. Unlike Rimes, McCann's focus has been on the country market exclusively, favoring the more upbeat side of the country sound.

Born in Puyallup, Washington, McCann came to a singing career naturally. At age four, she made her first appearance on stage with her father Pat's country band, the Southlanders. By eight, she was regularly singing with the group at their weekend engagements at the local Eagles Club. Her selections with the Southlanders included such modern country favorites as Kathy Mattea's "18 Wheels And A Dozen Roses" and the Judds' "Grandpa (Tell Me 'Bout The Good Ol' Days)," as well as standards like Patsy Cline's "Crazy" and "Sweet Dreams." Word began to spread about McCann's precocious talent, which led to Los Angeles-based manager Kasey Walker coming to see her perform. After years of managing actors and directors, Walker was tiring of the business and reluctant to take on a new client. Her

feelings changed once she heard McCann, however. "She got up and sang and, literally, my mouth dropped open," Walker told *Los Angeles Times* writer Jerry Crowe. "Even at nine, she was brilliant. Her voice had such a natural country feel to it."

Walker began to assemble a team of highly regarded music business professionals to work on the young singer's behalf, including attorney Ken Hertz and agent Rob Light. From there, Walker arranged for McCann, then aged 12, to perform at the Palomino in North Hollywood, California, a landmark country music venue. Around this same time, McCann entered a country music youth talent contest in Las Vegas, and found herself competing against LeAnn Rimes for singing honors. Rimes ended up winning an award for best female vocalist, while McCann took the prize for best female entertainer.

McCann's talent was evident enough to secure her a recording contract with Asylum Records at age 13. Rather than release an album as soon as possible, the decision was made to wait until she was fully ready to record. "We all decided that we didn't want to rush into things," McCann said in an interview with Mike Greenblatt of *Modern Screen's Country Music*. "We had a record deal with Asylum two and a half years before we started cutting songs. Asylum co-president Kyle Lehning told the *Los Angeles Times* that "though her [McCann's] voice was wonderful, she just didn't have it all there ... I didn't feel like Lila was somebody who at the time could sing about mature subjects and have anybody really buy into it. So there was a lot of thought that went into the choice of material." In the meantime, LeAnn Rimes recorded and released her own debut album in 1996, which proved to be phenomenally successful.

Mark Spiro, a songwriter and producer who had worked with such artists as Julian Lennon and Boyz II Men, was chosen to guide McCann in the studio. Spiro co-wrote much of the material McCann recorded for her debut album, which was eventually titled *Lila* and released in 1998. The first single from the album, "Down Came A Blackbird," was an unusual blend of bluegrass and rap elements and brought McCann a modest hit. Her next release, "I Wanna Fall In Love," was a more conventional upbeat tune that rose to the top of the country charts. Though two more singles, "Almost Over You" and "Yippy Ky Yay" performed less well, *Lila* went on to earn gold record certification. This led to McCann's 1998 Academy of Country Music award nomination for best new female vocalist.

Because of their ages, comparisons between McCann and Rimes in the media were inevitable. For her part, McCann tried to downplay any similarities between

For the Record . . .

Born December 4, 1981 in Puyallup, WA.

Began performing with her father's band The Southlanders, 1985; signed with Asylum Records, 1995; released debut album *Lila*, 1998; released *Something In The Air* in 1999.

Awards: platinum record for contribution to *Hope Floats* soundtrack album, 1998.

Addresses: *Record company* —Asylum, Elektra Entertainment Group, a division of Warner Communications Inc., 75 Rockefeller Plaza, New York, NY 10019. *Management*—Walker Management, 12021 Wilshire Blvd., Suite 911, Los Angeles, CA 90025. *Fan Club*—Lila McCann Fan Club, 3800A Bridgeport Way West, Suite 533, University Place, WA 98466.

them. As she told *People*, "the only thing we really have in common is our ages. As far as the music goes, or our lifestyles, we're pretty different. She's out on the road all the time, and most of the time I'm still home at school." Stories about McCann in the press emphasized her life as a typical Seattle, Washington area high school student apart from her singing career. Keeping her touring and recording to weekends during the school year, she managed to maintain a B-average as a sophomore. As a member of her school's cheerleading squad, she participated in a national championship competition in the fall of 1998 in Orlando, Florida.

McCann kept her career momentum running smoothly by appearing in an episode of the popular television series *Walker, Texas Ranger* in 1998. That same fall she received even greater exposure by recording the song "To Get Me To You" for the soundtrack for the film *Hope Floats*. Also important were her appearances as part of the 1998 George Strait Chevy Truck Country Music Festival, featuring her on a touring concert bill, which also included Tim McGraw, Faith Hill and John Michael Montgomery.

Something In The Air, McCann's second CD, was released in 1999. For this album, McCann and producer Mark Spiro built on the strengths of *Lila* while allowing for a more mature focus in the songwriting. While much of the material was by Spiro or outside writers, McCann did co-write two songs, "I Reckon I Will" and "Can You Hear Me." "With You," the first single, was an immediate hit, rising to Number One on the country charts. *Something In The Air* revealed the now 17 year-old singer to be an evolving artist just beginning to stretch out and make full use of her talents. "This time, just because I had spent more time in the studio, I knew better what I was doing," McCann said of *Somethng In The Air* in an interview with *Country Weekly*. "It was fun, too because I am a little older ... I mean, we didn't go way over into the divorce scene or anything, but... we got to grow up a little bit!"

McCann worked to maintain a balance between her burgeoning musical career and the pressures of teenage life as she approached her senior year in high school. She told *Country Weekly* that "I do want to go to college, but as soon as I get out of high school I want to do music full-time for a while. I think I'm going to wait about three years, because I really would like to produce and write a lot more."

Selected discography

Lila (includes "Down Came A Blackbird" and "I Wanna Fall In Love"), Asylum, 1998.
(Contributor) *Hope Floats* (soundtrack), Capitol, 1998.
Something In The Air (included "With You"), Asylum, 1999.

Sources

Billboard, February 13, 1999.
Country Weekly, March 23, 1999.
Los Angeles Times, February 7, 1998.
Modern Screen's Country Music, April 1999.
People, June 29, 1998.

Additional information was provided by Asylum publicity materials, 1999.

—*Barry Alfonso*

Jo Dee Messina

Singer, songwriter

Country singer and songwriter Jo Dee Messina enjoyed a trio of successive number one hits on Hot Country Singles & Tracks from her second album, *I'm Alright*, released in 1998. She became the first female solo artist to score three consecutive multiple-week number one hits from one album since *Billboard*'s country album chart debuted in 1964. The high-spirited, jocular redhead was nominated for six Kahlua Boston Music Awards, a distinction traditionally earned by rock artists. She was nominated for Act of the Year and Outstanding Album, Female Vocalist, Single ("Bye Bye"), Video ("I'm Alright"), and Country Act. After hearing of the award nominations, she told *Billboard*'s Chuck Taylor, "I had to check my messages twice because I didn't believe it." She was also nominated for CMT's Female Vocalist of the Year, and for a Horizon Award. Messina's songs demonstrate a sassy, upbeat muscularity, and are designed to strike a familiar chord or two in the listener. *Entertainment Weekly* said, "(Messina has) a style that blends the vocal cadences of Reba McEntire with the lyrical worldliness of K.T. Oslin." Her album *I'm Alright* went gold and platinum, and she won the Top New Female Vocalist award at the American Country Music Awards in 1999.

Messina was born Jo Dee Marie Messina on August 25, 1970, in Framington, Massachusetts. She was raised in Holliston, Massachusetts, by Vincent and Mary Messina, and had two sisters, Terese and Marianne, as well as a brother named Vincent. Her early musical influences include the Judds, Reba McEntire, Deana Carter, Dolly Parton, Loretta Lynn, Hank Williams, Jr., Patsy Cline, and Tim McGraw. She performed in plays in the Boston area as a child, and starting at the age of 14, sang in local country bars. By the age of 16 she was performing every weekend in the Jo Dee Messina Band, which included her brother on drums and one of her sisters on bass guitar. Although she was a good student in school, she was sometimes called to the principal's office for falling asleep in class due playing late night sessions. Messina knew at a young age that music was her calling, and at the age of 19 she left home for Nashville.

Messina then competed in talent contests and sent her demo tape to various industry executives. While at the Fan Fair in the mid-1990s, she approached an executive at Curb Records and said, "What you guys really need over there is a redhead." Just as the executive was about to reply, producer James Stroud approached Messina, said he had heard her demo tape, and lauded it to the skies. She was soon signed to Curb and her self-titled debut album was released in 1996, produced by Tim McGraw and Byron Gallimore. Two of her debut release's singles topped the charts: "Heads Carolina, Tails California" (written by Tom Nichols and Mark Sanders) and

Photo by John Basemore. AP/Wide World Photos. Reproduced by permission.

For the Record . . .

Born Jo Dee Marie Messina on August 25, 1970, in Framington, MA; daughter of Vincent and Mary Messina; two sisters, Terese and Marianne, brother Vincent.

Performed in plays in the Boston area as a child; sang in local country bars at age 14; left went to Nashville, 1986; competed in talent contests and sent her demo tape to various industry executives; signed to Curb Records, released *Jo Dee Messina*, 1996 (included "Heads Carolina, Tails California," and "You're Not In Kansas Anymore"); released *I'm Alright*, 1998; became the first female solo artist to score three consecutive multiple-week number one hits from one album since *Billboard*'s country album chart debuted in 1964; *I'm Alright* went gold and platinum; toured for several months during 1999 with the George Strait Country Music Festival.

Awards: Top New Female Vocalist, American Country Music Awards, 1999.

Addresses: Record company—Curb Records, 3907 West Alameda, Burbank, CA 91505; (818) 843-2872. *Internet*—http://www.curb.com

"You're Not In Kansas Anymore." Messina performed 215 shows in 1996, and told *Country Spotlight* reporter Susanna Scott that the best gift from a fan she ever received was a stuffed white horse that neighed when tilted, which was left on the stage by a five year old. When Scott asked her what piece of advice she would most like to impart to her fans, Messina said, "Don't give up."

She took her own advice to heart and stayed the difficult course. Taylor wrote, "(Messina) has seen her share of industry heartache, starting with a label deal that promised to make her dreams come true and then went sour when management shifted." She signed to Curb, but saw her finances dry up between hits and came close to losing her home and car and declaring bankruptcy. She spent almost a year finding the right songs and sound for her 1998 follow-up release, *I'm Alright*, which eventually made her one of the genuine country artist success stories of the 1990s. Robynn James, publicity director of

country WYYD/WJLM in the Lynchburg/Roanoke, Virginia, area told Taylor in 1999, "There are so many female singers at country radio now, and it's become all the more of a challenge to break through the pack." Messina told Taylor that the struggle was well worth the ride. "I don't know anything else besides country music. I'll always do some kind of music, whether it's writing or doing demos or commercials. It just runs through my veins."

Messina's 1998 release, *I'm Alright,* highlights a selection of songs about personal strength and survival. She told Taylor, "I have to be able to relate to what I sing and know what the song is saying. As a singer, you're painting a picture, and you can't sing it if you don't know what it looks or feels like." Jaymes added, "It seems like every record we get from her is stronger and stronger. When you think she can't get any better, she comes out with something superior." Mike Brophy, publicity director of WKLP Boston told *Billboard*,s Taylor, "The beauty of her music is that it's upbeat and positive. From a programming perspective, it's easier to put on that kind of music than slow, sad songs."

Messina's band members include Ralph Friedrichsen on bass guitar and vocals; Tim Haires on drums; Pete Jeffrey on keyboards, vocals, and as bandleader; Stacy Kostes on acoustic guitar and vocals; Allen Love on pedal steel; and Tony Obrohta on lead guitar and vocals. Messina, who has a tenacious, feisty, and dynamic personality, has some clearly defined goals set for her future: she wants to meet Bonnie Raitt, perform with an orchestra, write an entire album, and have Shania Twain cut one of her songs. She toured for several months during 1999 with the George Strait Country Music Festival, and appeared on *CBS This Morning* on April 28, 1999. She told Taylor, "Every day is a reward. It's all about getting out and meeting as many fans as I can and giving a little bit back to the people who've put me where I'm at. I'm very grateful for it all."

Selected discography

"Heads Carolina, Tails California," Curb Records, 1996.
Jo Dee Messina, Curb Records, 1996.
I'm Alright, Curb Records, 1998.

Sources

Periodicals

Billboard, March 5, 1999.
Entertainment Weekly, March 27, 1998; April 12, 1996.

Online

http://members.aol.com/JoDeeFan8/Index.html
"Jo Dee Messina Biography," http://www.curb.com (September 24, 1999).

—*B. Kimberly Taylor*

Pat Metheny

Guitar, composer

Multi-Grammy-winning jazz fusion guitarist and band leader Pat Metheney, noted for expanding the jazz envelope over the course of the 1970s, '80s, and '90s, incorporates elements of pop music, traditional jazz, new technology, and rock into jazz fusion music, and delivers them in a textured, atmospheric style. He told *Billboard*'s Bradley Bambarger about the Pat Metheney Group's 1999 release *Imaginary Day*, "Our past albums have always had a couple nine- or ten-minute songs that really try to take you somewhere, but with [*Imaginary Day*] we wanted to explore that territory from beginning to end. When I first took what became the title track to the band, I described it as a Chinese opera/blues with a Miles (Davis) "Filles De Kilimanjaro" interlude. Maybe that's indicative of where we're at." Other Pat Metheney Group members include co-composer and keyboardist Lyle Mays, bassist Steve Rodby, and drummer Paul Wertico. Bambarger went on to say that *Imaginary Day's* "intricate composition is wedded to spirited improvisation, yielding a far-reaching stylistic hybrid. It's music rooted in jazz but not limited to any preconceptions of how a jazz band should sound—in league with the legacy of fusion pioneers Weather Report but more evolved and more even more electric." Metheney's music is based on the principle of playing bebop: employing chord changes and then improvising on the changes. Bambarger wrote, ""The Metheney Group has always been at the forefront of technology.... But one especially charged new track, "The Roots of Coincidence," even finds common ground with the likes of Nine Inch Nails." Metheney told Bambarger, "We question ourselves less and less about idiom as we go on."

Metheney was born Patrick Bruce Metheney on August 12, 1954, in Lee's Summit, Missouri, where he was raised. He came from a musical family; his grandfather, father, mother, and older brother all played the trumpet, and marching band was their music of choice. Country and western music was pervasive in Lee's Summit as Metheney was growing up, yet he enjoyed a wide range of music, including the Beatles, the Beach Boys, and Miles Davis. At age 12 Metheney discovered the massive talent of Ornette Coleman when he found an album of his for 50 cents in a record store cut-out bin. He later told *Down Beat* magazine, "I thought it was the greatest thing I ever heard in my life." Metheney began listening to jazz music when he was a child and developed a great respect for the music's history. He told *Down Beat,* "If you're 15 and you want to be a jazz musician, you've still got to go back to 1900 and start checking it all out.... you have to have a thorough understanding of the tradition in order to consider going one step further."

By the age of 15, Metheney was proficient at both the trumpet and the guitar, and by the time he was a senior

Born Patrick Bruce Metheney on August 12, 1954, in Lee's Summit, MO; *Education:* Attended the University of Miami briefly before moving to Boston to take a teaching assistantship at the Berklee College of Music with jazz vibraphonist Gary Burton.

Proficient at trumpet and guitar by age 15; balanced playing in Kansas City, MO, jazz bands and school marching band before joining Burton's band in 1974; musical director and guitarist for the Pat Metheny Group, 1978—; worked with keyboardist Lyle Mays and Brazilian percussionist Nana Vasconcelos on the albums *As Falls Wichita, So Falls Wichita Falls*, 1981, and *Offramp*, 1982; recorded and toured with Ornette Coleman on *Song X*, 1986, and with Charlie Hayden and Dewey Redman on *80/81* and *Rejoicing*; released *As Falls Wichita, So Falls Wichita Falls*, 1981; used a home computer as a composing tool and experimented with guitar synthesizers during the early 1980s; toured as part of the backup band for singer/songwriter Joni Mitchell's Shadows and Light tour; scored the film soundtracks for *The Falcon and the Snowman, Twice in a Lifetime, Orphans, Lemon Sky, Adieux,* and *Big Time*; inducted into the Hall of Fame in 1994; scored the music for the films *Cinema Paradiso* and *Passagio Per Il Paradiso*.

Awards: Grammy Awards as composer or solo artist 1982, 1990, and 1992; with Pat Metheny Group in 1983,1984, 1987, 1989, 1993, 1885, and 1998; with Charlie Haden, 1997.

Addresses: *Record company*—Warner Brothers Records, 3300 Warner Boulevard, Burbank, CA 91505-4694, (818) 846-9090; 75 Rockefeller Plaza, New York, NY 10019; 1815 Division Street, P.O. Box 120897, Nashville, TN 37212, (615) 320-7525; *Internet*—http:www.wbr.com.

in high school, he was balancing his time between jazz performances with small bands in nearby Kansas City and playing the French horn in half-time marching band shows for school credit. After high school he attended the University of Miami briefly before moving to Boston to take a teaching assistantship at the Berklee College of Music with jazz vibraphonist Gary Burton. In 1974 Burton invited Metheney to join his band; Metheney stayed in the band for three years, and recorded three albums. Then in 1977 Metheney began to organize and tour with his own band. A 1984 *Down Beat* review described Metheney's music as a balance of three parts, "the first being his own irrepressible Midwestern lyricism, the second a penchant for Brazilian rhythms, and the third the wild card of Ornette Coleman's jagged, insular logic."

Metheney's work with keyboardist Lyle Mays and Brazilian percussionist Nana Vasconcelos on the albums *As Falls Wichita, So Falls Wichita Falls* and *Offramp* illustrated Metheney's lyricism and penchant for exotic rhythms. His flowing, melodic style was also emphasized in his straight-ahead jazz performances with Ornette Coleman on *Song X*, and with Coleman alumni Charlie Hayden and Dewey Redman on *80/81* and *Rejoicing*. The 1981 release *As Falls Wichita, So Falls Wichita Falls* established Metheney as a unique, vibrant new voice in jazz because of his focus on the texture of a song's improvisation rather than the more linear approach of improvising on a song's harmony. On the groundbreaking release, Mays, a multi-keyboardist and composer, moved from stunning solos to lush musical environments that enhanced Metheney's guitar work. Vasconcelos's drums and simple acoustic instruments offered an earthy rhythmic backdrop, providing a grounding effect for the electronic sound.

During the early 1980s Metheney used a home computer as a composing tool and experimented with guitar synthesizers. The advent of the Synclavier—an instrument with a built-in 32-track digital memory and the ability to create practically any sound for an instrument—altered Metheney's way of working; he used it in the studio for nearly all his composing and in performance to create a wide range of sounds for his guitar. On many of his recordings, his guitar adopts tones which hearken back to the trumpet playing of his youth. Metheney achieved the sounds of various horns on his guitar which, in part, attributed to his reputation as an innovative composer, multi-faceted producer, and guitar synthesizer pioneer.

In 1986 Metheney was presented with the opportunity to perform and tour with the idol of his youth, Ornette Coleman; they recorded the album *Song X* in 1986. Metheney's rounded tones and melodic sensibilities contrasted nicely with Coleman's hard-edged angular logic, and the result was successful. By the late 1980s, Metheney had toured as part of the backup band for singer/songwriter Joni Mitchell's Shadows and Light tour, scored the film soundtracks for *The Falcon and the Snowman, Twice in a Lifetime, Orphans, Lemon Sky, Adieux,* and *Big Time*, and had garnered four Grammy Awards from more than a dozen albums.

In 1997, Metheney received a declaration from the governor of Missouri proclaiming February 25th as Charlie Hayden/Pat Metheney Day in honor of their release *Beyond the Missouri Sky—Short Stories by Charlie Hayden and Pat Metheney.* Throughout the 1990s, Metheney continued his prodigious output and garnered Grammy Awards as a composer in 1990 and a solo artist in 1992; and with the Pat Metheny Group in 1993, 1995, and 1998. Metheney was inducted into the Hall of Fame in 1994, and scored the music for the lauded films *Cinema Paradiso* and *Passagio Per Il Paradiso.* Within the brackets of musical history, Metheney stands to be one of the great innovators in the pioneering jazz tradition.

Selected discography

Ring (Gary Burton Quintet), ECM, 1974.
Dreams So Real (Gary Burton Quintet), ECM, 1975.
Works, ECM, 1975.
Bright Size Life, ECM, 1975.
Works 11, ECM, 1976.
Passengers, ECM, 1976.
Watercolors, ECM, 1977.
Pat Metheney Group, ECM, 1978.
American Garage, ECM, 1979.
80/81, ECM, 1980.
As Falls Wichita, So Falls Wichita Falls, ECM, 1981.
Offramp, ECM, 1982.
Rejoicing, ECM, 1983.
First Circle, ECM, 1985.
Song X (with Ornette Coleman), Geffen, 1986.
Still Life (Talking), Geffen, 1987.
Travels, ECM, 1987.
Letter From Home, ECM, 1989.
Reunion, ECM, 1990.

Question and Answer, ECM, 1990.
Secret Story, ECM, 1993.
The Road to You, ECM, 1994.
We Live Here, ECM, 1995.
Quartet, Geffen, 1997.
Beyond The Missouri Sky—Short Stories by Charlie Hayden and Pat Metheney, ECM, 1997.
Imaginary Day, Warner Brothers, 1999.

Sources

Books

Contemporary Musicians, volume 2, Gale Research, 1990.

Periodicals

Audio, October, 1986.
Billboard, October 11, 1998.
Down Beat, August 1986; June 1986; April 1986; January 1985; May 1984; November 1982; October 1982.
High Fidelity, January 1985; September 1981.
New Republic, May 30, 1983.
Newsweek, April 14, 1986.
Rolling Stone, May 9, 1985.
Stereo Review, September 1982; November 1981.

Online

"Pat Metheney Group," http://www.wbr.com (September 1999).
"Grammy Awards," *The Recording Academy,* http://www.grammy.com/awards/ (September 15, 1999).

—B. Kimberly Taylor

Mojave 3

Rock band

Drawing upon both American country and British folk roots for inspiration, Mojave 3 has impressed listeners and critics alike with their moody, atmospheric sound. Formed from the remnants of the British group Slowdive, the band turned away from surging electric pop/rock towards a softer acoustic focus. Mojave 3's lyrics touch upon themes of thwarted love and loneliness, combining well with the quietly brooding ambiance of their music. Echoes of Bob Dylan, Neil Young and Gram Parsons are present in their songs, influences that the band proudly acknowledges.

Mojave 3 was launched in 1995, when singer/guitarist Neil Halstead, singer/bassist Rachel Goswell and drummer Ian McCutcheon regrouped after the breakup of their previous band, Slowdive. Formed in 1989 in England's Thames Valley area, Slowdive was part of a wave of British bands that included Ride, Pale Saints, and Swervedriver. Emphasizing feedback and effects-laden electric guitar sounds, these groups were tagged with the "shoegazer" label, a reference to the motionless, trance-like mood of their songs. After several years of popularity in the early 1990s, such groups fell out of favor, and Slowdive suffered from a backlash in the British music press. Following the 1995 release of Slowdive's third CD, Pygmalion, the band's three core members disbanded in favor of adopting a new name and musical identity. Regarding his shift in direction, Halstead said in a 4AD/Sire press biography that he "wanted to do something more with song structure, and something more acoustic-based. We didn't talk about it much before we recorded, it was just that I'd changed by the time I wrote those songs."

The music that Halstead and Goswell began creating after leaving Slowdive had a melancholy quality that was suggestive of stark, wide-open landscapes. Appropriately, they decided to name their new band after the Mojave desert, the vast Southern California landscape where one of their musical heroes, country-rock artist Gram Parsons, died in 1973. Adding keyboardist Christopher Andrews and slide guitarist Simon Rowe, Mojave 3 recorded a six-song demo tape over a two-day period and went looking for a recording contract. "Some of the demo recordings ended up on the final release," Halstead told writer Berett Atwood in an interview for *Billboard.* "We couldn't go into the studio to re-create them if we wanted to. There was an atmosphere and soul to the original sessions that can't be duplicated."

By the end of 1995, Mojave 3 had joined the roster of 4AD, the British label known for such highly-regarded artists as the Cocteau Twins and This Mortal Coil. Their debut CD for the label, *Ask Me Tomorrow,* appeared in January, 1996 to an encouraging reception. In place of the thickly-applied guitar sounds that Slowdive favored, keyboard-based textures highlighted "Love Songs On The Radio" and other tracks. The overall mood of the album was bittersweet and reflective, somewhat suggestive of Mazzy Star, Cowboy Junkies and similar dark-tinged rock units. Halstead and Goswell were quick to point out in interviews that Mojave 3 was a distinct departure from their previous group."We changed the name because the new songs are so different than the work we had done as Slowdive," Goswell told *Billboard.* "We didn't want to bring any prejudices against Slowdive to the new material."

Mojave 3 embarked on tours in both Britain and the United States in 1996 before returning to the studio. Chief songwriter Halstead began composing material with a more pronounced American country influence, harkening back to the homespun pathos of Hank Williams and George Jones. The poetic folk/rock of Bob Dylan's mid-1960s albums was another key reference point. The Dylan influence was underscored in part by newly-recruited member Alan Forester, who had replaced Andrews on keyboards. "Just the instrumentation, just the Hammond organs really adds that element..." Halstead said in an interview with Jack Rabid in *The Big Take-Over;* "as soon as Alan started in the band, he started whacking out these Hammond riffs, it was just great. I like the sound of those [Dylan] records, everything sort of going off and you got the Hammond and all these counter melodies."

Augmented by veteran British pedal-steel guitarist B.J. Cole, Mojave 3 recorded their second album at their home studio in Cornwall, England. The resulting album, *Out Of Tune,* took the group further into country music terrain while adding some brighter shadings to their sound. One track, "Some Kinda Angel," demonstrated that the band was capable of delivering an upbeat rock tune when in the mood. More than balancing the lighter moments, though, were such wistful ruminations as "All Your Tears," "Keep it All Hid" and "To Whom Should I Write." Halstead sang lead on all tracks, with Goswell providing her trademark harmonies. Reviews of *Out Of Tune* were generally positive. *Rolling Stone* reviewer James Hunter called the album "stunning, an unerring collection of floating, giant little moments," while *Spin* critic Joshua Clover hailed it as a "campfire micromaster-

piece." A dissenting voice came from Eric Broome in *Allstar*, who wrote that *Out Of Tune*'s tracks "sustain a lovely atmosphere, but by the sixth or seventh song, the laconic energy level begins to grate."

With two albums behind them, Mojave 3 defined themselves as a stripped-down, thoughtful group capable of extending their sound without losing their identity. For his part, Halstead seemed content to continue making music for a faithful cult audience. "I don't think we are doing anything terribly original," Halstead said modestly in an interview with *Rolling Stone Online.* "... I think we're getting better known; I mean, I think we've always had that sort of core fan base. I don't think it will ever be crazy."

Selected discography

Ask Me Tomorrow, 4AD, 1996.
Out Of Tune, 4AD/Sire, 1999.

Sources

Books

Larkin, Colin, editor, *The Encyclopedia of Popular Music,* Muze, 1998.

Periodicals

Big Take-Over, Summer, 1999.
Billboard, December 9, 1995.
Rolling Stone, April 1, 1999.

Online

Allstar, http://www.allstarmag.com (January 14, 1999).
Rolling Stone Online, http://www.rollingstone.com (January 14, 1999).

Additional information was provided by 4AD/Sire publicity materials, 1999.

—*Barry Alfonso*

Monica

Singer

The young chanteuse named Monica needed no last name to distinguish her, as word of her talent emerged in the music press during the mid-1990s. Her first recording, released when she was only 14 years old, sealed her reputation as a talented singing sensation. Despite her youth and the rapid rise of her career, Monica amazed the music world with the strength of her voice. Even as a young teen-ager she drew praise from critics, who compared her powerful voice to R&B legends such as Aretha Franklin, Whitney Houston, and Anita Baker.

With "Don't Take It Personal (Just One Of Dem Days)" in 1996 Monica became the youngest artist ever to top the *Billboard* R&B singles chart. Her first album, *Miss Thang,* appeared shortly after the hit single, and by the time she turned 16 the recording had gone double-platinum. When she released her second album, *The Boy Is Mine,* in 1997 the title song was already a chart-topping hit.

Monica Arnold was in born in College Park, Georgia in October of 1980. Her father, M.C. Arnold, Jr., left the family when Monica was only four years old. Monica's mother Marilyn, an airline employee, supported the family on her own until 1993 when she married the Reverend Edward Best. Monica first sang in her church choir when she was barely out of infancy. Stories hold that she made her singing debut at age two when her mother, a member of the church choir, allowed the toddler to join the group.

Most agree at any rate that by the age of four Monica was a bona fide member of the choir at Jones Chapel United Methodist Church in Newman, Georgia. Outside of Church, Monica was too shy to perform in front of anyone, including her friends. Yet she was completely enamored of singing and turned everyday objects—even pencils—into microphone props. She lived all of her young life in College Park until she was literally "discovered" as a pre-teen in a talent contest.

Monica was only ten years old when she first entered a talent contest, after years of singing in the choir and alone in her room. Two years later she took first prize in a contest, winning $1,000 for her rendition of the Whitney Houston hit, "The Greatest Love of All." Her performance solicited a standing ovation from the crowd, including record producer Dallas Austin. An associate of superstar singers including Madonna and TLC, Austin was impressed when he heard the youngster. He signed Monica to a recording contract with Rowdy Records in 1992.

Her life assumed a whirlwind pace as she attended high school at Atlanta Country Day School and fulfilled her agreement under Austin's contract with Rowdy Records. Despite her extreme youth Monica immediately began work on her *Miss Thang* album, which was two years in production. At 14 she completed her first chart-topping hit, "Don't Take It Personal (Just One Of Dem Days)." She graduated from high school at age 16 with a solid 4.0 grade point average, despite the demands of her recording schedule, public appearances, and touring engagements that included a ten-week concert tour in the spring and summer of 1996.

In October of 1997, after the demise of Rowdy Records, Monica signed with Arista Records. Her tall, striking appearance garnered her further work for modeling and acting assignments—all before she turned 17 years old. Along with her manager, rap singer Queen Latifah, Monica appeared on the Fox sit-com *Living Single,* and she appeared on the *Tonight Show*, as well.

Monica's second album with Austin, 1998s *The Boy Is Mine*, held the number one spot on *Billboard*'s chart for two months. The album included the hit single "The Boy Is Mine," a duet with fellow teenaged R&B star Brandy that debuted at number one and stayed there for six uninterrupted weeks. The two young singers performed the duet to a live audience for the fist time at the 1998 MTV Awards in Los Angeles amid rumors of an embittered rivalry between the superstars. The words of the duet, which imply that there is a love triangle going on

her grandmother in College Park. In music, Monica found an escape from the painful circumstance of living life away from her father. She developed an extremely close bond with her mother, and in time developed acute sensitivity to her mother's burden of raising five children alone. As word of Monica's fame spread, she reconciled with her father.

Selected discography

Miss Thang, 1995.
"Don't Take It Personal (Just One of Dem Days)," 1996.
(with Brandy) "The Boy Is Mine," 1997.
(contributor) *Space Jam* (soundtrack), 1997.
The Boy Is Mine (includes "Street Symphony" with the Atlanta Symphony Orchestra), Arista, 1998.

Sources

Ebony, September 1998.
Essence, October 1998.
Jet, October 5, 1998.
Newsweek, July 27, 1998.
Rolling Stone, December 24, 1998.
People, April 22, 1996; August 3, 1998.

—*Gloria Cooksey*

between the two singers, were misconstrued by eager fans who believed that the song told a personal story about Monica and Brandy. Although rumors persisted, both women asserted a sense of individual confidence and denied that there could be anything but mutual respect between the two.

After becoming famous, Monica continued to live with her mother and stepfather, younger brother Montez, and

Little Brother Montgomery

Piano

Little Brother Montgomery was one of the most versatile pianists to emerge from the blues. Although he never achieved the fame of musicians like Roosevelt Sykes, Sunnyland Slim, or Otis Spann—all of whose playing was shaped early on by contact with Montgomery—he was as comfortable playing New Orleans jazz or boogie-woogie as straight blues. His career in music stretched from the earliest years of recorded blues in the 1920s until the mid-1980s. But his playing, in particular his unaccompanied piano work, possesses a timelessness, a virtuosity, a serenity rare in any music. Little Brother Montgomery performances, right up until his death in 1985, were much more than mere blues shows. They transported the listener back to the New Orleans of the 1920s and made that old music sound as fresh as when it was first invented.

Eurreal Montgomery was the fifth of ten children—five girls and five boys—born to Harper and Dicy Montgomery. The family home in Kentwood Louisiana was located in the middle of timber country, and Harper ran a honky-tonk where logging workers gathered on weekends to drink, dance, gamble and listen to music. Most all of the Montgomerys were musical. Harper played clarinet, and Dicy played accordion and organ. Eurreal's brothers and sisters all learned to play piano to one degree or another. His brother Tollie made a record with him in the 1960s and brother Joe followed Eurreal to Chicago and performed regularly there in clubs and on record in the 1950s and 1960s. Little Brother—Eurreal was called by that name almost from birth—taught himself to play simple "three finger blues, as he called them, on a piano his father bought the family. "From then on," he told his biographer Karl Gert zur Heide, "I just created simple things on my own until later I got large enough and went to hear older people play.... like Rip Top, Loomis Gibson, Papa Lord God."

Montgomery had plenty of opportunity to hear older musicians. Most of them passed regularly through Kentwood and played at his father's honky-tonk. He decided at a young age that he wanted to be a piano player like them and he was an eager pupil. He would stand with them as they played rags, early blues and popular songs of the time, watch what they did with their fingers, and then imitate it himself. He was especially fond of the blues pieces they played; he copied them and modified them into pieces that would later become regular parts of his repertoire. A common feature of most of these proto-blues was a rollicking walking bass carried on by the left hand. Not much later the style would be called boogie-woogie; in the 1910s, however, it went by another name. "They used to call boogie piano Dudlow Joes," bassist Willie Dixon told Gert zur Heide, "I didn't hear it called boogie till long after. If a guy played boogie piano they'd say he was a Dudlow player."

Montgomery must have been a fast learner. He claimed that he quit seventh grade, left home at the age of eleven and began playing piano for a living wherever he could. His first job was in a juke joint in Holton, Louisiana where he was paid $8 a week plus room and board. He worked there for six months, playing and singing from seven until ten thirty on weekday evenings, and the whole night through on weekends. Feeling more confident, he left Holton and worked for six months at a "cabaret" in Plasquemine, Louisiana, where he earned $10 a night plus room and board. After that, he then moved on to Ferriday, Louisiana where he was paid $15 a night plus room and board. Within a year the pre-teen had doubled his earning power. More importantly, in Ferriday he made the acquaintance of two older piano players, Long Tall Friday and Dehlco Robert.

Friday, Robert, and Montgomery began working together perfecting a new blues that involved interplay of the left and right hand, that could produce either simple or complex music. What began as music that could be performed by a player without a great deal of technical skill, changed into "the hardest barrelhouse blues of any blues in history," as Montgomery described them to Gert zur Heide, "because you have to keep two different times going in each hand." The three friends called the new form "the Forty Fours." Later it would be transformed into one of Montgomery's biggest hits, "Vicksburg Blues."

Montgomery played in and around Ferriday until the flood of 1922 put parts of the city under eight feet of water. For the next year or so, probably in an automobile he purchased, he played his way through Louisiana, Mississippi and Arkansas. In 1923 he returned home to Kentwood for a time, then moved to New Orleans, where jazz was being born. The city was full of hundreds of piano players, all competing to be the best, at least in their wards. In the mid-1920s, Montgomery toured Louisiana with a variety of bands, his own and others, including the renowned Buddy Petit's. He played with Sunnyland Slim and guitarist Skip James. In 1928, Montgomery was hired by Clarence Desdune's Dixieland Revelers, a dance band. It was a challenging gig for him as Desdune's band played entirely from sheet music. Montgomery had a reputation as a formidable pianist but he was a blues pianist and was not adept at sight-reading. But he was a quick study here, as well, and with help from another band member was soon able to fake all the tunes in Parker's repertoire.

At the end of 1928, Montgomery quit the Revelers and moved up to Chicago. He made a name for himself playing rent parties—house parties put on in black neighborhoods to raise money to pay the rent. "I played house rent parties practically every night in the week for different people," Montgomery told Gert zur Heide. Chicago was becoming as hot a jazz town as New Orleans, but all party-goers let Montgomery play at the rent parties was blues and boogie-woogie. While in Chicago he

caught the attention of the Paramount record company. In late 1930, he accompanied Minnie Hicks on two songs and recorded about a half dozen sides of his own, including the greatly evolved version of the old Forty Fours, "Vicksburg Blues." The song was one of the most popular blues of its day, widely imitated by bluesmen; in 1935, Montgomery released his own imitation, "Vicksburg Blues No. 2." He recorded two records for Melotone in Chicago at the beginning of 1931, but as the Great Depression grew worse, he pulled up stakes and returned to New Orleans.

In New Orleans he formed his own band, the Southland Troubadors, which toured the South and parts of the Midwest including Illinois, Wisconsin, Michigan, Minnesota, and Iowa. Before long the group grew to ten pieces. They usually publicized their gigs with short radio concerts and earned such high pay touring that they turned down offers to record. Although the group existed until the late 1940s, Montgomery left in 1939. In summer 1935 he began recording for Bluebird Records, when he cut two records of his own and played on six others. The following summer he set a kind of record at the Bluebird studios, recording 23 sides in a single day, and those were part of 37 in all that he played on!

Around the time World War II started Montgomery paid a visit to his parents and then moved north to Chicago where he took off his travelling shoes—most of the time—and remained for the rest of his career. After the war, he began playing "old-time jazz" with musicians such as Baby Dodds and Lonnie Johnson. In 1948, he took part in a Carnegie Hall reunion concert by the Kid Ory Band. He played the Chicago club circuit regularly and was said to have some 1,000 songs committed to memory. As electric post-war blues took hold in Chicago, Montgomery was an active session musician. He appeared on some of the influential mid-fifties record made by Otis Rush, and played piano on one of Buddy Guy's first big hits, his 1960 remake of Montgomery's "First Time I Met The Blues."

He continued making records his entire life, both blues and early jazz. In 1969, he and his second wife Janet Floberg, founded their own record label, FM. The first single the company released was a remake of "Vicksburg Blues," sung by Jeanne Carroll. A biography, Gert zur Heide's *Deep South Piano: The Story of Little Brother Montgomery*, based on interviews with Montgomery, was published in 1970. Later in life, he expanded briefly into theater with a role in a staged biography of Bessie Smith. He continued performing and recording practically right up to his death on September 6, 1985 of congestive heart failure.

Selected discography

Tasty Blues, Original Blues Classics, 1960.
Chicago: The Living Legends (South Side Blues), Original
    Blues Classics, 1962, reissued 1993 CD.
Goodbye Mister Blues, Delmark, 1973-76.
At Home, Earwig, 1990.
Complete Recorded Works (1930-1936), Document, 1991.

Sources

Books

Erlewene, Michael, Vladímir Bogdana, Chris Woodstra, and
    Cub Koda, *All Music Guide to the Blues*, San Francisco,
    Freeman Books, 1996.
Gert zur Heide, Karl, *Deep South Piano: The Story of Little
    Brother Montgomery*, Blues Paperbacks, 1970.
Palmer, Robert, *Deep Blues*, Viking Press, 1981.

Periodicals

Down Beat, December 1985.

—*Gerald E. Brennan*

Oakland Interfaith Gospel Choir

Gospel choir

For over a decade the Oakland Interfaith Gospel Choir earned national recognition for its powerful and energetic interpretations of traditional spirituals and contemporary gospel songs. Under the direction of Terrance Kelly the choir imparted its message of hope, joy, unity and justice via numerous live performances from San Francisco to Canada and Australia.

Founded in Berkeley, California, the choir extended its audience through recordings with gospel stars like Tramaine Hawkins, and jazz and pop artists such as Linda Ronstadt and Peter Gabriel. It was profiled on CBS' *Sunday Morning with Charles Kuralt* and in the award-winning documentary *This is Our Story, This is Our Song* by film director Skip Brown. By 1999 the Oakland Interfaith Gospel Choir had produced two recordings and received the Gospel Academy Award for Best Community Choir of the Year for the fifth time.

The Oakland Interfaith Gospel Choir had its origins at the acclaimed Cazadero Jazz Camp, sponsored by the city

Photograph by Jim Yudelson. Reproduced by permission of The Oakland Interfaith Gospel Choir.

For the Record . . .

Members include 55 vocalists; **David Belove**, bass; **Rahsaan Ellison**, keyboards; **Ben Heveroh**, keyboards; **Terrance Kelly** (born October 29, 1962 in Oakland, CA), director; former accompanists include **Juan Forte**, drums; **Ellen Hoffman**, keyboards; **Ed Kelly**, keyboards; **Troy Lampkin**, bass.

Founded in 1986; performances in churches and at benefit events in the San Francisco, CA area; performed with the Duke Ellington orchestra at the Duke Ellington's Concert of Sacred Music, 1990; performed with jazz saxophonist Pharaoh Sanders at Oakland's Calvin Simmons Theater, 1990; first performances abroad in Vancouver, Canada, 1995; performed at the International Music Festival in Sydney, Australia, 1997; recorded backup vocals for Tramaine Hawkins, Take 6, The Clark Sisters, Walter Hawkins, The Dixie Hummingbirds, Linda Ronstadt, Peter Gabriel, Pharaoh Sanders, Stan Getz, John Denver, Malrena Shaw, and Jeffrey Osborne; released *The Oakland Interfaith Gospel Choir—Live!*, 1991; second album *We've Come a Mighty Long Way* recorded live at the First Congregational Church in Oakland, released December 1995.

Awards: Gospel Academy Award for Best Community Choir of the Year, 1997 and 1999; Arts Organization of the Year Award from the Oakland Metropolitan Chamber of Commerce, 1998; Gold Award for promotion of cultural understanding through music at the International Music Festival in Sydney, Australia, 1997. Terrance Kelly: Emmy Award for arrangement of "Circle of Friends," 1995; Gospel Academy Award for "Best Director," 1997.

Addresses: *Management*—2421 Prince Street, Berkeley, CA 94705, (510) 848-3938. *E-mail*—admin@oigc.com.

of Berkeley, California. Gospel choir directress and pianist Faye Kelly taught a one-week gospel singing workshop at the camp. After Faye died her son Terrance Kelly took over the workshop. In 1986 some of the faculty members and workshop participants decided they wanted to turn this short but uplifting experience into a regular activity. The choir, christened the Oakland Interfaith Gospel Choir, took off.

Only three and a half years after the choir was founded it was being praised for its sound and symbolism alike,

both of which were influenced primarily by director Kelly. Kelly, the son of jazz pianist Ed Kelly and grandson of a preacher, took on the job after some eager gospel workshop participants had approached him. It seemed like an almost impossible goal: to teach white singers to sound like "real gospel" and make them sing their souls out even if they didn't believe in the same gods.

Kelly taught the choir about black singing—shouting, pronunciation, hand clapping and rocking—simply by doing it, and letting the choir imitate him. He rewrote some lyrics to make them more acceptable to the non-Christian choir members, telling the *New York Times* "Jesus every now and again is O.K. ... Jesus every breath is too much." Kelly's baritone voice, covering over three octaves, earned him reputation as one of the choir's soloists.

Over its history the choir numbered between 55 to 60 members from more than 20 different faiths including Jews, Buddhists, Roman Catholics, Rastafarians, and Baptists. In a 1989 *New York Times* article, soprano Sheila Daar explained the group's mission: "In a society where race and religion divide us, our message is it's possible to maintain your differences, yet come together." Kelly encouraged non-Christians to "mentally insert the name of [their] own God into the music," singer and producer Kathleen Enright told the *Daily Republic*.

Right from the beginning, the Oakland Interfaith Gospel Choir took its message not only to churches, but also to benefits on behalf of the homeless, children, victims of AIDS and Alzheimer's Disease, poor families, and even prisoners. The choir also performed with the Duke Ellington orchestra at the Duke Ellington's Concert of Sacred Music at San Francisco's Grace Cathedral in 1990. They performed at various other festivals including the 40th Annual Atlanta Arts Festival and the New Orleans Jazz Festival. At one notable performance in 1994, the choir accompanied a sermon by South African Bishop Tutu held at Grace Cathedral in San Francisco. Their first trip abroad took the choir to Canada in 1995 where it performed to large audiences in Vancouver.

Several pop and gospel stars took notice of the Oakland Interfaith Gospel Choir's stellar reputation. The group sang backup vocals on singer Linda Ronstadt's 1989 album *Cry Like a Rainstorm, Howl Like the Wind,* on gospel star Tramaine Hawkins' *Tramaine—ive* in 1990, and on Hammer's 1991 album *Too Legit To Quit,* all of which won Grammy Awards.

In 1990 the choir's fifth Christmas Concert—a sold-out performance with jazz saxophonist Pharaoh Sanders at Oakland's Calvin Simmons Theater—was recorded and released on tape. The choir's search for an appropriate record label proved to be difficult, however, as Christian labels could not be convinced to support the group's philosophy of religious tolerance. Ultimately the group decided to finance and produce their first album independently, and *The Oakland Interfaith Gospel Choir—Live!* was released in 1991.

"The sounds of praise hit like drumbeats, backed by a funky bass line and an organ that demands you to move," wrote Anita Amirrezvani of the Oakland Interfaith Gospel Choir in the *West Country Times*. Amirrezvani was not alone in her opinion, as the choir soon began building a reputation outside of San Francisco. In December of 1995 the choir released a second self-produced album, *We've Come a Mighty Long Way*.

Recorded live at the First Congregational Church in Oakland, the album's mix of traditional and contemporary gospel included classical as well as jazz arrangements, and ballads as well as rocking songs. Kelly wrote and arranged most of the music for both of the choir's albums, while his father was among the accompanists on organ and piano. In 1995, Kelly won an Emmy Award for his arrangement of "Circle of Friends," which the choir performed for a public service announcement on KGO Channel 7. Two years later he received the Best Director Award at the 27th Annual Gospel Academy Awards.

In 1996 the Oakland Interfaith Gospel Choir performed at the State of the World Forum in San Francisco, which was attended by several global leaders. The following year the choir performed in Australia for the first time at the International Music Festival in Sydney. While there they received a Gold Award for promotion of cultural understanding through music. In December 1997 the group was featured in *This Is Our Story, This is Our Song*, a one hour documentary by filmmaker Skip Brown. Originally aired on KGO TV, *This Is Our Story, This is Our Song* later received a Bronze Apple Award from the National Educational Media Network.

Selected discography

The Oakland Interfaith Gospel Choir—Live!, Oakland Interfaith Gospel Choir, 1991.
We've Come a Mighty Long Way, Oakland Interfaith Gospel Choir, 1995.

Appears on

Linda Ronstadt, *Cry Like a Rainstorm, Howl Like the Wind*, Wea/Elektra Entertainment, 1989.
Hammer, *Too Legit To Quit*, Emd/Capitol, 1991.
Tramaine Hawkins, *Tramaine—Live*, Sparrow Records, 1990.

Sources

Daily Republic, February 28, 1997.
Diablo, December 1996.
New York Times, December 25, 1989.
Oakland Tribune, December 1, 1991; November 27.
San Francisco, December 1998, p. 67.
West Country Times (Oakland, CA), December 1, 1995.

Additional information for this profile was provided by publicity materials of the Oakland Interfaith Gospel Choir and by choir member Kathleen Enright.

—Evelyn Hauser

Beth Orton

Singer, songwriter

Beth Orton emerged from the British trip-hop dance scene as a singer/songwriter who directed her talents toward making amplified folk music in a refreshingly different vein. Orton, who lent vocal tracks for the likes of William Orbit and the Chemical Brothers prior to her solo career, found her way to the forefront of a new wave that *Village Voice* writer Julie Taraska termed "pastoral electronica … an amalgamation of '60s folk and processed beats." Orton's cheerless but haunting voice and songs about morbidity and tragic romances, and earned a slew of critical accolades for her two albums, 1997's *Trailer Park* and her 1999 release *Central Reservation.* As an article in *Rolling Stone* noted, "Orton weaves English folk, confessional songwriting, and high-tech arrangements into a modern rhythmic approach."

Orton was born in 1970 in Norfolk, a city in the east of England, but moved to the London area with her family as a young teen. Always fascinated by words and the English language, she wrote poetry and stories from a young age. As an adult she worked in a pub for a time, and began her own catering company for film sets that she called Fat Beth's Lunchbox. From her parents she inherited an appreciation for a wide range of music including Sixties-era folk ensembles. From her rebellious older brothers she gleaned an awareness of punk, but Orton turned her creative energies toward a career in the theater. "I had a huge love of music, but it was something I never thought I was worthy of," Orton told *Billboard*'s Dylan Siegler.

She appeared in London productions after studying drama, and even toured Russia "as a spitting, corseted whore in a play about Arthur Rimbaud," wrote Murphy Williams in *Harper's Bazaar.* In a hip London bar one night in 1989 she met ambient electronica producer William Orbit. Sitting on the barstool next to Orton at Quiet Storm, Orbit was struck by Orton's speaking voice, and convinced her to join him in the studio. They recorded "Don't Wanna Know About Evil" together, a cover from 1970s folk singer John Martyn. Orton then went on to work with several other acts including the Chemical Brothers on their groundbreaking 1995 LP *Exit Planet Dust* and the trip-hop act Red Snapper. "When I started singing, I just couldn't stop," Orton told Siegler. "Music satisfied this need in me—it was the expression I was looking for."

The exposure to studios and songwriters inspired Orton to begin writing her own songs. As she did so, a friend introduced her to the work of legendary, though somewhat forgotten, Chicago jazz singer Terry Callier. *Village Voice* writer Natasha Stovall explained that Callier's music had achieved a cultish fandom among London

For the Record . . .

Born December 1970 in Norfolk, England.

Once ran a film-set catering business; stage actress in London, England, late 1980s; recorded "Don't Wanna Know about Evil" with William Orbit as Spill; recorded with Chemical Brothers and Red Snapper; solo debut *Trailer Park* released in late 1996 on the Heavenly/ DeConstruction label.

Awards: *Trailer Park* named one of the ten best albums of 1997 by *Rolling Stone* magazine.

Addresses: *Home*—London, England. *Record Company*—Arista Records, 6 W. 57th St., New York NY 10019.

music scenesters by that point. "Callier's '60s and '70s recordings cook soul, folk, jazz, love, politics, and religion," wrote Stovall, and "guided by his example, Orton mixed her emotive free-associations and creamy melodies down into laid-back turntable soundscapes" that became her debut album, *Trailer Park.*

Released in the U.K. in 1996 and on the Heavenly/ DeConstruction label the following year in the United States, *Trailer Park* was somewhat of a departure from the production-heavy blips and beeps of William Orbit. The album instead featured Orton using a folk guitar but backing it with dance beats. The album was produced by highly regarded studio whiz Victor Van Vught, who had worked with Nick Cave, and Andrew Weatherall.

A single from *Trailer Park*, "She Cries Your Name," was released but Orton did not tour in support of it, though she did open some dates for the Beautiful South, John Cale and John Martyn. In a talk with *Billboard* writer Paul Sexton in late 1996, Orton agreed with the difficulty of neatly categorizing her style. "Folk, jazz, and hiphop all rolled into one," she theorized, adding, "at the end of the day, it's just good taste. People used to say you couldn't do a folk song with hip-hop. I know it's all the rage now, but I swear, four years ago you couldn't get anybody to do it."

Critical reception for *Trailer Park* was enthusiastic. "Teetering between a songwriter's linear development and electronica's conscious fragmentation, *Trailer Park* incorporates the sum total of Orton's experience: the lyrics and melodies she writes on acoustic guitar and the processing and effects of studio engineers," noted Taraska in the *Village Voice*. *Rolling Stone*'s Rob Sheffield called Orton's debut "one of those rare albums you could play for absolutely anyone and know they'd like it." By 1999, *Trailer Park* had snowballed into an underground success in the United States, selling over 90,000 copies.

Orton eventually did begin making live forays into North America, and found a warm reception in cities like Chicago and San Francisco. She also spent time on the Lilith Fair touring festival in 1998, where she met one of her more famous fans, Emmylou Harris. Returning to the studio she rehired Van Vught along with David Roback of Mazzy Star for her 1999 release *Central Reservation*. This time, however, Orton wrote nearly everything herself. Some of the tracks reflected her own circumstances—both of her parents had passed away—and musically, she headed in a different direction that distanced her from the intense beats of the electronica movement. In place of heavy drum loops was a greater emphasis on the guitar, the piano and conga drums.

Central Reservation also included several notable guest collaborators or performers. Ben Harper helped out on its first single, "Stolen Car," while New Orleans bluesman Dr. John and Callier appeared on other tracks. Dr. John had been working in the same studio complex and liked her work so much that he offered his services. Ben Watt from Everything but the Girl also made an appearance on the record.

Orton won wide critical acclaim for *Central Reservation*. "From a universe of elements, Orton has cobbled together on *Central Reservation* a sound both trippy and straightforward," opined Stovall in the *Village Voice*. Regarding Orton's progression as a songwriter and musician, Stovall wrote that she displays "an almost mystical relationship with sounds and words ... *Central Reservation* bypasses the cortex and goes straight for raw nerves; perhaps that's why Orton doesn't print out her lyrics, because you have to hear them to understand."

Billboard's Siegler also found *Central Reservation* a solid example of a developing artist. "The orchestration is lusher, the vocals are more dynamic and confident, and the artist's game of genre hopscotch is intact," Siegler declared. Writing in *Newsweek*, Karen Schoemer termed the record "a glorious accomplishment ... her songs drift along on oceans of strings, with brushed and Stax-style organ adding cushions of soul." *Rolling Stone* writer was no less impressed writing, "*Central Reservation* generates a special buzz of its own."

Selected discography

Trailer Park, Heavenly/DeConstruction, 1996.
Central Reservation, Heavenly/DeConstruction, 1999.

Sources

Billboard, December 14, 1996; February 13, 1999.
Esquire, February 1999.
Harper's Bazaar, September 1998.
Newsweek, March 15, 1999.
Rolling Stone, December 24, 1998; March 18, 1999;
Village Voice, May 13, 1997; April 13, 1999.

—*Carol Brennan*

Maria João Pires

Piano

Portuguese pianist and musical purist Maria João Pires performs intimate renditions of classical compositions with an exquisitely fluid style. She is best known for her performances of Beethoven, Mozart, Chopin, and Schumann. Pires, a child prodigy, gave her first recital at age four and went on to perform a Mozart concerto at age five. She studied with some of the greatest teachers of the twentieth century, and her perennial collaborations with symphony orchestras around the world are greeted with enthusiasm. Equally acclaimed are her chamber music renditions most notably in a trio, with cellist Jian Wang and Augustin Dumay on violin.

Pires, who was born in Lisbon, Portugal on July 23, 1944, began to play the piano at age three. She studied with Professor Campos Coelho at the Lisbon Academy of Music between 1953-60, and graduated at age 16. During that same time, she studied technique and theory with Francine Benoit. Afterward, she won a Gulbenkian scholarship and went to Munich to study with Rösl Schmidt at Staatliche Hochschule für Musik (Musikhochschule de Munich). She also studied in Hannover with Karl Engel.

In 1970, Pires took the first prize at the Beethoven Bicentennial International Competition in Brussels. That distinction brought her international notoriety, and soon she was in demand to perform outside of her native Portugal. Initially, she performed in Spain and in Germany but soon expanded the scope of her tours. She traveled throughout Europe, and into Africa, and Japan She debuted in London in 1986 accompanied by violinist Augustin Dumay, and she made her North American debut that same year, with the Montreal Symphony Orchestra in Canada. In 1987, Pires participated in the inaugural tour of the Gustav Mahler Youth Orchestra with Claudio Abbado. She performed with that group in Hamburg, Paris, and Amsterdam. The following year, she performed her debut tour of the United States. In 1989 she signed an exclusive contract with Deutsche Grammophon, and in 1990 she performed again with Abbado—this time with the Wiener Philharmoniker—at the Salzburg Easter Festival.

Over time Pires gained respect worldwide as a soloist with the finest orchestras in the world. She appeared regularly with the Berlin Philharmonic, the Boston Symphony Orchestra, the Royal Concertgebouw of Holland, the London Philharmonic, and Orchestre de Paris among others. In April of 1995, she toured the United States with Concertgebouw of Holland, under Riccardo Chailly as director. Among their performances were Richard Strauss's Ein Heldenleben at the Kennedy Center.

Pires appeared at the Edinburgh Festival in August and September of 1998, and in September of that year Deutsche Grammophon announced that Pires would perform in a new program of on-board concerts in conjunction with Seabourn Cruise Line. The concerts, scheduled for exotic ports of call, included an appearance by Pires in the first program of the series, performing on board during a transatlantic crossing destined for her hometown of Lisbon in April of 1999. That year she was to appear at Salzburg Mozartwoche with the Berlin Philharmonic. Additionally she was scheduled for multiple appearances with the Boston Symphony, including two shows at Carnegie Hall. Also on her itinerary was an appearance with the Minnesota Orchestra and concerts in the Orient, along with chamber music concerts in Europe and the United States—her Atlanta debut was scheduled for April of 1999 at the Clayton College & State University.

In addition to her work as an orchestral soloist, she is equally acclaimed for her chamber performances, and frequently performs accompanied by violinist Augustin Dumay. Pires and Dumay have performed together throughout much of Europe including Spain, Holland, Belgium, Switzerland, and Germany. They performed in Japan in 1992 and again in 1994. The duo frequently performs in trio with cellist Jian Wang, and in 1998 the three of them toured the Orient.

For the Record . . .

Born July 23, 1944 in Lisbon, Portugal. *Education:* Lisbon Academy of Music; studied with Campos Coelho, Francine Benoit, Rösl Schmidt, Karl Engel.

Recital debut, age 4; performed Mozart concerto at age 5; early tours of Europe; international tours, 1970—; British and North American debuts, 1986; U.S. debut, 1988. Repertoire of Mozart, Schubert, Schumann, Beethoven, Chopin; exclusive contract with Deutsche Grammophon

Awards: First Prize, Beethoven International Bicentennial Competition, Brussels, 1970; Edison Prize; Grand Prix International du Disque Français, L'Academie Charles Cros, 1996, 1997.

Addresses: *Agent*—Askonas Holt Limited Lonsdale Chambers, 27 Chancery Lane, London WC2A 1PF.

Pires admittedly concentrated a significant proportion of her repertoire on chamber scores, often to the exclusion of some of the more flamboyant concerti of Tchaikovsky or Rachmaninoff. She attributed her preference to the fact that she was not born with the large hands and long slender fingers stereotypical of a pianist. Indeed her hands are surprisingly small, yet she makes no bother of the fact, and instead plays music that is appropriate for her personal physical design. Among her most popular recordings are the complete nocturnes of Chopin and her many Mozart concertos. Pires takes credit for popularizing the works of Chopin and for providing new insight into his compositions, which for many years were subjected to stagnant, mechanical performances that lacked in-depth interpretation. Her *CHOPIN: the Complete Nocturnes* reached number one on the popular music charts very soon after its release in 1997. Allen Linkowski of *American Record Guide* called Pires "[A]n exquisite Chopinist," and said of her Chopin Nocturnes a "reviewer's dream."

In addition to her renditions of the works of Chopin, Pires's best performances include compositions by Beethoven, Mozart, Schubert, and Schumann. Critics applaud Pires for her clarity and interpretive phrasing. Brian Hunt in the *Daily Telegraph* said of her Mozart Piano Trios with Dumay and Wang, "[She has] illuminat-ing phrasing, animated line and golden touch." She is undeniably one of the great pianists of the late twentieth century. She is respected as a rare artist who plays strictly out of affection for the music and out of love for her instrument. Pires also teaches music herself and counts the 1991 Lara Haskil Competition finalist, Emmanuel Strosser of Strasbourg, among her students.

Apart from her accomplishments on the concert stage, Pires is the mother of four grown daughters, and she has five grandchildren. During the mid-1990s she adopted an infant boy, named Claudio, with whom she spends great deal of time, taking him along with her on tour whenever possible. Pires related the story of how she came to be Claudio's mother, explaining that he caught her attention as a newborn in the hospital where one of Pires's own daughters was delivering a child. Claudio's mother disappeared shortly after his birth. Pires adopted the boy when it became evident that she would never return and that the child was completely abandoned. She brought him to live with her on her farm which is located in a remote area about one hour's drive from Lisbon.

Although much of her land is reserved to grow olives for oil, Pires is extremely self-sufficient and grows her daily fare as well. She is unusually caring and warm as a person and opens her home to young musicians and other artists, in order to provide an informal setting for them to relax and discuss whatever problems are tugging at their minds. It is her goal to bring teachers and students back to the roots of their purpose as musicians. Pires admits that she has been saddened by the commercialism of the music world and by the young artists who are lacking in dreams of the beauty of the music for its own sake. Too many musicians, she believes, come into their careers because of external motivation. Too many musicians play ultimately to please their parents or for monetary gain, and this is a source of sadness to Pires. The rendition of the music and not the public performance, she believes, should be the musician's purpose. Pires was quoted in the *Jerusalem Post,* "Being on stage is the consequence of a life's work and not a goal in itself."

Selected discography

Chopin, the Complete Nocturnes, Deutsche Grammophon, 1997.
BACH: Partita No. 1, English Suite No. 3, French Suite No. 2.
(with Augustin Dumay and Jian Wang) *BRAHMS: Piano Trios Nos. 1 & 2.*

(with Augustin Dumay) *BRAHMS: Violin Sonatas.*

(with Emmanuel Krivine and the Chamber Orchestra of Europe) *CHOPIN: Concerto for Piano and Orchestra No. 1 in E minor.*

(with André Previn and the Royal Philharmonic Orchestra) *CHOPIN: Piano Concerto No. 2.*

(with Augustin Dumay) *GRIEG: Violin Sonatas Nos. 1-3.*

Le Voyage Magnifique.

(with Claudio Abbado and the Wiener Philharmoniker) *MOZART: Piano Concertos Nos. 14 & 26.*

(with Claudio Abbado and the Chamber Orchestra of Europe) *MOZART: Piano Concertos Nos. 17 & 21.*

MOZART: The Piano Sonatas.

MOZART: Violin Sonatas

(with Christine Schäfer, Claudio Abbado, and the Berlin Philharmonic) *MOZART: Non temer, amato bene.*

SCHUBERT: Impromptus.

SCHUBERT: Piano Sonata.

(with Douglas Boyd on oboe) *SCHUMANN: Adagio und Allegro op. 70, Romances op. 94—Fantasiestücke op. 73.*

Sources

Periodicals

American Record Guide, May 1, 1997.
Daily Telegraph, October 11, 1997, p. 12,
Jerusalem Post, June 10, 1997, p. 7.
St. Louis Post-Dispatch, February 20, 1997.
USA Today, March 18, 1995.

Online

"Askonas Holt Limited,—Maria Joāo Pires," http://www.holt.co.uk/artists/pire.htm (May 24, 1999).

"Maria Joāo Pires," http://www.dgclassics.com/artists/pires/pires.html (June 24, 1999).

"Maria Joāo Pires plays Chopin's First Piano Concerto," http://www.dgclassics.com/news/1980902.html (June 24, 1999).

—Gloria Cooksey

The Pretty Things

Rock band

Though never widely known in the United States, The Pretty Things have achieved legendary status in their native Britain after more than 30 years of existence. Through sheer tenacity the band has survived numerous career missteps and line-up changes to enjoy a creative upswing in the late 1990s. Initially notorious for their raw R&B sound and wild off-stage antics, The Pretty Things went on to record an impressive, if often overlooked, body of work that compares favorably with that of their British Invasion rock peers. Among other things, they are credited with inspiring the raw garage rock sound of the mid-Sixties and with releasing the first ever rock opera on album.

The Pretty Things trace their origins back to Sidcup Art College in Kent, England, where singer Phil May and guitarist Mick Taylor took part in lunchtime jam sessions. Another participant was guitarist Keith Richards, who recruited Taylor as a member of Little Boy Blue & the Blue Boys, an early version of the Rolling Stones. Rather than stick with the Stones, Taylor decided to form his own group in 1963 with May, recruiting rhythm guitarist Brian Pendleton, bassist John Stax and drummer Vivian Prince to complete the line-up. Taking their name from R&B pioneer Bo Diddley's song "Pretty Thing," the group took its place beside the Stones, the Animals, the Yardbirds and other young R&B-inspired British combos of the era.

The Pretty Things began to play venues around London and quickly attracted attention. Besides their raucous sound, the band became notorious for their unruly behavior and unkempt appearance. From the start, the band's music was more raw and aggressive than that of their peers. "What we wanted was something for a new generation, some musical identity," said May in a 1999 interview with *Discoveries*. "We'd found the music, and when we started playing it at the art school, that became our music. We weren't trying to be disrespectful to it, just do it our way. It was almost like thrash R&B. It was faster, but it had to be faster."

Signing a recording contract with Fontana Records, The Pretty Things released their debut single "Rosalyn" in June 1964. This hard-charging tune reached number 41 on the British singles charts. That single paved the way for the band's follow-up release, "Don't Bring Me Down," a number ten hit later that year. Their debut album, *The Pretty Things*, was released in 1965 and rose to number 6 on the British album charts.

Controversy surrounded The Pretty Things, even as they performed to ecstatic audiences in Britain and continental Europe. The band's fondness for wrecking hotels and smashing equipment led to their being blacklisted from numerous venues—even being barred from entering Australia and New Zealand. Perhaps the most outrageous member was drummer Prince, who left the band in 1965 after a fight aboard an airplane in Australia resulted in bad publicity.

Get The Picture, the band's second album, was released in late 1965. Featuring more original material than their debut album, the album veered away from R&B and towards a more acoustic rock sound. Though it contained the British hit "Midnight To Six Man," the album was not successful. Line-up changes followed, with Wally Allen replacing Stax on bass and John Povey added on keyboards. The Pretty Things tried again in 1967 with *Emotions*, a more mature effort that emphasized acoustic guitar and vocal harmonies. Unfortunately, the band felt that the album was marred by string arrangements added without their approval. The album failed to generate much interest, and the Pretty Things parted ways with Fontana soon after its release.

The Pretty Things' next album, *S.F. Sorrow*, appeared on the Harvest label in Britain in late 1968. Based on a short story by May and recorded over a 18-month period, the album is considered to be the first true rock opera. Held together by narration, the interrelated songs featured psychedelic effects that were a far cry from the band's R&B roots. Bad luck plagued the band once again, however. By the time *S.F. Sorrow* was released in the U.S. on the Motown distributed Rare Earth label in 1969, The Who had already released their own rock opera Tommy. As a result The Pretty Things were regarded as imitators rather than innovators, and *S.F. Sorrow* died in the marketplace.

In late 1969, Taylor exited the band, leaving May as the remaining original member. With Victor Unitt brought in on guitar, the Pretty Things released *Parachute* in 1970. Continuing the band's experimental streak, this sonically diverse work was named Record of the Year by *Rolling Stone*. Sales of *Parachute* were disappointing, and the band's fortunes seemed to be at a low ebb. In June, 1970 they broke up, only to reform not long afterwards with May at the helm once again. This new line-up released *Freeway Madness* on Warner Brothers in 1972, again to limited response.

Matters began to improve when heavy metal superstars Led Zeppelin took an interest in the Band. Signing with Zeppelin's Swan Song label the band ventured into a more commercially viable hard rock sound. Released in 1974, *Silk Torpedo* reflected this direction. Such songs as "Joey" and "Singapore Silk Torpedo" gained FM airplay, while lengthy U.S. tour helped to raise their profile further. But their next Swan Song release, 1976's *Savage Eye*, failed to perform as well as its predecessor. Dissention within the band's ranks led May to quit later that year, which brought The Pretty Things to an end for the second time. May went on to lead a band called the Fallen Angels, while the remaining members continued on as Metropolis. Neither project attracted much interest.

In 1980, May and Taylor rejoined forces to launch The Pretty Things yet again. The no-frills sound and jittery rhythms of new wave rock influenced the resulting Warner Brothers album, Cross Talk. "With *Cross Talk*, we just wanted to make a record that we could stand up and play, so there was no clever production," May told *Discoveries*. "So it was slimmed-down, just a straightforward bunch of songs." Despite this attempt to keep up with the times, the album didn't find a large audience. However, the renewed partnership of May and Taylor held together throughout the 1980s, resulting in sporadic live shows and a number of recordings with a changing roster of bandmates.

With the help of manager and sometime drummer Mark St. John, The Pretty Things worked to acquire legal rights to their old recordings. By the late 1990s, they had regained ownership of their first five albums, which were reissued through the British label Snapper. At the same time, the 1966 edition of the group—May, Taylor, John Povey, Skip Allen and Wally Waller—had re-formed and was actively recording and performing. One highpoint was a performance of *S.F. Sorrow* in its entirety at Abbey Road Studios in September, 1998, broadcast live over the World Wide Web and later released on CD as *Resurrection*.

All of this activity served as a lead up to the March 1999 release of *...Rage Before Beauty*, a CD of new recordings that was praised by critics as a strong return to form. In reviewing the album for *Rolling Stone*, critic David Fricke noted that "the [Pretty Things] revisit the Bo Diddley beat and recount old war stories the same way they lived 'em—with pride, without apology."

Selected discography

The Pretty Things, Fontana, 1965; reissued, Snapper Music, 1998.
Get The Picture, Fontana, 1965; reissued, Snapper Music, 1998.
Emotions, Fontana, 1967; reissued, Snapper Music, 1998.
S.F. Sorrow, Fontana, 1968 (U.K. only); Rare Earth, 1969 (U.S.); reissued, Snapper Music, 1998.
Silk Torpedo, Swan Song, 1974; reissued, Snapper Music, 1998.

Savage Eye, Swan Song, 1976; reissued, Snapper Music, 1998.
Resurrection, Snapper Music, 1999.
...Rage Before Beauty, Snapper Music, 1999.

Sources

Books

Bonds, Ray , *The Harmony Illustrated Encyclopedia Of Rock*, Harmony Books, 1982.
Pareles, Jon, ed., *The Rolling Stone Encyclopedia Of Rock & Roll*, Rolling Stone Press, 1983.
Rees, Dafydd and Crampton, Luke, *Encyclopedia Of Rock Stars*, DK Publishing, 1996.

Periodicals

Billboard, March 13, 1999.
Discoveries, June 1999.
Rolling Stone, April 1, 1999.

Online

The Snapper Connection, www.mindspring.com/~us00091/snapper.htm. (May 16, 1999).

—*Barry Alfonso*

Propellerheads

Electronica band

For the pair of English DJs, who evolved into big-beat electronica purveyors known as the Propellerheads, merging late nineties British dance music with the funk of early eighties American hip-hop and James Bond movie music, yielded critical accolades and transatlantic success. The band's 1998 debut, *decksanddrumsandrockandroll*, featured witty film dialogue samples buried under rapid-fire bass rhythms and a barrage of guitars, organ, and synthesized washes of chords. The Propellerheads also won praise for their unusual and intense live performances. *Billboard*'s Larry Flick summed the duo's music as, "a synergistic union that results in richly cinematic electronic soundscapes that are steeped in rugged hip-hop and funk—with a healthy sense of humor."

The Propellerheads are Alex Gifford, born in the mid-1960s, and Will White, a decade Gifford's junior. Gifford spent his formative years steeped in the music of James Brown, Parliament, and Booker T and the MGs, and as an adult became a session musician, engineer and producer. For a time, he worked at Peter Gabriel's Real World Studios in Bath, England as a songwriter and producer. Gifford began writing and setting down his own tracks in the early 1990s while working as a DJ in Bath dance clubs. One night he passed one of his tapes on to White, another local DJ.

White, who loved the Eighties rap acts like UTFO and KRS-One during his formative years, was also an ac-complished drummer. He was stunned by Gifford's mix of samples and heavy-duty, rap-sampled beats. The two soon began working together in White's basement to see if adding live drums, a bass line and various digital elements to the mix of song samples would work. As Gifford said in the DreamWorks biography, "Will's drumming is all about grooves.... He'll just sit on the groove, and then he'll play the beat backwards. It's like you've got two copies of the groove, and he'll just stick one a half beat out, like you would if you were DJing hip-hop style. It's wicked."

The sonic impact of their configurations would earn the duo immense praise, initially on the local level. They began releasing singles on their own under the name Propellerheads—borrowing the Silicon Valley term for computer nerds—and friends in Bath began pestering them to move out of the basement and into the live arena. At first, Gifford and White were not enthusiastic about doing so, but a club-owner friend put their name on some flyers announcing a gig, which forced them to create a live act.

The Propellerheads performances evolved into a barrage of sound that utilized four turntables with Gifford alternating between a bass and his Hammond organ, and White on drums with both spinning their songs on a homemade vinyl format known as an acetate. "Our show has developed this way because we felt there was no point in taking a bunch of studio equipment on the road," Gifford explained in the biography. "It's boring and it's not particularly visual. We figured if we put all the studio sounds on acetates, and called them up whenever we needed them, we could treat the show like a DJ set and make it more interactive."

Appropriately, the Propellerheads were soon signed to the independent British label Wall of Sound. Their first record, the EP *Dive!*, was issued in 1996, and they realized they'd hit upon a solid groove when the title song was purchased by Adidas for an ad campaign. *Take California* and *Spybreak!*, both EPs, followed featuring biting, oddball samples of film dialogue and galloping bass lines modeled after the 1960s spy-film music that Gifford had always loved.

The soundtrack composers from that era—Lalo Schifrin, John Barry, Henry Mancini, and Michele Legrand are some of the best known names in the genre—combined traditional orchestral arrangements with more contemporary pop and R&B-based rhythms. "It's the title sequences that move me most," Gifford explained in the press biography. "Like in a French film from the '60s that opens with a couple walking on a beach. Suddenly, a helicopter is flying around them and they're being shot at.

I love the sort of music that would accompany that scene. We're just trying to do soundtracks without the films."

One of the latter-day Bond movie composers, David Arnold, was so taken by the Propellerheads' spin on the form that he invited them to create a track for the 1997 album, *Shaken and Stirred: The David Arnold 007 Project*. Arnold also included one of their songs in a chase sequence in the Bond film *Tomorrow Never Dies*. For the album, Gifford and White wrote the song "On Her Majesty's Secret Service," a classic Bond-esque number that became a massive radio hit in England. The song also attracted the attention of the American record label DreamWorks, owned in part by Hollywood movie mogul Steven Spielberg. Signed to the label, Gifford and White decided to remix several of the tracks that had been released on their first Propellerheads LP for the U.K., *decksanddrumsandrockandroll*, adding more of a hip-hop flavor and a few new tracks.

Decksanddrumsandrockandroll—whose title paid homage to a 1978 Ian song, "Sex and Drugs and Rock and Roll"—debuted in the U.S. in early 1998 not long after Gifford and White impressed music industry insiders at the South by Southwest conference in Austin, Texas. The American version included "On Her Majesty's Secret Service" as well as another of the band's European hits, "History Repeating," which featured Shirley Bassey, the glamorous torch singer from Wales who sang the title songs to several Bond films, including *Goldfinger*. "It was a total fluke," Gifford told *Billboard* writer

Larry Flick. "We never in a million years thought she'd actually show up and record with us."

The Propellerheads' American debut also featured collaborative tracks done with De La Soul, "360 Degrees (Oh Yeah?)," and Jungle Brothers. Critical reception was somewhat wary, but generally favorable. Gina Arnold, writing in the on-line magazine *Salon*, called the Shirley Bassey collaboration "thus far the most mainstream-sounding techno recording on the market.... it may well become the 'Walk This Way' of electronica." *People* reviewer Steve Dougherty described *decksanddrumsandrockandroll* as "13 hyperkinetic, hypnotic sound collages and dance tracks." Writing in the *Village Voice*, R.J. Smith described the Propellerheads' sound as "not precisely funky, but it moves the body with an accretion of beat overkill, volume, and wit that is impeccably on-time."

Selected discography

Dive!, EP, Wall of Sound, 1996.
Take California, Wall of Sound, 1996.
Spybreak!, EP, Wall of Sound, 1997.
(contributor) *Shaken and Stirred: The David Arnold 007 Project*, Sire, 1997.
Propellerheads, DreamWorks, 1997.
decksanddrumsandrockandroll, DreamWorks, 1998.

Sources

Periodicals

Billboard, March 21, 1998; April 4, 1998.
New Musical Express, January 24, 1998;l April 30, 1998.
People, May 4, 1998.
Rolling Stone, April 16, 1998.
Village Voice, March 31, 1998.

Online

"Decksanddrumsandrockandroll," *Salon*, http://www.salon.com, (April 7, 1998).

Additional information for this profile was provided by Wall of Sound and DreamWorks Records, publicity materials, 1999.

—Carol Brennan

Thomas Quasthoff

Opera singer

Bass-baritone Thomas Quasthoff demonstrated an aptitude and appreciation for music before the age of one. According to *People* magazine's Patrick Rogers, he lay in the children's ward of a hospital in Germany near his home in Hildesheim, where nurses played recorded music to calm the young patients. The following day, Quasthoff was singing one of the melodies and the nurses informed his mother that he had musical talent. New York Philharmonic guest conductor Sir Colin Davis said, "[Quasthoff] is one of the great bass-baritones of our time. To me, he is a lesson in life." Quasthoff told Rogers, "I don't like recording. I love audiences," and by the time Quasthoff was thirty nine years old in 1999 with more than twenty CDs to his credit, it was clear that this star of the classic music realm was equally loved by his audiences.

Quasthoff was born on November 9, 1959 near the industrial city of Hildesheim in the Hannover region of Germany, where his father, Hans, worked as a civil servant. His mother, Brigitte, was a homemaker who took the drug thalidomide for morning sickness when pregnant with him. As a result of the drug, Quasthoff's hands are attached to his shoulders and he stands barely four feet tall. As an infant, he spent a year and a half in a plaster body cast that helped straighten his twisted feet. At age six, he was placed in a hospital for mentally and physically disabled children by German authorities, but eventually—after a prolonged battle—his father persuaded authorities to allow Quasthoff to live at home. When speaking with Rogers, he explained how he seemed unfazed by these early experiences: He said, "I learned to look around and realize there are people whose situation is worse than mine."

When Quasthoff was thirteen, he was refused a place at a school for the performing arts because it was physically impossible for him to play the piano. Though always small in stature, Quasthoff has always had a sturdy, exuberant personality and strong sense of self. His older brother, Michael, a journalist living in Hannover, told Rogers that his brother was never shy or timid. When other children taunted him because of his birth defects, he held his own. Michael said; "One couldn't exactly call him shy. He had such a big mouth, he didn't put up with much." Quasthoff's parents began recording his renditions of pop songs when he was still in diapers. His hopes for a musical career, however, were temporarily dashed when his application to the Hannover Hochschule fur Musik und Theater was rejected because of his disability. Resilient and determined, his parents arranged for daily lessons in Hannover with concert singer Charlotte Lehmann, a well-known soprano, with whom he studied voice for 17 years. Quasthoff gives her full credit for his extraordinary technical proficiency. He also studied music theory with Professor Ernst Huber-Contwig. Quasthoff's first big break came in 1988 when he received Germany's prestigious ARD International Musical Competition, spurring a rush of concert bookings and recording deals. Oregon Bach Festival conductor Helmuth Rilling heard him perform in Germany and thought, "Outstanding voice, outstanding person," and invited him to sing at the annual summer event in Eugene, OR in 1995. Quasthoff held on to his day job for a while, however, until his confidence grew. He continued to work as a popular Hannover radio announcer for six more years after that turning point in Munich.

Quasthoff rose to the apex of the musical world by utilizing his remarkably resonant voice. A *Wall Street Journal* reviewer described his delivery as "Gutsy, declamatory...," and *Tower of Babel* reviewer Pat Barnes described his voice as "large and resonant, both on top and on the bottom. He is in complete control of this voice, both in its shading and its dynamic effect, which he uses to its full advantage in the interpretation of songs.... ["Des Knaben Wunderhorn" was] sung with rollicking humor—chilling in its impact—phrasing and diction were exceptional." Quastoff recorded "Des Knaben Wunderhorn" for the first time with mezzo-soprano Anne Sofie von Otter and the Berlin Philharmonic, conducted by Claude Abbado, and Byrnes described it as "an exciting debut from a wonderful artist".

Born on November 9, 1959 near Hildesheim in Germany; son of Hans (a civil servant) and Brigitte Quasthoff (a homemaker); brother Michael a journalist. *Education:* Studied voice with concert singer Charlotte Lehmann for 17 years; studied music theory with Professor Ernst Huber-Contwig.

Radio announcer in Hannover; performed at venues across the globe, beginning in the early-to-mid 1990s; taught special master classes; professor for life at the Musikakademie in Detmold, Germany; released many recordings including *Carl Loewe: Ballads,* EMI, 1989; *Robert Schumann: Dichterliebe, Liederkreis Op. 39,* RCA, 1992; *Franz Schubert: Goethr-Lieder,* RCA, 1994; *Wolfgang Amadeus Mozart: Mozart Arias,* RCA, 1994; *Ludwig von Beethoven-fidelio,* RCA, 1995; *Georg Frideric Handel: The Messiah,* Hanssler Classic, 1997; *Gustav Mahler: Des Knaben Wunderhorn,* Duetsche Grammophone Gesellschaft, 1998; *Krzysztof Penderecki: Credo,* Hanssler Classic, 1998; *Franz Schubert: Winterreise,* RCA, 1998.

Awards: ARD International Musical Competition in 1998.

Addresses: *Record company*—Deutsche Grammophone, 825 Eighth Avenue, New York, NY 10019; (212) 333-8000.

Quasthoff, who resides in Hannover, discovered that his frequent concerts in the U.S. have left him appreciative of Americans. He told Rogers, "Americans respect accomplishment," and he recalled that a German critic once referred to him as a "gnome". Quasthoff, however, is not the type of person to let thoughtless slights deter him from happiness. He also told Rogers, "I think it's important to accept your disability. If you don't love people—and that includes yourself—you shouldn't be in this business." In April of 1999, he sang works by Bach and Mozart with the Los Angeles Chamber Orchestra, and has a seemingly limitless career ahead of him. His versatility and gusto, combined with his obvious enjoyment of the material, render him a memorable, unique performer. He has been undaunted by hurdles that would have left most people back at the starting gate decades ago, and his prolific output serves to underscore his success.

Since 1988, when he earned first prize in voice at Munich's ARD music competition—the same competition that earlier launched the career of Americana soprano Jessye Norman—Quasthoff has been winning over audiences. *Time* magazine's Elizabeth Gleick wrote of Quasthoff, "He is ... poised on the brink of world renown....With an impish sense of humor and an almost boisterous conviviality, Quasthoff presents a picture of a man who has never struggled—and indeed, he lives alone, and often travels alone, needing little or no assistance. Beyond such nuts and bolts, though, there is the all-important matter of soul—and Quasthoff has that in abundance." In addition to performing, Quasthoff teaches special master classes and has been made a professor for life at the Musikakademie in Detmold. In a beautiful twist of fate, the conservatory that turned him away as a child later invited him to do a temporary instructorship, which he graciously accepted.

Selected discography

Carl Loewe: Ballades, EMI, 1989.
Robert Schumman: Dichterliebe, Liederkreis Op. 39, RCA, 1992.
Franz Schubert: Goethe-Lieder, RCA, 1993.
Wolfgang Amadeus Mozart: Mozart Arias, RCA, 1994.
Ludwig von Beethoven—Fidelio, RCA, 1995.
Georg Frideric Handel: The Messiah, Hanssler Classic, 1997.
Gustav Mahler: Des Knaben Wunderhorn, Deutsche Grammophone Gesellschaft, 1998.
Krzysztof Penderecki: Credo, Hanssler Classic, 1998.
Franz Schubert: Winterreise, RCA, 1998.

Sources

Periodicals

People, March 8, 1999.
Time, June 30, 1997.

Online

"Thomas Quasthof Biography," http:www.ping.be/gopera/quasthoff (September 24, 1999).
"New York Philharmonc Review," *Tower of Babel Review,* http://www.towerofbabel.com/sections/music/baton/reviews/nyphilharmonic/111298 September 24, 1999).

—B. Kimberly Taylor

Ralph Sharon Quartet

Jazz group

Pianist/bandleader/arranger/composer Ralph Sharon has peformed and recorded with some of the most significant jazz artists of the last half century. Though primarily known to his musician peers and jazz aficianados, his career has been associated with that of such famous jazz and pop talents as Tony Bennett, Count Basie, Duke Ellington, Rosemary Clooney, Mel Torme and many others. Sharon's work has spanned the close of the big band era through bebop's formative years and into the present day. As a bandleader, his recording history has continued over some 50 years and, in the 1990s, saw an upswing with the release of his composer tribute CD series.

Born Septrember 17, 1923, in London, Sharon was first schooled in music by his American-born mother, who had previously played organ in silent movie theaters. As he grew older, he became attracted to jazz and, in particular, the innovative bebop sounds coming out of the United States during the late 1940s. His professional debut as a pianist was with British bandleader Ted Heath in 1946. A few years later, he also played piano with Frank Weir's jazz orchestra, a group which also included soon-to-be-famous pianist George Shearing on accordion. In addition, he recorded with saxophonist Ronnie Scott's Esquire Five in 1948. Readers of *Melody Maker* chose Sharon as Britain's number one pianist four years in a row, which lead to his participation in the magazine's All Stars group in 1951-1952. By 1948 he was also leading his own sextet, which included percussionist Victor Feldman, later a well-known session musician in the United States. This group released several recordings on the Melodisc label, including "There's A Small Hotel" and "Blue Moon."

Despite his rapid rise in the British jazz ranks, Sharon felt restricted by the music scene there and longed to work with American bebop players. In the fall of 1953, he emigrated to the United States, sharing quarters with clarinet player Tony Scott in New York. "The music I heard [in New York] was much more advanced than in England" he told *Contemporary Musicians* in a telephone interview. "I'd never heard this stuff in person, and it just blew me away. Tony was very much into bebop, and he would take me up to Minton's [a famous Harlem jazz club] to sit in. That's where I got my eduation."

Sharon formed a new version of his sextet and began recording for the Rama label in the mid-1950s. In 1954, he released his *Jazz Around The World* album, which featured such notables as bassist Charles Mingus, drummer Kenny Clarke, saxophonist Eli "Lucky" Thompson and guitarist Joe Puma interpreting Sharon's compositions. Switching to Bethlehem Records, he continued in a bebop-influenced direction with his 1956 *Ralph Sharon Trio* album. He also recorded with jazz vocalist Chris Connor on the Bethlehem label from 1955-1957. Another Bethlehem project brought him into the studio in 1956 with singer Mel Torme as part of an all-jazz musician version of *Porgy And Bess.*

In 1957, Sharon took on the duties of pianist and bandleader for singer Tony Bennett, which would prove to be a long and productive association. It seemed an unlikely pairing at the start, given Sharon's bebop affinities and Bennett's mainstream pop background. "I'd just gotten a call out of the blue, asking if I'd like to play with Tony," Sharon told *Contemporary Musicians.* "To me, he was just a pop singer, and I didn't know much about him. But I said that I'd like to try it, I went and played for him, and he hired me. I showed him different sorts of beats, different ways of phrasing, and he took to it immediately. All of a sudden, he was getting into a jazz feeling. I found it exciting, and he did, too." Sharon encouraged Bennett to work with jazz musicians, which led to sessions with bandleader Count Basie. The resulting album, *Bennett/Basie,* was released by Columbia Records in 1958 and featured Sharon as arranger and pianist. The late 1950s also found Sharon sitting in with the Duke Ellington Orchestra on piano when Bennett shared the concert bill with the famed jazz group on tour.

At first, Columbia was somewhat concerned to see Bennett heading in jazz direction under Sharon's influence. As it turned out, Bennett recorded some of his most enduring hits after Sharon became his musical director. Among them was "I Left My Heart In San Francisco," which reached number 19 in 1962 and went on to become one of Bennett's signature songs. In an interview with *Billboard*'s Jim Bessman, Sharon recalled that "A couple friends gave me a bunch of songs they wrote, and I put them in a drawer, and two years later I was looking for a shirt and found 'I Left My Heart In San Francisco.' A week later we were in Hot Springs, Arkansas and I look at it and called Tony and said, 'We're going to San Francisco next. I've got a tune here that it might be a good idea to do'." A few years later, Sharon heard a tune called "If I Ruled The World" in a performance of the musical *Pickwick* in London. Bennett and Sharon slowed down the song's tempo, recorded it and scored a number 34 hit single in 1965.

Taking a break from working with Bennett in 1965, Sharon signed on as singer Rosemary Clooney's accompanyist two years later. He also launched a new version of his own band, which he had put on hold after starting his job with Bennett. With Jay Cave on bass and Christy Fabbo on drums, he signed with the Chess-distributed Argo label in the late 1960s and released his *Two A.M.*

album. Sharon described the music on this LP to *Contemporary Musicians* as having "a melodic bop influence, not too far-out." Around this time, he began his service as pianist and bandleader for Robert Goulet, best-known as an interpreter of such Broadway show tunes as "Camelot" and "The Impossible Dream." Sharon recorded several albums with Goulet for Columbia in the early 1970s, and also released several albums with his own band on that label during those years as well, including *The Ralph Sharon Trio Plays The Tony Bennett Songbook*.

Sharon's tenure with Goulet lasted into the late 1970s. At that point, he joined forces with Bennett once again. "I'd been in touch with Tony the whole time," Sharon said of the years that the two were apart. "Torri Zito [Bennett's arranger after Sharon] wanted to get off the road, so Tony asked me to come back, and I was happy to. I was back doing music with a jazz kind of feel, thank God." With Sharon once again in the bandleader's role, Bennett enjoyed a renewed popularity in the 1990s, earning a gold album with *Tony Bennett Unplugged* in 1995.

Meanwhile, Sharon began recording with a trio once more after signing with Britain's Horatio Nelson Records. Joining him were bassist Lenny Bush and drummer Jack Parnell, the latter a bandmate of Sharon's during his stint with Ted Heath. In 1989, he began releasing a series of songwriter tribute albums for the label, all titled with the prefix *The Magic Of....*, starting with a recording of George Gershwin material. Similar albums interpreting the works of Cole Porter, Jerome Kern, Richard Rodgers and Irving Berlin followed. In explaining his series to *Billboard*, he said, "I like to take famous popular composers whom I admire and investigate their particular body of work. I try to choose tunes that show off the different angles and atttudes that they have on a song—and that I can put a jazz feeling into."

Sharon continued this series on the American label DRG, beginning with 1995's *The Ralph Sharon Trio Swings The Sammy Cahn Songbook*, which featured veteran saxophonist Gerry Mulligan as a guest player. Next came *Portrait Of Harold Arlen* in 1996, followed by albums celebrating the songs of Harry Warren and Frank Loesser in 1997 and 1999 respectively. Sharon's DRG incarnation of his trio, which included bassist Paul Langosch and drummer Clayton Cameron, was expanded into a quartet with the addition of guitarist Gray Sargeant on the Loesser tribute album.

After five decades in the music world, Sharon found that his brand of jazz was finally reaching a larger audience. "It used to be that, when you said you were a jazz musician, you didn't get much of a response," he told

Contemporary Musicians. "Now there's a lot more appreciation. I'm not the kind of musician who just plays for himself. I've always tried to find something that would be of interest to people...I still want to entertain them."

Selected discography

Jazz Around The World, Rama, 1954.
The Ralph Sharon Trio, Bethlehem, 1956.
The Magic Of George Gershwin, Horatio Nelson, 1989.
The Ralph Sharon Trio Swings The Sammy Cahn Songbook, DRG, 1995.
The Ralph Sharon Trio Plays The Harry Warren Songbook, DRG, 1997.
The Ralph Sharon Quartet Plays The Frank Loesser Songbook, DRG, 1999.

Sources

Books

Feather, Leonard, *The New Edition of The Encyclopedia Of Jazz,* Horizon, 1960.
Kernfeld, Barry, editor, *The New Grove Dictionary of Jazz,* Macmillan, 1988.

Periodicals

Billboard, March 13, 1999.

Additional information was obtained from telephone interviews with Sharon in August of 1999.

—*Barry Alfonso*

Rasputina

Cello group

Rasputina started as The Ladies' Cello Society in Brooklyn, New York, in 1996 when cellists Melora Creager, Julia Kent, and Carpella Parvo decided to see in what new directions they could take an instrument traditionally associated with classical music. As a counterpoint to this modernity, the women don Victorian corsets for concerts and draw lyrical inspiration from fables and archaic medical practices. The online publication *babysue* described the group as "three cellists who perform wearing turn of the century underwear. Your first reaction might be that this is a gimmick, but upon closer observation it becomes obvious that Rasputina is a band with an incredible amount of substance and style."

Creager, credited with founding the group and who regularly acts as its spokesperson, decided one day being a cellist was a dorky pursuit and stopped playing. Years later she made her living as a jewelry designer, but friends in rock groups kept pestering her to play with them. Among those groups were The Pixies and Nirvana. "Somewhere along the way," Brad Tyer wrote in a 1997 *Houston Press* article, "she decided that rock's guitar hegemony made no sense. The cello, she thought, was a much more evocative instrument, capable of conveying a greater range of feeling, especially if you were un-stuffy enough to run the thing through a flange box, distortion pedals and lots of reverb, as might suit the mood."

Agnieszka Rybska joined the group in 1996, with Norman Block adding drums. *Thanks for the Ether*, their debut album, was released in 1996 on Columbia Records. They performed with artists including Porno for Pyros and Bob Mould. In late 1998, Rybska was on maternity leave from the group and was replaced by Nana, a French "tap dancing, singing cellist type," according to the band's official website. It is unclear whether this is a temporary arrangement."[Nana] is wacky, blonde and foreign, just like Agnieszka."

Each cellist had extensive formal musical training prior to forming the group. "We all played since we were little girls. It was encouraged in our families," explains the band through a question and answer section on its official website. "Julia studied so hard in college that she got tired of it, but then she missed it. Melora brought her cello with her to art school in New York and played in weird performance art things."

Critics don't know quite what to make of Rasputina. They have been dubbed pop, rock, punk rock , goth and the closest invented moniker to corral them is the newly minted "darkwave." This term, coined around 1999, is used to describe brooding music which draws inspiration from and which is a cross-pollination of Medieval, Celtic, tribal, techno and neo-classical music as performed by artists such as Rhea's Obsession, Switchblade Symphony, Black Tape for a Blue Girl, and Cranes. Rasputina members say they're simply "a goddamn cello band."

Although seemingly allied with the goth/glam rock crowd, the trio maintains a following with classical music fans. "People who are specifically cellists of all different ages will make a point to see us," said Creager. "They love it, because they know exactly what we're doing ... playing the cello. But I think the classical music world is a pretty tight and closed thing. I've never been involved in it. I don't even know if they know of us, because for us to perform and put out records in a rock world. ... I don't know that anyone crosses over at all."

Their musical interests aren't neatly cross-stitched but a sonic crazy quilt. Band members say they listen to music by such diverse artists and groups as Cab Calloway, The Andrews Sisters, 16 Horsepower, Nick Drake, Ozzy Osborne, Ween, and Queen. The band wrote that a soundtrack of their life would include "Minnie the Moocher's Wedding Day," by Cab Calloway, Queen's "I'm In Love With My Car, "River Man" by Nick Drake, the Cheap Trick classic "I Want You to Want Me," the Pachelbel Canon, "Jesus' Blood Never Failed Me Yet" by

Ganin Bryer, Black Sabbath's "Iron Man," "Rocket Man" by Elton John, and David Bowie's "Life on Mars." "I'm drawn to these kinds of sarcastic, coy, cloying songs," Creager told allstar of the inclusion of Lesley Gore's hit, "You Don't Own Me," on *How We Quit the Forest*. "It's more about the music to me, but I like those snotty words."

The rock world hasn't been as accepting of hard rocking girls with attitude as it has boys with guitars and Rasputina has actively tried to subvert that. Band members contend most rock music is made by "interchangeable white boy bands." Even in this enlightened era, according to an opinion posted by the band on its website, it is "like a communist country where you can only get one brand of cereal. Boys," Creager told the *Houston Press* in 1997, "usually start bands to meet girls, or because they're fans, but this is about expression and satisfaction, and about empowerment, even though I hate that word."

Rasputina gained notoriety for touring as an opening act for the controversial Marilyn Manson in the late 1990s. Touring with Marilyn Manson was said to have made Rybska "more existential," while Creager became "more introverted." Their latest press materials hint at "the physical attacks ... suffered at the hands of Marilyn Manson's audience, which is to [sic] lurid to get into just now." In sum, the band found touring "a hard thing to do, but you really get good at it. The worst part was how boring and isolating it was during the day."

In that spare time, "Melora likes to write stories, draw, embroider, and try to get people to take her out for sushi. Agnieszka was setting diamonds in her off-time. Nana takes dancing class and goes to France. Julia keeps what she does a secret." Reading is also a favored pastime with Creager and Kent favoring the work of the late Angela Carter, known for her offbeat exploration of the fabulous and fables from a feminist perspective. But the women of Rasputina are usually practicing or rehearsing if not performing. "We have a really strong general work ethic because it takes a lot of work just to be sounding good on the cello, you know," said Creager in a 1997 with *babysue*. "It's not an easy instrument. We enjoy it to torture ourselves and overwork...."

Selected discography

Thanks for the Ether, Columbia, 1996.
Transylvanian Regurgitations (EP), Columbia, 1997.
How We Quit the Forest, Columbia, 1998.
(contributor four-CD compilation) *The Black Bible,* Cleopatra Records.

Sources

Periodicals

Billboard, July 4, 1998.
CMJ, April 1999.
Houston Press, March 20 - 26, 1997.

Online

AllStar, July 9, 1998 <http://www4.rocktropolis.com/allstar/database/news/9807/09/story4.asp">

Additional information provided by Columbia Records publicity materials, 1999, and materials from the official Rasputina site on the World Wide Web.

—*Linda Dailey Paulson*

Ray Condo and His Ricochets

Western swing band

Ray Condo and His Ricochets didn't always play the songs that they looked like they should have been playing. Dressed like country music stars from the 1950s, they played plenty of western swing and rockabilly tunes, but mixed in jazz and blues, as well. Performing few compositions of their own, their repertoire consisted of well-known and obscure songs covering a wide range of popular American music styles from the first sixty years of the twentieth century. Describing his band to Joel Bernstein of *Country Standard Time*, Condo referred to legendary figures from country-western, jazz, and western swing, saying they sound like "Hank Williams having a drink with Billie Holiday, and Bob Wills is the bartender."

While remaining faithful to the spirit of the old songs they played, Condo and His Ricochets put their signature sound on each tune. Discussing the band's approach to the music, Condo told Rich Kienzle of *Country Music,* "We've never been purists. We're not afraid of mixing things in. But I think the archival approach to our music is really important." Steel guitar player Jimmy Roy and guitarist Steven Nikleva arranged the songs for the band, and Roy's instrument makes a unique contribution to the band's sound. Although the non-pedal steel guitar is a staple of country music, it's a stranger in a strange land in the jazz and blues songs Ray Condo and His Ricochets play. Even on the western swing pieces, Roy's steel guitar takes on a different role than usual, playing the part that has traditionally belonged to the fiddle. Condo told Dave Howell of the Allentown, Pennsylvania *Morning Call* what makes the steel guitar important to the Ricochets' sound: "The steel guitar was the first synthesizer. Although it's used a lot in country, it really hasn't been fully exploited."

Ray Condo and His Ricochets were formed in Vancouver, British Columbia, where Condo, the band's lead singer and saxophonist, first met Roy in the 1980s. The two didn't join forces until much later, though. Condo, born near Montreal and raised in Ottawa, began his musical career as a rock guitarist in the 1960s. He went on to play punk rock for a time, before turning his hand to rockabilly. In 1984, he joined forces with stand-up rockabilly bassist Clive Jackson to form Ray Condo and His Hardrock Goners, who put out three albums and toured extensively throughout Canada and Europe.

Meanwhile, Roy met guitarist Nikleva in Vancouver, where he was in a western swing band. In 1990 the two of them, along with drummer Steve Taylor, helped form a honky-tonk revival band called Jimmy Roy's Five Star Hillbillies. When Condo's and Roy's bands came to an end in 1995 they got together with Jackson, Nikleva, and Taylor, to form Ray Condo and His Ricochets. The band wasted no time, releasing their fist album later that year. When *Swing, Brother, Swing* came out on the small Vancouver label East Side, it caught the attention of Jeff Richardson, owner of Joaquin Records in San Francisco. For years Richardson had been reissuing old western swing recordings, but had never thought of releasing a current artist's material before hearing Condo and His Ricochets. After licensing the album from East Side, Richardson decided the album need some changes. Condo told Bernstein, "Jeff thought it was a little too mellow. We added half a dozen tunes (while removing others) to make it more upbeat."

When the new version of *Swing, Brother, Swing* came out in 1996, it attracted critical attention for the band's innovative take on a wide variety of old material. The album includes tunes by Count Basie, Carl Perkins, and Stuff Smith. In a review in the *Village Voice,* Robert Christgau wrote, "They take over the material so completely that it's hard to tell whether the songs were this good to begin with, and beside the point to care." Condo and His Ricochets followed up quickly with their the release of *Door to Door Maniac* in 1997, and once again the band attracted attention and praise for their diversity of material. John Wooley wrote in the *Tulsa World,* "Condo and the boys cast their net wide and haul in plenty of gems." While their sound remained the same, their second album brought a personnel change, with John Cody playing drums on some tracks before officially replacing Taylor in the band in February of 1997.

For the Record . . .

Members include **John Cody** (joined group, 1997), drums; **Ray Condo** (born Ray Trombley, 1950, Hull, Quebec, Canada), vocals and saxophone; **Clive Jackson**, bass; **Steven Nikleva,** guitar; **Jimmy Roy**, steel guitar; **Steve Taylor** (left group, 1997), drums.

Grouped formed in Vancouver, Canada, 1995; released debut album *Swing, Brother, Swing* on East Side, 1995; signed with Joaquin Records and released revised version of *Swing, Brother, Swing,* 1996; released *Door to Door Maniac,* 1997.

Addresses: *Record Company*—Joaquin Records, 254 Scott St., San Francisco, CA 94117.

Along with critical praise, Condo and His Ricochets' albums have done well on the Americana charts, which measures sales and airplay of alternative country music. Still, sales have been modest when compared to more mainstream country bands. The band prefers staying outside of the Nashville country music industry, though, so that they can keep their own sound. Roy told Kienzle, "When you hear a country band, they're actually a rock band." Condo added his own thoughts about what would happen to the band if they went to a major label: "They'd have a new marketing term for us. They'd call it 'Hick Hop'."

Although the Ricochets released two albums in two years, performing live remained more important to them than recording in a studio. Condo told Bernstein, "Real music is live. Recordings are only documents." To that end, they have toured extensively throughout the United States, Canada, and Europe. They have played at such shrines of western swing as Cain's Ballroom in Tulsa, and have opened for country music stars such as Buck Owens. In 1997 the popular swing revival band Squirrel Nut Zippers invited Condo and His Ricochets to open their shows for two weeks. The band appreciated the opportunity to introduce the songs they play to a new, young audience. Condo told Chris Dickinson of the *St. Louis Post-Dispatch,* "I think Americans should know their grand-dads were rocking too."

Condo took heart in the popularity of bands like the Squirrel Nut Zippers, who revived pre-rock era musical styles for audiences too young to remember them. Condo told the *Pittsburgh Post-Gazette,* "This is really interesting because it really is cross-generational, from 18 to 68¼. Maybe by the end of the century, we all want to see what really is worth keeping and what ain't." On stage and in the studio Ray Condo and His Ricochets have energetically expressed their opinions on that issue.

Selected discography

Swing, Brother, Swing, Joaquin, 1996.
Door to Door Maniac, Joaquin, 1997.

Sources

Country Music, January-February, 1998.
Country Standard Time, December 1997.
Morning Call, (Allentown, PA), April 25, 1997.
Pittsburgh Post-Gazette, May 5, 1998.
St. Louis Post-Dispatch, August 22, 1996.
Tulsa World, July 10, 1998.
Village Voice, May 27, 1997.

—Lloyd Hemingway

André Rieu

Violin, conductor

A versatile violinist and spirited conductor, André Rieu capitalized on his classical music training and natural charisma to successfully recreate the uplifting atmosphere of the nineteenth- century Viennese dance halls for twentieth-century audiences worldwide. Rieu's unique classical style evolved around the notion that the audience must be involved in order to appreciate the music. Although the inspiration for his innovative musical presentations reached back over 100 years, his style was frequently categorized as "crossover" music because it combined the revered scores of the classical composers with a more informal performance atmosphere characteristic of popular music.

Rieu was born in Maastricht, Holland. His father conducted the Limburg Symphony Orchestra of Holland and the Leipzig Opera. Classical music permeated the Rieu household, and the Rieu children were well versed in the works of the great composers. André Rieu and his numerous siblings were heavily involved in musical training. Each displayed some talent and learned to play an instrument. Rieu himself developed into an accomplished violinist. As his understanding and appreciation of music grew, he developed a special fondness for the rhythms of the great Viennese waltzes. The waltzes, he maintained, stirred his emotions and created euphoria, so it was natural that he would devote his career to that style of music.

Rieu attended the Royal Conservatory in Brussels. After graduation he played in various Dutch symphony orchestras, including a term with the classical Limburg Symphony. Despite his appreciation and love for classical music, he grew increasingly disenchanted by the orchestral environment so familiar to his upbringing. He developed a dislike for the stiff and formal format that created a chasm between the performers and the audience. Rieu's frustration over the classical music format inspired him to assemble an orchestra of his own choosing and to seek his own method of presentation.

Began Encouraging Audience Participation

During the late 1980s, Rieu recorded with a variety of instrumental groups of his own selection, among them the Maastricht Salon Orchestra. During those early years he engrossed himself in conducting music and playing his violin. He was shy on stage and conversed rarely with the audience. As a result his performances took the traditional bent that he disliked so much, yet Rieu continued his efforts to remove the emotional distance that alienated the audience from the music and from the musicians. In search of a resolution, Rieu turned to the tradition of Johann Strauss II who is universally acknowledged as the King of the Waltz. Strauss, a violinist like Rieu, habitually performed facing his public; he created a festive atmosphere for his listeners, and encouraged them to dance and to enjoy each waltz. During a 1996 interview with Scott Simon for National Public Radio, Rieu called the waltz "stehgeig," a slang term that describes when a piece of music is assimilated totally into the performance medium. Rieu restructured his own performances according to the Strauss prescription, and quickly met with success. He assembled a new group of Dutch local instrumentalists and dubbed the ensemble the Johann Strauss Orchestra. Together Rieu and the Johann Strauss Orchestra, which consisted of two to three dozen performing musicians at any given time, developed a classical repertoire that emphasized lively dance music, polkas, and waltzes. One particular performance, during the early 1990s, in Harlingen, Holland, made a lasting impression on a music executive who was in attendance, and by 1994 Rieu was under contract with Mercury Holland Records. "[Rieu's] concerts are incredible—he faces the audience, and within a short while everyone is up out of their chairs waltzing," PolyGram Holland president Theo Roos told *Billboard*.

Mercury Holland wasted no time and released *Strauss & Co.*, Rieu's first album with the Strauss Orchestra, in September of 1994. Rieu made promotional appearances in Germany and developed a following very quickly. The CD entered the market as popular music and sold with ease, over half a million copies, including over 655,000 in Holland alone. Additionally, 55,000 copies sold in Belgium by June of 1995. For 19 weeks *Strauss & Co.* topped the Dutch album charts, and the record made a showing on the German charts. *Strauss & Co.* included tracks by Dmitri Shostakovich, Johann Strauss, Franz Lehar, and others. The album featured two singles that rose into the top ten ratings: Strauss's "No House but Strauss," and "The Second Waltz" of Shostakovich. Mercury ultimately released the album in South Africa, in the Philippines, and in Malaysia.

Found Commercial Success

In 1996, Rieu toured throughout Europe, to Germany, France, and Austria. He released a new album, *From Holland with Love,* that held strong at the number one position on the Dutch music charts for a solid year. A music video was released, and the CD went platinum eight times, prior to its American release later in 1996. Rieu also spent much of his time during that summer as a featured celebrity on PBS fund-raising specials. His album, *From Holland with Love,* was offered to viewers as an incentive for pledge donations, and the recording was among the most requested items during the pledge broadcast. Rieu donated his time once again for that same cause during March of 1997. *From Holland with Love* was released ultimately in over two dozen countries around the world and was among 96 albums to be certified as "Platinum Europe" recordings under a new program from Sony Music Entertainment Europe. Sony's platinum collection of million-selling albums were publicly acknowledged on June 27, 1996. Six months later, on January 28, 1997, *The Vienna I Love* was released on the Philips label. That album hit number three on the *Billboard* classical album chart, and a music video was also released. Rieu not only made a name for himself in the music world, but he also earned the gratitude of the European music industry which recognized and appreciated the impact of his popularity in spurring record sales in the European market.

In October of 1997, *Time* reported that Rieu had two albums on the *Billboard* classical music charts while another seemed likely to enter. *The Vienna I Love,* featuring waltzes, marches, and operatic airs, had climbed to number two while *From Holland with Love* held at number eight. As *Strauss Gala* remained poised to enter the charts, Terry Teachout of *Time* dubbed Rieu the "superstar nobody knows." Indeed Rieu's recordings rivaled those of the major classical stars for positions on the charts, including tenor Luciano Pavarotti and soprano Katherine Battle.

In the fall of 1997, Rieu released a Christmas album; creatively marketed in collaboration with the Dutch postal service which offered a free CD sampler from the album, as a premium with the purchase of Christmas stamps. Rieu and his orchestra also filmed a Christmas special that year, entitled *André Rieu: The Christmas I Love*, that aired on American public television in November of 1997. Rieu's first official tour of North America during that same year took him to Detroit, Philadelphia, Washington, and a number of other cities, including a sold-out concert at Boston Symphony Hall.

In January of 1998, Rieu received the Gold and Silver Harps award "Export Prize" from Conamus, for sales and other achievements by Dutch artists. Four months later *Billboard* reported that worldwide sales of Rieu's records exceeded 4.5 million. On December 17, 1998, a report of the year-end Billboard Music Charts from United Press International showed *The Vienna I Love* at number eight and *In Concert* at number ten among the year's classical album releases, based on retail sales.

In the spring of 1998, Rieu and the Johann Strauss Orchestra made an encore tour of the United States. They played the Universal Amphitheater in Universal City, Concord Pavilion in the San Francisco Bay area, and other large capacity theaters. Rieu's plans for 1999 included a June concert, scheduled for the Olympic Stadium in Munich, where he would perform with Michael Jackson, Pavarotti, and Montserrat Caballe, in a relief effort for Kosovo refugees.

Concert-goers Extraordinaire

Rieu's live concerts attract a spectrum of fans, typically ranging in age from 16 to 65 years old. Members of the audience can be seen in any manner of attire, from formal black tie , to T-shirt and tennis shoes. Rieu himself dresses in tails and wears his hair long. The Johann Strauss Orchestra, also dressed elegantly, appear to enjoy every moment of each performance. Rieu's warm demeanor habitually sets the audience to tapping its collective feet, if not dancing in the aisles outright. Rieu is not himself a dancer; he does not waltz and prefers it that way. Regardless he captured and held the interest of the mainstream public with his classical music repertoire, a feat accomplished by only a very few artists. Rieu's phenomenal success is not an accident; he is considered an excellent conductor, a talented violinist, and a great showman. According to Joshua Kosman of the *San Francisco Chronicle,* Rieu's performances are demanding and require hard work, " ... to sustain the illusion of spontaneous fun." Critics concur that Rieu's handsome face considerably enhances his talent and personal charm. Rieu in turn rejects any attempt to dissect his popularity. He attributes his success to the entire "package" of his performance and presentation.

Critical comparisons have likened Rieu to countless notable personalities but rarely become tiresome because of the extensive diversity. In a single breath the *Boston Globe* compared Rieu to singer Tom Jones, leading man Mel Gibson, swing band leader Spike Jones, fictional muscleman Conan the Barbarian, and the flamboyant pianist Liberace. The *Los Angeles Times* called Rieu the "Pied Piper of light classical music." Comparisons with television band leader Lawrence Welk also apply. The tongue-in-cheek nicknames bestowed upon Rieu vary drastically, from "waltzmeister" to the "schmaltz of waltz," while few refute the de facto appellation "New Waltz King," an allusion to his predecessor, Johann Strauss II.

Rieu is married and has two sons. The family lives in Holland, and it is there that Rieu recruits local talent for membership in the Johann Strauss Orchestra. He takes a personal approach to selecting the musicians—congeniality is the utmost priority; virtuoso musical skills are a plus.

Selected discography

Singles

"No House but Strauss," Mercury Holland, 1994.
"The Second Waltz," Mercury Holland, 1994.

Albums

Strauss & Co., Mercury Holland, 1994.
Strauz Gala, Multidisk, 1995.
In Concert, Mercury, 1996.
From Holland with Love, Mercury Holland, 1996.
The Vienna I Love, Phillips, 1997.
The Christmas I Love, 1997.
André Rieu in Concert, Philips, 1998.
Valses, PolyGram, 1998.
Live Gala Evening, Koch International, 1998.
On the Beautiful Blue Danube, Delta, 1998.
Emperor Waltz, Delta, 1998,
Tales from the Vienna Woods, Delta, 1998.
Great Waltzes, Delta, 1998.

Romantique, Philips/PolyGram, 1998.
Romantic Moments, PolyGram, 1999.

Sources

Periodicals

Billboard, June 10, 1995, pp. 46; June 16, 1995, p. 43;
    September 23, 1995, p. 66; May 18, 1996, p. 4; July 27,
    1996, p.56; March 8, 1997, p.15; May 30, 1998, p. 69.
Boston Globe, November 13, 1997.
Europe, September 1995, p. 42.
Los Angeles Times, May 1, 1998.
Orange County Register (Santa Ana, CA), April 28, 1998.
San Francisco Chronicle, April 30, 1998, p. E1.
Time, October 6, 1997, p. 101(2).

Online

"A brief history of André Rieu and the Orchestra," available
    at http://www.pukkie.demon.nl/rieu/special.htm (March
    19, 1999).

Additional information was taken from a National Public
Radio interview with André Rieu on April 6, 1996.

—*Gloria Cooksey*

Gabrielle Roth

Band leader, dancer

Gabrielle Roth makes records that people can move to. The sound of Roth and her band, The Mirrors, ranges from world music to urban street beat to the chant of Buddhist mantras. Regardless of the individual genre explored by her band, one thing remains the same; for Roth, the beat is everything. Roth herself is not a musician. But she has been the creative force behind more than ten albums recorded by the Mirrors since 1986. The guiding principle behind all her work is her theory of the Five Rhythms that are fundamental to all aspects of life. Roth has become internationally known for her courses on personal growth and awareness which take the Five Rhythms as a starting point and enable individuals to open themselves up—and dance. "Her methods," wrote Hal Zina Bennett in the magazine *Body Mind Spirit*, "can be used by anyone, dancer or non-dancer; it is a 'Western Zen,' integrating spirituality with everyday life." Roth's workshops are held regularly throughout North America and Europe. Her music, in particular the more hardcore sounds featured on the album Zone Unknown, have been played in dance clubs on both sides of the Atlantic.

Gabrielle Roth grew up on the East Coast. Possessed by "a hunger for rituals of spirit," as she described it in her book *Sweat Your Prayers,* she became fascinated by the two poles of body and spirit represented by ballet and religion. She was seven when she glimpsed a ballerina through the window of a dance school and made up her

mind that that was what she wanted to do. She got a hold of a book that illustrated the basic ballet positions and started practicing them at home in her room. Eventually her parents allowed her to take a real ballet class. Religion held just as large a place in her young life. On Sundays, she hid in the bushes outside the local fundamentalist church, enraptured by the passionate rhythms of preaching and singing. On weekdays, she attended Roman Catholic schools, where the nuns indoctrinated her in suspicion, if not outright loathing, for the body she wanted to dance with.

She continued dancing through college, to rock 'n roll as well as ballet, until an old knee injury reared its ugly head. Doctors told her she would never dance again. Thunderstruck but resigned to their professional opinion, Roth gave up dancing. "I had been cruelly cut off from a deep and beautiful part of myself," she later wrote in her book. She was thrown into a deep depression. At loose ends, she retreated to Big Sur, California, to participate in group therapy at the famous Esalen Institute. Before long, she had joined the institute's staff as a masseuse. When director Fritz Perls discovered Roth had once taught movement therapy in a mental hospital, he asked her to teach it to Esalen therapy groups. Slowly she was moving back toward her real passion.

The turning point came one evening at an institute social event. Live percussionists were pounding out rhythms so irresistible Roth found herself on the dance floor in spite of her knee. The music took over completely. By the time she came back to herself she was exhausted and drenched in sweat. Her knee had never been treated, but it turned out to be perfectly sound. Time had cured her wound. She later said that the experience taught her that humans have a natural craving for ecstatic experience and one way of satisfying it was through dance, which by and large had been repressed by centuries of control. She devoted herself, she says in her book, to uncovering "the flow of each person's energy." That would be the key to her emerging knowledge.

The form the knowledge eventually took was the Five Rhythms. Roth explained the connection with dance in an interview with Amazon.com. "The language of movement is rhythm. Rhythm is our mother tongue, and everything is moving in a beat, in a pulse, in a pattern, in a cycle, in a wave. I began to notice that as people surrendered to their dance, their soul became more visible. And when that energy was visible, one could see the patterns of rhythm that were natural to the soul. These five rhythms are Flowing, Staccato, Chaos, Lyrical, and Stillness. And each one is like a state of being."

For the Record . . .

Recording artist, author, theater director, and dance teacher; has released 12 albums with The Mirrors including *Totem*, 1986; *Zone Unknown*, 1997; *Refuge*, 1998 ; founded Raven Recording with husband Robert Ansell, late 1980s; published two books: *Maps to Ecstasy*, 1993, and *Sweat Your Prayers*, 1997; videos include *I Dance The Body Electric*, 1993, and *The Wave: Ecstatic Dance for Body and Soul*, 1994; has conducted workshops in spirituality and the body for over 35 years.

Addresses: *Record company*—Raven Recordings, PO Box 2034, Red Bank, NJ 07701, (973) 642-1979, *email*—ravenrec@panix.com; *website*—http://ravenrecording.com; *Public Relations*—Musik International, 154 Betasso Road, Boulder, CO 80302, (303) 813-1179; *email*—musikint@aol.com.

Her book *Sweat Your Prayers* is an extended look at the meaning and expression of the Five Rhythms. She tends to give them metaphorical descriptions—Flowing is like a field of wheat which a breeze blows over, for example. The most succinct summation appears on the jacket of the book: "FLOWING holds the feminine mysteries, STACCATO explores the masculine mysteries. In CHAOS, we are challenged to integrate these principles into the stream of personal energy. LYRICAL is the rhythm of trance and self-realization. In STILLNESS, the mother of all rhythms, we seek the emptiness within us and take refuge in it." Roth believes that each person was born with a "home base" rhythm, the fingerprint rhythm that characterizes him or her. It's the rhythm we usually exist in, the one we feel most comfortable with. It is important, in Roth's system, to work through the others to open up repressed feelings and to awaken our minds to hidden experience. Dance is the most natural path to this awareness. It uses the body to reach the body and puts us closer to the archetypes associated with each of the five rhythms.

The albums of Gabrielle Roth and the Mirrors are a further exploration of the Five Rhythms. The main purpose of the music is to get you on your feet and moving to the beat. But the records are also a guided tour through the rhythms, an exploration of the self. As such, the beat varies from record to record, or even from song to song. *Zone Unknown* has a distinctly urban flavor; its tracks explore the rhythms Flowing, Staccato and Chaos.

Tongues has more of a world beat sound that moves through the Five Rhythms. The meditative *Stillpoint* concentrates exclusively on Stillness.

Because rhythm is the principle element in all of Roth's work, the beat is the thread that binds all her records. The recording process begins with a drummer, a live drummer, as Roth refuses to use drum machines. That initial rhythm is usually one whose dancability has been proven in one of her workshops or performances. Other percussion is then layered on one instrument at a time, each new player responding to what has already been played. Before a track is cut, Roth has a general idea of what she wants. However, once recording is underway the spirit of the song and the musicians takes over and there is no way to know with precision where they will end up. It is a method that involves much trial and error and a good deal of music is eventually discarded. The result is determined by something like guided serendipity.

On her most recent album, *Refuge*, released in 1998, Roth collaborated with Boris Grebenshikov, once the leader of Aquarium, a leading underground band in the Soviet Union. The record is a 60-plus minute foray into the chants of Tibetan Buddhism. In a press release accompanying *Refuge,* Grebenshikov spoke of his sense of the far-reaching effect of the religion. "On *Refuge* I wanted to share this feeling by taking the mantras from their usual monasterial context—deep overtone chanting vocal and incense—and placing them in a more accessible format without losing their motivation or innate being." The result is an exploration of Stillness which relies on the hypnotic qualities of Grebenshikov's voice and accented by steady, regular drumming.

Roth sees her music as pure dance music and it has become popular in some European rave clubs. But dance will always be more than mere entertainment for her—it is a way of life, a path to self-discovery.

Selected discography

with The Mirrors

Totem, Raven Recording, 1986.
Initiation, Raven Recording, 1988.
Bones, Raven Recording, 1989.
Ritual, Raven Recording, 1990.
Waves, Raven Recording, 1991.
Trance, Raven Recording, 1992.
Luna, Raven Recording, 1994.
Tongues, Raven Recording, 1995.
Endless Wave, Raven Recording, 1996.
Stillpoint, Raven Recording, 1996.

Zone Unknown, Raven Recording, 1997.
Refuge, Raven Recording, 1998.

Books

Sweat Your Prayers, Putnam Books, 1997.
Maps to Ecstasy, Nataraj Publishing, 1993.

Videos

The Wave: Ecstatic Dance for Body and Soul, Raven Recording, 1994.
I Dance The Body Electric, Raven Recording, 1993.

Sources

Books

Roth, Gabrielle, *Sweat Your Prayers*, Putnam Books, 1997.

Periodicals

Body Mind Spirit, March-April, 1998.
Women's Sports and Fitness, January-February, 1999.

Additional information was provided by Raven Recording publicity materials, 1999.

—*Gerald E. Brennan*

Tom Russell

Singer, songwriter

A fascination with American folk culture and traditional music has been the hallmark of singer/songwriter Tom Russell's career. From his recording debut in the mid-1970s onwards, he has grown into the role of a musical storyteller, focusing in particular on America's working class and its struggles. Russell has cultivated an international following for his literate, well-crafted songs, which draw upon both country and acoustic folk styles for inspiration. Besides releasing 14 albums of original material, his compositions have been recorded by Nanci Griffith, Johnny Cash, Suzy Bogguss, Ian Tyson, Jerry Jeff Walker and other respected artists.

A Los Angeles native, Russell felt drawn to America's folk music heritage while still a child. "As a kid, I was interested in early folk songs," he told *Contemporary Musicians* in a telephone interview. "The first songs I heard from my brother were the cowboy ballads like 'Sam Bass' and 'Jesse James,' the ones that were really polished by being handed down over and over. I was so intrigued with how somebody could keep your attention with a narrative through seven or eight verses, whereas very rarely was I as moved by contemporary love songs or pop songs, until they became arty with Dylan or the Beatles."

Russell began performing in 1971 in Vancouver, Canada, where he played country music with various bands in local clubs. "We were backing topless dancers, strip-pers, female impersonators, dog acts and sword swallowers," he recalled in a Hightone Records press biography. From there, he moved to Austin, Texas, in 1974 to take part in the burgeoning country music scene there. Forming a duo with singer/keyboardist Patricia Hardin, he began to perform his own original songs. Russell and Hardin went on to record a pair of albums for the small Demo Records label—*Ring Of Bone* and *Wax Museum*, released in 1976 and 1978, respectively. These albums were critically well-received, but sales were minimal. The duo broke up in San Francisco in 1979.

Putting music aside for a time, Russell moved to New York and pursued fiction writing, securing a deal with the William Morris Agency to help place his manuscripts. When this failed to yield results, he took to driving a taxicab to earn a living. One of his fares was Grateful Dead lyricist Robert Hunter, who encouraged him to resume songwriting after hearing some of his material. By the mid-1980s, he was performing once again, this time in tandem with guitarist Andrew Hardin. Venturing into Europe, he was particularly well-received in Norway, and began to build a loyal audience there through repeated visits.

Russell began to record again, releasing his first album as a solo artist, *Heart On A Sleeve*, in 1984. Several more albums followed, including *Road To Baymon* and *Poor Man's Dream.* These song collections were in a country-rock vein, although Russell's version of this musical style was uniquely his own. His emphasis on writing about downtrodden American characters in real-life terms led him back to traditional Western music. *Cowboy Real*, released by Philo Records in 1991, started Russell in a new artistic direction that lasted for the next several years.

During this period, Russell enjoyed success as a collaborator with other singer/songwriters, most notably folk artist Nanci Griffith and cowboy balladeer Ian Tyson. "Outbound Plane," a song co-written by Russell and Griffith, became a top ten country hit for singer Suzy Bogguss in 1993. A Russell/Tyson collaboration, the Western-themed "Navajo Rug," was selected as the 1987 Country Music Association single of the year.

A more unlikely partnership came when Russell joined forces with Barrence Whitfield, a flamboyant R&B vocalist. "He's sort of a modern Little Richard," Russell said of Whitfield to *Contemporary Musicians*. "He wanted to do something country-oriented, so he contacted me, and what we came up with was this real eclectic, good-timey blend of roots music." The pair released their *Hillbilly Voodoo* CD on the East Side Digital label in 1993,

For the Record . . .

Born March 5, 1950, in Los Angeles, CA.

Began performing in 1971; released two albums on Demo Records as part of duo with Patricia Hardin, 1976 and 1978; released first solo album, *Heart On A Sleeve*, 1984; had hit single as co-writer of Suzy Bogguss single "Outbound Plane," 1993; collaborated on two albums with singer Barrence Whitfield, 1993 and 1994; signed with Hightone, released *Rose of The San Juaquin*, 1995; co-produced and performed on *Tulare Dust: A Songwriters Tribute To Merle Haggard*, 1995; released *The Man From God Knows Where*, 1999.

Awards: CMA award for Single Of The Year for "Navajo Rug," 1987; ASCAP Country Award for "Outbound Plane," 1993.

Addresses: *Record company*—Hightone Records, 220 4th St., Oakland, CA 94607. *Newsletter*—Dark Angel, P.O. Box 16083, Shawnee, KS 66203. *Website*—www.tomrussell.com.

followed by *Cowboy Mambo* in 1994. Russell joined forces with fellow singer/songwriter Dave Alvin in 1994 to co-produce *Tulare Dust: A Songwriters' Tribute To Merle Haggard* for Hightone Records. This album featured a number of artists interpreting Haggard's classic country tunes, including Russell himself. *Tulare Dust* went on to top the Americana radio format charts. Russell's association with Hightone continued when he released *The Rose Of San Joaquin*, a contemporary folk/country album, on that label in 1995.

Yet another rewarding collaboration for Russell during this period was with Canadian singer/songwriter Sylvia Fricker, former wife of Ian Tyson. In addition to co-writing songs with Fricker, he also collaborated with her on *And Then I Wrote: The Songwriter Speaks*, an anthology of quotes by songwriters about various aspects of their craft. Music remained Russell's main career, and he began working on a major song cycle dealing with American history in the early 1990s. Before this was completed, he released a pair of albums on Hightone featuring re-recordings of earlier songs, *The Long Way Around* and *Song Of The West*. From there, he concentrated on the ambitious work that would eventually be released as *The Man From God Knows Where* in 1999.

As he worked on the project, Russell delved deeper into the stories of his immigrant ancestors from Ireland and Norway. "After reading the diaries of my great grandfathers, the soundscapes and poetic ideas faded, blending into the real voices of my ancestors," he wrote in an essay included in Hightone press materials. "I read between the lines; added a touch of rhyme. I drew them out." Several songs dealt with Russell's father Charlie, a salesman and colorful character who had seen the highs and lows of the American dream during his lifetime. "I couldn't have written about my father until he passed away in 1997," he told *Contemporary Musicians*. "I'd had a lot of resentment towards him, and it enabled me to go back and deal with it. It's been therapeutic for me as a writer."

The Man From God Knows Where was recorded in a seventeenth-century baronial home in Norway under the auspices of a Norwegian record company, KKV. Besides Russell, the cast of featured vocalists on the album included American folk singers Iris DeMent and Dave Van Ronk, Irish artist Delores Keane, and Norwegian performers Sondre Bratland and Kari Bremnes. A sampling of poet Walt Whitman's voice taken from an 1890s-era wax cylinder recording was also included. Hightone released the album in the United States in March of 1999 to a favorable response. In its review, *Atlantic Monthly* gave warm praise to Russell, "whose reach is both wide and deep, balancing the grand sweep of history with individual tragedies of his ancestors broken on the frontier. Gary von Tersch of the *San Francisco Chronicle* felt that the album "should be required listening for every American history student."

Russell toured actively after *The Man From God Knows Where* was released, and looked forward to his next recording project. In his *Contemporary Musicians* interview, he reaffirmed his bond with his audience. "They're eclectic," he said. "You can go to one of my concerts and they'll be quite a few young people who may be discovering Hank Williams or Dave Alvin or Tom Russell, and then there's the older audience that was into folk music in the '60s. It's not a pop audience that's coming because this is getting a tremendous amount of radio airplay. It's the people who really want to seek out alternative roots music."

Selected discography

(with Patricia Hardin) *Ring Of Bone* and *Wax Museum* (reissue on one CD), Dark Angel, 1994.
Heart On A Sleeve, Bear Family, 1984.
Cowboy Real, Philo, 1991.

Rose Of The San Joaquin, Hightone, 1995.
The Long Way Around, Hightone, 1997.
Song Of The West, Hightone, 1997.
The Man From God Knows Where, Hightone, 1999.

Sources

Books

Tyson, Sylvia, *And Then I Wrote: The Songwriter Speaks*,
  Arsenal-Pulp Press, 1995.

Periodicals

Atlantic Monthly, April 1999.
Billboard, February 27, 1999.
San Francisco Chronicle, March 14, 1999.

Additional information was obtained from Hightone Records
and from a phone interview with Russell in April 1999.

—*Barry Alfonso*

Rusted Root

Rock group

Photo by Jack Hanrahan. AP/Wide World Photos. Reproduced by permission.

Rusted Root's tribal, drum enthused songs with melodic harmonies give the six-member group a uniquely earthy sound. The group counts African, Middle Eastern, and Latin American themes among its influences and uses them to form the music's spiritual center. Rusted Root has gained the attention of such big-name acts as Robert Plant and Jimmy Page, The Grateful Dead, The Allman Brothers, Sting, and The Dave Matthews Band, all of which the group has toured with.

Rusted Root got its start when lead singer and song writer Michael Glabicki and Liz Berlin, percussionist and vocals, discovered a mutual appreciation for interesting musical instruments after meeting at a political rally in Pittsburgh, Pennsylvania. They combined their vocal talents and looked for other musicians with similar styles. They found bassist Patrick Norman and Jim Dovonan at the University of Pittsburgh. Donovan was studying classical drumming while Norman was a jazz enthusiast. Now calling themselves Rusted Root, the band entered a local music contest and came in fourth out of more than 100 hopefuls. In 1993, Jim DiSpirito, an ethnomusicologist and percussionist who studied music in India, joined the band. By this time, Rusted Root had already developed a club following.

A unique quality about Rusted Root is each member's ability to play a variety of instruments like flute, penny whistle, acoustic guitar, banjo, mandolin, and hundreds of percussion toys like a washboard or bongos. According to Glabicki in an article in *Musician* magazine, "Switching instruments can give you a feel for how people perceive what you're doing, and help you understand what they need from you, and give everyone else an understanding of what you want out of a song… It's healthy to change things up like that." It is reported that Rusted Root uses up to 60 different musical instruments in a single show. Such diverse talent allows the band to pursue their successful global sound by playing Latin, African, and Middle Eastern rhythms, among other culturally diverse sounds. The band has been favorably compared to David Byrne, Peter Gabriel, and Arrested Development. Liz Berlin explained why Rusted Root sound the way they do in an interview with National Public Radio: "(We're) trying to create something we couldn't hear elsewhere. (We were) just trying to make sounds that I wasn't hearing that I wanted to hear." With heavy emphasis on percussion and harmonies, the band has released four albums since their inception in 1990 and a couple of EPs. The band has toured extensively around the country, often sharing the stage with performers like Hot Tuna and The Allman Brothers. They describe their sound as "body moving music." Rusted Root's combination of intriguing lyrics with difficult and intense songs allow them to be at the forefront of a new musical genre, a new world beat, so to speak.

As an offering to their loyal and growing fan base, Rusted Root released *Cruel Sun,* a self-produced effort on the Blue Duck label in 1990. The album was soon heard on more than the local college radio stations; it went on to sell more than 100,000 copies. The album and their performances quickly caught the attention of record executives at Mercury. Rusted Root released their major label debut, *When I Woke,* in 1994. The album was recorded live in six weeks in the inspirational Toad Hall in Pasadena, California, with all members playing together and doing very few takes. *When I Woke* has reconditioned versions of songs off *Cruel Sun* like "Cat Turned Blue" and "Back to Earth." The album, produced with Bill Bottrell (Tom Petty and Sheryl Crow), has gone on to sell over two million copies. According to one online review, "*When I Woke* will conjure up memories of early Jefferson Airplane, will swing you like Poi Dog Pondering, and will command your attention like The Talking Heads." One prize from the album is the eight-minute "Cruel Sun," an enchanting and arousing ensemble with flutes and acoustic guitar. "Drum Trip" is an excellent example of

the band's ability to cross international lines with musical notes and words. Glabicki has been described as having "fluid, expressive vocals (that) soar above melodies and wriggle between rhythms with both grace and power." By his own words, Glabicki calls his music "very visual, and I am trying to explain what I see in my head."

Many Rusted Root song lyrics are hard to decipher, as on *When I Woke.* Glabicki admits in a web page review that many times, there are no words at all, just syllables "that sound right with the music." A prime example of syllable lyrics is "Send Me On My Way." According to legend, Glabicki just never quite got around to replacing the syllables he injected into the music. Some of the songs are just chants, and usually the entire band joins in on the vocals. "Drum Trip" is an excellent example of the band's ability to cross international borders with musical notes and words.

The sophomoric effort *Remember* was released on the Mercury label in 1996 after being recorded at the famed Skywalker Ranch, owned by movie producer George Lucas. It was produced with the help of ex-Talking Head member Jerry Harrison. Harrison had also worked with Live and Crash Test Dummies. The hit single "Virtual Reality" can also be found on the *Twister* soundtrack. Rusted Root has been featured on other movie and TV soundtracks, including *Home for the Holidays* and the children's film Mathilda.

In 1998, the band returned to their roots by recording their third album for Mercury in their hometown of Pittsburgh. Pat Moran and Susan Rogers, who have collectively worked with such heavy hitters as Robert Plant, Iggy Pop, Prince and David Bryne, among others, produced their self-titled album. The third album offers a rousing rendition of the Rolling Stone classic "You Can't Always Get What You Want," which they recorded with Hot Tuna. Rusted Root met up with Hot Tuna while on tour with the Furthur Festival. Rusted Root often played the classic Rolling Stones "You Can't Always Get What You Want" at the end of their set and it became a tradition.

Rusted Root has toured often and extensively since its infancy. Early on in their musical career Rusted Root was "discovered" by legendary musical giants, like Jimmy Page and Robert Plant, and invited to tour along. They have been seen on tour with big-name acts like the Allman Brothers, Phish, Toad the Wet Sprocket, and Jewel. The band was also part of various summer tours packages like the Furthur Fest and spent two years touring with the Horde Fest. "It's kind of cool to be out there, just playing with Jimmy Page and Robert Plant, the Allman Brothers and the Grateful Dead. It's kind of a trip ... to like see these people you kind of grew up with and you're having conversations and jammin' with," Glabicki said on National Public Radio.

In the nine years since they began exploding on the live circuit, Rusted Roots has developed a strong following of fans, something akin to Grateful Dead fans. That could be because Rusted Root sometimes jams like the Grateful Dead in a long, continuous exploration into sounds and styles. "I've never actually seen a (Grateful Dead) show, and don't know any of the albums," reported Jim Donovan in an Internet interview at pweb.netcom.com. "We're not in any way, shape or form the Grateful Dead, nor claim to be, or sound anything like them—just one listen and you will know that—but they had a great idea about community and we are trying to establish something similar to that, in that we like to bring people together for a common thing … that being the music." Rusted Root had the honor of opening for the Dead at their final show before Jerry Garcia died, at the Three Rivers Stadium in Pittsburgh. "While their live shows don't have the same what-will-they-play-next? variation as Phish or the Grateful Dead, they do consistently crank out powerful performances. Their multi-layered rhythm section bangs away on a variety of odd-shaped percussion instruments while the bass drum holds it all together by thudding away every single beat," wrote Glenn Ricci in an online music review at http://members.tripod.com.

Even as their music gets the blood pumping and the feet going, the band will not tolerate slam dancing or moshing during their performances. Rusted Root reportedly walked off the stage at a 1994 show with the Violent Femmes because the crowd was too chaotic. Often times, Glabicki will ask the audience to "take a deep breath and move back three steps" so no one will get injured.

Because of their global perspective, Rusted Root is very world-friendly. Many of their lyrics, if you can decipher them, deal with environmental issues or social issues. During tours, the band will often ask fans to bring in donations for a local food bank. Their web site offers links to eco-friendly web sites, like Greenpeace, and some of the band's merchandise—T-shirts and hats— are made from hemp. It is their way, said Patrick

Norman, of educating people on important issues, other than what is going on in their small corner of the world. For Rusted Root, with their global tribe of fans and music, that isn't a difficult thing to do.

Selected discography

Cruel Sun, Blue Duck, 1990.
When I Woke, Mercury/Polygram, 1994.
Remember, Mercury/Polygram, 1996.
Rusted Root, Mercury/Polygram, 1998.

Sources

Periodicals

Iowa State Daily, November 12, 1996.
Michigan Daily, November 10, 1998.
Musician, April 1999.
Newsday, August 19, 1996; July 2, 1998.

Online

"Rusted Root Interview," http://pweb.netcome.com /~jwjenks/mikejim.html(April 13, 1999).
"Rusted Root: 'When I Wokr'," http://members.tripod.com/~agentile/articles/wiw-review-4html (April 13, 1999).
"Rusted Root," *iMusic Indie Showcase,* http://imusic.com/showcase (April 13, 1999)
"Rusted Root Bio," http://dead.net/cavenWeb/furthur/rustedrootbio.html (April 13, 1999).
"Rusted Root Articles," *Iowa State Daily,* http://www.publlic.istate.edu (April 13, 1999).
"Rusted Root," http://www.mercuryrecords.com/merc...tists/rusted_root/rusted_root.html (April 13, 1999).
"Rusted Root Contact," http://rustedroot.com/rootcontact.html (April 13, 1999).

Additional information was taken from a National Public Radio interview with Rusted Root, September 15, 1995.

—Gretchen A. Van-Monette

Rebecca St. James

Singer, songwriter

Australian-born Rebecca St. James has stood apart from her peers in contemporary Christian music by virtue of both her youth and her uncompromising evangelical focus. Beginning her recording career at age 16, she has gained an international following for her energetic, highly contemporary sound. The dance grooves and European-style techno-pop arrangements of St. James's CDs are all utilized in the service of an up-front Christian message of faith and morality. Her mixture of ministry and entertainment has won her recognition as an up-and-coming evangelist as well as a recording artist and touring performer. According to *Christianity Today*, "Rebecca St. James has been described as part Amy Grant, part Mother Teresa, and part Billy Graham—with some smoke and lasers thrown in."

St. James is explicit about using her music to stir the religious fervor of her audiences. Her concerts combine a sophisticated pop/rock stage show with preaching and question-and-answer sessions. Performing with a Bible in hand, she reads from scripture between songs and calls out to Christians to renew their faith. As she told interviewer Liz Kelly in *CCM*, "I really feel that I am called—and hey, I may be wrong—to encourage believers to be radical about their faith, to be bold ... I can't convince some 16-year-old, non-Christian guy to come and listen to my music, but if I can encourage believers to reach out to the world about the love of Christ... who knows? Revival could break out." Christian author Joshua Harris is among those who have praised St. James's commitment to her message, commenting in *Charisma* that "A lot of Christian music artists are shying away, not wanting to 'preach' to people. But Rebecca is very vocal and very real. People come to her concerts not just for the music but because they feel connected to her."

The call to musical missionary service has been a part of St. James's life since childhood. Her father, David Smallbone, helped to nurture her talent while working as a Christian concert promoter in Sydney, Australia. By age 13, she was singing on tour in her native country with international gospel star Carman. Further breakthroughs as a singer were interrupted when her family lost their home and savings after a failed concert venture. Moving to the United States and settling near Nashville, the Smallbones took on house cleaning and yard work jobs to make ends meet. "Sometimes we didn't know where the next meal was coming from," St. James told *Charisma* writer Lindy Warren. "We'd just pray as a family and have devotions, and people would drop groceries on our doorstep, give us furniture or send us checks in the mail that would just cover our bills. I can say to my peers, 'I've seen God at work.'"

Surviving through such hard times with her family, St. James rebounded and signed a recording contract at age 16 with Nashville-based ForeFront Records. Her 1994 self-titled debut album established her as a dynamic young Christian singer/songwriter and earned her a Dove Award nomination from the Gospel Music Association for New Artist of the Year. *God*, her second album, was released in 1996 and won her further recognition and acclaim, selling over 350,000 copies and receiving both a Grammy Award nomination for Best Rock/Gospel Album and a Dove Award nomination for Female Vocalist of the Year. 1998 saw the release of her third album, *Christmas*.

From the start, St. James has avoided diluting her gospel message for a wider audience. Her musical thrust, though, has become more experimental, taking on the computerized sheen of 1990s dance/pop and alternative rock with the help of producer Tedd T. and engineer Julian Kindred. Her 1998 release, *Pray*, was a pronounced leap in this direction, surrounding such songs as "Mirror" (a number one Christian pop radio hit), "Love To Love You" and the title track with drum loops and synthesizer flourishes. "I actually quite like the contradiction of having music that's [techno-sounding] with lyrics that are so straight ahead, so simple," she told *CCM*. "In the Christian life there are lots of contradictions to the world.... I love the contradictions of the world to God's way, so in a way I'm kind of pulling from that."

As St. James's recording career has taken off, she's used her growing celebrity to spread Christian teachings

For the Record . . .

Born July 26, 1977 in Sydney, Australia; daughter of David and Hellen Smallbone; five siblings.

Performed on tour with Carman in Australia, 1990; moved to Nashville, TN, with her family, 1991; released self-titled debut album on ForeFront, 1994; released *God*, 1996 published book *40 Days With God*, 1996; released *Christmas*, 1997; published book *You're The Voice - 40 More Days With God*, 1997; released *Pray*, 1998.

Addresses: *Record company*—ForeFront, 201 Seaboard Lane, Franklin, TN 37067.

sage because so many people think they're alone and that they are the only ones taking that stand when really there are thousands out there who are committed to the same thing, to wait."

Holding true to her beliefs while basking in the glory of popularity has been an ongoing challenge for St. James. "I'm not entirely comfortable on stage," she confessed to Tom Neven of *Christian Entertainment*. "I never set out to be a pop star." The content of her music, rather than the trappings of fame, have continued to be her stated focus. As she told *CCM,* "I have people come up to me and say, 'Thank you for putting my prayers into song.' That's cool to me. That's successful songwriting to me, or success in being faithful to hear from God."

Selected discography

Rebecca St. James, ForeFront, 1994.
God, ForeFront, 1996.
Christmas, ForFront, 1997.
Pray, ForeFront, 1998.

Books

40 Days With God, Thomas Nelson Publishing, 1996.
You're The Voice - 40 More Days With God, Thomas Nelson Publishing, 1997.

Sources

CCM, November 1998.
Charisma, April 1999.
Christian Entertainment, August 11, 1998.
Christian Single, August 1997.
Christianity Today, November 11, 1996.

Additional information was provided by ForeFront publicity materials.

—*Barry Alfonso*

beyond music. Her youth-oriented devotional book *40 Days With God* was issued by Nashville-based Thomas Nelson Publishing in 1996, followed in 1997 by *You're The Voice - 40 More Days With God.* She has also served as spokesperson for the *Promise Bible For Students* and, with her family, has established the charity organization Compassion International. For such efforts, she was recognized as one of the "Top 50 Up and Coming Evangelical Leaders Under 40" by *Christianity Today* in 1996.

St. James's tours have been family affairs, with her brothers Daniel, Ben, Joel, Josh and Luke helping out with stage managing, lighting, background singing and other duties. The Smallbone family remains a close-knit one, and the values of parents David and Helen have been embraced by Rebecca. During concerts and interviews, she has spoken freely about her lifestyle, particularly regarding dating and marriage. "I get a lot of feedback when I talk about [how] true love waits and virginity and [the fact that] I'm going to stay a virgin until I'm married," she told Deborah Evans Price in *Christian Single.* "I think people find hope in that mes-

Sebadoh

Indie rock group

Tracing the history of Sebadoh is akin to unraveling a complex cloth. Structured with an eclectic musical warp and weft, the only constant in the group is founder Lou Barlow. Sebadoh is credited with bringing lo-fi music to prominence in the 1990s, but their sound has evolved into a mature indie rock.

Founded in 1987 in Amherst, Massachusetts, Sebadoh is the brainchild of Barlow, who *Magnet* called "one of indie-pop's most talented tunesmiths." During his days performing as bassist for Dinosaur Jr., Barlow experimented with personalized songwriting and four-track recording as a creative outlet. He welcomed artistic tensions in Dinosaur Jr. With help from Eric Gaffney on drums, Sebadoh made two cassettes of bedroom-recorded folk songs and shopped them around to area record stores. The idea behind this low-tech approach to creating an album, Jason Loewenstein said in *Scene*, was that "... people could take heart in getting a guitar and starting a revolution." Homestead added the group to its roster in 1989 with the release of a CD combining these cassette recordings called *The Freed Weed*.

Barlow remained in Dinosaur Jr. and relations between he and J. Macius,—Dinosaur Jr. front man—were strained at best. A 1996 *Magnet* article described the relationship as having ultimately retreated to "a crabbed, wordless place." Barlow said, "After our first tour things were never the same between us. He just couldn't handle every-

one's personal quirks and he was really unforgiving. He never understood the beauty of tolerance. Me and J just sort of stopped talking after that." Tensions came to a head onstage. Macius, irritated with Barlow, hit him with a guitar during a Connecticut performance. Macius abruptly fired Barlow in 1989, leaving Barlow free to record and perform with Sebadoh. Rather than hearing the news from Macius, Barlow learned he'd been canned via MTV News; he was told falsely by Macius that the group was breaking up. He would later sue to recover his royalties from the group.

Sebadoh recruited Jason Loewenstein from Dissident Voices as bassist for *Sebadoh III*. The addition of Loewenstein started a musical give-and-take between members that created what is best described as a hardcore punk sound. This was fueled by Barlow's anger at Macius as much as their own fondness for "musical terrorism." Growing internal tensions made for additional unrest. Sebadoh's music during this time was described in *Magnet* as "the unlikely intersections of folk, punk and pot—ranging from screeching sludgefest to winsome folk rock—and slowly but surely, Barlow went from being known as the guy who got thrown out of Dinosaur Jr. to the guy who writes those incredibly beautiful songs on the Sebadoh records."

Sub Pop Records signed the group away from Homestead in 1992. Soon after, relations with Gaffney became strained. Gaffney wavered and wanted to stop touring. He quit the band three times between 1990 and 1993, and was temporarily replaced by drummer Bob Fay, but eventually returned again. According to *Magnet*, "The final straw came in the form of a letter Gaffney sent to Barlow and Loewenstein informing them that he would no longer tour, and asking for a third of all future recording budgets so that he could record his songs separately. 'We were just like, "He doesn't want to be in the band? F--- him,"' says Barlow incredulously." Barlow says that he has tried to find Gaffney and give him his share of royalties. Gaffney left in 1994 after recording *Bubble and Scrape* and was replaced permanently by Fay.

Harmacy was released in 1997. *Stereo-Type*'s Jack Rabid called it Sebadoh's "finest hour" with "delicate, beautiful pop moments. Rabid went on to say "*Harmacy* caught fire in the press, but to the surprise of everyone, the LP failed to root in radio or on MTV, leaving the band in big fish/small pondville." The band seemed to go through drummers likes a '90s indie rock version of Spinal Tap. Fay was sacked just prior to the recording of *The Sebadoh* and Russ Pollard became drummer. It is an issue Barlow doesn't like to discuss, knowing all too well the pain of being fired himself. Rather than dwell on Fay's departure, he told the *Houston Press* that Pollard's

---

Members include **Lou Barlow** (group founder; married: Kathleen Billus), vocals and guitar; **Bob Fay** (joined 1990, fired 1998); **Eric Gaffney** (1987-1993), drums; **Jason Loewenstein** (joined group in 1989), bass, drums; **Russ Pollard** (joined group 1998), drums.

Group founded in Amherst, Massachusetts, 1987, by Lou Barlow with Eric Gaffney; Jason Loewenstein later added to line up; released two self-produced cassettes; signed by Homestead, 1989; after a couple of releases, group was signed by Sub Pop Records in 1992; released *Smash Your Head on the Punk Rock*, 1992; Gaffney left group and was replaced; group recorded *Bakesale*, 1994, and *Harmacy*, 1996; Fay fired, 1998; Pollard joined band, 1998; released *The Sebadoh*, 1999.

Addresses: *Record company*—Sub Pop Records, 1932 First Avenue, Suite 1103, Seattle, WA 98101; *Publicity*—Girlie Action Media, Inc., 270 Lafayette Street, Suite 1302, New York, NY 10012.

contributions to the group "made something that could have sputtered to a stop find a new life."

Barlow said that he and Sebadoh have been evolving and growing up. "I feel like I've gone through musical puberty in the last year," he is quoted as saying in record company publicity materials announcing the release of *The Sebadoh*. "Rather than being this center of confusion maybe I'd rather be a center of inspiration." At least one newspaper headline—which appeared in Cleveland's *Scene*—summed up how critics view this older, getting wiser group: "Folk Terrorists Find Peace: Sebadoh survives near-breakups and cleans up its act." Critic Marc Lefkowitz called *The Sebadoh* their "most accomplished collaborative effort to date" and said that the group "after ten years of slogging out punk for punk's sake ... has made a subtle but conscious shift toward a more textured and, I daresay, commercial sound."

Influences and groups the band enjoy range widely. They include Brazilian metal band Sepultura, 1970s easy rockers Bread, The Byrds, and the Eagles, as well as an unlikely mix of Mission of Burma, Gang of Four, Devo, The Minutemen, Theolonious Monk, Stereolab, Kraftwerk, and Harry Partch.

Group members, as if not prolific enough in their recording with Sebadoh, also regularly play in side projects including Folk Implosion, Sentridoh, Sparcalepsy, and Deluxxe Folk Implosion, among others. Barlow's stint with Folk Implosion resulted in his penning most of the songs for the 1995 film soundtrack, *Kids*. "Natural One" became a hit.

The Sebadoh doesn't seem to indicate Sebadoh has abandoned its punk sensibilities, the group is simply refining them. "I'm kind of sick of yelling," Loewenstein told Jane Ratcliff of the *Detroit News*. "It really came down to technical stuff—like I couldn't hear myself in the monitors on stage so I'd have to yell. Now we have to play nice places so I can sing." Houston Press writer Jason Simutis explained the often hard to describe group succinctly. "Each Sebadoh release is an amalgam of noises, some midtempo indie rock and a small percentage of intimate, crushing love songs written by Barlow .... The tunes also are less and less lo-fi in fits and starts. Sensitive bookish indie-rock boys and girls eat it up, making Sebadoh a star of the underground."

Selected discography

The Freed Weed, Homestead, 1989.
Sebadoh III, Homestead, 1991.
Smash Your Head on the Punk Rock, Sub Pop Records 1992.
(contributor) *Afternoon Delight* (compilation), Sub Pop Records 1992.
Bubble and Scrape, Sub Pop Records, 1993.
(contributor) *Curtis W. Pitts: Sub Pop Employee of the Month* (compilation), Sub Pop Records, 1993.
Bakesale, Sub Pop Records, 1994.
(contributor) *KRCW Rare Air, Volume 2* (compilation), Mammoth, 1995.
Harmacy, Sub Pop Records, 1996.
The Sebadoh, Sub Pop Records, 1999.

Sources

Books

Erlewine, Michael, Vladimir Bogdanov, and Chris Woodstra, editors., *All Music Guide to Rock: The Best CDs, Albums & Tapes: Rock, Pop, Soul, R&B and Rap,* Miller Freeman Books, 1995.

Periodicals

Detroit Free Press, March 5, 1999.
Detroit News, March 5, 1999.

Houston Press, March 18, 1999.
Huh, September 1996.
Magnet, October-November 1996.
Request, October 1996.
Scene (Cleveland,OH), March 4, 1999.
Stereo-Type (Kingston,PA), March 1999.

Additional information provided by Sub Pop Records publicity materials, 1999.

—*Linda Dailey Paulson*

Bola Sete

Guitar

Bola Sete's career in music was artistic and spiritual journey that began in dire physical poverty, moved through success as a popular musician in his homeland Brazil and the United States, until the discovery of yoga and meditation put him in touch with the deep personal and traditional wellsprings from which he fashioned guitar music uniquely his own. Bola Sete has been called a jazz musician. But the music he created in the last decade and a half of his life had little in common with the harmonic or improvisational structures of jazz. He has been called a father of New Age Music. But while he certainly provided an inspiration for artists such as George Winston, Sete's music has a raw, virile power missing in nearly all New Age compositions. As with all performers who create ineffable music out of the personal vocabulary of their lives and experiences, it is better simply to *hear* Bola Sete's than to try to force it into meaningless categories.

Bola Sete was born Djalma de Andrade, the one son in a family of seven children. The family was black and poor, and they didn't always have enough food. But there was an abundance of music. Nearly every family member played an instrument, and on Sundays they would get together and play. While one such family jam session was in progress, six-year-old Djalma was told to go to bed. When he climbed in he found a *cavaquinho*, a Brazilian stringed instrument very similar to a ukulele, that someone had laid there. It was the right size for a child's hands. Djalma was able to work out a couple chords himself, his uncle showed him some others. Before long, he had his own *cavaquinho*. When he was nine, he was given a guitar for Christmas.

When Djalma was ten, he was taken in by foster parents, a well-to-do married couple. They taught Djalma and their other foster children proper manners, sent him to high school, and introduced him to classical music. He was performing with a semi-professional group that played Brazilian folk music and sambas when World War Two broke out. His foster parents sent him into hiding in the Brazilian interior so he would not be conscripted into the military. All the time he continued to play guitar, adding folk songs and classical pieces to his growing repertoire. When he returned to Rio at the end of the war, his foster parents wanted him to pursue a career in law. He had his sights set on becoming a musician, however, and attended first the National School of Music in Rio, then the conservatory in Sao Paolo where the guitar teachers were better. While he was in school, he performed regularly with the Brazilian national radio, playing whatever music was set in front of him, and in the process learning to sight read as easily as others read newspapers or magazines.

Life in South America was booming—for the upper classes, at least—after the war, and Djalma had no trouble finding work playing in the scores of night clubs and hotels opening in Brazil and Uruguay. He was playing with a swing-style dance band and with a smaller group within the band, performances that were often arduous. He described the work in *Down Beat*: "The band would play a tune, then the quartet, then the band, then the quartet—for an hour without stopping. Then finally we'd get a 20-minute break. I play the amplified guitar with the quartet, then turn off the volume and play rhythm guitar with the big band. No stopping. Hard work." The experience with the radio and the big band paid off. Individuals in the music business took notice and set him up with his own sextet. The coal black Djalma fronted a combo of white musicians, and led to his new name. In Brazilian billiards the seven ball—or *bola sete*—is the black ball. He didn't care for name Bola Sete because it called attention to his blackness.

Sete toured Europe with the sextet, and when he returned to Brazil he formed a new one which was soon playing at hotels throughout Latin America, Harley Watson attended one show, and by 1959, he would be manager of the Palace Hotel in San Francisco. Bola Sete was hired to play the Tudor Room, the Palace's new cocktail lounge. He played weekends, Thursday through Saturday, five until nine in the evening, fighting the noise from the bar and the kitchen. Occasionally he would just practice

For the Record . . .

Born Djalma de Andrade, July 16, 1923, Rio de Janeiro, Brazil; (died February 14, 1987, Greenbrae, CA); married Anne Hurd, 1969. *Education:* Attended National School of Music, Rio de Janeiro, Brazil; Conservatory of Music, Sao Paulo, Brazil.

Received first guitar for Christmas, 1932; played in semi-professional bands around Rio, 1940-41; toured Europe and Latin America with two sextets, middle to late 1940s; played regularly at Tudor Room, Palace Hotel in San Francisco; met and recorded with Dizzy Gillespie, 1962; first appeared at Monterey Jazz Festival, 1962; signed with Fantasy Records, 1963; joined Vince Guaraldi, 1964; formed own Brazilian trio, 1967; *Ocean* sessions at Fantasy studios, 1972; released *Ocean*, Takoma Records, 1975; released *Jungle Suite*, Jungle Cat Records, 1985.

scales for the indifferent crowd. One night in 1962, however, Dizzy Gillespie came to dinner at the Palace and heard Sete play. When his sets had ended for the night, Sete would head over to the Black Hawk where Gillespie's group was performing. After his San Francisco show was over Gillespie sent word to Sete inviting the guitarist to play on his forthcoming album, *New Wave.* The following September, Gillespie arranged for Sete to perform at the Monterey Jazz Festival.

Sete's popularity was growing. He returned to San Francisco and played for audiences who were interested in listening to his music. Fantasy Records signed him to a recording contract and Fantasy's Max Weiss hatched the idea of joining Sete with the Vince Guaraldi Trio, whom Weiss managed. It was an inspired combination. They made their first public appearance on March 6, 1964 and for the three years played to enthusiastic crowds throughout the country. *Down Beat* described a typical concert in the mid-1960s: "First comes the Vince Guaraldi trio [playing ballads]....With no fanfare at all, Sete appears on stand, ensconces himself on a stool out front ... and makes the group a bossa nova quartet for a while....The other musicians then leave the stand to Sete, and he launches into a solo set....[bassist Monty] Budwig and [drummer Colin] Bailey rejoin the guitarist....Guaraldi returns to piano bench almost unnoticed. Then in a leap of rushing excitement, he is back in the ball game and into a solo of much freshness and imagination."

In 1967, Sete left Guaraldi and put together his own Brazilian trio with Sebastiao Neto and drummer Paulhino. When the group broke up later in the 1960s, Sete was middle-aged, overweight, and at a crossroads. He stopped performing and started meditating and doing hatha yoga regularly. He gave up his meat and potatoes diet and became a vegetarian. The regimen not only enabled him to drop fifty pounds, he was also able to better control his asthma which had been aggravated by years of night club smoke. In 1969 he proposed marriage to his friend of seven years, Anne. She had turned down his proposal earlier in the year. But he explained to her that the rigid physical discipline he had undertaken broke through the armor around his heart. It would soon help him produce the most amazing music of his career as well.

He returned to music in 1970, touring Mexico—where he was extremely popular—with Stan Getz and other jazz artists. In 1972, he put together a quintet and cut another album, *Shebaba,* for Fantasy. With rock topping the charts and fusion taking over jazz, Sete's soft Brazilian sound was predestined to flop. Financial problems finally led him to break the group up and for a couple years he toured California colleges as a solo act.

Troubled increasingly by his asthma, Sete experimented with different positions. He noticed that the traditional classical guitar position—sitting on a stool, hunched over the guitar, right foot propped up on wooden block—impaired his breathing after a while. He taught himself to play sitting in the full lotus position used in yoga, with legs crossed and spine perfectly straight, and believed that the position enabled him to act better as a channel for the music he was creating. He played a series of concerts with John Handy, sitar player Ali Akbar Khan, percussionist Zhakir Hussein, and others, entirely in the lotus position. And like his entire life, Sete practiced four to six hours a day, six days a week.

Around 1974, guitarist John Fahey saw Sete performing his solo act in a club in San Francisco. Greatly impressed, Fahey contacted Sete and asked if he would be interested in recording for Fahey's Takoma label. Sete offered a set of tapes he had recorded for Fantasy in 1972. The music was a mixture of Brazilian folk music, classical guitar, and jazz standards. Fantasy hadn't known what to make of it and Sete had ended up buying the session tapes back from the label. Fahey released part of them in 1975 as *Ocean*. While not a popular success, the album was immensely influential among musicians. Fahey began performing his own versions of the *Ocean* pieces on his records and in concert. Pianist George Winston, the Windham Hill label's first star artist, was also taken by Sete's album and played the pieces on his records. His influence on Windham Hill artists—the label eventually re-released *Ocean* as well—have led some to call Sete the father of New Age music. But the different strains running through the performance's on the album add up to music far richer and more complex than any simple label can do justice to.

By the early 1980s, public performing had become such of a strain on Sete's health that he gave it up completely. He continued to practice, however, and to compose. Around 1984 he went into the studio one last time and cut *Jungle Suite* for George Winston's Dancing Cat label. Sete got all the music onto tape in a single take, a remarkable achievement until one considers that he had been rehearsing it daily for years and probably knew that his fragile health would give only one opportunity to do it. Interestingly, for *Jungle Suite* Sete replaced the gut strings on his classical guitar with steel strings to get a crisper sound. It was the last album he released. Thanks to the beta recorder George Winston gave him, which Sete used to set up a home studio, a good deal of unreleased solo music exists which his widow Anne Sete hopes one day to release on CD. She already plans to re-release Sete's last two albums in the fall of 1999: the complete *Ocean* sessions, including eight never-before-released tracks, under the title *Ocean Memories,* and *Jungle Suite,* with one bonus track, under the title *Guitar Moon Suite.* Both albums were produced by George Winston.

Bola Sete suffered from lung cancer most of the last decade of his life. He fought it with yoga and meditation, controlling his labored breathing with pranayama techniques. He continued to practice and play guitar in his home until his death on February 14, 1987.

Selected discography

Bossa Nova, Original Jazz Classics, 1962.
Bola Sete Bossa Nova, Fantasy, 1963.
Tour De Force Fantasy, 1964.
(/w Vince Guaraldi), *Live at El Matador,* Fantasy, 1966.
The Imcomparable Bola Sete, Fantasy, 1965.
Autentico, Fantasy, 1966.
Bola Sete at the Monterey Jazz Festival, Verve, 1967.
The Solo Guitar of Bola Sete, Fantasy, 1966.
Autentico Original Jazz Classics, 1966.
Shebaba, Fantasy 1969.
Workin' on a Groovy Thing, Paramount, 1970.
Ocean Vol. 1 Takoma, 1975 (re-released by Windham Hill 1980).
Jungle Suite, Dancing Cat Records, 1985.
(with Vince Guaraldi) *From All Sides,* reissued by Original Jazz Classics, 1998
Ocean Memories, Samba Moon Records, 1999.
Guitar Moon Suite, Samba Moon Records, 1999.

Videos

Carlos Santana Influences: Wes Montgomery, Gabor Szabo, Bola Sete, DCI Music Video, 1998.

Sources

Billboard March 14, 1987
Down Beat February 25, 1965; July 14, 1967; May 1987.

Additional information kindly supplied by Anne Sete.

—Gerald E.Brennan

Silk

R&B vocal group

The five-member male R&B vocal group Silk hit the music scene in 1992 with the single "Freak Me" from their first album, *Lose Control*. Produced by R&B legend Keith Sweat, the record achieved multi-platinum status. Though "Freak Me" was a hit, the group had to virtually reintroduce itself to the R&B market when it released its third album, *Tonight*, in 1999.

Silk formed in the early 1990s in Atlanta, Georgia, although the five members of the group essentially grew up together. Several members of the team—Timothy Cameron (Timzo), Jimmy Gates Jr. (Jimmy), Gary Glenn (Big G), Gary Jenkins (Lil' G), and Johnathen Rasboro (John John)—actually went to high school together. The five friends were influenced by such acts as gospel's Kirk Franklin, pop stars Stevie Wonder and Michael Jackson, rocker Prince and controversial rapper Tupac. Silk made a name for itself on its first outing for its catchy five-way harmonies and sexually suggestive material. They earned an ardent following in the R&B/Urban Contemporary market, particularly among women. "They fit nicely into what I call the 'lover man' category of artists like Usher, Tyrese, and Ginuwine," HMV media store urban music buyer Roberto Gooden told *Billboard* in 1999.

Being discovered by producer Keith Sweat was a coup for Silk. Sweat initially signed them to his own Keia record label, a subsidiary of Elektra Records, and re- leased Silk's debut album *Lose Control* in 1992. Sweat's title of producer gave the unknown group an advance in credibility. Silk earned fans and sold records with its overt and aggressive sexuality. The record rose to number one quickly on the *Billboard* top R&B albums chart. The album sold 1.8 million copies and produced three R&B top ten hits in the United States, including "Freak Me," which spent eight weeks at number one in 1993. Before its second release, *Silk*, in 1995, the group made the switch to Elektra, where they thought they could reach beyond such overtly sexual material as "Freak Me," and ultimately reach a bigger audience.

On *Silk*, the group made a departure from its libido-based songs. But, among fans of the group's first record, the release didn't fare well. Although it did achieve gold status in sales, even Silk's Gary Jenkins knew, "the public may not have been ready for the change in our approach," he told *Billboard* in 1999. So after touring and taking some time off to "regroup," Silk pulled together again to record its third release, *Tonight*.

Because of the different responses they received to *Lose Control* and *Silk*, the group knew they would have to consciously push their third record in the direction they wanted it to go. "We felt like we needed to go back to the mind frame we had on our first record," Gary Jenkins told *Billboard*. The group "went back to the more sexual, sensual kind of entity our fans want from us." But they felt, too, that their third—while bringing back the sexual overtones—was still a well-balanced album. "Even though we're know for our sexual and sensual themes, we want to show people that there are different aspects to us beyond the 'Freak Me'[theme]," Jenkins said. Gary Glenn felt the group was ready to keep working on *Tonight* until it felt right to them and had the makings of a strong R&B release. "R&B has gone through so many different modes in the past few years," Gary Glenn said in the group's Elektra publicity material. "We wanted to come out with guns blazing. We have a rear sound. Innocent in a way, but we still can make the kind of record people will be making babies to, if you know what I mean."

All the members of Silk have cited gospel and strong family and moral values as driving forces in their lives. "Family is important to us," Johnathen Rasboro said in the Elektra publicity material. "Family and the importance of getting an education, we try to instill that in our fans wherever we go." The paradox of religion and the sexual content of their music was clear, but Jimmy Gates Jr. tried to address it. "Everything has its place," he said. "We sing about love and relationships. I don't think you'd want to hear a Silk record if we strayed too far from what has always given R&B its strength."

For the Record . . .

Members include **Timothy Cameron** (Timzo), vocals; **Jimmy Gates Jr.** (Jimmy), vocals; **Gary Glenn** (Big G), vocals; **Gary Jenkins** (Lil' G), vocals; **Johnathen Rasboro** (John John), vocals.

Group formed in Atlanta, GA, c. 1990; released debut album, *Lose Control,* 1992; single "Freak Me" was number one on the Billboard R&B chart for eight weeks in 1993; released *Silk,* 1995; released *Tonight,* 1999.

Awards: *Lose Control* achieved multi-platinum status; *Silk* achieved gold status.

Addresses: *Record company*—Elektra Records, 75 Rockefeller Plaza, New York, NY 10019.

To compete well in the R&B arena, Silk had to be very aware of marketing, or at least hire someone to be aware of it for them. They met Sonja Norwood, of Norwood & Norwood Management, Inc., in 1996 while on tour with Keith Sweat and Norwood's daughter, teen pop sensation Brandy. Norwood took them on before the release of *Tonight* in 1999. The group sought longevity in a constantly changing industry and a market that is flooded with new groups. Jenkins had a vision of how Silk wanted to model its career, he told *Billboard,* "We look at a group like the Temptations as an example of how a group can find a niche and stick to it."

After its third release, and a conscious effort to create a sound that would fit into the sexy R&B genre and fare well with fans, the group's future looked strong. "The group is coming back with a bang," Niecy Davis, operations manager at WBLX, a Mobile, Alabama, radio station told *Billboard.* "The new single is getting a great response from our listeners because it's really a 'chick' song and their audience is mostly female, 18-34."

Selected discography

Lose Control, Elektra, 1992.
Silk, Elektra, 1995.
Tonight, Elektra, 1999.

Sources

Periodicals

Billboard, February 27, 1999; March 13, 1999.

Online

"Silk," *Elektra Records*, http://www.webobjects.elektra.com (May 13, 1999).
"Silk," *CD Now*, http://www.cdnow.com (April 29, 1999).

Additional information was provided by Elektra Records publicity materials, 1999.

—Brenna Sanchez

Sixpence None the Richer

Pop group

Photo by Randee St. Nicholas. Reproduced by permission.

Sixpence None the Richer was already on its third full-length album by the time the catchy single "Kiss Me" began climbing the charts in 1999, a fact that surely surprised many mainstream pop listeners. The group—which includes lead singer Leigh Nash (formerly Leigh Bingham), drummer Dale Baker, bassist Justin Cary, and guitarist Matt Slocum—had already gained popularity as a Christian pop-alternative act when "Kiss Me" landed on episodes of popular youth shows *Dawson's Creek* and *Party of Five,* and the high school film *She's All That.*

Sixpence None the Richer got its start in 1991 after Nash and Slocum met at a church the two attended in New Braunfels, Texas. Nash grew up listening to Patsy Cline and other older country music, and started singing in church as a youth. Slocum likewise got an early introduction to music, starting with piano lessons as a child. It wasn't until he got a guitar for Christmas, though, shortly before his 15th birthday, that his interest in music gelled into something serious. When en route to a church retreat, Slocum (four years Nash's senior) gave Nash a tape of a song he wrote. As a 17-year-old Nash (then Bingham) recalled in a 1994 interview with *The Lighthouse*, "We were on the way to a church retreat, on this church bus, and he came back and asked me to listen to 'Trust,' which was on this little demo tape, with this other person singing on it, and just wanted to know what I thought of it. And, of course, I loved it."

Taking their name from the C.S. Lewis story *Mere Christianity,* the band connected with drummer Dale Baker near Austin, Texas, when Slocum was a college music student and Nash was still in high school. A self-recorded demo drew attention to the band (whose wispy pop is most often compared to influences like 10,000 Maniacs and the Innocence Mission), and led to its first record contract.

The band learned some hard lessons about the music business early in its career. Sixpence None the Richer inked a deal with Nashville independent label R.E.X. Records in 1992 and started out promisingly enough, playing clubs and opening for acts such as 10,000 Maniacs and the Smithereens. While on R.E.X., the band released three albums—the acclaimed *The Fatherless and the Widow* in 1993, Dove award winner *This Beautiful Mess* in 1995, and *Tickets for a Prayer Wheel* in 1995—before watching their career stall when the financially-troubled label shuttered its doors. The band reportedly spent a year wrangling with the label's corporate parent before it was freed to sign in 1997 with a new independent label, Nashville-based Squint Entertainment. The band, which moved its base from Texas to Nashville in 1996, became the flagship act for the label, run by producer and filmmaker Steve Taylor.

In November of 1997, Sixpence None the Richer released its self-titled Squint debut, an album that featured the work of legendary producer Bob Clearmountain. The album slowly but steadily attracted interest and praise from both critics and audiences. In a 1999 *Request* review, Jim Meyer wrote of Slocum, the group's songwriter, that the "classically trained rocker skillfully adds a symphonic grace to his gently moving pop songs," while Lou Carlozo called the album "breathtaking" in a 1998 *Chicago Tribune* review. Doug Brumley of *Nashville Scene* had equally high praise for what he dubbed the band's "literate art-pop," and wrote that "Slocum's pensive lyrics reference works by W.H. Auden and Pablo Neruda, while layered instrumentation mixes string arrangements, pedal steel, and hurdy gurdy with catchy guitar riffs and Leigh Nash's bold yet coyly appealing vocals." *Sixpence None the Richer* was nominated for a Grammy award, and the band was selected to play on the Lillith Fair tour in 1998, an event which helped introduce the act to more listeners.

Though *Sixpence None the Richer* garnered much critical success, it was "Kiss Me" that got a spotlight trained on the band. A top five hit on a number of different charts, the song found its way into the animated MTV show *Daria,* the NBC show *Providence,* the soap opera *The Young and the Restless,* and the NBC movie *Vanished Without a Trace.* Certified gold in March of 1999, the song also landed the band performance spots on *The Tonight Show, Late Night with Conan O'Brien, Live with Regis and Kathie Lee,* and the *Late Show with David Letterman,* among others. Having played with performers ranging from The Wallflowers to Smash Mouth and Brian Setzer to Cher, the band was slated to play several dates on the 1999 Lillith Fair tour.

Even in the midst of their success, some band members have found time to participate in other projects. Slocum, who studied cello in college, played the instrument on Natalie Imbruglia's *Left of the Middle* album, and Nash was the celebrity host of an episode of cable music network VH1's *Women First* that aired in March of 1999.

Sixpence None the Richer has also benefited from the solid working relationship between Nash and Slocum. In interviews, Slocum has consistently praised Nash's singing, a favor Nash has returned. As she told Deborah Evans Price in a 1998 *Billboard* interview, "I'm his biggest fan. I love singing his songs."

In spite of their fan base in the Christian community and the spiritual nature of many of their songs, Sixpence has been somewhat resistant to the "Christian rock" tag. As Slocum noted in a 1998 interview in the *Kane County Chronicle,* "We don't really want the label 'Christian band,' because it is a label that has become meaningless. It is more of a marketing thing; it doesn't really have to do with your faith. We don't want to exclude anyone. We want to make music for everyone, not just for a subculture."

Though still a young band, Sixpence None the Richer has made a powerful impression on some music industry veterans. "Their songs immediately jumped out as something refreshingly different and quite appealing to me," Clearmountain told Price in 1998. "I found myself totally mesmerized by Leigh Nash's dreamy yet provocative vocals.... Having come up with a fantastic album, I believe they've embarked on a potentially long and extremely successful career."

Selected discography

The Fatherless and the Widow, R.E.X. Records, 1993.
This Beautiful Mess, R.E.X. Records, 1995.
Tickets for a Prayer Wheel, R.E.X. Records, 1995.
Sixpence None the Richer, Squint Entertainment, 1997.

Sources

Periodicals

Album Network, May 22, 1998.

Austin American Statesman, December 17, 1998.

Austin Chronicle, May 22, 1998.

Billboard, April 4, 1998; July 4, 1998; August 22, 1998; December 12, 1998; April 3, 1999.

Chicago Tribune, August 2, 1998.

CMJ New Music Report, February 23, 1998; April 20, 1998.

Detroit Free Press, August 28, 1998.

Detroit News, August 27, 1998.

Entertainment Today, September 17, 1998; February 19, 1999.

Gavin, September 18, 1998; December 18, 1998.

HITS, September 25, 1998.

Kane County Chronicle (Illlinois), November 27, 1998.

Los Angeles Times, May 1, 1999.

Nashville Scene, December 17, 1998.

Performing Songwriter, November 1998.

Request, March 1999.

Spin, June 1999.

Spot Magazine (Ohio), December 24, 1998.

Tennessean, February 2, 1999; February 3, 1999.

Online

"Sixpence None the Richer," http://www.suite101.com/article.cfm/christian_music/4056.

"Sixpence None the Richer" (originally from *The Lighthouse,* January 1994), http://tlem.netcentral.net/old/sixpence_ntr_9401.html.

Additional information was provided by Squint Entertainment publicity materials, 1999.

—*K. Michelle Moran*

Will Smith

Rap singer

AP/Wide World Photos. Reproduced by permission.

As the rapping half of DJ Jazzy Jeff and the Fresh Prince, Will Smith achieved almost overnight stardom after the duo's debut album was released by Jive Records in 1987. Platinum-level record sales proved to be only the beginning of the Philadelphia-born artist's phenomenally rewarding multi-media career. Smith managed to parlay his G-rated rap appeal into a starring role in the long-running *Fresh Prince of Bel-Air* television series and also into box-office success with such films as *Independence Day* and *Men In Black*. Even as his screen career was reaching new heights, he returned to recording as a solo rap artist with a multi-platinum 1997 release, *Big Willie Style*.

Though critics often dismissed his recordings as "cute" and "lightweight," Smith had little trouble connecting with a multi-racial audience from his first hit single "Parents Just Don't Understand" onwards. He made no apologies for avoiding profanity and violent themes in his recordings, preferring to concentrate on romance and ordinary teenage troubles. In reviewing their first three albums, critic Paul Evans wrote in *The Rolling Stone Album Guide* that Smith and his partner Jeffrey Townes were "clean-cut and ingratiating ... turning out credible grooves for the pre-teen set." In contrast to the angry, often politically controversial records by NWA, Public Enemy and similar artists, Smith and Townes offered a family-friendly version of hip-hop that appealed to millions in the United States and abroad.

Born September 25, 1968, in Philadelphia, Pennsylvania, Smith grew up in a middle-class household and learned the value of education and discipline in his early years. While still in elementary school, he showed an interest in music and took piano lessons. By age 12, he was listening to early rap recordings and beginning to try out his own rhyming skills. While performing at a house party in 1981, he met Townes and soon formed a performing partnership with him. Smith adopted the performing name "Fresh Prince" after his grade school teachers began calling him "Prince" because of his charming personality and "regal attitude."

Recording in Townes's basement, DJ Jazzy Jeff and the Fresh Prince began experimenting with soundtrack samples and drums loops, crafting a fast-paced, distinctive sound. Their debut single "Girls Ain't Nothing But Trouble" was released in 1986 on the small Word-up label, reaching number 81 on the R&B charts. After a dispute with Word-up over royalties, the duo signed with Jive Records, who released their *Rock This House* album in 1987. A year later, they scored their first big pop radio breakthrough with "Parents Just Don't Understand," a

For the Record . . .

Born Willard C. Smith II, September 25, 1968, in Philadelphia, PA; son of Willard C. Smith Sr. (a refrigeration engineer) and Caroline (a school board employee); married Sheree Zampino, 1992 (divorced, 1995); married Jada Pinkett, 1997; children: Willard C. Smith III, (from first marriage), born 1992; Jaden Christopher Syre Smith, (from second marriage), born 1998.

Began performing as rap singer c. 1980; formed duo DJ Jazzy Jeff and the Fresh Prince with Jeffrey Townes, 1981; released debut single "Girls Ain't Nothing But Trouble" on Word-up label, 1986; signed with Jive and released *Rock The House*, 1987; recorded further albums on Jive, 1988-1993; began first season of television series *Fresh Prince of Bel-Air*, 1990; left *Fresh Prince*, starred in films *Independence Day* in1996, *Men In Black*, 1997; released title song from *Men in Black* soundtrack,1997; released solo debut album on Columbia, *Big Willie Style*, 1998.

Awards: Grammy Award for Best Rap Performance, "Parents Just Don't Understand," 1988; Grammy Award for Best Rap Performance by a Duo or Group, "Summertime," 1991; NAACP Image Award for Outstanding Rap Artist, "Summertime," 1991: MTV Music Award for Best Video From a Film, "Men In Black," 1997; NAACP Image Award for Outstanding Rap Artist, "Men In Black," 1997; Grammy Award for Best Rap Solo Performance, "Men In Black," 1998; MTV Video Music Award for Rap Video, "Gettin' Jiggy Wit It," 1998.

Addresses: *Record company*—Columbia Records, 550 Madison Ave., New York, NY 10022-3211; *Fan mail*— Creative Artists Agency, 9830 Wilshire Blvd., Beverly Hills, CA 90212.

number 12 hit that eventually became a certified-gold single.

Putting aside plans to attend Massachusetts Institute of Technology on a scholarship, Smith plunged into his rap career full-time, continuing his hitmaking streak with such singles as "A Nightmare On My Street" and a re-recorded version of "Girls Ain't Nothing But Trou-

ble." 1988 saw the release of *He's The D.J., I'm The Rapper,* which went on reach the triple-platinum sales level. "Parents Just Don't Understand" went on to earn DJ Jazzy Jeff and the Fresh Prince a 1988 Grammy Award for Best Rap Performance, the first ever given in this category. Their next album, 1989's *... And In This Corner*, surpassed the platinum sales level and yielded the single "I Think I Can Beat Mike Tyson."

A new opportunity presented itself to Smith when he met Warner Brothers Records executive Benny Medina in December, 1989. Seeking a star for a TV situation comedy concept, Medina interested Smith in the lead role in the series that would eventually be aired by NBC-TV as *The Fresh Prince of Bel-Aire*. Broadcast from 1990 through 1996, the series enjoyed high ratings and made Smith into a multi-media celebrity. He received a Golden Globe nomination for best performance by an actor in a television series in 1992, with *The Fresh Prince of Bel-Aire* winning an award for best comedy series at the NAACP Image Awards that same year. The series increased in ratings in its later years, but Smith decided to leave the show at the end of its sixth season in favor of new challenges.

Smith continued his partnership with Townes during his days with *The Fresh Prince of Bel-Air*, releasing the albums *Homebase* and *Code Red* in 1991 and 1993, respectively. The duo scored a particularly big success in 1991 with "Summertime," a number one R&B and number four pop hit that went on to be awarded a Grammy for Best Rap Performance by a Duo or Group. Further high-charting singles continued, including "Ring My Bell" later on in 1991 and "Boom! Shake The Room" in 1993, the latter a number one hit in Britain. Nevertheless, he decided to put aside his rap career in favor of acting after he began to win motion picture roles. His most notable early film was 1993's *Six Degrees Of Separation*, which cast him as a gay street hustler opposite Stockard Channing and Donald Sutherland and earned him largely favorable reviews.

Smith's winning streak as a screen actor began with *Bad Boys,* a 1995 action film that received largely negative reviews but became a notable box-office success. His next role was as a fighter pilot in the science fiction thriller *Independence Day,* a huge hit with both film-goers and the critics that became the highest-grossing film of 1996. A year later, Smith co-starred with Tommy Lee Jones in *Men In Black,* a sci-fi excursion with a comedic twist that again set box-office records. 1998's *Enemy of the State* saw him in a more serious action role, while 1999's *Wild, Wild West* was a special effects-laden, tongue-in-cheek film vehicle similar in tone to *Men In Black.*

During this period, Smith refrained from recording. In interviews, he expressed concern over the violence associated with the hip-hop scene. "That was a large part of why I didn't make a record," he said in an interview found on his official website. "It was like I don't even wanna rhyme. I made records in my crib. I thought that if this what the world is going to, then I don't think there's any place for me." In the end, it was the popularity of *Men In Black* that helped to encourage Smith to launch himself as a solo rap recording artist. The film soundtrack's title number earned him a number one single in both the United States and Britain, and earned him a Grammy for Best Rap Solo Performance in 1998. Signing with Columbia Records, he released his solo debut *Big Willie Style* in 1997. The CD was both in keeping with Smith's smooth, broad-appeal style of his earlier days and reflective of a greater maturity and self-reflection. Such tracks as "Gettin' Jiggy Wit It" and "Miami" were infectious, playful numbers, while "Just The Two Of Us" found Smith rapping about fatherhood in highly personal terms. Though Townes produced several songs, the album's sonic polish was largely the work of the Trackmasters production team. *Big Willie Style* went on to sell 8,000,000 copies, proving that Smith had lost none of his touch as a rapper.

By any measure, Smith has enjoyed exceptional success and had a major impact on popular culture in the 1990s. In interviews, his outlook on life and his career seems as positive and confident as his work as a rap artist. As he told Lynn Hirschberg in a *Vanity Fair* interview, "I look at my neighborhood—I know personally 15 people who could do exactly what I'm doing right now. But they're scared to take that shot. If they give me the position, I'll shoot my shot. The only thing that can go wrong is, I miss. And if I miss, I'll shoot again."

Selected discography

with DJ Jazzy Jeff and The Fresh Prince

Rock The House, Jive, 1987.
He's The D.J., I'm The Rapper, Jive, 1988.
And In This Corner..., Jive, 1989
Homebase, Jive, 1991.
Code Red, Jive, 1993.

solo

Big Willie Style, Columbia, 1997.

Sources

Books

DeCurtis, Anthony and Henke, James, editors, *The Rolling Stone Album Guide,* Random House, 1992.
Larkin, Colin, *The Encyclopedia of Popular Music,* Muze, 1998.

Periodicals

Ebony, July 1999.
Teen People, August 1999.
Vanity Fair, October 1990.

Online

E!Online, http://www.eonline.com (May 21, 1999).
Wall of Sound, http://wallofsound.go.com (May 21, 1999).

Additional information was provided by Will Smith publicity materials, 1999.

—*Barry Alfonso*

Sonic Youth

Rock group

More than image, style, or even substance, the punk rock movement of the mid 1970s challenged the mainstream musical establishment. It was in the years following this movement and during Sonic Youth's beginning in 1978-79 that no wave rock—named for its lack of discernible musical influences—began evolving into 1990s grunge. Sonic Youth embodied the sound and attitude of the popular new genre and the group quickly became one of rock's most successful and highly acclaimed bands.

According to Ira Robbins, "latter day rock and roll revolutionaries have shown a marked tendency toward swift burnout. They reveal their raw vision to the world, but the world, being the philistine place that it is, turns away; the musicians move on. Sonic Youth, unlike so many of the noise bands that formed in New York at the beginning of the eighties, had the fortitude to hold on long enough to develop its ideas well beyond the original stances. As a result, the quartet has gotten better and better, moving from cacophony to chilling beauty, arising from the underground to become its emissaries to the

Photo by B.C. Kagan. Michael Ochs Archive. Reproduced by permission.

real rock world .... More than just updating the noise rock innovations of Jimi Hendrix or the Velvet Underground, Sonic Youth took them some place fresh."

Sonic Youth was formed in New York City in the early 1980s, when Thurston Moore met Lee Ranaldo. They were both involved in musical collaborations with guitarist and composer Glenn Branca at the time. In 1981, the two guitarists, Moore and Ranaldo, united with bassist and art school graduate Kim Gordon and drummer Richard Edson to create Sonic Youth.

They signed to Branca's Neutral label and before the band had released their first record. Edson left the group and was replaced by drummer Bob Bert. In 1982, Sonic Youth released their debut mini-album entitled *Sonic Youth*. It was followed the next year by *Confusion is Sex*. The early Sonic Youth records were characterized by large amounts of distortion and feedback which was

the result of Moore's and Ranaldo's penchant for tuning their guitars to various "hot rodded tunings." They also chose to play their instruments with drumsticks and screwdrivers. Death, urban decay, and the squalidness of life were the issues that Moore and his soon-to-be-wife Gordon mined for lyric inspiration. As Moore told the *Boston Phoenix*, "when we started we were being very reactionary, pulling against the norm at the time [and] trying to bring back and update the elements we liked that came out of bands like the Stooges and the MC5."

They slowly started to build a loyal cult following that spawned such hardcore contemporaries as the Meat Puppets, the Minutemen, and Black Flag among others. A European tour produced the 1983 German-only release *Kill Yr Idols* which was an EP of distorted soundscapes. The following year, Sonic Youth released *Sonic Death* which featured performances from their European tour. This album was released on Moore's Ecstatic Peace label.

By 1985, Sonic Youth began to change its sound somewhat as they toyed with sound dynamics, more unusual tunings, and song stylings. Also at this time, the band began to send out demo tapes to various independent labels. They were eventually signed to Blast First in England and to Homestead in America. They then released *Bad Moon Rising*, about which the *New Rolling Stone Encyclopedia of Rock and Roll* said "hit on a direction that incorporated swirling Branca style guitar textures into more traditional pop-based song structures." At the beginning of 1986, Sonic Youth had a new American label—the Black Flag bankrolled SST—and a new drummer, Steve Shelley, who replaced Bert. They began to work on their next album *E.V.O.L*, or love spelled backwards. The next year saw the release of *Sister*, which served as the musical primer for such bands as Sebadoh and Pavement.

Another label change, this time to Enigma, followed in 1988. At this time, the band decided to engage in a side project called Ciccone Youth. The resulting album, the *Whitey Album,* featured covers of Madonna songs, thus giving the band their pseudonym. Also that same year, Sonic Youth released their critically acclaimed classic underground album *Daydream Nation*. This album further elaborated on the theme of alienation which pervaded the two previous Sonic Youth releases. *Daydream Nation* contained the song "Teen Age Riot" which shot to the number one spot on the British independent singles chart and the American alternative singles chart.

They continued to travel the globe throughout the late 1980s, and with 1990 fast approaching, it was time for Sonic Youth to move on yet again. They left both their English label, Blast First, and their American label,

Enigma, and signed on to the major label DGC. 1990 heralded Sonic Youth's major label debut, *Goo,* which featured the hit single "Kool Thing," a collaboration between Gordon and Public Enemy's Chuck D. The album introduced the band to a wider, more mainstream audience in America. This increase in popularity helped Sonic Youth become the opening act for Neil Young on his tour. Two years later, the group released *Dirty.* The album was more politically charged than any of their previous work, due in part to its release during an American election year. On *Dirty,* there was a song denouncing the southern Senator Jesse Helms called "Chapel Hill" as well as a tune called "Youth Against Fascism."

Additional tours preceded 1994's *Experimental Jet Set, Trash and No Star* which was the first Sonic Youth album to make its way into the top 40 albums chart in America. Their continued success helped Sonic Youth become the headlining act at Lollapalooza in 1995 and to tour with R.E.M. The following year, they released *Washing Machine.*

In 1998, Sonic Youth released *A Thousand Leaves,* the first record to be solely recorded in their own studio. As Moore stated in the Sonic Youth DGC web site, "in an attempt to make our LPs dateable, we'll now include an answer song to some aspect of popular culture on each LP. We're not, as some people maintain, obsessed with pop culture, so much as we're obsessed with its possibilities for stratification and dateability."

Selected discography

Sonic Youth, Neutral, 1982.
Confusion is Sex, Neutral, 1983.
Kill Yr Idols, Zensor, 1983.
Sonic Death, Ecstatic Peace, 1984.
Bad Moon Rising, Homestead, 1985.

E.V.O.L, SST, 1986.
Sister, SST, 1987.
(as Ciccone Youth)*Whitey Album,* Enigma, 1988.
Daydream Nation, Enigma, 1988.
Goo, DGC, 1990.
Dirty, DGC, 1992.
Experimental Jet Set Trash and No Star, DGC, 1994.
Screaming Fields of Sonic Love, DGC, 1995.
Washing Machine, DGC, 1996.
A Thousand Leaves, DGC, 1998.

Sources

Books

Contemporary Musicians, vol. 9, Gale.
Robbins, Ira, editor, *Trouser Press Guide to 90s Rock,* Fireside, 1997.
Robbins, Ira, editor, *Trouser Press Record Guide,* fourth edition, Macmillan, 1991.
Romanowski, Patricia and Holly George Warren, eds., *New Rolling Stone Encyclopedia of Rock and Roll,* Fireside, 1995.

Periodicals

Boston Phoenix, July 17, 1992.
Musician, September 1992.
People, May 11, 1998.

Online

"Sonic Youth Biography," www.allmusic.com/cg/x.dll?p+amg&sql=B5474 (April 16, 1999).
"Sonic Youth," *Geffen Records Artist Page,* www.geffen.com/sonic-youth/bio/index.html (April 16, 1999).

—*Mary Alice Adams*

Kim Stockwood

Singer, songwriter

Canadian pop singer/songwriter Kim Stockwood was first propelled into the international spotlight with the global popularity of the humorous single "Jerk," from her debut album *Bonavista* in 1995, and she continued to engage listeners with her sophomore release, *12 Years Old* in 1999. Stephen Cooke of the *Halifax Herald* described her work as "irresistible" and "unabashed," and her dazzling personality proved to be as compelling and entertaining as her music. She landed her first record contract without a demo tape; she simply jumped up on a piano stool in the office of Mike McCarty, president of EMI Publishing, and belted out two singles, while scuffing his piano stool with her cowboy boots in the process. She was immediately signed to the EMI label, and proceeded to pour her heart and soul into two albums with favorable results. She told *Billboard*'s Larry LeBlanc, "[*12 Years Old*] is a really smart record with some good pop tunes. Since my first album, I've written with so many people and written so much on my own. I'm pretty proud where I've come to [as a songwriter]."

Stockwood was raised in St. John's, Newfoundland, and earned a bachelor of arts degree in English in 1986 from Memorial University in her hometown. She was coaxed into performing for amateur night in 1988 at the folk club Bridget's, in St. John's, and sang songs by Sinead O'Connor, Velvet Underground, and Patsy Cline. Her performance that evening so impressed the club's owner that he asked her to return and to perform again. She soon put together a band in order to work weekends at local bars, and performed cover songs along with a few of her own original songs. She told LeBlanc, "In the beginning, after a couple of Guinnesses, I'd sing Patsy Cline and Elvis Presley.... In the past couple of years, I've done ok (touring). I've been able to pay my phone bill."

Stockwood moved to Toronto in 1993 to further her career, and within two months of relocating, she landed a deal with EMI Music Publishing Canada. She was signed with EMI Music Canada within a year. Her career break has been attributed to her "whirling dervish" personality, since she landed a deal without a demo tape and spent only one hour with a music executive at EMI. It's the kind of break that many musicians dream of, yet few would be confident enough to attempt. Stockwood's exuberant personality also landed her a spot as a host for 1997's pre-Juno awards ceremony, as well as a spot as a correspondent for CTV's E channel. Stockwood's debut release for EMI, *Bonavista*, turned to gold and contained four high-charting singles, including the single "Jerk." The song was popular on the music charts in Thailand, Hong Kong, Singapore, New Zealand, Malaysia, Poland, the United States, Switzerland, and Sweden. Stockwood earned a 1996 Juno nomination for Best New Artist, and emerged as a new artist with songwriting depth and passion, as well as an expressive, talented vocalist. *Bonavista* sparked excitement, due to its eclectic mix of pop ballads, country, and country-rock fusion. Her sophomore release, *12 Years Old*, was generally hailed a more cohesive and coherent effort, and emphasized the vulnerability we all retain and feel most acutely at the age of twelve. Stockwood's sophomore release is a significant creative step forward from her debut, when she viewed herself more as a singer than singer/songwriter. She told LeBlanc, "The first album was all over the place."

Stockwood's longtime writing partner, Naoise Sheridan, accredits Stockwood with having an intuitive sense of a hook, and the Stockwood/Sheridan collaboration resulted in five hit singles on *Bonavista*; "Enough Love" was the winner of a Socan Airplay Award. Sheridan is credited with writing seven of the tracks on *12 Years Old*. Stockwood's debut release *Bonavista* was produced by Michael Phillip Wojewoda (Barenaked Ladies, Blue Rodeo, Ashely MacIsaac), and *12 Years Old* was produced by Wojewoda, with the exception of the title track, which was produced by English songwriter/producer Peter Vettese (Annie Lennox, Seal, The Cure) and Mike Shipley (Aerosmith, Shania Twain, Joni Mitchell). In addition, Randy Bachman and pop artist Glen Tillbrook of Squeeze collaborated with Stockwood on *12 Years Old*, as did New York City-based songwriter Abenna

For the Record . . .

Born and raised in St. John's, Newfoundland, Canada. *Education:* Memorial University in St. John's, bachelor of arts degree in English, 1986.

Began singing on amateur night in a local bar in St. John's in 1988; put together a band and performed locally in St. John's; moved to Toronto, 1993; signed with EMI Music Canada within two months without a demo tape; released *Bonavista,* 1995; single "Jerk" from the album became a popular international hit; hosted 1997's pre-Juno awards ceremony; worked as a correspondent for CTV's E channel; opened Van Morrison's Maritime Concerts in 1998; released *12 Years Old,* 1999.

Awards: Winner of a 1996 Socan Airplay Award for "Enough Love."

Addresses: *Record company*—EMI Music Canada, 3109 American Drive, Mississauga, Ontario Canada L4V 1B2; fax (905) 677-1651.

LeBlanc, "Musically the track is so different from the rest of the album, but the song is very personal to me."

Stockwood opened Van Morrison's Maritime Concerts in 1998, and the two musicians struck up an unlikely friendship. Stockwood anticipated touring more extensively to support *12 Years Old* throughout 1999, and has proven to be adept at knowing exactly how to cater to an audience. Whether any of the tracks on *12 Years Old* will also become international hits remained to be seen shortly after its release in 1999, but Stockwood acknowledged that the effervescent "Puzzle Girl," written with Sheridan, is the most likely follow-up track to the earlier success of "Jerk". She told *Billboard's* LeBlanc she was somewhat apprehensive of its release due to the fact that it's a mainstream pop single, and she wants to be remembered for her more substantial, in-depth material. She said, "(The label and management) think 'Puzzle Girl' is a hit, but a lot of great songs are on (*12 Years Old*). The song should be on the album, but I want to be remembered for more." Considering how quickly Stockwood has adapted and learned as her career has blossomed, she will no doubt have ample time in the future to present new material and to continue to write songs that reflect her honest, open heart.

Frempong (Vanessa Williams). The musical tone of *12 Years Old* ranges from bubbly pop to languid, romantic love songs, and twangy country-inspired ballads.

Cooke wrote, "The not-so-secret 'hidden track' (*on 12 Years Old*), 'Will I Ever,' that appears unannounced at the disc's end...(is) an unabashed paean to her homeland and family, complete with cameos by her grandparents on accordion and harmonica." The Celtic-styled "Will I Ever" was written with Bachman, and features her father, Leslie, on accordion, her 85-year old grandmother Blanch Stockwood on harmonica, and assorted dear friends and family members singing backup. She told

Selected discography

Bonavista, EMI Music Canada, 1995.
12 Years Old, EMI Music Canada, 1999.

Sources

Billboard, February 27, 1999.
Calgary Sun, July 8, 1997.
Halifax Herald, April 22, 1999.
Toronto Sun, March 30, 1999.

—B. Kimberly Taylor

Sweet Honey In The Rock

A cappella group

Sweet Honey In The Rock, the all-female Grammy Award-winning a cappella quintet, has uplifted and energized audiences from Australia to Zimbabwe with its creatively interpreted and perfectly intoned mix of traditional black spirituals and freedom songs, as well as a wealth of their own compositions. Sweet Honey's artistic style was best described in "A Tribute," a song celebrating the first 20-years of the group's history: "'Great Black Music' is what we sing/A cappella style with a political ring/Using work songs, spirituals,/Gospel and blues/The styles of African, jazz/And love songs, too/There are no limits/To the sounds we produce/In a social commentary/To express our views." According to Sweet Honey's Web site, the five African American women see themselves as "artists and cultural activists [who] compose, arrange and perform songs with strong messages about the world we live in and the ever expanding range of issues" concerning them. The five vocalists enhance their sound with hand-held percussion instruments. Since 1980, they have integrated a sign-language interpreter so the deaf community could also enjoy their performances. Sweet Honey In The Rock has recorded two albums for children. In 1998, the group celebrated its 25th anniversary with the release of their 15th album simply titled *twenty-five.*

Bernice Johnson Reagon, vocal director for the D.C. Black Repertory Theater and civil rights activist, founded the gospel ensemble in 1973. She created a workshop in a cappella gospel singing envisioning a mixed group of singers. The first rehearsal was attended by just four women, but the full sound they created together was so stirring that a new concept was born. Reagon provided the group with a wealth of traditional songs, which she knew from her childhood in Southwest Georgia singing in her father's community's Baptist church, a church that didn't have a piano until she was eleven. Reagon was also the driving force behind the group's social and political agenda. Before she moved to Washington D.C. to pursue a doctorate at Howard University, Reagon actively participated in the civil rights movement while studying at Albany State College. There she was a founding member of the SNCC (Student Nonviolent Coordinating Committee), and the Freedom Singers, a group that traveled across the country.

Sweet as Honey

The first song the new group learned was "Sweet Honey In The Rock." As Jim Bessman wrote in the liner notes to the group's album *twenty-five,* the song was based on a religious parable that "told of a land so rich that when rocks were cracked open, honey flowed from them." The symbolism seemed to incorporate perfectly the main characteristics of African-American women—to be sweet as honey but strong as a rock. Sweet Honey In The Rock made its first public appearance at Howard University in Washington D.C. in November of 1973.

Right from the beginning, the group devoted much of its work to specific goals, mainly striving for peace, justice, and freedom. It was Reagon's philosophy—later explained by her daughter Toshi in *twenty-five*'s liner notes—that "music is first a means of communicating to and about one's community, then a method of historical documentation, and only lastly a mode of entertainment." This philosophy formed the basis of the typical Sweet Honey style which is soothing and agitating at the same time. In numerous performances the vocal group supported disarmament, the liberation of the African peoples, the Reverend Jesse Jackson's organization PUSH, and especially the women's movement. For example, Sweet Honey performed at the June 12 Rally for Disarmament in New York City in 1982, at the United Nations Decade for Women Conference in Nairobi, Kenya, in 1985, at Nelson and Winnie Mandela Welcome Rallies in New York City, Washington, DC, and Oakland, California, in 1990, and the International Women's Conference in Bejing, China, in 1995. Sweet Honey has traveled extensively abroad and performed at numerous national and international festivals and community events as well as on various college campuses in the United States. According to Dan DeLuca of the *Philadelphia*

For the Record . . .

Members include **Ysaye Maria Barnwell** vocals, percussion; **Nitanju Bolade Casel**, vocals, percussion; **Aisha Kahlil**, vocals, percussion; **Carol Maillard,** vocals, percussion; **Bernice Johnson Reagon**, vocals, percussion; **Shirley Childress Saxton,** sign language interpreter. Former members include **Helena Coleman**, vocals; **Ingrid Ellis**, vocals; **Geraldine Hardin,** vocals; **Ayodele Harrington**, vocals; **Evelyn Maria Harris** vocals; **Rosie Lee Hooks**, vocals; **Patricia Johnson**, vocals; **Tulani Jordan Kinard**, vocals; **Akua Opokuwaa**, vocals; **Louise Robinson**, vocals; **Laura Sharp**, vocals; **Tia Juana Starks**, vocals; **Dianaruthe Wharton**, vocals; **Yasmeen Williams**, vocals.

Formed in 1973 by Bernice Johnson Reagon; released first album *Sweet Honey In The Rock,* Flying Fish, 1976; released second album *B'Lieve I'll Run On...See What the End's Gonna Be*, Redwood Records, 1978; album named "Best Women's Album" by the National Association of Independent Record Distributors, 1979; performed at the United Nations Decade for Women conference in Nairobi, Kenya, 1985; performed at a concert to observe the first national holiday celebration of Martin Luther King Jr.'s 60th birthday broadcast by PBS, 1989; released first children's album *All for Freedom,* Music for Little People, 1989; performed at Nelson and Winnie Mandela Welcome Rallies in New York City, Washington DC and Oakland, CA, 1990; released 20th anniversary album *Still On the Journey*, 1993; published book by and about the group *We Who Believe in Freedom*, 1993; released second children's album *I Got Shoes*, 1994; International Women's Conference, Bejing, China, 1995; released 25th anniversary album *twenty-five*, 1998; international tours and performances in Australia, Brazil, Cuba, Europe, Haiti, Japan, and Russia; contributions to numerous films and television documentaries.

Awards: Best Gospel Album of 1985; Washington Area Music Awards, Best Ethnic Group, 1987; Best Gospel 1987, 1988, 1989; Grammy Award, Traditional Folk, for "A Vision Shared," 1988; Best Gospel Music in the Mid-Atlantic, 1993; Top awards from The Contemporary A Cappella Society of America, 1993, 1994.

Addresses: *Office*—P.O. Box 77442, Washington, D.C. 20013-8442; *Website*—http://www.sweethoney.com.

Inquirer the group inspired "droves of all-women a cappella groups" such as Philadelphia's NaNiKha and Belgium's Zap Mama.

As recording artists, Sweet Honey In The Rock proved to be successful as well as productive. The group's first album *Sweet Honey In The Rock* was released on the Flying Fish label in 1976. *B'Lieve I'll Run On...See What the End's Gonna Be*, the group's second album released by Redwood Records in 1978, was named "Best Women's Album" by the National Association of Independent Record Distributors in 1979. During the 1980s the group produced six albums, five of which contained a mix of traditional material and their own compositions. *Feel Something Drawing Me On* of 1985 was the exception. It contained exclusively sacred music—nineteenth century congregational and traditional songs. In 1989, their first best-of album, *Breaths,* was released.

Strong as a Rock

In 1991, Sweet Honey received a Grammy Award in the Traditional Folk Category for their interpretations of Leadbelly songs "Sylvie" and "Gray Goose" on the 1988 Smithsonian Folkways album *A Vision Shared: A Tribute To Woody Guthrie and Leadbelly*. Two years later they celebrated twenty successful years as a group and released their anniversary album *Still On the Journey*. "When the women of Sweet Honey do let loose their impassioned voices of protest on the righteous shout 'In the Morning When I Rise' and Len Chandler's determined vow 'I'm Going to Get My Baby Out of Jail,' they come on with the riveting intensity of five earthshaking earth mothers, beautiful and proud, still struggling but unbowed," commented Dan DeLuca in the *Philadelphia Inquirer* on two of the album's songs. In addition to socially critical songs and African American traditional songs, the album also contained a love song, "Stay," by group member Carol Maillard, and a history in rap style, "Tribute," by Sweet Honey member Nitanju Bolade Casel describing the group's purpose and history in a rhyming narrative. The lyrics also play around the group's name and mention all the twenty women who were part of Sweet Honey during its first twenty years. In the twentieth year of Sweet Honey's existence, the group received an award for "Best Gospel Music in the Mid-Atlantic" and awards from the Contemporary A Cappella Society of America.

A collection of 28 essays was published in a book entitled *We Who Believe in Freedom* by Anchor Books in 1993. In addition to a chronicle of the group written by its founder and pieces written by current and former group members who reflected on their personal Sweet

Honey In The Rock experience, the book also included essays by Alice Walker, Angela Davis, and Toshi Reagon, the daughter of Bernice Johnson Reagon who co-produced many of the group's albums together with her mother.

Sweet Honey's endurance may be due to the fact that every group member, in addition to their collective musical work, leads a full life and their various individual experiences enrich the group. Founder and group leader Bernice Johnson Reagon, a divorced mother of two adult children, has worked as a music consultant, composer, performer, producer and actress. In 1989, Reagon received a MacArthur Fellowship "genius grant" for her life work. With the money, she was able to finance the award-winning 26-part series on NPR, *Wade in the Water: African American Sacred Music Traditions,* which aired in 1994. She organized a traveling exhibition with the same name while she was a curator for the Smithsonian Institution's National Museum of American History. Reagon has also authored and edited books as well as CD-collections of African-American sacred music and freedom songs.

Ysaye M. Barnwell worked as an actress and a commissioned composer for dance, choral, film, and video projects, and conducted "Singing in the African American Tradition"- workshops in the United States, Great Britain and Australia. Nitanju Bolade Casel studied, performed, and organized cultural events in Dakar, Senegal before joining Sweet Honey In The Rock. A professional dancer, she has taught dance classes in schools and had her own performance art production company together with Aisha Kahlil, another Sweet Honey member. Kahlil, an experienced professional singer with excellent credentials, in particular in blues singing, also specialized in teaching the integration of traditional and contemporary forms of music, dance, and theater. Founding member Carol Maillard who re-joined the group in 1989 has also been an active theater actress, vocal coach, and revue producer.

Just the Beginning

The year 1998 earmarked Sweet Honey's 25th anniversary. WGBS-TV for PBS produced the series "The African Americans" about American slavery, with the sound score by Bernice Joynson Reagon featuring Sweet Honey In the Rock. Members of the group also appeared in the movie *Beloved* and on its score. The 13 tracks on their fifteenth album simply titled *twenty-five* captures the essence of Sweet Honey in the Rock's work over a quarter of a century. It is a mix of traditional

African American spirituals such as a contemporary arrangment by Carol Maillard of the old spiritual "Motherless Chil'," the wordless "Chant" of a Central African rain forest tribe, classic freedom songs such as Bob Marley's "Redemption Song," arranged by Aisha Kahlil, and a broad array of their own compositions addressing social issues as well as the ups and downs of human—especially women's—existence. In Michelle Lancaster's "Battered Earth" the five singers draw a picture of our planet running away in order to survive; "Run" by Nitanju Bolade Casel tells the story of a female victim of domestic violence fleeing her home; "Greed" attempts to address one of the biggest issues of our time, one which songwriter Reagon called "a poison rising in this land;" "Forever Love" is a doo-wop jazz love ballad; and the 1928 classic "I was Standing By The Bedside Of A Neighbor" by gospel composer Thomas Andrew Dorsey is a reminder that all human beings will face death one day.

twenty-five was the first album produced by group member Ysaye M. Barnwell. The album was also an enhanced CD which simultaneously functions as a CD-ROM, providing extensive information about Sweet Honey In The Rock, including biographies of each member, digital images of the group, book excerpts, lyrics, background information about the songs and links to the Internet about the issues each song addressed. Barnwell also wrote the last track called "Hope," a chant stating the group's philosophy and future outlook: "If we want hope to survive in this world today/then every day we've got to pray on/work on/teach on/fight on/sing on."

Selected discography

Sweet Honey In The Rock, Flying Fish, 1976.
B'Lieve I'll Run On...See What the End's Gonna Be, Redwood Records, 1978.
Good News, Flying Fish, 1981.
We All...Everyone, Flying Fish, 1983.
The Other Side, Flying Fish, 1985.
Feel Something Drawing Me On, Flying Fish, 1985.
Live at Carnegie Hall, Flying Fish, 1988.
All for Freedom, Music for Little People, 1989.
Breaths-Best of Sweet Honey In The Rock, Cooking Vinyl, 1989.
In This Land, EarthBeat! Music, 1992.
Still on the Journey, EarthBeat! Music, 1993.
I Got Shoes, Music for Little People, 1994.
Sacred Ground, EarthBeat! Music, 1995.
Selections 1976-1988 (two CD-set), Rounder Records, 1997.
twenty-five (enhanced CD) (includes "Battered Earth," "Run," "Greed," "Hope," "Forever Love"), Rykodisc, 1998.

Selected Writings

We Who Believe in Freedom, Anchor Books, 1993.
Continuum, Third World Press, 1998.
Barnwell, Ysaye M., *No Mirrors in My Nana's House*, Harcourt Brace, 1998.

Sources

Books

Contemporary Musicians, Vol. 1, Gale Research, 1989.

Periodicals

Billboard, October 10, 1998; October 31, 1998, p. 39.
Democrat, February 25, 1999.
Philadelphia Inquirer, April 8, 1994, p 14.
Publishers Weekly, August 24, 1998, p. 28.

Additional information for this profile was provided by publicity materials of Sweet Honey In The Rock and from the liner notes of the albums *Still on the Journey* and *...twenty-five.*

—Evelyn Hauser

Steve Taylor

Singer, songwriter

Since the early 1980s, Steve Taylor has stood out among contemporary Christian musicians by virtue of his acerbic songs and brash stage persona. During the course of his career, Taylor has been called "evangelical rock's court jester" by *Newsweek*, "a gospel Elvis Costello" by *USA Today* and a "satanic influence upon the lives of young people" by evangelist Bob Jones III. Amidst all the controversy, he has released a series of recordings that have matched sharp-edged lyrics to a wide variety of rock and pop sonic styles. After more than a decade as a recording artist, the late 1990s found Taylor taking on the role of record company executive as well.

Roland Stephen Taylor came to the gospel music world in part through his family. Born in Brawley, California, he grew up in the Denver area, the son of a Baptist minister. His first artistic involvements included playing bass in local bands and dabbling in acting. Though his parents didn't allow him to listen to pop radio until his mid-teens, he became an avid punk and new wave rock fan by the time he entered Biola College in Southern California. "What was interesting was that The Clash and Sex Pistols were great at pointing out all the problems of the world, but they were short on solutions," Taylor told the *Nashville Scene*. "So I figured, 'Well, if I'm a Christian, I think I know absolute truth—why would I not want to write songs with that same kind of conviction, and yet offer some hope?' "

After unsuccessful attempts at interesting Los Angeles-based record companies in his brand of Christian rock, Taylor returned to Denver and worked with local musicians. In 1982, a performance at the annual Christian Artists Retreat in Estes Park, Colorado, helped to launch him as a songwriter and performer. The highlight of this concert was Taylor's "I Want To Be A Clone," a punk-flavored tune ridiculing Christian conformity. The song went on be the title track of Taylor's debut EP, released in 1983 by Sparrow Records. Influenced by the frenetic new wave sounds of the time, *I Want To Be A Clone* garnered praise for its fresh intelligence and spirit. "Steve's magic lies in that he makes us want to go out in left field, as far as he wants to take us," said the Christian music publication *CCM*.

Taylor followed up his first release with a full-length album, *Meltdown*, on Sparrow in 1983. The songs built on the strengths of *I Want To Be A Clone* while expanding the range of lyrical targets. One song, "We Don't Need No Colour Code," was an attack on the policies of conservative Bob Jones University, while tracks such as "Meat The Press" and "Am I In Sync" aimed at secular targets. Touring and favorable reviews helped *Meltdown* sell over 150,000 copies, a high figure for a Christian music album. While some in the gospel music community found his work too outspoken and radical, Taylor connected with many younger listeners with both his music and message. *Meltdown* went on to earn nominations for both a Grammy and for the Christian music industry's Dove Award.

In 1985, Taylor released *On The Fritz* to further acclaim. This time, he enlisted Ian McDonald from the British band Foreigner to co-produce the album. Though his sound was gaining more mainstream rock polish, Taylor's songs continued to deal with current issues in an often scathingly sarcastic way. His belief system as reflected in his lyrics was complicated, not entirely left or right-wing. On his next album, 1987's *I Predict 1990*, he raised controversy with "I Blew Up The Clinic Real Good," an ironic sketch of a anti-abortion extremist. Some listeners thought the song was in favor of abortion clinic bombings, and the fallout led to the cancellation of an Australian tour.

By the late 1980s, Taylor began to feel that the Christian music world was becoming restrictive, and he suspended his career as a solo artist. As he recalled to the *Nashville Scene*, "I had sort of hit a glass ceiling, and the choice was either do another album that was more geared toward the Church, and was musically more accessible, or just do something else." After moving to Nashville, Taylor decided to lead

For the Record . . .

Born December 9, 1957, in Brawley, CA.

Began performing as singer/songwriter in 1982; released first EP *I Want To Be A Clone* on Sparrow in 1983; released first album *Meltdown* in 1984; formed band Chagall Guevara, released self-titled album on MCA, 1991; returned to solo career, released *Squint* CD on Warner Alliance, 1993, and *Movies From The Soundtrack* video in 1994; founded record company Squint Entertainment, 1997.

Addresses: *Record company*—Squint Entertainment, P.O. Box 90394, Nashville, TN 37209

a band and venture into the secular rock marketplace. Together with guitarists L. Arthur Nichols and Dave Perkins, bassist Wade Jaynes and drummer Mike Mead, he formed Chagall Guevara and secured a contract with MCA Records.

Released in 1991, Chagall Guevara emphasized biting guitar sounds and clattering rhythms as a setting for Taylor's darkly comic lyrics. While the band acknowledged the Christian message in its material, the reach of the album's music was clearly for a wider audience. But despite such strong rock tunes as "Violent Blue" and "Escher's World," Chagall Guevara failed to become a commercial success. "Probably the fatal flaw of Chagall Guevara is that we weren't actually being driven by any sense of mission, outside of being a successful band," Taylor said in an interview with *TLeM Christian Music Resources* web site, " and that ended up being not enough to keep me going."

Taylor returned to Christian music in 1993 with the release of his *Squint* album on the Warner Alliance label. At times moody and aggressive in sound, the songs on this release revealed a more mature collection of songs with a sharper focus. The album's closing track, "Cash Cow," found Taylor stretching out to offer a mini-rock opera with a Biblical setting. Even more ambitious than *Squint* was a video project launched about the same time, which took Taylor to such exotic locales as Vietnam, Nepal and the United Arab Emirates for shooting sites. The results were released as the Warner Alliance video *Movies From The Soundtrack* in 1994.

Taylor rounded out his association with Warner Alliance with the release of *Liver*, a live album that included songs from his earliest recordings up through *Squint*. His next move was an unexpected one. Dissatisfied with his experience with established record companies, he decided to start his own. With the backing of Gaylord Entertainment—the parent company of gospel label Word Music—Taylor launched Squint Entertainment in 1997 and set up offices in Nashville. Rather than using the company to advance his own recording career, he has helped to guide a number of Christian-oriented artists to success. The most notable of these has been the band Sixpence None The Richer, whose single "Kiss Me" became a number one pop radio hit in May of 1999. Another Squint act, The Insyders, became the first group to ever top both Soundscan's Rock/Alternative chart and its Praise and Worship chart.

Through it all, Taylor has maintained his commitment to spreading the Christian message in unconventional ways to the world at large. "I was raised in an environment free from hypocrisy, so I don't have a chip on my shoulder," he stated in a *Tulsa World* interview. "My motivation is to see that the church is what Jesus had in mind and to challenge people outside the church to see that maybe Christianity is different from what they think it is."

Selected discography

I *Want To Be A Clone*, Sparrow, 1983.
Meltdown, Sparrow, 1984.
On The Fritz, Sparrow, 1985.
I Predict 1990, Myrrh, 1987.
(with Chagall Guevara) *Chagall Guevara*, MCA, 1991.
Squint, Warner Alliance, 1993.
Liver, Warner Alliance, 1995.

Sources

CCM, January 1983.
Chicago Tribune, April 14, 1985.
Denver Post, May 13, 1984.
Los Angeles Times, May 7, 1988.
Nashville Scene, April 22, 1999.
Tulsa World, June 17, 1985.
USA Today, January 8, 1986.

Additional information was provided by TLeM Christian Music Resources site on the World Wide Web.

—*Barry Alfonso*

Yuri Temirkanov

Conductor

Celebrated conductor Yuri Temirkanov brought his talents from the former Soviet Union through Europe, and to the United States. In 1999, he accepted a position as the principal conductor of the Baltimore Symphony Orchestra while retaining simultaneous positions as the principal conductor of the St. Petersburg Philharmonic Orchestra and the Royal Philharmonic Orchestra of London. Temirkanov is recognized globally as a precise orchestral conductor, highly knowledgeable of musical composition and intuitive in his direction.

Temirkanov was born Yuri Khatuyevich Temirkanov on December 10, 1938, in Nalchik, the capitol city of the southern Russian republic of Kabardino-Balkaria, on the Northern slopes of the Caucasus Mountains. He was born to Khatu Sagidovich Temirkano and Polina Petrovna Temirkanova. Khatu Temirkano was the minister of culture for the republic. The family lived in Nalchik until 1941, when Khatu Temirkano was executed during the German invasion. Just prior to his death, the composer Sergei Prokofieff and his future wife, Mira Mendelson, lived for a time with Temirkanov's family. Prokofieff was involved in writing the score of *War and Peace* at the time.

At the command of the Soviet regime, Temirkanov began to study music at age nine. It was the young boy's teacher who selected the violin as Termirkanov's instrument. At age 13 he went to Leningrad, sent by his teacher, to the School for Talented Children. Temirkanov studied both viola and violin and went on to the Leningrad Conservatory (Conservatoire). He graduated in a violin program there in 1962. Temirkanov came to consider Leningrad as home since he moved there at age 13. Beginning in 1961, he played violin with the Leningrad Philharmonic Orchestra until 1966. Between 1966 and 1968, he was a conductor for the Maly Theatre and Opera studio in Leningrad. During much of that time he continued at the Conservatoire in a post-graduate program of conducting, while working under Evgeny Mravinsky as an assistant conductor with the Leningrad Philharmonic Orchestra. Temirkanov graduated in conducting in 1965, and debuted with the Leningrad Opera that same year.

From 1968 until 1977, Temirkanov led the Leningrad Symphony (a different group from Mravinsky's Leningrad Philharmonic). He then took over as the chief conductor of the Kirov Opera and Ballet Company in 1977. His most memorable operatic productions included Shchedrin's *Dead Souls,* Tchaikovsky's *Queen of Spades* and *Eugene Onegin* at Kirov; as well as *Porgy and Bess* earlier at Maly. Temirkanov made his recording debut in 1973, performing *Rachmaninoff: Symphony No. 2* with the Royal Philharmonic, a popular rendition that was re-released in 1998 on compact disc. *American*

Born Yuri Khatuyevich Temirkanov, December 10, 1938, in Nalchik, Kabardino-Balkaria (Russian republic); son of Khatu Sagidovich Temirkanov and Polina Petrovna Temirkanova; married Irina Guseva (died 1997); one son, Vladimir. *Education*: Leningrad Conservatoire, graduated 1962 and 1965.

First violinist, Leningrad Philharmonic Orchestra, 1961-66; conductor, Maly Theatre and Opera Studio, Leningrad, 1966-68; chief conductor, Leningrad Symphony Orchestra, 1968-76; Kirov Opera and Ballet Company, 1976-88; professor, Leningrad Conservatoire, 1979-88; artistic director, Leningrad Philharmonia Orchestra (later St. Petersburg Philharmonia), 1988–; signed with BMG/RCA, 1988; chief conductor, London Philharmonic Orchestra, 1992–; music director, Baltimore Symphony Orchestra, 1999–; principal guest conductor, Royal Philharmonic Orchestra, Danish National Radio Symphony Orchestra, and Philadelphia Orchestra; guest conductor numerous countries; opera productions: *Porgy and Bess*; *Peter the Great*; *Dead Souls*; *Queen of Spades*, *Eugene Onegin*, 1979.

Awards: First Prize, U.S.S.R. All-Union Conductors' Competition, 1966; Moscow National Conducting Competition Winner, 1967; Glinka Prize, U.S.S.R State Prize, 1976, 1985; U.S.S.R. People's Artist, 1981.

Addresses: *Business*—State Philharmonia, Mikhailovskaya 2, St. Petersburg, Russia; c/o Baltimore Symphony Orchestra, Joseph Meyerhoff Symphony Hall, 1212 Cathedral Street, Baltimore, MD 21201.

Record Guide's Philip Haldeman called the performance "warmer [and] more passionate" than other interpretations. In 1979 Temirkanov joined the faculty of the Leningrad Conservatoire as a professor and served there until 1988. In 1979, he was named the principal guest conductor of the Royal Philharmonic of London, and in 1988 he assumed a position as the chief conductor and artistic director of the Leningrad Philharmonic, behind his mentor, Mravinsky. Temirkanov retained his position with that orchestra throughout the 1990s. In 1992 he added to his credits the title of chief conductor of the London Royal Philharmonic Orchestra, an organization which he formerly led as principal guest conductor.

Baltimore Symphony and Orchestras Worldwide

Temirkanov's made his conducting debut with the Baltimore Symphony Orchestra in 1992 and began a lasting affiliation with that organization. He returned in 1995, 1996, and 1998. In 1999 he assumed a position as the music director of the orchestra, and later that year he was appointed to succeed David Zinman as principal conductor of the Baltimore Symphony. In addition to his permanent positions, Termirkanov was named to a host of guest conductor positions, including principal guest conductor of the Philadelphia Orchestra and the Danish National Radio Symphony Orchestra. He served as guest conductor to orchestras around the world, including the Berlin Philharmonic, Vienna Philharmonic, L'Orchestre de Paris, the Dresden Staatskapelle, the Royal Concertgebouw of Amsterdam, as well as orchestras in Scandinavia and in Sweden in 1968. Additionally he has held positions in the United States—in New York, Philadelphia, Boston, Chicago, Cleveland, San Francisco, and Los Angeles since 1981.

In 1988, under an exclusive contract to BMG/RCA Records, Temirkanov recorded the Stravinsky ballets and Tchaikovsky symphonies with the Royal Philharmonic Orchestra. His other sound recordings included performances of Shostakovich and Prokofieff, Rachmaninoff, Ravel, and Sibelius with the St. Petersburg Philharmonic. He is well known for his performances on four continents, including Europe, South America, Japan, and other Asian countries. A critically acclaimed tour to the United States took him to Philadelphia, Cincinnati, San Francisco, and Minneapolis. Although audiences worldwide appreciate his presentations and interpretations of the works of the great Russian composers, Temirkanov is equally at ease with the music of non-Russian composers. He avers wholeheartedly that music is an international phenomenon that should not be compartmentalized by nationality.

Accomplishments and Awards

Temirkanov came to the conductor's post of the Leningrad Orchestra in 1968. His appointment followed 50 years of leadership by Mravinsky, a brilliant conductor who brought that orchestra into its standing as a world-class organization even amid the turmoil of World War II. Mravinsky led the orchestra until his death in 1989. Temirkanov patiently resurrected the long-lost vigor of the famed musicians and restored the orchestra to its legendary brilliance. In 1991 Temirkanov was quoted in *American Record Guide* as saying, "Mravinsky was the one who made the orchestra's name. [It was my job] ... to persuade the musicians to trust me." Under

Temirkanov's leadership the orchestra was revitalized and took on new qualities. In 1991, following the dissolution of the Soviet Union, the official name of the city of Leningrad was restored by popular vote to St. Petersburg. Temirkanov restored the name of the Philharmonic to follow suit, and the orchestra again became known as the St. Petersburg Philharmonic Orchestra. The collapse of the Soviet regime brought new freedom for musicians to travel freely abroad without the overbearing security and surveillance tactics characteristic of the old government. Since that time Temirkanov has retained his Russian citizenship, but has performed as much as possible in the United States. Regretfully he acknowledged that the situation in Russia resulted from the poor civic and economic climate of his motherland following the political upheaval of the 1990s. Many Russian musicians were unemployed during the 1990s, while others who were fortunate enough to secure work were paid only rarely, if ever. Temirkanov and the St. Petersburg Philharmonic were among the fortunate few to secure rewarding assignments. They received a commission from RCA Victor in 1995 to create a restored soundtrack for the early film classic, *Alexander Nevsky*. Stalin originally produced the film in 1938, the year of Temirkanov's birth. Ironically the movie was released as a propaganda vehicle to warn of the looming danger of a German invasion—the very circumstance that became a tragic reality in 1941 when Temirkanov was three years old. *Stereo Review* compared the luster of the completed stereo soundtrack led by Temirkanov to the restoration of Michelangelo's Sistine Chapel ceiling in Vatican City.

In 1995 Temirkanov conducted the San Francisco Orchestra through the Prokofieff soundtrack of the Sergei Eisenstein epic, *Ivan the Terrible. American Record Guide* critic Marilyn Tucker, called the music "extraordinary," and said that "Temirkanov sketched the scenes with a brush that painted up the immense scale and vitality of both the film and the music."

Temirkanov has been the recipient of numerous awards and prizes, even during the years of repressive rule by the Soviet government. In 1966 he won first prize in the All Soviet-Union Conductors' Competition, and he was named the winner of the Moscow National Conducting Competition in 1967. Temirkanov received the Glinka Prize, a State Prize awarded by the former Soviet Union, in 1976 and in 1985. In 1981 he was also named the People's Artist of the Soviet Union.

Temirkanov has one son, Vladimir, who plays violin for St. Petersburg Philharmonic. Temirkanov's wife, Irina Guseva, died in 1997.

Selected discography

Tchaikovsky: Nutcracker, RCA Victor, 1995.
(with St. Petersburg Philharmonic Orchestra) *Shostakovich: Symphony No. 7 "Leningrad,"* RCA Victor, 1996.
(with the Royal Philharmonic Orchestra) *Rachmaninoff: Symphony No. 2* 1998.
(with the St. Petersburg Philharmonic Orchestra) *Rachmaninoff, Symphony No. 2.*
(with the New York Philharmonic Orchestra) *Rimsky-Korsakov, Scheherazade / Russian Easter Overture.*
(with St. Petersburg Philharmonic Orchestra, with Itzhak Perlman, Yo-Yo Ma, Jessye Norman) *Tchaikovsky Gala.*

Sources

Periodicals

American Record Guide, January-February 1996; January-February 1998; March –April 1998.
San Francisco Chronicle, November 16, 1997.
Stereo Review, May 1995.
Washington Post, April 18, 1999.

Online

"Gramophone Chat Transcript," http://www.gramophone.co.uk/chats.html (March 19, 1999).

—*Gloria Cooksey*

Tom Petty and the Heartbreakers

Rock band

AP/Wide World Photos. Reproduced by permission.

After nearly twenty-five years and twelve albums together, Tom Petty and the Heartbreakers have not only maintained their creativity and friendship, they have all but out lived most other rock bands. The release of *Echo* in 1999 proves that Tom Petty and the Heartbreakers, according to *Houston Chronicle* reporter Bruce Westbrook, "[are] no burned-out gang of geezers going through the motions, but a tight professional band bolstered by Petty's reliably strong material."

Tom Petty was born October 20, 1950, the son of a Gainesville, Florida homemaker and insurance salesman. His parents learned early on that Petty was a rebel. At age four, he insisted on going to town alone—and he did. By age 11, after visiting Elvis Presley on the set of *Follow That Dream*, Petty knew his dream was to become a rock and roll rebel. Petty's father Earl recalled on VH-1's *Behind the Music* that he bought Petty a Sears and Roebuck guitar for twenty-eight dollars and, "he lived with that guitar, day and night." Petty formed his first band, the Sun Downers, in ninth grade. The band played at teen dances and parties for two years. After the Sun Downers broke up Petty joined the Epics, and then Mudcrutch. Two other members of Mudcrutch, guitarist Mike Campbell and keyboardist Benmont Tench, would help Petty start the Heartbreakers in 1974.

In the fall of 1976, Tom Petty and the Heartbreakers released their self-titled debut album on Shelter Records—which was then sold to ABC records. Petty described the album to *Rolling Stone* reporter Fred Schruers as, "a floodgate of influences of everything we'd ever admired and against what we thought was wrong with the music of the time." The album was not an instant hit in the United States, but the song "Anything that's Rock 'n Roll" generated a huge fan reaction in England. Petty and the Heartbreakers opened for guitarist Nils Lofgren for several dates throughout England.

A few months later the band opened for the new wave band Blondie at the infamous Whiskey A Go-Go in Los Angeles. That was the break Petty and the Heartbreakers needed to catch the attention of American audiences. By the spring of 1978 the single "Breakdown" from their debut album jumped into the Top 40. That summer, Petty and the Heartbreakers released their second album, *You're Gonna Get It*. The album was certified gold, but after ABC records sold Shelter to MCA, Petty was infuriated. Long time manager Tony Dimitkides told *Behind the Music* that Petty was "not gonna be sold like a piece of meat."

Petty thought that he and the band should have control over their copyrights and royalty rates. MCA thought that the band should uphold their original contract with Shelter Records—which Mudcrutch, not Petty and the Heart-

breakers, signed—and sued Petty. Petty held his ground, telling *Behind the Music*, "the power we have is that we don't play." MCA countered by issuing subpoenas for all of Petty's notes and lyrics that he and the band were working on. Continuing to stand firm, Petty devised a novel defense; he would declare bankruptcy, thus voiding the band's contract with MCA. Petty told *Behind the Music*, "I was pretty full of myself. I'd just fought the record industry and won."

In 1979, after signing with Backstreet Records, ironically a label affiliated with MCA, Petty and the Heartbreakers released their breakthrough album, *Damn the Torpedoes*. This album included the hit singles, "Refuge," "Don't Do Me Like That," and "Here Comes My Girl." Minneapolis *Star Tribune* writer Neal Justin called *Damn the Torpedoes*, "an awesome collection of one pop classic after another." With the success of that album Tom Petty and the Heartbreakers became hugely popular.

However, another battle with MCA loomed. MCA decided that it would raise the price of the band's next album, *Hard Promises*, from $8.98 to $9.98. Petty was livid because, as he told Schruers, "I never did this to make money." Petty publicly announced his outrage of the price hike, and MCA backed down. *Hard Promises*, as Justin noticed was "one of the first times Petty takes the part of narrator, singing in third person about lovable losers." *Hard Promises* sold 1.5 million copies on the strength of the hit single, "The Waiting."

Smashed Band and Hand

In 1982, Petty and the Heartbreakers followed up *Hard Promises* with *Long After Dark*, which included the smash hit, "You Got Lucky." However, bassist Ron Blair—tired of touring—had quit the band and was replaced by Howie Epstein. For the next year and a half, Petty and the Heartbreakers toured non-stop to support *Long After Dark*. Finally off the road by late 1983, Petty decided to record the next album *Southern Accents* at his new home studio with no producer. Having no producer is like having no captain to steer a ship. The recording sessions became, as Petty recalled on *Behind the Music*, "an ongoing party _ and drugs had entered the picture._ [it was like] opening the devil's door a bit." Thus, Petty and the Heartbreakers disappeared behind this devil's door for a year until a punch was heard around the world.

In 1984, as the *Southern Accents* recording sessions dragged on, Petty lost his cool. He punched a wall with his left hand, and as he told *Behind the Music*, "pulverized it.... to powder." Doctors believed Petty would never play guitar again and the Heartbreakers began calling Petty, "L.V." or Lead Vocalist. However, after surgery and nine months of physical therapy, Petty regained his ability to play. In the spring of 1985, Petty and the Heartbreakers began touring to support *Southern Accents*. Justin called the album, "a rich autobiographical project that marks Petty's most mature moments as a songwriter and singer."

Southern Accents included the singles "Rebels" and "Don't Come Around Here No More." The latter inspired an *Alice in Wonderland* themed music video that won Petty and the Heartbreakers an MTV Music Video Award. In 1985, Petty and the Heartbreakers performed at the first Farm Aid concert to support American farmers, backing up Bob Dylan. This performance led to a two year tour with the rock legend and a live album, *Pack Up the Plantation* as well as another smash single, "Jammin' Me" for the band's 1987 album *Let Me Up (I've Had Enough)*.

Took a Solo Flight

In the summer of 1987, Petty met producer and ex-Electric Light Orchestra leader Jeff Lynne. Together—without the Heartbreakers—they began writing "Free Fallin'," and in 1989 Petty released his first solo album, *Full Moon Fever*. The band was not happy. Guitarist Mike Campbell told *Rolling Stone* reporter Schruers that, "groups are a very complicated thing. It's like a family, it's like a business relationship, it's a very emotional thing. You care about each other, and you tug just like brothers; you're jealous, and then you love each other."

Things became even more complicated when Petty joined Lynne, Roy Orbison, Bob Dylan and George Harrison as a member of the Traveling Wilburys. In 1988 the Traveling Wilburys released their debut album, *The Traveling Wilburys, Vol. One*, and in 1990 won a Grammy for Best Rock Performance by Duo/Group for the hit single, "Handle With Care." Questions regarding the band's fate remained unanswered when, in 1990, the Traveling Wilburys recorded their second album, *The Traveling Wilburys, Vol. 3* and Petty began to record another solo album, *Into the Great Wide Open*.

That album became a group album, however, as Petty and the Heartbreakers regrouped and began touring. *Into the Great Wide Open*, with its hit single "Learning to Fly," went platinum in 1991. In 1993, Petty and the Heartbreakers released *Greatest Hits*, which included two new songs—one of which, "Mary Jane's Last Dance," earned

the band another MTV Video Award. In 1994, drummer Stan Lynch, amidst rising tensions, left the band.

In 1994, Petty signed with Warner Brothers and released his second solo album, *Wildflowers*, which included the hit "Free Fallin'." Commenting on *Wildflowers*, *Newsweek*'s Schoemer wrote, "[Petty] captures people at their most confused, frightened or revealing moments. Sleazy guys pick on innocent girls; solid marriages go awry; friends let friends down, and still despair gives way to renewal." That same year a tribute album to Petty and the Heartbreakers, *You Got Lucky*, was released. Petty told *Rolling Stone*'s Schruers that he was "very flattered, very moved" by this cover album of the band's songs. Petty rejoined the Heartbreakers in 1995 to compile Playback, a boxed set of the band's hits. However, it would be the next album, *Songs and Music From the Motion Picture She's the One* that would pull together Petty and the Heartbreakers for good.

Echoed Longevity

In 1996 Petty began writing a single song for the film, *She's the One*. Fifteen songs later, Petty and the Heartbreakers had recorded their eleventh album, *Songs and Music From the Motion Picture She's the One*. Petty had found a new love for his band, as he told *Denver Post* reporter G. Brown, "They really make my work enjoyable and effortless. It was a healing experience for us, to be in there all involved together and feeling good about what we were doing." Petty continued, "I don't know if I'll make many more solo albums. I'm content to be in the group and do that for awhile. I've had my flings. I've come back to my old sweetheart."

In 1999, the band followed up the soundtrack with *Echo*. Petty told the *Boston Globe*'s Steve Morse that, "we set out to make a rock 'n roll record this time _ we have such a good little rock 'n roll band, and I wanted to get them on record doing what they do best." Petty also continued his rebel ways when he refused to increase the cost of concert tickets, and by offering *Echo*'s first single, "Free Girl Now," on the MP3 format which internet users could download for free. Warner Brothers, however, did not pick a fight with Petty.

Producer Jimmy Iovine told *Behind the Music* that Petty is "one of the most consistent songwriters I've ever laid eyes on" while Producer Rick Rubin stated, "you don't really see great rock bands anymore, and they [Petty and the Heartbreakers] are a great rock band." Petty himself believed, " I know I'm better at what I do than I was when I was younger as a band we're better." To the question of how long Tom Petty and the Heartbreakers would continue making albums, Petty told *Behind the Music*, "I used to say that we'd quit when we got to be 40 [now] lookin' down the barrel at 50. I don't have any intention of quitting."

Selected discography

Tom Petty and the Heartbreakers, Shelter, 1976.
You're Gonna Get It, Shelter, 1978.
Damn the Torpedoes, MCA (Backstreet), 1979.
Long After Dark, MCA (Backstreet), 1982.
Southern Accents, MCA (Backstreet), 1985.
Pack Up the Plantation- Live!, MCA (Backstreet), 1985.
Let Me Up (I've Had Enough), MCA, 1987.
Into the Great Wide Open, MCA, 1991.
Greatest Hits, MCA, 1993.
Playback (boxed set), MCA, 1995.
Echo, Warner Bros., 1999.

Tom Petty solo albums

Full Moon Fever, MCA, 1989.
Wildflowers, Warner Bros., 1994.

Sources

Books

Contemporary Musicians, Vol. 9, Gale Research.

Periodicals

Boston Globe, April 9, 1999.
Denver Post, September 1, 1996.
Houston Chronicle, April 11, 1999.
Newsweek, November 7, 1994.
Rolling Stone, May 4, 1995.
Star Tribune (Minneapolis, MN), September 8, 1995.

Online

"Tom Petty," *Rolling Stone Network: Random Notes*, www.RollingStone.com (May 19, 1999).
"Tom Petty and the Heartbreakers," www.tompetty.com/cmp/biomain.html (May 4, 1999).
"Tom Petty," www.wallofsound.com (May 4, 1999).

—*Ann M. Schwalboski*

Underworld

Techno rock group

For the British ensemble Underworld, merging past and present—as well as chilly synthesizer-driven nuances with genuine emotive soul into futuristic rhythms—has resulted in a critically praised and commercially viable series of records. The band, wrote Barry Walters in *Rolling Stone,* "create darkly physical grooves that seduce psyche, body and soul without resorting to instant hooks or easily understood concepts." Though they gained fame when two of their songs were included in the hit 1996 film *Trainspotting,* the forming members of Underworld, Karl Hyde and Rick Smith, had been making music together for several years already. Both were accomplished songwriters and engineers who were well-versed in cutting-edge electronic instrumentation and production styles.

Hyde and Smith met at an art college in Cardiff, Wales, England, around 1980. Hyde has played guitar since the age of eleven and been in numerous bands, while the Welsh-born Smith was raised in a household headed by his minister father, and was heavily influenced by gospel music as a result. Smith also played the piano, and as

Photo by Hamish Brown. Reproduced by permission, V2 Records.

For the Record . . .

Members include **Darren Emerson** (born c. 1971), turntables; **Karl Hyde** (born c. 1958), guitars, vocals; and **Rick Smith** (born c. 1960, in Wales, England), keyboards.

Hyde and Smith were signed to CBS Records in the early 1980s as the band Freur; formed Underworld MK1, c. 1988; released two albums before disbanding; formed current version of band with Emerson, 1991.

Addresses: *Record company*—V2 Records, 14 E. 4th St., 3rd Floor, New York NY 10012.

a teen became a fan of the legendary 1970s German band Kraftwerk, who pioneered synthesizer music. In 1981 Hyde and Smith formed a moody, drum machine-based act they called Freur, and were signed to CBS Records. Their haunting, darkly spiraling 1983 single, "Doot Doot," charted well in the United Kingdom, was a huge hit in Italy, and even found its way into the alternative radio scene in North America.

Hyde and Smith were uninterested in becoming the next Depeche Mode. They remained in Wales, against industry advice, spent their advance on a car, and were soon dropped by CBS. From there, the duo formed Underworld MK1, which allowed them to pursue another musical direction that featured far less electronic-based instrumentation and leaned heavily toward funk. After a record deal with Sire and two albums—*Underneath the Radar,* released in 1988, and 1989's *Change the Weather*—they had achieved minor success in Australia, and were invited to open on the farewell tour for the Eurythmics in the late 1980s. They played to huge stadium crowds, and the experience left a negative impression on the pair. "Within three dates, it was like, `This is *awful,*'" Smith told *Urb* writer Tamara Palmer. "This is really awful. I stood in front of like 30,000 people. It was nice for five seconds, and after that it was awful."

Underworld Comes Together

After parting ways with Sire, Hyde became a guitar player for hire and toured with Iggy Pop for a time. He also spent a great deal of time in New York City, where he used to frequent a bar called Jackie 60 with Deborah Harry of Blondie. Meanwhile, Smith relocated to the Essex town of Romford, England, where he met 20-year-old Darren Emerson, a successful money-markets trader who also worked as a part-time DJ. At the time, the acid-house music scene had firmly taken hold in England, and Smith and Emerson began setting down tracks in the studio that merged the darkly electronic vibe of Freur with the more danceable rhythms of the first formation of Underworld. Hyde returned from touring and joined them in the studio.

"Mother Earth" was the first single the threesome cut together, created solely for Emerson's DJ set in a local club. "That was our outlet," Hyde told *Raygun* magazine. "We didn't have radio or any system for playing live; Darren was our shop window." Both "Mother Earth" and "Dirty" were released under the name Lemon Interrupt because of contractual issues with Sire over the Underworld MK1 name. At the time, Hyde and Smith also formed Tomato, an art collective/graphic design firm that over the decade evolved into art and music installation projects as well.

Their first record as Underworld, "Mmmm Skyscraper I Love You," became a huge underground hit in England, and they were soon signed to a label called Junior Boy's Own, a subsidiary of London Records. Another record, "Rez," was also a massive club hit. Both tracks were included on their 1994 debut, *dubnobasswithmyheadman,* an album termed by *Raygun* as rife "with electronic melodies so warm you could curl up inside them, and rhythms so powerful and methodical that they left you with no option but letting it all out." Underworld also made an impact with their live performances, shows that merged Emerson's DJ talents with Hyde and Smith's years of performing, and featured spectacular visual shows created by the Tomato creative collective as well. *Request* magazine declared that "the album crystallized a moment. The group's mix of live instrumentation and back house rhythms appealed to both dance and rock audiences, while its stunning live gigs, including one 14-hour long improvisation performance, solidified its reputation."

"A Very London Sound"

Underworld's second album, *Second Toughest in the Infants,* was released in 1996. It incorporated the burgeoning jungle beat flavors then sweeping the British music scene, gained serious critical approval, and managed to sell a respectable 87,000 copies in the U.S. alone. Reviewing it for the *Village Voice,* Ben Williams declared it to be "an album that manages to be as accomplished as the first while expanding upon its sound." Williams went on to note that as a band, "Underworld finds poignancy in the ambience of modern urban life, sculpting its repetitive blips and pulses into a seamless sonic flow that turns mechanical banality into emotional gold." Williams continued, "This is a very London sound, one of tube stations and corner-shops and dingy cafes: rain-soaked, gray, yet at times possessed of a still, tragic beauty that contradicts the constant forward motion of its rhythms."

Underworld were one of the first techno acts to integrate lyrics into their songs, though, as *Raygun* noted, "Hyde's fragmented poetry won't stand up to any logic test, although, in a way, abstraction seems the sensible stylistic match for a genre that's not big on meaning or interpretation." As Hyde explained in the same article, "I respond with the recording of the voice to the groove; the music comes first always."

Trainspotting Soundtrack Success

Though the original British release of *Second Toughest in the Infants* did not include the track "Born Slippy," the song was integrated into the American version released later that year as a result of its inclusion on the soundtrack to the 1996 cult favorite *Trainspotting*. The film, by director Danny Boyle, was a success on both sides of the Atlantic for its wry, often painfully comical depiction of a group of Scottish drug addicts. "Born Slippy" was released in England in the spring of 1995, and after it became indelibly associated with the successful film and best-selling soundtrack, went on to sell over a million copies. It was also named single of the year by several British music magazines, and finally brought the band greater recognition in North America.

Fittingly, Underworld's next effort received a massive marketing push from their label, now tied with New York City's V2 Records. *Beaucoup Fish* was written in fits and starts, as midway though the recording process, the band was compelled to honor a commitment to do a European tour. They used the opportunity to try out the songs live, and found the strategy resulted in a far different sound in the end. "It made us cut out much of the frou-frou and get rid of a lot of the unnecessary padding," Hyde told *Billboard*'s Dylan Siegler.

At the Forefront of Electronica

Released in the spring of 1999, *Beaucoup Fish* was a massive critical success stateside. The first single, "Cups," was singled out for particular praise. "They re-engineer the old-school Detroit-style synth that swerves through 'Cups' until it sounds sleek enough for a BMW commercial—then chop it down into pseudo-Latin breaks and icy chunks of melody," wrote *Details*' Pat Blashill, while *Entertainment Weekly*'s David Browne called its dozen minutes "something we've long been waiting for— the `Free Bird' of electronica!"

In his review, Browne praised the band for progressing creatively over the past five years. "*Beaucoup Fish* feels like a stimulating new beginning. Wipe away its dusting of frost and you'll encounter mystery, beauty, and alluring rhapsodies, with the warm, pulsating beats serving as the music's heart." Browne also wrote of the backlash against electronica, heralded as the next big thing, and noted that "no one should have ever expected such amelodic music to top anything." The critic termed *Beaucoup Fish* a record that proves "how many more places this music can wander, how it can grow and reinvent itself."

Reinvention and artistic progression have been constant in Hyde and Smith's career since their days together as Freur. "We embrace a lot of the sounds and rhythms that go on around us,"
Hyde told *Rolling Stone* writer Todd Roberts. "I think that's a way forward [for music]. I'd like to think that people are opening their minds a lot more."

Selected discography

(as Underworld MK1) *Underneath the Radar,* Sire, 1988.
(as Underworld MK1) *Change the Weather,* Sire, 1989.
dubnobasswithmyheadman, Junior Boy's Own, 1994.
Second Toughest in the Infants, Junior Boy's Own, 1996.
Pearl's Girl (EP), Junior Boy's Own, 1996.
Beaucoup Fish, Junior Boy's Own/V2, 1999.

Sources

Billboard, November 23, 1996, pp. 13, 20; March 20, 1999, pp. 11, 80.
Details, February 1999, p. 69.
Entertainment Weekly, April 4, 1999.
Raygun, March 1999.
Request, April 1999.
Rolling Stone, October 3, 1996, p. 32; April 29, 1999, p. 68.
Spin, April 1999.
Urb, January/February 1999.
Village Voice, May 21, 1996, p. 57.

—*Carol Brennan*

Vanessa-Mae

Violin

Andrew Wong/Archive Photos, Inc. Reproduced by permission.

Prodigious violinist Vanessa-Mae Nicholson performed with the London Philharmonia at age ten before attending the Royal College of Music in London. By age 14 she had released three CDs and signed a contract with a major recording company. Even as an adolescent she was uniquely adept in her ability to alternate between performing classical selections on an eighteenth-century acoustical violin and playing modern music on a high-tech electric jazz model violin. Vanessa-Mae has called her musical style "techno-acoustic fusion."

Vanessa-Mae was born Vanessa-Mae Vanakorn in Singapore on October 27, 1978, and growing up took inspiration from the fact that she shared the same birth date as Italian violinist Niccolo Paganini, though born 196 years after the famed musician. Although her parents divorced when she was very young, her mother remarried soon after, to Graham Nicholson, an attorney and a member of England's distinguished Freshfields law firm. Graham Nicholson adopted the budding violinist as his own daughter, and moved the family to England when Vanessa-Mae was four years old. She grew up in London, and it was Great Britain that provided her a national identity.

Vanessa-Mae played the piano as a toddler and began to study the violin at age five. She was only eight years old when she traveled to Beijing to study with Lin Yao Ji in the Yankelevich violin method. Vanessa-Mae finished the Yankelevich course, a two-year curriculum, in a brief six months. By the time she returned home she had made a decision to play the violin professionally. As Vanessa-Mae embarked on her quest, she was encouraged and assisted by her mother, Pamela Soei Luang (Tan) Nicholson, the owner of a private recording label and music agency. A musician in her own right, Pamela Nicholson was a semi-professional concert pianist, who on occasion accompanied her daughter's violin playing.

Young Vanessa-Mae made a formal concert debut as a soloist with the London Philharmonia at age ten, but it was not until one year after her concert debut that she enrolled at the Royal College of Music in London, where she studied with Felix Andrievsky. Vanessa-Mae attended Francis Holland girls' school for a liberal education, but soon dropped out of the school in order to devote more time to her musical studies and her career. Vanessa-Mae by that time was already a veteran of the recording studio, having released three albums on her mother's personal record label. Vanessa-Mae distinguished herself with her very first recordings, renditions of violin concertos by Tchaikovsky and Beethoven. She was the youngest artist to ever record those compositions. By age 14, she was an accomplished professional, having completed her first international tour as a featured soloist with the London Mozart Players. She then signed a recording contract with EMI Records. During those years, despite the demands of her career, she continued her traditional school curriculum under the guidance of private tutors.

Vanessa-Mae, who loved classical music as a child, was nevertheless enthralled by Michael Jackson and other popular artists of her generation. When she signed with EMI she retained the right to control her performance content, in order to accommodate her diverse musical interests. She refused to limit her selections to classical compositions exclusively. Instead she embarked on a career of crossover techno-fusion musical styles. At that time, under the artistic direction of producer Mel Bush, she emerged with a new visual image as an ingenue—more mature, and in abject contrast from the little girl persona of her earlier public performances. She then set out on her first tour of the United Kingdom, performing in her own style: Shostakovich in tandem with popular music, including selections by The Artist Formerly Known as Prince. She also appeared as a solo artist at the Royal Festival Hall that year. Vanessa-Mae released her first EMI album, *The Violin Player,* at age 16. The album it hit number eleven on the British charts and sold over two million copies. One selection from the album, "Toccata and Fugue in D Minor," became a hit single for Vanessa-Mae and remained on the top 40 charts for several weeks.

As a teen-ager performing in a grown-up arena, Vanessa-Mae's talent was frequently overshadowed by her youthful, seemingly suggestive wardrobe, as well as by certain choreography that she performed while playing her violin during her performances and in rock-video style recordings. The visual images of Vanessa-Mae's performances, in fact, generated considerable controversy and raised eyebrows. Many critics labeled her style as sexually aggressive. Cries of exploitation accompanied the release of her now-famous wet T-shirt video that was made when the violinist was 15 years old. In the controversial video, Vanessa-Mae emerged from the Mediterranean Sea in a soaking wet white sheath gown, so lightweight that it was barely visible. Some observers suggested that the performance approached being pornographic. Vanessa-Mae responded to the critics and assured the public that she had complete artistic control over her own image. She defended her video to the press with cool articulation. She reiterated that she maintained a presence in the cutting room when the tape was finalized, and that she had total control over the images that were released in the finished product. She further asserted that she enjoyed creating the video and noted that classical divas traditionally perform in provocative gowns. Vanessa-Mae was quoted by Scot Duncan of the *Orange Country Register* as saying, "Let's face it, I go into the classical department of record stores and I see a lot of grown women in low-cut gowns and flaunty dresses."

Vanessa-Mae celebrated the release of her first album on the EMI label with a promotional debut tour of the United States. Among her many tour stops was an appearance on the "Tonight Show," as well as stops at Chicago's Wrigley Field and Comiskey Park during the 1995 World Series play offs to perform the national anthem. Vanessa-Mae's style is unusual and unpredictable, and for many of her fans, the highlight of her 1995 tour was a memorable concert at New York City's Times Square. During the finale of the concert, Vanessa-Mae leaped onto the roof of a taxicab without missing a note on her violin. On another occasion early in 1997, Vanessa-Mae performed at St. Moritz, where she arrived in a hang-glider.

Musically Vanessa-Mae is equally unpredictable, often juxtaposing incongruous styles. When she performed a unique arrangement of the Scottish air, "I'm a Doun for Lack of Johnny," she featured African drums in the background. Her recording of that particular composition, under the title "Scottish Fantasy," came to typify the eclectic quality that characterized many of her selections. Vanessa-Mae's versatile style made it necessary for her to learn to perform on more than one instrument. For purely classical selections, she bows on a Guadagnini violin that dates back to 1761, a gift that she received when she was ten years old. For her unique techno-fusion adaptations of classic and popular compositions, she employs a MIDI configuration on an angular white electric violin. Her repertoire varies from Brahms, Paganini, Kreisler and Ravel, to syncopated upbeat rhythms.

Vanessa-Mae made her first formal concert tour of the United States in 1996 at age 18. Her mother provided piano accompaniment for some of the performances. Later that summer Vanessa-Mae performed at a reunification concert in Hong Kong, where she offered a rendition of "Happy Valley—the Reunification Overture," a composition of her own creation. She performed at a conference of economic ministers in France that same year, and in 1998 she performed at Buckingham Palace, to an assembly of heads of state who were in attendance at an Asia-Europe Meeting. Her performance at the Royal Albert Hall was well received.

Vanessa-Mae enjoys entertaining, and she embellished her 1998 album *Storm* with her own singing. She contemplates the possibility of a second career as a supermodel. Indeed she is easy to recognize and possesses striking, exotic features inherited from her Chinese mother and Thai father. She loves to read and plans to attend a university; she has a number of interests that she hopes to pursue academically. Until she finalizes her future plans, Vanessa-Mae hopes to maintain a busy schedule, perform continually, and tour often. She tenaciously guards her privacy when dealing with the press.

Selected discography

Singles

"Toccata and Fugue in D Minor," EMI Angel, 1995.

Albums

The Violin Player, EMI Angel, 1995.
Storm, Virgin, 1998.
The Original Four Seasons, Angel, 1999.

Sources

Billboard, March 4, 1995; October 5, 1996; May 3, 1997; March 21, 1998.
Daily News (Los Angeles), November 28, 1996.
Los Angeles Times, December 2, 1996.
Orange County Register, July 28, 1995.
Time, December 11, 1995.
Wall Street Journal, April 12, 1995; April 10, 1998.

—*Gloria Cooksey*

Waddy Wachtel

Guitar, producer, songwriter

Robert "Waddy" Wachtel has played and worked with a who's who of rock throughout his years as a session musician—Bob Dylan, The Everly Brothers, Iggy Pop, Keith Richards, Linda Ronstadt, and Warren Zevon, among many other musicians and vocalists. In the 1984 book *The Guitar,* Wachtel's sound was described as "the churning, badass end of the guitar's spectrum of sounds," and he was said to have the ability to play "fullblown gutsy raunch or sweet Mexican-flavored licks with equal ease. He is a high-energy player." Wachtel's talent has placed him in the company of esteemed session guitarists Ry Cooder, David Lindley and Lowell George. His behind the scenes contributions include credits as producer and songwriter.

Wachtel toured with The Everly Brothers, but began gaining attention as a session artist after backing Carole King during the recording and subsequent tour supporting her *Thoroughbred* album in the 1970s. He is credited with being one of a group of musicians in Los Angeles that gave rock songs recorded in the 1970s and 1980s a decidedly raucous Southern California flair. Dave DiMartino, in *Singer-Songwriters: Pop Music's Performer-Composers, from A to Zevon,* called them "the L.A. session-musician 'mafia' that dominated most recordings of the genre and era." These musicians included Andrew Gold, a multi-instrumental musician; Russ Kunkle, drums; Leland Sklar, bass; Jai Winding on piano; and a group of backing singers including Glenn Frey, J.D. Souther, Linda Ronstadt and Wendy Waldman.

Wachtel appeared on numerous rock recordings in the late 1970s and early 1980s. Frequent associates were Ronstadt, Karla Bonoff, and Zevon. "Poor, Poor Pitiful Me" was included on Zevon's 1976 self-titled album, a song which was covered successfully by Ronstadt a year later on her *Simple Dreams* album. Wachtel appears on both recordings. In 1978, again with Zevon, Wachtel worked on the *Excitable Boy* album. With Zevon he penned the classic "Werewolves of London" and co-produced the album with Jackson Browne.

During the early 1980s Wachtel began working with Stevie Nicks after she embarked on a solo career apart from Fleetwood Mac. Wachtel created the memorable guitar sound on her hit "Edge of Seventeen." He also played guitar on her subsequent recordings *The Wild Heart* and *Rock a Little.*

Wachtel was among the session musicians hired by Bob Seger in 1983 to record *The Distance.* Seger had long been recording as Bob Seger & The Silver Bullet Band. This album was issued as a Bob Seger & The Silver Bullet Band project, but other musicians were brought in. Using

Born May 24, 1947, in New York, NY; married to Annie Wachtel.

Started career as touring musician with the Everly Brothers; worked as a studio musician and became noticed in 1970s after working and touring with Carole King; made notable recordings with artists Linda Ronstadt, Warren Zevon and Stevie Nicks through the 1980s; worked as producer with artists including Zevon, Ronstadt, The Church, George Thorogood and others into the late 1990s, as well as continuing work as a studio musician; as a songwriter, Wachtel penned songs recorded by Zevon, Ronstadt, and the duet "Her Town Too" recorded by J.D. Souther and James Taylor.

Addresses: *Management*—Nick M. Ben-Meir, 652 N. Doheny Dr., Los Angeles, CA 90069.

musicians-for-hire was said to have upset Silver Bullet Band guitarist Drew Abbott, causing him to quit the band. Other artists with whom Wachtel has worked include the Motels, Rod Stewart, Spinal Tap, Ron Wood, and Bonnie Raitt.

What is a studio musician? As explained by Richie Unterberger in his essay in *All Music Guide to Rock: The Best CDs, Albums & Tapes: Rock, Pop, Soul, R&B and Rap,* these are musicians "who are not stars in their own right, but have done much to shape the course of rock music. Even today, when most session musicians are routinely credited on album jackets, they enjoy far less recognition that the performers they back in the studio. ... Session players are credited on most album sleeves these days, it's true, but the level of public recognition remains much lower than artists that work under their own name."

Wachtel is perhaps best known for his enduring association with Keith Richards, with whom he has played guitar, written music, and co-produced recordings during Richards's creative breaks from The Rolling Stones. The duo met in the mid-1970s and worked together on a single track on Tom Waits' *Bone Machine.* Soon after, Richards decided to go solo.

Richards assembled an eclectic group of musicians in the late 1980s including Wachtel, Ivan Neville, and Steve Jordan. His backing band became known as X-Pensive Winos after they were seen drinking an expensive vintage wine behind some speakers during a studio session. For 1988's *Talk is Cheap,* Wachtel played guitars and served as the album's production consultant. With Richards, Wachtel and Steve Jordan collaborated on production of the 1992 *Main Offender* album on which Wachtel also played guitars and piano, sang backing vocals, and assisted with songwriting. "...Waddy was a great breakthrough," Richards said in the 1998 Victor Bokris biography *Keith Richards: The Biography.* "He's got a better and mathematical brain than Steve [Jordan] or I have."

Wachtel produced the 1997 George Thorogood recording *Rockin' My Life Away.* Wachtel reportedly had gone to see Thorogood play and subsequently decided he wanted to work with him. "Waddy Wachtel, as you know, has this great body of work from the '70s, '80s and '90s. He's everybody's guy. It came to my attention that he wanted to work with me. I never knew about his work until he worked with Keith Richards," said Thorogood in an online interview. "I said 'Keith with a studio musician? I don't know about that.' But Waddy is a unique case and I went to see the Expensive (sic) Winos live and he supplied the guitar on that tour. I said 'okay, this is kinda funky, this makes it.' I met him and the problem was shutting the two of us up (laughter) to get us to play the music. It was like finding this long lost soul brother that you'd lost around 13 or 14 years of age. His whole childhood was mirrored of mine, completely. The difference between us is that he mastered the guitar. He's another genius."

Wachtel reunited with Ronstadt 1998 to play on her album *We Ran.* He also co-wrote and produced "I Go To Pieces," and wrote and produced "Damage." "[T]he two happiest parts of making this album were reuniting with Bernie [Leadon of The Eagles] and working again with Waddy Wachtel," said Ronstadt. "It was Waddy who first taught me how to phrase rock n' roll. He taught me how to find dynamics in all that howling and swirling of those coliseums we played in." In addition to touring coliseums with Ronstadt, Wachtel supported many musicians on the road whose albums he appeared on including Zevon, James Taylor, and Nicks.

Whether it is punchy riffs, raw energy, or musical embroidery, Wachtel has provided accompaniment and support to rock's elite for more than three decades. "That was why people would hire me," Wachtel told *Musician*'s David Simons in 1999, "because they needed that rock & roll statement." Watchel shows no signs of slowing down. He broadened his resume further in the late 1990s when he was hired as musical director for comic Adam Sandler.

Selected discography

(with Karla Bonoff)

Karla Bonoff, Columbia, 1977.
Restless Nights, Columbia, 1979.
Wild Heart of the Young, Columbia, 1982.

(with Stevie Nicks)

Bella Donna, WEA, 1981.
The Wild Heart, 1983.
Rock a Little, EMI, 1985.

(with Keith Richards and the X-Pensive Winos)

Talk is Cheap, Virgin, 1988.
Live at the Hollywood Palladium (Dec. 15, 1988), Virgin, 1991.
Main Offender, Virgin, 1992.

(with Linda Ronstadt)

Simple Dreams, Asylum, 1977
Living in the U.S.A., Asylum, 1978.
Mad Love, Asylum, 1980.
Get Closer, Asylum, 1982.
We Ran, Elektra, 1998.

(with James Taylor)

In the Pocket, Warner Brothers, 1976.
Flag, CBS, 1979.
Dad Loves His Work, CBS, 1981.

(with Warren Zevon)

Warren Zevon, Asylum, 1976.
*Excitable Boy,*Asylum, 1978.
Bad Luck Streak in Dancing School, Asylum, 1980.
The Envoy, Asylum, 1982.
Mr. Bad Example, Giant, 1991.

(with The Church)

Starfish (includes "Under the Milky Way," co-producer), Arista, 1988.
Gold Afternoon Fix, 1991.

(with others)

Circle of Souls, *Hands of Faith,* Hollywood, 1991.
Gilby Clarke, *Pawn Shop Guitars,* Virgin, 1994.
Bryan Ferry, *The Bride Stripped Bare,* Reprise, 1978.
George Thorogood, *Rockin' My Life Away,* EMI, 1997.

Sources

Books

Bacon, Tony, editor, *1000 Great Guitarists,* GPI Books/Miller Freeman Books, 1994.
Bokris, Victor, *Keith Richards: The Biography,* De Capo Press, 1998.
Booth, Stanley, *Keith Richards: Standing in the Shadows,* St. Martin's Press.
DiMartino, Dave, *Singer-Songwriters: Pop Music's Performer-Composers, from A to Zevon,* Billboard Books, 1994.
Erlewine, Michael, Vladimir Bogdanov, and Chris Woodstra, editors, *All Music Guide to Rock: The Best CDs, Albums & Tapes: Rock, Pop, Soul, R&B and Rap,* Miller Freeman Books, 1995.
Santoro, Gene, editor, *The Guitar,* Quarto Marketing, Ltd., 1984.

Periodicals

Billboard Daily Music Update, May 4, 1998.
Entertainment Weekly, July 29, 1994
Los Angeles Times, October 16, 1998.
Musician, April 1999.
Playboy, December 1990.

Online

Elektra Online, http://www.elektra.com/retro/ronstadt/index.html
George Thorogood Interview, http://www.rocknet.com/may97/georget.html

Additonal information was taken from liner notes by Kurt Loder for the X-Pensive Winos, 1991, and provided by Waddy Wachtel.

—*Linda Dailey Paulson*

Jody Watley

Singer, songwriter

AP/Wide World Photos. Reproduced by permission.

Jody Watley is the rare performer who measures success in terms of happiness. As a singer, dancer, songwriter, and producer, she typifies the complete artist of the 1990s. Watley was already a 15-year veteran of television, recording, and performing when she won the Grammy Award for Best New Artist in 1987.

Watley was born in Chicago around 1960. Her family lived for a time in Kansas City, Missouri, but Watley was raised for the most part in Los Angeles. She was born into a family with show business ties. Her father was an Episcopalian radio evangelist and a disk jockey; her mother was a piano player and singer. Among her family's most cherished friends were popular performers Joe Tex, Sam Cooke, and Jackie Wilson. Wilson, in fact, was Watley's godfather.

During the early 1970s when Watley was only 14 years old, she landed a steady job on the *Soul Train* television show. On *Soul Train,* Watley partnered with Jeffrey Daniel, who later joined Watley as a member of the R&B trio Shalamar. The two worked well together, choreographing their own wild and daring dance routines. Cornelius was so impressed that he encouraged Watley, a 17-year-old high school graduate, to pursue a career in the performing arts. Watley, who graduated high school with honors, fully intended to enroll in college, but knew instinctively that her future was in songwriting and singing. With the endorsement of Cornelius, she was hard-pressed to ignore what she perceived as her destiny. Also with Cornelius' encouragement, Watley was instrumental in establishing Shalamar. The group consisted of Watley, Howard Hewett, and her *Soul Train* partner, Daniels. Watley remained with Shalamar for seven years during the late 1970s and into the 1980s. In 1984 she left the group to expand her personal artistic talents. She was concerned about her stereotypical function in the group as a "sexy girl" instead of a serious singer, and she aspired to write and perform her own songs.

With Shalamar in her past, Watley spent some time working as a model in England. On her return to Los Angeles, she became professionally involved with André Cymone, a bass player, and former band member with The Artist Formerly Known as Prince. Watley and Cymone established a working relationship with former Diana Ross producer, Bernard Edwards. She wrote and collaborated with Cymone in a creative effort that resulted in several albums and hit singles. Watley's brother, John, was also involved as her tour manager. Watley signed a contract with MCA, and the success of her debut solo album *Jody Watley* won her the Grammy Award for Best New Artist in 1987. Among the selections on that album was the number one "smash" hit "Looking for a New Love."

For the Record . . .

Born January 30, c. 1960, in Chicago, IL; married André Cymone; divorced; one daughter, Lauren; one son, Arie.

Soul Train dancer, c. 1970; member of Shalamar, late 1970s; MCA records solo artist, 1987-1993; established Avitone record label, 1995; Atlantic Records, 1998–; established Divine Management.

Awards: Grammy Award for Best New Artist, 1987.

Addresses: *Record company*—Atlantic Recording Corp., 1290 Avenue of the Americas, New York, NY 10104.

Watley's next album, *Larger than Life* in 1989, featured the ballad "Real Love" which earned gold record status. The album also included a collection of dance tunes with a rousing beat. Her third album, comprised of an assortment of ballads, was the vehicle that established Watley as a serious singer. The soulful selections silenced those skeptics who compartmentalized her style and labeled her a songstress of the faded disco era. By 1993, Watley had released five albums on the MCA label, including her fifth and final MCA release, *Intimacy,* on which she co-wrote seven of the album's ten songs. Watley's solo career completed its metamorphosis in the 1990s. She shed her image as a "disco-dolly" and "pony-girl," diverging exclusively toward introspective and romantic moods. In 1991 President George Bush extended an invitation to Watley to sing at a White House ceremony at the Kennedy Center in 1992. Watley accepted, and she used the opportunity to voice her opinions on racial bigotry.

After leaving MCA, Watley launched her own record label, *Avitone,* and went on to produce her own album, *Affection,* in 1995. Additionally she directed and released a video for *Affection.* She signed with Atlantic Records in 1998, and by 1999 her solo career credits entailed six top ten singles and two platinum albums. Watley was heard singing along with a collection of other popular artists on the *Dr. Dolittle* movie soundtrack. She also sang on various soundtrack recordings for *Beverly Hills 90210, White Men Can't Jump,* and the AIDS benefit album *Band-Aid.* She appeared live on Black Entertainment's (BET) Planet Groove and made a round of talk show visits in anticipation of her first Atlantic release. With the release of her first album from Atlantic Records, Watley also established a management company called Divine.

It came as a surprise to many who followed Watley's career that her working relationship with Cymone transcended their professional life. The couple was married for three years before they revealed that fact to the public. According to Watley, the secrecy was intended in part to protect Cymone's privacy in the wake of her own soaring stardom. The couple has two children—a daughter, Lauren, born in the early 1980s, and a son, Arie, born in 1992. Watley and Cymone were married for approximately ten years. They divorced near the end of 1995.

Watley confronts the issue of a pending reunion between herself and the other Shalamar singers from time to time, but her attitude suggests that the group is a thing of the past and should not be resurrected. Motherhood demands much of her time, and her career outlets continue to unfold. Svelte and health-conscious, she filmed a fitness video in 1990, entitled *Jody Watley: Dance to Fitness.* In 1996, she signed with the famous Ford Modeling Agency and accepted an exclusive contract to model Sack's Fifth Avenue's Winter Coat wardrobe. Two years later she modeled for a (partially nude) six-page spread in the April 1998 issue of *Playboy* magazine.

Selected discography

Jody Watley, MCA, 1987.
Larger Than Life, MCA 1989.
You Wanna Dance with Me? 1989.
Affairs of the Heart, MCA, 1991.
Intimacy, MCA, 1993.
Remixes of Love (Japanese release), 1994.
Affection, Avitone/Bellmark, 1995.
Greatest Hits, 1996.
Flower, Atlantic, 1998.

Sources

Periodicals

Billboard, December 20, 1998.
Ebony, November 1993, p. 36.
Essence, March 1994, p. 62.
Jet, August 7, 1995, p. 34.
People, October 16, 1995, p. 96; March 11, 1996, p. 116; May 25, 1997, p. 21; April 6, 1998, p. 23.

Online

"Jody Watley Discography," and "Jody Biography" available at http://www.americamodels.com/jodywatley/ (May 25, 1999).

—*Gloria Cooksey*

Wendy O. Williams and The Plasmatics

Punk-Metal rock group

When dominitrix-dressed diva Wendy O. Williams burst on to the music scene with the Plasmatics in 1978, she further confused the average citizen and delighted and titillated fans with her no-holds-barred approach to creating a sonic spectacle. Straddling punk and heavy metal music, the Plasmatics were seemingly as much performance artists as musicians. Williams unleashed raw sexual energy in maiming guitars and cars with a heavy artillery including sledgehammers and chainsaws and matched those actions with equally raw raucous vocals.

Born in Rochester, New York, Williams began performing in dance recitals as a child, which led to an appearance on Howdy Doody. She also studied clarinet at the Eastman School of Music. According to some, Williams was reportedly wild since childhood—kicked out of her Brownie troop for flirting with boys and arrested at 15 for nude sunbathing on a public beach. As a teen, she dropped out of high school her junior year and hitchhiked to Colorado with cash saved from a Dunkin' Donuts job. There, she experimented with drugs and had a string of odd jobs. Later, she moved to Fort Lauderdale and worked as a lifeguard and sailing instructor. She also sold macrame bikinis she had made as well. Williams traveled around Europe from 1974-76 before returning to New York City.

The Plasmatics were formed by Rod Swenson, whom Williams met while working as a live sex show performer in "Captain Kink's Sex Fantasy Theatre." Swenson was Captain Kink, a Yale graduate who produced and promoted live sex shows. He had also completed videos for Patti Smith and The Ramones. His experience working on those videos inspired him to create his own band and decided Williams should front his concept of a punk band. Swenson essentially created the Plasmatics around her. He was the group's manager and lyricist, and would become Williams' life-long companion. Original members included Richie Stotts, who played lead guitar for the group, O. Chosei Funahara, bassist, Stu Deutsch on drums, and Williams, who wailed on saxophone as well as chainsaw and sledgehammer. Williams told *People* in an 1983 interview, "I was an outcast, a loner. I never felt like I fit." Wes Beech joined the Plasmatics as rhythm guitarist soon after they formed. The group made its debut at the legendary New York nightclub CBGB's in July of 1978.

In their first incarnation, *Trouser Press* described the group as "mere artless gimmickry" in which "Wendy O. Williams hoarsely talks/shouts/heavy-breathes lyrics jumbling the psychotronic film aesthetic (sex, violence, gratuitous grotesqueries) accompanied by a band playing with no subtlety whatever at punk speed and vol-

For the Record . . .

Members include **Wendy O. Williams**, born, Rochester, NY, 1949, (died April 6, 1998, Storrs, CT, of a self-inflicted gunshot wound), vocals, saxophone, chainsaw, sledgehammer; **Jean Beauvoir**, (group member from 1980-81), bass; **Wes Beech**, (group member from 1978-87), rhythm guitar; **Ray Callahan**, drums; **Stu Deutsch**, (group member from 1978-80), drums; **O. Chosei Funahara**, (group member from 1978-80), bass; **Tony Petri**, drums; **Joey Reese**, (died 1994), drums; **Chris "Junior" Romanelli**, (group member from 1981-87) bass and keyboards; **Richie Stotts**, (group member from 1978-83) guitar; **T.C. Tolliver**, drums.

Group formed by Rod Swenson in 1978; debuted at New York's CBGB's, July of 1978; released debut album, *New Hope for the Wretched,* Stiff America Records, 1980, released *Beyond the VAlley of 1984,* Stiff Amarica Records, 1981, released *Metal Priestess,* Stiff America Records, 1981, released *Coup d'Etat,* Capitol Records, 1982; Williams released first solo album *W.O.W.,* Passport, 1984; released rap album *Deffest and Baddest,* as Ultrafly and the Hometown Girls, Profile/Sledgehammer, 1988; Plasmatics disband, 1984; Williams and remaining Plasmatics continue to record and perform under her name; Williams stopped performing, late 1980s.

ume." It also described their debut album, *New Hope for the Wretched* as "entertaining for its sheer crassness perhaps, though hardly listenable."

Always provocative, Williams' stage antics seemed to draw more attention than the music. *Billboard*'s Chris Morris wrote that the group was known "less for its in-your-face, punk-derived music than for the onstage antics of its statuesque vocalist." Her notable stage stunts included shredding cars or demolishing guitars with chainsaws. Williams went so far as to blow up a car in the studios of the *Tomorrow with Tom Snyder* television program. For a video, she jumped off the roof of a moving school bus just prior to it crashing through a wall of television sets. For these sorts of stunts, she was often labeled a nihilist. "It's not that I don't value my life," she told *People* in 1983. "It's just that I love taking chances, testing myself, stepping over the line. It's fun. It's a turn-on."

Williams' also trod a thin line between provocative and obscene in her on stage gesticulations. She was arrested on charges of obscenely fondling a sledgehammer during a 1981 Milwaukee concert and was charged with obscenity in Cleveland when she covered herself in shaving cream and performed simulated sexual acts. Charges were dropped on the former and she was acquitted on the latter charges. Williams was also sentenced to a year of supervision and a $35 fine for beating a freelance photographer in Chicago who dared snap her picture as she jogged.

Williams never deviated from her character. She was seemingly always coiffed in a bleached-white mohawk with electrical tape strategically covering her nipples. Her attire and demeanor were apparently not that different from her domintrix days in the skin trade. Not to be outdone, Stotts often showed up in drag. His costumes included nurses' uniforms and tutus.

During this time, the Plasmatics recorded as well as toured. *Trouser Press* described *Beyond the Valley of 1984* as "quite listenable, if only intermittently memorable. Swenson's lyrics aspire to nightmares of apocalypse and superhuman lust and degradation. The music is heavier, but clearer and not without flashes of finesse."

The Plasmatics were more than a punk band. They became media stars with cameos in film as well as appearances on talk and variety shows throughout the early 1980s. Williams' first non-porn role was in a B-flick called *Reform School Girls. People* reviewer David Hutchings wrote in 1986 that "the film's one true inspiration is to cast nihilist rocker Wendy O. Williams as the foul-mouthed cellblock leader. Playing what must be the eldest juvenile offender on record, Williams emotes by gnashing her teeth, flexing her tattooed biceps and bulging out of her underwear. When she turns terminatrix and goes on a demolition derby rampage inside the reformatory, the film heats up. Unfortunately it also ends."

As a group, the Plasmatics even reportedly appeared on the oft-maligned musical variety show *Sold Gold* as well as *The Joan Rivers Show* and *SCTV*. Williams continued to be typecast in roles on television shows such as *MacGyver*, where she played a biker mama opposite Dick Butkus, and *The New Adventures of Beans Baxter*, in which she played a bikini-wearing terrorist. More in line with her musical persona, Williams guest-hosted MTV's *Headbangers' Ball* in the late 1980s.

The band went through numerous personnel changes throughout these years. Williams, Stotts and manager/

lyricist Swenson were seemingly the only constants. Tony Petri of Twisted Sister fame, for example, played with the band in 1981, but did not record with them. The group disbanded in 1984 when Stotts left the group. Although the Plasmatics were no more, remaining group members continued to perform and record under Wendy O. Williams' name. The band also shifted from punk to metal. The *W.O.W.* album, the first of these non-Plasmatic Williams projects, was produced by Gene Simmons and also features guest performances by his KISS colleagues. Williams received a Grammy nomination for best female rock vocal of 1984.

Williams recorded a few more albums, the last of which was a foray into rap in 1988 under the unlikely moniker Ultrafly and the Hometown Girls. She and Swenson continued to live together and moved to Connecticut in 1991. She became a licensed wildlife animal rehabilitator, acting on a life-long interest in caring for creatures, but seemingly remained unhappy. She purportedly also worked at a natural foods co-op near her home.

Swenson and others who knew Williams as a youth and adult told *People* on various occasions she was nothing like her onstage persona— reserved and meek. She was the last girl her high school guidance counselor expected to become a stripper. "When people met her offstage, they couldn't believe it," said Swenson in 1998. "She was sweet and shy...very vulnerable and so sensitive." Williams was also said to have been a dedicated vegetarian, mindfully health conscious. He also said Williams attempted suicide twice before she successfully killed herself April 6, 1998 with a self-inflicted gunshot to the head. Swenson found her body in the woods near their home. Williams "left behind a cryptic note that read, in part, 'For me, much of the world makes no sense, but my feelings about what I am doing ring loud and clear to an inner ear and a place where there is no self, only calm.'"

Selected discography

New Hope for the Wretched, Stiff America Records, 1980.
Beyond the Valley of 1984, Stiff America Records, 1981.
Metal Priestess, (EP) Stiff America Records, 1981
Coup d'Etat, Capitol Records, 1982.

Wendy O. Williams

W.O.W. Passport, 1984.
Kommander of Kaos, Gigasaurus/Sledgehammer, 1986.
(Contributor) *Reform School Girls* (soundtrack), Rhino Records, 1986
Maggots: The Record, Profile Records, 1987.

as Ultrafly and the Hometown Girls

Deffest and Baddest, Profile/Sledgehammer, 1988.

Sources

Books

Romanowski, Patricia, and Holly George-Warren, Editors, *The New Rolling Stone Encyclopedia of Rock & Roll*, Fireside/Simon & Schuster, Inc., 1995.

Periodicals

Billboard, April 18, 1998.
People, July 25, 1983; September 15, 1986; July 20, 1987; July 2, 1990; April 27, 1998.

Additional information provided by *Trouser Press* website as well as various Plasmatics and Wendy O. Williams fan sites on the World Wide Web.

—*Linda Dailey Paulson*

Paul Westerberg

Singer, songwriter

AP/Wide World Photos. Reproduced by permission.

Paul Westerberg and the band The Replacements—or as they are fondly referred to, the Mats—made a serious impression on the punk and alternative rock music scene during the 1980s. Now well after The Replacements' end, Westerberg is enjoying success as a solo songwriter and performer. After three solo albums, Westerberg has managed to prove that a brash punker can grow up and continue as a songwriter.

With a guitar purchased from his older sister for eight dollars, Westerberg began making music and composing lyrics as a teenager. Co-founded with other Minneapolis teens, Tommy and Bob Stinston, and Chris Mars, The Replacements began rehearsing and performing in 1979 and continued until 1991. According to a Replacements website, www.novia.net/mats, "The band earned a reputation for being one of the finest and unpredictable live acts on the 1980s indie scene by juxtaposing cathartic, punk-influenced shows with drunken tomfoolery. But their ace in the hole was front man, Paul Westerberg, who managed to perfectly articulate the ambivalence and alienation of growing up."

In 1989, Paul Westerberg and his band The Replacements were recognized as one of rock's greatest groups, with *Rolling Stone* magazine naming their 1984 album *Let It Be* as one of the 15 greatest albums of the decade. The Replacements were recognized by Nirvana, who named them as influences. The Mats were also an inspiration for numerous bands that came out of Minneapolis in the 1980s, including Husker Du. After years of serious partying on and off tours, the end of The Replacements came in Chicago on July 4, 1991, with an announcement to the crowd after their final show. After nine albums, thousands of tour dates and countless bar gigs, the band disintegrated and individual musicians began their own solo paths, Westerberg included. But true Replacement fans may have had an indication that the end was near. As The Replacements began to dissolve, Westerberg "took over" the last couple of albums, essentially making them his own.

Westerberg's first solo album, *14 Songs,* was released on Warner Bros./Reprise Records in 1993. The recording was considered a strong first album, but didn't receive the social and professional kudos Westerberg desired. Most fans were expecting a Replacements album filled with ripping guitar chords and raunchy lyrics. Instead, Westerberg offered them a deep and introspective album. While touring to support his first true solo album, "the audience was far more interested in singing along to songs like "Kiss Me on the Bus" and "I'll Be You…", two popular songs from his previous band, then to some of his newer work, according to an article in *Newsweek.* Although the article goes on to say that Westerberg has an "unfettered writing style that makes him one of alternative rock's biggest influences," his first solo album did not do that well with the press and fans.

According to a 1996 interview with Erik Philbrook, found on the ASCAP website, www. ascap.com, Westerberg was nervous about the release of his first solo album. "When The Replacements ended and I made *14 Songs*, I was very nervous because suddenly I was out on my own and I didn't have that role as leader of the group to fall back on. I really played up the fact that I was a songwriter… I sort of went back to the days before I had the band and eased into what I am now. I am a musician. I do write good songs. I'm comfortable with what I am and I think people will get it," Westerberg said.

His second solo album, *Eventually*, came out in 1996. Again, Replacement fans were disappointed because the album was a deep and introspective work and they wanted to hear Westerberg as he used to sound—loud, brash and angry. But he had matured and so had his music. Westerberg also produced *Eventually* and almost had help from Pearl Jam producers Brendan O'Brien, but the pairing didn't work and Westerberg finished the recording with Lou Giordano.

In between his first two albums, Westerberg wrote and recorded songs for various movie and television show soundtracks, including the movies *Singles,* "Dyslexic Heart," and *Tank Girl,* as well as for the television series *Melrose Place* and *Friends.* Westerberg didn't completely leave his Replacement roots behind him. Along with his musician wife, Laura Lindeen, he recorded a seven-inch single and an EP using the alter ego, "Grandpa Boy." His fans, though, knew who he was and enjoyed the album put out on the Soundproof/Monolyth label. Westerberg

played all the instruments on the album. Those "Grandpa Boy" tracks were a way for Westerberg to "become more fearless in my art," and a way to gain personal satisfaction rather than mass endorsement, according to the *Minneapolis Star Tribune.*

If he hadn't done Grandpa Boy, who knows where Westerberg, or his music, would be. "It was necessary to do that (Grandpa Boy), or *Suicaine* (Gratification, his third album) might have spiraled down to the point where I couldn't finish it," he is quoted as saying in a *Toronto Sun* interview. Westerberg's third album, *Suicaine Gratification*, attained some critical success since its release in 1999. Westerberg had a new contract with Capitol Records, after impressing Capitol president, Gary Gersh. According to an interview on a Paul Westerberg website, http://members.aol.com/paulspage, "Gary Gersh's commitment as president (of Capitol), who is going to personally oversee my record and my career, was hard to turn down. I mean, I had fans at every other (record) label, but they weren't all necessarily the presidents of the label. I felt that having the most powerful guy at the label interested in my career would be the smart move to make."

According to a *Gannett News Service* article, "In many ways, however, it is his best music in years. Westerberg sounds more relaxed and less defined by expectations, which, ironically, lets him sound more like himself." Westerberg finally found his own voice, one that isn't being related to his previous works with The Replacements. The album was produced by Don Was, who had success with "mature" musicians like Bone Raitt, Bob Dylan, and the Rolling Stones.

In an interview with the *Minneapolis Star Tribune*, Was said about Westerberg, "If I could have worked with John Lennon at his creative peak, that's what Paul Westerberg reminds me of. He doesn't want to repeat anything anyone has done before; he makes sure the mikes in the studio are not set up the same way they were the week before. Nothing with him is rote." Although Was helped with Westerberg's third album, he wasn't the songwriter's first choice. Westerberg originally wanted Quincy Jones, but Was, recognizing a great musician when he heard one, began getting involved with the production, at the same time staying out of the way. "The influence of producer Don Was is clearly felt here," writes Mike Meyer with *University Wire* in 1999, "as the tracks have a definite classic rock feel, more in the veins of Tom Petty or the Rolling Stones." In fact, The Replacements opened for Tom Petty and the Heartbreakers.

"I knew they were great songs and if there was any plan, it was to stay out of the way of the songs," Was told the

Minneapolis Star Tribune. Was did include some subtle accompanists, including a French horn and an accordion. Most of the songs off of *Suicaine Gratification* are deeply personal, dealing with Westerberg's alcohol abuse and the birth of his son. Almost the entire album was recorded in his basement in Minneapolis.

Westerberg found his niche within the "pop music" genre. According to Jeffery Puckett, with the *Gannett News Service*, "Westerberg has given up completely on rock'n'roll as abandon, and the hardest track here "Looking Out Forever," is essentially a pop song." Not everyone was pleased with Westerberg's rebirth as a pop song writer. Thor Christensen, reviewing *Suicaine Gratification* for the *Dallas Morning News* wrote, "A lot of skeptics dismiss ex-Replacements leader Paul Westerberg as the punk-rock Paul McCartney— an artist whose solo career is a disgrace to his storied past. The assessment isn't entirely off-base." According to an article in the *Ottawa Sun*, Westerberg said "I don't want to drown myself out any more. For years I played in a loud rock band it's like 'Hell, they're not going to hear me anyway." Westerberg told the *Minneapolis Star Tribune*, "I guess I am proud that I followed the muse where it took me, which is a very solitary, dark place."

"Westerberg's greatest strength has always been his lyrics, which normally convey his time-worn wisdom about life and especially love in just about the most artistic way possible," compliments Mike Meyer with *CD Review*, about *Suicaine Gratification*. "Aching, sometimes confused, it's a new effort for Westerberg, and the ideal backdrop for some of the best words he's ever come up with," admires the *Toronto Sun.* Dave Pirner, from Soul Asylum, contributed to the album, along with singer and Grammy-winner Shawn Colvin.

Westerberg admits to being clinically depressed during the writing and recording of *Suicaine Gratification,* and those feelings show themselves bluntly on the album. He has since begun to take anti-depressant drugs to combat his depression. "There was a lot of sorrow on this record, and it wasn't pretend," Westerberg recounts in an interview in the *Toronto Sun.* Never a big fan of touring, or the life behind touring, Westerberg took his time in following up his solo albums with tours. In fact, Westerberg doesn't like leaving his hometown of Minneapolis. "I was probably 36 when I started recording this album,

(Suicaine Gratification) and it dawned on me that I don't know what (kids) want—I'm a fool even to guess. So I have to do what I want at the risk of being considered a has-been, on old man or whatever. When they rediscover me when they're 25, they'll see that I was very cool."

Selected discography

"Dyslexic Heart," *Singles* soundtrack, 1992.
14 Songs, Warner Bros./Reprise Records, 1993.
"A Star is Bored", *Melrose Place* soundtrack, Giant, 1994.
"Sunshine", *Friends* soundtrack, Reprise, 1994.
Eventually, Reprise Records, 1996.
Grandpa Boy, Soundproof/Monolyth, 1997.
Suicaine Gratification, Capitol Records, 1999.

Sources

Periodicals

Dallas Morning News, August 10, 1997.
Gannett News Service, February 26, 1999.
Minneapolis Star Tribune, February 21, 1999.
Newsday, August 8, 1993; August 3, 1996; February 14, 1999.
Ottawa Sun, February 21, 1999.
St. Louis Post-Dispatch, June 28, 1996.
Time, June 6, 1993.
Toronto Sun, February 21, 1999
University Wire, February 5, 1999.
Wisconsin State Journal, October 15, 1993.

Online

http://hiponline.com (April 21, 1999).
http://hollywoodandvine.com (June 1, 1999).
http://members.aol.com/paulspage (April 16, 1999).
http://metroactive.com (June 1, 1999).
http://www.ascap.com/playback (June 1, 1999).
http://www.mtv.com/news (April 21, 1999).
http://www.novia.net (June 1, 1999).
http://www.addicted.com (April 21, 1999).
http://www.playboy.com (April 16, 1999).
http://www.wwwebworld.com (April 21, 1999).

—*Gretchen Van Monette*

Paul Williams

Songwriter, actor, singer

Multitalented entertainer Paul Williams is an award-winning songwriter, as well as an actor and singer. He is best known for his many popular tunes including the score of the film *A Star is Born*. Williams, who also wrote "We've Only Just Begun" and other top-selling hit songs of the 1970s and 1980s, has appeared in a number of motion pictures and starred on Broadway during his career. He is also known for his charming and witty personality. In the mid-1990s, Williams spent much of his time writing country music songs in Nashville.

Williams was born Paul Hamilton Williams, Jr., on September 19, 1940, in Omaha, Nebraska. He was the son of the late Bertha Mae and Paul Williams, Sr. Williams's father was an architectural engineer, and his mother was a homemaker. Childhood unfortunately was not a carefree time for Williams. The family relocated often, and Williams, who was small in stature, changed schools frequently as a result. That combination of circumstances set him apart from classmates and often caused him to be the butt of cruel jokes. Williams was only 13 when his father died in an auto accident. He subsequently left Nebraska and went to live with his aunt and uncle in Long Beach, California.

Williams was drawn to show business even as an adolescent. At Woodrow Wilson High School in Long Beach, he joined the thespian club and acted in school plays. After graduation he moved for a time to Albuquerque, New Mexico, where he earned a solid reputation as an actor at the local community theater. Eventually he returned to Southern California to pursue a career in motion pictures, an effort that kept him occupied during much of the 1960s. He also started his own band, and the group released an album on the Warner Brothers label. Although he secured many small acting roles, he failed to achieve movie stardom. Equally disappointing was the success of his band, which never developed mass appeal. His early film appearances included *Planet of the Apes* in 1967, *Watermelon Man* in 1970, and an adaptation of the *Phantom of the Opera* called *Phantom of the Paradise,* for which he also wrote the score in 1974.

Williams' true talent was his ability to write touching, often romantic song lyrics. His career as a songwriter solidified rapidly over a simple advertising jingle that he wrote for a bank commercial. The jingle, a collaborative effort between Williams and composer Roger Nichols, caught the ear of an up-and-coming singing duo called The Carpenters, comprised of Richard Carpenter and his sister, the late Karen Carpenter. The Carpenters recorded the song, called "We've Only Just Begun," and in 1970 it climbed the charts to become their second major hit. The recycled bank jingle turned solid gold for The Carpenters, and it became one of their most popular recordings ever. "We've Only Just Begun" went on to sell over 2.5 million copies in the first two years of its release. The songwriting team of Nichols and Williams continued working together and found more success. They went on to write additional hits for Richard and Karen Carpenter, along with other new songs that were popularized by such artists as Johnny Mathis, Anne Murray, Three Dog Night, Bobby Sherman, and the Monkees.

Career Blossomed

The popularity of the Williams and Nichols songwriting team opened new doors for Williams as an individual creative talent and performer. Many of the tunes penned by Williams throughout his career became memorable hits. In 1971 he made a trip to Paris where he contributed the lyrics for Michel Colombier's pop symphony, *Wings.* Upon his return, he collaborated with Barbra Streisand on the soundtrack of *A Star Is Born* which included the best-selling song "Evergreen." The song won an Academy Award for song of the year in 1976. Additionally, *A Star Is Born* won two Golden Globe awards for Williams: one for the movie score, and another for the movie's hit theme song, "Evergreen." Williams' songs were heard in other movies including *Cinderella Liberty* in 1973, *The Day of the Locust* in 1975, and *Bugsy Malone* in 1976. Williams scored the Muppets' movie in the 1970s and the

Muppets' Christmas special, "A Christmas Carol," in 1993. Williams also wrote songs for the television series "The Love Boat" which aired from 1977-86.

Williams, a talented musician with a witty personality, plays the piano and the guitar. His name recognition grew when Williams began making personal appearances and performing his own hit songs. He appeared frequently on the *Tonight Show*, made appearances on *Midnight Special*, and released a number of solo albums on Herb Alpert's A&M label. Williams proved himself to be a talented comedian and he resumed his acting career in a number of memorable movie appearances, including a recurring role as a harried bootlegger in a series of *Smokey and the Bandit* movies with Burt Reynolds in 1977, 1980, and 1983.

Williams dramatic talents unfolded on Broadway in 1989 when he portrayed Truman Capote in *Tru.* He played the Capote character once more in 1990 on NBC's *People Like Us.* He later appeared in the film *Seventh Veil,* which was filmed in 1998. Additional television performances included a role in the pilot film of ABC's *The Fall Guy,* which aired from 1981-86. Williams also starred in an ongoing role on the afternoon soap opera *The Bold and the Beautiful* for several months in the late 1990s.

Time Out for Help

Around 1980, the talented and plucky songwriter began a decade-long plunge into the world of substance abuse. The descent lasted until September of 1989 when he realized the severity of his addiction. Williams took it upon himself to call a psychiatrist and committed himself to a month-long rehabilitation program in Los Angeles. Williams took his private drug battle seriously and vowed to control his addiction for the rest of his life. He successfully reversed the direction of his life, and later put his efforts to work as an accredited counselor to assist others like himself who battle addiction. He became intensely involved in counseling work. Undeterred by past indiscretions, he moved forward optimistically in the companionship of his wife Hilda Keenan Williams, a former agent whom he married in 1993. Williams set out to make amends for his past follies and wanted in particular to reconcile with his two children from a former marriage who were nearly grown by that time.

Once an avid race car driver, Williams greatest pleasures involve simpler pursuits. He enjoys reading mystery stories and caring for a couple of pet rabbits. He maintains a high profile in the Musicians Assistance Program. As a member of the board and counselor for the group, Williams generously donates his time by traveling and lecturing about the evils of addiction. He also maintains a position on the board of the National Council of Alcoholism and Drug Dependence.

On to Nashville

With a renewed spirit Williams went on to revive his career in the mid-1990s. By 1999 Williams was an established fixture in Nashville. He wrote new songs, went into contract negotiations with Atlantic records, and he established and operated a music publishing company that kept him constantly in transit between his home in Los Angeles and temporary accommodations in Tennessee. Williams' "You're Gone," was a hit song for the Diamond Rio Band. Likewise "Party On," recorded by Neil McCoy, was a hit on the country charts.

Williams is a member of the American Society of Composers, Authors, and Publishers and a trustee of the National Academy of Recording Arts and Sciences.

During the late 1990s, Williams testified before a congressional hearing in Nashville regarding copyright legislation that would affect the music industry.

Selected discography

"Out in the Country," 1969.
Someday Man, Warner Brothers, 1970.
"We've Only Just Begun," 1970.
Just an Old-fashioned Love Song, 1971.
"Rainy Days and Mondays," 1971.
"An Old Fashioned Love Song," 1972.
Life Goes On, 1972.
"Evergreen," 1976.
Classics, 1977.
"The Rainbow Connection," 1979.
Crazy for Loving You, 1981.

Sources

Periodicals

Billboard, February 13, 1999, p. 65.
People, December 21, 1998, p. 133.

Online

http://www.ifco.org/starstats/W-Z/paul_williams_ss.shtml.

—*Gloria Cooksey*

Cassandra Wilson

Singer, composer

Vocalist Cassandra Wilson emerged in the 1980s as a fresh, young jazz talent whose performances solicited comparisons with the greatest jazz divas of the twentieth century. Yet Wilson ultimately defied labels as she traded the sultry and sophisticated image of past jazz and blues singers to project a much simpler image that was less flamboyant and more "down home." She was acclaimed for her crossover talents when she branched into reggae, R&B, hip-hop, and folk. "Cassandra Wilson transcends category and defies convention," said Joy Bennett Kinnon of *Ebony*.

Wilson was born Cassandra Marie Fowlkes, in Jackson, Mississippi, on December 4, 1955. She was raised in a close-knit, middle class family. Her father, Herman Fowlkes, was a professional musician. Initially he played bass but went on to learn the cello, violin, guitar, and saxophone. He put his musical career on hold around the time that his third child and only daughter, Cassandra, was born. After Wilson's birth, her father changed careers and worked as a postman, but music remained his fondest interest. Wilson idolized her father who played endless hours of jazz music on the family hi-fi. The sounds of Betty Carter, Sarah Vaughan, and Nancy Wilson filled the Fowlkes' household. Wilson's grandmother, who sang zealously in church, also influenced the young girl's attitudes. Although her grandmother passed away when Wilson was an 12 years old, Wilson fondly recalled "sleeping on her couch … and the curtains blowing over me at night. I remember that as being a truly magical feeling. There was a train would come by every night, and I'd hear the whistle blow. That is the sweetest memory I have," she confided to George Tate of *Essence*.

Wilson's fervor for jazz was further aroused as a young child when she developed a childhood "crush" on Miles Davis after hearing his album, *Sketches of Spain*. Shortly afterward she began to study classical piano, and she took up playing the guitar at the age of nine. During her high school years in the 1960s, Wilson nurtured a keen interest in the music styles of Bob Dylan, Judy Collins, and others popular folk singers of the era. Joni Mitchell provided particular inspiration for Wilson who soon began writing her own songs in the folk tradition while she was in high school. Because of her diverse interests and her affinity for folk music, Wilson never came to see herself as a jazz singer in the traditional sense. Public opinion differed, however, as Wilson's musical career unfolded.

Jazz Jamming after College

Wilson put great importance on education. Her mother, a career schoolteacher, encouraged her daughter to obtain a higher education and to nurture a backup career apart from music—a precarious profession that offered little security. After high school Wilson attended Milsap College and later completed her curriculum in mass communication at Jackson State. Even as a college student, Wilson aspired to a musical career, and she was singing professionally by 1975.

Wilson sang with the Black Arts Music Society in Jackson and studied with drummer Alvin Fielder before setting out for New Orleans in 1981. There she worked as an assistant public affairs director at a television station and decided to pursue a career in television, but she never abandoned her deep love of music and her desire to continue singing professionally. In New Orleans she continued her musical studies with saxophone player Earl Turbinton and worked with jazz patriarch Ellis Marsalis. One year later, in 1982, she moved to New York City where she joined a group of jazz players called M-Base and did a lot of "jazz jamming." In the company of her avant-garde musical cohorts, including M-Base leader and jazz saxophone player Steve Coleman, Wilson became immersed in the culture of the local musicians. She later worked with the Black Rock Coalition (B.R.C.), and recorded her first album in 1985. She continued to perform and recorded more albums, with M-Base, B.R.C, and Coleman, but it was her solo album, *Blue Skies,* in 1988 that became her vehicle to recognition and stardom. Wilson's throaty voice came through in "Blue Skies." Critics praised the solo effort and compared her style to that of Betty Carter.

Crossover Stardom

As the 1980s came to a close Wilson signed with EMI records and expanded her repertoire to embrace a wide spectrum of music. Her jazz-inspired renditions extended from adaptations of works by Joni Mitchell and Van Morrison, to funk-based rhythms. Her reputation as a crossover artist flourished, and her universal musical styles transcended the generations. The strength of Wilson's voice, combined with her flexibility and propensity to "cross over" into non-jazz compositions, generated a following within the music niches of younger listeners.

In 1995 Wilson embarked on a six-week European tour, with a side trip to Rio. She undertook a promotional tour for her album *Blue Light 'til Dawn* in April of 1996. At JVC Jazz Festival in New York that year she performed on the strength of her own reputation, as an established star in her own right. Also in that year she joined in with assorted artists including Q-tip and D'Angelo in performing cameos for The Roots on *illadelph halflife,* on DGC Records. In late summer that year she opened for Ray Charles at Radio City Music Hall. Additionally, Wilson collaborated from time to time with Benin folk musician Angelique Kidjo, including a performance at the Montreaux Jazz Festival, and the two contributed cameos to each other's albums.

Wilson's partiality for 1960s music came through in her album *New Moon Daughter* which included selections from Joni Mitchell and the Monkees that were adapted to Wilson's uniquely jazz-based improvisational style. Gene Santoro said about the release of *Nation* in 1996 that Wilson "may well have locked up the title 'Chanteuse of the Nineties.' She is the direct descendant of Billie Holiday and Dinah Washington." Santoro said in 1999 that Wilson and her instrumentalists forego the "microphone in front of a kickass big band or an intimate piano trio. Instead, they create a rural, bluesy atmosphere, a studio back porch of acoustic guitars and bass, gently persistent percussion and odd daubs of color, like a floating steel guitar or a skirling fiddle. The dense arrangements sway to allow improvised solos and ideas into radically revamped material ranging from Son House's raw country blues to The Monkees' 'Last Train to Clarksville.'"

In 1997, Wilson toured in Wynton Marsalis' Pulitzer Prize winning jazz opera, *Blood on the Fields,* a composition that she had interpreted earlier in a National Public Radio broadcast performance in 1994. A recording of the opera, taped in 1995, was released in 1997. That year in the JVC Jazz Festival in New York City she performed at Carnegie Hall. In 1998 she played at the Lincoln Center along with Marsalis and his group.

A Tribute to Miles Davis

The late Miles Davis undoubtedly held the greatest influence on Wilson's music outside of her family. In 1989, during her early days as a recording artist, Wilson was thrilled to perform as the opening act for Davis at the JVC Jazz Festival in Chicago. Although she never had the opportunity to meet and speak with Davis, she produced an album, *Traveling for Miles,* released in 1999, as a tribute to him. The album developed from a series of jazz concerts that she performed at Lincoln Center in November of 1997 in Davis honor. The album included three selections based on Davis own compositions, in which Wilson adapted the original themes. She balanced the selections on the album with four original compositions of her own, including the title song, "Traveling Miles," to keep the album fresh and interesting. Four other songs on the album were either recorded by or associated with Davis during his lifetime. *Traveling for Miles* was a milestone production for Wilson. Her backup artists on the Davis album included Regina Carter on violin, Steve Coleman on alto saxophone, Stefon Harris on vibes, and Dave Holland on bass. Wilson adapted, arranged, wrote, produced, and for the first time in her life conducted the music on *Traveling for Miles.* She promoted the album by means of a 24-city tour that took her to a number of out-of-the-way locations in Vermont, New Hampshire, South Carolina, and Tennessee.

Wilson was married briefly to Anthony Wilson from 1981 to 1983. She has one son, Jeris, born in the late 1980s. The two live in Harlem, New York, in an apartment that once belonged to jazz great Duke Ellington. Wilson and Jeris travel together frequently whenever Jeris' school schedule allows.

Selected discography

Point of View, JMT, 1986.
Days Aweigh, JMT, 1987.
Blue Skies, JMT, 1988.
She Who Weeps, JMT, 1991.
After the Beginning Again, JMT, 1991.
Blue Light 'Til Dawn, Blue Note, 1993.

No Prima Donna: the Songs of Van Morrison, 1994.
After the Beginning Again, JMT/Verve 1994.
New Moon Daughter, Blue Note, 1996.
Traveling for Miles, Blue Note, 1999
(with Jacky Terrasson) *Rendezvous,* Blue Note, 1997.
(with New Air) *Air Show No. 1,* Black Saint.
(with Jim DeAngelis and Tony Signs) *Straight from the Top,* Statiras.

with Steve Coleman

Motherland Pulse, JMT, 1985.
World Expansion, JMT.
On the Edge of Tomorrow, JMT.

with M-Base

Anatomy of a Groove, DIW/Columbia.
Dance to the Drums Again, DIW/Columbia, 1993.

Sources

Books

Erlewine, Michael, exec. ed., *All Music Guide to Jazz,* Miller Freeman Books, 1998.
Larkin, Colin, ed., *The Guiness Encyclopedia of Popular Music,* Guinness Publishing, reprinted 1994.

Periodicals

Billboard, March 6, 1999, p. 11.
Down Beat, January 1995, p. 22; July 1995, p. 13; November 1996, p. 66.
Ebony, December 1996, p. 62.
Essence, July 1996, p. 60.
Nation, April 15, 1996, p. 33; April 19, 1999, p. 40.
Newsweek, April 5, 1999, p. 72.
People, March 11, 1996, p. 25.
Time, March 11, 1996, p. 69.
U.S. News & World Report, February 3, 1997, p. 91.

—*Gloria Cooksey*

XTC

Rock band

British group XTC garnered a cult following that some music scribes contend rivals only the devotion of Grateful Dead's "deadheads." The group was centered around the songwriting team of Andy Partridge and Colin Moulding. Before the group was known as XTC, it was Star Park and Helium Kidz. Partridge was at the helm during those early incarnations in the early 1970s. Moulding joined the Swindon, England based group in 1973 when they became Helium Kidz, as did Terry Chambers. In 1975 there was a move afoot to abandon glitter rock and change the group's name. Keyboardist John Perkins was added to the group, and was replaced by Barry Andrews in 1977 before XTC began recording.

The following year, XTC signed with Virgin Records and released their debut album. *White Music* reached number 38 on the U.K. album charts. Andrews stayed with the group long enough to record their first American album, *Drums and Wires*. While most of XTC's recorded output would be considered pop/rock they were originally associated with both punk and new wave. "The best thing about punk," Partridge said in a 1999 *Boston Globe* interview, "was it had a timeless quality all music should have—which is anyone can do it." Partridge's band was only nominally a punk group, but he was there when it was first gestating, and he, too, was learning how to play music on the job. "It's not about musical ability; it's about doing it. It's about the fire in your belly and saying, 'I could do that.'"

In its early years, XTC toured almost endlessly. That all changed in 1982 when Partridge fell ill from a combination of fatigue and stage fright. He reportedly suffered from stomach ulcers, as well. The band bailed out of their U.S. tour after a San Diego show, and all remaining tour dates were cancelled. He announced that the band would continue to record and shoot promotional videos, but would no longer perform live. Partridge spent the next year in seclusion. "I don't like it," Partridge said of touring in a 1999 interview. "I don't feel the need to do it. I got that out of my system in my 20s."

In 1986 XTC entered the studio with producer Todd Rundgren to record *Skylarking*. Despite widely reported tension between Rundgren and Partridge, the album proved to be the group's breakthrough recording. *Skylarking* saw XTC take the plunge into pool of psychedelic pop that they had merely dipped their toes into on their previous two releases, *Mummer* in 1983 and *The Big Express* in 1984. Ironically the song that pushed *Skylarking*—and XTC—into the limelight, "Dear God," was initially left off the album. Originally released as the flipside of the single "Grass," subsequent pressings of *Skylarking* included the track after it was discovered by a college disc jockey and received more airplay than its

A-side. Their next album, 1989s *Oranges & Lemons*, was also heartily embraced by U.S. college radio. Bolstered by the strength of its first single, "The Mayor of Simpleton," *Oranges & Lemons* was hailed as the top college album that year. The infectious, melodic "The Mayor of Simpleton" reached number 72 on *Billboard*'s Hot 100 and number one on its Modern Rock Tracks chart.

Riding the crest of their two biggest recordings to date, XTC then hit a series of setbacks. According to Kyle Swenson writing in *Guitar Player*, "After releasing the acclaimed *Nonsuch* in 1992, which when to the top of college charts, the band became embroiled in legal difficulties with Virgin Records, and refused to enter the studio to track any music. During their self-imposed studio exile, bandmates Andy Partridge and Colin Moulding wrote enough songs to spill into the next decade. 'By the time we got out of our legal mess and were able to record what we wanted,' says Partridge, 'we had 42 songs.' This project became *Apple Venus, Volumes I and II*. Splitting their material into two releases had one

advantage: Partridge and Moulding were able to indulge their cravings for acoustic/orchestral sounds on the first album, and then resume traveling their longtime electro-pop path on the second.

Because the pair chose to record the orchestral songs first, Dave Gregory left during recording *Apple Venus, Volume I*. "T
Guitar Player, "is that he left before we made the album he wanted to make. He was much miffed that we always asked him to play keyboards. We'd always say, 'This needs a piano,' and then we'd look around the room and our eyes would slowly land on Dave. He got sick of being the piano player by default."

Partridge said the songwriting during the band's legal problems and absence from recording was cathartic. "In the past six years," he told *Billboard*'s Dylan Siegler in early 1999, "I got divorced; I was prevented from legally doing my art; an infection burst my ear drum; I felt betrayed, rejected, and useless. And I found all of it vastly inspirational." The string of tribulations seemed to have only strengthened Partridge's resolve, "The older and more ornery we got about the music we wanted to do, the more entrenched we got in the craftsmanship side of it," he explained to Siegler. "It was like this: We wanted to make our chair the best chair that ever was, and our former label [Virgin] wanted us to knock out cheap plastic chairs and 'Have you got a few tables and a settee as well.'"

Although XTC never became the massively successful band that many critics and fans believed they should have, it wasn't for a lack of strong pop songs. As Stephen Thomas Erlewine wrote in the *All Music Guide*, "XTC's lack of commercial success isn't because their music isn't accessible—their bright occasionally melancholic, melodies flow with more grace than most—it has more to do with the group constantly being out of step with the times. However, the band has left behind a remarkably rich and varied series of albums that make a convincing argument that XTC is the great lost pop band."

Selected discography

Go 2, Geffen, 1978.
White Music, Geffen, 1978.
Drums And Wires
Black Sea
English Settlement
Waxworks: Some Singles 1977-1982
Mummer
Skylarking
Oranges & Lemons

Nonsuch (includes "My Bird Performs"), Geffen, 1992.
Rag 'N' Bone Buffet, Geffen, 1990.
Transistor Blast—The Best of the BBC Sessions (four-CD set of radio performances, 1977 to 1989) TVT Records, 1998.
Apple Venus, Volume I, TVT Records, 1999.

as The Dukes of Stratosphear

25 O'Clock (EP), Virgin UK, 1985.
Psonic Psunspot, Geffen, 1987.
Chips from the Chocolate Fireball, Geffen, 1987.

Sources

Books

Buckley, Jonathan and Mark Ellingham, eds., *Rock: The Rough Guide*, Penguin Books USA, Inc., 1996.

Erlewine, Michael, et. al., editors, *All Music Guide*, third edition, Miller Freeman Books, 1997.
Romanowski, Patricia, and Holly George-Warren, Editors, *The New Rolling Stone Encyclopedia of Rock & Roll*, Fireside/Simon & Schuster, Inc., 1995.

Periodicals

Billboard, February 13, 1999.
Boston Globe, March 14, 1999.
Guitar Player, April 1999.

Online

"XTC," http://www.allmusic.com (April 16, 1999).
"XTC Artist Biography," http://imusic.com/showcase/rock/xtc.html (April 16, 1999).

—Linda Dailey Paulson

Cumulative Indexes

Cumulative Subject Index

Volume numbers appear in **bold.**

A cappella
Brightman, Sarah **20**
Bulgarian State Female Vocal Choir, The **10**
Golden Gate Quartet **25**
Nylons, The **6**
Sweet Honey In The Rock **26**
Take 6 **6**
Zap Mama **14**

Accordion
Buckwheat Zydeco **6**
Chenier, C. J. **15**
Chenier, Clifton **6**
Queen Ida **9**
Richard, Zachary **9**
Rockin' Dopsie **10**
Simien, Terrance **12**
Sonnier, Jo-El **10**
Yankovic, "Weird Al" **7**

Ambient/Rave/Techno
2 Unlimited **18**
Agust, Daniel
    See Gus Gus
Aphex Twin **14**
Arni, Stefen
    See Gus Gus
Chemical Brothers **20**
Deep Forest **18**
Emerson, Darren
    See Underworld
Front Line Assembly **20**
Gifford, Alex
    See Propellerheads
Gus Gus **26**
Hafdis, Huld
    See Gus Gus
Hyde, Karl
    See Underworld
Jonsson, Magnus
    See Gus Gus
Kjartansson, Siggi
    See Gus Gus
KMFDM **18**
Kraftwerk **9**
Legowitz, Herr
    See Gus Gus
Lords of Acid **20**
Man or Astroman? **21**
Orb, The **18**
Propellerheads **26**
Shadow, DJ **19**
Stefansson, Baldur
    See Gus Gus
Smith, Rick
    See Underworld
Thorarinsson, Biggi
    See Gus Gus
Underworld **26**
White, Will
    See Propellerheads

Bandoneon
Piazzolla, Astor **18**
Saluzzi, Dino **23**

Banjo
Boggs, Dock **25**
Bromberg, David **18**
Clark, Roy **1**
Crowe, J.D. **5**
Eldridge, Ben
    See Seldom Scene, The
Fleck, Bela **8**
    Also see New Grass Revival, The
Hartford, John **1**
Johnson, Courtney
    See New Grass Revival, The
McCoury, Del **15**
Piazzolla, Astor **18**
Scruggs, Earl **3**
Seeger, Pete **4**
    Also see Weavers, The
Skaggs, Ricky **5**
Stanley, Ralph **5**
Watson, Doc **2**

Bass
Brown, Ray **21**
Bruce, Jack
    See Cream
Carter, Ron **14**
Chambers, Paul **18**
Clarke, Stanley **3**
Collins, Bootsy **8**
Dixon, Willie **10**
Entwistle, John
    See Who, The
Fender, Leo **10**
Haden, Charlie **12**
Hill, Dusty
    See ZZ Top
Hillman, Chris
    See Byrds, The
    Also see Desert Rose Band, The
Johnston, Bruce
    See Beach Boys, The
Jones, John Paul
    See Led Zeppelin
Kaye, Carol **22**
Lake, Greg
    See Emerson, Lake & Palmer/Powell
Laswell, Bill **14**
Love, Laura **20**
Mann, Aimee **22**
McBride, Christian **17**
McCartney, Paul **4**
    Also see Beatles, The
McVie, John
    See Fleetwood Mac
Meisner, Randy
    See Eagles, The
Mingus, Charles **9**
Ndegéocello, Me'Shell **18**

Porter, Tiran
    See Doobie Brothers, The
Rutherford, Mike
    See Genesis
Schmit, Timothy B.
    See Eagles, The
Shakespeare, Robbie
    See Sly and Robbie
Simmons, Gene
    See Kiss
Sting **19**
    Earlier sketch in CM **2**
Sweet, Matthew **9**
Vicious, Sid
    See Sex Pistols, The
    Also see Siouxsie and the Banshees
Was, Don **21**
    Also see Was (Not Was)
Waters, Roger
    See Pink Floyd
Watt, Mike **22**
Weymouth, Tina
    See Talking Heads
Whitaker, Rodney **20**
Wyman, Bill
    See Rolling Stones, The

Big Band/Swing
Andrews Sisters, The **9**
Arnaz, Desi **8**
Bailey, Pearl **5**
Basie, Count **2**
Beiderbecke, Bix **16**
Bennett, Tony **16**
    Earlier sketch in CM **2**
Berrigan, Bunny **2**
Blakey, Art **11**
Brown, Lawrence **23**
Calloway, Cab **6**
Carter, Benny **3**
Chenille Sisters, The **16**
Cherry Poppin' Daddies **24**
Clooney, Rosemary **9**
Cody, John
    See Ray Condo and His Ricochets
Como, Perry **14**
Condo, Ray
    See Ray Condo and His Ricochets
Cugat, Xavier **23**
Dorsey Brothers, The **8**
Dorsey, Jimmy
    See Dorsey Brothers, The
Dorsey, Tommy
    See Dorsey Brothers, The
Eckstine, Billy **1**
Eldridge, Roy **9**
Ellington, Duke **2**
Ferguson, Maynard **7**
Fitzgerald, Ella **1**
Fountain, Pete **7**
Getz, Stan **12**
Gillespie, Dizzy **6**

Goodman, Benny **4**
Henderson, Fletcher **16**
Herman, Woody **12**
Hines, Earl "Fatha" **12**
Jackson, Clive
    See Ray Condo and His Ricochets
Jacquet, Illinois **17**
James, Harry **11**
Jones, Spike **5**
Jordan, Louis **11**
Krupa, Gene **13**
Lee, Peggy **8**
McKinney's Cotton Pickers **16**
Miller, Glenn **6**
Nikleva, Steven
    See Ray Condo and His Ricochets
Norvo, Red **12**
Parker, Charlie **5**
Prima, Louis **18**
Puente, Tito **14**
Ray Condo and His Ricochets **26**
Rich, Buddy **13**
Rodney, Red **14**
Roomful of Blues **7**
Roy, Jimmy
    See Ray Condo and His Ricochets
Scott, Jimmy **14**
Severinsen, Doc **1**
Shaw, Artie **8**
Sinatra, Frank **1**
Squirrel Nut Zippers **20**
Stafford, Jo **24**
Strayhorn, Billy **13**
Taylor, Steve
    See Ray Condo and His Ricochets
Teagarden, Jack **10**
Torme, Mel **4**
Vaughan, Sarah **2**
Welk, Lawrence **13**
Whiteman, Paul **17**

Bluegrass
Auldridge, Mike **4**
Bluegrass Patriots **22**
Clements, Vassar **18**
Country Gentlemen, The **7**
Crowe, J.D. **5**
Flatt, Lester **3**
Fleck, Bela **8**
    Also see New Grass Revival, The
Gill, Vince **7**
Grisman, David **17**
Hartford, John **1**
Krauss, Alison **10**
Louvin Brothers, The **12**
Martin, Jimmy **5**
    Also see Osborne Brothers, The
McCoury, Del **15**
McReynolds, Jim and Jesse **12**
Monroe, Bill **1**
Nashville Bluegrass Band **14**
New Grass Revival, The **4**
Northern Lights **19**
O'Connor, Mark **1**
Osborne Brothers, The **8**
Parsons, Gram **7**
    Also see Byrds, The
Reverend Horton Heat **19**
Scruggs, Earl **3**
Seldom Scene, The **4**
Skaggs, Ricky **5**
Stanley Brothers, The **17**
Stanley, Ralph **5**
Stuart, Marty **9**

Watson, Doc **2**
Wiseman, Mac **19**

Blues
Allison, Luther **21**
Ayler , Albert **19**
Bailey, Pearl **5**
Baker, Ginger **16**
    Also see Cream
Ball, Marcia **15**
Barnes, Roosevelt, "Booba" **23**
Berry, Chuck **1**
Bill Wyman & the Rhythm Kings **26**
Bland, Bobby "Blue" **12**
Block, Rory **18**
Blood, Sweat and Tears **7**
Blues Brothers, The **3**
Boggs, Dock **25**
Brooker, Gary
    See Bill Wyman & the Rhythm Kings
Broonzy, Big Bill **13**
Brown, Clarence "Gatemouth" **11**
Brown, Ruth **13**
Burdon, Eric **14**
    Also see War
    Also see Animals
Cale, J. J. **16**
Charles,, Ray **24**
    Earlier sketch in CM **1**
Clapton, Eric **11**
    Earlier sketch in CM **1**
    Also see Cream
    Also see Yardbirds, The
Collins, Albert **4**
Cray, Robert **8**
Davis, Reverend Gary **18**
Diddley, Bo **3**
Dixon, Willie **10**
Dr. John **7**
Dupree, Champion Jack **12**
Earl, Ronnie **5**
    Also see Roomful of Blues
Estes, John **25**
Fabulous Thunderbirds, The **1**
Fame, Georgie
    See Bill Wyman & the Rhythm Kings
Fuller, Blind Boy **20**
Fulson, Lowell **20**
Gatton, Danny **16**
Guy, Buddy **4**
Handy, W. C. **7**
Hawkins, Screamin' Jay **8**
Healey, Jeff **4**
Holiday, Billie **6**
Hooker, John Lee **26**
Hooker, John Lee **1**
Hopkins, Lightnin' **13**
House, Son **11**
Howlin' Wolf **6**
James, Elmore **8**
James, Etta **6**
Jefferson, Blind Lemon **18**
Johnson, Blind Willie **26**
Johnson, Lonnie **17**
Johnson, Robert **6**
Jon Spencer Blues Explosion **18**
Joplin, Janis **3**
King, Albert **2**
King, B. B. **1**
King, Freddy **17**
Leadbelly **6**
Led Zeppelin **1**
Lewis, Furry **26**
Little Feat **4**

Little Walter **14**
Lockwood, Robert, Jr. **10**
Mayall, John **7**
McClennan, Tommy **25**
McClinton, Delbert **14**
McDowell, Mississippi Fred **16**
McLean, Dave **24**
McTell, Blind Willie **17**
Memphis Jug Band **25**
Memphis Minnie **25**
Montgomery, Little Brother **26**
Muldaur, Maria **18**
Patton, Charley **11**
Plant, Robert **2**
    Also see Led Zeppelin
Professor Longhair **6**
Raitt, Bonnie **23**
    Earlier sketch in CM **3**
Redding, Otis **5**
Reed, Jimmy **15**
Rich, Charlie **3**
Robertson, Robbie **2**
Robillard, Duke **2**
Roomful of Blues **7**
Rush, Otis **12**
Shaffer, Paul **13**
Shines, Johnny **14**
Skeete, Beverley
    See Bill Wyman & the Rhythm Kings
Smith, Bessie **3**
Snow, Phoebe **4**
Spann, Otis **18**
Sunnyland Slim **16**
Sykes, Roosevelt **20**
Taj Mahal **6**
Tampa Red **25**
Taylor, Koko **10**
Thornton, Big Mama **18**
Toure, Ali Farka **18**
Turner, Big Joe **13**
Ulmer, James Blood **13**
Van Zandt, Townes **13**
Vaughan, Jimmie **24**
Vaughan, Stevie Ray **1**
Waits, Tom **1**
Walker, T-Bone **5**
Wallace, Sippie **6**
Washington, Dinah **5**
Waters, Ethel **11**
Waters, Muddy **24**
    Earlier sketch in CM **4**
Wells, Junior **17**
Weston, Randy **15**
Whitfield, Mark **18**
Whitley, Chris **16**
Whittaker, Hudson **20**
Williams, Joe **11**
Williamson, Sonny Boy **9**
Wilson, Gerald **19**
Winter, Johnny **5**
Witherspoon, Jimmy **19**
Wyman, Bill
    See Bill Wyman & the Rhythm Kings
    See Rolling Stones, The
ZZ Top **2**

Cajun/Zydeco
Ball, Marcia **15**
Brown, Clarence "Gatemouth" **11**
Buckwheat Zydeco **6**
Chenier, C. J. **15**
Chenier, Clifton **6**
Doucet, Michael **8**
Landreth, Sonny **16**

Queen Ida **9**
Richard, Zachary **9**
Rockin' Dopsie **10**
Simien, Terrance **12**
Sonnier, Jo-El **10**

Cello
Block, Norman
    See Rasputina
Casals, Pablo **9**
Creager, Melora
    See Rasputina
DuPré, Jacqueline **26**
Gray, Walter
    See Kronos Quartet
Harrell, Lynn **3**
Jeanrenaud, Joan Dutcher
    See Kronos Quartet
Kent, Julia
    See Rasputina
Ma, Yo Yo **24**
    Earlier sketch in CM **2**
Nana
    See Rasputina
Parvo, Carpella
    See Rasputina
Rasputina **26**
Rostropovich, Mstislav **17**
Rybska, Agnieszka
    See Rasputina

Children's Music
Bartels, Joanie **13**
Cappelli, Frank **14**
Chapin, Tom **11**
Chenille Sisters, The **16**
Harley, Bill **7**
Lehrer, Tom **7**
Nagler, Eric **8**
Penner, Fred **10**
Raffi **8**
Rosenshontz **9**
Sharon, Lois & Bram **6**

Christian Music
4Him **23**
Anointed **21**
Ashton, Susan **17**
Audio Adrenaline **22**
Avalon **26**
Baker, Dale
    See Sixpence None the Richer
Cary, Justin
    See Sixpence None the Richer
Champion, Eric **21**
Chapman, Steven Curtis **15**
Cloud, Jeff
    See Joy Electric
dc Talk **18**
Duncan, Bryan **19**
Eskelin, Ian **19**
Grant, Amy **7**
Hassman, Nikki
    See Avalon
Jars of Clay **20**
Joy Electric **26**
Keaggy, Phil **26**
Kelly, Sean
    See Sixpence None the Richer
King's X **7**
Martin, Ronnie
    See Joy Electric
McBrayer, Jody
    See Avalon

Nash, Leigh
    See Sixpence None the Richer
Newsboys, The **24**
Paliotta, Cherie
    See Avalon
Paris, Michael
    See Avalon
Paris, Twila **16**
Patti, Sandi **7**
Petra **3**
Point of Grace **21**
Potter, Janna
    See Avalon
Rice, Chris **25**
Sixpence None the Richer **26**
Slocum, Matt
    See Sixpence None the Richer
Smith, Michael W. **11**
St. James, Rebecca **26**
Stryper **2**
Taylor, Steve **26**
Waters, Ethel **11**

Clarinet
Adams, John **8**
Bechet, Sidney **17**
Braxton, Anthony **12**
Brötzmann, Peter **26**
Byron, Don **22**
Dorsey, Jimmy
    See Dorsey Brothers, The
Fountain, Pete **7**
Goodman, Benny **4**
Herman, Woody **12**
Russell, Pee Wee **25**
Shaw, Artie **8**
Stoltzman, Richard **24**

Classical
Ameling, Elly **24**
Anderson, Marian **8**
Arrau, Claudio **1**
Austral, Florence **26**
Baker, Janet **14**
Bernstein, Leonard **2**
Boulez, Pierre **26**
Boyd, Liona **7**
Bream, Julian **9**
Britten, Benjamin **15**
Bronfman, Yefim **6**
Canadian Brass, The **4**
Carter, Ron **14**
Casals, Pablo **9**
Chang, Sarah **7**
Clayderman, Richard **1**
Cliburn, Van **13**
Copland, Aaron **2**
Davis, Anthony **17**
Davis, Chip **4**
DuPré, Jacqueline **26**
Dvorak, Antonin **25**
Fiedler, Arthur **6**
Fleming, Renee **24**
Galway, James **3**
Gardiner, John Eliot **26**
Gingold, Josef **6**
Gould, Glenn **9**
Gould, Morton **16**
Hampson, Thomas **12**
Harrell, Lynn **3**
Hayes, Roland **13**
Hendricks, Barbara **10**
Herrmann, Bernard **14**
Hinderas, Natalie **12**

Horne, Marilyn **9**
Horowitz, Vladimir **1**
Jarrett, Keith **1**
Kennedy, Nigel **8**
Kissin, Evgeny **6**
Kronos Quartet **5**
Kunzel, Erich **17**
Lemper, Ute **14**
Levine, James **8**
Liberace **9**
Ma, Yo Yo **24**
    Earlier sketch in CM **2**
Marsalis, Wynton **6**
Mascagni, Pietro **25**
Masur, Kurt **11**
McNair, Sylvia **15**
McPartland, Marian **15**
Mehta, Zubin **11**
Menuhin, Yehudi **11**
Midori **7**
Mutter, Anne-Sophie **23**
Nyman, Michael **15**
Ott, David **2**
Parkening, Christopher **7**
Perahia, Murray **10**
Perlman, Itzhak **2**
Phillips, Harvey **3**
Pires, Maria João **26**
Quasthoff, Thomas **26**
Rampal, Jean-Pierre **6**
Rangell, Andrew **24**
Rieu, André **26**
Rostropovich, Mstislav **17**
Rota, Nino **13**
Rubinstein, Arthur **11**
Salerno-Sonnenberg, Nadja **3**
Salonen, Esa-Pekka **16**
Schickele, Peter **5**
Schuman, William **10**
Segovia, Andres **6**
Shankar, Ravi **9**
Solti, Georg **13**
Stern, Isaac **7**
Stoltzman, Richard **24**
Sutherland, Joan **13**
Takemitsu, Toru **6**
Temirkanov, Yuri **26**
Thibaudet, Jean-Yves **24**
Tilson Thomas, Michael **24**
Toscanini, Arturo **14**
Upshaw, Dawn **9**
Vanessa-Mae **26**
Vienna Choir Boys **23**
von Karajan, Herbert **1**
Weill, Kurt **12**
Wilson, Ransom **5**
Yamashita, Kazuhito **4**
York, Andrew **15**
Zukerman, Pinchas **4**

Composers
Adams, John **8**
Allen, Geri **10**
Alpert, Herb **11**
Anderson, Wessell **23**
Anka, Paul **2**
Atkins, Chet **5**
Bacharach, Burt **20**
    Earlier sketch in CM **1**
Badalamenti, Angelo **17**
Beiderbecke, Bix **16**
Benson, George **9**
Berlin, Irving **8**
Bernstein, Leonard **2**

Blackman, Cindy 15
Bley, Carla 8
Bley, Paul 14
Boulez, Pierre 26
Braxton, Anthony 12
Brickman, Jim 22
Britten, Benjamin 15
Brubeck, Dave 8
Burrell, Kenny 11
Byrne, David 8
　　Also see Talking Heads
Byron, Don 22
Cage, John 8
Cale, John 9
Casals, Pablo 9
Clarke, Stanley 3
Coleman, Ornette 5
Cooder, Ry 2
Cooney, Rory 6
Copeland, Stewart 14
　　Also see Police, The 20
Copland, Aaron 2
Crouch, Andraé 9
Curtis, King 17
Davis, Anthony 17
Davis, Chip 4
Davis, Miles 1
de Grassi, Alex 6
Dorsey, Thomas A. 11
Dvorak, Antonin 25
Elfman, Danny 9
Ellington, Duke 2
Eno, Brian 8
Enya 6
Esquivel, Juan 17
Evans, Bill 17
Evans, Gil 17
Fahey, John 17
Foster, David 13
Frisell, Bill 15
Frith, Fred 19
Galás, Diamanda 16
Garner, Erroll 25
Gillespie, Dizzy 6
Glass, Philip 1
Golson, Benny 21
Gould, Glenn 9
Gould, Morton 16
Green, Benny 17
Grusin, Dave 7
Guaraldi, Vince 3
Hamlisch, Marvin 1
Hammer, Jan 21
Hancock, Herbie 8
Handy, W. C. 7
Hargrove, Roy 15
Harris, Eddie 15
Hartke, Stephen 5
Henderson, Fletcher 16
Herrmann, Bernard 14
Hunter, Alberta 7
Ibrahim, Abdullah 24
Isham, Mark 14
Jacquet, Illinois 17
Jarre, Jean-Michel 2
Jarrett, Keith 1
Johnson, James P. 16
Jones, Hank 15
Jones, Howard 26
Jones, Quincy 20
　　Earlier sketch in CM 2
Joplin, Scott 10
Jordan, Stanley 1
Kenny G 14

Kenton, Stan 21
Kern, Jerome 13
Kitaro 1
Kottke, Leo 13
Lacy, Steve 23
Lateef, Yusef 16
Lee, Peggy 8
Legg, Adrian 17
Lewis, Ramsey 14
Lincoln, Abbey 9
Lloyd, Charles 22
Lloyd Webber, Andrew 6
Loesser, Frank 19
Loewe, Frederick
　　See Lerner and Loewe
Mancini, Henry 20
　　Earlier sketch in CM 1
Marsalis, Branford 10
Marsalis, Ellis 13
Martino, Pat 17
Mascagni, Pietro 25
Masekela, Hugh 7
McBride, Christian 17
McPartland, Marian 15
Menken, Alan 10
Metheny, Pat 26
　　Earlier sketch in CM 2
Miles, Ron 22
Mingus, Charles 9
Moby 17
Monk, Meredith 1
Monk, Thelonious 6
Montenegro, Hugo 18
Morricone, Ennio 15
Morton, Jelly Roll 7
Mulligan, Gerry 16
Nascimento, Milton 6
Newman, Randy 4
Nyman, Michael 15
Oldfield, Mike 18
Orff, Carl 21
Osby, Greg 21
Ott, David 2
Palmieri, Eddie 15
Parker, Charlie 5
Parks, Van Dyke 17
Perez, Danilo 25
Peterson, Oscar 11
Piazzolla, Astor 18
Ponty, Jean-Luc 8
Porter, Cole 10
Post, Mike 21
Previn, André 15
Puente, Tito 14
Pullen, Don 16
Reich, Steve 8
Reinhardt, Django 7
Ritenour, Lee 7
Roach, Max 12
Rollins, Sonny 7
Rota, Nino 13
Sakamoto, Ryuichi 19
Salonen, Esa-Pekka 16
Sanders, Pharoah 16
Satie, Erik 25
Satriani, Joe 4
Schickele, Peter 5
Schuman, William 10
Shankar, Ravi 9
Shaw, Artie 8
Shorter, Wayne 5
Silver, Horace 19
Solal, Martial 4
Sondheim, Stephen 8

Sousa, John Philip 10
Story, Liz 2
Strauss, Richard 25
Stravinsky, Igor 21
Strayhorn, Billy 13
Styne, Jule 21
Summers, Andy 3
　　Also see Police, The
Sun Ra 5
Takemitsu, Toru 6
Talbot, John Michael 6
Tatum, Art 17
Taylor, Billy 13
Taylor, Cecil 9
Tesh, John 20
Thielemans, Toots 13
Threadgill, Henry 9
Tilson Thomas, Michael 24
Towner, Ralph 22
Tyner, McCoy 7
Vangelis 21
Was, Don 21
　　Also see Was (Not Was)
Washington, Grover, Jr. 5
Weill, Kurt 12
Weston, Randy 15
Whelan, Bill 20
Whiteman, Paul 17
Williams, John 9
Wilson, Cassandra 12
Wilson, Cassandra 26
Winston, George
Winter, Paul 10
Worrell, Bernie 11
Yanni 11
Yeston, Maury 22
York, Andrew 15
Young, La Monte 16
Zappa, Frank 17
　　Earlier sketch in CM 1
Zimmerman, Udo 5
Zorn, John 15

Conductors
Bacharach, Burt 20
　　Earlier sketch CM 1
Bernstein, Leonard 2
Boulez, Pierre 26
Britten, Benjamin 15
Casals, Pablo 9
Copland, Aaron 2
Davies, Dennis Russell 24
Domingo, Placido 20
　　Earlier sketch in CM 1
Evans, Gil 17
Fiedler, Arthur 6
Gardiner, John Eliot 26
Gould, Morton 16
Herrmann, Bernard 14
Ibrahim, Abdullah 24
Jarrett, Keith 1
Jones, Hank 15
Kunzel, Erich 17
Levine, James 8
Mancini, Henry 20
　　Earlier sketch in CM 1
Marriner, Neville 7
Mascagni, Pietro 25
Masur, Kurt 11
Mehta, Zubin 11
Menuhin, Yehudi 11
Nero, Peter 19
Previn, André 15
Rampal, Jean-Pierre 6

Rieu, André **26**
Rostropovich, Mstislav **17**
Salonen, Esa-Pekka **16**
Schickele, Peter **5**
Solti, Georg **13**
Strauss, Richard
Temirkanov, Yuri **26**
Tilson Thomas, Michael **24**
Toscanini, Arturo **14**
Valdes, Chuco **25**
von Karajan, Herbert **1**
Welk, Lawrence **13**
Williams, John **9**
Zukerman, Pinchas **4**

Contemporary Dance Music
Abdul, Paula **3**
Aphex Twin **14**
Bee Gees, The **3**
B-52's, The **4**
Brown, Bobby **4**
Brown, James **2**
C + C Music Factory **16**
Cherry, Neneh **4**
Clinton, George **7**
Craig, Carl **19**
Deee-lite **9**
De La Soul **7**
Depeche Mode **5**
Earth, Wind and Fire **12**
English Beat, The **9**
En Vogue **10**
Erasure **11**
Eurythmics **6**
Exposé **4**
Fox, Samantha **3**
Fun Lovin' Criminals **20**
Gang of Four **8**
Hammer, M.C. **5**
Harry, Deborah **4**
    Also see Blondie
Ice-T **7**
Idol, Billy **3**
Jackson, Janet **16**
    Earlier sketch in CM **3**
Jackson, Michael **17**
    Earlier sketch in CM **1**
    Also see Jacksons, The
James, Rick **2**
Jones, Grace **9**
Madonna **16**
    Earlier sketch in CM **4**
Massive Attack **17**
Moby **17**
M People **15**
New Order **11**
Orbital **20**
Peniston, CeCe **15**
Pet Shop Boys **5**
Pizzicato Five **18**
Portishead **22**
Prince **14**
    Earlier sketch in CM **1**
Queen Latifah **6**
Rodgers, Nile **8**
Salt-N-Pepa **6**
Shadow, DJ **19**
Shamen, The **23**
Simmons, Russell **7**
Soul II Soul **17**
Sugar Ray **22**
Summer, Donna **12**
Technotronic **5**
TLC **15**

Tricky **18**
2 Unlimited **18**
Vasquez, Junior **16**
Village People, The **7**
Was (Not Was) **6**
Waters, Crystal **15**
Young M.C. **4**

Contemporary Instrumental/New Age
Ackerman, Will **3**
Arkenstone, David **20**
Clinton, George **7**
Collins, Bootsy **8**
Davis, Chip **4**
de Grassi, Alex **6**
Enigma **14**
Enya **6**
Esquivel, Juan **17**
Hedges, Michael **3**
Isham, Mark **14**
Jarre, Jean-Michel **2**
Kitaro **1**
Kronos Quartet **5**
Legg, Adrian **17**
Roth, Gabrielle **26**
Sete, Bola **26**
Story, Liz **2**
Summers, Andy **3**
    Also see Police, The
Tangerine Dream **12**
Tesh, John **20**
Winston, George **9**
Winter, Paul **10**
Yanni **11**

Cornet
Armstrong, Louis **4**
Beiderbecke, Bix **16**
Cherry, Don **10**
Handy, W. C. **7**
Oliver, King **15**
Vaché, Jr., Warren **22**

Country
Acuff, Roy **2**
Akins, Rhett **22**
Alabama **21**
    Earlier sketch in CM **1**
Anderson, John **5**
Arnold, Eddy **10**
Asleep at the Wheel **5**
Atkins, Chet **26**
Atkins, Chet **5**
Auldridge, Mike **4**
Autry, Gene **25**
    Earlier sketch in CM **12**
Barnett, Mandy **26**
Bellamy Brothers, The **13**
Berg, Matraca **16**
Berry, John **17**
Black, Clint **5**
BlackHawk **21**
Blue Rodeo **18**
Boggs, Dock **25**
Bogguss, Suzy **11**
Bonamy, James **21**
Boone, Pat **13**
Boy Howdy **21**
Brandt, Paul **22**
Brannon, Kippi **20**
Brooks & Dunn **25**
    Earlier sketch in CM **12**
Brooks, Garth **25**
    Earlier sketch in CM **8**

Brown, Junior **15**
Brown, Marty **14**
Brown, Tony **14**
Buffett, Jimmy **4**
Byrds, The **8**
Cale, J. J. **16**
Campbell, Glen **2**
Carter, Carlene **8**
Carter, Deana **25**
Carter Family, The **3**
Cash, Johnny **17**
    Earlier sketch in CM **1**
Cash, June Carter **6**
Cash, Rosanne **2**
Chapin Carpenter, Mary **25**
    Earlier sketch in CM **6**
Chesney, Kenny **20**
Chesnutt, Mark **13**
Clark, Guy **17**
Clark, Roy **1**
Clark, Terri **19**
Clements, Vassar **18**
Cline, Patsy **5**
Cody, John
    See Ray Condo and His Ricochets
Condo, Ray
    See Ray Condo and His Ricochets
Coe, David Allan **4**
Collie, Mark **15**
Confederate Railroad **23**
Cooder, Ry **2**
Cowboy Junkies, The **4**
Crawford, Randy **25**
Crowe, J. D. **5**
Crowell, Rodney **8**
Cyrus, Billy Ray **11**
Daniels, Charlie **6**
Davis, Linda **21**
Davis, Skeeter **15**
Dean, Billy **19**
DeMent, Iris **13**
Denver, John **22**
    Earlier sketch in CM **1**
Desert Rose Band, The **4**
Diamond Rio **11**
Dickens, Little Jimmy **7**
Diffie, Joe **10**
Dixie Chicks **26**
Dylan, Bob **21**
    Earlier sketch in CM **3**
Earle, Steve **16**
Erwin, Emily
    See Dixie Chicks
Estes, John **25**
Flatt, Lester **3**
Flores, Rosie **16**
Ford, Tennessee Ernie **3**
Foster, Radney **16**
Frizzell, Lefty **10**
Gayle, Crystal **1**
Germano, Lisa **18**
Gill, Vince **7**
Gilley, Mickey **7**
Gilmore, Jimmie Dale **11**
Gordy, Jr., Emory **17**
Greenwood, Lee **12**
Griffith, Nanci **3**
Haggard, Merle **2**
Hall, Tom T. **4**
Hall, Tom T. **26**
Harris, Emmylou **4**
Hartford, John **1**
Hay, George D. **3**
Herndon, Ty **20**

Hiatt, John **8**
Highway 101 **4**
Hill, Faith **18**
Hinojosa, Tish **13**
Howard, Harlan **15**
Jackson, Alan **25**
   Earlier sketch in CM **7**
Jackson, Clive
   See Ray Condo and His Ricochets
Jennings, Waylon **4**
Jones, George **4**
Judd, Wynonna
   See Wynonna
   See Judds, The
Judds, The **2**
Keith, Toby **17**
Kentucky Headhunters, The **5**
Kershaw, Sammy **15**
Ketchum, Hal **14**
Kristofferson, Kris **4**
Lamb, Barbara **19**
Lang, kd **25**
   Earlier sketch in CM **4**
Lawrence, Tracy **11**
LeDoux, Chris **12**
Lee, Brenda **5**
Little Feat **4**
Little Texas **14**
Louvin Brothers, The **12**
Loveless, Patty **21**
   Earlier sketch in CM **5**
Lovett, Lyle **5**
Lynch, Laura
   See Dixie Chicks
Lynn, Loretta **2**
Lynne, Shelby **5**
Macy, Robin
   See Dixie Chicks
Maines, Natalie
   See Dixie Chicks
Mandrell, Barbara **4**
Mattea, Kathy **5**
Mavericks, The **15**
McBride, Martina **14**
McCann, Lila **26**
McClinton, Delbert **14**
McCoy, Neal **15**
McCready, Mindy **22**
McEntire, Reba **11**
McGraw, Tim **17**
Messina, Jo Dee **26**
Miller, Roger **4**
Milsap, Ronnie **2**
Moffatt, Katy **18**
Monroe, Bill **1**
Montgomery, John Michael **14**
Morgan, Lorrie **10**
Murphey, Michael Martin **9**
Murray, Anne **4**
Nelson, Willie **11**
   Earlier sketch in CM **1**
Newton-John, Olivia **8**
Nikleva, Steven
   See Ray Condo and His Ricochets
Nitty Gritty Dirt Band, The **6**
O'Connor, Mark **1**
Oak Ridge Boys, The **7**
Oslin, K. T. **3**
Owens, Buck **2**
Parnell, Lee Roy **15**
Parsons, Gram **7**
   Also see Byrds, The
Parton, Dolly **24**
   Earlier sketch in CM **2**

Pearl, Minnie **3**
Pierce, Webb **15**
Price, Ray **11**
Pride, Charley **4**
Rabbitt, Eddie **24**
   Earlier sketch in CM **5**
Raitt, Bonnie **3**
Ray Condo and His Ricochets **26**
Raye, Collin **16**
Reeves, Jim **10**
Restless Heart **12**
Rich, Charlie **3**
Richey, Kim **20**
Ricochet **23**
Rimes, LeAnn **19**
Robbins, Marty **9**
Rodgers, Jimmie **3**
Rogers, Kenny **1**
Rogers, Roy **24**
   Earlier sketch in CM **9**
Roy, Jimmy
   See Ray Condo and His Ricochets
Sawyer Brown **13**
Scruggs, Earl **3**
Scud Mountain Boys **21**
Seals, Dan **9**
Seidel, Martie
   See Dixie Chicks
Shenandoah **17**
Skaggs, Ricky **5**
Sonnier, Jo-El **10**
Statler Brothers, The **8**
Stevens, Ray **7**
Stone, Doug **10**
Strait, George **5**
Stuart, Marty **9**
Sweethearts of the Rodeo **12**
Taylor, Steve
   See Ray Condo and His Ricochets
Texas Tornados, The **8**
Tillis, Mel **7**
Tillis, Pam **25**
   Earlier sketch in CM **8**
Tippin, Aaron **12**
Travis, Merle **14**
Travis, Randy **9**
Tritt, Travis **7**
Tubb, Ernest **4**
Tucker, Tanya **3**
Twain, Shania **17**
Twitty, Conway **6**
Van Shelton, Ricky **5**
Van Zandt, Townes **13**
Wagoner, Porter **13**
Walker, Clay **20**
Walker, Jerry Jeff **13**
Wariner, Steve **18**
Watson, Doc **2**
Wells, Kitty **6**
West, Dottie **8**
White, Lari **15**
Whitley, Keith **7**
Williams, Don **4**
Williams, Hank, Jr. **1**
Williams, Hank, Sr. **4**
Williams, Lucinda **24**
Willis, Kelly **12**
Wills, Bob **3**
Wynette, Tammy **24**
   Earlier sketch in CM **2**
Wynonna **11**
   Also see Judds, The
Yearwood, Trisha **25**
   Earlier sketch in CM **10**

Yoakam, Dwight **21**
   Earlier sketch in CM **1**
Young, Faron **7**

Dobro
Auldridge, Mike **4**
   Also see Country Gentlemen, The
   Also see Seldom Scene, The
Burch, Curtis
   See New Grass Revival, The
Knopfler, Mark **25**
   Also see Dire Straits
   Earlier sketch in CM **3**
Whitley, Chris **16**

Drums
Aronoff, Kenny **21**
   See **Percussion**
Colaiuta, Vinnie **23**
Starr, Ringo **24**

Dulcimer
Ritchie, Jean **4**

Fiddle
MacIsaac, Ashley **21**
   See **Violin**

Film Scores
Anka, Paul **2**
Bacharach, Burt **20**
   Earlier sketch in CM **1**
Badalamenti, Angelo **17**
Berlin, Irving **8**
Bernstein, Leonard **2**
Blanchard, Terence **13**
Britten, Benjamin **15**
Byrne, David **8**
   Also see Talking Heads
Cafferty, John
   See Beaver Brown Band, The
Cahn, Sammy **11**
Cliff, Jimmy **8**
Copeland, Stewart **14**
   Also see Police, The
Copland, Aaron **2**
Crouch, Andraé **9**
Dibango, Manu **14**
Dolby, Thomas **10**
Donovan **9**
Eddy, Duane **9**
Elfman, Danny **9**
Ellington, Duke **2**
Ferguson, Maynard **7**
Froom, Mitchell **15**
Gabriel, Peter **16**
   Earlier sketch in CM **2**
   Also see Genesis
Galás, Diamanda **16**
Gershwin, George and Ira **11**
Gould, Glenn **9**
Grusin, Dave **7**
Guaraldi, Vince **3**
Hamlisch, Marvin **1**
Hancock, Herbie **8**
Harrison, George **2**
Hayes, Isaac **10**
Hedges, Michael **3**
Herrmann, Bernard **14**
Isham, Mark **14**
Jones, Quincy **20**
   Earlier sketch in CM **2**
Knopfler, Mark **25**
   Earlier sketch in CM **3**
   Also see Dire Straits

Lennon, John **9**
  Also see Beatles, The
Lerner and Loewe **13**
Loesser, Frank **19**
Mancini, Henry **20**
  Earlier sketch in CM **1**
Marsalis, Branford **10**
Mayfield, Curtis **8**
McCartney, Paul **4**
  Also see Beatles, The
Menken, Alan **10**
Mercer, Johnny **13**
Metheny, Pat **26**
  Earlier sketch in CM **2**
Montenegro, Hugo **18**
Morricone, Ennio **15**
Nascimento, Milton **6**
Nilsson **10**
Nyman, Michael **15**
Parks, Van Dyke **17**
Peterson, Oscar **11**
Porter, Cole **10**
Previn, André **15**
Reznor, Trent **13**
Richie, Lionel **2**
Robertson, Robbie **2**
Rollins, Sonny **7**
Rota, Nino **13**
Sager, Carole Bayer **5**
Sakamoto, Ryuichi **18**
Schickele, Peter **5**
Shankar, Ravi **9**
Taj Mahal **6**
Waits, Tom **12**
  Earlier sketch in CM **1**
Weill, Kurt **12**
Williams, John **9**
Williams, Paul **26**
Williams, Paul **5**
Willner, Hal **10**
Young, Neil **15**
  Earlier sketch in CM **2**

Flugelhorn
Sandoval, Arturo **15**
Mangione, Chuck **23**

Flute
Anderson, Ian
  See Jethro Tull
Galway, James **3**
Lateef, Yusef **16**
Mangione, Chuck **23**
Mann, Herbie **16**
Najee **21**
Nakai, R. Carlos **24**
Rampal, Jean-Pierre **6**
Ulmer, James Blood **13**
Wilson, Ransom **5**

Folk/Traditional
Altan **18**
America **16**
Anonymous 4 **23**
Arnaz, Desi **8**
Baez, Joan **1**
Belafonte, Harry **8**
Black, Mary **15**
Blades, Ruben **2**
Bloom, Luka **14**
Blue Rodeo **18**
Boggs, Dock **25**
Brady, Paul **8**
Bragg, Billy **7**

Bromberg, David **18**
Buckley, Tim **14**
Buffalo Springfield **24**
Bulgarian State Female Vocal Choir, The **10**
Byrds, The **8**
Campbell, Sarah Elizabeth **23**
Caravan **24**
Carter Family, The **3**
Chandra, Sheila **16**
Chapin, Harry **6**
Chapman, Tracy **20**
  Earlier sketch in CM **4**
Chenille Sisters, The **16**
Cherry, Don **10**
Chieftains, The **7**
Childs, Toni **2**
Clannad **23**
Clegg, Johnny **8**
Cockburn, Bruce **8**
Cohen, Leonard **3**
Collins, Judy **4**
Colvin, Shawn **11**
Cotten, Elizabeth **16**
Crosby, David **3**
  Also see Byrds, The
Cruz, Celia **22**
  Earlier sketch in CM **10**
de Lucia, Paco **1**
DeMent, Iris **13**
Donovan **9**
Dr. John **7**
Drake, Nick **17**
Driftwood, Jimmy **25**
Dylan, Bob **3**
Elliot, Cass **5**
Enya **6**
Estefan, Gloria **15**
  Earlier sketch in CM **2**
Fahey, John **17**
Fairport Convention **22**
Feliciano, José **10**
Galway, James **3**
Germano, Lisa **18**
Gibson, Bob **23**
Gilmore, Jimmie Dale **11**
Gipsy Kings, The **8**
Gorka, John **18**
Griffin, Patty **24**
Griffith, Nanci **3**
Grisman, David **17**
Guthrie, Arlo **6**
Guthrie, Woody **2**
Hakmoun, Hassan **15**
Hardin, Tim **18**
Harding, John Wesley **6**
Hartford, John **1**
Havens, Richie **11**
Henry, Joe **18**
Hinojosa, Tish **13**
Ian and Sylvia **18**
Ian, Janis **24**
Iglesias, Julio **20**
  Earlier sketch in CM **2**
Incredible String Band **23**
Indigo Girls **20**
  Earlier sketch in CM **3**
Ives, Burl **12**
Khan, Nusrat Fateh Ali **13**
Kingston Trio, The **9**
Klezmatics, The **18**
Kottke, Leo **13**
Kuti, Fela **7**
Ladysmith Black Mambazo **1**
Larkin, Patty **9**

Lavin, Christine **6**
Leadbelly **6**
Lightfoot, Gordon **3**
Los Lobos **2**
Makeba, Miriam **8**
Mamas and the Papas **21**
Masekela, Hugh **7**
McKennitt, Loreena **24**
McLean, Don **7**
Melanie **12**
Mitchell, Joni **17**
  Earlier sketch in CM **2**
Moffatt, Katy **18**
Morrison, Van **24**
  Earlier sketch in CM **3**
Morrissey, Bill **12**
N'Dour, Youssou **6**
Nascimento, Milton **6**
Near, Holly **1**
O'Connor, Sinead **3**
Ochs, Phil **7**
Odetta **7**
Parsons, Gram **7**
  Also see Byrds, The
Paxton, Tom **5**
Pentangle **18**
Peter, Paul & Mary **4**
Pogues, The **6**
Prine, John **7**
Proclaimers, The **13**
Rankins, The **24**
Redpath, Jean **1**
Ritchie, Jean, **4**
Roches, The **18**
Rodgers, Jimmie **3**
Russell, Tom **26**
Sainte-Marie, Buffy **11**
Santana, Carlos **1**
Seeger, Peggy **25**
Seeger, Pete **4**
  Also see Weavers, The
Selena **16**
Shankar, Ravi **9**
Simon and Garfunkel **24**
Simon, Paul **16**
  Earlier sketch in CM **1**
  Also see Simon and Garfunkel
Snow, Pheobe **4**
Steeleye Span **19**
Story, The **13**
Sweet Honey in the Rock **1**
Taj Mahal **6**
Thompson, Richard **7**
Tikaram, Tanita **9**
Toure, Ali Farka **18**
Van Ronk, Dave **12**
Van Zandt, Townes **13**
Vega, Suzanne **3**
Wainwright III, Loudon **11**
Walker, Jerry Jeff **13**
Watson, Doc **2**
Weavers, The **8**
Whitman, Slim **19**

French Horn
Ohanian, David
  See Canadian Brass, The

Funk
Bambaataa, Afrika **13**
Brand New Heavies, The **14**
Brown, James **2**
Burdon, Eric **14**
  Also see War
  Also see Animals

Clinton, George **7**
Collins, Bootsy **8**
Fishbone **7**
Gang of Four **8**
Jackson, Janet **16**
    Earlier sketch in CM **3**
Khan, Chaka **19**
    Earlier sketch in CM **9**
Mayfield, Curtis **8**
Meters, The **14**
Ohio Players **16**
Parker, Maceo **7**
Prince **14**
    Earlier sketch in CM **1**
Red Hot Chili Peppers, The **7**
Sly and the Family Stone **24**
Stone, Sly **8**
    Also see Sly and the Family Stone
Toussaint, Allen **11**
Worrell, Bernie **11**

Funky
Avery, Teodross **23**
Cloud, Jeff
    See Joy Electric
Front 242 **19**
Jamiroquai **21**
Joy Electric **26**
Martin, Ronnie
    See Joy Electric
Wu-Tang Clan **19**

Fusion
Anderson, Ray **7**
Avery, Teodross **23**
Beck, Jeff **4**
    Also see Yardbirds, The
Clarke, Stanley **3**
Coleman, Ornette **5**
Corea, Chick **6**
Davis, Miles **1**
Fishbone **7**
Hancock, Herbie **8**
Harris, Eddie **15**
Johnson, Eric **19**
Lewis, Ramsey **14**
Mahavishnu Orchestra **19**
McLaughlin, John **12**
Metheny, Pat **26**
    Earlier sketch in CM **2**
O'Connor, Mark **1**
Ponty, Jean-Luc **8**
Reid, Vernon **2**
Ritenour, Lee **7**
Shorter, Wayne **5**
Summers, Andy **3**
    Also see Police, The
Washington, Grover, Jr. **5**

Gospel
4Him **23**
Allman, Chris
    See Greater Vision
Anderson, Marian **8**
Armstrong, Vanessa Bell **24**
Baylor, Helen **20**
Belove, David
    See Oakland Interfaith Gospel Choir
Boone, Pat **13**
Brown, James **2**
Caesar, Shirley **17**
Carter Family, The **3**
Charles, Ray **1**
Cleveland, James **1**

Cooke, Sam **1**
    Also see Soul Stirrers, The
Crouch, Andraé **9**
Dorsey, Thomas A. **11**
Ellison, Rahsaan
    See Oakland Interfaith Gospel Choir
Five Blind Boys of Alabama **12**
Ford, Tennessee Ernie **3**
Forte, Juan
    See Oakland Interfaith Gospel Choir
Franklin, Aretha **17**
    Earlier sketch in CM **2**
Franklin, Kirk **22**
Golden Gate Quartet **25**
Greater Vision **26**
Green, Al **9**
Griffin, Rodney
    See Greater Vision
Hawkins, Tramaine **17**
Heveroh, Ben
    See Oakland Interfaith Gospel Choir
Hoffman, Ellen
    See Oakland Interfaith Gospel Choir
Houston, Cissy **26**
    Earlier sketch in CM **6**
Jackson, Mahalia **8**
Johnson, Blind Willie **26**
Kee, John P. **15**
Kelly, Ed
    See Oakland Interfaith Gospel Choir
Kelly, Terrance
    See Oakland Interfaith Gospel Choir
Knight, Gladys **1**
Lampkin, Troy
    See Oakland Interfaith Gospel Choir
Little Richard **1**
Louvin Brothers, The **12**
Mighty Clouds of Joy, The **17**
Oak Ridge Boys, The **7**
Oakland Interfaith Gospel Choir **26**
Paris, Twila **16**
Pickett, Wilson **10**
Presley, Elvis **1**
Redding, Otis **5**
Reese, Della **13**
Robbins, Marty **9**
Smith, Michael W. **11**
Soul Stirrers, The **11**
Sounds of Blackness **13**
Staples, Mavis **13**
Staples, Pops **11**
Sweet Honey In The Rock **26**
Take 6 **6**
Trammell, Mark
    See Greater Vision
Waldroup, Jason
    See Greater Vision
Waters, Ethel **11**
Watson, Doc **2**
Williams, Deniece **1**
Williams, Marion **15**
Winans, The **12**
Wolfe, Gerald
    See Greater Vision
Womack, Bobby **5**

Guitar
Abercrombie, John **25**
Ackerman, Will **3**
Adé, King Sunny **18**
Allison, Luther **21**
Allman, Duane
    See Allman Brothers, The
Alvin, Dave **17**

Atkins, Chet **26**
    Earlier sketch in CM **5**
Autry, Gene **25**
    Earlier sketch in CM **12**
Barnes, Roosevelt "Booba" **23**
Baxter, Jeff
    See Doobie Brothers, The
Beauvoir, Jean
    See Wendy O. Williams and the
Plasmatics
Beck **18**
Beck, Jeff **4**
    Also see Yardbirds, The
Beech, Wes
    See Wendy O. Williams and the
Plasmatics
Belew, Adrian **5**
Benson, George **9**
Berry, Chuck **1**
Berry, John **17**
Bettencourt, Nuno
    See Extreme
Betts, Dicky
    See Allman Brothers, The
Block, Rory **18**
Bloom, Luka **14**
Boyd, Liona **7**
Bream, Julian **9**
Bromberg, David **18**
Brooks, Garth **25**
    Earlier sketch in CM **8**
Brown, Junior **15**
Buck, Peter
    See R.E.M.
Buckingham, Lindsey **8**
    Also see Fleetwood Mac
Burrell, Kenny **11**
Callahan, Ray
    See Wendy O. Williams and the
Plasmatics
Campbell, Glen **2**
Carter, Deana **25**
Chapin-Carpenter, Mary **25**
    Earlier sketch in CM **6**
Chaquico, Craig **23**
Chesney, Kenny **20**
Chesnutt, Mark **13**
Christian, Charlie **11**
Clapton, Eric **11**
    Earlier sketch in CM **1**
    Also see Cream
    Also see Yardbirds, The
Clark, Roy **1**
Cockburn, Bruce **8**
Collie, Mark **15**
Collins, Albert **19**
    Earlier sketch in CM **4**
Cooder, Ry **2**
Cotten, Elizabeth **16**
Cray, Robert **8**
Cropper, Steve **12**
Dale, Dick **13**
Daniels, Charlie **6**
Davis, Reverend Gary **18**
de Grassi, Alex **6**
de Lucia, Paco **1**
Del Rubio Triplets **21**
Denver, John **22**
    Earlier sketch in CM **1**
Deutsch, Stu
    See Wendy O. Williams and the
Plasmatics
Di Meola, Al **12**
Dickens, Little Jimmy **7**

Diddley, Bo **3**
DiFranco, Ani **17**
Drake, Nick **17**
Earl, Ronnie **5**
    Also see Roomful of Blues
Eddy, Duane **9**
Edge, The
    See U2
Ellis, Herb **18**
Emmanuel, Tommy **21**
Etheridge, Melissa **16**
    Earlier sketch in CM **4**
Fahey, John **17**
Fankhauser,, Merrell **24**
Feliciano, José **10**
Fender, Leo **10**
Flatt, Lester **3**
Flores, Rosie **16**
Ford, Lita **9**
Frampton, Peter **3**
Frehley, Ace
    See Kiss
Fripp, Robert **9**
Frisell, Bill **15**
Frith, Fred **19**
Fuller, Blind Boy **20**
Fulson, Lowell **20**
Funahara, O. Chosei
    See Wendy O. Williams and the
    Plasmatics
Garcia, Jerry **4**
    Also see Grateful Dead, The
Gatton, Danny **16**
George, Lowell
    See Little Feat
Gibbons, Billy
    See ZZ Top
Gibson, Bob **23**
Gil, Gilberto **26**
Gill, Vince **7**
Gilmour, David
    See Pink Floyd
Gorka, John **18**
Green, Grant **14**
Green, Peter
    See Fleetwood Mac
Guy, Buddy **4**
Hackett, Bobby **21**
Haley, Bill **6**
Hall, Tom T. **26**
Hardin, Tim **18**
Harper, Ben **17**
Harrison, George **2**
Hatfield, Juliana **12**
    Also see Lemonheads, The
Havens, Richie **11**
Healey, Jeff **4**
Hedges, Michael **3**
Hendrix, Jimi **2**
Hepcat, Harry **23**
Hillman, Chris
    See Byrds, The
    Also see Desert Rose Band, The
Hitchcock, Robyn **9**
Holly, Buddy **1**
Hooker, John Lee **1**
Hooker, John Lee **26**
Hopkins, Lightnin' **13**
Howlin' Wolf **6**
Hunter, Charlie **24**
Iommi, Tony
    See Black Sabbath
Ives, Burl **12**

Jackson, Alan **25**
    Earlier sketch in CM **7**
James, Elmore **8**
James, Skip **24**
Jardine, Al
    See Beach Boys, The
Jean, Wyclef **22**
Jefferson, Blind Lemon **18**
Jewel **25**
Jobim, Antonio Carlos **19**
Johnson, Blind Willie **26**
Johnson, Eric **19**
Johnson, Lonnie **17**
Johnson, Robert **6**
Jones, Brian
    See Rolling Stones, The
Jordan, Stanley **1**
Kantner, Paul
    See Jefferson Airplane
Keaggy, Phil **26**
Keith, Toby **17**
King, Albert **2**
King, B. B. **1**
King, B.B. **24**
King, Freddy **17**
Klugh, Earl **10**
Knopfler, Mark **25**
    Earlier sketch in CM **3**
    Also see Dire Straits
Kottke, Leo **13**
Landreth, Sonny **16**
Larkin, Patty **9**
Leadbelly **6**
Legg, Adrian **17**
Lennon, John **9**
    Also see Beatles, The
Lindley, David **2**
Lockwood, Robert, Jr. **10**
Loeb, Lisa **19**
Lofgren, Nils **25**
Marr, Johnny
    See Smiths, The
    See The The
Martino, Pat **17**
Matthews, Eric **22**
May, Brian
    See Queen
Mayfield, Curtis **8**
McClinton, Delbert **14**
McCoury, Del **15**
McDowell, Mississippi Fred **16**
McGuinn, Roger
    See Byrds, The
McLachlan, Sarah **12**
McLaughlin, John **12**
McLean, Dave **24**
McLennan, Grant **21**
McReynolds, Jim
    See McReynolds, Jim and Jesse
McTell, Blind Willie **17**
Metheny, Pat **26**
    Earlier sketch in CM **2**
Mitchell, Joni **17**
    Earlier sketch in CM **2**
Mo', Keb' **21**
Montgomery, Wes **3**
Morrissey, Bill **12**
Muldaur, Maria **18**
Nugent, Ted **2**
Oldfield, Mike **18**
Owens, Buck **2**
Page, Jimmy **4**
    Also see Led Zeppelin
    Also see Yardbirds, The

Parkening, Christopher **7**
Parnell, Lee Roy **15**
Pass, Joe **15**
Patton, Charley **11**
Perkins, Carl **9**
Perry, Joe
    See Aerosmith
Petri, Tony
    See Wendy O. Williams and the
    Plasmatics
Petty, Tom **9**
Phair, Liz **14**
Phillips, Sam **12**
Powell, Baden, **23**
Prince **14**
    Earlier sketch in CM **1**
Raitt, Bonnie **23**
    Earlier sketch in CM **1**
Ray, Amy
    See Indigo Girls
Redbone, Leon **19**
Reed, Jimmy **15**
Reese, Joey
    See Wendy O. Williams and the
    Plasmatics
Reid, Vernon **2**
    Also see Living Colour
Reinhardt, Django **7**
Richards, Keith **11**
    Also see Rolling Stones, The
Richman, Jonathan **12**
Ritenour, Lee **7**
Robbins, Marty **9**
Robertson, Robbie **2**
Robillard, Duke **2**
Rodgers, Nile **8**
Romanelli, Chris "Junior"
    See Wendy O. Williams and the
    Plasmatics
Rush, Otis **12**
Saliers, Emily
    See Indigo Girls
Sambora, Richie **24**
Santana, Carlos **19**
    Earlier sketch in CM **1**
Satriani, Joe **4**
Scofield, John **7**
Segovia, Andres **6**
Sete, Bola **26**
Sharrock, Sonny **15**
Shepherd, Kenny Wayne **22**
Shines, Johnny **14**
Simon, Paul **16**
    Earlier sketch in CM **1**
Skaggs, Ricky **5**
Slash
    See Guns n' Roses
Springsteen, Bruce **25**
    Earlier sketch in CM **6**
Stewart, Dave
    See Eurythmics
Stills, Stephen **5**
Stotts, Richie
    See Wendy O. Williams and the
    Plasmatics
Stuart, Marty **9**
Summers, Andy **3**
    Also see Police, The
Tampa Red **25**
Taylor, Mick
    See Rolling Stones, The
Thielemans, Toots **13**
Thompson, Richard **7**
Tippin, Aaron **12**

Tolliver, T.C.
  See Wendy O. Williams and the
Plasmatics
Toure, Ali Farka 18
Towner, Ralph 22
Townshend, Pete 1
Travis, Merle 14
Trynin, Jen 21
Tubb, Ernest 4
Ulmer, James Blood 13
Vai, Steve 5
Van Halen, Edward
  See Van Halen
Van Ronk, Dave 12
Vaughan, Jimmie 24
  Also see Fabulous Thunderbirds, The
Vaughan, Stevie Ray 1
Wachtel, Waddy 26
Wagoner, Porter 13
Waits, Tom 12
  Earlier sketch in CM 1
Walker, Jerry Jeff 13
Walker, T-Bone 5
Walsh, Joe 5
  Also see Eagles, The
Wariner, Steve 18
Waters, Muddy 24
Watson, Doc 2
Weir, Bob
  See Grateful Dead, The
Weller, Paul 14
White, Lari 15
Whitfield, Mark 18
Whitley, Chris 16
Whittaker, Hudson 20
Wilson, Brian 24
Wilson, Nancy
  See Heart
Winston, George 9
Winter, Johnny 5
Wiseman, Mac 19
Wray, Link 17
Yamashita, Kazuhito 4
Yarrow, Peter
  See Peter, Paul & Mary
Yoakam, Dwight 21
York, Andrew 15
Young, Angus
  See AC/DC
Young, Malcolm
  See AC/DC
Young, Neil 15
  Earlier sketch in CM 2
Zappa, Frank 17
  Earlier sketch in CM 1

Harmonica
Barnes, Roosevelt, "Booba" 23
Dylan, Bob 3
Guthrie, Woody 2
Horton, Walter 19
Lewis, Huey 9
Little Walter 14
McClinton, Delbert 14
Musselwhite, Charlie 13
Reed, Jimmy 15
Thielemans, Toots 13
Waters, Muddy 24
  Earlier sketch in CM 4
Wells, Junior 17
Williamson, Sonny Boy 9
Wilson, Kim
  See Fabulous Thunderbirds, The

Wonder, Stevie 17
  Earlier sketch in CM 2
Young, Neil 15
  Earlier sketch in CM 2

Heavy Metal
AC/DC 4
Aerosmith 22
  Earlier sketch in CM 1
Alice in Chains 10
Anthrax 11
Black Sabbath 9
Blue Oyster Cult 16
Cinderella 16
Circle Jerks 17
Danzig 7
Deep Purple 11
Def Leppard 3
Dokken 16
Faith No More 7
Fishbone 7
Ford, Lita 9
Guns n' Roses 2
Iron Maiden 10
Judas Priest 10
Kilgore 24
King's X 7
Kiss 25
  Earlier sketch in CM 5
L7 12
Led Zeppelin 1
Megadeth 9
Melvins 21
Metallica 7
Mötley Crüe 1
Motörhead 10
Nugent, Ted 2
Osbourne, Ozzy 3
Pantera 13
Petra 3
Queensryche 8
Reid, Vernon 2
  Also see Living Colour
Reznor, Trent 13
Roth, David Lee 1
  Also see Van Halen
Sepultura 12
Skinny Puppy 17
Slayer 10
Soundgarden 6
Spinal Tap 8
Stryper 2
Suicidal Tendencies 15
Tool 21
Warrant 17
Wendy O. Williams and The Plasmatics 26
White Zombie 17
Whitesnake 5
Williams, Wendy O.
  See Wendy O. Williams and the
Plasmatics

Humor
Borge, Victor 19
Coasters, The 5
Dr. Demento 23
Jones, Spike 5
Lehrer, Tom 7
Pearl, Minnie 3
Russell, Mark 6
Sandler, Adam 19
Schickele, Peter 5
Shaffer, Paul 13
Spinal Tap 8

Stevens, Ray 7
Yankovic, "Weird Al" 7

Inventors
Fender, Leo 10
Harris, Eddie 15
Paul, Les 2
Scholz, Tom
  See Boston
Teagarden, Jack 10
Theremin, Leon 19

Jazz
Abercrombie, John 25
Adderly, Cannonball 15
Allen, Geri 10
Allison, Mose 17
Anderson, Ray 7
Armstrong, Louis 4
Art Ensemble of Chicago 23
Avery, Teodross 23
Bailey, Mildred 13
Bailey, Pearl 5
Baker, Anita 9
Baker, Chet 13
Baker, Ginger 16
  Also see Cream
Barbieri, Gato 22
Basie, Count 2
Bechet, Sidney 17
Beiderbecke, Bix 16
Belle, Regina 6
Bennett, Tony 16
  Earlier sketch in CM 2
Benson, George 9
Berigan, Bunny 2
Blackman, Cindy 15
Blakey, Art 11
Blanchard, Terence 13
Bley, Carla 8
Bley, Paul 14
Blood, Sweat and Tears 7
Brand New Heavies, The 14
Braxton, Anthony 12
Bridgewater, Dee Dee 18
Brötzmann, Peter 26
Brown, Clifford 24
Brown, Lawrence 23
Brown, Ray 21
Brown, Ruth 13
Brubeck, Dave 8
Burrell, Kenny 11
Burton, Gary 10
Calloway, Cab 6
Cameron, Clayton
  See Ralph Sharon Quartet
Canadian Brass, The 4
Carter, Benny 3
  Also see McKinney's Cotton Pickers
Carter, Betty 6
Carter, James 18
Carter, Regina 22
Carter, Ron 14
Chambers, Paul 18
Charles, Ray 1
Cherry, Don 10
Christian, Charlie 11
Clarke, Stanley 3
Clements, Vassar 18
Clooney, Rosemary 9
Cole, Holly 18
Cole, Nat King 3
Coleman, Ornette 5
Coltrane, John 4

Connick, Harry, Jr. **4**
Corea, Chick **6**
Crawford, Randy **25**
Culp, Dennis
  See Five Iron Frenzy
Davis, Anthony **17**
Davis, Miles **1**
DeJohnette, Jack **7**
Di Meola, Al **12**
Dietrich, Marlene **25**
Dirty Dozen **23**
Dunham, Nathanel "Brad"
  See Five Iron Frenzy
Eckstine, Billy **1**
Eldridge, Roy **9**
  Also see McKinney's Cotton Pickers
Ellington, Duke **2**
Ellis, Herb **18**
Evans, Bill **17**
Evans, Gil **17**
Ferguson, Maynard **7**
Ferrell, Rachelle **17**
Fitzgerald, Ella **1**
Five Iron Frenzy **26**
Flanagan, Tommy **16**
Fleck, Bela **8**
  Also see New Grass Revival, The
Fountain, Pete **7**
Frisell, Bill **15**
Galway, James **3**
Garner, Erroll **25**
Getz, Stan **12**
Gillespie, Dizzy **6**
Goodman, Benny **4**
Gordon, Dexter **10**
Grappelli, Stephane **10**
Green, Benny **17**
Green, Grant **14**
Guaraldi, Vince **3**
Hackett, Bobby **21**
Haden, Charlie **12**
Hampton, Lionel **6**
Hancock, Herbie **25**
Hancock, Herbie **8**
Hardcastle, Paul **20**
Hargrove, Roy **15**
Harris, Eddie **15**
Harris, Teddy **22**
Hawkins, Coleman **11**
Hawkins, Erskine **19**
Hedges, Michael **3**
Henderson, Fletcher **16**
Henderson, Joe **14**
Herman, Woody **12**
Hines, Earl "Fatha" **12**
Hirt, Al **5**
Hoerig, Keith
  See Five Iron Frenzy
Holiday, Billie **6**
Horn, Shirley **7**
Horne, Lena **11**
Humes, Helen **19**
Hunter, Alberta **7**
Hunter, Charlie **24**
Ibrahim, Abdullah **24**
Incognito **16**
Isham, Mark **14**
Israel "Cachao" Lopez **14**
Jackson, Milt **15**
Jacquet, Illinois **17**
James, Boney **21**
James, Harry **11**
Jarreau, Al **1**
Jarrett, Keith **1**

Jensen, Ingrid **22**
Jobim, Antonio Carlos **19**
Johnson, James P. **16**
Johnson, Lonnie **17**
Johnston, Sonnie
  See Five Iron Frenzy
Jones, Elvin **9**
Jones, Hank **15**
Jones, Philly Joe **16**
Jones, Quincy **20**
  Earlier sketch in CM **2**
Jones, Thad **19**
Jordan, Stanley **1**
Kennedy, Nigel **8**
Kenny G **14**
Kenton, Stan **21**
Kerr, Scott
  See Five Iron Frenzy
Kirk, Rahsaan Roland **6**
Kitt, Eartha **9**
Klugh, Earl **10**
Kronos Quartet **5**
Krupa, Gene **13**
Laine, Cleo **10**
Langosch, Paul
  See Ralph Sharon Quartet
Lateef, Yusef **16**
Lee, Peggy **8**
Lewis, Ramsey **14**
Lincoln, Abbey **9**
Lloyd, Charles **22**
Lovano, Joe **13**
Mahavishnu Orchestra **19**
Mahogany, Kevin **26**
Mancini, Henry **20**
  Earlier sketch in CM **1**
Mangione, Chuck **23**
Manhattan Transfer, The **8**
Mann, Herbie **16**
Marsalis, Branford **10**
Marsalis, Ellis **13**
Marsalis, Wynton **20**
  Earlier sketch in CM **6**
Martino, Pat **17**
Masekela, Hugh **7**
McBride, Christian **17**
McFerrin, Bobby **3**
McKinney's Cotton Pickers **16**
McLaughlin, John **12**
McPartland, Marian **15**
McRae, Carmen **9**
Metheny, Pat **26**
  Earlier sketch in CM **2**
Mingus, Charles **9**
Monk, Thelonious **6**
Montgomery, Wes **3**
Morgan, Frank **9**
Morton, Jelly Roll **7**
Mulligan, Gerry **16**
Najee **21**
Nascimento, Milton **6**
Navarro, Fats **25**
Norvo, Red **12**
O'Day, Anita **21**
Oliver, King **15**
Ortega, Leonor "Jeff"
  See Five Iron Frenzy
Orgega, Micah
  See Five Iron Frenzy
Palmer, Jeff **20**
Palmieri, Eddie **15**
Parker, Charlie **5**
Parker, Maceo **7**
Pass, Joe **15**

Paul, Les **2**
Pepper, Art **18**
Perez, Danilo **25**
Peterson, Oscar **11**
Ponty, Jean-Luc **8**
Powell, Bud **15**
Previn, André **15**
Professor Longhair **6**
Puente, Tito **14**
Pullen, Don **16**
Ralph Sharon Quartet **26**
Rampal, Jean-Pierre **6**
Redman, Joshua **25**
  Earlier sketch in CM **12**
Reeves, Dianne **16**
Reid, Vernon **2**
  Also see Living Colour
Reinhardt, Django **7**
Rich, Buddy **13**
Roach, Max **12**
Roberts, Marcus **6**
Robillard, Duke **2**
Rodney, Red **14**
Rollins, Sonny **7**
Roper, Reese
  See Five Iron Frenzy
Russell, Pee Wee **25**
Saluzzi, Dino
Sanborn, David **1**
Sanders, Pharoah **16**
Sandoval, Arturo **15**
Santana, Carlos **19**
  Earlier sketch in CM **1**
Sargeant, Gray
  See Ralph Sharon Quartet
Sharon, Ralph
  See Ralph Sharon Quartet
Schuur, Diane **6**
Scofield, John **7**
Scott, Jimmy **14**
Scott-Heron, Gil **13**
Severinsen, Doc **1**
Sharrock, Sonny **15**
Shaw, Artie **8**
Shorter, Wayne **5**
Silver, Horace **19**
Simone, Nina **11**
Solal, Martial **4**
Strayhorn, Billy **13**
Summers, Andy **3**
  Also see Police, The
Sun Ra **5**
Take 6 **6**
Tatum, Art **17**
Taylor, Billy **13**
Taylor, Cecil **9**
Teagarden, Jack **10**
Terry, Clark **24**
Thielemans, Toots **13**
Threadgill, Henry **9**
Torme, Mel **4**
Tucker, Sophie **12**
Turner, Big Joe **13**
Turtle Island String Quartet **9**
Tyner, McCoy **7**
Ulmer, James Blood **13**
US3 **18**
Valdes, Chuco **25**
Vaughan, Sarah **2**
Verdecchio
  See Five Iron Frenzy
Walker, T-Bone **5**
Washington, Dinah **5**
Washington, Grover, Jr. **5**

Weather Report **19**
Webb, Chick **14**
Weston, Randy **15**
Whitaker, Rodney **20**
Whiteman, Paul **17**
Whitfield, Mark **18**
Whittaker, Rodney **19**
Williams, Joe **11**
Wilson, Cassandra **12**
Wilson, Cassandra **26**
Wilson, Nancy **14**
Winter, Paul **10**
Witherspoon, Jimmy **19**
Young, La Monte **16**
Young, Lester **14**
Zorn, John **15**

Juju
Adé, King Sunny **18**

Keyboards, Electric
Aphex Twin **14**
Bley, Paul **14**
Brown, Tony **14**
Chemical Brothers **20**
Corea, Chick **6**
Davis, Chip **4**
Dolby, Thomas **10**
Emerson, Keith
  See Emerson, Lake & Palmer/Powell
Eno, Brian **8**
Foster, David **13**
Froom, Mitchell **15**
Hammer, Jan **21**
Hancock, Herbie **25**
Hancock, Herbie **8**
Hardcastle, Paul **20**
Jackson, Joe **22**
  Earlier sketch in CM **4**
Jarre, Jean-Michel **2**
Jones, Booker T. **8**
Kitaro **1**
Man or Astroman? **21**
Manzarek, Ray
  See Doors, The
McDonald, Michael
  See Doobie Brothers, The
McVie, Christine
  See Fleetwood Mac
Orbital **20**
Palmer, Jeff **20**
Pierson, Kate
  See B-52's, The
Sakamoto, Ryuichi **19**
Shaffer, Paul **13**
Sun Ra **5**
Waller, Fats **7**
Wilson, Brian
  See Beach Boys, The
Winwood, Steve **2**
  Also see Spencer Davis Group
  Also see Traffic
Wonder, Stevie **17**
  Earlier sketch in CM **2**
Worrell, Bernie **11**
Yanni **11**

Liturgical Music
Cooney, Rory **6**
Talbot, John Michael **6**

Mandolin
Bromberg, David **18**
Bush, Sam
  See New Grass Revival, The

Duffey, John
  See Seldom Scene, The
Grisman, David **17**
Hartford, John **1**
Lindley, David **2**
McReynolds, Jesse
  See McReynolds, Jim and Jesse
Monroe, Bill **1**
Rosas, Cesar
  See Los Lobos
Skaggs, Ricky **5**
Stuart, Marty **9**

Musicals
Allen, Debbie **8**
Allen, Peter **11**
Andrews, Julie **4**
Andrews Sisters, The **9**
Bacharach, Burt **20**
  Earlier sketch in CM **1**
Bailey, Pearl **5**
Baker, Josephine **10**
Berlin, Irving **8**
Brightman, Sarah **20**
Brown, Ruth **13**
Buckley, Betty **16**
  Earlier sketch in CM **1**
Burnett, Carol **6**
Carter, Nell **7**
Channing, Carol **6**
Chevalier, Maurice **6**
Crawford, Michael **4**
Crosby, Bing **6**
Curry, Tim **3**
Davis, Sammy, Jr. **4**
Day, Doris **24**
Garland, Judy **6**
Gershwin, George and Ira **11**
Hamlisch, Marvin **1**
Horne, Lena **11**
Johnson, James P. **16**
Jolson, Al **10**
Kern, Jerome **13**
Laine, Cleo **10**
Lerner and Loewe **13**
Lloyd Webber, Andrew **6**
LuPone, Patti **8**
Masekela, Hugh **7**
Menken, Alan **10**
Mercer, Johnny **13**
Moore, Melba **7**
Patinkin, Mandy **20**
  Earlier sketch in CM **3**
Peters, Bernadette **7**
Porter, Cole **10**
Robeson, Paul **8**
Rodgers, Richard **9**
Sager, Carole Bayer **5**
Shaffer, Paul **13**
Sondheim, Stephen **8**
Styne, Jule **21**
Waters, Ethel **11**
Weill, Kurt **12**
Yeston, Maury **22**

Oboe
Lateef, Yusef **16**

Opera
Adams, John **8**
Ameling, Elly **24**
Anderson, Marian **8**
Austral, Florence **26**

Baker, Janet **14**
Bartoli, Cecilia **12**
Battle, Kathleen **6**
Blegen, Judith **23**
Bocelli, Andrea **22**
Bumbry, Grace **13**
Caballe, Monserrat **23**
Callas, Maria **11**
Carreras, José **8**
Caruso, Enrico **10**
Copeland, Stewart **14**
  Also see Police, The
Cotrubas, Ileana **1**
Davis, Anthony **17**
Domingo, Placido **20**
  Earlier sketch in CM **1**
Fleming, Renee **24**
Freni, Mirella **14**
Gershwin, George and Ira **11**
Graves, Denyce **16**
Hampson, Thomas **12**
Hendricks, Barbara **10**
Heppner, Ben **23**
Herrmann, Bernard **14**
Horne, Marilyn **9**
McNair, Sylvia **15**
Norman, Jessye **7**
Pavarotti, Luciano **20**
  Earlier sketch in CM **1**
Price, Leontyne **6**
Quasthoff, Thomas **26**
Sills, Beverly **5**
Solti, Georg **13**
Sutherland, Joan **13**
Te Kanawa, Kiri **2**
Toscanini, Arturo **14**
Upshaw, Dawn **9**
von Karajan, Herbert **1**
Weill, Kurt **12**
Zimmerman, Udo **5**

Percussion
Aronoff, Kenny **21**
Baker, Ginger **16**
  Also see Cream
Blackman, Cindy **15**
Blakey, Art **11**
Bonham, John
  See Led Zeppelin
Burton, Gary **10**
Collins, Phil **20**
  Earlier sketch in CM **2**
  Also see Genesis
Copeland, Stewart **14**
  Also see Police, The
DeJohnette, Jack **7**
Densmore, John
  See Doors, The
Dunbar, Aynsley
  See Jefferson Starship
  Also see Journey
  Also see Whitesnake
Dunbar, Sly
  See Sly and Robbie
Fleetwood, Mick
  See Fleetwood Mac
Hampton, Lionel **6**
Hart, Mickey
  See Grateful Dead, The
Henley, Don **3**
Jones, Elvin **9**
Jones, Kenny
  See Who, The
Jones, Philly Joe **16**

Jones, Spike **5**
Kreutzman, Bill
　See Grateful Dead, The
Krupa, Gene **13**
Mason, Nick
　See Pink Floyd
Moon, Keith
　See Who, The
Mo', Keb' **21**
N'Dour, Youssou **6**
Otis, Johnny **16**
Palmer, Carl
　See Emerson, Lake & Palmer/Powell
Palmieri, Eddie **15**
Peart, Neil
　See Rush
Powell, Cozy
　See Emerson, Lake & Palmer/Powell
Puente, Tito **14**
Rich, Buddy **13**
Roach, Max **12**
Sheila E. **3**
Starr, Ringo **10**
　Also see Beatles, The
Walden, Narada Michael **14**
Watts, Charlie
　See Rolling Stones, The
Webb, Chick **14**

Piano
Allen, Geri **10**
Allison, Mose **17**
Amos, Tori **12**
Arrau, Claudio **1**
Bacharach, Burt **20**
　Earlier sketch in CM **1**
Ball, Marcia **15**
Basie, Count **2**
Berlin, Irving **8**
Blake, Eubie **19**
Bley, Carla **8**
Bley, Paul **14**
Borge, Victor **19**
Brendel, Alfred **23**
Brickman, Jim **22**
Britten, Benjamin **15**
Bronfman, Yefim **6**
Brubeck, Dave **8**
Bush, Kate **4**
Carpenter, Richard **24**
Charles, Ray **24**
　Earlier sketch in CM **1**
Clayderman, Richard **1**
Cleveland, James **1**
Cliburn, Van **13**
Cole, Nat King **3**
Collins, Judy **4**
Collins, Phil **20**
　Earlier sketch in CM **2**
　Also see Genesis
Connick, Harry, Jr. **4**
Crouch, Andraé **9**
Davies, Dennis Russell **24**
DeJohnette, Jack **7**
Domino, Fats **2**
Dr. John **7**
Dupree, Champion Jack **12**
Ellington, Duke **2**
Esquivel, Juan **17**
Evans, Bill **17**
Evans, Gil **17**
Feinstein, Michael **6**
Ferrell, Rachelle **17**
Flack, Roberta **5**

Flanagan, Tommy **16**
Frey, Glenn **3**
Galás, Diamanda **16**
Garner, Erroll **25**
Glass, Philip **1**
Gould, Glenn **9**
Green, Benny **17**
Grusin, Dave **7**
Guaraldi, Vince **3**
Hamlisch, Marvin **1**
Hancock, Herbie **25**
Hancock, Herbie **8**
Harris, Teddy **22**
Helfgott, David **19**
Henderson, Fletcher **16**
Hinderas, Natalie **12**
Hines, Earl "Fatha" **12**
Horn, Shirley **7**
Hornsby, Bruce **25**
　Earlier sketch in CM **3**
Horowitz, Vladimir **1**
Ibrahim, Abdullah **24**
Jackson, Joe **22**
　Earlier sketch in CM **4**
James, Skip **24**
Jarrett, Keith **1**
Joel, Billy **12**
　Earlier sketch in CM **2**
John, Elton **20**
　Earlier sketch in CM **3**
Johnson, James P. **16**
Jones, Hank **15**
Jones, Howard **26**
Joplin, Scott **10**
Kenton, Stan **21**
Kissin, Evgeny **6**
Levine, James **8**
Lewis, Jerry Lee **2**
Lewis, Ramsey **14**
Liberace **9**
Little Richard **1**
Manilow, Barry **2**
Marsalis, Ellis **13**
Matthews, Eric **22**
McDonald, Michael
　See Doobie Brothers, The
McPartland, Marian **15**
McRae, Carmen **9**
McVie, Christine
　See Fleetwood Mac
Milsap, Ronnie **2**
Mingus, Charles **9**
Monk, Thelonious **6**
Montgomery, Little Brother **26**
Morton, Jelly Roll **7**
Nero, Peter **19**
Newman, Randy **4**
Palmieri, Eddie **15**
Perahia, Murray **10**
Perez, Danilo **25**
Peterson, Oscar **11**
Pires, Maria João **26**
Post, Mike **21**
Powell, Bud **15**
Pratt, Awadagin **19**
Previn, André **15**
Professor Longhair **6**
Puente, Tito **14**
Pullen, Don **16**
Rangell, Andrew **24**
Rich, Charlie **3**
Roberts, Marcus **6**
Rubinstein, Arthur **11**
Russell, Mark **6**

Schickele, Peter **5**
Sedaka, Neil **4**
Shaffer, Paul **13**
Solal, Martial **4**
Solti, Georg **13**
Spann, Otis **18**
Story, Liz **2**
Strayhorn, Billy **13**
Sunnyland Slim **16**
Sykes, Roosevelt **20**
Tatum, Art **17**
Taylor, Billy **13**
Taylor, Cecil **9**
Thibaudet, Jean-Yves **24**
Tilson Thomas, Michael **24**
Tyner, McCoy **7**
Valdes, Chuco **25**
Vangelis **21**
Waits, Tom **12**
　Earlier sketch in **1**
Waller, Fats **7**
Weston, Randy **15**
Wilson, Brian **24**
Wilson, Cassandra **12**
Winston, George **9**
Winwood, Steve **2**
　Also see Spencer Davis Group
　Also see Traffic
Wonder, Stevie **17**
　Earlier sketch in CM **2**
Wright, Rick
　See Pink Floyd
Young, La Monte **16**

Piccolo
Galway, James **3**

Pop
10,000 Maniacs **3**
A-ha **22**
Abba **12**
Abdul, Paula **3**
Adam Ant **13**
Adams, Bryan **20**
　Earlier sketch in CM **2**
Adams, Oleta **17**
Air Supply **22**
All Saints **25**
All-4-One **17**
Alpert, Herb **11**
America **16**
Amos, Tori **12**
Anderson, Laurie **25**
　Earlier sketch in CM **1**
Andrews, Christopher
　See Mojave **3**
Andrews Sisters, The **9**
Arden, Jann **21**
Arena, Tina **21**
Armatrading, Joan **4**
Arnold, Eddy **10**
Artifacts **23**
Astley, Rick **5**
Atkins, Chet **5**
Avalon, Frankie **5**
B-52's, The **4**
Bacharach, Burt **20**
　Earlier sketch in CM **1**
Backstreet Boys **21**
Badu, Erykah **26**
Bailey, Pearl **5**
Baker, Arthur **23**
Baker, Dale
　See Sixpence None the Richer

Bananarama **22**
Bangles **22**
Basia **5**
Beach Boys, The **1**
Beatles, The **2**
Beaver Brown Band, The **3**
Bee Gees, The **3**
Belly **16**
Bennett, Tony **16**
  Earlier sketch in CM **2**
Benson, George **9**
Benton, Brook **7**
Better Than Ezra **19**
Blige, Mary J. **15**
Blondie **14**
Blood, Sweat and Tears **7**
Blue Rodeo **18**
BoDeans, The **20**
  Earlier sketch in CM **3**
Bolton, Michael **4**
Boo Radleys, The **21**
Booker T. & the M.G.'s **24**
Boone, Pat **13**
Boston **11**
Bowie, David **23**
  Earlier sketch in CM **1**
Boyz II Men **15**
Bragg, Billy **7**
Branigan, Laura **2**
Braxton, Toni **17**
Brickell, Edie **3**
Brooks, Garth **25**
  Earlier sketch in CM **8**
Brown, Bobby **4**
Brown, Foxy **25**
Browne, Jackson **3**
Bryson, Peabo **11**
Buckingham, Lindsey **8**
  Also see Fleetwood Mac
Buckley, Tim **14**
Buffett, Jimmy **4**
Burdon, Eric **14**
  Also see War
  Also see Animals
Burroughs, William S. **26**
Cabaret Voltaire **18**
Campbell, Glen **2**
Campbell, Tevin **13**
Captain Beefheart and the Magic Band **26**
Cardigans **19**
Carey, Mariah **20**
  Earlier sketch in CM **6**
Carlisle, Belinda **8**
Carnes, Kim **4**
Carpenter, Richard **24**
Carpenters, The **13**
Cary, Justin
  See Sixpence None the Richer
Case, Peter **13**
Chandra, Sheila **16**
Chapin, Harry **6**
Chapin-Carpenter, Mary **25**
  Earlier sketch in CM **6**
Chapman, Tracy **20**
  Earlier sketch in CM **4**
Charlatans, The **13**
Charles, Ray **24**
  Earlier sketch in CM **1**
Checker, Chubby **7**
Cher **1**
Cherry, Neneh **4**
Cherry Poppin' Daddies **24**
Chicago **3**
Chilton, Alex **10**

Clapton, Eric **11**
  Earlier sketch in CM **1**
  Also see Cream
  Also see Yardbirds, The
Clayderman, Richard **1**
Clooney, Rosemary **9**
Cloud, Jeff
  See Joy Electric
Coasters, The **5**
Cocker, Joe **4**
Cocteau Twins, The **12**
Cole, Lloyd **9**
Cole, Nat King **3**
Cole, Natalie **21**
  Earlier sketch in CM **1**
Cole, Paula **20**
Collins, Judy **4**
Collins, Phil **20**
  Earlier sketch in CM **2**
  Also see Genesis
Color Me Badd **23**
Colvin, Shawn **11**
Commodores, The **23**
Como, Perry **14**
Connick, Harry, Jr. **4**
Cooke, Sam **1**
  Also see Soul Stirrers, The
Cope, Julian **16**
Cornershop **24**
Costello, Elvis **12**
  Earlier sketch in CM **2**
Cranberries, The **14**
Crash Test Dummies **14**
Crenshaw, Marshall **5**
Croce, Jim **3**
Crosby, David **3**
  Also see Byrds, The
Crow, Sheryl **18**
Crowded House **12**
Cure, The **20**
  Earlier sketch in CM **3**
D'Arby, Terence Trent **3**
Daltrey, Roger **3**
  Also see Who, The
Darin, Bobby **4**
Dave Clark Five, The **12**
Davies, Ray **5**
Davis, Sammy, Jr. **4**
Davis, Skeeter **15**
Day, Doris **24**
Dayne, Taylor **4**
DeBarge, El **14**
Del Amitri **18**
Del Rubio Triplets **21**
Denver, John **1**
Depeche Mode **5**
Des'ree **15**
Des'ree **24**
Devo **13**
Diamond, Neil **1**
Dietrich, Marlene **25**
Dion **4**
Dion, Celine **25**
Dion, Céline **12**
Doc Pomus **14**
Donovan **9**
Doobie Brothers, The **3**
Doors, The **4**
Droge, Pete **24**
Dubstar **22**
Duran Duran **4**
Dylan, Bob **21**
  Earlier sketch in CM **3**
Eagles, The **3**

Earth, Wind and Fire **12**
Easton, Sheena **2**
Edmonds, Kenneth "Babyface" **12**
Electric Light Orchestra **7**
Elfman, Danny **9**
Elliot, Cass **5**
En Vogue **10**
Enigma **14**
Estefan, Gloria **15**
  Earlier sketch in CM **2**
Eurythmics **6**
Everly Brothers, The **2**
Everything But The Girl **15**
Exposé **4**
Fabian **5**
Fatboy Slim **22**
Feliciano, José **10**
Ferguson, Maynard **7**
Ferry, Bryan **1**
Fiedler, Arthur **6**
Fine Young Cannibals **22**
Fisher, Eddie **12**
Fitzgerald, Ella **1**
Flack, Roberta **5**
Fleetwood Mac **5**
Fogelberg, Dan **4**
Fordham, Julia **15**
Forrester, Alan
  See Mojave 3
Foster, David **13**
Four Tops, The **11**
Fox, Samantha **3**
Frampton, Peter **3**
Francis, Connie **10**
Franklin, Aretha **17**
  Earlier sketch in CM **2**
Frey, Glenn **3**
  Also see Eagles, The
Garbage **25**
Garfunkel, Art **4**
Gaye, Marvin **4**
Gayle, Crystal **1**
Geldof, Bob **9**
Genesis **4**
Gershwin, George and Ira **11**
Gibson, Debbie **1**
  See Gibson, Deborah
Gibson, Deborah **24**
  See Gibson, Debbie
Gifford, Alex
  See Propellerheads
Gift, Roland **3**
Gil, Gilberto **26**
Gin Blossoms **18**
Ginsberg, Allen **26**
Go-Go's, The **24**
Gong **24**
Goodman, Benny **4**
Gordy, Berry, Jr. **6**
Goswell, Rachel
  See Mojave 3
Grant, Amy **7**
Grebenshikov, Boris **3**
Green, Al **9**
Guthrie, Arlo **6**
Hall & Oates **6**
Halstead, Neil
  See Mojave 3
Hammer, M.C. **5**
Hancock, Herbie **8**
Hanson **20**
Harding, John Wesley **6**
Harrison, George **2**
  Also see Beatles, The

Harry, Deborah **4**
  Also see Blondie
Hawkins, Sophie B. **21**
Healey, Jeff **4**
Henley, Don **3**
  Also see Eagles, The
Herman's Hermits **5**
Hill, Lauryn **25**
Hitchcock, Robyn **9**
Holland-Dozier-Holland **5**
Hootie and the Blowfish **18**
Horne, Lena **11**
Hornsby, Bruce **25**
  Earlier sketch in CM **3**
Houston, Cissy **26**
Houston, Whitney **25**
  Earlier sketch in CM **8**
Human League, The **17**
Humperdinck, Engelbert **19**
Ian, Janis **5**
Idol, Billy **3**
Iglesias, Julio **20**
  Earlier sketch in CM **2**
Incubus **23**
Indigo Girls **20**
  Earlier sketch in CM **3**
Ingram, James **11**
Ink Spots, The **23**
Isaak, Chris **6**
Isley Brothers, The **8**
Jackson, Janet **16**
  Earlier sketch in CM **3**
Jackson, Joe **22**
  Earlier sketch in CM **4**
Jackson, Michael **17**
  Earlier sketch in CM **1**
  Also see Jacksons, The
Jacksons, The **7**
Jam, Jimmy, and Terry Lewis **11**
James **12**
James, Harry **11**
James, Rick **2**
Jarreau, Al **1**
Jayhawks, The **15**
Jefferson Airplane **5**
Jesus Jones **23**
Jewel **25**
Jodeci **13**
Joel, Billy **12**
  Earlier sketch in CM **2**
Johansen, David **7**
John, Elton **20**
  Earlier sketch in CM **3**
Johnston, Freedy **20**
Jolson, Al **10**
Jones, Howard **26**
Jones, Quincy **20**
  Earlier sketch in CM **2**
Jones, Rickie Lee **4**
Jones, Tom **11**
Joplin, Janis **3**
Joy Electric **26**
Kaye, Carol **22**
Keaggy, Phil **26**
Kelly, Sean
  See Sixpence None the Richer
Khan, Chaka **19**
  Earlier sketch in CM **9**
King, Ben E. **7**
King, Carole **6**
Kiss **25**
  Earlier sketch in CM **5**
Kitt, Eartha **9**
Knight, Gladys **1**

Knopfler, Mark **25**
  Earlier sketch in CM **3**
  Also see Dire Straits
Kool & the Gang **13**
Kraftwerk **9**
Kristofferson, Kris **4**
LaBelle, Patti **8**
Lang, kd **25**
  Earlier sketch in CM **4**
Lauper, Cyndi **11**
Lee, Brenda **5**
Leiber and Stoller **14**
Lemper, Ute **14**
Lennon, John **9**
  Also see Beatles, The
Lennon, Julian **2**
Lennon, Julian **26**
Lennox, Annie **18**
Lewis, Huey **9**
Liberace **9**
Lightfoot, Gordon **3**
Lightning Seeds **21**
  Also see Eurythmics, The
Lisa Lisa **23**
Loeb, Lisa **19**
Loggins, Kenny **20**
  Earlier sketch in CM **3**
Lovett, Lyle **5**
Lowe, Nick **25**
  Earlier sketch in CM **6**
Lush **13**
Lynne, Jeff **5**
MacColl, Kirsty **12**
Madonna **16**
  Earlier sketch in CM **4**
Mamas and the Papas **21**
Mancini, Henry **20**
  Earlier sketch in CM **1**
Manhattan Transfer, The **8**
Manilow, Barry **2**
Marley, Bob **3**
Marley, Ziggy **3**
Marsalis, Branford **10**
Martin, Dean **1**
Martin, George **6**
Martin, Ricky **26**
Martin, Ronnie
  See Joy Electric
Marx, Richard **21**
  Earlier sketch in CM **3**
Mathis, Johnny **2**
Mazzy Star **17**
McCartney, Paul **4**
  Also see Beatles, The
McCutcheon, Ian
  See Mojave 3
McFerrin, Bobby **3**
McLachlan, Sarah **12**
McLean, Don **7**
McLennan, Grant **21**
Medley, Bill **3**
Melanie **12**
Merchant, Natalie **25**
Michael, George **9**
Midler, Bette **8**
Mighty Mighty Bosstones **20**
Mike & the Mechanics **17**
Miller, Mitch **11**
Miller, Roger **4**
Milli Vanilli **4**
Mills Brothers, The **14**
Minnelli, Liza **19**
Mitchell, Joni **17**
  Earlier sketch in CM **2**

Mojave 3 **26**
Money, Eddie **16**
Monica **26**
Monkees, The **7**
Montand, Yves **12**
Moore, Chante **21**
Morcheeba **25**
Morissette, Alanis **19**
Morrison, Jim **3**
Morrison, Van **24**
  Earlier sketch in CM **3**
Morrissey **10**
Mouskouri, Nana **12**
Moyet, Alison **12**
Murray, Anne **4**
Myles, Alannah **4**
N Sync **25**
Nash, Leigh
  See Sixpence None the Richer
Neville, Aaron **5**
  Also see Neville Brothers, The
Neville Brothers, The **4**
New Kids on the Block **3**
Newman, Randy **4**
Newton, Wayne **2**
Newton-John, Olivia **8**
Nicks, Stevie **25**
  Also see Fleetwood Mac
  Earlier sketch in CM **2**
Nilsson **10**
Nitty Gritty Dirt Band **6**
No Doubt **20**
Nyro, Laura **12**
O'Connor, Sinead **3**
Oak Ridge Boys, The **7**
Ocasek, Ric **5**
Ocean, Billy **4**
Odds **20**
Oldfield, Mike **18**
Orchestral Manoeuvres in the Dark **21**
Orlando, Tony **15**
Orton, Beth **26**
Osborne, Joan **19**
Osmond, Donny **3**
Page, Jimmy **4**
  Also see Led Zeppelin
  Also see Yardbirds, The
Page, Patti **11**
Parks, Van Dyke **17**
Parsons, Alan **12**
Parton, Dolly **2**
Pendergrass, Teddy **3**
Peniston, CeCe **15**
Penn, Michael **4**
Pet Shop Boys **5**
Peter, Paul & Mary **4**
Phillips, Sam **12**
Piaf, Edith **8**
Pizzicato Five **18**
Plant, Robert **2**
  Also see Led Zeppelin
Pointer Sisters, The **9**
Porter, Cole **10**
Prefab Sprout **15**
Presley, Elvis **1**
Priest, Maxi **20**
Prince **14**
  Earlier sketch in CM **1**
Proclaimers, The **13**
Prodigy **22**
Propellerheads **26**
Pulp **18**
Queen **6**
R.E.M. **25**
  Earlier sketch in CM **5**

Rabbitt, Eddie **5**
Raitt, Bonnie **3**
Rea, Chris **12**
Redding, Otis **5**
Reddy, Helen **9**
Reeves, Martha **4**
Republica **20**
Richard, Cliff **14**
Richie, Lionel **2**
Riley, Teddy **14**
Robbins, Marty **9**
Robinson, Smokey **1**
Rogers, Kenny **1**
Rolling Stones **3**
Ronstadt, Linda **2**
Ross, Diana **1**
Roth, David Lee **1**
  Also see Van Halen
Rowe, Simon
  See Mojave **3**
Roxette **23**
Ruffin, David **6**
RuPaul **20**
Sade **2**
Sager, Carole Bayer **5**
Sainte-Marie, Buffy **11**
Sanborn, David **1**
Seal **14**
Seals & Crofts **3**
Seals, Dan **9**
Secada, Jon **13**
Sedaka, Neil **4**
Selena **16**
Shaffer, Paul **13**
Shamen, The **23**
Sheila E. **3**
Shirelles, The **11**
Shonen Knife **13**
Siberry, Jane **6**
Simon, Carly **22**
  Earlier sketch in CM **4**
Simon, Paul **16**
  Earlier sketch in CM **1**
Sinatra, Frank 23
  Earlier sketch in CM **1**
Sixpence None the Richer **26**
Slocum, Matt
  See Sixpence None the Richer
Smiths, The **3**
Snow, Pheobe **4**
Sobule, Jill **20**
Sonny and Cher **24**
Soul Coughing **21**
Sparks **18**
Spector, Phil **4**
Spice Girls **22**
Springfield, Dusty **20**
Springfield, Rick **9**
Springsteen, Bruce **25**
  Earlier sketch in CM **6**
Squeeze **5**
Stafford, Jo **24**
Stansfield, Lisa **9**
Starr, Ringo **24**
  Earlier sketch in CM **10**
Steely Dan **5**
Stereolab **18**
Stevens, Cat **3**
Stewart, Rod **20**
  Earlier sketch in CM **2**
  Also see Faces, The
Stills, Stephen **5**
Sting **19**
  Earlier sketch in CM **2**
  Also see Police, The

Stockwood, Kim **26**
Story, The **13**
Straw, Syd **18**
Streisand, Barbra **2**
Suede **20**
Summer, Donna **12**
Sundays, The **20**
Supremes, The **6**
Surfaris, The **23**
Sweat, Keith **13**
Sweet, Matthew **9**
SWV **14**
Talk Talk **19**
Talking Heads **1**
Taylor, James **25**
  Earlier sketch in CM **2**
Taylor, Steve **26**
Tears for Fears **6**
Teenage Fanclub **13**
Temptations, The **3**
The The **15**
They Might Be Giants **7**
Thomas, Irma **16**
Three Dog Night **5**
Tiffany **4**
Tikaram, Tanita **9**
Timbuk 3 **3**
TLC **15**
Toad the Wet Sprocket **13**
Tony! Toni! Toné! **12**
Torme, Mel **4**
Townshend, Pete **1**
  Also see Who, The
Turner, Tina **1**
  Also see Ike & Tina Turner
Valli, Frankie **10**
Vandross, Luther **2**
Vanessa-Mae **26**
Vega, Suzanne **3**
Velocity Girl **23**
Vinton, Bobby **12**
Walsh, Joe **5**
Warnes, Jennifer **3**
Warwick, Dionne **2**
Was (Not Was) **6**
Washington, Dinah **5**
Waters, Crystal **15**
Watley, Jody **26**
  Earlier sketch in CM **9**
Webb, Jimmy **12**
Weird Al" Yankovic **7**
Weller, Paul **14**
White, Will
  See Propellerheads
Who, The **3**
Williams, Andy **2**
Williams, Dar **21**
Williams, Deniece **1**
Williams, Joe **11**
Williams, Lucinda **24**
  Earlier sketch in CM **10**
Williams, Paul **26**
Williams, Paul **5**
Williams, Robbie **25**
Williams, Vanessa **10**
Williams, Victoria **17**
Wilson, Brian **24**
  Also see Beach Boys, The
Wilson, Jackie **3**
Wilson Phillips **5**
Winwood, Steve **2**
  Also see Spencer Davis Group
  Also see Traffic
Womack, Bobby **5**

Wonder, Stevie **17**
  Earlier sketch in CM **2**
Young M.C. **4**
Young, Neil **15**
  Earlier sketch in CM **2**

Producers
Ackerman, Will **3**
Afanasieff, Walter **26**
Albini, Steve **15**
Alpert, Herb **11**
Austin, Dallas **16**
Baker, Anita **9**
Bass, Ralph **24**
Benitez, Jellybean **15**
Bogaert, Jo
  See Technotronic
Brown, Junior **15**
Brown, Tony **14**
Browne, Jackson **3**
Burnett, T Bone **13**
Cale, John **9**
Clark, Dick **25**
Clarke, Stanley **3**
Clinton, George **7**
Collins, Phil **2**
  Also see Genesis
Combs, Sean "Puffy" **25**
  Earlier sketch in CM **16**
Costello, Elvis **2**
Cropper, Steve **12**
Crowell, Rodney **8**
Dixon, Willie **10**
DJ Premier
  See Gang Starr
Dolby, Thomas **10**
Dozier, Lamont
  See Holland-Dozier-Holland
Dr. Dre **15**
  Also see N.W.A.
Dupri, Jermaine **25**
  Earlier sketch in CM **2**
Edmonds, Kenneth "Babyface" **12**
Enigma **14**
Eno, Brian **8**
Ertegun, Ahmet **10**
Ertegun, Nesuhi **24**
Foster, David **13**
Fripp, Robert **9**
Froom, Mitchell **15**
Gabler, Milton **25**
Gordy, Jr., Emory **17**
Gray, F. Gary **19**
Grusin, Dave **7**
Hardcastle, Paul **20**
Holland, Brian
  See Holland-Dozier-Holland
Holland, Eddie
  See Holland-Dozier-Holland
Jackson, Millie **14**
Jam, Jimmy, and Terry Lewis **11**
Jones, Booker T. **8**
Jones, Quincy **20**
  Earlier sketch in CM **2**
Jordan, Montell **26**
Jourgensen, Al
  See Ministry
Krasnow, Bob **15**
Lanois, Daniel **8**
Laswell, Bill **14**
Leiber and Stoller **14**
Lillywhite, Steve **13**
Lynne, Jeff **5**
Marley, Rita **10**

Martin, George **6**
Master P **22**
Mayfield, Curtis **8**
McKnight, Brian **22**
McLaren, Malcolm **23**
Miller, Mitch **11**
Osby, Greg **21**
Parks, Van Dyke **17**
Parsons, Alan **12**
Post, Mike **21**
Prince **14**
    Earlier sketch in CM **1**
Queen Latifah **24**
    Earlier sketch in CM **6**
Riley, Teddy **14**
Robertson, Robbie **2**
Rodgers, Nile **8**
Rubin, Rick **9**
Rundgren, Todd **11**
Shocklee, Hank **15**
Simmons, Russell **7**
Skaggs, Ricky **5**
Spector, Phil **4**
Sure!, Al B. **13**
Sweat, Keith **13**
Swing, DeVante
    See Jodeci
Too $hort **16**
Toussaint, Allen **11**
Tricky **18**
Vandross, Luther **2**
Vasquez, Junior **16**
Vig, Butch **17**
Wachtel, Waddy **26**
Walden, Narada Michael **14**
Was, Don **21**
Watt, Mike **22**
Wexler, Jerry **15**
Whelan, Bill **20**
Willner, Hal **10**
Wilson, Brian **24**
    Also see Beach Boys, The
Winbush, Angela **15**
Woods-Wright, Tomica **22**

Promoters
Clark, Dick **25**
    Earlier sketch in CM **2**
Geldof, Bob **9**
Graham, Bill **10**
Hay, George D. **3**
Simmons, Russell **7**

Ragtime
Johnson, James P. **16**
Joplin, Scott **10**

Rap
2Pac **17**
Anthony, Marc **19**
Arrested Development **14**
Austin, Dallas **16**
Bambaataa, Afrika **13**
Basehead **11**
Beastie Boys **25**
    Earlier sketch in CM **8**
Biz Markie **10**
Black Sheep **15**
Bone Thugs-N-Harmony **18**
Busta Rhymes **18**
Campbell, Luther **10**
Cherry, Neneh **4**
Combs, Sean "Puffy **25**
    Earlier sketch in CM **16**

Common **23**
Coolio **19**
Cypress Hill **11**
Das EFX **14**
De La Soul **7**
Digable Planets **15**
Digital Underground **9**
DJ Jazzy Jeff and the Fresh Prince **5**
DMX **25**
Dr. Dre **15**
    Also see N.W.A.
Dupri, Jermaine **25**
Eazy-E **13**
    Also see N.W.A.
EPMD **10**
Eric B. and Rakim **9**
Evans, Faith **25**
Franti, Michael **16**
Fugees, The **17**
Gang Starr **13**
Geto Boys, The **11**
Goodie Mob **24**
Grandmaster Flash **14**
Gravediggaz **23**
Hammer, M.C. **5**
Heavy D **10**
House of Pain **14**
Ice Cube **25**
    Earlier sketch in CM **10**
Ice-T **7**
Insane Clown Posse **22**
Jackson, Millie **14**
Kane, Big Daddy **7**
Kid 'n Play **5**
Knight, Suge **15**
Kool Moe Dee **9**
Kris Kross **11**
KRS-One **8**
L.L. Cool J. **5**
Last Poets **21**
Love, G. **24**
Master P **22**
MC 900 Ft. Jesus **16**
MC Breed **17**
MC Lyte **8**
MC Serch **10**
N.W.A. **6**
Nas **19**
Naughty by Nature **11**
Notorious B.I.G. **20**
P.M. Dawn **11**
Pharcyde, The **17**
Public Enemy **4**
Queen Latifah **24**
    Earlier sketch in CM **6**
Rage Against the Machine **18**
Riley, Teddy **14**
Rubin, Rick **9**
Run-D.M.C. **25**
    Earlier sketch in CM **4**
Salt-N-Pepa **6**
Scott-Heron, Gil **13**
Shaggy **19**
Shanté **10**
Shocklee, Hank **15**
Simmons, Russell **7**
Sir Mix-A-Lot **14**
Smith, Will **26**
Snoop Doggy Dogg **17**
Snow **23**
Spearhead **19**
Special Ed **16**
Sure!, Al B. **13**
TLC **15**

Tone-L c **3**
Too $hort **16**
Tribe Called Quest, A **8**
Tricky **18**
US3 **18**
Usher **23**
Vanilla Ice **6**
Wu-Tang Clan **19**
Yo Yo **9**
Young M.C. **4**

Record Company Executives
Ackerman, Will **3**
Alpert, Herb **11**
Blackwell, Chris **26**
Brown, Tony **14**
Busby, Jheryl **9**
Chess, Leonard **24**
Combs, Sean "Puffy" **25**
    Earlier sketch in CM **16**
Davis, Chip **4**
Davis, Clive **3**
Ertegun, Ahmet **10**
Foster, David **13**
Gabriel, Peter **16**
    Earlier sketch in CM **2**
    Also see Genesis
Geffen, David **8**
Gordy, Berry, Jr. **6**
Hammond, John **6**
Harley, Bill **7**
Harrell, Andre **16**
Jam, Jimmy, and Terry Lewis **11**
Knight, Suge **15**
Koppelman, Charles **14**
Krasnow, Bob **15**
LiPuma, Tommy **18**
Madonna **16**
    Earlier sketch in CM **4**
Marley, Rita **10**
Martin, George **6**
Mayfield, Curtis **8**
Mercer, Johnny **13**
Miller, Mitch **11**
Mingus, Charles **9**
Near, Holly **1**
Ostin, Mo **17**
Penner, Fred **10**
Phillips, Sam **5**
Reznor, Trent **13**
Rhone, Sylvia **13**
Robinson, Smokey **1**
Rubin, Rick **9**
Simmons, Russell **7**
Spector, Phil **4**
Teller, Al **15**
Too $hort **16**
Wexler, Jerry **15**
Woods-Wright, Tomica **22**

Reggae
Bad Brains **16**
Big Mountain **23**
Black Uhuru **12**
Burning Spear **15**
Cliff, Jimmy **8**
Dube, Lucky **17**
Inner Circle **15**
Israel Vibration **21**
Marley, Bob **3**
Marley, Rita **10**
Marley, Ziggy **3**
Mystic Revealers **16**
Skatalites, The **18**

Sly and Robbie **13**
Steel Pulse **14**
Third World **13**
Tosh, Peter **3**
UB40 **4**
Wailer, Bunny **11**

Rhythm and Blues/Soul
Aaliyah **21**
Abdul, Paula **3**
Adams, Oleta **17**
Alexander, Arthur **14**
All-4-One **17**
Austin, Dallas **16**
Badu, Erykah **26**
Baker, Anita **9**
Baker, LaVern **25**
Ball, Marcia **15**
Ballard, Hank **17**
Basehead **11**
Belle, Regina **6**
Berry, Chuck **1**
Blackstreet **23**
Bland, Bobby "Blue" **12**
Blessid Union of Souls **20**
Blige, Mary J. **15**
Blues Brothers, The **3**
Bolton, Michael **4**
Booker T. & the M.G.'s **24**
Boyz II Men **15**
Brandy **19**
Braxton, Toni **17**
Brown, James **16**
    Earlier sketch in CM **2**
Brown, Ruth **13**
Brownstone **21**
Bryson, Peabo **11**
Burdon, Eric **14**
    Also see War
    Also see Animals
Busby, Jheryl **9**
C + C Music Factory **16**
Cameron, Timothy
    See Silk
Campbell, Tevin **13**
Carey, Mariah **20**
    Earlier sketch in CM **6**
Carr, James **23**
Charles, Ray **24**
    Earlier sketch in CM **1**
Cole, Natalie **21**
    Earlier sketch in CM **1**
Color Me Badd **23**
Commodores, The **23**
Cooke, Sam **1**
    Also see Soul Stirrers, The
Crawford, Randy **25**
Cropper, Steve **12**
Curtis, King **17**
D'Angelo **20**
D'Arby, Terence Trent **3**
Dawn, Sandra
    See Platters, The
DeBarge, El **14**
Des'ree **15**
Dibango, Manu **14**
Diddley, Bo **3**
Domino, Fats **2**
Dr. John **7**
Dru Hill **25**
Earth, Wind and Fire **12**
Edmonds, Kenneth "Babyface" **12**
En Vogue **10**
Evora, Cesaria **19**

Fabulous Thunderbirds, The **1**
Four Tops, The **11**
Fox, Samantha **3**
Franklin, Aretha **17**
    Earlier sketch in CM **2**
Gates, Jimmy Jr.
    See Silk
Gaye, Marvin **4**
Gill, Johnny **20**
Gordy, Berry, Jr. **6**
Green, Al **9**
Guthrie, Gwen **26**
Hall & Oates **6**
Hayes, Isaac **10**
Hill, Lauryn **25**
Hodge, Alex
    See Platters, The
Holland-Dozier-Holland **5**
Houston, Whitney **25**
    Earlier sketch in CM **8**
Howland, Don **24**
Hurt, Mississippi John **24**
Ike and Tina Turner **24**
Incognito **16**
Ingram, James **11**
Isley Brothers, The **8**
Jackson, Freddie **3**
Jackson, Janet **3**
Jackson, Michael **17**
    Earlier sketch in CM **1**
    Also see Jacksons, The
Jackson, Millie **14**
Jacksons, The **7**
Jam, Jimmy, and Terry Lewis **11**
James, Etta **6**
Jenkins, Gary
    See Silk
Jodeci **13**
John, Willie **25**
Jones, Booker T. **8**
Jones, Grace **9**
Jones, Quincy **20**
    Earlier sketch CM **2**
Jordan, Louis **11**
Jordan, Montell **26**
Kelly, R. **19**
Khan, Chaka **19**
    Earlier sketch CM **9**
King, B. B. **24**
King, Ben E. **7**
Knight, Gladys **1**
Kool & the Gang **13**
LaBelle, Patti **8**
Los Lobos **2**
Love, G. **24**
Lynch, David
    See Platters, The
Martha and the Vandellas **25**
Maxwell **22**
Mayfield, Curtis **8**
McKnight, Brian **22**
McPhatter, Clyde **25**
Medley, Bill **3**
Meters, The **14**
Milli Vanilli **4**
Mills, Stephanie **21**
Mo', Keb' **21**
Monica **26**
Monifah **24**
Moore, Chante **21**
Moore, Melba **7**
Morrison, Van **24**
    Earlier sketch in CM **3**
Ndegéocello, Me'Shell **18**

Nelson, Nate
    See Platters, The
Neville, Aaron **5**
    Also see Neville Brothers, The
Neville Brothers, The **4**
O'Jays, The **13**
Ocean, Billy **4**
Ohio Players **16**
Otis, Johnny **16**
Pendergrass, Teddy **3**
Peniston, CeCe **15**
Perry, Phil **24**
Pickett, Wilson **10**
Platters, The **25**
Pointer Sisters, The **9**
Price, Lloyd **25**
Priest, Maxi **20**
Prince **14**
    Earlier sketch in CM **1**
Rainey, Ma **22**
Rasboro, Johnathen
    See Silk
Rawls, Lou **19**
Redding, Otis **5**
Reed, Herbert
    See Platters, The
Reese, Della **13**
Reeves, Martha **4**
Richie, Lionel **2**
Riley, Teddy **14**
Robi, Paul
    See Platters, The
Robinson, Smokey **1**
Ross, Diana **6**
    Also see Supremes, The
Ruffin, David **6**
    Also see Temptations, The
Sam and Dave **8**
Scaggs, Boz **12**
Secada, Jon **13**
Shai **23**
Shanice **14**
Shirelles, The **11**
Shocklee, Hank **15**
Silk **26**
Sledge, Percy **15**
Sly & the Family Stone **24**
Soul II Soul **17**
Spinners , The **21**
Stansfield, Lisa **9**
Staples, Mavis **13**
Staples, Pops **11**
Stewart, Rod **20**
    Earlier sketch in CM **2**
    Also see Faces, The
Stone, Sly **8**
Subdudes, The **18**
Supremes, The **6**
    Also see Ross, Diana
Sure!, Al B. **13**
Sweat, Keith **13**
SWV **14**
Taylor, Zola
    See Platters, The
Temptations, The **3**
Third World **13**
Thomas, Irma **16**
Thornton, Big Mama **18**
TLC **15**
Tony! Toni! Toné! **12**
Toussaint, Allen **11**
Turner, Sonny
    See Platters, The

Turner, Tina **1**
  Also see Ike & Tina Turner
Vandross, Luther **24**
  Earlier sketch in CM **2**
Was (Not Was) **6**
Waters, Crystal **15**
Watley, Jody **9**
Wexler, Jerry **15**
White, Karyn **21**
Williams, Deniece **1**
Williams, Tony
  See Platters, The
Williams, Vanessa **10**
Wilson, Jackie **3**
Winans, The **12**
Winbush, Angela **15**
Womack, Bobby **5**
Wonder, Stevie **17**
  Earlier sketch in CM **2**
Zhane **22**

Rock
  10,000 Maniacs **3**
  311 **20**
  AC/DC **4**
  Adam Ant **13**
  Adams, Bryan **20**
    Earlier sketch in CM **2**
  Aerosmith **22**
    Earlier sketch in CM **3**
  Afghan Whigs **17**
  Agust, Daniel
    See Gus Gus
  Alan, Skip
    See Pretty Things, The
  Alarm **2**
  Albini, Steve **15**
  Alder, John "Twink"
    See Pretty Things, The
  Alexander, Arthur **14**
  Alice in Chains **10**
  Alien Sex Fiend **23**
  Allen, Wally
    See Pretty Things, The
  Allman Brothers, The **6**
  Alvin, Dave **17**
  America **16**
  American Music Club **15**
  Andrews, Barry
    See XTC
  Andrews, Christopher
    See Mojave 3
  Animals **22**
  Anthrax **11**
  Aquabats **22**
  Archers of Loaf **21**
  Arnie, Stefan
    See Gus Gus
  Art of Noise **22**
  Audio Adrenaline **22**
  Aztec Camera **22**
  Babes in Toyland **16**
  Baccus, Richard
    See D Generation
  Bad Brains **16**
  Bad Company **22**
  Badfinger **23**
  Baker, Ginger **16**
    Also see Cream
  Ballard, Hank **17**
  Band, The **9**
  Barenaked Ladies **18**

Barlow, Lou **20**
  Also see Sebadoh
Barr, All
  See Dropkick Murphys
Barton, Rick
  See Dropkick Murphys
Basehead **11**
Bass, Lance
  See N'Sync
Beach Boys, The **1**
Beastie Boys, The **25**
  Earlier sketch in CM **8**
Beat Farmers, The **23**
Beatles, The **2**
Beaver Brown Band, The **3**
Beck **18**
Beck, Jeff **4**
  Also see Yardbirds, The
Belew, Adrian **5**
Belly **16**
Ben Folds Five **20**
Benatar, Pat **8**
Berlin, Liz
  See Rusted Root
Berry, Chuck **1**
Bert, Bob
  See Sonic Youth
Bettie Serveert **17**
Bevis Frond **23**
Biafra, Jello **18**
Big Audio Dynamite **18**
Big Head Todd and the Monsters **20**
Bill Wyman & the Rhythm Kings **26**
Bjork **16**
Black Crowes, The **7**
Black Flag **22**
Black, Frank **14**
Black, Jimmy Carl
  See Captain Beefheart and His Magic
Band
Black Sabbath **9**
Blackman, Cindy **15**
Blair, Ron
  See Tom Petty and the Heartbreakers
Blakely, Paul
  See Captain Beefheart and His Magic
Band
Blind Melon **21**
Block, Norman
  See Rasputina
Blondie **14**
Blood, Sweat and Tears **7**
Blue Oyster Cult **16**
Blue Rodeo **18**
Blues Traveler **15**
Blur **17**
BoDeans, The **20**
  Earlier sketch in CM **3**
Bon Jovi **10**
Boston **11**
Boston, Mark
  See Captain Beefheart and His Magic
Band
Bottom, Roddy
  See Imperial Teen
Bowie, David **23**
  Earlier sketch in CM **1**
Brad **21**
Bragg, Billy **7**
Breeders **19**
Brickell, Edie **3**
Brooker, Gary
  See Bill Wyman & the Rhythm Kings

Brooks, Stuart
  See Pretty Things, The
Browne, Jackson **3**
Buckingham, Lindsey **8**
  Also see Fleetwood Mac
Buckley, Tim **14**
Buffalo Springfield **24**
Buffalo Tom **18**
Burdon, Eric **14**
  Also see War
  Also see Animals
Burnett, T Bone **13**
Bush **18**
Butthole Surfers **16**
Buynak, John
  See Rusted Root
Buzzcocks, The **9**
Byrds, The **8**
Byrne, David **8**
  Also see Talking Heads
Cadogan, Kevin
  See Third Eye Blind
Cale, J. J. **16**
Cale, John **9**
Camel **21**
Campbell, Mike
  See Tom Petty and the Heartbreakers
Captain Beefheart **10**
Captain Beefheart and the Magic Band **26**
Caravan **24**
Cardigans **19**
Cars, The **20**
Casey, Ken
  See Dropkick Murphys
Catherine Wheel **18**
Cave, Nick **10**
Chambers, Terry
  See XTC
Charlatans, The **13**
Charm Farm **20**
Chasez, Joshua Scott "JC"
  See N'Sync
Cheap Trick **12**
Cher **1**
Chicago **3**
Chumbawamba **21**
Church, The **14**
Cinderella **16**
Circle Jerks, The **17**
Clapton, Eric **11**
  Earlier sketch in CM **1**
  Also see Cream
  Also see Yardbirds, The
Clash, The **4**
Clemons, Clarence **7**
Clinton, George **7**
Close, Bill
  See Dropkick Murphys
Coasters, The **5**
Cochrane , Tom **22**
Cocker, Joe **4**
Collective Soul **16**
Collingwood, Chris
  See Fountains of Wayne
Collins, Phil **2**
  Also see Genesis
Compulsion **23**
Congo Norvell **22**
Cooder, Ry **2**
  Also see Captain Beefheart and His Magic
Band
Cooke, Sam **1**
  Also see Soul Stirrers, The
Cooper, Alice **8**

Cope, Julian **16**
Costello, Elvis **12**
  Earlier sketch in CM **2**
Cotton, Jeff
  See Captain Beefheart and His Magic
Band
Cougar, John(ny)
  See Mellencamp, John
Counting Crows **18**
Cracker **12**
Cramps, The **16**
Cranberries, The **14**
Crash Test Dummies **14**
Creager, Melora
  See Rasputina
Cream **9**
Creedence Clearwater Revival **16**
Crenshaw, Marshall **5**
Crosby, David **3**
  Also see Byrds, The
Crosby, Stills, and Nash **24**
Crow, Sheryl **18**
Crowded House **12**
Cult, The **16**
Cure, The **20**
  Earlier sketch in CM **3**
Currie, Kevin
  See Supertramp
Curry, Tim **3**
Curve **13**
D Generation **26**
D'Arby, Terence Trent **3**
Dale, Dick **13**
Daltrey, Roger **3**
  Also see Who, The
Damon and Naomi **25**
Dandy Warhols, The
Daniels, Charlie **6**
Danzig **7**
Dave Clark Five, The **12**
Dave Matthews Band **18**
Davies, Ray **5**
Davies, Richard (Rick)
  See Supertramp
dc Talk **18**
de Burgh, Chris **22**
Dead Can Dance **16**
Dead Milkmen **22**
Deep Purple **11**
Def Leppard **3**
Deftones **22**
Del Amitri **18**
Depeche Mode **5**
Devo **13**
Diddley, Bo **3**
DiFranco, Ani **17**
Dinosaur Jr. **10**
Dire Straits **22**
DiSpirito, Jim
  See Rusted Root
Doc Pomus **14**
Dog's Eye View **21**
Dokken **16**
Donovan, Jim
  See Rusted Root
Doobie Brothers, The **3**
Doors, The **4**
Dreamtheater **23**
Dropkick Murphys **26**
Duran Duran **4**
Dylan, Bob **3**
Eagles, The **3**
Echobelly **21**
Eddy, Duane **9**

Edson, Richard
  See Sonic Youth
Edwards, Gordon
  See Pretty Things, The
Einstürzende Neubauten **13**
Electric Light Orchestra **7**
Elliot, Cass **5**
Emerson, Darren
  See Underworld
Emerson, Lake & Palmer/Powell **5**
Emmet Swimming **24**
English Beat, The **9**
Eno, Brian **8**
Epstein, Howie
  See Tom Petty and the Heartbreakers
Erickson, Roky **16**
Erner, Jeff "The Shark"
  See Dropkick Murphys
Escovedo, Alejandro **18**
Estrada, Roy
  See Captain Beefheart and His Magic
Band
Etheridge, Melissa **16**
  Earlier sketch in CM **4**
Eurythmics **6**
Everclear **18**
Extreme **10**
Faces, The **22**
Fairport Convention **22**
Faith No More **7**
Faithfull, Marianne **14**
Fall, The **12**
Fame, Georgie
  See Bill Wyman & the Rhythm Kings
Farrell, Frank
  See Supertramp
Fatone, Joey
  See 'NSync
Fay, Bob
  See Sebadoh
Feldman, Eric Drew
  See Captain Beefheart and His Magic
Band
Ferry, Bryan **1**
fIREHOSE **11**
Fishbone **7**
Five Iron Frenzy **26**
Flaming Lips **22**
Fleetwood Mac **5**
Flores, Rosie **16**
Fogelberg, Dan **4**
Fogerty, John **2**
  Also see Creedence Clearwater Revival
Foo Fighters **20**
Ford, Frankie
  See Pretty Things, The
Ford, Lita **9**
Foreigner **21**
Forrester, Alan
  See Mojave 3
Fountains of Wayne **26**
Four Seasons, The **24**
Fowler, Bruce
  See Captain Beefheart and His Magic
Band
Fox, Samantha **3**
Frampton, Peter **3**
Frankie Lymon and The Teenagers **24**
Franti, Michael **16**
French, John
  See Captain Beefheart and His Magic
Band
Frey, Glenn **3**
  Also see Eagles, The

Front 242 **19**
Froom, Mitchell **15**
Fu Manchu **22**
Fugazi **13**
Gabriel, Peter **16**
  Earlier sketch in CM **2**
  Also see Genesis
Gaffney, Eric
  See Sebadoh
Gang of Four **8**
Garcia, Jerry **4**
  Also see Grateful Dead, The
Gatton, Danny **16**
Genesis **4**
Geraldine Fibbers **21**
Ghost **24**
Gift, Roland **3**
Gin Blossoms **18**
Glabicki, Michael
  See Rusted Root
Glitter, Gary **19**
Goo Goo Dolls, The **16**
Gordon, Kim
  See Sonic Youth
Goswell, Rachel
  See Mojave 3
Graham, Bill **10**
Grant Lee Buffalo **16**
Grateful Dead **5**
Grebenshikov, Boris **3**
Green Day **16**
Gregory, Dave
  See XTC
Griffin, Patty **24**
Guess Who **23**
Guided By Voices **18**
Guns n' Roses **2**
Gus Gus **26**
Gwar **13**
Hagar, Sammy **21**
Hagen, Nina **25**
Hall & Oates **6**
Halstead, Neil
  See Mojave 3
Handley, Jerry
  See Captain Beefheart and His Magic
Band
Hargreaves, Brad
  See Third Eye Blind
Harkelroad, Bill
  See Captain Beefheart and His Magic
Band
Harper, Ben **17**
Harrison, George **2**
  Also see Beatles, The
Harry, Deborah **4**
  Also see Blondie
Hart, Mark
  See Supertramp
Harvey, Polly Jean **11**
Hassman, Nikki **26**
Hatfield, Juliana **12**
  Also see Lemonheads, The
Hayden, Victor
  See Captain Beefheart and His Magic
Band
Healey, Jeff **4**
Helliwell, John
  See Supertramp
Helmet **15**
Hendrix, Jimi **2**
Henley, Don **3**
  Also see Eagles, The
Henry, Joe **18**

Hepner, Rich
  See Captain Beefheart and His Magic Band
Hiatt, John 8
Hodgson, Roger 26
  Also see Supertramp
Hoffman, Sam
  See Captain Beefheart and His Magic Band
Hole 14
Holland-Dozier-Holland 5
Hooters 20
Hootie and the Blowfish 18
Huld, Hafdis
  See Gus Gus
Hyde, Karl
  See Underworld
Idol, Billy 3
Imperial Teen 26
Ingber, Elliot
  See Captain Beefheart and His Magic Band
INXS 21
  Earlier sketch in CM 2
Iron Maiden 10
Isaak, Chris 6
Jackson, Joe 22
  Earlier sketch in CM 4
Jackyl 24
Jagger, Mick 7
  Also see Rolling Stones, The
Jane's Addiction 6
Jars of Clay 20
Jayhawks, The 15
Jefferson Airplane 5
Jenkins, Stephan
  See Third Eye Blind
Jesus and Mary Chain, The 10
Jesus Lizard 19
Jethro Tull 8
Jett, Joan 3
Jimmie's Chicken Shack 22
Joel, Billy 12
  Earlier sketch in CM 2
Johansen, David 7
John, Elton 20
  Earlier sketch in CM 3
Jon Spencer Blues Explosion 18
Jonsson, Magnus
  See Gus Gus
Joplin, Janis 3
Journey 21
Joy Division 19
Judas Priest 10
Kelly, Matt
  See Dropkick Murphys
Kennedy, Nigel 8
Kent, Julia
  See Rasputina
Kidjo, Anjelique 17
King Crimson 17
King Missile 22
Kinks, The 15
Kirkpatrick, Chris
  See N'Sync
Kiss 25
  Earlier sketch in CM 5
Kiss 25
Kjartansson, Siggi
  See Gus Gus
KMFDM 18
Knopfler, Mark 25
  Earlier sketch in CM 3
  Also see Dire Straits

Korn 20
Kravitz, Lenny 26
  Earlier sketch in CM 5
Krupse, Richard
  See Rammstein
L7 12
Landers, Paul
  See Rammstein
Landreth, Sonny 16
Led Zeppelin 1
Lee, Ben 26
Legowitz, Herr
  See Gus Gus
Leiber and Stoller 14
Lemonheads, The 12
Lennon, John 9
  Also see Beatles, The
Lennon, Julian 2
Less Than Jake 22
Letters to Cleo 22
Lindemann, Till
  See Rammstein
Lindley, David 2
Linkous, Mark 26
Little Feat 4
Little Texas 14
Live 14
Living Colour 7
Loewenstein, Jason
  See Sebadoh
Lofgren, Nils 25
Loggins, Kenny 20
  Earlier sketch in CM 3
Lorenz, Flake
  See Rammstein
Los Lobos 2
Love and Rockets 15
Love Spit Love 21
Lowe, Nick 25
  Earlier sketch in CM 6
Lucas, Gary
  See Captain Beefheart and His Magic Band
Luna 18
Luscious Jackson 19
Lush 13
Lydon, John 9
  Also see Sex Pistols, The
Lynch, Stan
  See Tom Petty and the Heartbreakers
Lynne, Jeff 5
Lynyrd Skynyrd 9
MacIsaac, Ashley 21
Madder Rose 17
Malin, Jesse
  See D Generation
Marilyn Manson 18
Martensen, Vic
  See Captain Beefheart and His Magic Band
Martin, George 6
Martinez, Cliff
  See Captain Beefheart and His Magic Band
Marx, Richard 3
May, Phil
  See Pretty Things, The
MC5, The 9
McCartney, Paul 4
  Also see Beatles, The
McClinton, Delbert 14
McColgan, Mike
  See Dropkick Murphys
McCutcheon, Ian
  See Mojave 3

McKee, Maria 11
McMurtry, James 10
Meat Loaf 12
Meat Puppets, The 13
Megadeth 9
Mekons, The 15
Mellencamp, John 20
  Earlier sketch in CM 2
Metallica 7
Midnight Oil 11
Mighty Mighty Bosstones 20
Mike & the Mechanics 17
Miller, Robert
  See Supertramp
Miller, Steve 2
Ministry 10
Moby Grape 12
Mojave 3 26
Money, Eddie 16
Moody Blues, The 18
Moon, Doug
  See Captain Beefheart and His Magic Band
Moore, Thurston
  See Sonic Youth
Morphine 16
Morrison, Jim 3
  Also see Doors, The
Morrison, Van 24
  Earlier sketch in CM 3
Mötley Crüe 1
Motörhead 10
Mould, Bob 10
Moulding, Colin
  See XTC
Mudhoney 16
Muldaur, Maria 18
Murphy, Peter 22
Myles, Alannah 4
Nana
  See Rasputina
Nelson, Rick 2
New York Dolls 20
Newman, Randy 4
Newsboys, The 24
Nicks, Stevie 25
  Earlier sketch in CM 2
  Also see Fleetwood Mac
Nirvana 8
Norman, Patrick
  See Rusted Root
NRBQ 12
'NSync 25
Nugent, Ted 2
O'Connor, Sinead 3
Oasis 16
Ocasek, Ric 5
Offspring 19
Ono, Yoko 11
Orbison, Roy 2
Osbourne, Ozzy 3
Our Lady Peace 22
Page, Jimmy 4
  Also see Led Zeppelin
  Also see Yardbirds, The
Palmer, Richard
  See Supertramp
Palmer, Robert 2
Pantera 13
Parker, Graham 10
Parker, Maceo 7
Parsons, Alan 12
Parsons, Gram 7
  Also see Byrds, The

Partridge, Andy
    See XTC
Parvo, Carpella
    See Rasputina
Pavement 14
Pearl Jam 12
Pearls Before Swine 24
Pendleton, Brian
    See Pretty Things, The
Pere Ubu 17
Perkins, Carl 9
Perkins, John
    See XTC
Perko, Lynn
    See Imperial Teen
Petty, Tom 9
    Also see Tom Petty and the Heartbreakers
Phillips, Sam 5
Phish 25
    Earlier sketch in CM 13
Pigface 19
Pink Floyd 2
Pixies, The 21
Plant, Robert 2
    Also see Led Zeppelin
Pogues, The 6
Poi Dog Pondering 17
Poison 11
Police, The 20
Pollard, Russ
    See Sebadoh
Pop, Iggy 23
    Earlier sketch in CM 1
Porter, Jody
    See Fountains of Wayne
Povey, John
    See Pretty Things, The
Presley, Elvis 1
Pretenders, The 8
Pretty Things, The 26
Primal Scream 14
Primus 11
Prince 14
    Earlier sketch in CM 1
Prince, Vivian
    See Pretty Things, The
Prine, John 7
Proclaimers, The 13
Prong 23
Pulp 18
Pyro, Howie
    See D Generation
Quasi 24
Queen 6
Queensryche 8
Quicksilver Messenger Service 23
R.E.M. 25
    Earlier sketch in CM 5
Radiohead 24
Rage Against the Machine 18
Raitt, Bonnie 23
    Earlier sketch in CM 3
Rammstein
Ramones, The 9
Rasputina 26
Red Hot Chili Peppers, The 7
Redd Kross 20
Redus, Richard
    See Captain Beefheart and His Magic
Band
Reed, Lou 16
    Earlier sketch in CM 1
    Also see Velvet Underground, The
Reef 24

Reid, Vernon 2
    Also see Living Colour
Renaldo, Lee
    See Sonic Youth
REO Speedwagon 23
Replacements, The 7
Residents, The 14
Reverend Horton Heat 19
Reznor, Trent 13
Richards, Keith 11
    Also see Rolling Stones, The
Richman, Jonathan 12
Riedel, Oliver
    See Rammstein
Rizzo, Joe
    See D Generation
Robertson, Robbie 2
Rolling Stones, The 23
    Earlier sketch in CM 3
Rollins, Henry 11
Roth, David Lee 1
    Also see Van Halen
Rowe, Simon
    See Mojave 3
Rubin, Rick 9
Rundgren, Todd 11
Rush 8
Rusted Root 26
Rybska, Agnieszka
    See Rasputina
Ryder, Mitch 11
Sage, Danny
    See D Generation
Salazar, Arion
    See Third Eye Blind
Sambora, Richie 24
Santana, Carlos 19
    Earlier sketch in CM 1
Satriani, Joe 4
Scaggs, Boz 12
Schlessinger, Adam
    See Fountains of Wayne
Schneider, Christoph
    See Rammstein
Schwartz, Will
    See Imperial Teen
Scorpions, The 12
Screaming Trees 19
Scud Mountain Boys 21
Seal 14
Sebadoh 26
Seger, Bob 15
Sepultura 12
Sex Pistols, The 5
Shadows, The 22
Shaffer, Paul 13
Shannon, Del 10
Shelly, Steve
    See Sonic Youth
Shocked, Michelle 4
Shonen Knife 13
Shudder to Think 20
Siebenberg, Bob
    See Supertramp
Silver Apples 23
Silverchair 20
Simon and Garfunkel 24
Simon, Carly 4
Simon, Paul 16
    Earlier sketch in CM 1
    Also see Simon and Garfunkel
Simple Minds 21
Siouxsie and the Banshees 8

Skeete, Beverley
    See Bill Wyman & the Rhythm Kings
Skinny Puppy 17
Slayer 10
Sleater-Kinney 20
Smashing Pumpkins 13
Smith, Patti 17
    Earlier sketch in CM 1
Smith, Rick
    See Underworld
Smithereens, The 14
Smiths, The 3
Snouffer, Alex
    See Captain Beefheart and His Magic
Band
Snyder, Richard
    See Captain Beefheart and His Magic
Band
Social Distortion 19
Son Volt 21
Sonic Youth 26
    Earlier sketch in CM 9
Soul Asylum 10
Soundgarden 6
Sparks 18
Specials, The 21
Spector, Phil 4
Spencer Davis Group 19
Spin Doctors 14
Spinal Tap 8
Spirit 22
Sponge 18
Springsteen, Bruce 25
    Earlier sketch in CM 6
Squeeze 5
Stefansson, Baldur
    See Gus Gus
Starr, Ringo 24
    Earlier sketch in CM 10
    Also see Beatles, The
Stax, John
    Also see Beatles, The
Stebbins, Jone
    See Imperial Teen
Steeleye Span 19
Steely Dan 5
Steppenwolf 20
Stevens, Cat 3
Stewart, Rod 2
Stills, Stephen 5
Sting 19
    Earlier sketch in CM 2
Stone Roses, The 16
Stone, Sly 8
Stone Temple Pilots 14
Straw, Syd 18
Stray Cats, The 11
Stryper 2
Sublime 19
Sugarcubes, The 10
Suicidal Tendencies 15
Summers, Andy 3
    Also see Police, The
Superdrag 23
Supertramp 25
Surfin' Pluto 24
T. Rex 11
Taylor, Mick
    Also see Beatles, The

Taylor, Steve **26**
Tears for Fears **6**
Teenage Fanclub **13**
Television **17**
Tench Benmont
    See Tom Petty and the Heartbreakers
Tepper, Jeff "Morris"
    See Captain Beefheart and His Magic Band
Tesla **15**
Texas Tornados, The **8**
The The **15**
They Might Be Giants **7**
Thin Lizzy **13**
Third Eye Blind **25**
Thomas, John
    See Captain Beefheart and His Magic Band
Thompson, Dougie
    See Supertramp
Thompson, Richard **7**
Thorarinsson, Biggi
    See Gus Gus
Thornburg, Lee
    See Supertramp
Three Dog Night **5**
Throwing Muses **15**
Timberlake, Justin
    See N'Sync
Timbuk 3 **3**
Toad the Wet Sprocket **13**
Tolson, Peter
    Also see Beatles, The
Tom Petty and the Heartbreakers **26**
Tool **21**
Townshend, Pete **1**
    Also see Who, The
Traffic **19**
Tragically Hip, The **18**
Treadmill Trackstar **21**
Tripp, Art
    See Captain Beefheart and His Magic Band
Trynin, Jen **21**
Tsunami **21**
Turner, Tina **1**
    Also see Ike & Tina Turner
Tuxedomoon **21**
U2 **12**
    Earlier sketch in CM **2**
Ulmer, James Blood **13**
Underworld **26**
Unitt, Victor
    Also see Beatles, The
Urge Overkill **17**
Uriah Heep **19**
Vai, Steve **5**
Valens, Ritchie **23**
Valli, Frankie **10**
Van Halen **25**
    Earlier sketch in CM **8**
Van Vliet, Don (Capt. Beefheart)
    See Captain Beefheart and His Magic Band
Vaughan,, Jimmie **24**
Vaughan, Stevie Ray **1**
Velvet Underground, The **7**
Ventures **19**
Veruca Salt **20**
Verve Pipe, The **20**
Verve, The **18**
Vincent, Gene **19**
Violent Femmes **12**

Waits, Tom **12**
    Earlier sketch in CM **1**
Wallflowers, The **20**
Walsh, Joe **5**
    Also see Eagles, The
Walsh, Marty
    See Supertramp
War **14**
Warrant **17**
Weezer **20**
Weller, Paul **14**
Wendy O. Williams and The Plasmatics **26**
Wertz, Jenn
    See Rusted Root
Westerberg, Paul **26**
Whalley, Dennis
    See Captain Beefheart and His Magic Band
White Zombie **17**
Whitesnake **5**
Whitley, Chris **16**
Who, The **3**
Wildwood, Michael
    See D Generation
Williams, Robert
    See Captain Beefheart and His Magic Band
Wilson, Brian **24**
    Also see Beach Boys, The
Winter, Johnny **5**
Winthrop, Dave
    See Supertramp
Winwood, Steve **2**
    Also see Spencer Davis Group
    Also see Traffic
Wolf, Peter **25**
Wray, Link **17**
Wyatt, Robert **24**
Wyman, Bill
    See Bill Wyman & the Rhythm Kings
    See Rolling Stones
X **11**
XTC **26**
    Earlier sketch in CM **10**
Yardbirds, The **10**
Yes **8**
Yo La Tengo **24**
Young, Brian
    See Fountains of Wayne
Young, Neil **15**
    Earlier sketch in CM **2**
Youth, Todd
    See D Generation
Zappa, Frank **17**
    Earlier sketch in CM **1**
Zevon, Warren **9**
Zombies, The **23**
ZZ Top **2**

Rock and Roll Pioneers
Ballard, Hank **17**
Berry, Chuck **1**
Clark, Dick **25**
    Earlier sketch in CM **2**
Darin, Bobby **4**
Diddley, Bo **3**
Dion **4**
Domino, Fats **2**
Eddy, Duane **9**
Everly Brothers, The **2**
Francis, Connie **10**
Glitter, Gary **19**
Haley, Bill **6**
Hawkins, Screamin' Jay **8**

Holly, Buddy **1**
James, Etta **6**
Jordan, Louis **11**
Lewis, Jerry Lee **2**
Little Richard **1**
Nelson, Rick **2**
Orbison, Roy **2**
Otis, Johnny **16**
Paul, Les **2**
Perkins, Carl **9**
Phillips, Sam **5**
Presley, Elvis **1**
Professor Longhair **6**
Sedaka, Neil **4**
Shannon, Del **10**
Shirelles, The **11**
Spector, Phil **4**
Twitty, Conway **6**
Valli, Frankie **10**
Wilson, Jackie **3**
Wray, Link **17**

Saxophone
Adderly, Cannonball **15**
Anderson, Wessell **23**
Ayler , Albert **19**
Barbieri, Gato **22**
Bechet, Sidney **17**
Braxton, Anthony **12**
Brötzmann, Peter **26**
Carter, Benny **3**
    Also see McKinney's Cotton Pickers
Carter, James **18**
Chenier, C. J. **15**
Clemons, Clarence **7**
Coleman, Ornette **5**
Coltrane, John **4**
Curtis, King **17**
Desmond, Paul **23**
Dibango, Manu **14**
Dorsey, Jimmy
    See Dorsey Brothers, The
Getz, Stan **12**
Golson, Benny **21**
Gordon, Dexter **10**
Harris, Eddie **15**
Hawkins, Coleman **11**
Henderson, Joe **14**
Herman, Woody **12**
Hodges, Johnny **24**
Jacquet, Illinois **17**
James, Boney **21**
Kenny G **14**
Kirk, Rahsaan Roland **6**
Koz, Dave **19**
Lacy, Steve **23**
Lateef, Yusef **16**
Lloyd, Charles **22**
Lopez, Israel "Cachao" **14**
Lovano, Joe **13**
Marsalis, Branford **10**
Morgan, Frank **9**
Mulligan, Gerry **16**
Najee **21**
Osby, Greg **21**
Parker, Charlie **5**
Parker, Maceo **7**
Pepper, Art **18**
Redman, Joshua **25**
    Earlier sketch in CM **12**
Rollins, Sonny **7**
Russell, Pee Wee **25**
Sanborn, David **1**
Sanders, Pharoah **16**

Shorter, Wayne **5**
Threadgill, Henry **9**
Washington, Grover, Jr. **5**
Winter, Paul **10**
Young, La Monte **16**
Young, Lester **14**
Zorn, John **15**

Sintir
Hakmoun, Hassan **15**

Songwriters
2Pac **17**
Acuff, Roy **2**
Adams, Bryan **20**
  Earlier sketch in CM **2**
Adams, Yolanda **23**
Afanasieff, Walter **26**
Aikens, Rhett **22**
Albini, Steve **15**
Alexander, Arthur **14**
Allen, Peter **11**
Allison, Mose **17**
Alpert, Herb **11**
Alvin, Dave **17**
Amos, Tori **12**
Anderson, Ian
  See Jethro Tull
Anderson, John **5**
Anka, Paul **2**
Armatrading, Joan **4**
Astbury, Ian
  See Cult, The
Atkins, Chet **26**
Atkins, Chet **5**
Autry, Gene **25**
  Earlier sketch in CM **12**
Bacharach, Burt **20**
  Earlier sketch in CM **1**
Badu, Erykah **26**
Baez, Joan **1**
Baker, Anita **9**
Balin, Marty
  See Jefferson Airplane
Barlow, Lou **20**
Barrett, (Roger) Syd
  See Pink Floyd
Basie, Count **2**
Becker, Walter
  See Steely Dan
Beckley, Gerry
  See America
Belew, Adrian **5**
Benton, Brook **7**
Berg, Matraca **16**
Berlin, Irving **8**
Berry, Chuck **1**
Bjork **16**
  Also see Sugarcubes, The
Black, Clint **5**
Black, Frank **14**
Blades, Ruben **2**
Blige, Mary J. **15**
Bloom, Luka **14**
Bono
  See U2
Brady, Paul **8**
Bragg, Billy **7**
Brandt, Paul **22**
Brickell, Edie **3**
Brokop, Lisa **22**
Brooke, Jonatha
  See Story, The
Brooks, Garth **25**

Earlier sketch in CM **8**
Brown, Bobby **4**
Brown, James **16**
  Earlier sketch in CM **2**
Brown, Junior **15**
Brown, Marty **14**
Browne, Jackson **3**
Buck, Peter
  See R.E.M.
Buck, Robert
  See 10,000 Maniacs
Buckingham, Lindsey **8**
  Also see Fleetwood Mac
Buckley, Jeff **22**
Buckley, Tim **14**
Buffett, Jimmy **4**
Bunnell, Dewey
  See America
Burdon, Eric **14**
  Also see War
  Also see Animals
Burnett, T Bone **13**
Burning Spear **15**
Burroughs, William S. **26**
Bush, Kate **4**
Byrne, David **8**
  Also see Talking Heads
Cahn, Sammy **11**
Cale, J. J. **16**
Cale, John **9**
Calloway, Cab **6**
Campbell, Sarah Elizabeth **23**
Captain Beefheart **10**
Cardwell, Joi **22**
Carlisle, Bob **22**
Carter, Carlene **8**
Carter, Deana **25**
Cash, Johnny **17**
  Earlier sketch in CM **1**
Cash, Rosanne **2**
Cetera, Peter
  See Chicago
Chandra, Sheila **16**
Chapin, Harry **6**
Chapin-Carpenter, Mary **25**
  Earlier sketch in CM **6**
Chapman, Steven Curtis **15**
Chapman, Tracy **4**
Chaquico, Craig **23**
Charles, Ray **24**
  Earlier sketch in CM **1**
Chenier, C. J. **15**
Childs, Toni **2**
Chilton, Alex **10**
Clapton, Eric **11**
  Earlier sketch in CM **1**
  Also see Cream
  Also see Yardbirds, The
Clark, Guy **17**
Clements, Vassar **18**
Cleveland, James **1**
Clinton, George **7**
Cochrane, Tom **23**
Cockburn, Bruce **8**
Cohen, Leonard **3**
Cole, Lloyd **9**
Cole, Nat King **3**
Collie, Mark **15**
Collins, Albert **4**
Collins, Judy **4**
Collins, Phil **2**
  Also see Genesis
Cooder, Ry **2**

Cooke, Sam **1**
  Also see Soul Stirrers, The
Cooper, Alice **8**
Cope, Julian **16**
Corgan, Billy
  See Smashing Pumpkins
Costello, Elvis **12**
  Earlier sketch in CM **2**
Cotten, Elizabeth **16**
Crenshaw, Marshall **5**
Croce, Jim **3**
Crofts, Dash
  See Seals & Crofts
Cropper, Steve **12**
Crosby, David **3**
  Also see Byrds, The
Crow, Sheryl **18**
Crowe, J. D. **5**
Crowell, Rodney **8**
Daniels, Charlie **6**
Davies, Ray **5**
  Also see Kinks, the
de Burgh, Chris **22**
DeBarge, El **14**
DeMent, Iris **13**
Denver, John **22**
  Earlier sketch in CM **1**
Des'ree **15**
Diamond, Neil **1**
Diddley, Bo **3**
Difford, Chris
  See Squeeze
DiFranco, Ani **17**
Dion **4**
Dixon, Willie **10**
DMX **25**
Doc Pomus **14**
Domino, Fats **2**
Donelly, Tanya
  See Belly
  Also see Throwing Muses
Donovan **9**
Dorsey, Thomas A. **11**
Doucet, Michael **8**
Dozier, Lamont
  See Holland-Dozier-Holland
Drake, Nick **17**
Dube, Lucky **17**
Duffy, Billy
  See Cult, The
Dulli, Greg **17**
  See Afghan Whigs, The
Dylan, Bob **21**
  Earlier sketch in CM **3**
Earle, Steve **16**
Edge, The
  See U2
Edmonds, Kenneth "Babyface" **12**
Eitzel, Mark
  See American Music Club
Elfman, Danny **9**
Ellington, Duke **2**
Emerson, Keith
  See Emerson, Lake & Palmer/Powell
Emmanuel, Tommy **21**
English, Michael **23**
Enigma **14**
Erickson, Roky **16**
Ertegun, Ahmet **10**
Escovedo, Alejandro **18**
Estefan, Gloria **15**
  Earlier sketch in CM **2**
Etheridge, Melissa **16**
  Earlier sketch in CM **4**

Everly, Don
   See Everly Brothers, The
Everly, Phil
   See Everly Brothers, The
Fagen, Don
   See Steely Dan
Faithfull, Marianne **14**
Ferry, Bryan **1**
Flack, Roberta **5**
Flatt, Lester **3**
Fogelberg, Dan **4**
Fogerty, John **2**
   Also see Creedence Clearwater Revival
Fordham, Julia **15**
Foster, David **13**
Frampton, Peter **3**
Franti, Michael **16**
Frey, Glenn **3**
   Also see Eagles, The
Fripp, Robert **9**
Frizzell, Lefty **10**
Gabriel, Peter **16**
   Earlier sketch in CM **2**
   Also see Genesis
Garcia, Jerry **4**
   Also see Grateful Dead, The
Gaye, Marvin **4**
Geldof, Bob **9**
George, Lowell
   See Little Feat
Gershwin, George and Ira **11**
Gibb, Barry
   See Bee Gees, The
Gibb, Maurice
   See Bee Gees, The
Gibb, Robin
   See Bee Gees, The
Gibbons, Billy
   See ZZ Top
Gibson, Bob **23**
Gibson, Debbie **1**
Gift, Roland **3**
Gill, Vince **7**
Gilley, Mickey **7**
Gilmour, David
   See Pink Floyd
Goffin-King **24**
Gold, Julie **22**
Goodman, Benny **4**
Gordy, Berry, Jr. **6**
Gorka, John **18**
Grant, Amy **7**
Green, Al **9**
Greenwood, Lee **12**
Griffin, Patty **24**
Griffith, Nanci **3**
Guthrie, Arlo **6**
Guthrie, Gwen **26**
Guthrie, Woodie **2**
Guy, Buddy **4**
Hagen, Nina **25**
Haggard, Merle **2**
Hall, Daryl
   See Hall & Oates
Hall, Tom T. **4**
Hall, Tom T. **26**
Hamlisch, Marvin **1**
Hammer, M.C. **5**
Hammerstein, Oscar
   See Rodgers, Richard
Hancock, Herbie **25**
Hardin, Tim **18**
Harding, John Wesley **6**
Harley, Bill **7**

Harper, Ben **17**
Harris, Emmylou **4**
Harrison, George **2**
   Also see Beatles, The
Harry, Deborah **4**
   Also see Blondie
Hart, Lorenz
   See Rodgers, Richard
Hartford, John **3**
Hatfield, Juliana **12**
   Also see Lemonheads, The
Hawkins, Screamin' Jay **8**
Hayes, Isaac **10**
Healey, Jeff **4**
Hedges, Michael **3**
Hendrix, Jimi **2**
Henley, Don **3**
   Also see Eagles, The
Henry, Joe **18**
Hersh, Kristin
   See Throwing Muses
Hiatt, John **8**
Hidalgo, David
   See Los Lobos
Hill, Lauryn **25**
Hillman, Chris
   See Byrds, The
   Also see Desert Rose Band, The
Hinojosa, Tish **13**
Hitchcock, Robyn **9**
Holland, Brian
   See Holland-Dozier-Holland
Holland, Eddie
   See Holland-Dozier-Holland
Holly, Buddy **1**
Hornsby, Bruce **25**
   Earlier sketch in CM **3**
Howard, Harlan **15**
Hutchence, Michael
   See INXS
Hynde, Chrissie
   See Pretenders, The
Ian, Janis **5**
Ice Cube **25**
   Earlier sketch in CM **10**
Ice-T **7**
Idol, Billy **3**
Isaak, Chris **6**
Jackson, Alan **25**
   Earlier sketch in CM **7**
Jackson, Janet **16**
   Earlier sketch in CM **3**
Jackson, Joe **22**
   Earlier sketch in CM **4**
Jackson, Michael **17**
   Earlier sketch in CM **1**
   Also see Jacksons, The
Jackson, Millie **14**
Jagger, Mick **7**
   Also see Rolling Stones, The
Jam, Jimmy, and Terry Lewis **11**
James, Rick **2**
Jarreau, Al **1**
Jennings, Waylon **4**
Jett, Joan **3**
Jewel **25**
Joel, Billy **12**
   Earlier sketch in CM **2**
Johansen, David **7**
John, Elton **20**
   Earlier sketch in CM **3**
Johnson, Lonnie **17**
Johnson, Matt
   See The The

Jones, Brian
   See Rolling Stones, The
Jones, George **4**
Jones, Mick
   See Clash, The
Jones, Quincy **20**
   Earlier sketch in CM **2**
Jones, Rickie Lee **4**
Joplin, Janis **3**
Jordan, Montell **26**
Judd, Naomi
   See Judds, The
Kane, Big Daddy **7**
Kantner, Paul
   See Jefferson Airplane
Kee, John P. **15**
Keith, Toby **17**
Kelly, R. **19**
Ketchum, Hal **14**
Khan, Chaka **19**
   Earlier sketch in CM **9**
King, Albert **2**
King, B. B. **1**
King, Ben E. **7**
King, Carole **6**
King, Freddy **17**
Kirkwood, Curt
   See Meat Puppets, The
Knopfler, Mark **25**
   Earlier sketch in CM **3**
   Also see Dire Straits
Kottke, Leo **13**
Kravitz, Lenny **26**
Kravitz, Lenny **5**
Kristofferson, Kris **4**
L.L. Cool J **5**
Lake, Greg
   See Emerson, Lake & Palmer/Powell
Landreth, Sonny **16**
Lang, K. D. **25**
   Earlier sketch in CM **4**
Larkin, Patty **9**
Lavin, Christine **6**
LeDoux, Chris **12**
Lee, Ben **26**
Lee, Peggy **8**
Lehrer, Tom **7**
Leiber and Stoller **14**
Lennon, John **9**
   Also see Beatles, The
Lennon, Julian **2**
Lennon, Julian **26**
Lewis, Huey **9**
Lightfoot, Gordon **3**
Linkous, Mark **26**
Little Richard **1**
Llanas, Sammy
   See BoDeans, The
Loeb, Lisa **23**
Loggins, Kenny **20**
   Earlier sketch in CM **3**
Love, Courtney
   See Hole
Love, Laura **20**
Loveless, Patty **5**
Lovett, Lyle **5**
Lowe, Nick **25**
   Earlier sketch in CM **6**
Lydon, John **9**
   Also see Sex Pistols, The
Lynn, Loretta **2**
Lynne, Jeff **5**
Lynne, Shelby **5**

Lynott, Phil
  See Thin Lizzy
MacColl, Kirsty **12**
MacDonald, Barbara
  See Timbuk 3
MacDonald, Pat
  See Timbuk 3
Madonna **16**
  Earlier sketch in CM **4**
Manilow, Barry **2**
Mann, Aimee **22**
Mann, Billy **23**
Manzarek, Ray
  See Doors, The
Marley, Bob **3**
Marley, Ziggy **3**
Marx, Richard **3**
Mattea, Kathy **5**
May, Brian
  See Queen
Mayfield, Curtis **8**
MC 900 Ft. Jesus **16**
MC Breed **17**
McCartney, Paul **4**
  Also see Beatles, The
McClinton, Delbert **14**
McCoury, Del **15**
McCulloch, Ian **23**
McDonald, Michael
  See Doobie Brothers, The
McGuinn, Roger
  See Byrds, The
McLachlan, Sarah **12**
McLaren, Malcolm **23**
McLean, Don **7**
McLennan, Grant **21**
McMurtry, James **10**
McTell, Blind Willie **17**
McVie, Christine
  See Fleetwood Mac
Medley, Bill **3**
Melanie **12**
Mellencamp, John **20**
  Earlier sketch in CM **2**
Mercer, Johnny **13**
Merchant, Natalie
  See 10,000 Maniacs
Merchant, Natalie **25**
Mercury, Freddie
  See Queen
Messina, Jo Dee **26**
Michael, George **9**
Miller, Roger **4**
Miller, Steve **2**
Milsap, Ronnie **2**
Mitchell, Joni **17**
  Earlier sketch in CM **2**
Moffatt, Katy **18**
Morrison, Jim **3**
Morrison, Van **24**
  Earlier sketch in CM **3**
Morrissey **10**
Morrissey, Bill **12**
Morton, Jelly Roll **7**
Mould, Bob **10**
Moyet, Alison **12**
Nascimento, Milton **6**
Ndegéocello, Me'Shell **18**
Near, Holly **1**
Nelson, Rick **2**
Nelson, Willie **11**
  Earlier sketch in CM **1**
Nesmith, Mike
  See Monkees, The

Neville, Art
  See Neville Brothers, The
Newman, Randy **4**
Newmann, Kurt
  See BoDeans, The
Nicks, Stevie **25**
  Earlier sketch in CM **2**
  Also see Fleetwood Mac
Nilsson **10**
Nugent, Ted **2**
Nyro, Laura **12**
O'Connor, Sinead **3**
Oates, John
  See Hall & Oates
Ocasek, Ric **5**
Ocean, Billy **4**
Ochs, Phil **7**
Odetta **7**
Orbison, Roy **2**
Orton, Beth **26**
Osbourne, Ozzy **3**
Oslin, K. T. **3**
Owens, Buck **2**
Page, Jimmy **4**
  See Led Zeppelin
  Also see Yardbirds, The
Palmer, Robert **2**
Paris, Twila **16**
Parker, Graham **10**
Parks, Van Dyke **17**
Parnell, Lee Roy **15**
Parsons, Gram **7**
  Also see Byrds, The
Parton, Dolly **24**
  Earlier sketch in CM **2**
Paul, Les **2**
Paxton, Tom **5**
Peniston, CeCe **15**
Penn, Michael **4**
Perez, Louie
  See Los Lobos
Perkins, Carl **9**
Perry, Joe
  See Aerosmith
Petty, Tom **9**
  Also see Tom Petty & the Heartbreakers
Phair, Liz **14**
Phillips, Sam **12**
Pickett, Wilson **10**
Pierson, Kate
  See B-52's, The
Plant, Robert **2**
  Also see Led Zeppelin
Pop, Iggy **1**
Porter, Cole **10**
Price, Lloyd **25**
Prince **14**
  Earlier sketch in CM **1**
Prine, John **7**
Professor Longhair **6**
Rabbitt, Eddie **24**
  Earlier sketch in CM **5**
Raitt, Bonnie **23**
  Earlier sketch in CM **3**
Ray, Amy
  See Indigo Girls
Rea, Chris **12**
Redding, Otis **5**
Reddy, Helen **9**
Reed, Lou **16**
  Earlier sketch in CM **1**
  Also see Velvet Underground, The
Reid, Charlie
  See Proclaimers, The

Reid, Craig
  See Proclaimers, The
Reid, Vernon **2**
  Also see Living Colour
Rice, Chris **25**
Rich, Charlie **3**
Richards, Keith **11**
  Also see Rolling Stones, The
Richey, Kim **20**
Richie, Lionel **2**
Richman, Jonathan **12**
Riley, Teddy **14**
Ritchie, Jean **4**
Robbins, Marty **9**
Roberts, Brad
  See Crash Test Dummies
Robertson, Robbie **2**
Robillard, Duke **2**
Robinson, Smokey **1**
Rodgers, Jimmie **3**
Rodgers, Richard **9**
Roland, Ed
  See Collective Soul
Roth, David Lee **1**
  Also see Van Halen
Russell, Mark **6**
Rutherford, Mike
  See Genesis
Ryder, Mitch **23**
Sade **2**
Sager, Carole Bayer **5**
Saliers, Emily
  See Indigo Girls
Sandman, Mark
  See Morphine
Sangare, Oumou **22**
Satriani, Joe **4**
Scaggs, Boz **12**
Schneider, Fred III
  See B-52's, The
Scott-Heron, Gil **13**
Scruggs, Earl **3**
Seal **14**
Seals, Dan **9**
Seals, Jim
  See Seals & Crofts
Secada, Jon **13**
Sedaka, Neil **4**
Seeger, Pete **4**
  Also see Weavers, The
Seger, Bob **15**
Shannon, Del **10**
Sheila E. **3**
Shepherd, Kenny Wayne **22**
Shocked, Michelle **4**
Siberry, Jane **6**
Simmons, Gene
  See Kiss
Simmons, Patrick
  See Doobie Brothers, The
Simon, Carly **22**
  Earlier sketch in CM **4**
Simon, Paul **16**
  Earlier sketch in CM **1**
Skaggs, Ricky **5**
Sledge, Percy **15**
Slick, Grace
  See Jefferson Airplane
Smith, Patti **17**
  Earlier sketch in CM **1**
Smith, Robert
  See Cure, The
  Also see Siouxsie and the Banshees

Smith, Will **26**
   Also see DJ Jazzy Jeff and the Fresh
Prince **5**
Snoop Doggy Dogg **17**
Sondheim, Stephen **8**
Spector, Phil **4**
Springsteen, Bruce **25**
   Earlier sketch in CM **6**
St. James, Rebecca **26**
Stanley, Paul
   See Kiss
Stanley, Ralph **5**
Starr, Ringo **10**
   Also see Beatles, The
Stevens, Cat **3**
Stevens, Ray **7**
Stewart, Dave
   See Eurythmics, The
Stewart, Rod **20**
   Earlier sketch in CM **2**
   Also see Faces, The
Stills, Stephen **5**
Sting **19**
   Earlier sketch in CM **2**
   Also see Police, The
Stipe, Michael
   See R.E.M.
Stockwood, Kim **26**
Strait, George **5**
Straw, Syd **18**
Streisand, Barbra **2**
Strickland, Keith
   See B-52's, The
Strummer, Joe
   See Clash, The
Stuart, Marty **9**
Styne, Jule **21**
Summer, Donna **12**
Summers, Andy **3**
   Also see Police, The
Sure!, Al B. **13**
Sweat, Keith **13**
Sweet, Matthew **9**
Swing, DeVante
   See Jodeci
Taj Mahal **6**
Taupin, Bernie **22**
Taylor, James **25**
   Earlier sketch in CM **2**
Taylor, Koko **10**
Taylor, Steve **26**
Thompson, Richard **7**
Thornton, Big Mama **18**
Tikaram, Tanita **9**
Tilbrook, Glenn
   See Squeeze
Tillis, Mel **7**
Tillis, Pam **25**
   Earlier sketch in CM **8**
Timmins, Margo
   See Cowboy Junkies, The
Timmins, Michael
   See Cowboy Junkies, The
Tippin, Aaron **12**
Tone-L c **3**
Torme, Mel **4**
Tosh, Peter **3**
Toussaint, Allen **11**
Townshend, Pete **1**
   Also see Who, The
Travis, Merle **14**
Travis, Randy **9**
Treadmill Trackstar **21**

Tricky **18**
Tritt, Travis **7**
Trynin, Jen **21**
Tubb, Ernest **4**
Twain, Shania **17**
Twitty, Conway **6**
Tyler, Steve
   See Aerosmith
Vai, Steve **5**
   Also see Whitesnake
Van Halen, Edward
   See Van Halen
Van Ronk, Dave **12**
Van Shelton, Ricky **5**
Van Zandt, Townes **13**
Vandross, Luther **24**
   Earlier sketch in CM **2**
Vedder, Eddie
   See Pearl Jam
Vega, Suzanne **3**
Wachtel, Waddy **26**
Wagoner, Porter **13**
Waits, Tom **12**
   Earlier sketch in CM **1**
Walden, Narada Michael **14**
Walker, Jerry Jeff **13**
Walker, T-Bone **5**
Waller, Fats **7**
Walsh, Joe **5**
   Also see Eagles, The
Wariner, Steve **18**
Warren, Diane **21**
Waters, Crystal **15**
Waters, Muddy **4**
Waters, Roger
   See Pink Floyd
Watley, Jody **26**
Watt, Mike **22**
Webb, Jimmy **12**
Weill, Kurt **12**
Weir, Bob
   See Grateful Dead, The
Welch, Bob
   See Fleetwood Mac
Weller, Paul **14**
West, Dottie **8**
Westerberg, Paul **26**
White, Karyn **21**
White, Lari **15**
Whitley, Chris **16**
Whitley, Keith **7**
Williams, Dar **21**
Williams, Deniece **1**
Williams, Don **4**
Williams, Hank, Jr. **1**
Williams, Hank, Sr. **4**
Williams, Lucinda **10**
Williams, Lucinda **24**
   Earlier sketch in CM **10**
Williams, Paul **26**
Williams, Paul **5**
Williams, Victoria **17**
Wills, Bob **6**
Wilson, Brian **24**
   Also see Beach Boys, The
Wilson, Cindy
   See B-52's, The
Wilson, Ricky
   See B-52's, The
Winbush, Angela **15**
Winter, Johnny **5**
Winwood, Steve **2**
   Also see Spencer Davis Group
   Also see Traffic

Womack, Bobby **5**
Wonder, Stevie **17**
   Earlier sketch in CM **2**
Wray, Link **17**
Wyatt, Robert **24**
Wynette, Tammy **24**
   Earlier sketch in CM **2**
Yearwood, Trisha **25**
   Earlier sketch in CM **10**
Yoakam, Dwight **21**
   Earlier sketch in CM **1**
Young, Angus
   See AC/DC
Young, Neil **15**
   Earlier sketch in CM **2**
Zappa, Frank **17**
   Earlier sketch in CM **1**
Zevon, Warren **9**

Trombone
Anderson, Ray **7**
Brown, Lawrence **23**
Dorsey, Tommy
   See Dorsey Brothers, The
Miller, Glenn **6**
Teagarden, Jack **10**
Turre, Steve **22**
Watts, Eugene
   See Canadian Brass, The

Trumpet
Alpert, Herb **11**
Armstrong, Louis **4**
Baker, Chet **13**
Berigan, Bunny **2**
Blanchard, Terence **13**
Brown, Clifford **24**
Cherry, Don **10**
Coleman, Ornette **5**
Davis, Miles **1**
Eldridge, Roy **9**
   Also see McKinney's Cotton Pickers
Ferguson, Maynard **7**
Gillespie, Dizzy **6**
Hargrove, Roy **15**
Hawkins, Erskine **19**
Hirt, Al **5**
Isham, Mark **14**
James, Harry **11**
Jensen, Ingrid **22**
Jones, Quincy **20**
   Earlier sketch in CM **2**
Jones, Thad **19**
Loughnane, Lee **3**
Marsalis, Wynton **20**
   Earlier sketch in CM **6**
Masekela, Hugh **7**
Matthews, Eric **22**
Mighty Mighty Bosstones **20**
Miles, Ron **22**
Mills, Fred
   See Canadian Brass, The
Navarro, Fats **25**
Oliver, King **15**
Rodney, Red **14**
Romm, Ronald
   See Canadian Brass, The
Sandoval, Arturo **15**
Severinsen, Doc **1**
Terry, Clark **24**

Tuba
Daellenbach, Charles
   See Canadian Brass, The
Phillips, Harvey **3**

Vibraphone

Burton, Gary **10**
Hampton, Lionel **6**
Jackson, Milt **15**
Norvo, Red **12**

Viola

Dutt, Hank
  See Kronos Quartet
Jones, Michael
  See Kronos Quartet
Killian, Tim
  See Kronos Quartet
Menuhin, Yehudi **11**
Zukerman, Pinchas **4**

Violin

Acuff, Roy **2**
Anderson, Laurie **25**
  Earlier sketch in CM **1**
Bell, Joshua **21**
Bromberg, David **18**

Bush, Sam
  See New Grass Revival, The
Carter, Regina **22**
Chang, Sarah **7**
Clements, Vassar **18**
Coleman, Ornette **5**
Cugat, Xavier **23**
Daniels, Charlie **6**
Doucet, Michael **8**
Germano, Lisa **18**
Gingold, Josef **6**
Grappelli, Stephane **10**
Gray, Ella
  See Kronos Quartet
Harrington, David
  See Kronos Quartet
Hartford, John **1**
Hidalgo, David
  See Los Lobos
Kennedy, Nigel **8**
Krauss, Alison **10**

Lamb, Barbara **19**
Lewis, Roy
  See Kronos Quartet
Marriner, Neville **7**
Menuhin, Yehudi **11**
Midori **7**
Mutter, Anne-Sophie **23**
O'Connor, Mark **1**
Perlman, Itzhak **2**
Ponty, Jean-Luc **8**
Rieu, André **26**
Salerno-Sonnenberg, Nadja **3**
Shallenberger, James
  See Kronos Quartet
Sherba, John
  See Kronos Quartet
Skaggs, Ricky **5**
Stern, Isaac **7**
Vanessa-Mae **26**
Whiteman, Paul **17**
Wills, Bob **6**
Zukerman, Pinchas **4**

Cumulative Musicians Index

Volume numbers appear in **bold.**

10,000 Maniacs **3**
2 Unlimited **18**
23, Richard
  See Front 242
2Pac **17**
  Also see Digital Underground
3-D
  See Massive Attack
311 **20**
A-ha **22**
Aaliyah **21**
Abba **12**
Abbott, Jacqueline
  See Beautiful South
Abbott, Jude
  See Chumbawamba
Abbruzzese, Dave
Abdul, Paula **3**
Abercrombie, John **25**
Abong, Fred
  See Belly
Abrahams, Mick
  See Jethro Tull
Abrams, Bryan
  See Color Me Badd
Abrantes, Fernando
  See Kraftwerk
AC/DC **4**
Ace of Base **22**
Ackerman, Will **3**
Acland, Christopher
  See Lush
Acuff, Roy **2**
Acuna, Alejandro
  See Weather Report
Adam Ant **13**
Adamendes, Elaine
  See Throwing Muses
Adams, Bryan **20**
  Earlier sketch in CM **2**
Adams, Clifford
  See Kool & the Gang
Adams, Craig
  See Cult, The
Adams, Donn
  See NRBQ
Adams, John **8**
Adams, Mark
  See Specials, The
Adams, Oleta **17**
Adams, Terry
  See NRBQ
Adams, Victoria
  See Spice Girls
Adams, Yolanda **23**
Adcock, Eddie
  See Country Gentleman, The
Adderly, Cannonball **15**
Adderly, Julian
  See Adderly, Cannonball
Adé, King Sunny **18**
Adler, Steven
  See Guns n' Roses

Aerosmith **22**
  Earlier sketch in CM **3**
Afanasieff, Walter **26**
Afghan Whigs **17**
Afonso, Marie
  See Zap Mama
AFX
  See Aphex Twin
Air Supply **22**
Ajile
  See Arrested Development
Akingbola, Sola
  See Jamiroquai
Akins, Rhett **22**
Alabama **21**
  Earlier sketch in CM **1**
Alarm **22**
Albarn, Damon
  See Blur
Albert, Nate
  See Mighty Mighty Bosstones
Alberti, Dorona
  See KMFDM
Albini, Steve **15**
Albuquerque, Michael de
  See Electric Light Orchestra
Alder, John
  See Gong
Alexakis, Art
  See Everclear
Alexander, Arthur **14**
Alexander, Tim
  See Asleep at the Wheel
Alexander, Tim "Herb"
  See Primus
Ali
  See Tribe Called Quest, A
Alice in Chains **10**
Alien Sex Fiend **23**
Alkema, Jan Willem
  See Compulsion
All Saints **25**
All-4-One **17**
Allcock, Martin
  See Fairport Convention
  See Jethro Tull
Allen, April
  See C + C Music Factory
Allen, Chad
  See Guess Who
Allen, Daevid
  See Gong
Allen, Dave
  See Gang of Four
Allen, Debbie **8**
Allen, Duane
  See Oak Ridge Boys, The
Allen, Geri **10**
Allen, Johnny Ray
  See Subdudes, The
Allen, Papa Dee
  See War

Allen, Peter **11**
Allen, Red
  See Osborne Brothers, The
Allen, Rick
  See Def Leppard
Allen, Ross
  See Mekons, The
Allison, Luther **21**
Allison, Mose **17**
Allman Brothers, The **6**
Allman, Duane
  See Allman Brothers, The
Allman, Gregg
  See Allman Brothers, The
Allsup, Michael Rand
  See Three Dog Night
Alpert, Herb **11**
Alphonso, Roland
  See Skatalites, The
Alsing, Pelle
  See Roxette
Alston, Andy
  See Del Amitri
Alston, Shirley
  See Shirelles, The
Altan **18**
Alvin, Dave **17**
  Also see X
Am, Svet
  See KMFDM
Amato, Dave
  See REO Speedwagon
Amedee, Steve
  See Subdudes, The
Ameling, Elly **24**
Ament, Jeff
  See Pearl Jam
America **16**
American Music Club **15**
Amon, Robin
  See Pearls Before Swine
Amos, Tori **12**
Anastasio, Trey
  See Phish
Anderson, Al
  See NRBQ
Anderson, Andy
  See Cure, The
Anderson, Brett
  See Suede
Anderson, Cleave
  See Blue Rodeo
Anderson, Emma
  See Lush
Anderson, Gladstone
  See Skatalites, The
Anderson, Ian
  See Jethro Tull
Anderson, Jhelisa
  See Shamen, The
Anderson, John **5**
Anderson, Jon
  See Yes

Anderson, Keith
  See Dirty Dozen
Anderson, Laurie 25
  Earlier sketch in CM 1
Anderson, Marian 8
Anderson, Pamela
  See Incognito
Anderson, Ray 7
Anderson, Signe
  See Jefferson Airplane
Anderson, Wessell 23
Andersson, Benny
  See Abba
Andes, Mark
  See Spirit
Andes, Matt
  See Spirit
Andes, Rachel
  See Spirit
Andrews, Barry
  See XTC
Andrews, Julie 4
Andrews, Laverne
  See Andrews Sisters, The
Andrews, Mark
  See Dru Hill
Andrews, Maxene
  See Andrews Sisters, The
Andrews, Patty
  See Andrews Sisters, The
Andrews, Revert
  See Dirty Dozen
Andrews Sisters, The 9
Andy, Horace
  See Massive Attack
Anger, Darol
  See Turtle Island String Quartet
Angus, Colin
  See Shamen, The
Animals 22
Anka, Paul 2
Anointed 21
Anonymous 4 23
Anonymous, Rodney
  See Dead Milkmen
Anselmo, Philip
  See Pantera
Ant, Adam
  See Adam Ant
Anthony, Larry
  See Dru Hill
Anthony, Marc 19
Anthony, Michael
  See Van Halen
Anthony, Michael
  See Massive Attack
Anthrax 11
Anton, Alan
  See Cowboy Junkies, The
Antoni, Mark De Gli
  See Soul Coughing
Antunes, Michael
  See Beaver Brown Band, The
Aphex Twin 14
Appice, Vinnie
  See Black Sabbath
Appleton, Natalie
  See All Saints
Appleton, Nicole
  See All Saints
Aquabats 22
Araya, Tom
  See Slayer
Archers of Loaf 21
Arden, Jann 21

Ardolino, Tom
  See NRBQ
Arellano, Rod
  See Aquabats
Arena, Tina 21
Argent, Rod
  See Zombies, The
Arkenstone, David 20
Arm, Mark
  See Mudhoney
Armatrading, Joan 4
Armerding, Jake
  See Northern Lights
Armerding, Taylor
  See Northern Lights
Armstrong, Billie Joe
  See Green Day
Armstrong, Louis 4
Armstrong, Vanessa Bell 24
Arnaz, Desi 8
Arnold, Eddy 10
Arnold, Kristine
  See Sweethearts of the Rodeo
Aronoff, Kenny 21
Arrau, Claudio 1
Arrested Development 14
Art Ensemble of Chicago, The 23
Art of Noise 22
Arthurs, Paul
  See Oasis
Artifacts 23
Ash, Daniel
  See Love and Rockets
Ashcroft, Richard
  See Verve, The
Ashford, Rosalind
  See Martha and the Vandellas
Ashton, Susan 17
Asleep at the Wheel 5
Astbury, Ian
  See Cult, The
Astley, Rick 5
Astro
  See UB40
Asuo, Kwesi
  See Arrested Development
Atkins, Chet 26
  Earlier sketch in CM 5
Atkinson, Paul
  See Zombies, The
Atkinson, Sweet Pea
  See Was (Not Was)
Audio Adrenaline 22
Auf Der Maur, Melissa
  See Hole
Augustyniak, Jerry
  See 10,000 Maniacs
Auldridge, Mike 4
  Also see Country Gentlemen, The
  Also see Seldom Scene, The
Austin, Cuba
  See McKinney's Cotton Pickers
Austin, Dallas 16
Austral, Florence 26
Autry, Gene 25
  Earlier sketch in CM 12
Avalon 26
Avalon, Frankie 5
Avery, Eric
  See Jane's Addiction
Avery, Teodross 23
Avory, Mick
  See Rolling Stones, The
Avory, Mick
  See Kinks, The

Ayers, Kevin
  See Gong
Aykroyd, Dan
  See Blues Brothers, The
Ayler, Albert 19
Ayres, Ben
  See Cornershop
Azorr, Chris
  See Cherry Poppin' Daddies
Aztec Camera 22
B, Daniel
  See Front 242
B-52's, The 4
B-Real
  See Cypress Hill
Baah, Reebop Kwaku
  See Traffic
Babatunde, Don
  See Last Poets
Babes in Toyland 16
Babjak, James
Babyface
  See Edmonds, Kenneth "Babyface"
Bacharach, Burt 20
  Earlier sketch in CM 1
Bachman, Eric
  See Archers of Loaf
Bachman, Randy
  See Guess Who
Backstreet Boys 21
Bad Brains 16
Bad Company 22
Bad Livers, The 19
Badalamenti, Angelo 17
Badfinger 23
Badger, Pat
  See Extreme
Badrena, Manola
  See Weather Report
Badu, Erykah 26
Baez, Joan 1
Bailey, Keith
  See Gong
Bailey, Mildred 13
Bailey, Pearl 5
Bailey, Phil
  See Earth, Wind and Fire
Bailey, Victor
  See Weather Report
Baker, Anita 9
Baker, Arthur 23
Baker, Bobby
  See Tragically Hip, The
Baker, Chet 13
Baker, Ginger 16
  Also see Cream
Baker, Janet 14
Baker, Jon
  See Charlatans, The
Baker, Josephine 10
Baker, LaVern 25
Balakrishnan, David
  See Turtle Island String Quartet
Balch, Bob
  See Fu Manchu
Balch, Michael
  See Front Line Assembly
Baldursson, Sigtryggur
  See Sugarcubes, The
Baldwin, Donny
  See Starship
Baliardo, Diego
  See Gipsy Kings, The
Baliardo, Paco
  See Gipsy Kings, The

Baliardo, Tonino
  See Gipsy Kings, The
Balin, Marty
  See Jefferson Airplane
Ball, Marcia **15**
Ballard, Florence
  See Supremes, The
Ballard, Hank **17**
Balsley, Phil
  See Statler Brothers, The
Baltes, Peter
  See Dokken
Balzano, Vinnie
  See Less Than Jake
Bambaataa, Afrika **13**
Bamonte, Perry
  See Cure, The
Bananarama **22**
Bancroft, Cyke
  See Bevis Frond
Band, The **9**
Bangles **22**
Banks, Nick
  See Pulp
Banks, Peter
  See Yes
Banks, Tony
  See Genesis
Baptiste, David Russell
  See Meters, The
Barbarossa, Dave
  See Republica
Barbata, John
  See Jefferson Starship
Barber, Keith
  See Soul Stirrers, The
Barbero, Lori
  See Babes in Toyland
Barbieri, Gato **22**
Bardens, Peter
  See Camel
Barenaked Ladies **18**
Bargeld, Blixa
  See Einstürzende Neubauten
Bargeron, Dave
  See Blood, Sweat and Tears
Barham, Meriel
  See Lush
Barile, Jo
  See Ventures, The
Barker, Paul
  See Ministry
Barker, Travis Landon
  See Aquabats
Barlow, Barriemore
  See Jethro Tull
Barlow, Lou **20**
  Also see Dinosaur Jr.
Barlow, Tommy
  See Aztec Camera
Barnes, Danny
  See Bad Livers, The
Barnes, Micah
  See Nylons, The
Barnes, Roosevelt "Booba" **23**
Barnett, Mandy **26**
Barnwell, Duncan
  See Simple Minds
Barnwell, Ysaye Maria
  See Sweet Honey in the Rock
Barr, Ralph
  See Nitty Gritty Dirt Band, The
Barre, Martin
  See Jethro Tull

Barrere, Paul
  See Little Feat
Barrett, (Roger) Syd
  See Pink Floyd
Barrett, Dicky
  See Mighty Mighty Bosstones
Barrett, Robert
  See Goodie Mob
Barron, Christopher
  See Spin Doctors
Barrow, Geoff
  See Portishead
Bartels, Joanie **13**
Bartholomew, Simon
  See Brand New Heavies, The
Bartoli, Cecilia **12**
Barton, Lou Ann
  See Fabulous Thunderbirds, The
Bartos, Karl
  See Kraftwerk
Basehead **11**
Basher, Mick
  See X
Basia **5**
Basie, Count **2**
Bass, Colin
  See Camel
Bass, Lance
  See 'N Sync
Bass, Ralph **24**
Batchelor, Kevin
  See Big Mountain
  See Steel Pulse
Batel, Beate
  See Einstürzende Neubauten
Batiste, Lionel
  See Dirty Dozen
Batoh, Masaki
  See Ghost
Batoh, Masaki
  See Pearls Before Swine
Battin, Skip
  See Byrds, The
Battle, Kathleen **6**
Bauer, Judah
  See Jon Spencer Blues Explosion
Baumann, Peter
  See Tangerine Dream
Bautista, Roland
  See Earth, Wind and Fire
Baxter, Adrian
  See Cherry Poppin' Daddies
Baxter, Jeff
  See Doobie Brothers, The
Bayer Sager, Carole
  See Sager, Carole Bayer
Baylor, Helen **20**
Baynton-Power, David
  See James
Bazilian, Eric
  See Hooters
Beach Boys, The **1**
Beale, Michael
  See Earth, Wind and Fire
Beard, Annette
  See Martha and the Vandellas
Beard, Frank
  See ZZ Top
Beasley, Paul
  See Mighty Clouds of Joy, The
Beastie Boys **25**
  Earlier sketch in CM **8**
Beat Farmers **23**
Beatles, The **2**

Beauford, Carter
  See Dave Matthews Band
Beautiful South **19**
Beaver Brown Band, The **3**
Bechet, Sidney **17**
Beck **18**
Beck, Jeff **4**
  Also see Yardbirds, The
Beck, William
  See Ohio Players
Becker, Walter
  See Steely Dan
Beckford, Theophilus
  See Skatalites, The
Beckley, Gerry
  See America
Bee Gees, The **3**
Beers, Garry Gary
  See INXS
Behler, Chuck
  See Megadeth
Beiderbecke, Bix **16**
Belafonte, Harry **8**
Belew, Adrian **5**
  Also see King Crimson
Belfield, Dennis
  See Three Dog Night
Bell, Andy
  See Erasure
Bell, Brian
  See Weezer
Bell, Derek
  See Chieftains, The
Bell, Eric
  See Thin Lizzy
Bell, Jayn
  See Sounds of Blackness
Bell, Joshua **21**
Bell, Melissa
  See Soul II Soul
Bell, Ronald
  See Kool & the Gang
Bell, Taj
  See Charm Farm
Belladonna, Joey
  See Anthrax
Bellamy Brothers, The **13**
Bellamy, David
  See Bellamy Brothers, The
Bellamy, Howard
  See Bellamy Brothers, The
Belle, Regina **6**
Bello, Elissa
  See Go-Go's, The
Bello, Frank
  See Anthrax
Belly **16**
Belushi, John
  See Blues Brothers, The
Ben Folds Five **20**
Benante, Charlie
  See Anthrax
Benatar, Pat **8**
Benckert, Vicki
  See Roxette
Benedict, Scott
  See Pere Ubu
Bengry, Peter
  See Cornershop
Benitez, Jellybean **15**
Bennett, Brian
  See Shadows, The
Bennett, Tony **16**
  Earlier sketch in CM **2**

Bennett-Nesby, Ann
   See Sounds of Blackness
Benson, George 9
Benson, Ray
   See Asleep at the Wheel
Benson, Renaldo "Obie"
   See Four Tops, The
Bentley, John
   See Squeeze
Benton, Brook 7
Bentyne, Cheryl
   See Manhattan Transfer, The
Berenyi, Miki
   See Lush
Berg, Matraca 16
Bergeson, Ben
   See Aquabats
Berggren, Jenny
   See Ace of Base
Berggren, Jonas
   See Ace of Base
Berggren, Linn
   See Ace of Base
Berigan, Bunny 2
Berkely, Anthony
   See Gravediggaz
Berlin, Irving 8
Berlin, Steve
   See Los Lobos
Berndt, Jay
   See Kilgore
Bernstein, Leonard 2
Berry, Bill
   See R.E.M.
Berry, Chuck 1
Berry, John 17
Berry, Robert
   See Emerson, Lake & Palmer/Powell
Berryhill, Bob
   See Surfaris, The
Bessant, Jack
   See Reef
Best, Nathaniel
   See O'Jays, The
Best, Pete
   See Beatles, The
Bettencourt, Nuno
   See Extreme
Better Than Ezra 19
Bettie Serveert 17
Bettini, Tom
   See Jackyl
Betts, Dicky
   See Allman Brothers, The
Bevan, Bev
   See Black Sabbath
   See Electric Light Orchestra
Bevis Frond 23
Bezozi, Alan
   See Dog's Eye View
Biafra, Jello 18
Big Audio Dynamite 18
Big Head Todd and the Monsters 20
Big Mike
   See GetoBoys, The
Big Money Odis
   See Digital Underground
Big Mountain 23
Bill Wyman & the Rhythm Kings 26
Bin Hassan, Umar
   See Last Poets
Bingham, John
   See Fishbone
Binks, Les
   See Judas Priest

Biondo, George
   See Steppenwolf
Birchfield, Benny
   See Osborne Brothers, The
Bird
   See Parker, Charlie
Birdsong, Cindy
   See Supremes, The
Birdstuff
   See Man or Astroman?
Biscuits, Chuck
   See Danzig
   See Social Distortion
Bishop, Michael
   See Gwar
Biz Markie 10
BizzyBone
   See Bone Thugs-N-Harmony
Bjelland, Kat
   See Babes in Toyland
Bjork, Brant
   See Fu Manchu
Björk 16
   Also see Sugarcubes, The
Black, Clint 5
Black Crowes, The 7
Black Flag 22
Black Francis
   See Black, Frank
Black, Frank 14
Black, Mary 15
Black Sabbath 9
Black Sheep 15
Black Uhuru 12
Black, Vic
   See C + C Music Factory
BlackHawk 21
Blackman, Cindy 15
Blackman, Tee-Wee
   See Memphis Jug Band
Blackmore, Ritchie
   See Deep Purple
Blackstreet 23
Blackwell, Chris 26
Blackwood, Sarah
   See Dubstar
Bladd, Stephen Jo
   See J. Geils Band
Blades, Ruben 2
Blake, Eubie 19
Blake, Norman
   See Teenage Fanclub
Blake, Tim
   See Gong
Blakey, Art 11
Blanchard, Terence 13
Bland, Bobby "Blue" 12
Blatt, Melanie
   See All Saints
Blegen, Jutith 23
Blessid Union of Souls 20
Bley, Carla 8
Bley, Paul 14
Blige, Mary J. 15
Blind Melon 21
Block, Rory 18
Blondie 14
Blood, Dave
   See Dead Milkmen
Blood, Sweat and Tears 7
Bloom, Eric
   See Blue Oyster Cult
Bloom, Luka 14
Blue, Buddy
   See Beat Farmers

Blue Oyster Cult 16
Blue Rodeo 18
Bluegrass Patriots 22
Blues, "Joliet" Jake
   See Blues Brothers, The
Blues Brothers, The 3
Blues, Elwood
   See Blues Brothers, The
Blues Traveler 15
Blunstone, Colin
   See Zombies, The
Blunt, Martin
   See Charlatans, The
Blur 17
Bob, Tim
   See Rage Against the Machine
Bocelli, Andrea 22
BoDeans, The 20
   Earlier sketch in CM 3
Boff, Richard
   See Chumbawamba
Bogaert, Jo
   See Technotronic
Bogdan, Henry
   See Helmet
Boggs, Dock 25
Bogguss, Suzy 11
Bogle, Bob
   See Ventures, The
Bohannon, Jim
   See Pearls Before Swine
Bolade, Nitanju
   See Sweet Honey in the Rock
Bolan, Marc
   See T. Rex
Bolton, Michael 4
Bon Jovi, Jon
   See Bon Jovi
Bon Jovi 10
Bonamy, James 21
Bone Thugs-N-Harmony 18
Bonebrake, D. J.
   See X
Bonham, John
   See Led Zeppelin
Bonnecaze, Cary
   See Better Than Ezra
Bonner, Leroy "Sugarfoot"
   See Ohio Players
Bono
   See U2
Bono, Sonny
   See Sonny and Cher
Bonsall, Joe
   See Oak Ridge Boys, The
Boo Radleys, The 21
Booker T. & the M.G.'s 24
Books
   See Das EFX
Boone, Pat 13
Booth, Tim
   See James
Boquist, Dave
   See Son Volt
Boquist, Jim
   See Son Volt
Bordin, Mike
   See Faith No More
Borg, Bobby
   See Warrant
Borge, Victor 19
Borowiak, Tony
   See All-4-One

Bostaph, Paul
  See Slayer
Boston **11**
Bostrom, Derrick
  See Meat Puppets, The
Bottum, Roddy
  See Faith No More
Bouchard, Albert
  See Blue Oyster Cult
Bouchard, Joe
  See Blue Oyster Cult
Bouchikhi, Chico
  See Gipsy Kings, The
Boulez, Pierre **26**
Bowen, Jimmy
  See Country Gentlemen, The
Bowens, Sir Harry
  See Was (Not Was)
Bowie, David **23**
  Earlier sketch in CM **1**
Bowie, Lester
  See Art Ensemble of Chicago, The
Bowman, Steve
  See Counting Crows
Box, Mick
  See Uriah Heep
Boy Howdy **21**
Boyd, Brandon
  See Incubus
Boyd, Eadie
  See Del Rubio Triplets
Boyd, Elena
  See Del Rubio Triplets
Boyd, Liona **7**
Boyd, Milly
  See Del Rubio Triplets
Boyle, Doug
  See Caravan
Boyz II Men **15**
Bozulich, Carla
  See Geraldine Fibbers
Brad **21**
Bradbury, John
  See Specials, The
Bradshaw, Tim
  See Dog's Eye View
Bradstreet, Rick
  See Bluegrass Patriots
Brady, Paul **8**
Bragg, Billy **7**
Bramah, Martin
  See Fall, The
Brand New Heavies, The **14**
Brandt, Paul **22**
Brandy **19**
Branigan, Laura **2**
Brannon, Kippi **20**
Brantley, Junior
  See Roomful of Blues
Braxton, Anthony **12**
Braxton, Toni **17**
Bream, Julian **9**
Breeders **19**
Brendel, Alfred **23**
Brennan, Ciaran
  See Clannad
Brennan, Enya
  See Clannad
Brennan, Maire
  See Clannad
Brennan, Paul
  See Odds
Brennan, Pol
  See Clannad

Brenner, Simon
  See Talk Talk
Brevette, Lloyd
  See Skatalites, The
Brickell, Edie **3**
Brickman, Jim **22**
Bridgewater, Dee Dee **18**
Briggs, David
  See Pearls Before Swine
Briggs, James Randall
  See Aquabats
Briggs, Vic
  See Animals
Bright, Garfield
  See Shai
Bright, Ronnie
  See Coasters, The
Brightman, Sarah **20**
Briley, Alex
  See Village People, The
Brindley, Paul
  See Sundays, The
Britten, Benjamin **15**
Brittingham, Eric
  See Cinderella
Brix
  See Fall, The
Brockenborough, Dennis
  See Mighty Mighty Bosstones
Brockie, Dave
  See Gwar
Brokop, Lisa **22**
Bromberg, David **18**
Bronfman, Yefim **6**
Brooke, Jonatha
  See Story, The
Brookes, Jon
  See Charlatans, The
Brooks & Dunn **25**
  Earlier sketch in CM **12**
Brooks, Baba
  See Skatalites, The
Brooks, Garth **25**
  Earlier sketch in CM **8**
Brooks III, Leon Eric "Kix"
  See Brooks & Dunn,
Broonzy, Big Bill **13**
Brotherdale, Steve
  See Joy Division
  See Smithereens, The
Brötzmann, Peter **26**
Broudie, Ian
  See Lightning Seeds
Brown, Bobby **4**
Brown, Brooks
  See Cherry Poppin' Daddies
Brown, Clarence "Gatemouth" **11**
Brown, Clifford **24**
Brown, Donny
  See Verve Pipe, The
Brown, Duncan
  See Stereolab
Brown, Foxy **25**
Brown, George
  See Kool & the Gang
Brown, Harold
  See War
Brown, Heidi
  See Treadmill Trackstar
Brown, Ian
  See Stone Roses, The
Brown, James **16**
  Earlier sketch in CM **2**
Brown, Jimmy
  See UB40

Brown, Junior **15**
Brown, Lawrence **23**
Brown, Marty **14**
Brown, Melanie
  See Spice Girls
Brown, Mick
  See Dokken
Brown, Morris
  See Pearls Before Swine
Brown, Norman
  See Mills Brothers, The
Brown, Rahem
  See Artifacts
Brown, Ray **21**
Brown, Ruth **13**
Brown, Selwyn "Bumbo"
  See Steel Pulse
Brown, Steven
  See Tuxedomoon
Brown, Tim
  See Boo Radleys, The
Brown, Tony **14**
Browne, Jackson **3**
  Also see Nitty Gritty Dirt Band, The
Brownstein, Carrie
  See Sleater-Kinney
Brownstone **21**
Brubeck, Dave **8**
Bruce, Dustan
  See Chumbawamba
Bruce, Jack
  See Cream
Bruford, Bill
  See King Crimson
  See Yes
Bruster, Thomas
  See Soul Stirrers, The
Bryan, David
  See Bon Jovi
Bryan, Karl
  See Skatalites, The
Bryan, Mark
  See Hootie and the Blowfish
Bryant, Elbridge
  See Temptations, The
Bryant, Jeff
  See Ricochet
Bryant, Junior
  See Ricochet
Bryson, Bill
  See Desert Rose Band, The
Bryson, David
  See Counting Crows
Bryson, Peabo **11**
Buchanan, Wallis
  See Jamiroquai
Buchholz, Francis
  See Scorpions, The
Buchignani, Paul
  See Afghan Whigs
Buck, Mike
  See Fabulous Thunderbirds, The
Buck, Peter
  See R.E.M.
Buck, Robert
  See 10,000 Maniacs
Buckingham, Lindsey **8**
  Also see Fleetwood Mac
Buckley, Betty **16**
  Earlier sketch in CM **1**
Buckley, Jeff **22**
Buckley, Tim **14**
Buckwheat Zydeco **6**
Budgie
  See Siouxsie and the Banshees

Buerstatte, Phil
See White Zombie
Buffalo Springfield 24
Buffalo Tom 18
Buffett, Jimmy 4
Bulgarian State Radio and Television Female
Vocal Choir, The
See Bulgarian State Female Vocal Choir,
The
Bulgarian State Female Vocal Choir, The 10
Bulgin, Lascelle
See Israel Vibration
Bullock, Craig
See Sugar Ray
Bumbry, Grace 13
Bumpus, Cornelius
See Doobie Brothers, The
Bunker, Clive
See Jethro Tull
Bunnell, Dewey
See America
Bunskoeke, Herman
See Bettie Serveert
Bunton, Emma
See Spice Girls
Burch, Curtis
See New Grass Revival, The
Burchill, Charlie
See Simple Minds
Burden, Ian
See Human League, The
Burdon, Eric
See Animals
Burdon, Eric 14
Also see War
Burgess, Paul
See Camel
Burgess, Tim
See Charlatans, The
Burke, Clem
See Blondie
Burkum, Tyler
See Audio Adrenaline
Burnett, Carol 6
Burnett, T Bone 13
Burnette, Billy
See Fleetwood Mac
Burnham, Hugo
See Gang of Four
Burning Spear 15
Burns, Bob
See Lynyrd Skynyrd
Burns, Karl
See Fall, The
Burr, Clive
See Iron Maiden
Burrell, Boz
See Bad Company
Burrell, Kenny 11
Burrell
See King Crimson
Burroughs, William S. 26
Burse, Charlie
See Memphis Jug Band
Burse, Robert
See Memphis Jug Band
Burton, Cliff
See Metallica
Burton, Gary 10
Burton, Tim
See Mighty Mighty Bosstones
Busby, Jheryl 9
Bush 18
Bush, Dave
See Fall, The

Bush, John
See Anthrax
Bush, Kate 4
Bush, Sam
See New Grass Revival, The
Bushwick, Bill
See Geto Boys, The
Busta Rhymes 18
Butler, Bernard
See Suede
Butler, Richard
See Love Spit Love
Butler, Terry "Geezer"
See Black Sabbath
Butler, Tim
See Love Spit Love
Butterfly
See Digable Planets
Butthole Surfers 16
Buttrey, Kenneth
See Pearls Before Swine
Buzzcocks, The 9
Byers, Roddy
See Specials, The
Byrds, The 8
Byrne, David 8
Also see Talking Heads
Byrne, Dermot
See Altan
Byrom, Larry
See Steppenwolf
Byron, David
See Uriah Heep
Byron, Don 22
Byron, Lord T.
See Lords of Acid
C + C Music Factory 16
Caballe, Monserrat 23
Cabaret Voltaire 18
Cachao
See Lopez, Israel "Cachao"
Cadogan, Kevin
See Third Eye Blind
Caesar, Shirley 17
Cafferty, John
See Beaver Brown Band, The
Caffey, Charlotte
See Go-Go's, The
Cage, John 8
Cahn, Sammy 11
Cain, Jonathan
See Journey
Calderon, Mark
See Color Me Badd
Cale, J. J. 16
Cale, John 9
Also see Velvet Underground, The
Calhoun, Will
See Living Colour
California, Randy
See Spirit
Calire, Mario
See Wallflowers, The
Callahan, Ken
See Jayhawks, The
Callas, Maria 11
Callis, Jo
See Human League, The
Calloway, Cab 6
Camel 21
Cameron, Duncan
See Sawyer Brown
Cameron, G. C.
See Spinners, The

Cameron, Matt
See Soundgarden
Campbell, Ali
See UB40
Campbell, Glen 2
Campbell, Kerry
See War
Campbell, Luther 10
Campbell, Martyn
See Lightning Seeds
Campbell, Phil
See Motörhead
Campbell, Robin
See UB40
Campbell, Sarah Elizabeth 23
Campbell, Tevin 13
Canadian Brass, The 4
Cantrell, Jerry
See Alice in Chains
Canty, Brendan
See Fugazi
Capaldi, Jim
See Traffic
Cappelli, Frank 14
Captain Beefheart and the Magic Band 26
Earlier sketch in CM 10
Caravan 24
Cardigans 19
Cardwell, Joi 22
Carey, Danny
See Tool
Carey, Mariah 20
Earlier sketch in CM 6
Carlisle, Belinda 8
Also see Go-Go's, The
Carlisle, Bob 22
Carlos, Bun E.
See Cheap Trick
Carlos, Don
See Black Uhuru
Carlson, Paulette
See Highway 101
Carnes, Kim 4
Carpenter, Bob
See Nitty Gritty Dirt Band, The
Carpenter, Karen
See Carpenters, The
Carpenter, Richard 24
Also see Carpenters, The
Carpenter, Stephen
See Deftones
Carpenters, The 13
Carr, Ben
See Mighty Mighty Bosstones
Carr, Eric
See Kiss
Carr, James 23
Carr, Martin
See Boo Radleys, The
Carr, Teddy
See Ricochet
Carrack, Paul
See Mike & the Mechanics
See Squeeze
Carreras, José 8
Carrigan, Andy
See Mekons, The
Carroll, Earl "Speedo"
See Coasters, The
Carruthers, John
See Siouxsie and the Banshees
Cars, The 20
Carter, A. P.
See Carter Family, The

Carter, Anita
  See Carter Family, The
Carter, Benny **3**
  Also see McKinney's Cotton Pickers
Carter, Betty **6**
Carter, Carlene **8**
Carter, Deana **25**
Carter Family, The **3**
Carter, Helen
  See Carter Family, The
Carter, James **18**
Carter, Janette
  See Carter Family, The
Carter, Jimmy
  See Five Blind Boys of Alabama
Carter, Joe
  See Carter Family, The
Carter, June **6**
  Also see Carter Family, The
Carter, Maybell
  See Carter Family, The
Carter, Nell **7**
Carter, Nick
  See Backstreet Boys
Carter, Regina **22**
Carter, Ron **14**
Carter, Sara
  See Carter Family, The
Carthy, Martin
  See Steeleye Span
Caruso, Enrico **10**
Casady, Jack
  See Jefferson Airplane
Casale, Bob
  See Devo
Casale, Gerald V.
  See Devo
Casals, Pablo **9**
Case, Peter **13**
Cash, Johnny **17**
  Earlier sketch in CM **1**
Cash, Rosanne **2**
Cassidy, Ed
  See Spirit
Catallo, Gene
  See Surfin' Pluto
Catallo, Shris
  See Surfin' Pluto
Cates, Ronny
  See Petra
Catherall, Joanne
  See Human League, The
Catherine Wheel **18**
Caustic Window
  See Aphex Twin
Cauty, Jimmy
  See Orb, The
Cavalera, Igor
  See Sepultura
Cavalera, Max
  See Sepultura
Cave, Nick **10**
Cavoukian, Raffi
  See Raffi
Cease, Jeff
  See Black Crowes, The
Cervenka, Exene
  See X
Cetera, Peter
  See Chicago
Chamberlin, Jimmy
  See Smashing Pumpkins
Chambers, Martin
  See Pretenders, The

Chambers, Paul **18**
Chambers, Terry
  See XTC
Champion, Eric **21**
Chance, Slim
  See Cramps, The
Chancellor, Justin
  See Tool
Chandler, Chas
  See Animals
Chandra, Sheila **16**
Chaney, Jimmy
  See Jimmie's Chicken Shack
Chang, Sarah **7**
Channing, Carol **6**
Chapin Carpenter, Mary **25**
  Earlier sketch in CM **6**
Chapin, Harry **6**
Chapin, Tom **11**
Chapman, Steven Curtis **15**
Chapman, Tony
  See Rolling Stones, The
Chapman, Tracy **20**
  Earlier sketch in CM **4**
Chaquico, Craig **23**
  Also see Jefferson Starship
Charlatans, The **13**
Charles, Ray **24**
  Earlier sketch in CM **1**
Charles, Yolanda
  See Aztec Camera
Charm Farm **20**
Chasez, Joshua Scott "JC"
  See 'N Sync
Che Colovita, Lemon
  See Jimmie's Chicken Shack
Chea, Alvin "Vinnie"
  See Take 6
Cheap Trick **12**
Checker, Chubby **7**
Cheeks, Julius
  See Soul Stirrers, The
Chemical Brothers **20**
Cheng, Chi
  See Deftones
Chenier, C. J. **15**
Chenier, Clifton **6**
Chenille Sisters, The **16**
Cher **1**
  Also see Sonny and Cher
Cherone, Gary
  See Extreme
Cherone, Gary
  See Van Halen
Cherry, Don **10**
Cherry, Neneh **4**
Cherry Poppin' Daddies **24**
Chesney, Kenny **20**
Chesnutt, Mark **13**
Chess, Leonard **24**
Chevalier, Maurice **6**
Chevron, Phillip
  See Pogues, The
Chicago **3**
Chieftains, The **7**
Childress, Ross
  See Collective Soul
Childs, Toni **2**
Chilton, Alex **10**
Chimes, Terry
  See Clash, The
Chin, Tony
  See Big Mountain

Chisholm, Melanie
  See Spice Girls
Chopmaster J
  See Digital Underground
Chrisman, Andy
  See FourHim
Christ, John
  See Danzig
Christian, Charlie **11**
Christina, Fran
  See Fabulous Thunderbirds, The
  See Roomful of Blues
Chuck D
  See Public Enemy
Chumbawamba **21**
Chung, Mark
  See Einstürzende Neubauten
Church, Kevin
  See Country Gentlemen, The
Church, The **14**
Cieka, Rob
  See Boo Radleys, The
Cinderella **16**
Cinelu, Mino
  See Weather Report
Cipollina, John
  See Quicksilver Messenger Service
Circle Jerks, The **17**
Cissell, Ben
  See Audio Adrenaline
Clannad **23**
Clapton, Eric **11**
  Earlier sketch in CM **1**
  Also see Cream
  Also see Yardbirds, The
Clark, Alan
  See Dire Straits
Clark, Dave
  See Dave Clark Five, The
Clark, Dick **25**
  Earlier sketch in CM **2**
Clark, Gene
  See Byrds, The
Clark, Graham
  See Gong
Clark, Guy **17**
Clark, Keith
  See Circle Jerks, The
Clark, Mike
  See Suicidal Tendencies
Clark, Roy **1**
Clark, Steve
  See Def Leppard
Clark, Terri **19**
Clark, Tony
  See Blessid Union of Souls
Clarke, "Fast" Eddie
  See Motörhead
Clarke, Bernie
  See Aztec Camera
Clarke, Michael
  See Byrds, The
Clarke, Stanley **3**
Clarke, Vince
  See Depeche Mode
  See Erasure
Clarke, William
  See Third World
Clash, The **4**
Clayderman, Richard **1**
Claypool, Les
  See Primus
Clayton, Adam
  See U2

Clayton, Sam
  See Little Feat
Clayton-Thomas, David
  SeeBlood, Sweat and Tears
Clean, Dean
  See Dead Milkmen
Cleaves, Jessica
  See Earth, Wind and Fire
Clegg, Johnny 8
Clements, Vassar 18
Clemons, Clarence 7
Cleveland, James 1
Cliburn, Van 13
Cliff, Jimmy 8
Clifford, Douglas Ray
  See Creedence Clearwater Revival
Cline, Nels
  See Geraldine Fibbers
Cline, Patsy 5
Clinton, George 7
Clivilles, Robert
  See C + C Music Factory
Clooney, Rosemary 9
Clouser, Charlie
  See Prong
Coasters, The 5
Cobain, Kurt
  See Nirvana
Cobham, Billy
  See Mahavishnu Orchestra
Cochran, Bobby
  See Steppenwolf
Cochrane, Tom 23
Cockburn, Bruce 8
Cocker, Jarvis
  See Pulp
Cocker, Joe 4
Cocking, William "Willigan"
  See Mystic Revealers
Coco the Electronic Monkey Wizard
  See Man or Astroman?
Cocteau Twins, The 12
Codenys, Patrick
  See Front 242
Codling, Neil
  See Suede
Coe, David Allan 4
Coffey, Jeff
  See Butthole Surfers
Coffey, Jr., Don
  See Superdrag
Coffie, Calton
  See Inner Circle
Cohen, Jeremy
  See Turtle Island String Quartet
Cohen, Leonard 3
Cohen, Porky
  See Roomful of Blues
Colaiuta, Vinnie 23
Colbourn, Chris
  See Buffalo Tom
Cole, David
  See C + C Music Factory
Cole, Holly 18
Cole, Lloyd 9
Cole, Nat King 3
Cole, Natalie 21
  Earlier sketch in CM 1
Cole, Paula 20
Cole, Ralph
  See Nylons, The
Coleman, Ornette 5
Collective Soul 16
Colletti, Dominic
  See Bevis Frond

Colley, Dana
  See Morphine
Collie, Mark 15
Collin, Phil
  See Def Leppard
Collins, Albert 19
  Earlier sketch in CM 4
Collins, Allen
  See Lynyrd Skynyrd
Collins, Bootsy 8
Collins, Chris
  See Dream Theater
Collins, Judy 4
Collins, Mark
  See Charlatans, The
Collins, Mel
  See Camel
  See King Crimson
Collins, Phil 20
  Earlier sketch in CM 2
  Also see Genesis
Collins, Rob
  See Charlatans, The
Collins, William
  See Collins, Bootsy
Colomby, Bobby
  See Blood, Sweat and Tears
Color Me Badd 23
Colt, Johnny
  See Black Crowes, The
Coltrane, John 4
Colvin, Shawn 11
Colwell, David
  See Bad Company
Combs, Sean "Puffy" 16
Comess, Aaron
  See Spin Doctors
Commodores, The 23
Common 23
Como, Perry 14
Compulsion 23
Confederate Railroad 23
Congo Norvell 22
Conneff, Kevin
  See Chieftains, The
Connelly, Chris
  See KMFDM
Connick, Harry, Jr. 4
Connolly, Pat
  See Surfaris, The
Connors, Marc
  See Nylons, The
Conti, Neil
  See Prefab Sprout
Conway, Billy
  See Morphine
Conway, Gerry
  See Pentangle
Cooder, Ry 2
Cook, Greg
  See Ricochet
Cook, Jeffrey Alan
  See Alabama
Cook, Paul
  See Sex Pistols, The
Cook, Stuart
  See Creedence Clearwater Revival
Cook, Wayne
  See Steppenwolf
Cooke, Sam 1
  Also see Soul Stirrers, The
Cool, Tre
  See Green Day
Coolio 19

Coomes, Sam
  See Quasi
Cooney, Rory 6
Cooper, Alice 8
Cooper, Jason
  See Cure, The
Cooper, Martin
  See Orchestral Manoeuvres in the Dark
Cooper, Michael
  See Third World
Cooper, Paul
  See Nylons, The
Cooper, Ralph
  See Air Supply
Coore, Stephen
  See Third World
Cope, Julian 16
Copeland, Stewart 14
  Also see Police, The
Copland, Aaron 2
Copley, Al
  See Roomful of Blues
Corea, Chick 6
Corella, Doug
  See Verve Pipe, The
Corgan, Billy
  See Smashing Pumpkins
Corina, Sarah
  See Mekons, The
Cornelius, Robert
  See Poi Dog Pondering
Cornell, Chris
  See Soundgarden
Cornershop 24
Cornick, Glenn
  See Jethro Tull
Corrigan, Brianna
  See Beautiful South
Cosper, Kina
  See Brownstone
Costello, Elvis 12
  Earlier sketch in CM 2
Coté, Billy
  See Madder Rose
Cotoia, Robert
  See Beaver Brown Band, The
Cotrubas, Ileana 1
Cotten, Elizabeth 16
Cotton, Caré
  See Sounds of Blackness
Cougar, John(ny)
  See Mellencamp, John
Coughlan, Richard
  See Caravan
Counting Crows 18
Country Gentlemen, The 7
Coury, Fred
  See Cinderella
Coutts, Duncan
  See Our Lady Peace
Coverdale, David
  See Whitesnake 5
Cowan, John
  See New Grass Revival, The
Cowboy Junkies, The 4
Cox, Andy
  See English Beat, The
  See Fine Young Cannibals
Cox, Terry
  See Pentangle
Coxon, Graham
  See Blur
Coyne, Mark
  See Flaming Lips

Coyne, Wayne
  See Flaming Lips
Cracker 12
Craig, Albert
  See Israel Vibration
Craig, Carl 19
Crain, S. R.
  See Soul Stirrers, The
Cramps, The 16
Cranberries, The 14
Crash Test Dummies 14
Crawford, Da'dra
  See Anointed
Crawford, Dave Max
  See Poi Dog Pondering
Crawford, Ed
  See fIREHOSE
Crawford, Michael 4
Crawford, Randy 25
Crawford, Steve
  See Anointed
Cray, Robert 8
Creach, Papa John
  See Jefferson Starship
Cream 9
Creedence Clearwater Revival 16
Creegan, Andrew
  See Barenaked Ladies
Creegan, Jim
  See Barenaked Ladies
Crenshaw, Marshall 5
Cretu, Michael
  See Enigma
Criss, Peter
  See Kiss,
Crissinger, Roger
  See Pearls Before Swine
Croce, Jim 3
Crofts, Dash
  See Seals & Crofts
Cronin, Kevin
  See REO Speedwagon
Cropper, Steve 12
Cropper, Steve
  See Booker T. & the M.G.'s
Crosby, Bing 6
Crosby, David 3
  Also see Byrds, The
  Also see Crosby, Stills, and Nash
Crosby, Stills, and Nash 24
Cross, Bridget
  See Velocity Girl
Cross, David
  See King Crimson
Cross, Mike
  See Sponge
Cross, Tim
  See Sponge
Crouch, Andraé 9
Crover, Dale
  See Melvins
Crow, Sheryl 18
Crowded House 12
Crowe, J. D. 5
Crowell, Rodney 8
Crowley, Martin
  See Bevis Frond
Cruikshank, Gregory
  See Tuxedomoon
Cruz, Celia 22
  Earlier sketch in CM 10
Cuddy, Jim
  See Blue Rodeo
Cugat, Xavier 23
Cult, The 16

Cumming, Graham
  See Bevis Frond
Cummings, Burton
  See Guess Who
Cummings, Danny
  See Dire Straits
Cummings, David
  See Del Amitri
Cunningham, Abe
  See Deftones
Cunningham, Ruth
  See Anonymous 4
Cuomo, Rivers
  See Weezer
Cure, The 20
  Earlier sketch in CM 3
Curless, Ann
  See Exposé
Curley, John
  See Afghan Whigs
Curran, Ciaran
  See Altan
Currie, Justin
  See Del Amitri
Currie, Kevin
  See Supertramp
Currie, Steve
  See T. Rex
Curry, Tim 3
Curtis, Ian
  See Joy Division
Curtis, King 17
Curve 13
Custance, Mickey
  See Big Audio Dynamite
Cuthbert, Scott
  See Everclear
Cutler, Chris
  See Pere Ubu
Cypress Hill 11
Cyrus, Billy Ray 11
D Generation 26
D.J. Lethal
  See House of Pain
D.J. Minutemix
  See P.M. Dawn
D'Angelo 20
D'Angelo, Greg
  See Anthrax
D'Arby, Terence Trent 3
Dacus, Donnie
  See Chicago
Dacus, Johnny
  See Osborne Brothers, The
Daddy G
  See Massive Attack
Daddy Mack
  See Kris Kross
Daellenbach, Charles
  See Canadian Brass, The
Dahlheimer, Patrick
  See Live
Daisley, Bob
  See Black Sabbath
Dale, Dick 13
Daley, Richard
  See Third World
Dall, Bobby
  See Poison
Dallin, Sarah
  See Bananarama
Dalton, John
  See Kinks, The
Dalton, Nic
  See Lemonheads, The

Daltrey, Roger 3
  Also see Who, The
Dammers, Jerry
  See Specials, The
Damon and Naomi 25
Dando, Evan
  See Lemonheads, The
Dandy Warhols 22
Danell, Dennis
  See Social Distortion
Daniels, Charlie 6
Daniels, Jack
  See Highway 101
Daniels, Jerry
  See Ink Spots
Danko, Rick
  See Band, The
Danny Boy
  See House of Pain
Danzig 7
Danzig, Glenn
  See Danzig
Darin, Bobby 4
Darling, Eric
  See Weavers, The
Darriau, Matt
  See Klezmatics, The
Darvill, Benjamin
  See Crash Test Dummies
Das EFX 14
Daugherty, Jay Dee
  See Church, The
Daulne, Marie
  See Zap Mama
Dave Clark Five, The 12
Dave, Doggy
  See Lords of Acid
Dave Matthews Band 18
Davenport, N'Dea
  See Brand New Heavies, The
Davidson, Lenny
  See Dave Clark Five, The
Davie, Hutch
  See Pearls Before Swine
Davies, Dave
  See Kinks, The
Davies, Dennis Russell 24
Davies, James
  See Jimmie's Chicken Shack
Davies, Ray 5
  Also see Kinks, The
Davies, Richard
  See Supertramp
Davies, Saul
  See James
Davis, Anthony 17
Davis, Brad
  See Fu Manchu
Davis, Chip 4
Davis, Clive 14
Davis, Gregory
  See Dirty Dozen
Davis, Jody
  See Newsboys, The
Davis, John
  See Superdrag
Davis, Jonathan
  See Korn
Davis, Linda 21
Davis, Michael
  See MC5, The
Davis, Miles 1
Davis, Reverend Gary 18
Davis, Sammy, Jr. 4

Davis, Santa
  See Big Mountain
Davis, Skeeter **15**
Davis, Spencer
  See Spencer Davis Group
Davis, Steve
  See Mystic Revealers
Davis, Zelma
  See C + C Music Factory
Dawdy, Cheryl
  See Chenille Sisters, The
Dawn, Sandra
  See Platters, The
Day, Doris **24**
Dayne, Taylor **4**
dc Talk **18**
de Albuquerque, Michael
  See Electric Light Orchestra
de Burgh, Chris **22**
de Coster, Jean Paul
  See 2 Unlimited
de Grassi, Alex **6**
de la Rocha, Zack
  See Rage Against the Machine
de Lucia, Paco **1**
de Prume, Ivan
  See White Zombie
de Young, Joyce
  See Andrews Sisters, The
De Borg, Jerry
  See Jesus Jones
De La Soul **7**
De La Luna, Shai
  See Lords of Acid
De Meyer, Jean-Luc
  See Front 242
De Oliveria, Laudir
  See Chicago
Deacon, John
  See Queen
Dead Can Dance **16**
Dead Milkmen **22**
Deakin, Paul
  See Mavericks, The
Deal, Kelley
  See Breeders
Deal, Kim
  See Breeders
  See Pixies, The
Dean, Billy **19**
DeBarge, El **14**
Dee, Mikkey
  See Dokken
  See Motörhead
Deee-lite **9**
Deep Forest **18**
Deep Purple **11**
Def Leppard **3**
Deftones **22**
DeGarmo, Chris
  See Queensryche
Deibert, Adam Warren
  See Aquabats
Deily, Ben
  See Lemonheads, The
DeJohnette, Jack **7**
Del Amitri **18**
Del Mar, Candy
  See Cramps, The
Del Rubio Triplets **21**
Delaet, Nathalie
  See Lords of Acid
DeLeo, Dean
  See Stone Temple Pilots

DeLeo, Robert
  See Stone Temple Pilots
DeLorenzo, Victor
  See Violent Femmes
Delp, Brad
  See Boston
DeMent, Iris **13**
Demento, Dr. **23**
Demeski, Stanley
  See Luna
Demos, Greg
  See Guided By Voices
Dempsey, Michael
  See Cure, The
Denison, Duane
  See Jesus Lizard
Dennis, Garth
  See Black Uhuru
Denny, Sandy
  See Fairport Convention
Densmore, John
  See Doors, The
Dent, Cedric
  See Take 6
Denton, Sandy
  See Salt-N-Pepa
Denver, John **22**
  Earlier sketch in CM **1**
Depeche Mode **5**
Derosier, Michael
  See Heart
Des'ree **24**
  Earlier sketch in CM **15**
Desaulniers, Stephen
  See Scud Mountain Boys
Deschamps, Kim
  See Blue Rodeo
Desert Rose Band, The **4**
Desmond, Paul **23**
Destri, Jimmy
  See Blondie
Deupree, Jerome
  See Morphine
Deutrom, Mark
  See Melvins
DeVille, C. C.
  See Poison
Devito, Tommy
  See Four Seasons, The
Devo **13**
Devoto, Howard
  See Buzzcocks, The
DeWitt, Lew C.
  See Statler Brothers, The
Dexter X
  See Man or Astroman?
Di Meola, Al **12**
Di'anno, Paul
  See Iron Maiden
Diagram, Andy
  See James
Diamond "Dimebag" Darrell
  See Pantera
Diamond, Mike
  See Beastie Boys, The
Diamond, Neil **1**
Diamond Rio **11**
Dibango, Manu **14**
Dick, Magic
  See J. Geils Band
Dickens, Little Jimmy **7**
Dickerson, B.B.
  See War
Dickinson, Paul Bruce
  See Iron Maiden

Dickinson, Rob
  See Catherine Wheel
Diddley, Bo **3**
Dietrich, Marlene **25**
Diffie, Joe **10**
Difford, Chris
  See Squeeze
DiFranco, Ani **17**
Digable Planets **15**
Diggle, Steve
  See Buzzcocks, The
Diggs, Robert
  See Gravediggaz
Digital Underground **9**
Dilworth, Joe
  See Stereolab
DiMant, Leor
  See House of Pain
DiMucci, Dion
  See Dion
DiNizo, Pat
  See Smithereens, The
Dinning, Dean
  See Toad the Wet Sprocket
Dinosaur Jr. **10**
Dio, Ronnie James
  See Black Sabbath
Dion **4**
Dion, Celine **25**
  Earlier sketch in CM **12**
Dire Straits **22**
Dirks, Michael
  See Gwar
Dirnt, Mike
  See Green Day
Dirty Dozen **23**
Dittrich, John
  See Restless Heart
Dixie Chicks **26**
Dixon, George W.
  See Spinners, The
Dixon, Jerry
  See Warrant
Dixon, Willie **10**
DJ Domination
  See Geto Boys, The
DJ Fuse
  See Digital Underground
DJ Jazzy Jeff and the Fresh Prince **5**
DJ Muggs
  See Cypress Hill
DJ Premier
  See Gang Starr
DJ Ready Red
  See Geto Boys, The
DJ Terminator X
  See Public Enemy
DMC
  See Run DMC
DMX **25**
Doc Pomus **14**
Doe, John
  See X
Dog's Eye View **21**
Dogbowl
  See King Missile
Doherty, Denny
  See Mamas and the Papas
Dokken **16**
Dokken, Don
  See Dokken
Dolby, Monica Mimi
  See Brownstone
Dolby, Thomas **10**

Dolenz, Micky
  See Monkees, The
Dombroski, Vinnie
  See Sponge
Domingo, Placido **20**
  Earlier sketch in CM **1**
Dominici, Charlie
  See Dream Theater
Domino, Fats **2**
Don, Rasa
  See Arrested Development
Donahue, Jerry
  See Fairport Convention
Donahue, Jonathan
  See Flaming Lips
Donald, Tony
  See Simple Minds
Donelly, Tanya
  See Belly
  See Breeders
  See Throwing Muses
Donohue, Tim
  See Cherry Poppin' Daddies
Donovan **9**
Donovan, Bazil
  See Blue Rodeo
Doobie Brothers, The **3**
Doodlebug
  See Digable Planets
Doors, The **4**
Dorge, Michel (Mitch)
  See Crash Test Dummies
Dorney, Tim
  See Republica
Dorough, Bob
  See Pearls Before Swine
Dorough, Howie
  See Backstreet Boys
Dorsey Brothers, The **8**
Dorsey, Jimmy
  See Dorsey Brothers, The
Dorsey, Thomas A. **11**
Dorsey, Tommy
  See Dorsey Brothers, The
Doth, Anita
  See 2 Unlimited
Dott, Gerald
  See Incredible String Band
Doucet, Michael **8**
Doughty, M.
  See Soul Coughing
Doughty, Neal
  See REO Speedwagon
Douglas, Jerry
  See Country Gentlemen, The
Dowd, Christopher
  See Fishbone
Dowling, Dave
  See Jimmie's Chicken Shack
Downes, Geoff
  See Yes
Downey, Brian
  See Thin Lizzy
Downie, Gordon
  See Tragically Hip, The
Downing, K. K.
  See Judas Priest
Doyle, Candida
  See Pulp
Dozier, Lamont
  See Holland-Dozier-Holland
Dr. Dre **15**
  Also see N.W.A.
Dr. John **7**

Drake, Nick **17**
Drake, Steven
  See Odds
Drayton, Leslie
  See Earth, Wind and Fire
Dream Theater **23**
Dreja, Chris
  See Yardbirds, The
Drew, Dennis
  See 10,000 Maniacs
Driftwood, Jimmy **25**
Droge, Pete **24**
Dropkick Murphys **26**
Drozd, Stephen
  See Flaming Lips
Dru Hill **25**
Drumbago,
  See Skatalites, The
Drumdini, Harry
  See Cramps, The
Drummond, Don
  See Skatalites, The
Drummond, Tom
  See Better Than Ezra
Dryden, Spencer
  See Jefferson Airplane
Dubbe, Berend
  See Bettie Serveert
Dube, Lucky **17**
Dubstar **22**
Dudley, Anne
  See Art of Noise
Duffey, John
  See Country Gentlemen, The
  See Seldom Scene, The
Duffy, Billy
  See Cult, The
Duffy, Martin
  See Primal Scream
Dufresne, Mark
  See Confederate Railroad
Duggan, Noel
  See Clannad
Duggan, Paidraig
  See Clannad
Duke, John
  See Pearls Before Swine
Dukowski, Chuck
  See Black Flag
Dulli, Greg
  See Afghan Whigs
Dumont, Tom
  See No Doubt
Dunbar, Aynsley
  See Jefferson Starship
  See Journey
  See Whitesnake
Dunbar, Sly
  See Sly and Robbie
Duncan, Bryan **19**
Duncan, Gary
  See Quicksilver Messenger Service
Duncan, Steve
  See Desert Rose Band, The
Duncan, Stuart
  See Nashville Bluegrass Band
Dunlap, Slim
  See Replacements, The
Dunn, Donald "Duck"
  See Booker T. & the M.G.'s
Dunn, Holly **7**
Dunn, Larry
  See Earth, Wind and Fire
Dunn, Ronnie Gene
  See Brooks & Dunn

Dunning, A.J.
  See Verve Pipe, The
DuPré, Jacqueline **26**
Dupree, Champion Jack **12**
Dupree, Jimmy
  See Jackyl
Dupri, Jermaine **25**
Duran Duran **4**
Durante, Mark
  See KMFDM
Duritz, Adam
  See Counting Crows
Durrill, Johnny
  See Ventures, The
Dutt, Hank
  See Kronos Quartet
Dvorak, Antonin **25**
Dyble, Judy
  See Fairport Convention
Dylan, Bob **21**
  Earlier sketch in CM **3**
Dylan, Jakob
  See Wallflowers, The
D'Amour, Paul
  See Tool
E., Sheila
  See Sheila E.
Eacrett, Chris
  See Our Lady Peace
Eagles, The **3**
Earl, Ronnie **5**
  Also see Roomful of Blues
Earle, Steve **16**
Earle, Steve
  See Afghan Whigs
Early, Ian
  See Cherry Poppin' Daddies
Earth, Wind and Fire **12**
Easton, Elliot
  See Cars, The
Easton, Sheena **2**
Eazy-E **13**
  Also see N.W.A.
Echeverria, Rob
  See Helmet
Echobelly **21**
Eckstine, Billy **1**
Eddy, Duane **9**
Eden, Sean
  See Luna
Edge, Graeme
  See Moody Blues, The
Edge, The
  See U2
Edmonds, Kenneth "Babyface" **12**
Edmonton, Jerry
  See Steppenwolf
Edwards, Dennis
  See Temptations, The
Edwards, Edgar
  See Spinners, The
Edwards, Gordon
  See Kinks, The
Edwards, John
  See Spinners, The
Edwards, Johnny
  See Foreigner
Edwards, Leroy "Lion"
  See Mystic Revealers
Edwards, Mark
  See Aztec Camera
Edwards, Michael James
  See Jesus Jones
Edwards, Mike
  See Electric Light Orchestra

Edwards, Nokie
　See Ventures, The
Edwards, Skye
　See Morcheeba
Efrem, Towns
　See Dirty Dozen
Ehran
　See Lords of Acid
Eid, Tamer
　See Emmet Swimming
Einheit, F.M.
　See KMFDM
Einheit
　See Einstürzende Neubauten
Einstürzende Neubauten **13**
Einziger, Michael
　See Incubus
Eisenstein, Michael
　See Letters to Cleo
Eitzel, Mark
　See American Music Club
Ekberg, Ulf
　See Ace of Base
Eklund, Greg
　See Everclear
El-Hadi, Sulieman
　See Last Poets
Eldon, Thór
　See Sugarcubes, The
Eldridge, Ben
　See Seldom Scene, The
Eldridge, Roy **9**
　Also see McKinney's Cotton Pickers
Electric Light Orchestra **7**
Elfman, Danny **9**
Elias, Manny
　See Tears for Fears
Ellefson, Dave
　See Megadeth
Ellington, Duke **2**
Elliot, Cass **5**
Elliot, Joe
　See Def Leppard
Elliott, Cass
　See Mamas and the Papas
Elliott, Dennis
　See Foreigner
Elliott, Doug
　See Odds
Ellis, Arti
　See Pearls Before Swine
Ellis, Bobby
　See Skatalites, The
Ellis, Herb **18**
Ellis, Terry
　See En Vogue
Elmore, Greg
　See Quicksilver Messenger Service
ELO
　See Electric Light Orchestra
Ely, John
　See Asleep at the Wheel
Ely, Vince
　See Cure, The
Emerson, Bill
　See Country Gentlemen, The
Emerson, Keith
　See Emerson, Lake & Palmer/Powell
Emerson, Lake & Palmer/Powell **5**
Emery, Jill
　See Hole
Emmanuel, Tommy **21**
Emmet Swimming **24**
En Vogue **10**

English Beat, The **9**
English, Michael **23**
English, Richard
　See Flaming Lips
Enigma **14**
Eno, Brian **8**
Enos, Bob
　See Roomful of Blues
Enright, Pat
　See Nashville Bluegrass Band
Entwistle, John
　See Who, The
Enya **6**
EPMD **10**
Erasure **11**
Eric B.
　See Eric B. and Rakim
Eric B. and Rakim **9**
Erickson, Roky **16**
Erikson, Duke
　See Garbage
Erlandson, Eric
　See Hole
Errico, Greg
　See Sly & the Family Stone
Errico, Greg
　See Quicksilver Messenger Service
Erskine, Peter
　See Weather Report
Ertegun, Ahmet **10**
Ertegun, Nesuhi **24**
Esch, En
　See KMFDM
Escovedo, Alejandro **18**
Eshe, Montsho
　See Arrested Development
Eskelin, Ian **19**
Esler-Smith, Frank
　See Air Supply
Esquivel, Juan **17**
Estefan, Gloria **15**
　Earlier sketch in CM **2**
Estes, Sleepy John **25**
Estrada, Roy
　See Little Feat
Etheridge, Melissa **16**
　Earlier sketch in CM **4**
Eurythmics **6**
Evan, John
　See Jethro Tull
Evans, Bill **17**
Evans, Dick
　See U2
Evans, Faith **25**
Evans, Gil **17**
Evans, Mark
　See AC/DC
Evans, 'Shane
　See Collective Soul
Evans, Tom
　See Badfinger
Everclear **18**
Everlast
　See House of Pain
Everly Brothers, The **2**
Everly, Don
　See Everly Brothers, The
Everly, Phil
　See Everly Brothers, The
Everman, Jason
　See Soundgarden
Everything But The Girl **15**
Evora, Cesaria **19**
Ewen, Alvin
　See Steel Pulse

Exkano, Paul
　See Five Blind Boys of Alabama
Exposé **4**
Extreme **10**
Ezell, Ralph
　See Shenandoah
Fabian **5**
Fabulous Thunderbirds, The **1**
Faces, The **22**
Fadden, Jimmie
　See Nitty Gritty Dirt Band, The
Fagan, Don
　See Steely Dan
Fahey, John **17**
Fahey, Siobhan
　See Bananarama
Fairport Convention **22**
Fairs, Jim
　See Pearls Before Swine
Faith No More **7**
Faithfull, Marianne **14**
Fakir, Abdul "Duke"
　See Four Tops, The
Falconer, Earl
　See UB40
Fall, The **12**
Fallon, David
　See Chieftains, The
Fältskog, Agnetha
　See Abba
Fambrough, Henry
　See Spinners, The
Fankhauser, Merrell **24**
Farley, J. J.
　See Soul Stirrers, The
Farndon, Pete
　See Pretenders, The
Farrar, Jay
　See Son Volt
Farrar, John
　See Shadows, The
Farrell, Frank
　See Supertramp
Farrell, Perry
　See Jane's Addiction
Farris, Dionne
　See Arrested Development
Farris, Tim
　See Israel Vibration
Farriss, Andrew
　See INXS
Farriss, Jon
　See INXS
Farriss, Tim
　See INXS
Fatboy Slim **22**
Fatone, Joey
　See 'N Sync
Fay, Johnny
　See Tragically Hip, The
Fay, Martin
　See Chieftains, The
Fearnley, James
　See Pogues, The
Fehlmann, Thomas
　See Orb, The
Feinstein, Michael **6**
Fela
　See Kuti, Fela
Felber, Dean
　See Hootie and the Blowfish
Felder, Don
　See Eagles, The
Feldman, Eric Drew
　See Pere Ubu

Feliciano, José **10**
Fender, Freddy
  See Texas Tornados, The
Fender, Leo **10**
Fennell, Kevin
  See Guided By Voices
Fennelly, Gere
  See Redd Kross
Fenwick, Ray
  See Spencer Davis Group
Ferguson, Jay
  See Spirit
Ferguson, Keith
  See Fabulous Thunderbirds, The
Ferguson, Maynard **7**
Ferguson, Neil
  See Chumbawamba
Ferguson, Steve
  See NRBQ
Ferrell, Rachelle **17**
Ferrer, Frank
  See Love Spit Love
Ferry, Bryan **1**
Ficca, Billy
  See Television
Fiedler, Arthur **6**
Fielder, Jim
  See Blood, Sweat and Tears
Fields, Johnny
  See Five Blind Boys of Alabama
Fier, Anton
  See Pere Ubu
Finch, Jennifer
  See L7
Fine Young Cannibals **22**
Finer, Jem
  See Pogues, The
Fink, Jr., Rat
  See Alien Sex Fiend
Finn, Micky
  See T. Rex
Finn, Neil
  See Crowded House
Finn, Tim
  See Crowded House
fIREHOSE **11**
Fishbone **7**
Fisher, Brandon
  See Superdrag
Fisher, Eddie **12**
Fisher, Jerry
  See Blood, Sweat and Tears
Fisher, John "Norwood"
  See Fishbone
Fisher, Phillip "Fish"
  See Fishbone
Fisher, Roger
  See Heart
Fishman, Jon
  See Phish
Fitzgerald, Ella **1**
Fitzgerald, Kevin
  See Geraldine Fibbers
Five Blind Boys of Alabama **12**
Five Iron Frenzy **26**
Flack, Roberta **5**
Flaming Lips **22**
Flanagan, Tommy **16**
Flannery, Sean
  See Cherry Poppin' Daddies
Flansburgh, John
  See They Might Be Giants
Flatt, Lester **3**
Flavor Flav
  See Public Enemy

Flea
  See Red Hot Chili Peppers, The
Fleck, Bela **8**
  Also see New Grass Revival, The
Fleetwood Mac **5**
Fleetwood, Mick
  See Fleetwood Mac
Fleischmann, Robert
  See Journey
Fleming, Renee **24**
Flemons, Wade
  See Earth, Wind and Fire
Flesh-N-Bone
  See Bone Thugs-N-Harmony
Fletcher, Andy
  See Depeche Mode
Fletcher, Guy
  See Dire Straits
Flint, Keith
  See Prodigy
Flores, Rosie **16**
Floyd, Heather
  See Point of Grace
Flür, Wolfgang
  See Kraftwerk
Flynn, Pat
  See New Grass Revival, The
Fogelberg, Dan **4**
Fogerty, John **2**
  Also see Creedence Clearwater Revival
Fogerty, Thomas
  See Creedence Clearwater Revival
Folds, Ben
  See Ben Folds Five
Foley
  See Arrested Development
Foo Fighters **20**
Forbes, Derek
  See Simple Minds
Forbes, Graham
  See Incredible String Band
Ford, Lita **9**
Ford, Mark
  See Black Crowes, The
Ford, Penny
  See Soul II Soul
Ford, Robert "Peg"
  See Golden Gate Quartet
Ford, Tennessee Ernie **3**
Fordham, Julia **15**
Foreigner **21**
Forsi, Ken
  See Surfaris, The
Fortune, Jimmy
  See Statler Brothers, The
Fortus, Richard
  See Love Spit Love
Fossen, Steve
  See Heart
Foster, David **13**
Foster, Malcolm
  See Pretenders, The
Foster, Paul
  See Soul Stirrers, The
Foster, Radney **16**
Fountain, Clarence
  See Five Blind Boys of Alabama
Fountain, Pete **7**
Fountains of Wayne **26**
Four Seasons, The **24**
Four Tops, The **11**
FourHim **23**
Fox, Lucas
  See Motörhead

Fox, Oz
  See Stryper
Fox, Samantha **3**
Foxwell Baker, Iain Richard
  See Jesus Jones
Frame, Roddy
  See Aztec Camera
Frampton, Peter **3**
Francis, Black
  See Pixies, The
Francis, Connie **10**
Francis, Mike
  See Asleep at the Wheel
Franke, Chris
  See Tangerine Dream
Frankenstein, Jeff
  See Newsboys, The
Frankie Lymon and The Teenagers **24**
Franklin, Aretha **17**
  Earlier sketch in CM **2**
Franklin, Elmo
  See Mighty Clouds of Joy, The
Franklin, Kirk **22**
Franklin, Larry
  See Asleep at the Wheel
Franklin, Melvin
  See Temptations, The
Franti, Michael **16**
Frantz, Chris
  See Talking Heads
Fraser, Elizabeth
  See Cocteau Twins, The
Frater, Shaun
  See Fairport Convention
Frazier, Stan
  See Sugar Ray
Fredriksson, Marie
  See Roxette
Freese, Josh
  See Suicidal Tendencies
Frehley, Ace
  See Kiss
Freiberg, David
  See Quicksilver Messenger Service
Freiberg, David
  See Jefferson Starship
French, Mark
  See Blue Rodeo
Freni, Mirella **14**
Freshwater, John
  See Alien Sex Fiend
Frey, Glenn **3**
  Also see Eagles, The
Fricker, Sylvia
  See Ian and Sylvia
Friedman, Marty
  See Megadeth
Friel, Tony
  See Fall, The
Fripp, Robert **9**
  Also see King Crimson
Frisell, Bill **15**
Frishmann, Justine
  See Suede
Frith, Fred **19**
Frizzell, Lefty **10**
Froese, Edgar
  See Tangerine Dream
Front 242 **19**
Front Line Assembly **20**
Froom, Mitchell **15**
Frusciante, John
  See Red Hot Chili Peppers, The
Fu Manchu **22**

Fugazi **13**
Fugees, The **17**
Fulber, Rhys
  See Front Line Assembly
Fuller, Blind Boy **20**
Fuller, Jim
  See Surfaris, The
Fulson, Lowell **20**
Fun Lovin' Criminals **20**
Fuqua, Charlie
  See Ink Spots
Furay, Richie
  See Buffalo Springfield
Furler, Peter
  See Newsboys, The
Furr, John
  See Treadmill Trackstar
Furuholmen, Magne
  See A-ha
Futter, Brian
  See Catherine Wheel
Gabay, Yuval
  See Soul Coughing
Gabler, Milton **25**
Gabriel, Peter **16**
  Earlier sketch in CM **2**
  Also see Genesis
Gadler, Frank
Gagliardi, Ed
  See Foreigner
Gahan, Dave
  See Depeche Mode
Gaines, Steve
  See Lynyrd Skynyrd
Gaines, Timothy
  See Stryper
Galás, Diamanda **16**
Gale, Melvyn
  See Electric Light Orchestra
Galea, Darren
  See Jamiroquai
Gallagher, Liam
  See Oasis
Gallagher, Noel
  See Oasis
Gallup, Simon
  See Cure, The
Galore, Lady
  See Lords of Acid
Galway, James **3**
Gambill, Roger
  See Kingston Trio, The
Gamble, Cheryl "Coko"
  See SWV
Gane, Tim
  See Stereolab
Gang of Four **8**
Gang Starr **13**
Gannon, Craig
  See Aztec Camera
Gano, Gordon
  See Violent Femmes
Garbage **25**
Garcia, Dean
  See Curve
Garcia, Jerry **4**
  Also see Grateful Dead, The
Garcia, Leddie
  See Poi Dog Pondering
Gardiner, John Eliot **26**
Gardner, Carl
  See Coasters, The
Gardner, Suzi
  See L7

Garfunkel, Art **4**
  Also see Simon and Garfunkel
Garland, Judy **6**
Garner, Erroll **25**
Garnes, Sherman
  See Frankie Lymon and The Teenagers
Garrett, Amos
  See Pearls Before Swine
Garrett, Peter
  See Midnight Oil
Garrett, Scott
  See Cult, The
Garvey, Steve
  See Buzzcocks, The
Gaskill, Jerry
  See King's X
Gatton, Danny **16**
Gaudio, Bob
  See Four Seasons, The
Gaudreau, Jimmy
  See Country Gentlemen, The
Gaugh, "Bud" Floyd, IV
  See Sublime
Gavurin, David
  See Sundays, The
Gay, Marc
  See Shai
Gayden, Mac
  See Pearls Before Swine
Gaye, Marvin **4**
Gayle, Crystal **1**
Gaynor, Mel
  See Simple Minds
Gayol, Rafael "Danny"
  See BoDeans
Geary, Paul
  See Extreme
Gee, Rosco
  See Traffic
Geffen, David **8**
Geils, J.
  See J. Geils Band
Geldof, Bob **9**
Genensky, Marsha
  See Anonymous 4
Genesis **4**
Gentling, Matt
  See Archers of Loaf
Gentry, Teddy Wayne
  See Alabama
George, Lowell
  See Little Feat
George, Rocky
  See Suicidal Tendencies
Georges, Bernard
  See Throwing Muses
Georgiev, Ivan
  See Tuxedomoon
Geraldine Fibbers **21**
Germano, Lisa **18**
Gerrard, Lisa
  See Dead Can Dance
Gershwin, George and Ira **11**
Gessle, Per
  See Roxette
GetoBoys, The **11**
Getz, Stan **12**
Ghost **24**
Giammalvo, Chris
  See Madder Rose
Gianni, Angelo
  See Treadmill Trackstar
Gibb, Barry
  See Bee Gees, The

Gibb, Maurice
  See Bee Gees, The
Gibb, Robin
  See Bee Gees, The
Gibbins, Mike
  See Badfinger
Gibbons, Beth
  See Portishead
Gibbons, Billy
  See ZZ Top
Gibbons, Ian
  See Kinks, The
Giblin, John
  See Simple Minds
Gibson, Bob **23**
Gibson, Debbie
  See Gibson, Deborah
Gibson, Deborah **24**
  Earlier sketch in CM **1**
Gibson, Wilf
  See Electric Light Orchestra
Gifford, Katharine
  See Stereolab
Gifford, Peter
  See Midnight Oil
Gift, Roland **3**
  Also see Fine Young Cannibals
Gil, Gilberto **26**
Gilbert, Gillian
  See New Order
Gilbert, Nicole Nicci
  See Brownstone
Gilbert, Ronnie
  See Weavers, The
Gilbert, Simon
  See Suede
Giles, Michael
  See King Crimson
Gilkyson, Tony
  See X
Gill, Andy
  See Gang of Four
Gill, Janis
  See Sweethearts of the Rodeo
Gill, Johnny **20**
Gill, Pete
  See Motörhead
Gill, Vince **7**
Gillan, Ian
  See Deep Purple
Gillespie, Bobby
  See Primal Scream
Gillespie, Dizzy **6**
Gilley, Mickey **7**
Gillian, Ian
  See Black Sabbath
Gillies, Ben
  See Silverchair
Gillingham, Charles
  See Counting Crows
Gilmore, Jimmie Dale **11**
Gilmour, David
  See Pink Floyd
Gin Blossoms **18**
Gingold, Josef **6**
Ginn, Greg
  See Black Flag
Ginsberg, Allen **26**
Gioia
  See Exposé
Gipp, Cameron
  See Goodie Mob
Gipsy Kings, The **8**

Giraudy, Miquitte
　See Gong
Gittleman, Joe
　See Mighty Mighty Bosstones
Glass, Eddie
　See Fu Manchu
Glass, Philip **1**
Glasscock, John
　See Jethro Tull
Glennie, Jim
　See James
Glitter, Gary **19**
Glover, Corey
　See Living Colour
Glover, Roger
　See Deep Purple
Go-Go's, The **24**
Gobel, Robert
　See Kool & the Gang
Godchaux, Donna
　See Grateful Dead, The
Godchaux, Keith
　See Grateful Dead, The
Godfrey, Paul
　See Morcheeba
Godfrey, Ross
　See Morcheeba
Goettel, Dwayne Rudolf
　See Skinny Puppy
Goffin, Gerry
　See Goffin-King
Goffin-King **24**
Gogin, Toni
　See Sleater-Kinney
Goh, Rex
　See Air Supply
Gold, Julie **22**
Golden Gate Quartet **25**
Golden, William Lee
　See Oak Ridge Boys, The
Golding, Lynval
　See Specials, The
Goldsmith, William
　See Foo Fighters
Goldstein, Jerry
　See War
Golson, Benny **21**
Gong **24**
Goo Goo Dolls, The **16**
Gooden, Ramone Pee Wee
　See Digital Underground
Goodie Mob **24**
Goodman, Benny **4**
Goodman, Jerry
　See Mahavishnu Orchestra
Goodridge, Robin
　See Bush
Gordon, Dexter **10**
Gordon, Dwight
　See Mighty Clouds of Joy, The
Gordon, Jim
　See Traffic
Gordon, Kim
　See Sonic Youth
Gordon, Mike
　See Phish
Gordon, Nina
　See Veruca Salt
Gordy, Berry, Jr. **6**
Gordy, Emory, Jr. **17**
Gore, Martin
　See Depeche Mode
Gorham, Scott
　See Thin Lizzy

Gorka, John **18**
Gorman, Christopher
　See Belly
Gorman, Steve
　See Black Crowes, The
Gorman, Thomas
　See Belly
Gosling, John
　See Kinks, The
Gossard, Stone
　See Brad
　See Pearl Jam
Gott, Larry
　See James
Goudreau, Barry
　See Boston
Gould, Billy
　See Faith No More
Gould, Glenn **9**
Gould, Morton **16**
Goulding, Steve
　See Poi Dog Pondering
Grable, Steve
　See Pearls Before Swine
Gracey, Chad
　See Live
Gradney, Ken
　See Little Feat
Graffety-Smith, Toby
　See Jamiroquai
Graham, Bill **10**
Graham, Glen
　See Blind Melon
Graham, Johnny
　See Earth, Wind and Fire
Graham, Larry
　See Sly & the Family Stone
Gramm, Lou
　See Foreigner
Gramolini, Gary
　See Beaver Brown Band, The
Grandmaster Flash **14**
Grant, Amy **7**
Grant, Bob
　See The Bad Livers
Grant Lee Buffalo **16**
Grant, Lloyd
　See Metallica
Grappelli, Stephane **10**
Grateful Dead, The **5**
Gratzer, Alan
　See REO Speedwagon
Gravatt, Eric
　See Weather Report
Gravediggaz **23**
Graves, Denyce **16**
Gray, Del
　See Little Texas
Gray, Ella
　See Kronos Quartet
Gray, F. Gary **19**
Gray, James
　See Spearhead
Gray, James
　See Blue Rodeo
Gray, Luther
　See Tsunami
Gray, Tom
　See Country Gentlemen, The
　See Seldom Scene, The
Gray, Walter
　See Kronos Quartet
Gray, Wardell
　See McKinney's Cotton Pickers

Greater Vision **26**
Grebenshikov, Boris **3**
Grech, Rick
　See Traffic
Greco, Paul
　See Chumbawamba
Green, Al **9**
Green, Benny **17**
Green, Carlito
　See Goodie Mob
Green, Charles
　See War
Green, David
　See Air Supply
Green Day **16**
Green, Grant **14**
Green, James
　See Dru Hill
Green, Karl Anthony
　See Herman's Hermits
Green, Peter
　See Fleetwood Mac
Green, Susaye
　See Supremes, The
Green, Willie
　See Neville Brothers, The
Greenhalgh, Tom
　See Mekons, The
Greensmith, Domenic
　See Reef
Greenspoon, Jimmy
　See Three Dog Night
Greenwood, Al
　See Foreigner
Greenwood, Gail
　See Belly
Greenwood, Jonny
　See Radiohead
Greenwood, Lee **12**
Greenwood, Colin
　See Radiohead
Greer, Jim
　See Guided By Voices
Gregg, Paul
　See Restless Heart
Gregory, Bryan
　See Cramps, The
Gregory, Dave
　See XTC
Gregory, Troy
　See Prong
Greller, Al
　See Yo La Tengo
Grey, Charles Wallace
　See Aquabats
Griffin, A.C. "Eddie"
　See Golden Gate Quartet
Griffin, Bob
　See BoDeans, The
Griffin, Kevin
　See Better Than Ezra
　See NRBQ
Griffin, Mark
　See MC 900 Ft. Jesus
Griffin, Patty **24**
Griffith, Nanci **3**
Grigg, Chris
　See Treadmill Trackstar
Grisman, David **17**
Grohl, Dave
　See Nirvana
Grohl, David
　See Foo Fighters
Grotberg, Karen
　See Jayhawks, The

Groucutt, Kelly
  See Electric Light Orchestra
Grove, George
  See Kingston Trio, The
Grover, Charlie
  See Sponge
Grundy, Hugh
  See Zombies, The
Grusin, Dave **7**
Guaraldi, Vince **3**
Guard, Dave
  See Kingston Trio, The
Gudmundsdottir, Björk
  See Björk
  Also see Sugarcubes, The
Guerin, John
  See Byrds, The
Guess Who **23**
Guest, Christopher
  See Spinal Tap
Guided By Voices **18**
Gunn, Trey
  See King Crimson
Guns n' Roses **2**
Gunther, Cornell
  See Coasters, The
Gunther, Ric
  See Bevis Frond
Guru
  See Gang Starr
Gus Gus **26**
Guss, Randy
  See Toad the Wet Sprocket
Gustafson, Steve
  See 10,000 Maniacs
Gut, Grudrun
  See Einstürzende Neubauten
Guthrie, Arlo **6**
Guthrie, Gwen **26**
Guthrie, Robin
  See Cocteau Twins, The
Guthrie, Woody **2**
Guy, Billy
  See Coasters, The
Guy, Buddy **4**
Guyett, Jim
  See Quicksilver Messenger Service
Gwar **13**
H.R.
  See Bad Brains
Hacke, Alexander
  See Einstürzende Neubauten
Hackett, Bobby **21**
Hackett, Steve
  See Genesis
Haden, Charlie **12**
Hadjopulos, Sue
  See Simple Minds
Hagar, Regan
  See Brad
Hagar, Sammy **21**
  Also see Van Halen
Hagen, Nina **25**
Haggard, Merle **2**
Hakim, Omar
  See Weather Report
Hakmoun, Hassan **15**
Hale, Simon
  See Incognito
Haley, Bill **6**
Haley, Mark
  See Kinks, The
Halford, Rob
  See Judas Priest

Hall & Oates **6**
Hall, Bruce
  See REO Speedwagon
Hall, Daryl
  See Hall & Oates
Hall, John S.
  See King Missile
Hall, Lance
  See Inner Circle
Hall, Randall
  See Lynyrd Skynyrd
Hall, Terry
  See Specials, The
Hall, Tom T. **26**
  Earlier sketch in CM **4**
Hall, Tony
  See Neville Brothers, The
Halliday, Toni
  See Curve
Halliwell, Geri
  See Spice Girls
Ham, Pete
  See Badfinger
Hamer, Harry
  See Chumbawamba
Hamilton, Arnold
  See Gravediggaz
Hamilton, Frank
  See Weavers, The
Hamilton, Katie
  See Treadmill Trackstar
Hamilton, Milton
  See Third World
Hamilton, Page
  See Helmet
Hamilton, Tom
  See Aerosmith
Hamlisch, Marvin **1**
Hammer, Jan **21**
  Also see Mahavishnu Orchestra
Hammer, M.C. **5**
Hammerstein, Oscar
  See Rodgers, Richard
Hammett, Kirk
  See Metallica
Hammon, Ron
  See War
Hammond, John **6**
Hammond-Hammond, Jeffrey
  See Jethro Tull
Hampson, Sharon
  See Sharon, Lois & Bram
Hampson, Thomas **12**
Hampton, Lionel **6**
Hancock, Herbie **25**
  Earlier sketch in CM **8**
Handy, W. C. **7**
Hanley, Kay
  See Letters to Cleo
Hanley, Steve
  See Fall, The
Hanna, Jeff
  See Nitty Gritty Dirt Band, The
Hannan, Patrick
  See Sundays, The
Hanneman, Jeff
  See Slayer
Hannibal, Chauncey "Black"
  See Blackstreet
Hannon, Frank
  See Tesla
Hansen, Mary
  See Stereolab
Hanson **20**

Hanson, Isaac
  See Hanson
Hanson, Paul
  See Gravediggaz
Hanson, Taylor
  See Hanson
Hanson, Zachary
  See Hanson
Hardcastle, Paul **20**
Hardin, Eddie
  See Spencer Davis Group
Hardin, Tim **18**
Harding, John Wesley **6**
Hardson, Tre "Slimkid"
  See Pharcyde, The
Hargreaves, Brad
  See Third Eye Blind
Hargrove, Kornell
  See Poi Dog Pondering
Hargrove, Roy **15**
Harket, Morten
  See A-ha
Harley, Bill **7**
Harley, Wayne
  See Pearls Before Swine
Harms, Jesse
  See REO Speedwagon
Harper, Ben **17**
Harper, Raymond
  See Skatalites, The
Harrell, Andre **16**
Harrell, Lynn **3**
Harrington, Carrie
  See Sounds of Blackness
Harrington, David
  See Kronos Quartet
Harris, Addie "Micki"
  See Shirelles, The
Harris, Damon Otis
  See Temptations, The
Harris, Eddie **15**
Harris, Emmylou **4**
Harris, Evelyn
  See Sweet Honey in the Rock
Harris, Gerard
  See Kool & the Gang
Harris, James
  See Echobelly
Harris, Jet
  See Shadows, The
Harris, Joey
  See Beat Farmers
Harris, Kevin
  See Dirty Dozen
Harris, Lee
  See Talk Talk
Harris, Mark
  See FourHim
Harris, Mary
  See Spearhead
Harris, R. H.
  See Soul Stirrers, The
Harris, Steve
  See Iron Maiden
Harris, Teddy **22**
Harrison, George **2**
  Also see Beatles, The
Harrison, Jerry
  See Talking Heads
Harrison, Nigel
  See Blondie
Harrison, Richard
  See Stereolab

Harry, Deborah **4**
 Also see Blondie
Hart, Chuck
 See Surfin' Pluto
Hart, Hattie
 See Memphis Jug Band
Hart, Lorenz
 See Rodgers, Richard
Hart, Mark
 See Crowded House
Hart, Mark
 See Supertramp
Hart, Mickey
 See Grateful Dead, The
Hart, Robert
 See Bad Company
Hart, Tim
 See Steeleye Span
Hartford, John **1**
Hartke, Stephen **5**
Hartley, Matthieu
 See Cure, The
Hartman, Bob
 See Petra
Hartman, John
 See Doobie Brothers, The
Hartnoll, Paul
 See Orbital
Hartnoll, Phil
 See Orbital
Harvey, Bernard "Touter"
 See Inner Circle
Harvey, Philip "Daddae"
 See Soul II Soul
Harvey, Polly Jean **11**
Harvie, Iain
 See Del Amitri
Harwood, Justin
 See Luna
Haseltine, Dan
 See Jars of Clay
Hashian
 See Boston
Haskell, Gordon
 See King Crimson
Haskins, Kevin
 See Love and Rockets
Haslinger, Paul
 See Tangerine Dream
Hassan, Norman
 See UB40
Hassman, Nikki
 Se e Avalon
Hastings, Jimmy
 See Caravan
Hastings, Pye
 See Caravan
Hatfield, Juliana **12**
 Also see Lemonheads, The
Hauser, Tim
 See Manhattan Transfer, The
Havens, Richie **11**
Hawes, Dave
 See Catherine Wheel
Hawkes, Greg
 See Cars, The
Hawkins, Coleman **11**
Hawkins, Erskine **19**
Hawkins, Nick
 See Big Audio Dynamite
Hawkins, Roger
 See Traffic
Hawkins, Screamin' Jay **8**
Hawkins, Sophie B. **21**

Hawkins, Taylor
 See Foo Fighters
Hawkins, Tramaine **17**
Hawkins, Xian
 See Silver Apples
Hay, George D. **3**
Hayes, Gordon
 See Pearls Before Swine
Hayes, Isaac **10**
Hayes, Roland **13**
Haynes, Gibby
 See Butthole Surfers
Haynes, Warren
 See Allman Brothers, The
Hays, Lee
 See Weavers, The
Hayward, David Justin
 See Moody Blues, The
Hayward, Richard
 See Little Feat
Headliner
 See Arrested Development
Headon, Topper
 See Clash, The
Healey, Jeff **4**
Heard, Paul
 See M People
Hearn, Kevin
 See Barenaked Ladies
Heart **1**
Heaton, Paul
 See Beautiful South
Heavy D **10**
Hecker, Robert
 See Redd Kross
Hedford, Eric
 See Blessid Union of Souls
Hedges, Eddie
 See Blessid Union of Souls
Hedges, Michael **3**
Heggie, Will
 See Cocteau Twins, The
Heidorn, Mike
 See Son Volt
Heitman, Dana
 See Cherry Poppin' Daddies
Helfgott, David **19**
Hell, Richard
 See Television
Hellauer, Susan
 See Anonymous 4
Hellerman, Fred
 See Weavers, The
Helliwell, John
 See Supertramp
Helm, Levon
 See Band, The
 Also see Nitty Gritty Dirt Band, The
Helmet **15**
Hemingway, Dave
 See Beautiful South
Hemmings, Paul
 See Lightning Seeds
Henderson, Andy
 See Echobelly
Henderson, Billy
 See Spinners, The
Henderson, Fletcher **16**
Henderson, Joe **14**
Hendricks, Barbara **10**
Hendrix, Jimi **2**
Henley, Don **3**
 Also see Eagles, The
Henrit, Bob
 See Kinks, The

Henry, Bill
 See Northern Lights
Henry, Joe **18**
Henry, Kent
 See Steppenwolf
Henry, Nicholas "Drummie"
 See Mystic Revealers
Hensley, Ken
 See Uriah Heep
Hepcat, Harry **23**
Heppner, Ben **23**
Herdman, Bob
 See Audio Adrenaline
Herman, Maureen
 See Babes in Toyland
Herman, Tom
 See Pere Ubu
Herman, Woody **12**
Herman's Hermits **5**
Herndon, Mark Joel
 See Alabama
Herndon, Ty **20**
Heron, Mike
 See Incredible String Band
Herrera, R. J.
 See Suicidal Tendencies
Herrlin, Anders
 See Roxette
Herrmann, Bernard **14**
Herron, Cindy
 See En Vogue
Hersh, Kristin
 See Throwing Muses
Hester, Paul
 See Crowded House
Hetfield, James
 See Metallica
Hetson, Greg
 See Circle Jerks, The
Hewson, Paul
 See U2
Hexum, Nick
 See 311
Hiatt, John **8**
Hickman, Johnny
 See Cracker
Hicks, Chris
 See Restless Heart
Hicks, Sheree
 See C + C Music Factory
Hidalgo, David
 See Los Lobos
Higgins, Jimmy
 See Altan
Higgins, Terence
 See Dirty Dozen
Highway 101 **4**
Hijbert, Fritz
 See Kraftwerk
Hill, Brendan
 See Blues Traveler
Hill, Dusty
 See ZZ Top
Hill, Faith **18**
Hill, Ian
 See Judas Priest
Hill, Lauryn **25**
 Also see Fugees, The
Hill, Scott
 See Fu Manchu
Hill, Stuart
 See Shudder to Think
Hillage, Steve
 See Orb, The

Hillage, Steve
  See Gong
Hillier, Steve
  See Dubstar
Hillman, Bones
  See Midnight Oil
Hillman, Chris
  See Byrds, The
  Also see Desert Rose Band, The
Hinderas, Natalie 12
Hinds, David
  See Steel Pulse
Hines, Earl "Fatha" 12
Hines, Gary
  See Sounds of Blackness
Hinojosa, Tish 13
Hirst, Rob
  See Midnight Oil
Hirt, Al 5
Hitchcock, Robyn 9
Hitchcock, Russell
  See Air Supply
Hitt, Bryan
  See REO Speedwagon
Hodge, Alex
  See Platters, The
Hodges, Johnny 24
Hodgson, Roger 26
  Also see Supertramp
Hodo, David
  See Village People, The
Hoenig, Michael
  See Tangerine Dream
Hoffman, Guy
  See BoDeans, The
  Also see Violent Femmes
Hoffman, Kristian
  See Congo Norvell
Hoffs, Susanna
  See Bangles
Hogan, Mike
  See Cranberries, The
Hogan, Noel
  See Cranberries, The
Hoke, Jim
  See NRBQ
Holder, Gene
  See Yo La Tengo
Hole 14
Holiday, Billie 6
Holland, Brian
  See Holland-Dozier-Holland
Holland, Bryan "Dexter"
  See Offspring
Holland, Dave
  See Judas Priest
Holland, Eddie
  See Holland-Dozier-Holland
Holland, Julian "Jools"
  See Squeeze
Holland-Dozier-Holland 5
Hollis, Mark
  See Talk Talk
Hollister, Dave
  See Blackstreet
Holly, Buddy 1
Holmes, Malcolm
  See Orchestral Manoeuvres in the Dark
Holmstrom, Peter
Holt, David Lee
  See Mavericks, The
Honeyman, Susie
  See Mekons, The
Honeyman-Scott, James
  See Pretenders, The

Hood, David
  See Traffic
Hook, Peter
  See Joy Division
  Also see New Order
Hooker, John Lee 26
  Earlier sketch in CM 1
Hoon, Shannon
  See Blind Melon
Hooper, Nellee
  See Soul II Soul
  Also see Massive Attack
Hooters 20
Hootie and the Blowfish 18
Hope, Gavin
  See Nylons, The
Hopkins, Doug
  See Gin Blossoms
Hopkins, Lightnin' 13
Hopkins, Nicky
  See Quicksilver Messenger Service
Hopwood, Keith
  See Herman's Hermits
Horn, Shirley 7
Horn, Trevor
  See Yes
Horne, Lena 11
Horne, Marilyn 9
Horner, Jessica
  See Less Than Jake
Hornsby, Bruce 25
  Earlier sketch in CM 3
Horovitz, Adam "King Ad-Rock"
  See Beastie Boys
Horowitz, Vladimir 1
Horton, Jeff
  See Northern Lights
Horton, Walter 19
Hossack, Michael
  See Doobie Brothers, The
Houari, Rachid
  See Gong
House, Kenwyn
  See Reef
House of Pain 14
House, Son 11
Houston, Cissy 26
  Earlier sketch in CM 6
Houston, Whitney 25
  Earlier sketch in CM 8
Howard, Harlan 15
Howe, Brian
  See Bad Company
Howe, Steve
  See Yes
Howell, Porter
  See Little Texas
Howland, Don 24
Howlett, Liam
  See Prodigy
Howlett, Mike
  See Gong
Howlin' Wolf 6
Hubbard, Greg "Hobie"
  See Sawyer Brown
Hubbard, Preston
  See Fabulous Thunderbirds, The
  Also see Roomful of Blues
Huber, Connie
  See Chenille Sisters, The
Hubrey, Georgia
  See Yo La Tengo
Hudson, Earl
  See Bad Brains

Hudson, Garth
  See Band, The
Huffman, Doug
  See Boston
Hughes, Bruce
  See Cracker
Hughes, Glenn
  See Black Sabbath
Hughes, Glenn
  See Village People, The
Hughes, Leon
  See Coasters, The
Human League, The 17
Humes, Helen 19
Humperdinck, Engelbert 19
Humphreys, Paul
  See Orchestral Manoeuvres in the Dark
Hunt, Darryl
  See Pogues, The
Hunter, Alberta 7
Hunter, Charlie 24
Hunter, Mark
  See James
Hunter, Shepherd "Ben"
  See Soundgarden
Hurley, George
  See fIREHOSE
Hurst, Ron
  See Steppenwolf
Hurt, Mississippi John 24
Hutchence, Michael
  See INXS
Hutchings, Ashley
  See Fairport Convention
  Also see Steeleye Span
Huth, Todd
  See Primus
Hütter, Ralf
  See Kraftwerk
Hutton, Danny
  See Three Dog Night
Huxley, Rick
  See Dave Clark Five, The
Hyatt, Aitch
  See Specials, The
Hyde, Michael
  See Big Mountain
Hyman, Jerry
  See Blood, Sweat and Tears
Hyman, Rob
  See Hooters
Hynde, Chrissie
  See Pretenders, The
Hyslop, Kenny
  See Simple Minds
Ian and Sylvia 18
Ian, Janis 24
  Earlier sketch in CM 5
Ian, Scott
  See Anthrax
Ibbotson, Jimmy
  See Nitty Gritty Dirt Band, The
Ibold, Mark
  See Pavement
Ibrahim, Abdullah 24
Ice Cube 25
  Earlier sketch in CM 10
  Also see N.W.A
Ice-T 7
Idol, Billy 3
Iglesias, Julio 20
  Earlier sketch in CM 2
Iha, James
  See Smashing Pumpkins
Ike and Tina Turner 24

Illsley, John
See Dire Straits
Imperial Teen 26
Incognito 16
Incredible String Band 23
Incubus 23
Indigo Girls 20
Earlier sketch in CM 3
Inez, Mike
See Alice in Chains
Infante, Frank
See Blondie
Ingram, Jack
See Incredible String Band
Ingram, James 11
Ink Spots 23
Inner Circle 15
Innes, Andrew
See Primal Scream
Innis, Dave
See Restless Heart
Insane Clown Posse 22
Interior, Lux
See Cramps, The
INXS 21
Earlier sketch in CM 2
Iommi, Tony
See Black Sabbath
Iron Maiden 10
Irons, Jack
See Red Hot Chili Peppers, The
Isaak, Chris 6
Isacsson, Jonas
See Roxette
Isham, Mark 14
Isles, Bill
See O'Jays, The
Isley Brothers, The 8
Isley, Ernie
See Isley Brothers, The
Isley, Marvin
See Isley Brothers, The
Isley, O'Kelly, Jr.
See Isley Brothers, The
Isley, Ronald
See Isley Brothers, The
Isley, Rudolph
See Isley Brothers, The
Israel Vibration 21
Ives, Burl 12
Ivey, Michael
See Basehead
Ivins, Michael
See Flaming Lips
J, David
See Love and Rockets
J. Geils Band 25
J.
See White Zombie
Jabs, Matthias
See Scorpions, The
Jackson 5, The
See Jacksons, The
Jackson, Al
See Booker T. & the M.G.'s
Jackson, Alan 25
Earlier sketch in CM 7
Jackson, Eddie
See Queensryche
Jackson, Freddie 3
Jackson, Jackie
See Jacksons, The
Jackson, Janet 16
Earlier sketch in CM 3

Jackson, Jermaine
See Jacksons, The
Jackson, Joe 22
Earlier sketch in CM 4
Jackson, Karen
See Supremes, The
Jackson, Mahalia 8
Jackson, Marlon
See Jacksons, The
Jackson, Michael 17
Earlier sketch in CM 1
Also see Jacksons, The
Jackson, Millie 14
Jackson, Milt 15
Jackson, Pervis
See Spinners , The
Jackson, Randy
See Jacksons, The
Jackson, Tito
See Jacksons, The
Jacksons, The 7
Jackyl 24
Jacobs, Christian Richard
See Aquabats
Jacobs, Jeff
See Foreigner
Jacobs, Parker
See Aquabats
Jacobs, Walter
See Little Walter
Jacox, Martin
See Soul Stirrers, The
Jacquet, Illinois 17
Jade 4U
See Lords of Acid
Jaffee, Rami
See Wallflowers, The
Jagger, Mick 7
Also see Rolling Stones, The
Jairo T.
See Sepultura
Jalal
See Last Poets
Jam, Jimmy
See Jam, Jimmy, and Terry Lewis
Jam, Jimmy, and Terry Lewis 11
Jam Master Jay
See Run DMC
James 12
James, Alex
See Blur
James, Andrew "Bear"
See Midnight Oil
James, Boney 21
James, Cheryl
See Salt-N-Pepa
James, David
See Spearhead
James, David
See Alien Sex Fiend
James, Doug
See Roomful of Blues
James, Elmore 8
James, Etta 6
James, Harry 11
James, Jesse
See Jackyl
James, John
See Newsboys, The
James, Onieda
See Spearhead
James, Richard
See Aphex Twin
James, Rick 2

James, Ruby
See Aztec Camera
James, Skip 24
James, Sylvia
See Aztec Camera
Jamiroquai 21
Jamison, Le Le
See Spearhead
Jane's Addiction 6
Janovitz, Bill
See Buffalo Tom
Jansch, Bert
See Pentangle
Jardine, Al
See Beach Boys, The
Jarman, Joseph
See Art Ensemble of Chicago, The
Jarobi
See Tribe Called Quest, A
Jarre, Jean-Michel 2
Jarreau, Al 1
Jarrett, Irwin
See Third World
Jarrett, Keith 1
Jars of Clay 20
Jasper, Chris
See Isley Brothers, The
Jaworski, Al
See Jesus Jones
Jay, Miles
See Village People, The
Jayhawks, The 15
Jayson, Mackie
See Bad Brains
Jazzie B
See Soul II Soul
Jean, Wyclef 22
Also see Fugees, The
Jeanrenaud, Joan Dutcher
See Kronos Quartet
Jeczalik, Jonathan
See Art of Noise
Jefferson Airplane 5
Jefferson, Blind Lemon 18
Jefferson Starship
See Jefferson Airplane
Jemmott, Gerald
See Pearls Before Swine
Jenifer, Darryl
See Bad Brains
Jenkins, Barry
See Animals
Jenkins, Stephan
See Third Eye Blind
Jennings, Greg
See Restless Heart
Jennings, Waylon 4
Jensen, Ingrid 22
Jerry, Jah
See Skatalites, The
Jessee, Darren
See Ben Folds Five
Jessie, Young
See Coasters, The
Jesus and Mary Chain, The 10
Jesus Jones 23
Jesus Lizard 19
Jethro Tull 8
Jett, Joan 3
Jewel 25
Jimenez, Flaco
See Texas Tornados, The
Jimmie's Chicken Shack 22
Joannou, Chris
See Silverchair

Jobim, Antonio Carlos **19**
Jobson, Edwin
  See Jethro Tull
Jodeci **13**
Joel, Billy **12**
  Earlier sketch in CM **2**
Joel, Phil
  See Newsboys, The
Johansen, David
  See New York Dolls
Johansen, David **7**
Johanson, Jai Johanny
  See Allman Brothers, The
Johansson, Glenn
  See Echobelly
Johansson, Lars-Olof
  See Cardigans
John, Elton **20**
  Earlier sketch in CM **3**
John, Little Willie **25**
Johns, Daniel
  See Silverchair
Johnson, Alphonso
  See Weather Report
Johnson, Blind Willie **26**
Johnson, Bob
  See Steeleye Span
Johnson, Brian
  See AC/DC
Johnson, Courtney
  See New Grass Revival, The
Johnson, Danny
  See Steppenwolf
Johnson, Daryl
  See Neville Brothers, The
Johnson, Eric **19**
Johnson, Eric
  See Archers of Loaf
Johnson, Gene
  See Diamond Rio
Johnson, Gerry
  See Steel Pulse
Johnson, James P. **16**
Johnson, Jerry
  See Big Mountain
Johnson, Lonnie **17**
Johnson, Matt
  See The The
Johnson, Mike
  See Dinosaur Jr.
Johnson, Ralph
  See Earth, Wind and Fire
Johnson, Robert **6**
Johnson, Scott
  See Gin Blossoms
Johnson, Shirley Childres
  See Sweet Honey in the Rock
Johnson, Tamara "Taj"
  See SWV
Johnson, Willie
  See Golden Gate Quartet
Johnston, Bruce
  See Beach Boys, The
Johnston, Freedy **20**
Johnston, Howie
  See Ventures, The
Johnston, Tom
  See Doobie Brothers, The
JoJo
  See Jodeci
Jolly, Bill
  See Butthole Surfers
Jolson, Al **10**
Jon Spencer Blues Explosion **18**

Jones, Adam
  See Tool
Jones, Benny
  See Dirty Dozen
Jones, Booker T. **8**
  Also see Booker T. & the M.G.'s
Jones, Brian
  See Rolling Stones, The
Jones, Busta
  See Gang of Four
Jones, Claude
  See McKinney's Cotton Pickers
Jones, Darryl
  See Rolling Stones, The
Jones, Davy
  See Monkees, The
Jones, Denise
  See Point of Grace
Jones, Elvin **9**
Jones, Geoffrey
  See Sounds of Blackness
Jones, George **4**
Jones, Grace **9**
Jones, Hank **15**
Jones, Howard **26**
Jones, Jab
  See Memphis Jug Band
Jones, Jamie
  See All-4-One
Jones, Jim
  See Pere Ubu
Jones, John Paul
  See Led Zeppelin
Jones, Kendall
  See Fishbone
Jones, Kenny
  See Faces, The
Jones, Kenny
  See Who, The
Jones, Marshall
  See Ohio Players
Jones, Maxine
  See En Vogue
Jones, Mic
  See Big Audio Dynamite
  Also see Clash, The
Jones, Michael
  See Kronos Quartet
Jones, Mick
  See Foreigner
Jones, Orville
  See Ink Spots
Jones, Philly Joe **16**
Jones, Quincy **20**
  Earlier sketch in CM **2**
Jones, Rickie Lee **4**
Jones, Robert "Kuumba"
  See Ohio Players
Jones, Ronald
  See Flaming Lips
Jones, Sandra "Puma"
  See Black Uhuru
Jones, Simon
  See Verve, The
Jones, Spike **5**
Jones, Stacy
  See Letters to Cleo
  See Veruca Salt
Jones, Steve
  See Sex Pistols, The
Jones, Terry
  See Point of Grace
Jones, Thad **19**
Jones, Tom **11**

Jones, Will "Dub"
  See Coasters, The
Joplin, Janis **3**
Joplin, Scott **10**
Jordan, Lonnie
  See War
Jordan, Louis **11**
Jordan, Montell **26**
Jordan, Stanley **1**
Jorgensor, John
  See Desert Rose Band, The
Joseph, Charles
  See Dirty Dozen
Joseph, Kirk
  See Dirty Dozen
Joseph-I, Israel
  See Bad Brains
Josephmary
  See Compulsion
Jourgensen, Al
  See Ministry
Journey **21**
Joy Division **19**
Joy Electric **26**
Joyce, Mike
  See Buzzcocks, The
  Also see Smiths, The
Judas Priest **10**
Judd, Naomi
  See Judds, The
Judd, Wynonna
  See Judds, The
  Also see Wynonna
Judds, The **2**
Juhlin, Dag
  See Poi Dog Pondering
Jukebox
  See Geto Boys, The
Jungle DJ "Towa" Towa
  See Deee-lite
Jurado, Jeanette
  See Exposé
Justman, Seth
  See J. Geils Band
K-Ci
  See Jodeci
Kabongo, Sabine
  See Zap Mama
Kahlil, Aisha
  See Sweet Honey in the Rock
Kain, Gylan
  See Last Poets
Kakoulli, Harry
  See Squeeze
Kale, Jim
  See Guess Who
Kalligan, Dick
  See Blood, Sweat and Tears
Kamanski, Paul
  See Beat Farmers
Kaminski, Mik
  See Electric Light Orchestra
Kamomiya, Ryo
  See Pizzicato Five
Kanal, Tony
  See No Doubt
Kanawa, Kiri Te
  See Te Kanawa, Kiri
Kane, Arthur
  See New York Dolls
Kane, Big Daddy **7**
Kane, Nick
  See Mavericks, The

Kannberg, Scott
  See Pavement
Kanter, Paul
  See Jefferson Airplane
Kaplan, Ira
  See Yo La Tengo
Karajan, Herbert von
  See von Karajan, Herbert
Karges, Murphy
  See Sugar Ray
Kath, Terry
  See Chicago
Kato, Nash
  See Urge Overkill
Katunich, Alex
  See Incubus
Katz, Simon
  See Jamiroquai
Katz, Steve
  See Blood, Sweat and Tears
Kaukonen, Jorma
  See Jefferson Airplane
Kavanagh, Chris
  See Big Audio Dynamite
Kay Gee
  See Naughty by Nature
Kay, Jason
  See Jamiroquai
Kay, John
  See Steppenwolf
Kaye, Carol 22
Kaye, Tony
  See Yes
Keaggy, Phil 26
Kean, Martin
  See Stereolab
Keane, Sean
  See Chieftains, The
Kee, John P. 15
Keelor, Greg
  See Blue Rodeo
Keenan, Maynard James
  See Tool
Keene, Barry
  See Spirit
Keifer, Tom
  See Cinderella
Keitaro
  See Pizzicato Five
Keith, Jeff
  See Tesla
Keith, Toby 17
Kelly, Betty
  See Martha and the Vandellas
Kelly, Charlotte
  See Soul II Soul
Kelly, Kevin
  See Byrds, The
Kelly, Rashaan
  See US3
Kemp, Rick
  See Steeleye Span
Kendrick, David
  See Devo
Kendricks, Eddie
  See Temptations, The
Kennedy, Delious
  See All-4-One
Kennedy, Frankie
  See Altan
Kennedy, Nigel 8
Kenner, Doris
  See Shirelles, The
Kenny, Bill
  See Ink Spots

Kenny, Clare
  See Aztec Camera
Kenny G 14
Kenny, Herb
  See Ink Spots
Kenton, Stan 21
Kentucky Headhunters, The 5
Kern, Jerome 13
Kerr, Jim
  See Simple Minds
Kershaw, Sammy 15
Ketchum, Hal 14
Key, Cevin
  See Skinny Puppy
Keyser, Alex
  See Echobelly
Khan, Chaka 19
  Earlier sketch in CM 9
Khan, Nusrat Fateh Ali 13
Khan, Praga
  See Lords of Acid
Kibble, Mark
  See Take 6
Kibby, Walter
  See Fishbone
Kick, Johnny
  See Madder Rose
Kid 'n Play 5
Kidjo, Anjelique 17
Kiedis, Anthony
  See Red Hot Chili Peppers, The
Kilbey, Steve
  See Church, The
Kilgallon, Eddie
  See Ricochet
Kilgore 24
Killian, Tim
  See Kronos Quartet
Kimball, Jennifer
  See Story, The
Kimball, Jim
  See Jesus Lizard
Kimble, Paul
  See Grant Lee Buffalo
Kincaid, Jan
  See Brand New Heavies, The
Kinchla, Chan
  See Blues Traveler
King Ad-Rock
  See Beastie Boys, The
King, Albert 2
King, Andy
  See Hooters
King, B.B. 24
  Earlier sketch in CM 1
King, Ben E. 7
King, Bob
  See Soul Stirrers, The
King, Carole 6
  Also see Goffin-King
King Crimson 17
King, Ed
  See Lynyrd Skynyrd
King, Freddy 17
King, Jon
  See Gang of Four
King, Jr., William
  See Commodores, The
King, Kerry
  See Slayer
King Missile 22
King, Philip
  See Lush
King's X 7

Kingston Trio, The 9
Kinks, The 15
Kinney, Sean
  See Alice in Chains
Kirk, Rahsaan Roland 6
Kirk, Richard H.
  See Cabaret Voltaire
Kirke, Simon
  See Bad Company
Kirkland, Mike
  See Prong
Kirkpatrick, Chris
  See 'N Sync
Kirkwood, Cris
  See Meat Puppets, The
Kirkwood, Curt
  See Meat Puppets, The
Kirtley, Peter
  See Pentangle
Kirwan, Danny
  See Fleetwood Mac
Kiss 25
  Earlier sketch in CM 5
Kisser, Andreas
  See Sepultura
Kissin, Evgeny 6
Kitaro 1
Kitsos, Nick
  See BoDeans
Kitt, Eartha 9
Klein, Danny
  See J. Geils Band
Klein, Jon
  See Siouxsie and the Banshees
Klezmatics, The 18
Klugh, Earl 10
Kmatsu, Bravo
  See Pizzicato Five
KMFDM 18
Knight, Gladys 1
Knight, Jon
  See New Kids on the Block
Knight, Jordan
  See New Kids on the Block
Knight, Larry
  See Spirit
Knight, Peter
  See Steeleye Span
Knight, Suge 15
Knighton, Willie
  See Goodie Mob
Knopfler, David
  See Dire Straits
Knopfler, Mark 25
  Earlier sketch in CM 3
  Also see Dire Straits
Know, Dr.
  See Bad Brains
Knowledge
  See Digable Planets
Knox, Nick
  See Cramps, The
Knox, Richard
  See Dirty Dozen
Knudsen, Keith
  See Doobie Brothers, The
Konietzko, Sascha
  See KMFDM
Konishi, Yasuharu
  See Pizzicato Five
Konto, Skip
  See Three Dog Night
Kool & the Gang 13
Kool Moe Dee 9

Kooper, Al
  See Blood, Sweat and Tears
Koppelman, Charles 14
Koppes, Peter
  See Church, The
Korn 20
Kottke, Leo 13
Kotzen, Richie
  See Poison
Kowalczyk, Ed
  See Live
Kraftwerk 9
Krakauer, David
  See Klezmatics, The
Kramer, Joey
  See Aerosmith
Kramer, Wayne
  See MC5, The
Krasnow, Bob 15
Krause, Bernie
  See Weavers, The
Krauss, Alison 10
Krauss, Scott
  See Pere Ubu
Kravitz, Lenny 26
  Earlier sketch in CM 5
Krawits, Michael
  See Pearls Before Swine
Krayzie Bone
  See Bone Thugs-N-Harmony
Krazy Drayz
  See Das EFX
Kretz, Eric
  See Stone Temple Pilots
Kreutzman, Bill
  See Grateful Dead, The
Krieger, Robert
  See Doors, The
Kriesel, Greg
  See Offspring
Kris Kross 11
Kristofferson, Kris 4
Krizan, Anthony
  See Spin Doctors
Kronos Quartet 5
Kropp, Mike
  See Northern Lights
KRS-One 8
Krukowski, Damon
  See Damon and Naomi
Krupa, Gene 13
Krusen, Dave
  See Pearl Jam
Kruspe, Richard
  See Rammstein
Kulak, Eddie
  See Aztec Camera
Kulick, Bruce
  See Kiss
Kunkel, Bruce
  See Nitty Gritty Dirt Band, The
Kunzel, Erich 17
Kurdziel, Eddie
  See Redd Kross
Kurihara, Michio
  See Ghost
Kuti, Fela 7
L.L. Cool J. 5
L7 12
LaBar, Jeff
  See Cinderella
LaBelle, Patti 8
LaBrie, James
  See Dream Theater

Lack, Steve
  See Veruca Salt
Lacy, Steve 23
Lady Miss Kier
  See Deee-lite
Ladybug
  See Digable Planets
Ladysmith Black Mambazo 1
Lafalce, Mark
  See Mekons, The
Lagerburg, Bengt
  See Cardigans, The
Laine, Cleo 10
Laine, Denny
  See Moody Blues, The
Laird, Rick
  See Mahavishnu Orchestra
Lake, Greg
  See Emerson, Lake & Palmer/Powell
  Also see King Crimson
Lally, Joe
  See Fugazi
LaLonde, Larry "Ler"
  See Primus
Lamb, Michael
  See Confederate Railroad
Lamble, Martin
  See Fairport Convention
Lamm, Robert
  See Chicago
Lancaster, Brian
  See Surfin' Pluto
Landers, Paul
  See Rammstein
Landreth, Sonny 16
Lane, Jani
  See Warrant
Lane, Jay
  See Primus
Lane, Ronnie
  See Faces, The
lang, k. d. 25
  Earlier sketch in CM 4
Langan, Gary
  See Art of Noise
Langford, Jon
  See Mekons, The
Langford, Willie
  See Golden Gate Quartet
Langley, John
  See Mekons, The
Langlois, Paul
  See Tragically Hip, The
Langston, Leslie
  See Throwing Muses
Lanier, Allen
  See Blue Oyster Cult
Lanker, Dustin
  See Cherry Poppin' Daddies
Lanois, Daniel 8
LaPread, Ronald
  See Commodores, The
Larkin, Patty 9
Larson, Chad Albert
  See Aquabats
Larson, Nathan
  See Shudder to Think
Last Poets 21
Laswell, Bill 14
Lataille, Rich
  See Roomful of Blues
Lateef, Yusef 16
Latimer, Andrew
  See Camel

Laughner, Peter
  See Pere Ubu
Lauper, Cyndi 11
Laurence, Lynda
  See Supremes, The
Lavin, Christine 6
Lavis, Gilson
  See Squeeze
Lawlor, Feargal
  See Cranberries, The
Lawrence, Tracy 11
Lawry, John
  See Petra
Laws, Roland
  See Earth, Wind and Fire
Lawson, Doyle
  See Country Gentlemen, The
Layzie Bone
  See Bone Thugs-N-Harmony
Le Mystère des VoixBulgares
  See Bulgarian State Female Vocal Choir,
  The
Leadbelly 6
Leadon, Bernie
  See Eagles, The
  Also see Nitty Gritty Dirt Band, The
Lear, Graham
  See REO Speedwagon
Leary, Paul
  See Butthole Surfers
Leavell, Chuck
  See Allman Brothers, The
LeBon, Simon
  See Duran Duran
Leckenby, Derek "Lek"
  See Herman's Hermits
Led Zeppelin 1
Ledbetter, Huddie
  See Leadbelly
LeDoux, Chris 12
Lee, Ben 26
Lee, Beverly
  See Shirelles, The
Lee, Brenda 5
Lee, Buddy
  See Less Than Jake
Lee, Garret
  See Compulsion
Lee, Geddy
  See Rush
Lee, Peggy 8
Lee, Pete
  See Gwar
Lee, Sara
  See Gang of Four
Lee, Stan
  See Incredible String Band
Lee, Tommy
  See Mötley Crüe
Lee, Tony
  See Treadmill Trackstar
Leeb, Bill
  See Front Line Assembly
Leen, Bill
  See Gin Blossoms
Leese, Howard
  See Heart
Legg, Adrian 17
Lehrer, Tom 7
Leiber and Stoller 14
Leiber, Jerry
  See Leiber and Stoller
LeMaistre, Malcolm
  See Incredible String Band

Lemmy
 See Motörhead
Lemonheads, The 12
Lemper, Ute 14
Lenear, Kevin
 See Mighty Mighty Bosstones
Lenners, Rudy
 See Scorpions, The
Lennon, John 9
 Also see Beatles, The
Lennon, Julian 26
 Earlier sketch in CM 2
Lennox, Annie 18
 Also see Eurythmics
Leonard, Glenn
 See Temptations, The
Lerner, Alan Jay
 See Lerner and Loewe
Lerner and Loewe 13
Lesh, Phil
 See Grateful Dead, The
Leskiw, Greg
 See Guess Who
Leslie, Chris
 See Fairport Convention
Less Than Jake 22
Lessard, Stefan
 See Dave Matthews Band
Letters to Cleo 22
Levene, Keith
 See Clash, The
Levert, Eddie
 See O'Jays, The
Leverton, Jim
 See Caravan
Levin, Tony
 See King Crimson
Levine, James 8
Levy, Andrew
 See Brand New Heavies, The
Levy, Ron
 See Roomful of Blues
Lewis, Furry 26
Lewis, Hambone
 See Memphis Jug Band
Lewis, Huey 9
Lewis, Ian
 See Inner Circle
Lewis, Jerry Lee 2
Lewis, Marcia
 See Soul II Soul
Lewis, Michael
 See Quicksilver Messenger Service
Lewis, Mike
 See Yo La Tengo
Lewis, Otis
 See Fabulous Thunderbirds, The
Lewis, Peter
 See Moby Grape
Lewis, Ramsey 14
Lewis, Roger
 See Dirty Dozen
 See Inner Circle
Lewis, Roger
Lewis, Roy
 See Kronos Quartet
Lewis, Samuel K.
 See Five Blind Boys of Alabama
Lewis, Shaznay T.
 See All Saints
Lewis, Terry
 See Jam, Jimmy, and Terry Lewis
Lhote, Morgan
 See Stereolab

Li Puma, Tommy 18
Libbea, Gene
 See Nashville Bluegrass Band
Liberace 9
Licht, David
 See Klezmatics, The
Lifeson, Alex
 See Rush
Lightfoot, Gordon 3
Lightning Seeds 21
Ligon, Willie Joe
 See Mighty Clouds of Joy, The
Liles, Brent
 See Social Distortion
Lilienstein, Lois
 See Sharon, Lois & Bram
Lilker, Dan
 See Anthrax
Lilley, John
 See Hooters
Lillywhite, Steve 13
Lincoln, Abbey 9
Lindemann, Till
 See Rammstein
Lindes, Hal
 See Dire Straits
Lindley, David 2
Linkous, Mark 26
Linna, Miriam
 See Cramps, The
Linnell, John
 See They Might Be Giants
Lipsius, Fred
 See Blood, Sweat and Tears
Lisa, Lisa 23
Little Feat 4
Little, Keith
 See Country Gentlemen, The
Little, Levi
 See Blackstreet
Little Richard 1
Little Texas 14
Little Walter 14
Littrell, Brian
 See Backstreet Boys
Live 14
Living Colour 7
Llanas, Sam
 See BoDeans
Llanas, Sammy
 See BoDeans, The
Lloyd, Charles 22
Lloyd, Richard
 See Television
Lloyd Webber, Andrew 6
Locke, John
 See Spirit
Locking, Brian
 See Shadows, The
Lockwood, Robert, Jr. 10
Lodge, John
 See Moody Blues, The
Loeb, Lisa 23
Loewe, Frederick
 See Lerner and Loewe
Lofgren, Nils 25
Loggins, Kenny 20
 Earlier sketch in CM 3
Lombardo, Dave
 See Slayer
London, Frank
 See Klezmatics, The
Lopes, Lisa "Left Eye"
 See TLC

Lopez, Israel "Cachao" 14
Lord, Jon
 See Deep Purple
Lords of Acid 20
Lorenz, Flake
 See Rammstein
Loria, Steve
 See Spirit
Lorson, Mary
 See Madder Rose
Los Lobos 2
Los Reyes
 See Gipsy Kings, The
Loughnane, Lee
 See Chicago
Louison, Steve
 See Massive Attack
Louris, Gary
 See Jayhawks, The
Louvin Brothers, The 12
Louvin, Charlie
 See Louvin Brothers, The
Louvin, Ira
 See Louvin Brothers, The
Lovano, Joe 13
Love and Rockets 15
Love, Courtney
 See Hole
Love, G. 24
Love, Gerry
 See Teenage Fanclub
Love, Laura 20
Love, Mike
 See Beach Boys, The
Love, Rollie
 See Beat Farmers
Love Spit Love 21
Loveless, Patty 21
 Earlier sketch in CM 5
Lovering, David
 See Cracker
 Also see Pixies, The
Lovett, Lyle 5
Lowe, Chris
 See Pet Shop Boys
Lowe, Nick 25
 Earlier sketch in CM 6
Lowell, Charlie
 See Jars of Clay
Lowery, David
 See Cracker
Lozano, Conrad
 See Los Lobos
Lucas, Trevor
 See Fairport Convention
Luccketta, Troy
 See Tesla
Lucia, Paco de
 See de Lucia, Paco
Luciano, Felipe
 See Last Poets
Luke
 See Campbell, Luther
Lukin, Matt
 See Mudhoney
Luna 18
Lupo, Pat
 See Beaver Brown Band, The
LuPone, Patti 8
Lush 13
Luttell, Terry
 See REO Speedwagon
Lydon, John 9
 Also see Sex Pistols, The

Lyfe, DJ
  See Incubus
Lymon, Frankie
  See Frankie Lymon and The Teenagers
Lynch, David
  See Platters, The
Lynch, Dermot
  See Dog's Eye View
Lynch, George
  See Dokken
Lyngstad, Anni-Frid
  See Abba
Lynn, Lonnie Rashid
  See Common
Lynn, Loretta 2
Lynne, Jeff 5
  Also see Electric Light Orchestra
Lynne, Shelby 5
Lynott, Phil
  See Thin Lizzy
Lynyrd Skynyrd 9
Lyons, Leanne "Lelee"
  See SWV
M People 15
M.C. Hammer
  See Hammer, M.C.
M.C. Ren
  See N.W.A.
Ma, Yo-Yo 24
  Earlier sketch in CM 2
MacColl, Kirsty 12
MacDonald, Eddie
  See Alarm
Macfarlane, Lora
  See Sleater-Kinney
MacGowan, Shane
MacIsaac, Ashley 21
Mack Daddy
  See Kris Kross
MacKaye, Ian
  See Fugazi
Mackey, Steve
  See Pulp
MacNeil, Michael
  See Simple Minds
MacPherson, Jim
  See Breeders
Madan, Sonya Aurora
  See Echobelly
Madder Rose 17
Madonna 16
  Earlier sketch in CM 4
Mael, Ron
  See Sparks
Mael, Russell
  See Sparks
Magehee, Marty
  See FourHim
Maghostut, Malachi Favors
  See Art Ensemble of Chicago, The
Maginnis, Tom
  See Buffalo Tom
Magnie, John
  See Subdudes, The
Magoogan, Wesley
  See English Beat, The
Maher, John
  See Buzzcocks, The
Mahogany, Kevin 26
Mahoney, Tim
  See 311
Maida, Raine
  See Our Lady Peace
Maimone, Tony
  See Pere Ubu

Maïtra, Shyamal
  See Gong
Makeba, Miriam 8
Malcolm, Hugh
  See Skatalites, The
Malcolm, Joy
  See Incognito
Male, Johnny
  See Republica
Malherbe, Didier
  See Gong
Malins, Mike
  See Goo Goo Dolls, The
Malkmus, Stephen
  See Pavement
Malley, Matt
  See Counting Crows
Mallinder, Stephen
  See Cabaret Voltaire
Malmsteen, Yngwie 24
Malo, Raul
  See Mavericks, The
Malone, Tom
  See Blood, Sweat and Tears
Malone, Tommy
  See Subdudes, The
Mamas and the Papas 21
Man or Astroman? 21
Mancini, Henry 20
  Earlier sketch in CM 1
Mandrell, Barbara 4
Maness, J. D.
  See Desert Rose Band, The
Mangione, Chuck 23
Manhattan Transfer, The 8
Manilow, Barry 2
Mann, Aimee 22
Mann, Billy 23
Mann, Herbie 16
Manson, Shirley
  See Garbage
Manuel, Richard
  See Band, The
Manzarek, Ray
  See Doors, The
March, Kevin
  See Shudder to Think
Marie, Buffy Sainte
  See Sainte-Marie, Buffy
Marilyn Manson 18
Marini, Lou, Jr.
  See Blood, Sweat and Tears
Marker, Steve
  See Garbage
Marley, Bob 3
Marley, Rita 10
Marley, Ziggy 3
Marr, Johnny
  See Smiths, The
  Also see The The
Marriner, Neville
Mars, Chris
  See Replacements, The
Mars, Derron
  See Less Than Jake
Mars, Mick
  See Mötley Crüe
Marsalis, Branford 10
Marsalis, Ellis 13
Marsalis, Wynton 20
  Earlier sketch in CM 6
Marsh, Ian Craig
  See Human League, The
Marshal, Cornel
  See Third World

Marshall, Jenell
  See Dirty Dozen
Martha and the Vandellas 25
Martin, Barbara
  See Supremes, The
Martin, Carl
  See Shai
Martin, Christopher
  See Kid 'n Play
Martin, Dean 1
Martin, Dewey
  See Buffalo Springfield
Martin, George 6
Martin, Greg
  See Kentucky Headhunters, The
Martin, Jim
  See Faith No More
Martin, Jimmy 5
  Also see Osborne Brothers, The
Martin, Johnney
  See Mighty Clouds of Joy, The
Martin, Phonso
  See Steel Pulse
Martin, Ricky 26
Martin, Sennie
  See Kool & the Gang
Martin, Tony
  See Black Sabbath
Martinez, Anthony
  See Black Flag
Martinez, S. A.
  See 311
Martini, Jerry
  See Sly & the Family Stone
Martino, Pat 17
Marvin, Hank B.
  See Shadows, The
Marx, Richard 21
  Earlier sketch in CM 3
Mascagni, Pietro 25
Mascis, J
  See Dinosaur Jr.
Masdea, Jim
  See Boston
Masekela, Hugh 7
Maseo, Baby Huey
  See De La Soul
Masi, Nick
  See Four Seasons, The
Mason, Dave
  See Traffic
Mason, Nick
  See Pink Floyd
Mason, Steve
  See Jars of Clay
Mason, Terry
  See Joy Division
Masse, Laurel
  See Manhattan Transfer, The
Massey, Bobby
  See O'Jays, The
Massive Attack 17
Mastelotto, Pat
  See King Crimson
Master P 22
Masur, Kurt 11
Material
  See Laswell, Bill
Mathis, Johnny 2
Mathus, Jim
  See Squirrel Nut Zippers
Matlock, Glen
  See Sex Pistols, The
Mattacks, Dave
  See Fairport Convention

Mattea, Kathy **5**
Matthews Band, Dave
  See Dave Matthews Band
Matthews, Chris
  See Shudder to Think
Matthews, Dave
  See Dave Matthews Band
Matthews, Eric **22**
Matthews, Ian
  See Fairport Convention
Matthews, Quinn
  See Butthole Surfers
Matthews, Scott
  See Butthole Surfers
Matthews, Simon
  See Jesus Jones
Maunick, Bluey
  See Incognito
Maurer, John
  See Social Distortion
Mavericks, The **15**
Maxwell **22**
Maxwell, Charmayne
  See Brownstone
Maxwell, Tom
  See Squirrel Nut Zippers
May, Brian
  See Queen
Mayall, John **7**
Mayfield, Curtis **8**
Mays, Odeen, Jr.
  See Kool & the Gang
Mazelle, Kym
  See Soul II Soul
Mazibuko, Abednigo
  See Ladysmith Black Mambazo
Mazibuko, Albert
  See Ladysmith Black Mambazo
Mazzola, Joey
  See Sponge
Mazzy Star **17**
MC 900 Ft. Jesus **16**
MC Clever
  See Digital Underground
MC Eric
  See Technotronic
MC Lyte **8**
MC Serch **10**
MC5, The **9**
MCA
  See Yauch, Adam
McAloon, Martin
  See Prefab Sprout
McAloon, Paddy
  See Prefab Sprout
McArthur, Keith
  See Spearhead
McBrain, Nicko
  See Iron Maiden
McBrayer, Jody
  See Avalon
MC Breed **17**
McBride, Christian **17**
McBride, Martina **14**
McCabe, Nick
  See Verve, The
McCabe, Zia
McCall, Renee
  See Sounds of Blackness
McCann, Lila **26**
McCarrick, Martin
  See Siouxsie and the Banshees
McCarroll, Tony
  See Oasis

McCartney, Paul **4**
  Also see Beatles, The
McCarty, Jim
  See Yardbirds, The
McCary, Michael S.
  See Boyz II Men
McClary, Thomas
  See Commodores, The
McClennan, Tommy **25**
McClinton, Delbert **14**
McCluskey, Andy
  See Orchestral Manoeuvres in the Dark
McCollum, Rick
  See Afghan Whigs
McConnell, Page
  See Phish
McCook, Tommy
  See Skatalites, The
McCoury, Del **15**
McCowin, Michael
  See Mighty Clouds of Joy, The
McCoy, Neal **15**
McCracken, Chet
  See Doobie Brothers, The
McCready, Mike
  See Pearl Jam
McCready, Mindy **22**
McCulloch, Andrew
  See King Crimson
McCullough, Danny
  See Animals
McCuloch, Ian **23**
McD, Jimmy
  See Jimmie's Chicken Shack
McDaniel, Chris
  See Confederate Railroad
McDaniels, Darryl "D"
  See Run DMC
McDermott, Brian
  See Del Amitri
McDonald, Barbara Kooyman
  See Timbuk 3
McDonald, Ian
  See Foreigner
  Also see King Crimson
McDonald, Jeff
  See Redd Kross
McDonald, Michael
  See Doobie Brothers, The
McDonald, Pat
  See Timbuk 3
McDonald, Steven
  See Redd Kross
McDorman, Joe
  See Statler Brothers, The
McDougall, Don
  See Guess Who
McDowell, Hugh
  See Electric Light Orchestra
McDowell, Mississippi Fred **16**
McEntire, Reba **11**
McEuen, John
  See Nitty Gritty Dirt Band, The
McFarlane, Elaine
  See Mamas and the Papas
McFee, John
  See Doobie Brothers, The
McFerrin, Bobby **3**
McGee, Brian
  See Simple Minds
McGee, Jerry
  See Ventures, The
McGeoch, John
  See Siouxsie and the Banshees

McGinley, Raymond
  See Teenage Fanclub
McGinniss, Will
  See Audio Adrenaline
McGrath, Mark
  See Sugar Ray
McGraw, Tim **17**
McGuigan, Paul
  See Oasis
McGuinn, Jim
  See McGuinn, Roger
McGuinn, Roger
  See Byrds, The
McGuire, Mike
  See Shenandoah
McIntosh, Robbie
  See Pretenders, The
McIntyre, Joe
  See New Kids on the Block
McJohn, Goldy
  See Steppenwolf
McKagan, Duff
  See Guns n' Roses
McKay, Al
  See Earth, Wind and Fire
McKay, John
  See Siouxsie and the Banshees
McKean, Michael
  See Spinal Tap
McKee, Julius
  See Dirty Dozen
McKee, Maria **11**
McKeehan, Toby
  See dc Talk
McKenna, Greg
  See Letters to Cleo
McKennitt, Loreena **24**
McKenzie, Christina "Licorice"
  See Incredible String Band
McKenzie, Derrick
  See Jamiroquai
McKenzie, Scott
  See Mamas and the Papas
McKernarn, Ron "Pigpen"
  See Grateful Dead, The
McKinney, William
  See McKinney's Cotton Pickers
McKinney's Cotton Pickers **16**
McKnight, Brian **22**
McKnight, Claude V. III
  See Take 6
McLachlan, Sarah **12**
McLagan, Ian
  See Faces, The
McLaren, Malcolm **23**
McLaughlin, John **12**
  Also see Mahavishnu Orchestra
McLean, A. J.
  See Backstreet Boys
McLean, Dave **24**
McLean, Don **7**
McLennan, Grant **21**
McLeod, Rory
  See Roomful of Blues
McLoughlin, Jon
  See Del Amitri
McMeel, Mickey
  See Three Dog Night
McMurtry, James **10**
McNabb, Travis
  See Better Than Ezra
McNair, Sylvia **15**
McNeilly, Mac
  See Jesus Lizard

McNew, James
  See Yo La Tengo
McPartland, Marian 15
McPhatter, Clyde 25
McQuillar, Shawn
  See Kool & the Gang
McRae, Carmen 9
McReynolds, Jesse
  See McReynolds, Jim and Jesse
McReynolds, Jim
  See McReynolds, Jim and Jesse
McReynolds, Jim and Jesse 12
McShane, Ronnie
  See Chieftains, The
McShee, Jacqui
  See Pentangle
McTell, Blind Willie 17
McVie, Christine
  See Fleetwood Mac
McVie, John
  See Fleetwood Mac
McWhinney, James
  See Big Mountain
McWhinney, Joaquin
  See Clannad
  See Big Mountain
Mdletshe, Geophrey
  See Ladysmith Black Mambazo
Meat Loaf 12
Meat Puppets, The 13
Medley, Bill 3
Medlock, James
  See Soul Stirrers, The
Meehan, Tony
  See Shadows, The
Megadeth 9
Mehta, Zubin 11
Meine, Klaus
  See Scorpions, The
Meisner, Randy
  See Eagles, The
Mekons, The 15
Melanie 12
Melax, Einar
  See Sugarcubes, The
Mellencamp, John 20
  Earlier sketch in CM 2
Melvins 21
Memphis Jug Band 25
Memphis Minnie 25
Mendel, Nate
  See Foo Fighters
Mengede, Peter
  See Helmet
Menken, Alan 10
Menuhin, Yehudi 11
Menza, Nick
  See Megadeth
Mercer, Johnny 13
Merchant, Jimmy
  See Frankie Lymon and The Teenagers
Merchant, Natalie 25
  Also see 10,000 Maniacs
Mercier, Peadar
  See Chieftains, The
Mercury, Freddie
  See Queen
Mertens, Paul
  See Poi Dog Pondering
Mesaros, Michael
  See Smithereens, The
Messecar, Dek
  See Caravan

Messina, Jim
  See Buffalo Springfield
Messina, Jo Dee 26
Metallica 7
Meters, The 14
Methembu, Russel
  See Ladysmith Black Mambazo
Metheny, Pat 26
  Earlier sketch in CM 2
Meyer, Eric
  See Charm Farm
Meyers, Augie
  See Texas Tornados, The
Mhaonaigh, Mairead Ni
  See Altan
Michael, George 9
Michaels, Bret
  See Poison
Michel, Luke
  See Emmet Swimming
Michel, Prakazrel "Pras"
  See Fugees, The
Middlebrook, Ralph "Pee Wee"
  See Ohio Players
Middleton, Mark
  See Blackstreet
Midler, Bette 8
Midnight Oil 11
Midori 7
Mighty Clouds of Joy, The 17
Mighty Mighty Bosstones 20
Mike & the Mechanics 17
Mike D
  See Beastie Boys, The
Mikens, Dennis
  See Smithereens, The
Mikens, Robert
  See Kool & the Gang
Milchem, Glenn
  See Blue Rodeo
Miles, Chris
  See Northern Lights
Miles, Richard
  See Soul Stirrers, The
Miles, Ron 22
Millar, Deborah
  See Massive Attack
Miller, Charles
  See War
Miller, Glenn 6
Miller, Jacob "Killer" Miller
  See Inner Circle
Miller, Jerry
  See Moby Grape
Miller, Mark
  See Sawyer Brown
Miller, Mitch 11
Miller, Rice
  See Williamson, Sonny Boy
Miller, Robert
  See Supertramp
Miller, Roger 4
Miller, Steve 2
Milli Vanilli 4
Mills Brothers, The 14
Mills, Donald
  See Mills Brothers, The
Mills, Fred
  See Canadian Brass, The
Mills, Harry
  See Mills Brothers, The
Mills, Herbert
  See Mills Brothers, The

Mills, John, Jr.
  See Mills Brothers, The
Mills, John, Sr.
  See Mills Brothers, The
Mills, Mike
  See R.E.M.
Mills, Sidney
  See Steel Pulse
Mills, Stephanie 21
Milsap, Ronnie 2
Milton, Doctor
  See Alien Sex Fiend
Mingus, Charles 9
Ministry 10
Miss Kier Kirby
  See Lady Miss Kier
Mitchell, Alex
  See Curve
Mitchell, John
  See Asleep at the Wheel
Mitchell, Joni 17
  Earlier sketch in CM 2
Mitchell, Keith
  See Mazzy Star
Mitchell, Mitch
  See Guided By Voices
Mitchell, Roscoe
  See Art Ensemble of Chicago, The
Mittoo, Jackie
  See Skatalites, The
Mize, Ben
  See Counting Crows
Mizell, Jay
  See Run DMC
Mo', Keb' 21
Moby 17
Moby Grape 12
Modeliste, Joseph "Zigaboo"
  See Meters, The
Moerlen, Pierre
  See Gong
Moffatt, Katy 18
Moginie, Jim
  See Midnight Oil
Mohr, Todd
  See Big Head Todd and the Monsters
Mojave 3 26
Molland, Joey
  See Badfinger
Molloy, Matt
  See Chieftains, The
Moloney, Paddy
  See Chieftains, The
Monarch, Michael
  See Steppenwolf
Money B
  See Digital Underground
Money, Eddie 16
Monica 26
Monifah 24
Monk, Meredith 1
Monk, Thelonious 6
Monkees, The 7
Monroe, Bill 1
Montana, Country Dick
  See Beat Farmers
Montand, Yves 12
Montenegro, Hugo 18
Montgomery, John Michael 14
Montgomery, Little Brother 26
Montgomery, Wes 3
Monti, Steve
  See Curve
Montoya, Craig
  See Everclear

Montrose, Ronnie **22**
Moody Blues, The **18**
Moon, Keith
　See Who, The
Mooney, Tim
　See American Music Club
Moore, Alan
　See Judas Priest
Moore, Angelo
　See Fishbone
Moore, Archie
　See Velocity Girl
Moore, Chante **21**
Moore, Johnny "Dizzy"
　See Skatalites, The
Moore, Kevin
　See Dream Theater
Moore, LeRoi
　See Dave Matthews Band
Moore, Melba **7**
Moore, Sam
　See Sam and Dave
Moore, Thurston
　See Sonic Youth
Morand, Grace
　See Chenille Sisters, The
Moraz, Patrick
　See Moody Blues, The
　Also see Yes
Morcheeba **25**
Moreira, Airto
　See Weather Report
Morello, Tom
　See Rage Against the Machine
Moreno, Chino
　See Deftones
Moreve, Rushton
　See Steppenwolf
Morgan, Frank **9**
Morgan, Lorrie **10**
Morley, Pat
　See Soul Asylum
Morphine **16**
Morricone, Ennio **15**
Morris, Keith
　See Circle Jerks, The
Morris, Kenny
　See Siouxsie and the Banshees
Morris, Nate
　See Boyz II Men
Morris, Stephen
　See Joy Division
　Also see New Order
　Also see Pogues, The
Morris, Wanya
　See Boyz II Men
Morrison, Bram
　See Sharon, Lois & Bram
Morrison, Claude
　See Nylons, The
Morrison, Jim **3**
　Also see Doors, The
Morrison, Sterling
　See Velvet Underground, The
Morrison, Van **24**
　Earlier sketch in CM 3
Morrissett, Paul
　See Klezmatics, The
Morrissey **10**
　Also see Smiths, The
Morrissey, Bill **12**
Morrissey, Steven Patrick
　See Morrissey
Morton, Everett
　See English Beat, The

Morton, Jelly Roll **7**
Morvan, Fab
　See Milli Vanilli
Mosbaugh, Garth
　See Nylons, The
Mosely, Chuck
　See Faith No More
Moser, Scott "Cactus"
　See Highway 101
Mosher, Ken
　See Squirrel Nut Zippers
Mosley, Bob
　See Moby Grape
Moss, Jason
　See Cherry Poppin' Daddies
Mothersbaugh, Bob
　See Devo
Mothersbaugh, Mark
　See Devo
Mötley Crüe **1**
Motörhead **10**
Motta, Danny
　See Roomful of Blues
Mould, Bob **10**
Moulding, Colin
　See XTC
Mounfield, Gary
　See Stone Roses, The
Mouquet, Eric
　See Deep Forest
Mouskouri, Nana **12**
Mouzon, Alphonse
　See Weather Report
Moye, Famoudou Don
　See Art Ensemble of Chicago, The
Moyet, Alison **12**
Moyse, David
　See Air Supply
Mr. Dalvin
　See Jodeci
Mudhoney **16**
Mueller, Karl
　See Soul Asylum
Muir, Jamie
　See King Crimson
Muir, Mike
　See Suicidal Tendencies
Muldaur, Maria **18**
Mulholland, Dave
　See Aztec Camera
Mullen, Larry, Jr.
　See U2
Mullen, Mary
　See Congo Norvell
Mulligan, Gerry **16**
Murcia, Billy
　See New York Dolls
Murdock, Roger
　See King Missile
Murph
　See Dinosaur Jr.
Murphey, Michael Martin **9**
Murphy, Brigid
　See Poi Dog Pondering
Murphy, Dan
　See Soul Asylum
Murphy, Michael
　See REO Speedwagon
Murphy, Peter **22**
Murray, Anne **4**
Murray, Dave
　See Iron Maiden
Murray, Dee
　See Spencer Davis Group

Murray, Jim
　See Quicksilver Messenger Service
Mushroom
　See Massive Attack
Musselwhite, Charlie **13**
Mustaine, Dave
　See Megadeth
　Also see Metallica
Mutter, Anne-Sophie **23**
Mwelase, Jabulane
　See Ladysmith Black Mambazo
Mydland, Brent
　See Grateful Dead, The
Myers, Alan
　See Devo
Myles, Alannah **4**
Mystic Revealers **16**
Myung, John
　See Dream Theater
N.W.A. **6**
N'Dour, Youssou **6**
Nadirah
　See Arrested Development
Naftalin, Mark
　See Quicksilver Messenger Service
Nagler, Eric **8**
Najee **21**
Nakai, R. Carlos **24**
Nakamura, Tetsuya "Tex"
　See War
Nakatami, Michie
　See Shonen Knife
Narcizo, David
　See Throwing Muses
Nascimento, Milton **6**
Nash, Graham
　See Crosby, Stills, and Nash
Nashville Bluegrass Band **14**
Nastanovich, Bob
　See Pavement
Naughty by Nature **11**
Navarro, David
　See Jane's Addiction
Navarro Fats **25**
Nawasadio, Sylvie
　See Zap Mama
Ndegéocello, Me'Shell **18**
Ndugu
　See Weather Report
Near, Holly **1**
Neel, Johnny
　See Allman Brothers, The
Negron, Chuck
　See Three Dog Night
Negroni, Joe
　See Frankie Lymon and The Teenagers
Neil, Chris
　See Less Than Jake
Neil, Vince
　See Mötley Crüe
Nelson, Brian
　See Velocity Girl
Nelson, David
　See Last Poets
Nelson, Errol
　See Black Uhuru
Nelson, Nate
　See Platters, The
Nelson, Rick **2**
Nelson, Shara
　See Massive Attack
Nelson, Willie **11**
　Earlier sketch in CM 1
Nesbitt, John
　See McKinney's Cotton Pickers

Nesmith, Mike
  See Monkees, The
Ness, Mike
  See Social Distortion
Neufville, Renee
  See Zhane
Neumann, Kurt
  See BoDeans
Nevarez, Alfred
  See All-4-One
Neville, Aaron 5
  Also see Neville Brothers, The
Neville, Art
  See Meters, The
  Also see Neville Brothers, The
Neville Brothers, The 4
Neville, Charles
  See Neville Brothers, The
Neville, Cyril
  See Meters, The
  Also see Neville Brothers, The
Nevin, Brian
  See Big Head Todd and the Monsters
New Grass Revival, The 4
New Kids on the Block 3
New Order 11
New Rhythm and Blues Quartet
  See NRBQ
New York Dolls 20
Newman, Randy 4
Newmann, Kurt
  See BoDeans, The
Newsboys, The 24
Newson, Arlene
  See Poi Dog Pondering
Newton, Paul
  See Uriah Heep
Newton, Wayne 2
Newton-Davis, Billy
  See Nylons, The
Newton-John, Olivia 8
Nibbs, Lloyd
  See Skatalites, The
Nicholas, James Dean "J.D."
  See Commodores, The
Nicholls, Geoff
  See Black Sabbath
Nichols, Gates
  See Confederate Railroad
Nichols, Todd
  See Toad the Wet Sprocket
Nickerson, Charlie
  See Memphis Jug Band
Nicks, Stevie 25
  Earlier sketch in CM 2
  Also see Fleetwood Mac
Nico
  See Velvet Underground, The
Nicol, Simon
  See Fairport Convention
Nicolette
  See Massive Attack
Nielsen, Rick
  See Cheap Trick
Nilija, Robert
  See Last Poets
Nilsson 10
Nilsson, Harry
  See Nilsson
Nirvana 8
Nisbett, Steve "Grizzly"
  See Steel Pulse
Nishino, Kohji
  See Ghost

Nitty Gritty Dirt Band, The 6
No Doubt 20
Nobacon, Danbert
  See Chumbawamba
Nocentelli, Leo
  See Meters, The
Nolan, Jerry
  See New York Dolls
Nomiya, Maki
  See Pizzicato Five
Noone, Peter
  See Herman's Hermits
Norica, Sugar Ray
  See Roomful of Blues
Norman, Jessye 7
Norman, Jimmy
  See Coasters, The
Norris, Jean
  See Zhane
Northey, Craig
  See Odds
Norum, John
  See Dokken
Norvell, Sally
  See Congo Norvell
Norvo, Red 12
Notorious B.I.G. 20
Novoselic, Chris
  See Nirvana
Nowell, Bradley James
  See Sublime
NRBQ 12
'N Sync 25
Nugent, Ted 2
Nunn, Bobby
  See Coasters, The
Nutter, Alice
  See Chumbawamba
Nylons, The 18
Nyman, Michael 15
Nyolo, Sally
  See Zap Mama
Nyro, Laura 12
O'Brien, Darrin Kenneth
  See Snow
O'Brien, Derek
  See Social Distortion
O'Brien, Dwayne
  See Little Texas
O'Brien, Ed
  See Radiohead
O'Brien, Marty
  See Kilgore
O'Bryant, Alan
  See Nashville Bluegrass Band
O'Connell, Chris
  See Asleep at the Wheel
O'Connor, Billy
  See Blondie
O'Connor, Daniel
  See House of Pain
O'Connor, Mark 1
O'Connor, Sinead 3
O'Day, Anita 21
O'Donnell, Roger
  See Cure, The
O'Hagan, Sean
  See Stereolab
O'Hare, Brendan
  See Teenage Fanclub
O'Jays, The 13
O'Reagan, Tim
  See Jayhawks, The

O'Riordan, Cait
  See Pogues, The
O'Riordan, Dolores
  See Cranberries, The
Oak Ridge Boys, The 7
Oakes, Richard
  See Suede
Oakey, Philip
  See Human League, The
Oakland Interfaith Gospel Choir 26
Oakley, Berry
  See Allman Brothers, The
Oasis 16
Oates, John
  See Hall & Oates
Ocasek, Ric 5
Ocasek, Ric
  See Cars, The
Ocean, Billy 4
Oceans, Lucky
  See Asleep at the Wheel
Ochs, Phil 7
Odds 20
Odetta 7
Odmark, Matt
  See Jars of Clay
Ofwerman, Clarence
  See Roxette
Ofwerman, Staffan
  See Roxette
Ogino, Kazuo
  See Ghost
Ogletree, Mike
  See Simple Minds
Ogre, Nivek
  See Skinny Puppy
Ohanian, David
  See Canadian Brass, The
Ohio Players 16
Oje, Baba
  See Arrested Development
Olafsson, Bragi
  See Sugarcubes, The
Olander, Jimmy
  See Diamond Rio
Olaverra, Margot
  See Go-Go's, The
Oldfield, Mike 18
Oldham, Jack
  See Surfaris, The
Oldham, Sean
  See Cherry Poppin' Daddies
Olds, Brent
  See Poi Dog Pondering
Oliver, Joe
  See Oliver, King
Oliver, King 15
Olson, Jeff
  See Village People, The
Olson, Mark
  See Jayhawks, The
Olsson, Nigel
  See Spencer Davis Group
Onassis, Blackie
  See Urge Overkill
Ono, Yoko 11
Orange, Walter "Clyde"
  See Commodores, The
Orb, The 18
Orbison, Roy 2
Orbital 20
Orchestral Manoeuvres in the Dark 21
Orff, Carl 21
Orlando, Tony 15

Örn, Einar
  See Sugarcubes, The
Örnolfsdottir, Margret
  See Sugarcubes, The
Orr, Benjamin
  See Cars, The
Orr, Casey
  See Gwar
Orrall, Frank
  See Poi Dog Pondering
Orton, Beth **26**
Orzabal, Roland
  See Tears for Fears
Osborne, Bob
  See Osborne Brothers, The
Osborne Brothers, The **8**
Osborne, Buzz
  See Melvins
Osborne, Sonny
  See Osborne Brothers, The
Osbourne, Ozzy **3**
  Also see Black Sabbath
Osby, Greg **21**
Oskar, Lee
  See War
Oslin, K. T. **3**
Osman, Mat
  See Suede
Osmond, Donny **3**
Ostin, Mo **17**
Otis, Johnny **16**
Ott, David **2**
Our Lady Peace **22**
Outler, Jimmy
  See Soul Stirrers, The
Owen, Randy Yueull
  See Alabama
Owens, Buck **2**
Owens, Campbell
  See Aztec Camera
Owens, Henry
  See Golden Gate Quartet
Owens, Ricky
  See Temptations, The
Oyewole, Abiodun
  See Last Poets
P.M. Dawn **11**
Page, Jimmy **4**
  See Led Zeppelin
  Also see Yardbirds, The
Page, Patti **11**
Page, Steven
  See Barenaked Ladies
Paice, Ian
  See Deep Purple
Paliotta, Cherie
  See Avalon
Palmer, Bruce
  See Buffalo Springfield
Palmer, Carl
  See Emerson, Lake & Palmer/Powell
Palmer, Clive
  See Incredible String Band
Palmer, David
  See Jethro Tull
Palmer, Jeff **20**
Palmer, Keeti
  See Prodigy
Palmer, Phil
  See Dire Straits
Palmer, Richard
  See Supertramp
Palmer, Robert **2**

Palmer-Jones, Robert
  See King Crimson
Palmieri, Eddie **15**
Paluzzi, Jimmy
  See Sponge
Pamer, John
  See Tsunami
Pankow, James
  See Chicago
Panter, Horace
  See Specials, The
Pantera **13**
Papach, Leyna
  See Geraldine Fibbers
Pappas, Tom
  See Superdrag
Parazaider, Walter
  See Chicago
Paris, Twila **16**
Park, Cary
  See Boy Howdy
Park, Larry
  See Boy Howdy
Parkening, Christopher **7**
Parker, Charlie **5**
Parker, Graham **10**
Parker, Kris
  See KRS-One
Parker, Maceo **7**
Parker, Tom
  See Animals
Parkin, Chad
  See Aquabats
Parks, Van Dyke **17**
Parnell, Lee Roy **15**
Parsons, Alan **12**
Parsons, Dave
  See Bush
Parsons, Gene
  See Byrds, The
Parsons, Gram **7**
  Also see Byrds, The
Parsons, Ted
  See Prong
Parsons, Tony
  See Iron Maiden
Parton, Dolly **24**
  Earlier sketch in CM **2**
Partridge, Andy
  See XTC
Pasemaster, Mase
  See De La Soul
Pash, Jim
  See Surfaris, The
Pasillas, Jose
  See Incubus
Pass, Joe **15**
Passons, Michael
  See Avalon
Pastorius, Jaco
  See Weather Report
Paterson, Alex
  See Orb, The
Patinkin, Mandy **20**
  Earlier sketch CM **3**
Patti, Sandi **7**
Patton, Charley **11**
Patton, Mike
  See Faith No More
Paul, Alan
  See Manhattan Transfer, The
Paul III, Henry
  See BlackHawk
Paul, Les **2**

Paul, Vinnie
  See Pantera
Paulo, Jr.
  See Sepultura
Pavarotti, Luciano **20**
  Earlier sketch in CM **1**
Pavement **14**
Paxton, Tom **5**
Payne, Bill
  See Little Feat
Payne, Scherrie
  See Supremes, The
Payton, Denis
  See Dave Clark Five, The
Payton, Lawrence
  See Four Tops, The
Pearl Jam **12**
Pearl, Minnie **3**
Pearls Before Swine **24**
Pearson, Dan
  See American Music Club
Peart, Neil
  See Rush
Pedersen, Herb
  See Desert Rose Band, The
Peduzzi, Larry
  See Roomful of Blues
Peek, Dan
  See America
Peeler, Ben
  See Mavericks, The
Pegg, Dave
  See Fairport Convention
  Also see Jethro Tull
Pegrum, Nigel
  See Steeleye Span
Pelletier, Mike
  See Kilgore
Pence, Jeff
  See Blessid Union of Souls
Pendergrass, Teddy **3**
Pengilly, Kirk
  See INXS
Peniston, CeCe **15**
Penn, Michael **4**
Penner, Fred **10**
Pentangle **18**
Pepper, Art **18**
Perahia, Murray **10**
Pere Ubu **17**
Peretz, Jesse
  See Lemonheads, The
Perez, Danilo **25**
Perez, Louie
  See Los Lobos
Perkins, Carl **9**
Perkins, John
  See XTC
Perkins, Percell
  See Five Blind Boys of Alabama
Perkins, Steve
  See Jane's Addiction
Perlman, Itzhak **2**
Perlman, Marc
  See Jayhawks, The
Pernice, Joe
  See Scud Mountain Boys
Perry, Brendan
  See Dead Can Dance
Perry, Doane
  See Jethro Tull
Perry, Joe
  See Aerosmith
Perry, John G.
  See Caravan

Perry, Phil **24**
Perry, Steve
  See Cherry Poppin' Daddies
Perry, Steve
  See Journey
Perry, Virgshawn
  See Artifacts
Persson, Nina
  See Cardigans
Pet Shop Boys **5**
Peter, Paul & Mary **4**
Peters, Bernadette **7**
Peters, Dan
  See Mudhoney
Peters, Joey
  See Grant Lee Buffalo
Peters, Mike
  See Alarm
Petersen, Chris
  See Front Line Assembly
Peterson, Debbi
  See Bangles
Peterson, Garry
  See Guess Who
Peterson, Oscar **11**
Peterson, Vicki
  See Bangles
Petersson, Tom
  See Cheap Trick
Petra **3**
Petrucci, John
  See Dream Theater
Petty, Tom **9**
  Also see Tom Petty and the Heartbreakers
Pfaff, Kristen
  See Hole
Phair, Liz **14**
Phantom, Slim Jim
  See Stray Cats, The
Pharcyde, The **17**
Phelps, Doug
  See Kentucky Headhunters, The
Phelps, Ricky Lee
  See Kentucky Headhunters, The
Phife
  See Tribe Called Quest, A
Phil, Gary
  See Boston
Philbin, Greg
  See REO Speedwagon
Philips, Anthony
  See Genesis
Phillips, Chris
  See Squirrel Nut Zippers
Phillips, Chynna
  See Wilson Phillips
Phillips, Glenn
  See Toad the Wet Sprocket
Phillips, Grant Lee
  See Grant Lee Buffalo
Phillips, Harvey **3**
Phillips, John
  See Mamas and the Papas
Phillips, Mackenzie
  See Mamas and the Papas
Phillips, Michelle
  See Mamas and the Papas
Phillips, Sam **5**
Phillips, Sam **12**
Phillips, Shelley
  See Point of Grace
Phillips, Simon
  See Judas Priest

Phish **25**
  Earlier sketch in CM **13**
Phungula, Inos
  See Ladysmith Black Mambazo
Piaf, Edith **8**
Piazzolla, Astor **18**
Picciotto, Joe
  See Fugazi
Piccolo, Greg
  See Roomful of Blues
Pickering, Michael
  See M People
Pickett, Wilson **10**
Pierce, Charlie
  See Memphis Jug Band
Pierce, Marvin "Merv"
  See Ohio Players
Pierce, Webb **15**
Pierson, Kate
  See B-52's, The
Pilatus, Rob
  See Milli Vanilli
Pilson, Jeff
  See Dokken
Pinder, Michael
  See Moody Blues, The
Pine, Courtney
  See Soul II Soul
Pink Floyd **2**
Pinkus, Jeff
  See Butthole Surfers
Pinnick, Doug
  See King's X
Pires, Maria João **26**
Pirner, Dave
  See Soul Asylum
Pirroni, Marco
  See Siouxsie and the Banshees
Pixies, The **21**
Pizzicato Five **18**
Plakas, Dee
  See L7
Plant, Robert **2**
  Also see Led Zeppelin
Platters, The **25**
Ploog, Richard
  See Church, The
Pogues, The **6**
Poi Dog Pondering **17**
Poindexter, Buster
  See Johansen, David
Pointer, Anita
  See Pointer Sisters, The
Pointer, Bonnie
  See Pointer Sisters, The
Pointer, June
  See Pointer Sisters, The
Pointer, Ruth
  See Pointer Sisters, The
Pointer Sisters, The **9**
Poison **11**
Poison Ivy
  See Rorschach, Poison Ivy
Poland, Chris
  See Megadeth
Polce, Tom
  See Letters to Cleo
Police, The **20**
Pollard, Jim
  See Guided By Voices
Pollard, Robert, Jr.
  See Guided By Voices
Pollock, Courtney Adam
  See Aquabats

Polygon Window
  See Aphex Twin
Pomus, Doc
  See Doc Pomus
Ponty, Jean-Luc **8**
  Also see Mahavishnu Orchestra
Pop, Iggy **23**
  Earlier sketch in CM **1**
Popper, John
  See Blues Traveler
Porter, Cole **10**
Porter, George, Jr.
  See Meters, The
Porter, Tiran
  See Doobie Brothers, The
Portishead **22**
Portman-Smith, Nigel
  See Pentangle
Portnoy, Mike
  See Dream Theater
Posdnuos
  See De La Soul
Post, Louise
  See Veruca Salt
Post, Mike **21**
Potter, Janna
  See Avalon
Potts, Sean
  See Chieftains, The
Powell, Baden **23**
Powell, Billy
  See Lynyrd Skynyrd
Powell, Bud **15**
Powell, Cozy
  See Emerson, Lake & Palmer/Powell
Powell, Kobie
  See US3
Powell, Paul
  See Aztec Camera
Powell, William
  See O'Jays, The
Powers, Kid Congo
  See Congo Norvell
Prater, Dave
  See Sam and Dave
Prefab Sprout **15**
Presley, Elvis **1**
Pretenders, The **8**
Pretty Things, The **26**
Previn, André **15**
Price, Alan
  See Animals
Price, Leontyne **6**
Price, Lloyd **25**
Price, Louis
  See Temptations, The
Price, Mark
  See Archers of Loaf
Price, Ray **11**
Price, Rick
  See Electric Light Orchestra
Pride, Charley **4**
Priest, Maxi **20**
Prima, Louis **18**
Primal Scream **14**
Primettes, The
  See Supremes, The
Primus **11**
Prince **14**
  Earlier sketch in CM **1**
Prince Be
  See P.M. Dawn
Prince, Prairie
  See Journey
Prine, John **7**

Prior, Maddy
  See Steeleye Span
Proclaimers, The **13**
Prodigy **22**
Professor Longhair **6**
Prong **23**
Propatier, Joe
  See Silver Apples
Propellerheads **26**
Propes, Duane
  See Little Texas
Prout, Brian
  See Diamond Rio
Public Enemy **4**
Puccini, Giacomo **25**
Puente, Tito **14**
Puff Daddy
  See Combs, Sean "Puffy"
Pullen, Don **16**
Pulp **18**
Pulsford, Nigel
  See Bush
Pusey, Clifford "Moonie"
  See Steel Pulse
Pyle, Andy
  See Kinks, The
Pyle, Artemis
  See Lynyrd Skynyrd
Pyle, Pip
  See Gong
Q-Tip
  See Tribe Called Quest, A
Quaife, Peter
  See Kinks, The
Quasi **24**
Quasthoff, Thomas **26**
Queen **6**
Queen Ida **9**
Queen Latifah **24**
  Earlier sketch in CM **6**
Queensryche **8**
Querfurth, Carl
  See Roomful of Blues
Quicksilver Messenger Service **23**
R.E.M. **25**
  Earlier sketch in CM **5**
Rabbitt, Eddie **24**
  Earlier sketch in CM **5**
Rabin, Trevor
  See Yes
Radiohead **24**
Raffi **8**
Rage Against the Machine **18**
Raheem
  See GetoBoys, The
Rainey, Ma **22**
Rainey, Sid
  See Compulsion
Rainford, Simone
  See All Saints
Raitt, Bonnie **23**
  Earlier sketch in CM **3**
Rakim
  See Eric B. and Rakim
Raleigh, Don
  See Squirrel Nut Zippers
Ralph Sharon Quartet **26**
Ralphs, Mick
  See Bad Company
Rammstein **25**
Ramone, C. J.
  See Ramones, The
Ramone, Dee Dee
  See Ramones, The

Ramone, Joey
  See Ramones, The
Ramone, Johnny
  See Ramones, The
Ramone, Marky
  See Ramones, The
Ramone, Ritchie
  See Ramones, The
Ramone, Tommy
  See Ramones, The
Ramones, The **9**
Rampal, Jean-Pierre **6**
Ramsay, Andy
  See Stereolab
Ranaldo, Lee
  See Sonic Youth
Randall, Bobby
  See Sawyer Brown
Raney, Jerry
  See Beat Farmers
Rangell, Andrew **24**
Ranglin, Ernest
  See Skatalites, The
Ranken, Andrew
  See Pogues, The
Rankin, Cookie
  See Rankins, The
Rankin, Heather
  See Rankins, The
Rankin, Jimmy
  See Rankins, The
Rankin, John Morris
  See Rankins, The
Rankin, Raylene
  See Rankins, The
Ranking, Roger
  See English Beat, The
Rankins, The **24**
Rapp, Tom
  See Pearls Before Swine
Rarebell, Herman
  See Scorpions, The
Rasputina **26**
Ravel, Maurice **25**
Raven, Paul
  See Prong
Ray, Amy
  See Indigo Girls
Ray Condo and His Ricochets **26**
Raybon, Marty
  See Shenandoah
Raye, Collin **16**
Raymonde, Simon
  See Cocteau Twins, The
Rea, Chris **12**
Read, John
  See Specials, The
Reagon, Bernice Johnson
  See Sweet Honey in the Rock
Red Hot Chili Peppers, The **7**
Redd Kross **20**
Redding, Otis **5**
Reddy, Helen **9**
Redman, Don
  See McKinney's Cotton Pickers
Redman, Joshua **25**
  Earlier sketch in CM **12**
Redpath, Jean **1**
Reece, Chris
  See Social Distortion
Reed, Herbert
  See Platters, The
Reed, Jimmy **15**
Reed, Lou **16**
  Earlier sketch in CM **1**
  Also see Velvet Underground, The

Reef **24**
Reese, Della **13**
Reeves, Dianne **16**
Reeves, Jim **10**
Reeves, Lois
  See Martha and the Vandellas
Reeves, Martha **4**
  Also see Martha and the Vandellas
Reich, Steve **8**
Reid, Charlie
  See Proclaimers, The
Reid, Christopher
  See Kid 'n Play
Reid, Craig
  See Proclaimers, The
Reid, Delroy "Junior"
  See Black Uhuru
Reid, Don
  See Statler Brothers, The
Reid, Ellen Lorraine
  See Crash Test Dummies
Reid, Harold
  See Statler Brothers, The
Reid, Janet
  See Black Uhuru
Reid, Jim
  See Jesus and Mary Chain, The
Reid, Vernon **2**
  Also see Living Colour
Reid, William
  See Jesus and Mary Chain, The
Reifman, William
  See KMFDM
Reinhardt, Django **7**
Reitzell, Brian
  See Redd Kross
Relf, Keith
  See Yardbirds, The
Renbourn, John
  See Pentangle
Reno, Ronnie
  See Osborne Brothers, The
REO Speedwagon **23**
Replacements, The **7**
Republica **20**
Residents, The **14**
Restless Heart **12**
Revell, Adrian
  See Jamiroquai
Rex
  See Pantera
Reyes, Andre
  See Gipsy Kings, The
Reyes, Canut
  See Gipsy Kings, The
Reyes, Nicolas
  See Gipsy Kings, The
Reynolds, Nick
  See Kingston Trio, The
Reynolds, Robert
  See Mavericks, The
Reynolds, Sheldon
  See Earth, Wind and Fire
Reznor, Trent **13**
Rhodes, Nick
  See Duran Duran
Rhodes, Philip
  See Gin Blossoms
Rhodes, Todd
  See McKinney's Cotton Pickers
Rhone, Sylvia **13**
Rice, Chris **25**
Rich, Buddy **13**

Rich, Charlie **3**
Richard, Cliff **14**
Richard, Zachary **9**
Richards, Edward
  See Shamen, The
Richards, Keith **11**
  Also see Rolling Stones, The
Richardson, Geoffrey
  See Caravan
Richardson, Kevin
  See Backstreet Boys
Richey, Kim **20**
Richie, Lionel **2**
  Also see Commodores, The
Richling, Greg
  See Wallflowers, The
Richman, Jonathan **12**
Richrath, Gary
  See REO Speedwagon
Rick, Dave
  See King Missile
Ricochet **23**
Riebling, Scott
  See Letters to Cleo
Rieckermann, Ralph
  See Scorpions, The
Riedel, Oliver
  See Rammstein
Rieflin, William
  See Ministry
Rieu, André **26**
Riles, Kelly
  See Velocity Girl
Riley, Teddy "Street" **14**
  See Blackstreet
Riley, Timothy Christian
  See Tony! Toni! Toné!
Rippon, Steve
  See Lush
Ritchie, Brian
  See Violent Femmes
Ritchie, Jean **4**
Ritenour, Lee **7**
Roach, Max **12**
Roback, David
  See Mazzy Star
Robbins, Charles David
  See BlackHawk
Robbins, Marty **9**
Roberts, Brad
  See Crash Test Dummies
Roberts, Brad
  See Gwar
Roberts, Dan
  See Crash Test Dummies
Roberts, Ken
  See Charm Farm
Roberts, Marcus **6**
Roberts, Nathan
  See Flaming Lips
Robertson, Brian
  See Motörhead
  Also see Thin Lizzy
Robertson, Ed
  See Barenaked Ladies
Robertson, Robbie **2**
  Also see Band, The
Robeson, Paul **8**
Robi, Paul
  See Platters, The
Robie, Milton
  See Memphis Jug Band
Robillard, Duke **2**
  Also see Roomful of Blues

Robinson, Arnold
  See Nylons, The
Robinson, Chris
  See Black Crowes, The
Robinson, Cynthia
  See Sly & the Family Stone
Robinson, David
  See Cars, The
Robinson, Dawn
  See En Vogue
Robinson, R.B.
  See Soul Stirrers, The
Robinson, Rich
  See Black Crowes, The
Robinson, Romye "Booty Brown"
  See Pharcyde, The
Robinson, Smokey **1**
Roche, Maggie
  See Roches, The
Roche, Suzzy
  See Roches, The
Roche, Terre
  See Roches, The
Roches, The **18**
Rockenfield, Scott
  See Queensryche
Rocker, Lee
  See Stray Cats, The
Rockett, Rikki
  See Poison
Rockin' Dopsie **10**
Rodford, Jim
  See Kinks, The
Rodgers, Jimmie **3**
Rodgers, Nile **8**
Rodgers, Paul
  See Bad Company
Rodgers, Richard **9**
Rodney, Red **14**
Rodriguez, Rico
  See Skatalites, The
  Also see Specials, The
Rodriguez, Sal
  See War
Roe, Marty
  See Diamond Rio
Roeder, Klaus
  See Kraftwerk
Roeser, Donald
  See Blue Oyster Cult
Roeser, Eddie "King"
  See Urge Overkill
Roessler, Kira
  See Black Flag
Rogers, Dan
  See Bluegrass Patriots
Rogers, Kenny **1**
Rogers, Norm
  See Jayhawks, The
Rogers, Roy **24**
  Earlier sketch in CM **9**
Rogers, Willie
  See Soul Stirrers, The
Roland, Dean
  See Collective Soul
Roland, Ed
  See Collective Soul
Rolie, Gregg
  See Journey
Rolling Stones, The **23**
  Earlier sketch in CM **3**
Rollins, Henry **11**
  Also see Black Flag
Rollins, Sonny **7**

Rollins, Winston
  See Jamiroquai
Romano, Ruben
  See Fu Manchu
Romm, Ronald
  See Canadian Brass, The
Ronstadt, Linda **2**
Roomful of Blues **7**
Roper, De De
  See Salt-N-Pepa
Rorschach, Poison Ivy
  See Cramps, The
Rosas, Cesar
  See Los Lobos
Rose, Axl
  See Guns n' Roses
Rose, Johanna Maria
  See Anonymous 4
Rose, Michael
  See Black Uhuru
Rosen, Gary
  See Rosenshontz
Rosen, Peter
  See War
Rosenshontz **9**
Rosenthal, Jurgen
  See Scorpions, The
Rosenthal, Phil
  See Seldom Scene, The
Ross, Diana **1**
  Also see Supremes, The
Ross, Malcolm
  See Aztec Camera
Rossdale, Gavin
  See Bush
Rossi, John
  See Roomful of Blues
Rossington, Gary
  See Lynyrd Skynyrd
Rostill, John
  See Shadows, The
Rostropovich, Mstislav **17**
Rota, Nino **13**
Roth, C. P.
  See Blessid Union of Souls
Roth, David Lee **1**
  Also see Van Halen
Roth, Gabrielle **26**
Roth, Ulrich
  See Scorpions, The
Rotheray, Dave
  See Beautiful South
Rotsey, Martin
  See Midnight Oil
Rotten, Johnny
  See Lydon, John
  Also see Sex Pistols, The
Rourke, Andy
  See Smiths, The
Rowberry, Dave
  See Animals
Rowe, Dwain
  See Restless Heart
Rowlands, Bruce
  See Fairport Convention
Rowlands, Tom
  See Chemical Brothers
Rowntree, Dave
  See Blur
Roxette **23**
Rubin, Mark
  See Bad Livers, The
Rubin, Rick **9**
Rubinstein, Arthur **11**

Rucker, Darius
    See Hootie and the Blowfish
Rudd, Phillip
    See AC/DC
Rue, Caroline
    See Hole
Ruffin, David **6**
    Also see Temptations, The
Ruffin, Tamir
    See Dru Hill
Ruffy, Dave
    See Aztec Camera
Run DMC **25**
    Earlier sketch in CM **4**
Rundgren, Todd **11**
RuPaul **20**
Rush **8**
Rush, Otis **12**
Rushlow, Tim
    See Little Texas
Russell, Alecia
    See Sounds of Blackness
Russell, Graham
    See Air Supply
Russell, John
    See Steppenwolf
Russell, Mark **6**
Russell, Mike
    See Shudder to Think
Russell, Pee Wee **25**
Russell, Tom **26**
Rusted Root **26**
Rutherford, Mike
    See Genesis
    Also see Mike & the Mechanics
Rutsey, John
    See Rush
Ryan, David
    See Lemonheads, The
Ryan, Mark
    See Quicksilver Messenger Service
Ryan, Mick
    See Dave Clark Five, The
Ryder, Mitch **23**
    Earlier sketch in CM **11**
Ryland, Jack
    See Three Dog Night
Rzeznik, Johnny
    See Goo Goo Dolls, The
Sabo, Dave
    See Bon Jovi
Sade **2**
Sadier, Laetitia
    See Stereolab
Saffery, Anthony
    See Cornershop
Saffron,
    See Republica
Sager, Carole Bayer **5**
Sahm, Doug
    See Texas Tornados, The
Saint-Saëns, Camille **25**
Sainte-Marie, Buffy **11**
Sakamoto, Ryuichi **19**
Salazar, Arion
    See Third Eye Blind
Salerno-Sonnenberg, Nadja **3**
Saliers, Emily
    See Indigo Girls
Salisbury, Peter
    See Verve, The
    Also see Pizzicato Five
Salmon, Michael
    See Prefab Sprout

Saloman, Nick
    See Bevis Frond
Salonen, Esa-Pekka **16**
Salt-N-Pepa **6**
Saluzzi, Dino **23**
Sam and Dave **8**
Sam, Watters
    See Color Me Badd
Sambora, Richie **24**
    Also see Bon Jovi
Sammy, Piazza
    See Quicksilver Messenger Service
Sampson, Doug
    See Iron Maiden
Samuelson, Gar
    See Megadeth
Samwell-Smith, Paul
    See Yardbirds, The
Sanborn, David **1**
Sanchez, Michel
    See Deep Forest
Sanctuary, Gary
    See Aztec Camera
Sanders, Ric
    See Fairport Convention
Sanders, Steve
    See Oak Ridge Boys, The
Sandman, Mark
    See Morphine
Sandoval, Arturo **15**
Sandoval, Hope
    See Mazzy Star
Sands, Aaron
    See Jars of Clay
Sanford, Gary
    See Aztec Camera
Sangare, Oumou **22**
Sanger, David
    See Asleep at the Wheel
Santana, Carlos **20**
    Earlier sketch in CM **1**
Santiago, Herman
    See Frankie Lymon and The Teenagers
Santiago, Joey
    See Pixies, The
Saraceno, Blues
    See Poison
Sasaki, Mamiko
    See PulpSanders, Pharoah **16**
Satchell, Clarence "Satch"
    See Ohio Players
Satie, Erik **25**
Satriani, Joe **4**
Savage, Rick
    See Def Leppard
Savage, Scott
    See Jars of Clay
Sawyer Brown **13**
Sawyer, Phil
    See Spencer Davis Group
Saxa
    See English Beat, The
Saxon, Stan
    See Dave Clark Five, The
Scaccia, Mike
    See Ministry
Scaggs, Boz **12**
Scanlon, Craig
    See Fall, The
Scarface
    See Geto Boys, The
Schelhaas, Jan
    See Camel
    Also see Caravan

Schemel, Patty
    See Hole
Schenker, Michael
    See Scorpions, The
Schenker, Rudolf
    See Scorpions, The
Schenkman, Eric
    See Spin Doctors
Schermie, Joe
    See Three Dog Night
Scherpenzeel, Ton
    See Camel
Schickele, Peter **5**
Schlitt, John
    See Petra
Schloss, Zander
    See Circle Jerks, The
Schmelling, Johannes
    See Tangerine Dream
Schmid, Daniel
    See Cherry Poppin' Daddies
Schmit, Timothy B.
    See Eagles, The
Schmoovy Schmoove
    See Digital Underground
Schneider, Christoph
    See Rammstein
Schneider, Florian
    See Kraftwerk
Schneider, Fred III
    See B-52's, The
Schnitzler, Conrad
    See Tangerine Dream
Schock, Gina
    See Go-Go's, The
Scholten, Jim
    See Sawyer Brown
Scholz, Tom
    See Boston
Schon, Neal
    See Journey
Schramm, Dave
    See Yo La Tengo
Schrody, Erik
    See House of Pain
Schroyder, Steve
    See Tangerine Dream
Schulman, Mark
    See Foreigner
Schulz, Guenter
    See KMFDM
Schulze, Klaus
    See Tangerine Dream
Schuman, William **10**
Schuur, Diane **6**
Sclavunos, Jim
    See Congo Norvell
Scofield, John **7**
Scorpions, The **12**
Scott, George
    See Five Blind Boys of Alabama
Scott, Howard
    See War
Scott, Jimmy **14**
Scott, Ronald Belford "Bon"
    See AC/DC
Scott, Sherry
    See Earth, Wind and Fire
Scott-Heron, Gil **13**
Scruggs, Earl **3**
Scud Mountain Boys **21**
Seal **14**
Seales, Jim
    See Shenandoah

Seals & Crofts **3**
Seals, Brady
  See Little Texas
Seals, Dan **9**
Seals, Jim
  See Seals & Crofts
Seaman, Ken
  See Bluegrass Patriots
Sears, Pete
  See Jefferson Starship
Sebadoh **26**
Secada, Jon **13**
Secrest, Wayne
  See Confederate Railroad
Sedaka, Neil **4**
Seeger, Peggy **25**
Seeger, Pete **4**
  Also see Weavers, The
Seger, Bob **15**
Segovia, Andres **6**
Seldom Scene, The **4**
Selena **16**
Selway, Phil
  See Radiohead
Sen Dog
  See Cypress Hill
Senior, Milton
  See McKinney's Cotton Pickers
Senior, Russell
  See Pulp
Sensi
  See Soul II Soul
Sepultura **12**
Seraphine, Daniel
  See Chicago
Sermon, Erick
  See EPMD
Sete, Bola **26**
Setzer, Brian
  See Stray Cats, The
Severin, Steven
  See Siouxsie and the Banshees
Severinsen, Doc **1**
Sex Pistols, The **5**
Sexton, Chad
  See 311
Seymour, Neil
  See Crowded House
Shabalala, Ben
  See Ladysmith Black Mambazo
Shabalala, Headman
  See Ladysmith Black Mambazo
Shabalala, Jockey
  See Ladysmith Black Mambazo
Shabalala, Joseph
  See Ladysmith Black Mambazo
Shade, Will
  See Memphis Jug Band
Shadows, The **22**
Shaffer, Paul **13**
Shai **23**
Shakespeare, Robbie
  See Sly and Robbie
Shakur, Tupac
  See 2Pac
Shallenberger, James
  See Kronos Quartet
Shamen, The **23**
Shane, Bob
  See Kingston Trio, The
Shanice **14**
Shankar, Ravi **9**
Shannon, Del **10**
Shannon, Sarah
  See Velocity Girl

Shanté **10**
Shapiro, Jim
  See Veruca Salt
Shapps, Andre
  See Big Audio Dynamite
Sharon, Lois & Bram **6**
Sharp, Dave
  See Alarm
Sharpe, Matt
  See Weezer
Sharrock, Chris
  See Lightning Seeds
Sharrock, Sonny **15**
Shaw, Adrian
  See Bevis Frond
Shaw, Artie **8**
Shaw, Martin
  See Jamiroquai
Shea, Tom
  See Scud Mountain Boys
Shearer, Harry
  See Spinal Tap
Sheehan, Bobby
  See Blues Traveler
Sheehan, Fran
  See Boston
Sheila E. **3**
Shelley, Peter
  See Buzzcocks, The
Shelley, Steve
  See Sonic Youth
Shenandoah **17**
Shepherd, Kenny Wayne **22**
Sheppard, Rodney
  See Sugar Ray
Sherba, John
  See Kronos Quartet
Sherinian, Derek
  See Dream Theater
Sherman, Jack
  See Red Hot Chili Peppers, The
Shines, Johnny **14**
Shirelles, The **11**
Shirley, Danny
  See Confederate Railroad
Shively, William
  See Big Mountain
Shock G
  See Digital Underground
Shocked, Michelle **4**
Shocklee, Hank **15**
Shogren, Dave
  See Doobie Brothers, The
Shonen Knife **13**
Shontz, Bill
  See Rosenshontz
Shorter, Wayne **5**
  Also see Weather Report
Shovell
  See M People
Shudder to Think **20**
Siberry, Jane **6**
Sice
  See Boo Radleys, The
Sidelnyk, Steve
  See Aztec Camera
Siebenberg, Bob
  See Supertramp
Siegal, Janis
  See Manhattan Transfer, The
Sikes, C. David
  See Boston
Silk **26**
Sills, Beverly **5**
Silva, Kenny Jo
  See Beaver Brown Band, The

Silver Apples **23**
Silverchair **20**
Simien, Terrance **12**
Simins, Russell
  See Jon Spencer Blues Explosion
Simmons, Gene
  See Kiss
Simmons, Joe "Run"
  See Run DMC
Simmons, Patrick
  See Doobie Brothers, The
Simmons, Russell **7**
Simmons, Trinna
  See Spearhead
Simms, Nick
  See Cornershop
Simon and Garfunkel **24**
Simon, Carly **22**
  Earlier sketch in CM **4**
Simon, Paul **16**
  Earlier sketch in CM **1**
  See also Simon and Garfunkel
Simone, Nina **11**
Simonon, Paul
  See Clash, The
Simons, Ed
  See Chemical Brothers
Simple Minds **21**
Simpson, Denis
  See Nylons, The
Simpson, Derrick "Duckie"
  See Black Uhuru
Simpson, Mel
  See US3
Simpson, Ray
  See Village People, The
Simpson, Rose
  See Incredible String Band
Sims, David William
  See Jesus Lizard
Sims, Neil
  See Catherine Wheel
Sin, Will
  See Shamen, The
Sinatra, Frank **23**
  Earlier sketch in CM **1**
Sinclair, David
  See Camel
  See Caravan
Sinclair, Gord
  See Tragically Hip, The
Sinclair, Richard
  See Camel
  See Caravan
Sinfield, Peter
  See King Crimson
Singer, Eric
  See Black Sabbath
Singer, Eric
  See Kiss
Singh, Talvin
  See Massive Attack
Singh, Tjinder
  See Cornershop
Sioux, Siouxsie
  See Siouxsie and the Banshees
Siouxsie and the Banshees **8**
Sir Mix-A-Lot **14**
Sir Rap-A-Lot
  See Geto Boys, The
Sirois, Joe
  See Mighty Mighty Bosstones
Siverton
  See Specials, The
Sixpence None the Richer **26**

Sixx, Nikki
  See Mötley Crüe
Sixx, Roger
  See Less Than Jake
Skaggs, Ricky **5**
  Also see Country Gentlemen, The
Skatalites, The **18**
Skeoch, Tommy
  See Tesla
Skillings, Muzz
  See Living Colour
Skinny Puppy **17**
Sklamberg, Lorin
  See Klezmatics, The
Skoob
  See Das EFX
Slash
  See Guns n' Roses
Slayer **10**
Sleater-Kinney **20**
Sledd, Dale
  See Osborne Brothers, The
Sledge, Percy **15**
Sledge, Robert
  See Ben Folds Five
Slick, Grace
  See Jefferson Airplane
Slijngaard, Ray
  See 2 Unlimited
Sloan, Eliot
  See Blessid Union of Souls
Slovak, Hillel
  See Red Hot Chili Peppers, The
Sly & the Family Stone **24**
Sly and Robbie **13**
Small, Heather
  See M People
Smalls, Derek
  See Spinal Tap
Smart, Terence
  See Butthole Surfers
Smashing Pumpkins **13**
Smear, Pat
  See Foo Fighters
Smith, Adrian
  See Iron Maiden
Smith, Bessie **3**
Smith, Brad
  See Blind Melon
Smith, Chad
  See Red Hot Chili Peppers, The
Smith, Charles
  See Kool & the Gang
Smith, Curt
  See Tears for Fears
Smith, Debbie
  See Curve
  See Echobelly
Smith, Fran
  See Hooters
Smith, Fred
  See Television
Smith, Fred
  See Blondie
Smith, Fred
  See MC5, The
Smith, Garth
  See Buzzcocks, The
Smith, Joe
  See McKinney's Cotton Pickers
Smith, Kevin
  See dc Talk
Smith, Mark E.
  See Fall, The

Smith, Michael W. **11**
Smith, Mike
  See Dave Clark Five, The
Smith, Parrish
  See EPMD
Smith, Patti **17**
  Earlier sketch in CM **1**
Smith, Robert
  See Cure, The
  Also see Siouxsie and the Banshees
Smith, Robert
  See Spinners, The
Smith, Shawn
  See Brad
Smith, Smitty
  See Three Dog Night
Smith, Steve
  See Journey
Smith, Tweed
  See War
Smith, Wendy
  See Prefab Sprout
Smith, Will **26**
  Also see DJ Jazzy Jeff and the Fresh Prince
Smithereens, The **14**
Smiths, The **3**
Smyth, Gilli
  See Gong
Smyth, Joe
  See Sawyer Brown
Sneed, Floyd Chester
  See Three Dog Night
Snoop Doggy Dogg **17**
Snow **23**
Snow, Don
  See Squeeze
Snow, Phoebe **4**
Soan, Ashley
  See Del Amitri
Sobule, Jill **20**
Solal, Martial **4**
Soloff, Lew
  See Blood, Sweat and Tears
Solti, Georg **13**
Son Volt **21**
Sondheim, Stephen **8**
Sonefeld, Jim
  See Hootie and the Blowfish
Sonic Youth **26**
  Earlier sketch in CM **9**
Sonnenberg, Nadja Salerno
  See Salerno-Sonnenberg, Nadja
Sonni, Jack
  See Dire Straits
Sonnier, Jo-El **10**
Sonny and Cher **24**
Sorum, Matt
  See Cult, The
Sosa, Mercedes **3**
Soucie, Michael
  See Surfin' Pluto
Soul Asylum **10**
Soul Coughing **21**
Soul II Soul **17**
Soul Stirrers, The **11**
Soundgarden **6**
Sounds of Blackness **13**
Sousa, John Philip **10**
Southerland, Bill
  See Kilgore
Spampinato, Joey
  See NRBQ
Spampinato, Johnny
  See NRBQ

Spann, Otis **18**
Sparks **18**
Sparks, Donita
  See L7
Spearhead **19**
Special Ed **16**
Specials, The **21**
Spector, Phil **4**
Speech
  See Arrested Development
Spellman, Jim
  See Velocity Girl
Spence, Alexander "Skip"
  See Jefferson Airplane
  Also see Moby Grape
Spence, Cecil
  See Israel Vibration
Spence, Skip
  See Spence, Alexander "Skip"
Spencer, Jeremy
  See Fleetwood Mac
Spencer, Jim
  See Dave Clark Five, The
Spencer, Jon
  See Jon Spencer Blues Explosion
Spencer, Thad
  See Jayhawks, The
Spice Girls **22**
Spin Doctors **14**
Spinal Tap **8**
Spinners, The **21**
Spirit **22**
Spitz, Dan
  See Anthrax
Spitz, Dave
  See Black Sabbath
Sponge **18**
Spring, Keith
  See NRBQ
Springfield, Dusty **20**
Springfield, Rick **9**
Springsteen, Bruce **25**
  Earlier sketch in CM **6**
Sproule, Daithi
  See Altan
Sprout, Tobin
  See Guided By Voices
Squeeze **5**
Squire, Chris
  See Yes
Squire, John
  See Stone Roses, The
Squires, Rob
  See Big Head Todd and the Monsters
Squirrel Nut Zippers **20**
St. Hubbins, David
  See Spinal Tap
St. James, Rebecca **26**
St. John, Mark
  See Kiss
St. Marie, Buffy
  See Sainte-Marie, Buffy
St. Nicholas, Nick
  See Steppenwolf
Stacey, Peter "Spider"
  See Pogues, The
Stacy, Jeremy
  See Aztec Camera
Staehely, Al
  See Spirit
Staehely, J. Christian
  See Spirit
Stafford, Jo **24**
Staley, Layne
  See Alice in Chains

Staley, Tom
  See NRBQ
Stanier, John
  See Helmet
Stanley, Ian
  See Tears for Fears
Stanley, Paul
  See Kiss
Stanley, Ralph **5**
Stansfield, Lisa **9**
Staples, Mavis **13**
Staples, Neville
  See Specials, The
Staples, Pops **11**
Starcrunch
  See Man or Astroman?
Starling, John
  See Seldom Scene, The
Starr, Mike
  See Alice in Chains
Starr, Ringo **24**
  Earlier sketch in CM **10**
  Also see Beatles, The
Starship
  See Jefferson Airplane
Statler Brothers, The **8**
Stead, David
  See Beautiful South
Steaks, Chuck
  See Quicksilver Messenger Service
Steel, John
  See Animals
Steel Pulse **14**
Steele, Billy
  See Sounds of Blackness
Steele, David
  See English Beat, The
  Also see Fine Young Cannibals
Steele, Jeffrey
  See Boy Howdy
Steele, Michael
  See Bangles
Steely Dan **5**
Stefani, Gwen
  See No Doubt
Steier, Rick
  See Warrant
Stein, Chris
  See Blondie
Steinberg, Lewis
  See Booker T. & the M.G.'s
Steinberg, Sebastian
  See Soul Coughing
Stephenson, Van Wesley
  See BlackHawk
Steppenwolf **20**
Sterban, Richard
  See Oak Ridge Boys, The
Stereolab **18**
Sterling, Lester
  See Skatalites, The
Stern, Isaac **7**
Stevens, Cat **3**
Stevens, Ray **7**
Stevens, Roger
  See Blind Melon
Stevens, Vol
  See Memphis Jug Band
Stevenson, Bill
  See Black Flag
Stevenson, Don
  See Moby Grape
Steward, Pat
  See Odds

Stewart, Dave
  See Eurythmics
Stewart, Derrick "Fatlip"
  See Pharcyde, The
Stewart, Freddie
  See Sly & the Family Stone
Stewart, Ian
  See Rolling Stones, The
Stewart, Jamie
  See Cult, The
Stewart, John
  See Kingston Trio, The
Stewart, Larry
  See Restless Heart
Stewart, Rod **20**
  Earlier sketch in CM **2**
  Also see Faces, The
Stewart, Sylvester
  See Sly & the Family Stone
Stewart, Tyler
  See Barenaked Ladies
Stewart, Vaetta
  See Sly & the Family Stone
Stewart, William
  See Third World
Stewart, Winston "Metal"
  See Mystic Revealers
Stiff, Chris
  See Jackyl
Stills, Stephen **5**
  See Buffalo Springfield
  Also see Crosby, Stills, and Nash
Sting **19**
  Earlier sketch in CM **2**
  Also see Police, The
Stinson, Bob
  See Replacements, The
Stinson, Tommy
  See Replacements, The
Stipe, Michael
  See R.E.M.
Stockman, Shawn
  See Boyz II Men
Stockwood, Kim **26**
Stoll
  See Clannad
  See Big Mountain
Stoller, Mike
  See Leiber and Stoller
Stoltz, Brian
  See Neville Brothers, The
Stoltzman, Richard **24**
Stonadge, Gary
  See Big Audio Dynamite
Stone, Curtis
  See Highway 101
Stone, Doug **10**
Stone Roses, The **16**
Stone, Sly **8**
Stone Temple Pilots **14**
Stookey, Paul
  See Peter, Paul & Mary
Story, Liz **2**
Story, The **13**
Stradlin, Izzy
  See Guns n' Roses
Strain, Sammy
  See O'Jays, The
Strait, George **5**
Stratton, Dennis
  See Iron Maiden
Strauss, Richard **25**
Stravinsky, Igor **21**
Straw, Syd **18**

Stray Cats, The **11**
Strayhorn, Billy **13**
Street, Richard
  See Temptations, The
Streisand, Barbra **2**
Strickland, Keith
  See B-52's, The
Stringer, Gary
  See Reef
Strummer, Joe
  See Clash, The
Stryper **2**
Stuart, Mark
  See Audio Adrenaline
Stuart, Marty **9**
Stuart, Peter
  See Dog's Eye View
Stubbs, Levi
  See Four Tops, The
Styne, Jule **21**
Subdudes, The **18**
Sublime **19**
Such, Alec Jon
  See Bon Jovi
Suede **20**
Sugar Ray **22**
Sugarcubes, The **10**
Suicidal Tendencies **15**
Sulley, Suzanne
  See Human League, The
Sullivan, Jacqui
  See Bananarama
Sullivan, Kirk
  See FourHim
Summer, Donna **12**
Summer, Mark
  See Turtle Island String Quartet
Summers, Andy **3**
  Also see Police, The
Sumner, Bernard
  See Joy Division
  Also see New Order
Sun Ra **5**
Sundays, The **20**
Sunnyland Slim **16**
Super DJ Dmitry
  See Deee-lite
Superdrag **23**
Supertramp **25**
Supremes, The **6**
Sure!, Al B. **13**
Surfaris, The **23**
Surfin' Pluto **24**
Sutcliffe, Stu
  See Beatles, The
Sutherland, Joan **13**
Svenigsson, Magnus
  See Cardigans
Svensson, Peter
  See Cardigans
Svigals, Alicia
  See Klezmatics, The
Swarbrick, Dave
  See Fairport Convention
Sweat, Keith **13**
Sweet Honey In The Rock **26**
  Earlier sketch in CM **1**
Sweet, Matthew **9**
Sweet, Michael
  See Stryper
Sweet, Robert
  See Stryper
Sweethearts of the Rodeo **12**

Swing, DeVante
  See Jodeci
SWV **14**
Sykes, John
  See Whitesnake
Sykes, Roosevelt **20**
Sylvain, Sylvain
  See New York Dolls
T. Rex **11**
Tabac, Tony
  See Joy Division
Tabor, Ty
  See King's X
TAFKAP (The Artist Formerly Known as
  Prince)
  See Prince
Taggart, Jeremy
  See Our Lady Peace
Tait, Michael
  See dc Talk
Taj Mahal **6**
Tajima, Takao
  See Pizzicato Five
Takac, Robby
  See Goo Goo Dolls, The
Takanami
  See Pizzicato Five
Take 6 **6**
Takemitsu, Toru **6**
Takizawa, Taishi
  See Ghost
Talbot, John Michael **6**
Talcum, Joe Jack
  See Dead Milkmen
Talking Heads **1**
Tampa Red **25**
Tandy, Richard
  See Electric Light Orchestra
Tangerine Dream **12**
Taree, Aerle
  See Arrested Development
Tate, Geoff
  See Queensryche
Tatum, Art **17**
Taupin, Bernie **22**
Taylor, Andy
  See Duran Duran
Taylor, Billy **13**
Taylor, Cecil **9**
Taylor, Chad
  See Live
Taylor, Courtney
Taylor, Dave
  See Pere Ubu
Taylor, Dick
  See Rolling Stones, The
Taylor, Earl
  See Country Gentlemen, The
Taylor, James **25**
  Earlier sketch in CM **2**
Taylor, James "J.T."
  See Kool & the Gang
Taylor, John
  See Duran Duran
Taylor, Johnnie
  See Soul Stirrers, The
Taylor, Koko **10**
Taylor, Leroy
  See Soul Stirrers, The
Taylor, Melvin
  See Ventures, The
Taylor, Mick
  See Rolling Stones, The

Taylor, Philip "Philthy Animal"
  See Motörhead
Taylor, Roger Meadows
  See Queen
Taylor, Roger
  See Duran Duran
Taylor, Steve **26**
Taylor, Teresa
  See Butthole Surfers
Taylor, Zola
  See Platters, The
Te Kanawa, Kiri **2**
Teagarden, Jack **10**
Tears for Fears **6**
Technotronic **5**
Teenage Fanclub **13**
Television **17**
Teller, Al **15**
Temirkanov, Yuri **26**
Tempesta, John
  See White Zombie
Temple, Michelle
  See Pere Ubu
Temptations, The **3**
Tennant, Neil
  See Pet Shop Boys
Terminator X
  See Public Enemy
Terrell, Jean
  See Supremes, The
Terry, Boyd
  See Aquabats
Terry, Clark **24**
Tesh, John **20**
Tesla **15**
Texas Tornados, The **8**
Thacker, Rocky
  See Shenandoah
Thain, Gary
  See Uriah Heep
Thayil, Kim
  See Soundgarden
The The **15**
They Might Be Giants **7**
Thibaudet, Jean-Yves **24**
Thielemans, Toots **13**
Thin Lizzy **13**
Third Eye Blind **25**
Third World **13**
Thomas, Alex
  See Earth, Wind and Fire
Thomas, David
  See Pere Ubu
Thomas, David
  See Take 6
Thomas, David Clayton
  See Clayton-Thomas, David
Thomas, Dennis "D.T."
  See Kool & the Gang
Thomas, George "Fathead"
  See McKinney's Cotton Pickers
Thomas, Irma **16**
Thomas, Mickey
  See Jefferson Starship
Thomas, Olice
  See Five Blind Boys of Alabama
Thomas, Ray
  See Moody Blues, The
Thomas, Rozonda "Chilli"
  See TLC
Thompson, Chester
  See Weather Report
Thompson, Danny
  See Pentangle

Thompson, Dennis
  See MC5, The
Thompson, Dougie
  See Supertramp
Thompson, Les
  See Nitty Gritty Dirt Band, The
Thompson, Mayo
  See Pere Ubu
Thompson, Porl
  See Cure, The
Thompson, Richard **7**
  Also see Fairport Convention
Thomson, Kristin
  See Tsunami
Thorn, Christopher
  See Blind Melon
Thorn, Stan
  See Shenandoah
Thorn, Tracey
  See Everything But The Girl
  Also see Massive Attack
Thornalley, Phil
  See Cure, The
Thornburg, Lee
  See Supertramp
Thornhill, Leeroy
  See Prodigy
Thornton, Big Mama **18**
Thornton
  See Color Me Badd
Thornton, Willie Mae
  See Thornton, Big Mama
Threadgill, Henry **9**
Three Dog Night **5**
Throwing Muses **15**
Thunders, Johnny
  See New York Dolls
Tickner, George
  See Journey
Tiffany **4**
Tikaram, Tanita **9**
Tilbrook, Glenn
  See Squeeze
Tiller, Mary
  See Anointed
Tilley, Sandra
  See Martha and the Vandellas
Tillis, Mel **7**
Tillis, Pam **25**
  Earlier sketch in CM **8**
Tilson Thomas, Michael **24**
Timberlake, Justin
  See 'N Sync
Timbuk 3 **3**
Timmins, Margo
  See Cowboy Junkies, The
Timmins, Michael
  See Cowboy Junkies, The
Timmins, Peter
  See Cowboy Junkies, The
Timms, Sally
  See Mekons, The
Tinsley, Boyd
  See Dave Matthews Band
Tippin, Aaron **12**
Tipton, Glenn
  See Judas Priest
TLC **15**
Toad the Wet Sprocket **13**
Toback, Jeremy
  See Brad
Todd, Andy
  See Republica
Tolhurst, Laurence
  See Cure, The

Tolland, Bryan
  See Del Amitri
Toller, Dan
  See Allman Brothers, The
Tom Petty and the Heartbreakers **26**
Tone-Loc **3**
Tontoh, Frank
  See Aztec Camera
Tony K
  See Roomful of Blues
Tony! Toni! Toné! **12**
Too $hort **16**
Toohey, Dan
  See Guided By Voices
Took, Steve Peregrine
  See T. Rex
Tool **21**
Toomey, Jenny
  See Tsunami
Topham, Anthony "Top"
  See Yardbirds, The
Tork, Peter
  See Monkees, The
Torme, Mel **4**
Torres, Hector "Tico"
  See Bon Jovi
Toscanini, Arturo **14**
Tosh, Peter **3**
Toure, Ali Farka **18**
Tourish, Ciaran
  See Altan
Toussaint, Allen **11**
Towner, Ralph **22**
Townes, Jeffery
  See DJ Jazzy Jeff and the Fresh Prince
Townshend, Pete **1**
  Also see Who, The
Tragically Hip, The **18**
Travers, Brian
  See UB40
Travers, Mary
  See Peter, Paul & Mary
Travis, Merle **14**
Travis, Randy **9**
Treach
  See Naughty by Nature
Treadmill Trackstar **21**
Tribe Called Quest, A **8**
Tricky **18**
Tricky
  See Massive Attack
Trimm, Rex
  See Cherry Poppin' Daddies
Tritsch, Christian
  See Gong
Tritt, Travis **7**
Trotter, Kera
  See C + C Music Factory
Trucks, Butch
  See Allman Brothers, The
Trugoy the Dove
  See De La Soul
Trujillo, Robert
  See Suicidal Tendencies
Truman, Dan
  See Diamond Rio
Trynin, Jen **21**
Tsunami **21**
Tubb, Ernest **4**
Tubridy, Michael
  See Chieftans, The
Tucker, Corin
  See Sleater-Kinney

Tucker, Moe
  See Velvet Underground, The
Tucker, Sophie **12**
Tucker, Tanya **3**
Tufnel, Nigel
  See Spinal Tap
Tull, Bruce
  See Scud Mountain Boys
Turbin, Neil
  See Anthrax
Turgon, Bruce
  See Foreigner
Turner, Big Joe **13**
Turner, Erik
  See Warrant
Turner, Ike
  See Ike and Tina Turner
Turner, Joe Lynn
  See Deep Purple
Turner, Mike
  See Our Lady Peace
Turner, Sonny
  See Platters, The
Turner, Steve
  See Mudhoney
Turner, Tina **1**
  Also see Ike and Tina Turner
Turpin, Will
  See Collective Soul
Turre, Steve **22**
Turtle Island String Quartet **9**
Tutton, Bill
  See Geraldine Fibbers
Tutuska, George
  See Goo Goo Dolls, The
Tuxedomoon **21**
Twain, Shania **17**
Twist, Nigel
  See Alarm
Twitty, Conway **6**
Tyagi, Paul
  See Del Amitri
Tyler, Steve
  See Aerosmith
Tyner, McCoy **7**
Tyner, Rob
  See MC5, The
Tyson, Ian
  See Ian and Sylvia
Tyson, Ron
  See Temptations, The
U2 **12**
  Earlier sketch in CM **2**
UB40 **4**
Ulmer, James Blood **13**
Ulrich, Lars
  See Metallica
Ulvaeus, Björn
  See Abba
Um Romao, Dom
  See Weather Report
Underworld **26**
Unruh, N. U.
  See Einstürzende Neubauten
Uosikkinen, David
  See Hooters
Upshaw, Dawn **9**
Urge Overkill **17**
US3 **18**
Usher **23**
Utley, Adrian
  See Portishead
Vaché, Jr., Warren **22**

Vachon, Chris
  See Roomful of Blues
Vai, Steve **5**
  Also see Whitesnake
Valdès, Chucho **25**
Valens, Ritchie **23**
Valenti, Dino
  See Quicksilver Messenger Service
Valentine, Gary
  See Blondie
Valentine, Hilton
  See Animals
Valentine, Kathy
  See Go-Go's, The
Valentine, Rae
  See War
Valenzuela, Jesse
  See Gin Blossoms
Valli, Frankie **10**
  Also see Four Seasons, The
Valory, Ross
  See Journey
van Dijk, Carol
  See Bettie Serveert
Van Gelder, Nick
  See Jamiroquai
Van Halen, Alex
  See Van Halen
Van Halen **25**
  Earlier sketch in CM **8**
Van Halen, Edward
  See Van Halen
Van Hook, Peter
  See Mike & the Mechanics
Van Rensalier, Darnell
  See Shai
Van Ronk, Dave **12**
Van Shelton, Ricky **5**
Van Vliet, Don
  See Captain Beefheart
Van Zandt, Townes **13**
Van Zant, Johnny
  See Lynyrd Skynyrd
Van Zant, Ronnie
  See Lynyrd Skynyrd
Vandenburg, Adrian
  See Whitesnake
Vander Ark, Brian
  See Verve Pipe, The
Vander Ark, Brad
  See Verve Pipe, The
Vandross, Luther **24**
  Earlier sketch in CM **2**
Vanessa-Mae **26**
Vanilla Ice **6**
Vasquez, Junior **16**
Vaughan, Jimmie **24**
  Also see Fabulous Thunderbirds, The
Vaughan, Sarah **2**
Vaughan, Stevie Ray **1**
Vedder, Eddie
  See Pearl Jam
Vega, Bobby
  See Quicksilver Messenger Service
Vega, Suzanne **3**
Velocity Girl **23**
Velvet Underground, The **7**
Ventures, The **19**
Verlaine, Tom
  See Television
Verta-Ray, Matt
  See Madder Rose
Veruca Salt **20**
Verve Pipe, The **20**
Verve, The **18**

Vettese, Peter-John
See Jethro Tull
Vicious, Sid
See Sex Pistols, The
Also see Siouxsie and the Banshees
Vickrey, Dan
See Counting Crows
Victor, Tommy
See Prong
Vienna Boys Choir 23
Vig, Butch 17
Also see Garbage
Village People, The 7
Vincent, Gene 19
Vincent, Vinnie
See Kiss
Vinnie
See Naughty by Nature
Vinton, Bobby 12
Violent Femmes 12
Virtue, Michael
See UB40
Visser, Peter
See Bettie Serveert
Vito, Rick
See Fleetwood Mac
Vitous, Mirslav
See Weather Report
Voelz, Susan
See Poi Dog Pondering
Volz, Greg
See Petra
von Karajan, Herbert 1
Von, Eerie
See Danzig
Vox, Bono
See U2
Vudi
See American Music Club
Waaktaar, Pal
See A-ha
Wachtel, Waddy 26
Wade, Adam
See Shudder to Think
Wade, Chrissie
See Alien Sex Fiend
Wade, Nik
See Alien Sex Fiend
Wadenius, George
See Blood, Sweat and Tears
Wadephal, Ralf
See Tangerine Dream
Wagoner, Faidest
See Soul Stirrers, The
Wagoner, Porter 13
Wahlberg, Donnie
See New Kids on the Block
Wailer, Bunny 11
Wainwright III, Loudon 11
Waits, Tom 12
Earlier sketch in CM 1
Wakeling, David
See English Beat, The
Wakeman, Rick
See Yes
Walden, Narada Michael 14
Walford, Britt
See Breeders
Walker, Clay 20
Walker, Colin
See Electric
See King Crimson
Wallace, Richard
See Mighty Clouds of Joy, The

Wallace, Sippie 6
Waller, Charlie
See Country Gentlemen, The
Waller, Fats 7
Wallflowers, The 20
Wallinger, Karl 11
Wallis, Larry
See Motörhead
Walls, Chris
See Dave Clark Five, The
Walls, Denise "Nee-C"
See Anointed
Walls, Greg
See Anthrax
Walsh, Joe 5
Also see Eagles, The
Walsh, Marty
See Supertramp
Walters, Robert "Patch"
See Mystic Revealers
War 14
Ward, Andy
See Bevis Frond
See Camel
Ward, Bill
Ward, Michael
See Wallflowers, The
See Black Sabbath
Ware, Martyn
See Human League, The
Wareham, Dean
See Luna
Wariner, Steve 18
Warner, Les
See Cult, The
Warnes, Jennifer 3
Warrant 17
Warren, George W.
See Five Blind Boys of Alabama
Warren, Mervyn
Warwick, Clint
See Moody Blues, The
Warwick, Dionne 2
Was (Not Was) 6
Was, David
See Was (Not Was)
Was, Don 21
Also see Was (Not Was)
Wash, Martha
See C + C Music Factory
Washington, Chester
See Earth, Wind and Fire
Washington, Dinah 5
Washington, Grover, Jr. 5
Wasserman, Greg
See Offspring
Waters, Crystal 15
Waters, Ethel 11
Waters, Muddy 24
Earlier sketch in CM 4
Waters, Roger
See Pink Floyd
Watkins, Christopher
See Cabaret Voltaire
Watkins, Tionne "T-Boz"
See TLC
Watley, Jody 26
Earlier sketch in CM 9
Watson, Doc 2
Watson, Guy
See Surfaris, The
Watson, Ivory
See Ink Spots
Watt, Ben
See Everything But The Girl

Watt, Mike 22
Also see fIREHOSE
Watts, Bari
See Bevis Frond
Watts, Charlie
See Rolling Stones, The
Watts, Eugene
See Canadian Brass, The
Watts, Lou
See Chumbawamba
Watts, Raymond
See KMFDM
Watts, Todd
See Emmet Swimming
Weaver, Louie
See Petra
Weavers, The 8
Webb, Chick 14
Webb, Jimmy 12
Webb, Paul
See Talk Talk
Webber, Andrew Lloyd
See Lloyd Webber, Andrew
Webber, Mark
See Pulp
Webster, Andrew
See Tsunami
Wedgwood, Mike
See Caravan
Wedren, Craig
See Shudder to Think
Weezer 20
Weider, John
See Animals
Weiland, Scott
See Stone Temple Pilots
Weill, Kurt 12
Weir, Bob
See Grateful Dead, The
Weiss, Janet
See Quasi
Weiss, Janet
See Sleater-Kinney
Welch, Bob
Welch, Bruce
See Shadows, The
Welch, Mcguinness
See Fleetwood Mac
Also see Lords of Acid
Welch, Sean
See Beautiful South
Welk, Lawrence 13
Weller, Paul 14
Wells, Cory
See Three Dog Night
Wells, Junior 17
Wells, Kitty 6
Welnick, Vince
See Grateful Dead, The
Welty, Ron
See Offspring
Wenberg, Erik
See Emmet Swimming
Wendy O. Williams and The Plasmatics 26
West, Brian
See Cherry Poppin' Daddies
West, Dottie 8
West, Steve
See Pavement
Westerberg, Paul 26
Also see Replacements, The
Weston, Randy 15
Weston
See Orb, The

Wetton, John
  See King Crimson
Wexler, Jerry **15**
Weymouth, Tina
  See Talking Heads
Whalen, Katharine
  See Squirrel Nut Zippers
Wheat, Brian
  See Tesla
Wheeler, Audrey
  See C + C Music Factory
Wheeler, Caron
  See Soul II Soul
Wheeler, Harriet
  See Sundays, The
Wheeler, Robert
  See Pere Ubu
Whelan, Bill **20**
Whelan, Gavan
  See James
Whitaker, Rodney **20**
White, Alan
  See Oasis
  See Yes
White, Barry **6**
White, Billy
White, Chris
  See Dire Straits
  See Zombies, The
White, Clarence
  See Byrds, The
White, Dave
  See Warrant
White, Dennis
  See Charm Farm
  See Dokken
White, Freddie
  See Earth, Wind and Fire
White, Lari **15**
White, Mark
  See Mekons, The
White, Mark
  See Spin Doctors
White, Maurice
  See Earth, Wind and Fire
White, Ralph
  See Bad Livers, The
White, Roland
  See Nashville Bluegrass Band
White, Verdine
  See Earth, Wind and Fire
White Zombie **17**
Whitehead, Donald
  See Earth, Wind and Fire
Whiteman, Paul **17**
Whitesnake **5**
Whitfield, Mark **18**
Whitford, Brad
  See Aerosmith
Whitley, Chris **16**
Whitley, Keith **7**
Whittaker, Hudson **20**
Whitten, Chris
  See Dire Straits
Whitwam, Barry
  See Herman's Hermits
Who, The **3**
Wichnewski, Stephen
  See Yo La Tengo
Widenhouse, Je
  See Squirrel Nut Zippers
Wiedlin, Jane
  See Go-Go's, The
Wiggins, Dwayne
  See Tony! Toni! Toné!

Wiggins, Raphael
  See Tony! Toni! Toné!
Wiggs, Josephine
  See Breeders
Wikso, Ron
  See Foreigner
Wilborn, Dave
  See McKinney's Cotton Pickers
Wilburn, Ishmael
  See Weather Report
Wilcox, Imani
  See Pharcyde, The
Wilde, Phil
  See 2 Unlimited
Wilder, Alan
  See Depeche Mode
Wilk, Brad
  See Rage Against the Machine
Wilkeson, Leon
  See Lynyrd Skynyrd
Wilkie, Chris
  See Dubstar
Wilkinson, Geoff
  See US3
Wilkinson, Keith
  See Squeeze
Williams, Andy **2**
Williams, Boris
  See Cure, The
Williams, Cliff
  See AC/DC
Williams, Dana
  See Diamond Rio
Williams, Deniece **1**
Williams, Don **4**
Williams, Eric
  See Blackstreet
Williams, Fred
  See C + C Music Factory
Williams, Hank, Sr. **4**
Williams, Hank, Jr. **1**
Williams, James "Diamond"
  See Ohio Players
Williams, Joe **11**
Williams, John **9**
Williams, Lamar
  See Allman Brothers, The
Williams, Lucinda **24**
  Earlier sketch in CM **10**
Williams, Marion **15**
Williams, Milan
  See Commodores, The
Williams, Otis
  See Temptations, The
Williams, Paul **26**
  Earlier sketch in CM **5**
Williams, Phillard
  See Earth, Wind and Fire
Williams, Robbie **25**
Williams, Terry
  See Dire Straits
Williams, Tony
  See Platters, The
Williams, Vanessa **10**
Williams, Victoria **17**
Williams, Walter
  See O'Jays, The
Williams, Wilbert
  See Mighty Clouds of Joy, The
Williams, William Elliot
  See Artifacts
Williamson, Gloria
  See Martha and the Vandellas
Williamson, Robin
  See Incredible String Band

Williamson, Sonny Boy **9**
Willie D.
  See Geto Boys, The
Willis, Clarence "Chet"
  See Ohio Players
Willis, Kelly **12**
Willis, Larry
  See Blood, Sweat and Tears
Willis, Pete
  See Def Leppard
Willis, Rick
  See Foreigner
Willis, Victor
  See Village People, The
Willner, Hal **10**
Wills, Aaron (P-Nut)
  See 311
Wills, Bob **6**
Wills, Rick
  See Bad Company
Willson-Piper, Marty
  See Church, The
Wilmot, Billy "Mystic"
  See Mystic Revealers
Wilson, Anne
  See Heart
Wilson, Brian **24**
  Also see Beach Boys, The
Wilson, Carl
  See Beach Boys, The
Wilson, Carnie
  See Wilson Phillips
Wilson, Cassandra **26**
  Earlier sketch in CM **12**
Wilson, Chris
  See Love Spit Love
Wilson, Cindy
  See B-52's, The
Wilson, Dennis
  See Beach Boys, The
Wilson, Don
  See Ventures, The
Wilson, Eric
  See Sublime
Wilson, Jackie **3**
Wilson, Kim
  See Fabulous Thunderbirds, The
Wilson, Mary
  See Supremes, The
Wilson, Nancy **14**
  See Heart
Wilson, Orlandus
  See Golden Gate Quartet
Wilson, Patrick
  See Weezer
Wilson Phillips **5**
Wilson, Ransom **5**
Wilson, Ricky
  See B-52's, The
Wilson, Robin
  See Gin Blossoms
Wilson, Ron
  See Surfaris, The
Wilson, Shanice
  See Shanice
Wilson, Wendy
  See Wilson Phillips
Wilson-James, Victoria
  See Shamen, The
Wilton, Michael
  See Queensryche
Wimpfheimer, Jimmy
  See Roomful of Blues
Winans, Carvin
  See Winans, The

Winans, Marvin
  See Winans, The
Winans, Michael
  See Winans, The
Winans, Ronald
  See Winans, The
Winans, The **12**
Winbush, Angela **15**
Winfield, Chuck
  See Blood, Sweat and Tears
Winston, George **9**
Winter, Johnny **5**
Winter, Kurt
  See Guess Who
Winter, Paul **10**
Winthrop, Dave
  See Supertramp
Winwood, Muff
  See Spencer Davis Group
Winwood, Steve **2**
  Also see Spencer Davis Group
  Also see Traffic
Wiseman, Bobby
  See Blue Rodeo
WishBone
  See Bone Thugs-N-Harmony
Withers, Pick
  See Dire Straits
Wolf, Peter
  See J. Geils Band
Wolstencraft, Simon
  See Fall, The
Womack, Bobby **5**
Wonder, Stevie **17**
  Earlier sketch in CM **2**
Wood, Chris
  See Traffic
Wood, Danny
  See New Kids on the Block
Wood, Ron
  See Faces, The
  See Rolling Stones, The
Wood, Roy
  See Electric Light Orchestra
Woods, Gay
  See Steeleye Span
Woods, Terry
  See Pogues, The
Woodson, Ollie
  See Temptations, The
Woodward, Keren
  See Bananarama
Woody, Allen
  See Allman Brothers, The
Woolfolk, Andrew
  See Earth, Wind and Fire
Worley, Jeff
  See Jackyl
Worrell, Bernie **11**
Wray, Link **17**
Wreede, Katrina
  See Turtle Island String Quartet
Wren, Alan
  See Stone Roses, The
Wretzky, D'Arcy
  See Smashing Pumpkins
Wright, Adrian
  See Human League, The
Wright, David "Blockhead"
  See English Beat, The

Wright, Heath
  See Ricochet
Wright, Hugh
  See Boy Howdy
Wright, Jimmy
  See Sounds of Blackness
Wright, Norman
  See Country Gentlemen, The
Wright, Rick
  See Pink Floyd
Wright, Simon
  See AC/DC
Wright, Tim
  See Pere Ubu
Wurzel
  See Motörhead
Wyatt, Robert **24**
Wyman, Bill
  See Bill Wyman & The Rhythm Kings
  See Rolling Stones, The
Wynette, Tammy **24**
  Earlier sketch in CM **2**
Wynne, Philippe
  See Spinners, The
Wynonna **11**
  Also see Judds, The
X **11**
Xefos, Chris
  See King Missile
XTC **26**
  Earlier sketch in CM **10**
Ya Kid K
  See Technotronic
Yamamoto, Hiro
  See Soundgarden
Yamano, Atsuko
  See Shonen Knife
Yamano, Naoko
  See Shonen Knife
Yamashita, Kazuhito **4**
Yamauchi, Tetsu
  See Faces, The
Yamazaki, Iwao
  See Ghost
Yang, Naomi
  See Damon and Naomi
Yankovic, "Weird Al" **7**
Yanni **11**
Yardbirds, The **10**
Yarrow, Peter
  See Peter, Paul & Mary
Yates, Bill
  See Country Gentlemen, The
Yauch, Adam
  See Beastie Boys, The
Yearwood, Trisha **25**
  Earlier sketch in CM **10**
Yella
  See N.W.A.
Yes **8**
Yeston, Maury **22**
Yo La Tengo **24**
  Earlier sketch in CM **9**
Yoakam, Dwight **21**
  Earlier sketch in CM **1**
Yoot, Tukka
  See US3
York, Andrew **15**

York, John
  See Byrds, The
York, Pete
  See Spencer Davis Group
Yorke, Thom E.
  See Radiohead
Young, Adrian
  See No Doubt
Young, Angus
  See AC/DC
Young, Faron **7**
Young, Fred
  See Kentucky Headhunters, The
Young, Gary
  See Pavement
Young, Grant
  See Soul Asylum
Young, Jeff
  See Megadeth
Young, La Monte **16**
Young, Lester **14**
Young M.C. **4**
Young, Malcolm
  See AC/DC
Young, Neil **15**
  Earlier sketch in CM **2**
  Also see Buffalo Springfield
Young, Paul
  See Mike & the Mechanics
Young, Richard
  See Kentucky Headhunters, The
Young, Robert "Throbert"
  See Primal Scream
Yow, David
  See Jesus Lizard
Yseult, Sean
  See White Zombie
Yule, Doug
  See Velvet Underground, The
Zander, Robin
  See Cheap Trick
Zankey, Glen
  See Bluegrass Patriots
Zap Mama **14**
Zappa, Frank **17**
  Earlier sketch in CM **1**
Zawinul, Josef
  See Weather Report
Zender, Stuart
  See Jamiroquai
Zevon, Warren **9**
Zhane **22**
Zilinskas, Annette
  See Bangles
Zimmerman, Udo **5**
Zombie, Rob
  See White Zombie
Zombies, The **23**
Zoom, Billy
  See X
Zorn, John **15**
Zoyes, Dino
  See Charm Farm
Zuccaro, Steve
  See Charm Far
Zukerman, Pinchas **4**
Zulu, Ras I
  See Spearhead
ZZ Top **2**